You See, I Haven't Forgotten

YVES MONTAND

You See, I Haven't Forgotten

with Hervé Hamon
and Patrick Rotman

translated from the
French by Jeremy Leggatt

ALFRED A. KNOPF
New York
1992

THIS IS A BORZOI BOOK

PUBLISHED BY ALFRED A. KNOPF, INC.

 Published in the United States by Alfred A. Knopf, Inc., New York, and simultaneously in Canada by Random House of Canada Limited, Toronto. Distributed by Random House, Inc., New York.

Originally published in France as *Tu vois, je n'ai pas oublié* by Editions du Seuil et Editions Fayard, Paris, in 1990.

Library of Congress Cataloging-in-Publication Data

Montand, Yves, 1921–1991
[Tu vois, je n'ai pas oublié. English]
You see, I haven't forgotten / by Yves Montand with Hervé Hamon and Patrick Rotman. — 1st American ed.
p. cm.
Translation of: Tu vois, je n'ai pas oublié.
Includes index.
ISBN 0-679-41012-0
1. Montand, Yves, 1921–1991. 2. Singers—France—Biography.
I. Hamon, Hervé. II. Rotman, Patrick. III. Title.
ML420.M56A3 1992
782.42164'092—dc20
[B] 91-58647
CIP
M

Manufactured in the United States of America

First American Edition

Preface

A book by Montand, about Montand—and with him. Who can resist the story of his journey from the hills of his native Tuscany to New York's Metropolitan Opera House, from the Alcazar music hall in Marseilles to the studios of Hollywood, from the nightclubs of occupied France to Khrushchev's Kremlin?

We did not know Yves Montand personally when we wrote to him in 1988 to suggest that we write his biography. He called us to discuss it at once, and soon after he made up his mind: he would never write his memoirs, he told us, but he would tell us about himself, give us the run of his personal records, and reserve the right to withhold only those intimate secrets that every man is entitled to keep.

Nothing could take the place of the two hundred hours of interviews we had with him, or his reams of notes, diaries, and journals, and his carefully preserved and filed documents. It became a hybrid project, both biography and—at least we hope—more than biography; for it is also Yves Montand's autobiography, with him telling his story in his own words, throughout our text. But Montand's very availability raised an issue: How could we uncover the man without our being co-opted by his readiness to help? How could we tie the threads together without becoming entangled ourselves?

Our answer was to carry out parallel inquiries in traditional biographical style, interviewing witnesses, friends, colleagues, and acquaintances—including those not so friendly or no longer friendly—digging into every imaginable source, checking facts, dates, stories. As meticulously as we could, we weighed Montand's own recollections against our findings. We avoided skirting gray areas with words like "probably," and we have reported no conversation in the book unless we were told about it independently by our sources. We would like to express our heartfelt thanks to the many eyewitnesses who were kind enough to answer our questions; we list them in the Acknowledgments at the back of the book. All quotations not footnoted have been taken from our unpublished interviews.

Have we really come up with the "truth"? The reader must decide. Many sources told us to tread warily, warned us that Montand might react angrily to this or that analysis, description, or anecdote. That was the risk all three of us had to take. But Montand gave us a free hand throughout the writing of the book. His trust does us honor; it did not commit us.

And, in a way, every biography is a work of deception: Montand shared this conviction with us. Four hundred thirty-nine pages are inadequate to convey the density and texture of a life—especially one as rich as Montand's. We hope, at least, that we have been honest.

We have many debts we shall never be able to repay, but we would like to express our gratitude to Anne Sastourné, who transcribed our lengthy interviews with Yves Montand; to Diane d'Ormesson, who helped compile our data; to Anne Rousseau, who translated the 1956 Soviet press comment for us; and to Dominique de Libéra, who proofread the French book.

HERVÉ HAMON
PATRICK ROTMAN

You See, I Haven't Forgotten

Chapter 1

The thermal springs and steam-filled caves that attract visitors to health spas once justified the little Tuscan town of Monsummano in adding the word *"terme"* to its name. But Monsummano no longer looks like a thermal establishment; Montecatini Terme, only a few miles away, is one of Europe's biggest spas and a formidable rival.

Once upon a time, Monsummano Terme was called Monsummano Basso, to distinguish it from the upper village set higher on the mountainside. But today Monsummano Alto has disappeared. You have to explore around the eighteenth-century church and look very carefully before discovering, almost by chance, a plaque designating the Via Castello di Monsummano Alto, a narrow path that snakes up through olive groves. Down in the valley the Florence-Pisa *autostrada* teems with an unbroken flow of cars and trucks. After a few miles of what quickly turns into a rocky trail you are almost ready to give up. Suddenly the crumbling, overgrown walls of a five-sided stone tower, all that remain of the *castello,* come into view. A rough path leads up through the trees from the foot of the ruined keep for a couple of hundred yards, then opens out onto a small square bordered with houses. The stone façades look sound; the green shutters are closed. Nothing moves. Across from the houses is a Romanesque church: small, sturdy, huddled against its squat bell tower, waiting for a congregation that will never return. Over the first house on the left is an almost illegible sign whose faded letters proclaim it to be the café of Monsummano Alto. Grass grows in the cracks between the rocky paving stones of the square. Gaunt, quicksilver cats stalk careless birds.

The cemetery is on your right as you go back down from the *castello.* Many of the graves seem abandoned, their inscriptions attesting to distant deaths; others appear to be visited from time to time. In the middle of the cemetery stands a family marker scarcely deserving the name of monument. There are several marble plaques on its peeling walls: the best preserved of them, just to the left of the doorway, recalls the memory of the Livi family to the passerby.

Giovanni Livi was born on November 15, 1891. His father died two years later, at the age of twenty-five, his body found at the bottom of a hole he was digging to plant a cherry tree. Dead of exhaustion. With his twenty-two-year-old wife, Arduina, the young man left three boys, aged three, two, and one. Arduina, who was a beauty, abandoned these offspring a little later and ran off with a youth of eighteen. So Giovanni and his two brothers, Giuseppino and Virgilio, were raised by their grandfather Carlo, known to all as Carlino. Carlo could read and write: rare accomplishments for a peasant in those days. He was justly proud, and it won him fame tinged with a little jealousy in the village. He owned the works of Dante, Tasso, and Hugo, and he would read the stories in them to his grandchildren. Much later, Giovanni Livi said, "We worshiped him because of those wonderful tales."

But times were hard, and the Livis, like other peasants, hovered somewhere between poverty and total destitution. From the age of seven, Giovanni Livi worked in the fields. When it rained or snowed, he and his brothers attended Monsummano Alto elementary school—a schooling dependent on the weather, but a schooling nonetheless. His grandfather, a man of firm principles, extolled education and often told them: "The less you know, the stupider you sound."

Pepe Carlino's principles were respected. Virgilio, eldest of the three Livi sons, as a schoolboy built with his own hands a miniature wooden threshing machine. Proud of his grandson, Carlino entered it in a competition in Florence, where it won first prize. Virgilio later left for Livorno, where he became assistant manager of a truck factory. Giuseppino, the youngest of the three, had a fine voice. He learned to play the guitar and mandolin, and was soon in demand as a singer and player at local festivals.

Giovanni stayed on to work the soil. On his twentieth birthday the army called him up for a three-year stint. It was 1912, and Italy, hankering after empire, had dispatched forty thousand men to "pacify" Libya. Away from home for the first time, Giovanni Livi discovered the brutality of war. He came back a corporal, shaken, matured—and shattered by the experience of having to order his men to climb, one after another, into an observation post where, one after another, they were shot down.

In 1914, Giovanni married Giuseppina Simoni. If the history of the Livis is like something from a Zola novel, the Simonis were closer to Dickens. Their story begins with an abandoned child, named Olimpia by the nuns who took her in around 1850 (no one is sure of the exact date).

In Florence in those days, when girls in an orphanage reached adulthood they were placed on a kind of revolving roundabout, and farmers came to view them and to choose a bride. A young man named Leopoldo Simoni inspected Olimpia and saw that she was comely, that she looked strong enough to work in the fields, and, above all, that she looked like a good childbearer.

Leopoldo and Olimpia married and had ten children. Pious as any monk, Leopoldo feared that on Judgment Day he might be reproached with having engendered too few offspring. He farmed his landlord's fields in Monsummano Alto. The soil was poor, and, like all Italian tenant farmers, he handed over the best of his harvest to the landlord. Theirs was a grinding poverty. Among the stories passed down in the family is one of Leopoldo standing by the fire to dole out pieces of salt cod (all there was to eat) to his ten children, lined up before him in order of height. The second-to-last child, Giuseppina, born in 1893 when her mother was already forty-five, first met Giovanni Livi in school at Monsummano when bad weather made work in the fields impossible. In 1914, after Giovanni returned from Libya, she married him.

He was a stocky man of medium height, all muscle. What he lacked in education he made up for with the shrewdness and alert intelligence characteristic of those who work the land. Tuscans are a reserved, proud people who prefer listening to speaking. Polite but distant, they can often be sarcastic. Was it Giovanni's wit or his genuine goodness that attracted his old classmate Giuseppina—"Beppina"—whose oval face was of classic Florentine beauty?

Italy considerately delayed its entry into the Great War, which gave the couple time to conceive a child in peacetime. Lidia Fedora was born on March 25, 1915 (the family never called her by anything but her first name, later Gallicized to Lydia). Yet Giovanni and Giuseppina had not really planned to have her. Worse, they did not want to keep her. Lydia was forty-nine before she learned the family's shameful secret: that her mother had tried everything to abort, even jumping from a treetop, which knocked her out for half an hour. Lydia withstood it all. Of this inborn fighting spirit (for that is how the Livis see it), she has retained a strength, stubbornness, and will acknowledged by the entire family. In the Livi family, Lydia is a sacred figure, the saint of the clan.

Like every self-respecting Italian, Giovanni wanted a son. Once again he was drafted, but an eye disease contracted in Libya exempted him from the trenches. He took advantage of a furlough to sire Giuliano (Julien in French), who was born on November 2, 1917. In Petrograd the Bolsheviks had seized power. It was pure coincidence, but a whim of fate just the same. Julien Livi's whole life would be spent under the sign of the October Revolution.

Ivo was born on October 13, 1921, after an agonizing thirteen-hour labor. Little Lydia, six at the time, buried her face in her Aunt Marina's lap, her hands on her ears to cover her mother's screams. It took four men to hold Giuseppina down. The baby appeared around eleven in the evening; he weighed over twelve pounds. Lydia was allowed to go upstairs to the bedroom. According to custom, the eldest sister was always the first to kiss the newborn child. The baby was so big that she had to sit down in order to hold him in her arms.

Even today, Lydia weeps at the memory. Strangely enough, it was triggered all over again nearly seven decades later, when a young woman named Carole Amiel—the lover of that same baby brother—gave birth to a son. "I phoned Carole," Lydia recalls. "I said to her, 'I haven't seen your baby boy, but I'll describe him to you: he has long brown hair, he's pink, and he has a well-defined mouth.' I was describing my brother to her as I saw him the day he was born. She said: 'You are absolutely right!' " As Lydia wrote in a letter to her brother, Yves Montand, in 1987, "Everyone in and around Monsummano came to see you. They had never seen such a beautiful baby. I swear it is *true.*" She underlined "true" three times.

Giovanni had decided to name his latest child Ivo—an unusual name in Italy—because he wanted him to become a lawyer, and Ivo was the patron saint of defenders of the just (canonized in 1347 for accepting the worst kind of client—the destitute). Montand often joked about this with his father, the man he cherished above all others: how naive of him to think that a man might earn a living by using words! Why not put the words to music while you were about it? But we are getting ahead of our story—even though there are no surprises here.

On their strip of land, the Livis grew just enough to feed themselves. The children did not go hungry, but their staple food was polenta, the classic northern Italian cornmeal pudding. They also grew vegetables—beets, peas, and beans—which for want of anything better they made into a watery soup. On Sundays they baked bread and cooked the cheapest cuts of beef and pork, the kind butchers nowadays set aside for cats. If a child was sick, he was entitled to an egg. "Real" meat, a rare luxury, was served only on feast days.

"I don't remember suffering from hunger so much as from permanent frustration," says Julien Livi. "For example, we used to add a little oil to our polenta, but my mother flattened the spout on the oil can to prevent it from flowing too freely. It just gave you the illusion that you were adding oil. And for dessert, our biggest treat was baked chestnuts."

A sense of propriety is still highly prized in the Livi family. They are too proud to paint an excessively somber picture of living conditions that were, after all, shared by most of Tuscany's peasants in those days. Lydia prefers simply to recall the villagers' daily round: "You worked hard. You hacked at the earth with hoes, ten-year-olds dug up wild vegetables on all fours, my mother cut wheat with a sickle. One of our neighbors owned an ox which he sometimes lent out for plowing. Other peasants raised chickens and rabbits. Once a week they went down to the market in Monsummano Basso to sell their eggs and rabbits, which the women carried in huge baskets balanced on their heads. My mother looked magnificent, graceful, bolt upright. You bought salt in the local grocery-café; it was expensive and rationed. And you bought cod, dirt cheap. I never understood why we didn't eat our rabbits instead of selling them so we could buy cod. But that's how it was, that was the tradition. With salt cod you could make any kind of dish."

Life in the trenches during World War I threw millions of Italians together, yet social and regional divisions persisted. Almost half of the six hundred thousand killed at the front were of peasant stock. After this slaughter of the young, the survivors returned to a weakened, bruised country in which social injustices were accentuated by daily hardship. It was apparently on his return from the Great War that Giovanni Livi became a Socialist—or, at least, embraced Socialist ideas. With the carnage over, and the country laid waste by war, Italy's Socialist party now faced a fork in the road: the traditional direction of social and legal reform or the road of revolution, inspired by the Soviet example, which many Italians dreamed of emulating. The overwhelming majority of them opted for the latter course, proclaiming their support for the Russian Revolution and voting by acclamation to join the Third International, just founded in Moscow.

Subversion threatened in Germany, worker councils were forming in Hungary, and the Red Army was advancing on Warsaw. The east wind blowing across Europe was also sweeping down the boot of Italy. You had to be prudent about your choice of terms: calling yourself a Socialist in Italy in 1918 was declaring yourself a revolutionary. We do not know precisely what steps Giovanni Livi took to reach this point. Most likely, as was the case with millions of young people of his generation, the trauma of war was the catalyst for a young pacifist who, to all intents and purposes, had been under arms since 1911.

His son Julien confirms that when he was in the army, Giovanni Livi took part in political discussions. It seems likely that he encountered uniformed militants who brought shape and coherence to his confused intuitions. And the Socialist party was a powerful magnet. Although lacking a clearly defined program, it garnered a third of the votes in the 1919 election and sent 156 deputies to parliament, mainly from northern Italy, simply by preaching the revolutionary ideal. It also gained control of a third of Italy's communes, a third of the provincial legislatures, and eight thousand agricultural and industrial cooperatives. In 1920, it boasted 216,000 members. In the fall of that same year a wave of strikes paralyzed factories taken over by the workers. The agitation spread to the countryside. Peasants raised the red flag and demanded land. Terrified landowners looked around for support. Italy was on the brink of revolution.

At this stage, apparently, Giovanni Livi decided that his peasant days were over. He found work in a small shop that manufactured brooms. The business soon foundered, and Livi was fired; deciding to go into business for himself, he learned how to make his own brooms of sorghum grass, and he built a plank and tarred-roof shack in front of his house for a workshop.

A photograph taken in the summer of 1921 shows him in front of this "broom factory." Wearing a sturdy, voluminous apron, he holds one of his products across his knees. Around him are a dozen women and children. To fill in the space in front of the camera, the photographer has placed Julien and Lydia in the first row. Ivo is present but invisible, hidden behind Giovanni's shoulders, in Giuseppina's womb. None of the group looks unhappy, although expressions are serious and smiles rare (in those days a photograph was by definition a solemn event). The family expresses a kind of collective serenity, a collective dignity. They look equal to whatever might happen. This turned out to be a short-lived certainty, the briefest of respites before tribulations fell on Italy and the Livis.

On January 15, 1921, the Italian Socialist Party Congress convened at the Goldoni Theater in Livorno. Three factions met head-on. The first, very much in the minority, advocated reform and social democracy. The two others claimed allegiance to Communism and had already accepted the twenty-one harsh conditions laid down by Lenin for membership in the Third International. But envoys from Moscow, in particular Comrade Rakosi (he was to rule Stalinist Hungary in the 1950s), managed to drive a wedge between these two groups despite their close ideological kinship. The larger of the two movements, disavowed by Moscow, nevertheless unanimously reaffirmed its commitment to the Communist International and adopted the hammer and sickle—to which they added a book—as its emblem. This "unitarian" group kept the name Socialist party. The others, led by Antonio Gramsci, immediately founded the Italian Communist Party.

Giovanni Livi went with the last and most radical group and became a founder of the local Communist cell at Monsummano, attending all public meetings at the Casa del Popolo (community center) and handing out propaganda. On May Day they brought out the red flag and marched to the strains of "Bandiera rossa." This modest but regular activity won Giovanni a local reputation as a Communist militant.

The Livis' house was at the very top of the village, on the hill past the church. To reach it, you had to walk up a narrow, walled-in passageway. As he returned home one November evening in 1921, he was attacked by three men armed with bullwhips. Giovanni yelled, and despite a stunning blow to the nape of his neck he managed to drag himself to a circle of lamplight. The light saved him. "My mother and I heard him calling for help," Lydia remembers, "and then he appeared. His eyes were starting out of his head. There were purple marks like fat worms all over his face and neck. He looked insane. What shocked him the most was that he had recognized two of his attackers under the light—two former fellow Socialists who had joined Mussolini."

Benito Mussolini was the son of a Socialist blacksmith, and he had espoused his father's ideas. His antimilitarist activities—which landed him in prison during Italy's Libyan adventure—and his ferocious anticlericalism attracted the attention of Socialist leaders; in 1912 they invited him to Milan to run the party daily, *Avanti*. His fiery articles before the war proclaimed his uncompromising positions, opposed to reformism or any kind of compromise. When hostilities broke out, he first declared himself in favor of neutrality and then, in a complete about-face, argued for intervention. The party expelled him.

In 1919, in a hall borrowed from local industrialists and businessmen near the Piazza San Sepolcro in Milan, he and some fifty disciples founded the Italian Combat Groups (or Fasci). The Fascist party was born. Three years later, Mussolini seized power.

Yet Fascism's beginnings were painful. A mere 5,000 out of Milan's 268,000 voters supported the party in 1919, and by the end of the year, the Fascists had mustered only 17,000 followers. It was public reaction to the failure of the 1920 strikes that first assisted Mussolini's climb. Out in the countryside, the landowners joined forces and assembled *squadri*—armed gangs paid to block tenant-farmer claims. Quickly gaining ground, this rural Fascism soon trained its sights on the Socialists. Incidents of extreme brutality kept up throughout 1921.

Mussolini's men began their operations in the Po Valley and Tuscany. Their violence was directed particularly at institutions run by the reformist wing of the Socialist party—employment exchanges that organized regional economic life or cooperatives in which small peasants pooled their resources. Their favored form of action was the punitive expedition: radiating out from urban centers, they would ravage the countryside. Black Shirts would show up in a "red" township and vent their fury on anyone who resisted, assaulting employment exchanges, municipal buildings, cooperatives, community centers. They looted and burned. They also hunted down the red leaders to punish them and force them to recant in public. To humiliate them, they forced them to swallow draft after draft of resin oil. Lydia witnessed many such scenes: "It was horrible. The Fascists forced their victims to drink at gunpoint, surrounded by villagers who looked on without protesting. Children laughed because the victims begged for an end to be put to their suffering; they vomited all over their clothes and soiled themselves, and in this state they were pushed and kicked around the square until they shouted 'Viva Mussolini!' Once I even saw a priest subjected to this treatment."

So the attack on Giovanni Livi was not an isolated act, or the work of disturbed minds or of local rivals. As a notorious Communist militant, he was a natural target for the venom of Mussolini's supporters. But a family drama further complicated the political feud. For the local Fascist leader, the man who had probably ordered the attack against Giovanni, was his own brother-in-law.

Known to everyone as Gigi, Luigi was the oldest of the ten Simoni children. Like all the Simonis, he was tall; but unlike the others, he, being the eldest son, had received an education. As a young man he wanted to be a priest, but a voyage to Africa stripped him of his vocation, forcing him to trade his cassock for a uniform. When the Great War was over, thousands of young Italians, beaten and humiliated, returned with an unshakable hatred for the politicians who had sent them to the slaughter. They dreamed of a new order that would restore their pride, and applauded the legendary exploits of Gabriele D'Annunzio. These were the half-pay rejects who formed Mussolini's frontline troops.

Luigi Simoni followed this unremarkable path, the exact opposite of the one taken by his brother-in-law Giovanni Livi. The same village, the same upbringing, the same family, and the same poverty had engendered diametrically divergent destinies.

Big brother Gigi tried to convince his sister Giuseppina, a believer like himself, of the pernicious influence her Communist husband exerted over her children. Did not the Bolsheviks in Russia murder children? Were not these Livis creatures with neither faith nor morals? Had not Giovanni's mother (a whore!) abandoned him and his two brothers at a tender age to elope with a stranger? Giuseppina was terrified of her enormous, powerful elder brother and his black uniform and his squad of roughnecks. And even though she was half-convinced by his warnings, she resisted him, for she loved her Giovanni more than anything else. So Gigi's only recourse was intimidation and violence. And since blows had not worked . . .

One night in November 1921, with a strong wind moaning across the rooftops, Giovanni was awakened by a strange light glowing through his bedroom shutters. He leapt to the window: out in the yard, the little shack that did service as his broom factory was engulfed in flames, which were already licking at the front of the house. Through the smoke outside he caught glimpses of shadowy figures at work. He let out a cry of terror. "We were wrenched awake by my father's yell," recalls Julien Livi. "He grabbed all three of us"—Yves was one month old—"and clattered down the stairs, pushing my mother ahead with shouts of 'Beppina, *vai, vai* [get out]!' He got us clear of the house and handed us over to a neighbor. I was four and a half. Nearly seventy years later, I still hear my father's yells and see our house on fire. The sight and sounds have never left me. When I was a prisoner in Germany during the [Second World] war I witnessed the firebombing of Hamburg. The memory of our blazing house came back to me."

Raking through the embers of his workshop at first light, Giovanni Livi found a sign written with the pitch used to ignite the flames: *"A morte Communisti!"* Nobody claimed credit for the attack, but the signature was there. There is no proof that Uncle Gigi personally gave the order, but as head of the local *fascio* he could not have been ignorant of his followers' actions. A few days later, within earshot of a neighbor who had helped extinguish the blaze, he said, "We should have let them roast, and rid ourselves of this scum." The margin between intimidation and liquidation was dangerously narrow. Clearly, though, the deed fell short of the words. If they had wanted to murder the Livi family, the authors of the crime would have set fire to the house where the family lay sleeping, and not to the shack in front of it. The fire appeared, in fact, to be a last warning from Fascists blinded by tribal and ideological hatred.

In that autumn of 1921, the list of atrocities committed by Mussolini's Black Shirts lengthened. Many Socialist and Communist leaders were gunned down on their doorsteps. Many, to spare their families the sight, allowed themselves to be captured and liquidated in the countryside. In Tuscany, a region where more than half the farm population were peasant farmers, the local landowners readily called on Mussolini's squads. In Florence there were battles with bombs and guns—even machine guns. On March 4, in Siena, the Casa del Popolo was shelled and set on fire. In parliament, the Socialist deputy Giacomo Matteotti (who would be assassinated three years later) gave a frightening account of nocturnal rampages: "In the dead of night, truckloads of Fascists arrive in tiny villages, hamlets of barely a few hundred inhabitants. . . . Twenty or a hundred men armed with shotguns and revolvers approach a small house. They hail the local Party leader and order him to come out: 'If you do not, we will burn down the house with your wife and children inside!' If he opens the door they seize him, tie him up, throw him into a truck, and inflict the most savage tortures upon him. If he does not open up, instant execution."[1]

Employment exchanges in Lucca, Arezzo, and Grosseto had been gutted by flames during the previous spring. According to information gathered by the official historian of the Fascist party, in Tuscany alone eleven community centers, fifteen employment exchanges, seventy Communist or Socialist headquarters, and twenty-four workers clubs had been destroyed. Angelo Tasca, a founder of the Italian Communist Party, points out that these figures do not include thousands of punitive forays and acts of violence against isolated individuals. By the autumn of 1921, besides the Veneto region and the Po Valley, Fascist terror was striking throughout the greater part of Tuscany. Monsummano and the Livi family were at the heart of the storm, and the disaster that befell them was the common lot of anti-Fascists.

Nothing now seemed to stand in the way of Benito Mussolini. The parties of the left disintegrated under his constant attack or dissolved in internal fighting. At the Second Fascist Congress, in November 1921, Mussolini summed up his thinking in one sentence: "We are economic liberals—not political ones!"[2] By now, the "black" party had mustered 320,000 members. By the next spring, the figure would double. On October 26, 1922, twenty thousand Black Shirts marched on Rome and delivered an ultimatum to King Victor Emmanuel III. Two days later, Benito Mussolini was asked to form a government. Ivo Livi was a year old.

After the Fascist seizure of power, violence was institutionalized. Those who opposed Mussolini were systematically harassed until their position became unbearable. One day, more than a year later, Giovanni Livi was summoned to the Fascist headquarters under the eaves in the main square of Monsummano. Giovanni hesitated before complying. Convinced that his enemies intended to kill him, his wife begged him not to go. But the summons had made it clear that if he failed to appear, he would be shot down anyway. He walked to the *fascio,* where an official delivered an edifying speech: a man as brave and hardworking as Giovanni had his place

1. Parliamentary address, March 10, 1921, reprinted in *Critica Sociale,* no. 7.

2. Quoted in Pierre Milza and Serge Bernstein, *Le Fascisme italien* (Paris, 1980).

in the new Italy. They would help him build a much bigger workshop, of stone this time.

"What must I do?" asked Livi.

"All you have to do," said the Black Shirt, "is join our night expeditions."

Giovanni prudently asked for time to think. But, back at home, he knew he no longer had a choice. He had to leave. In a long talk with Beppina he told her of his decision: he would leave for America, where the family could join him as soon as possible.

"One evening, I remember, he kissed us all hard. He had tears in his eyes, although he was not an emotional man." Like Julien, then six, Lydia, who was nearly nine at the time, remembers that evening in the last days of January 1924. "It was dark and very cold. Mama and I clung to him and cried. He tore himself away and left on foot." Giovanni Livi made his getaway in secret, without applying for a visa. It seems likely that he took the train to within a short distance of the French frontier; there he had arranged to meet a *passeur*—a professional smuggler of refugees—who would take him across the mountainous terrain to France for 100 lire. Giovanni had borrowed 150 lire before leaving to meet this cost, first handing 15 lire to his wife.

They crossed at night. It was winter and the air was icy, and Giovanni, who had a bad cold, could not stop coughing. The *passeur* threatened to throw him down the mountain if he did not keep quiet. Eventually, on February 2, Giovanni Livi reached Marseilles. Before leaving Monsummano, he had lovingly packed Carlino's big, red-bound volume of Tasso into the skimpy bundle of belongings he brought away with him.

As far as he was concerned, Marseilles was merely a first step, for he was determined to go on to America. But when he applied at the U.S. consulate he learned that in the previous twenty-four hours all visas had been annulled and stringent restrictions imposed on entry to the United States. One day earlier, and Ivo Livi might have followed in the footsteps of De Niro, Sinatra, or Coppola. But Giovanni refused to lose heart. He had family in Marseilles, where his young Aunt Lizena had married an Italian named Parlanti. The couple took him in. He slept on a mat on their floor and got work doing the roughest manual labor. Finally, through his aunt's husband, the foreman in an olive-oil factory, he found regular employment. The job was hard and exhausting, but within three months Livi had a work permit and could write to his family to join him.

Once Giovanni had gone, life in Monsummano had become much harsher for his wife and children. They had literally nothing to eat. Kindhearted aunts "stole" cornmeal from their own homes and brought it to them in secret. Fifty years later, Marina Simoni, Giuseppina's twin sister, described the family's distress to an Italian magazine reporter: "My sister was struggling to raise her children. She had hardly any milk for Ivo, so I fed him myself. You can't imagine how ugly he was—a grownup's face, all wrinkles."

Several times at night there were violent knocks at the door: "*Carabinieri!* Open up!" The mother took refuge in the kitchen, hugging her children to her as men in black uniforms ripped mattresses apart and poked in every corner hoping to find a letter from Giovanni. Giuseppina never said a word. She drummed it into Lydia and Julien: even if they were threatened they must never tell an outsider where their father was.

One morning in May 1924, Giuseppina and her three children left their Monsummano home. As an adult, Ivo, who was two and a half, would remember nothing of the trip. Shooting a movie in Italy almost thirty years later, he returned to Monsummano Alto and looked over the village, then still inhabited. He visited the family's clay-and-gravel house, tested the red-tiled floors with his foot, ducked to avoid hitting his head on the beams. But he felt nothing specific, no shock of recognition. As described sixty-five years later by Lydia, the family's departure is like those yellowing photos in which immigrants, no matter who or where, smile painfully at the camera. The Livis did not have a suitcase, so Giuseppina piled their poor treasures into burlap sacks. Lydia held her brother Julien's hand, and Ivo, along with a package, was cradled in his mother's arms.

> Our family odyssey was a little bit like a Western. The people who crossed the United States in covered wagons, facing the worst difficulties, became tough and stubborn—under conditions like that you either make it through or die. All things being equal, it was the same with Italian peasants, or with peasants anywhere in the Mediterranean basin: if you weren't very tough you went under. Adversity in childhood almost always hardens you. For me, Italy is first of all my father's struggle, a struggle for survival that left its mark on all of us. But as a small child I learned about oppression, humiliation, struggle, and dignity. That was the entirety of my early life.
>
> Whenever I hear Italian spoken today I melt: it breaks down all my barriers, because I hear my father again. I am French, I have always felt profoundly French, but I take pleasure in having been born in Tuscany, in being thus linked to a great civilization, the civilization of Michelangelo, of Leonardo. I like the Italians' courtesy, their kindness, their elegance. Their arm waving and

tendency to boast annoys me a bit, but that's all superficial, conventional. There is integrity and real warmth behind the "macho" façade.

Giovanni was waiting at the Gare Saint-Charles. When he saw the fugitives, grimy, covered with soot, dragging bags too heavy for them to lift, he burst into tears. And when Ivo pushed away this strange man he had not seen for months, the tears flowed faster.

"My son doesn't know me any more," cried Giovanni.

Chapter 2

Marseilles in the 1920s was still a conglomerate city, a patchwork of juxtaposed villages. Sprawling over an area three times the size of Paris, it was a clutter of contrasting neighborhoods, a jigsaw puzzle with a hundred unmatched pieces. Some of these faced the sea and depended on fishing; others nestled in the hills, almost out of sight of the Mediterranean—a duality that expressed the twin destinies of a city responsive to the call of the open sea yet firmly rooted in its hinterland. Marseilles had grown by leaps and bounds, gobbling up the surrounding countryside and cutting off broad enclaves of still productive farmland. Each component hamlet had its own traditions, culture, and festivals—even its own eating habits. You were a native of Estaque or Belle-de-Mai first, and a native of Marseilles only second.

The Marseillais worked their fields without having to leave the city. You lived on your own home ground, almost on your own vegetable patch, and you kept a wary and aloof eye on the next-door neighbors. Going downtown to stroll along the Canebière, a natural frontier between the homes of the poor and the wealthy, or to kick around the Vieux Port, was a full-scale expedition. Whoever undertook it was hailed as an intrepid explorer.

But with the appearance and swift expansion of the electric streetcar system, all this changed. Emitting warning whoops as loud as the foghorns of the freighters in the port below, the cars hurtled around the steeply sloping streets in a clatter of metal. Their sides flaunted advertisements for Zan toothpaste or Rivoire & Carret noodles. They had no windshields; in winter their operators wore fur-lined capes. Soon you could ride across the whole city for a few pennies—or for nothing at all if, like the children, you clung to the sides of the cars.

Lydia Livi's first image of Marseilles was of a forest of hands and arms reaching up to the rear platform of a streetcar and clusters of urchins hanging on to the running boards. Fresh from the fields of Tuscany, the young woman had her initial view of the city through the windows of a straw-yellow tram that rocked and bucked along the rails as it climbed toward her new home. For Giovanni Livi had found not merely work but a house.

In fact, it was a cramped shanty close to collapse, lost in the hills of the Verduron-Haut neighborhood on the boulevard du Plateau, but to the immigrants it was a heaven-sent refuge. Best of all, there was running water at the kitchen washstand. Giovanni had worked hard to furnish their new home. In those days there was a store on the rue de la République called the Good Genie where, on producing evidence of a job, you were given credit (although buying on credit automatically doubled the price of every item). Livi had bought cots, a stove, pots and pans. He had even decorated the packing crates that did service as armoires and tables. All around the house was open scrubland, with olive trees and the scent of thyme to remind the young Tuscans of other, more familiar hills. And far to the south, to their astonishment, was a sparkling patch of blue sea, remote but strong-smelling even at that distance. Today that stretch is urban wasteland, buried beneath highways and low-income housing developments.

From October on, Lydia and Julien attended the Saint-Antoine elementary school, and after only a few months they had mastered French. Giovanni worked the night shift at the Darrier de Rouffio olive-oil factory on the boulevard Oddo; Giuseppina stayed at home to take care of Ivo. Julien remembers having to creep to school in the early-morning darkness down a trail winding between creaking tree trunks through a neighborhood known as the Devil's Mill, where nameless crimes had been committed years before. It was a relief to see the lights in the schoolhouse, though by early afternoon the terror of the return journey would be back.

Montand's memories of Verduron were only fragmentary: a watermelon cooling in a bowl of water; a small wooden mill his father built for him, whose wheel turned in the waters of a nearby spring; the mournful wailing of a neighborhood dog whose master beat it and kept it tied up. Black woolen stockings meant to protect his scab-covered legs. A parasol fir. And Mediterranean smells—mingled lavender and rosemary—exhaled by the vegetation and remembered across the intervening years. Scattered fragments, scarcely enough to re-create the substance of a life.

Soon Giovanni left the olive-oil factory. A man who owned a two-story house at 42 avenue Félix-Zaccola, in the neighborhood known as Les Crottes, agreed to let the ground floor to Livi and to advance him enough money to start his broom-making business again. This offer shattered the children's lives, for father and mother now left at dawn for the makeshift workshop, and the youngsters were alone all day long.

Ivo had been entered in kindergarten at Saint-Antoine. Only three, he was unable to manage the two-and-a-half-mile trip there and back. Going was no problem, since it was downhill, but on the way home in the evenings Lydia had to become a beast of burden. "Getting him back uphill from school was hard," she recalls. "He was big and heavy. He used to beg me to carry him, but I couldn't. So I worked out a way: I walked behind him and pushed." But it was all too much for him. In class, Ivo wept endlessly; when Lydia came to fetch him at the end of the day, tears had washed ravines down cheeks turned purple by the schoolyard dust. The Livis held a family counsel, and Giovanni, despair in his heart, decided that Lydia would attend school only halftime and look after her younger brother at home. For the Italian immigrant obsessed with the importance of learning (he himself was studying French at night school), the decision was wrenching. And it was not to be Lydia's last sacrifice. At the age of ten, she was already responsible for the family and entrusted with managing its skimpy resources.

Those were months of empty stomachs, for the brooms, Giovanni's constant concern, brought in little income. The children were hungry. Every account of Montand's life mentions the hardship suffered by him and his siblings in the days when a meal consisted of one fried egg shared among the three of them. Julien confirms it: "We would get a bowl of watered milk, more water than milk, with a few scraps of bread floating in it. I won't dwell on that shared egg. The story has been told too often, but it's true. My sister divided it up, and we used our bread to soak up the oil it was cooked in, turned yellowish from the yolk."

In 1927, the Livi clan moved to Les Crottes, for, thanks to a conversation overheard in the Spanish-run café next door, Giovanni had stumbled onto an apartment close to his workshop. A young man, Henri Bertolini, was willing to share his fairly spacious lodgings with an Italian family in return for cooked meals and part payment of the rent. The Livis therefore moved into 20 rue Saint-Jean-Baptiste (it was "secularized" during their stay there to rue Edgar Quinet). Les Crottes (the name means "droppings") was bathed in harsh, incurable gloom. Returning to it sixty years later, during the writing of this book, Lydia Livi prowled the mean streets, muttering, "It hasn't changed. Nothing has changed. I feel as if I just got here." In fact, the area surrounding the huddle of dwellings has undergone several alterations. The narrow *biau,* or drainage channel, that flowed close by, ferrying every kind of refuse in its leaden waters—where children used to play, not far from a foul-smelling chemical-fertilizer plant—has been covered over. Farther down the street, the children played out most of their adventures in a *bachas,* or vacant lot, which at night was peopled by mysterious noises and sometimes screams of terror, and was strictly out of bounds; today the spot is occupied by a railroad yard.

Sunless even when the sun was shining, dirt poor, Les Crottes was nevertheless a lively place, a private theater for the exclusive pleasure of its denizens. In summer, people sat outside on chairs by their front doors, enjoying the cool of the evening, keeping up conversations until the night turned chilly and they went to bed. At first Ivo was considered too young to come down and be with the grownups, but he would later remember voices and laughter from the narrow street outside rising through the open window as the shadows in his room deepened.

The rue Edgar Quinet ran between gutters brimming with doubtful-looking water. Today the house still has the same grayish façade, criss-crossed with fat drainpipes and pierced with the occasional narrow window. The Livi apartment, on the fourth floor, had three rooms. Ivo and Julien shared a bed in one half of a room that was divided by a sheet, while Lydia slept on the other side. When the family moved in, they had to wage a pitiless war of extermination on the bedbugs that swarmed from every crevice. Giuseppina, raised with vigilant Tuscan notions of cleanliness, had never set eyes on such creatures, and for a long while she was obsessed by them.

The toilets were out in the courtyard; every morning the neighbors took turns trooping downstairs and emptying their chamber pots. There was no electricity; light was provided by oil lamps.

The house stood at the corner of the rue Edgar Quinet and an alleyway called Antoine-Carial, where a small metal-box factory run by a man named Orienti employed twenty-five women. Every now and then a scream arose as a worker caught her finger in the machinery.

With the exception of Ivo, in kindergarten, the whole Livi family was now manufacturing brooms. To her teacher's distress, Lydia gave up school for good at the age of thirteen. Julien passed his high-school graduation exam with flying colors, and Giovanni, proud of this glittering achievement, took him on as a broom maker the moment his schooldays ended. Giuseppina, too, made brooms from the long sorghum grass stems, but she also looked after the house and took care of the young Bertolini, the landlord they had agreed to feed and keep in clean laundry. Bertolini had done his military service in the navy and gladly donated his old uniforms of coarse serge; Giuseppina cut them down for her sons. The rough cloth caused rashes and unbearable itching.

As time went on, the young man's presence became irksome. Lydia was growing up, and Giuseppina was worried that such close quarters might encourage intimacy. After two and a half years in Les Crottes, Giovanni found a small house in the Cabucelle neighborhood, and once more the Livis moved. Shortly afterward, Giovanni experienced the joy of a lifetime. On January 8, 1929, President Gaston Doumergue of France signed the Livi family's naturalization order. In conformity with French law, the decree was published in the *Journal Officiel* on January 20. At the age of eight, Ivo Livi had become a French citizen.

The impasse des Mûriers was an alleyway between little semidetached garden cottages, each with a small open space in front. The "garden" in front of number 7 was scarcely wider than a corridor in an apartment building. The house had four rooms. In the back, bedrooms looked onto a dirt mound that blocked out both view and light. But out front the former owners had rigged a miniature terrace covered with tar, which melted in summer. Modest though their dwelling was, with its postage-stamp patch of green, the Livis felt they had moved to another planet. Yet the alleyway was not paved, and in the absence of a drainage system children splashed about in the open channel dug out by wastewater. Much later, Montand could still remember the hearse that appeared at least once a month, strewn with white flowers, to take away the corpse of a child struck down by diphtheria.

The odd-numbered side of the alleyway ran alongside a big vacant lot. Across it was a small square boasting a modest little café—the Bar des Mûriers, which still stands today, and is the heart of neighborhood life. Beyond it, this somewhat rustic-looking enclave was hemmed in by factories. Fumes and smells of all kinds mingled with dust and industrial emissions to make a dense, grimy, thick atmosphere, a slurry, which became unendurable when stirred by the wind. Located at the very heart of this industrial conglomeration, the impasse des Mûriers seemed a fragile oasis indeed, its relative tranquillity ripped asunder at dawn by sirens summoning workers to the factories. It was the time of day when the working-class districts of Marseilles turned blue—the dark working-blue of the proletariat.

In the impasse des Mûriers, as in Les Crottes and Verduron, most of the inhabitants were immigrants. For years the city had owed its growth to the regular influx of imported workers on which its industries fed. "Marseilles," said one social historian, "teems with foreign denizens. Cosmopolitanism is its natural condition, inherent in the city's very nature, in its origins and in the tasks it performs."[1] At that time the ancient city

1. Gaston Rambert, *Marseille: La Formation d'une grande cité moderne* (Paris, 1934).

founded by Greek colonists boasted a population of 650,000, of which 250,000 were foreign-born. There were Greeks, Maltese, Spanish, Levantines, and even travelers come in from the northern cold, Britons and Germans; but the great majority of these fugitives from hunger, repression, or the need to remake their lives were Italian.

They would troop ashore on the quai de la Joliette, believing themselves en route for America (they rarely got there), or get off the train at the Gare Saint-Charles, or simply appear on the highway, dragging weary limbs and trailing their wrapped belongings. The first wave, swollen by destitution, broke over Marseilles at the end of the nineteenth century. By the eve of the First World War, one hundred thousand Italians were living in Marseilles, and an additional hundred thousand had just been naturalized. In all, almost a third of the city's population was of transalpine origin.

The Great War cut a terrible swathe through their ranks, for many new arrivals volunteered to fight in French uniform in hopes of being naturalized. One out of two lost their lives. At the end of the 1920s came the second immigrant wave, this time, as in the Livis' case, driven by political persecution. Marseilles became a refuge for Mussolini's victims and for scores of thousands of Armenians who had survived Turkey's genocidal policies.

The new arrivals tended to mingle with others from the same region. The *babis,* northern Italians, and the *nabos,* Italians from the south (*nabo* was derived from *Napoli*), piled up in successive surges of immigration and "colonized" whole neighborhoods. The Belle-de-Mai quarter was known as Little Italy, Saint-Mauron as Little Sicily. This massive presence triggered a powerful xenophobic reaction to the "Macaronis" who had come to steal jobs from "true" Frenchmen. But the kids, absorbed in their own world, were less aware of the racism around them.

> I had no real sense of being an immigrant. Of course, I heard occasional insults—"spaghetti eater" or "dirty macaroni"—but their real meaning and intention escaped me, went right over my head. I simply wondered, "What is that clown talking about?" At school we were all immigrants' children. There was no point in our teacher asking, "Who is French here?" All our names sounded foreign. Racism meant nothing concrete or comprehensible to me, nothing threatening, since all my pals were Italian, Armenian, Greek, or Spanish. Our neighborhood was a true melting pot. Nevertheless, some French people did behave in a racist fashion (although the expression didn't come along till later), sometimes very obviously. I remember a cop who lived not far from our house; his name was Coste, M. Coste. He wore fine lace-up boots

and a leather coat. When he cycled home at night, generally three sheets to the wind, he picked on anyone even slightly swarthy, hit them with his belt, insulted them. One day he was found lying out in the street, badly beaten up. The neighborhood had decided to inflict collective punishment.

Armenians lived in the house next door to the Livis—or, rather, in a shack they had built themselves, made up of two tiny but spotless rooms. The beds were simply planks nailed together, but Ivo, who had made friends with the children, was surprised to find a water carafe sitting on a hand-embroidered white tablecloth (an overturned soapbox served as the table). He quickly picked up a few words of Armenian, mainly those having to do with sex. Soon he knew enough to be able to sing Armenian songs (he remembered them for decades) and to understand their tales of genocide. In La Cabucelle people rubbed shoulders without thought or word of race, but there was still an unspoken pecking order among the different countries of origin. Ivo visited the Armenians, but they never came to his house. Giovanni, in fact, was not above considering his neighbors uncouth: some of them blew their noses without handkerchiefs and had other habits that shocked the Latins. On Saturdays, for example, the rickety shack that did service as their communal wash house was taken over by the men. Stark naked, they crouched modestly in big zinc tubs while their wives scrubbed their backs. The contrast between the white of those backs and the blue scars left by sacks of copra and cement, and the forearms burned brown by the sun, was startling.

The "Macaronis" had no intention of exhibiting themselves in this way. The Luchesis, the Lottis, the Innocentis, the Turchis, the Campaninis—all countrymen of the Livis, from Tuscany or Piedmont—kept their native customs intact. They liked to stroll to a neighbor's house for a game of cards, play bocci on the ground in front of the Bar des Mûriers, or engage in long Sunday discussions. Ivo stuck close by his father, listening to the terse political judgments regularly delivered by Luchesi, a tall, dry man with a small mustache and a wide-brimmed black felt hat.

"Bastards, every one of them," he would say. "They call themselves politicians? We should go to Paris and string them all up."

And Luchesi would glance for approval at Turchi, the wine merchant who understood nothing but had an opinion on everything. Giovanni Livi, who was listened to and respected for his gentle common sense, would interrupt to suggest that there might be solutions less extreme than hanging the elected representatives of the people. As the little group turned its gaze away from him, Luchesi, sensing that he was losing his hold, would fake a suffocating fit of coughing. His features purple, he thumped his chest with his fist, wheezing: "Don't worry, don't worry, it's just the gas." And at once the heroic *poilu,* gassed during the Great War, had his audience back in the palm of his hand. The scenario never varied; the same actors always played the same parts; everyone had a good time.

Ivo also admired Campanini, an old Tuscan who lived nearby. Huge, his ravaged features framed by elephantine ears, he hid two glittering eyes beneath the turned-down brim of a faded hat. Campanini always wore a heavy cord jacket, rose before anyone else, and breakfasted on onions or garlic and goat or Parmesan cheese. Montand remembered Campanini half a century later when he was putting together the character of Papet in *Jean de Florette* and *Manon of the Spring.*

Sundays were a different world. The factory sirens were still. Despite the unaccustomed silence, everyone, conditioned by a lifetime of early-morning awakenings, emerged from sleep at the same time as usual. But on Sundays you had time to laze in bed, to eat breakfast, or simply to talk. Sunday was also the day when workingmen took their baths. The Livis' small house had a washroom on the ground floor; the family took turns using it. Then the men put on white shirts and dark pants. Giovanni Livi looked especially dapper in a necktie and a pearl pin (artificial, of course). There was even a pen protruding from his breast pocket (although he possessed only the cap). He would stroll around the neighborhood like a prince, doffing his hat in greeting.

Sunday lunch was a solemn occasion for the Livi family, as it was for all the other Italians. At the bottom of his small garden Giovanni had built a hutch for a dozen rabbits and a half-dozen hens. These provided the basic raw ingredients for the Sunday feast, and Giuseppina had a thousand ways of cooking them. But the chosen animal was always stretched to cover several meals: Mama Livi served a cunning blend of breaded chicken morsels and vegetables, doing it so well that at the sight of the heaping golden helpings the diners briefly thought they were about to gorge themselves on poultry. The remains would be served at the evening meal and would add savor to the next day's soup—nothing was wasted. Sunday lunch naturally began with spaghetti, prepared by Papa Livi with the requisite solemnity and following an elaborate recipe Montand himself used throughout his life.

As befitted the head of the family, Giovanni monopolized the conversation at table. He often spoke of his determination to succeed, to struggle for something bigger and better than mere survival. The family's situation had improved since their days at Les Crottes. They never ran short of bread—the children wolfed it down in quantity. Montand has never shaken this habit, inculcated by need: he still eats bread with everything, even with pasta. During the week Giuseppina always made polenta, in enormous loaves sliced with a wire and seasoned with the remains of gravy or sauce. In short, they were no longer hungry. But deep down, Giovanni never stopped worrying. Despite this, the family's meals were merry. They joked, teased one another, laughed.

Montand would forever remain homesick for the warmth of those family gatherings. Twenty years later he tried to rekindle it by lodging Julien and his sister-in-law in his own house on the Place Dauphine in Paris. Steadfast and affectionate loyalty was always a Montand trait. Little Ivo—who never really went away—continued to need the protection of the nest; Montand's life and psyche were inseparable from this truth, and he drew astonishing strength and vitality from it, as well as a sudden fragility when the lifeline seemed to wear thin. Half a century later, Gérard Depardieu, his partner in *Jean de Florette,* felt the depth of these personal roots. "A character like Papet," he says, "comes from a long way back, and is nourished by all the experiences along the way. No one could have played the part as he did. When I met Montand I sensed in him what I had always missed—roots, a family, the permanence of a family. You sense a strength behind him, a survivor's strength. What touched me in Yves, what will always touch me, is the tribal loyalty. Montand is a real voyager. I mean, the child he once was has stayed alive within him."

> When I went back to the house on Sunday afternoons, around five, my mother would be standing over a mountain of laundry, ironing or darning. I sat down on a chair and watched her. It was the time when you begin to feel the sadness of the parting day. The vacation was over. Tomorrow the week would begin all over again. But sitting there with my mother, I felt happy. She would be in a gentle mood—most times she was abrupt and distracted. I still have inside me this vision of a beautiful face beginning to thicken with age, as she sang, "How our mother will weep when they murder her sons, dead for liberty."

The parents spoke Italian, and the children replied in French. Although the three young ones had quickly assimilated the new language, Giovanni had real difficulties, often wrongly using one word in place of another. As for Giuseppina, she Italianized the French language by tacking an *o* or an *i* on the end of every word. She called rabbit *lapino,* her version of the French word *lapin,* although the Italian for rabbit is *coniglio.* The name by which Ivo would later become famous was born of this rough-and-ready linguistic compromise. When supper was ready, Giuseppina would lean out the window to call her son in from playing in the street:

"Ivo, monta!"

What she was trying to say was "*Ivo, montes*" ("Come on up!"). But what stuck with the boy, heard across the roofs of Marseilles, was her stentorian Italian-French:

"Ivo, montaAAAA!"

Giovanni Livi was fiercely anticlerical; Giuseppina, deeply religious. But this union of hammer-and-sickle and crucifix—not uncommon in Italian families—went hand in hand with considerable tolerance. The three children had been baptized back in Tuscany (in deepest secret, Giuseppina had taken little Ivo to the priest wrapped in a dress she had embroidered herself; Valentin Giovanni Jacques Livi, Montand's son, wore that same christening dress at his baptism at the church of Saint-Germain-l'Auxerrois on March 27, 1989). Lydia had had her first communion at Monsummano before the family went into exile, for her mother believed that, as a consequence of the French Revolution, communion would be forbidden on French soil. Giovanni allowed his daughter to attend catechism classes in Marseilles, but one day the priest questioned the girl: Wasn't her father a red? Lydia said nothing, but from then on, of her own volition, she severed her ties with the Church.

The religious practices of the Livis, then, were moderate. Giovanni had no liking for the priesthood, but he opposed no one's beliefs. His wife never spoke of her faith but bore witness to it with furtive signs of the cross. Although she rarely went to church, she carried out her own personal rites, rooted in the Mediterranean soul: on All Saints' Day she set photos of family members recently deceased on the mantelpiece and lit two wicks floating in a bowl. The flames of memory flickered softly throughout the day.

Giuseppina was pious, austere, and literal-minded about her religion. Ivo was never initiated into the sacred mysteries, but he grew up with all the weight of Judeo-Christian guilt, all the pangs of original sin. More than anything else, sex was taboo.

> I must have been about four when, in all innocence, I discovered a girl's sex. We were sitting out in the schoolyard, both of us on our best behavior, and my hand came into contact with her little pussy. It was soft and nice, and we sat there smiling blissfully. Suddenly the teacher came out and yelled, "What are you up to?" I was very shaken, for I had no idea why she was so angry. But when teacher told my mother about our "crime," she grabbed my arm and shook me until I thought it would come off. "If you ever do that again," she said, "I'll tell Papa."

And a little later I was in the yard with a neighborhood kid from Les Crottes. We were examining penises. Mama saw me from the third-floor window. She leaned right out and yelled, "What are you doing? Come up this minute!" I obeyed, and she grabbed my ear and said, "One more time and I'll tell the police." I was six or seven, and once again I had no idea of the seriousness of my crime. But I was so scared that I came down with jaundice.

In the impasse des Mûriers a neighbor's daughter, Thérèse, agreed one day to let me feel her up in the corridor of our building, on condition that I buy her a chocolate bar with nut topping, which cost thirteen centimes. I accepted the terms. I no longer remember how I found the money, but I went to a candy store run by two plump sisters in black dresses who never sold anything because everything there was too expensive. I returned with my trophy and waited for an hour, but Thérèse never came down. I ate the chocolate myself. Perhaps, with my eight-year-old's wisdom, I realized that I had strayed into forbidden territory.

At home I never went naked in front of my father. You didn't talk about sex in Italian families. Never. Except to drive out sin: masturbation, which made you insane. One night, around the age of twelve, as I indulged in this hidden pleasure in the secret of my bed, I suddenly felt a sharp pain. My foreskin had slipped right down off the tip of my penis and refused to return. I began to panic, to blubber, not daring to whimper too loud, but soon the pain was unbearable and I let out a yell. My mother ran in and assessed the damage. She didn't say a word; she dashed to the kitchen for some oil, swabbed me down, and put things to rights. What shame, what embarrassment! Strangely enough, though, she didn't threaten me this time. Everything returned to normal. Well, not exactly, because after that brutal defrocking it was as if I had been circumcised. During the war I had the chance to appreciate just how much that accident might have cost me.

Ivo attended elementary school at 52 boulevard Viala; after the enforced academic retirement of Lydia and Julien, he was now the tribe's only hope (his father still saw him in a lawyer's robes). But he did not like school; he couldn't sit still and listen to someone talk. Since he was not permitted to leave, he daydreamed, with his gaze fixed on the teacher. The latter admitted to Lydia that he was baffled: "It's strange; he pays attention, no doubt about that. But he understands nothing, nothing at all."

Now it was Giovanni's turn to worry. "How is it you're so stupid, Ivo?"

"I don't know. I look at him while he's talking, and he thinks I understand, but I'm somewhere else, in Europe, in America. I don't remember anything, I get so bored."

"Ivo, if you don't try, you'll end up as poor as us, as unhappy. There'll be no way out."

"I'd like to like school, but I can't."

As an adult Montand believed that basic inequality begins there, between children who readily assimilate information and those who function differently, to whom a school bench is torture.

Ivo's mind was both elsewhere and busy. That same presence-absence that so disconcerted his teachers became a typical Montand characteristic, one that all his friends noted: a capacity for absenting himself in order to think about other things. He never stopped thinking and planning—an idea, an act, a show.

But Montand remembered the best of his teachers with gratitude. They were France's real soldiers between the wars—the teachers who smoothed the path into French life for the little immigrants flooding into their classrooms. M. Florian, an anarchist who faithfully celebrated each anniversary of the Paris Commune of 1871, used to pin large posters on the classroom walls. One of them depicted a pile of coffins higher than Mont Blanc, over the caption "The dead of the 1914–1918 war."

A second teacher, Bondu, a former infantryman, was determined to instill true republican spirit into his young charges. There was always a new phrase on the chalkboard whenever they entered his classroom. For example: "A spear thrust is nobler than a speech." The kids would scratch their heads uncomprehendingly. And Bondu would speak of the evils of libel, which could harm and even destroy a person. Sometimes he would bring a phonograph to help teach them how to distinguish among different musical instruments. Bondu, an archetypal teacher of the heroic age, even gave free private lessons to pupils who needed them. Ivo was one of these; he had to give up his Thursday afternoons (free time in France, where the school week ends at noon on Saturday) to go to the teacher's house, which was almost next door.

But Ivo was not cut out for studying, and as he grew older he preferred to seek his schooling in the streets and neighborhoods. On the way down to Calade there was an abandoned mansion on private grounds with an ornamental lake. The kids of La Cabucelle had chosen it for their escapades. Ivo Livi frequently pursued his "schooling" there. He inspected the old drawing rooms, the lofty, vandalized bedrooms. And he climbed to the very top of a tree, from which he could see the port, the sea, and the railway yards. Aloft one afternoon, he was startled to hear a sharp voice.

"What are you up to?"

His mother, skeptical about his devotion to school, had followed him. Slithering down with the speed of a squirrel, Ivo managed to dodge his mother.

"Just wait, I'm going to tell Papa!" she screamed.

That evening, Giovanni rolled ferocious eyes and pretended he was about to hit his worthless son (in fact, he never struck him). It would have taken more than that to keep Ivo in school. And now, at the age of ten, he had discovered a new and boundless playground: the port.

"She is a port," said one ecstatic aficionado, "and one of the fairest there is, renowned in every clime. Night and day, ships plow the most distant oceans in her behalf. She is a monarch of the main, a French lighthouse whose beacon floods the four corners of the earth with light. Her name is Marseilles."[2] Between the two world wars, the city, its prosperity long rooted in maritime trade, did indeed live and breathe through its port. Ships laden with cargoes from all over the world tied up at its miles of wharves. As early as the nineteenth century, a Marseilles reporter had noted that "Africa is its doorstep, Asia its outskirts, America its neighbor."[3]

From La Cabucelle, Ivo had to scramble down just a few hundred yards to sniff the exotic tang of the port. With his pal Marius Céréda, with whom he shared a desk at the back of the classroom and who was his companion in all his adventures, he roamed among bales off-loaded from the ships and watched the boiling activity at the Joliette docks, men and machines moving at a frenzied pace amid the moaning of foghorns and the dockers' yells. It is tempting to speculate about the two kids' dreams as the parting ships, so far away you would have sworn they were motionless, dropped slowly over the horizon.

Ivo and Marius concocted a thousand projects for flight to the open sea and the Statue of Liberty. They became skilled at their game, watching like hawks for the slightest lapse on the part of the men guarding the ships, alert for the right moment and the right place for slipping aboard. And, indeed, security was fairly slack—too many ships, too many warehouses, too many people. The boys broke into bunches of bananas still green and wrapped in straw, stole oranges and spices. Sometimes seamen caught them red-handed and gave chase, adding the thrill of pursuit to the boys' fun. The

2. Albert Londres, *Marseille: Porte du sud* (reprint: Marseilles, 1980).

3. Quoted in Philippe Joutard, "Marseille: Porte de l'Orient," *L'Histoire,* no. 69 (1984).

young pirates also watched for trucks loaded with unrefined sugar, which slowed down as they climbed the boulevard Barnabo toward the refinery; the boys swarmed over their sides, stabbing the sacks with knives and filling their pockets with the brown powder that spilled out. Needless to say, for children from La Cabucelle—children growing up in total destitution—such thievery seemed the finest and most legitimate of sports. "If it's there, take it" was their motto. A rough-and-ready system of ethics, perhaps, but on reflection Montand would feel that, all things considered, it was not a bad philosophy.

Ivo Livi and his friends took the most dangerous risks in their search for the ultimate thrill. And the best (or worst) of them all was the "tunnel game." You raced into the Mirabeau tunnel seconds before a train and ran like hell for the far end, without looking back. Behind you the locomotive spat and roared in a din amplified by the tunnel. The runner felt its hot breath. One slip on the gravel, one second's miscalculation, and you would be pulverized. But what a triumph to burst into the open at the end of the tunnel, conqueror of the murderous machine, and hurl yourself aside, breathless, gleeful, oblivious to the torrent of curses from the driver! Much later, the moviegoer Montand watched with an experienced eye as James Dean's car hurtled toward the cliff edge in *Rebel Without a Cause.* The best of scriptwriters, he concluded, was little more than a man remembering himself.

When he was not down in the port, Ivo Livi headed in the direction of the slaughterhouses. He was both fascinated and troubled by the sight of thousands of cattle running to meet their fate. The cattle came from North Africa; they were driven to the slaughterhouses on foot, prodded along by drovers. The slaughterers, wearing big gray smocks and cloth caps and carrying staves, were beefy, red-faced, loud-voiced men, who slapped the women working in the tripe section on the backside. Summer and winter, the women worked in the open, their arms up to the elbows in blood, intestines, and feces, amid warm steam and sickening smells. Ivo looked on in terror and fascination as the work of death proceeded: lambs whose bleating was like a baby's cry, pigs whose throats were slit just before they were thrust, still living, into tubs of boiling water, cows killed with poleaxes, horses with their heads covered by black hoods so that they would not skitter in terror as the hollow steel tube of the "gun" that drove a spike into their brains was set between their eyes. He heard the spasmodic scrape and rattle of hooves as the animal jerked and collapsed. At lunch hour the blood-spattered men wolfed down cold cuts and ham.

A lesson in humanity at the outset of the Depression . . .

Ivo Livi, a just-naturalized *babi,* was ten. He was learning about the world not from books but from the streets of Marseilles. He was growing up in the big extended "Macaroni" family that lived as closely as strands of spaghetti wrapped around a fork—by no means prisoners of their ghetto. And if the boy is father to the man, then Montand remained a child of La Cabucelle, even—perhaps especially—at the wheel of his Ferrari.

Early in 1930, a few months after the Livis had moved to the impasse des Mûriers, Giovanni decided to transport his broom factory there as well. He had left it at Les Crottes, but he no longer got along with Malberti, his landlord there. So he erected a hut in the garden of number 7 with a stove to smoke the sorghum stems. The whole family pitched in; it was hard work, and the sulfur vapors made it advisable to work outside as much as possible. Production struggled along, but Giovanni was not satisfied: he also wanted to start making brooms out of copra. He hired a capable woman who had learned the skill in a factory and paid her to train him. For a year, "Livi Enterprises" turned out sorghum and copra brooms, but it was slow, time-consuming work, done entirely by hand.

In 1931, Giovanni decided to move into higher gear. He called in an expert who quickly persuaded him to invest in better equipment. On the installment plan, Giovanni bought a magnificent machine that cost him 15,000 francs—a fortune, but he naturally hoped that it would soon pay for itself. Thinking big, and confident that success was just around the corner, he also bought a whole wagonload of sorghum. From a strictly commercial standpoint, it seemed a reasonable acquisition, for the price of sorghum was going up 50 percent a year. This time, Giovanni was sure he was about to hit the bull's-eye: "Just wait, Beppina, we're on our way, we're going to pay off all our debts, we're going to make money, the children will have everything they need." It was an optimistic view, and as the months went by Lydia heard it a lot. But Giovanni Livi, swept away by dreams of social improvement, or perhaps just of survival, failed to notice an event that had shaken America—the America he so desperately wanted to reach—and that would ruin him.

On October 23, 1929, as Wall Street's brokers helplessly watched the value of their shares plunge, they had no idea that the Black Thursday crash would have repercussions around the world, leading stage by stage to the deepest of depressions. It took two full years for the shock waves to reach France. But in September 1931, the devaluation of the pound triggered a currency collapse throughout the British Commonwealth, Latin America, and Scandinavia. Since the franc remained pegged to gold, the price of French products soared, along with the country's external trade deficit. In just eight months, between September 1931 and April 1932, industrial production fell off 17 percent and there was a rash of bankruptcies.[4] Giovanni had chosen the wrong time to go into debt.

It was a catastrophe. Giovanni was losing two francs on every broom he made, yet he had to honor his agreements and pay his suppliers. "It was terrible," Lydia Livi recalls. "My father was in despair. He paced around the house waving his arms. He had to return the machine, which he could no longer afford, but he still had to repay friends and acquaintances who had lent him small sums. He called them together and said, 'I've gone belly-up, but don't worry, we're going to carry on working, and every one of you will be repaid.' Every week Julien and I would deliver a small sum to one or two of them, usually just the interest payments."

Julien remembers the humiliation of having to go and hand over the few francs, perhaps a tenth of the sum owing, and the sarcasm and often xenophobic insults he had to take from some creditors. Once Yves Montand became a star and the constant target of requests for money, he found it hard to resist the tears of a mother begging him for help. It happened often, often enough to become tiresome; but almost every time, he would remember his father's debts and would give.

It was inevitable: In 1932, Giovanni Livi declared bankruptcy, with debts of 32,000 francs. The family was now without any means of support. At the same time, the Depression was filling the streets with unemployed men; the lines outside soup kitchens and unemployment offices grew longer and longer. The hungry organized in angry protest: In November 1933, "hunger marchers" left Lille to air their grievances in Paris, shouting for bread and work and singing "La Grève des ventres" ("The Strike of the Stomachs").[5] The average wage fell 15 percent. Between 1931 and 1935, the jobless rate doubled—but selectively, striking hardest at young people, women, and immigrants. Victims of the times, the last were also subjected to racist campaigns, for they were charged with "stealing Frenchmen's jobs." The Italians, as the most numerous minority, were particularly targeted. It was no good, the Livis waving their naturalization certificates: a piece of paper, whether or not it was stamped with the shield of the Republic, would not get them work or fill their stomachs.

Lydia saved the family.

For some time, she had been interested in hairdressing. She would cut the hair of her friends Riri and Lulu in a corner of the dining room, and in return they gave her a few francs, which allowed her to buy curling irons . . . and so it went. Word of her skill quickly spread, and the circle of her

4. Dominique Borne and Henri Dubief, *La Crise des années 30* (Paris, 1989).

5. Jean-Pierre Rioux, "Du pain, du sang et des rêves," *L'Histoire,* no. 58 (1983).

clients widened. Growing bolder, Lydia took a course at a hairdressers school, where you had to pay your guinea pig three francs an hour. It ate up all her savings, but she made progress and began to show true flair. Her reputation grew, and soon she was making a little money.

Julien found a job in a wharfside bar. Fifteen years old, he got up at 4:00 a.m. to pour drinks for longshoremen on the night shift; soon he knew them well. Like Lydia, he brought his pay home on Saturday evenings. As for Ivo, now eleven and a half, he left school without a backward glance and started work in a factory. It was Lydia who first heard of a job for him from a customer, Mme Guérin, whose husband manufactured noodles.

I had to lie about my birth date to get into the Guérin factory. They didn't hire under thirteen. Luckily I was very tall. My first job was to fill yellow cellophane bags with noodles. I sat in a cellar lit by a skylight, surrounded by piles of big jute sacks full of different kinds of pasta—shells, vermicelli, macaroni, spaghetti. I filled those little yellow bags ten hours a day. The biggest satisfaction came at the end of the week when I was handed an envelope with the fifty francs I had earned. The envelope was stuffed with coins, including one of the old-fashioned five-centime pieces with a hole in the center. I took the envelope home to my mother. She opened it and shook the contents on the table. Then she kissed me, pushed the small change over to me, and said, "That's for you!" And she added, half smiling, "Don't spend it all!"

Then I was promoted. I was transferred to the factory itself, among the women workers. The pasta was laid out in enormous drawers swept by a cross-ventilation system. Two of the women kept shifting the drawers around so that the pasta dried evenly.

I was their factotum. I moved packets of pasta around and swept up. The first step in the process was grinding the flour in enormous mills and turning it into dough. A male worker shoved the dough into a big cylinder, then a piston pushed it down, and it came out at the bottom in the form of shells, noodles, and so on. They fitted a different mold on the machine for each product. It was hard work. The man who put the dough in wore an undershirt and drank two or three liters of wine a day. He kept a cherrywood cigarette-holder in his mouth all day long. My job was to clean out the molds. On my first day, one of the women showed me some cockroaches around an electrical outlet above the vat where the noodles were left to soak. She handed me a glass of water.

Without thinking, I threw the water at the outlet to scare the roaches off and got a terrible shock. They were pleased as punch; they laughed. I began to hate them.

Ivo had been bored in school, but doing this painstaking, repetitive work, the twelve-year-old belatedly realized that classrooms had their point. Luckily, his boss, Raoul Guérin, a good man, perhaps a bit paternalistic, switched him to deliveries. Because of his height, Ivo was treated like a man. He had sought this promotion, but it proved to be an ordeal. At each stop he hoisted the heavy bags of pasta onto his back and sweated like a horse; but he gritted his teeth, determined not to show that the loads were too much for his skinny shoulders to bear.

He certainly no longer looked like a child. He had given up short pants while still at school. A photo from that period shows him with long pants on legs that seem endless. He is wearing a rather tight-fitting coat, with enormous hands sticking out of narrow sleeves. The scarf around his throat and the broad-brimmed cap give him the air of an outlaw.

When storekeepers offered the deliverymen a glass of pastis, Ivo Livi would have choked rather than refuse. His partner, Fouqué, the driver, took no notice of the boy, barely even speaking to him. When their work was done, he had no compunction about taking out an enormous sandwich stuffed with slices of ham and gulping it down beside Ivo—who would be chewing pieces of uncooked pasta, hard and tasteless—without ever offering him a bite.

One day, after two years of this life, Ivo's boss decided to dock from his pay the price of a demijohn of mineral water that Ivo had accidentally broken. Ivo fought back: he said that the demijohn was already cracked, that he had been jostled; he lost his temper and refused to pay what he considered an unjust penalty. He was fired. He was thirteen and a half, and out of work. But, as always, Lydia was there.

Lydia's salon was doing so well that it not only supported the family but generated enough money to pay off Giovanni's broom debts as well. Soon the little parlor they had fitted out in the house was no longer big enough. One of her customers, a maid who worked in the house across the street, told Lydia (conversations under the hair dryer were so instructive!) that the owner, a slaughterer at the abattoirs, might be willing to rent out space. At almost the same time, in December 1934, Lydia married André Ferroni, a worker at the sugar refinery; it was as Mme Ferroni that she signed the lease.

* * *

On December 13, 1982, Yves Montand returned to La Cabucelle. His great friend Jorge Semprun, the Spanish political author and screenwriter, went with him.

" 'How long has it been since you were last here?' I asked him.

"He shrugged, obviously in the grip of strong but suppressed feelings. 'I don't really know,' he said. 'Years, a whole lot of years!' "

The two men drove slowly through the neighborhood.

"He was looking at the low houses, the little yards leading off the lane. At first he had the feeling that nothing had changed. 'It's exactly the same,' he kept saying. But looking closer, trying to find the exact spot where he had lived, he lost his bearings. Suddenly everything looked different.

"He got out of the car.

"He was walking around with great strides, crossing from one sidewalk to the other, inspecting the impasse des Mûriers from every angle, looking up its nose, into its eyes, and sideways into its ears. He couldn't pinpoint the exact location of his childhood home.

"Suddenly he was sad and resentful. 'Come on, let's go,' he said. 'There's nothing to see here.'

"We got back into the car.

"Then, as we were leaving the impasse des Mûriers, he spotted a rectangle more faded than the masonry façade around it, just above a wall that had obviously been rebuilt. 'There!' he shouted."[6]

The paler rectangle that had caught Montand's attention had a faint inscription on it: "Coiffeuse Jacky." This sign had been repainted since Lydia's time, when it had read "Salon Lydia."

Once she had rented number 8, Lydia set up shop in an unused garage which she had repainted and tiled. Only nineteen, she had to dissociate herself from her family to obtain credit for the equipment she needed, for the name Livi was no longer creditworthy.

To cope with her growing clientele, Lydia asked the jobless Ivo to help her with shampoos (she had already hired her mother). Her little brother was now fourteen and growing fast: when agonizing spasms racked his spine and limbs, the doctor diagnosed growing pains and suggested that he remain on his back as much as possible. Ivo spent several days in bed, spoiled by everyone, then went back to his shampooing chores. Lydia was the next to fall ill—stricken by typhoid fever, which kept her from work for two months. But as soon as she was better she acquired the very latest mechanical marvel: an electric permanent-wave

6. Jorge Semprun, *Montand: La Vie continue* (Paris, 1983).

machine, with a helmet that fitted onto the customer's head. A special product was applied to the hair, which was rolled around aluminum curlers and then baked into place; it would keep its waves for at least six months. This was revolutionary technology, and to test it Lydia picked Ivo as her guinea pig. She prepared his hair, adjusted the machine, and plugged it in. The guinea pig at once began to scream and wave his arms and legs. "He was always playing the fool," says Lydia, "so I laughed when I saw him writhing and making faces. I told him to stop clowning and shook him by the shoulder—and got a shock. The current was running right through him . . . he was in the electric chair!" For a long time the permanent-wave machine was a family joke. No customer would ever understand the look that passed between sister and brother when they prepared to turn it on.

The assistant hairdresser's job was to pick up used towels, hair still clinging to them, brush them off in the next room, fold them carefully, and solemnly bring them back in as if they were clean linen. Mainly, though, he had to wash hair—the hair of supine women whom he would ordinarily never have approached, let alone touched.

> I received part of my sex education in my sister's salon. There is a Marseilles word, *espincher,* which means peeping without meaning to. Well, there I became a real Peeping Tom! I was the helper, the owner's kid brother, part of the scenery, and no one paid any attention to me, so I saw and heard everything. They would tell horrible stories about their husbands and lovers: "If he cheats on me, Lydia, you know what I'm going to do? Pour boiling oil in his ear while he's asleep." They thought they were unobserved; they were relaxed and dropped all modesty. They lay around in amazing positions.
>
> As I washed their hair, I massaged the backs of their necks. Their heads were thrown back, and I had a long plunging view down their necklines, and even farther, especially in summer, when their breasts had only a thin cotton covering. But the best was when I had to collect hairpins from the floor and scrambled about among their legs, with their feet on little footrests that made it easier for them to read under the dryer. Those legs would open and close unconsciously, which made it all the more exciting. I was fourteen, I didn't count, I was part of the furniture. It drove me crazy. One day a customer of around fifty actually put her hand on my crotch and said, "How nice your brother is." At once I heard my mother's voice: "Ivo, go and get me some number four shampoo." Yes, I learned a lot in my sister's salon.

The customers loved Ivo. He joked, laughed, and every now and then mimicked them. Then he would suddenly disappear: "Goodbye, ladies, it's teatime." In fact, the apprentice hairdresser raced to the Bar des Mûriers, thirty yards down the street. There a pretty barmaid named Bruna exerted a magnetic attraction on him—and not just on him. Plump, vivacious, high-spirited, Bruna was the life and soul of the bar, which belonged to her brother-in-law, a Piedmontese named Garone. He kept a watchful eye on her as she walked from table to table, flirting with one customer after another, crisscrossing the floor, repulsing advances. When the lunch-hour crowd filled the bar, Bruna had no time to linger, which is why resourceful Ivo chose the afternoon lull to venture his amorous approaches. They left her more or less indifferent. To the eighteen-year-old seductress, the Livi youngster was only a kid, and it amused her to see him eating his heart out for love.

After his midafternoon break he returned to the salon. His heart was not in hairdressing. His mind was miles away. His relations with Giuseppina were tense. She constantly nagged him, and even hit him with a broom (climbing on a chair, if necessary, to do so). Nevertheless, at his mother's urgent entreaty—she was anxious about his future and wanted him to learn a trade—the rebel agreed to attend professional hairdressing school. Two evenings a week he went into Marseilles to learn how to snip, curl, and wave. He liked it no better; indeed, he despised it as work unfit for a man. (Reflecting on it he told us he was wrong.) But the family was counting on him, so he conscientiously studied the nature of hair and different dyeing techniques. (Even late in life Montand could immediately detect a dye job on an entertainer or politician he saw on the TV screen.)

After a few months, Ivo took the exam for his professional barber's license. He needed someone to work on for the test, and a blond neighbor who worked in a shoe factory offered her own Harlow-like hair. Ivo gave her three successive waves and a platinum dye, using the "Maguy" technique. Whether it was his barbering talent or his model's resemblance to the Hollywood star, Ivo Livi came in first and won a medal. But his success did nothing to increase his enthusiasm for the trade he now feared would be his forever.

In just a few years, through endurance and hard work, Lydia had repaid every debt Giovanni had contracted while expanding his workshop. She had saved the family from destitution; even better, she provided a degree of well-being for her loved ones and herself. But Giovanni suffered. He was fully aware of the dimensions of the crisis he had led his family into, and his sense of guilt was only deepened by the fact that since his business failure he had been unable to find decent stable employment. These Depression years of crisis and forced inactivity were years of torment for the head of the clan—a man to whom dignity was everything. It was surely painful to be supported by his daughter (the Livi children do not like to discuss the subject). Luckily, Giovanni still had politics.

It was apparently in La Cabucelle that Giovanni Livi again made contact with Communists. Earlier, the fight for survival had filled his days, but in the early 1930s Comrade Livi, now past forty, became one of the Italian leaders of the Communist Party cell in La Cabucelle. He organized secret meetings in a bar called Chez Zitti, just across from the sugar refinery. The "Macaroni" Communists met in the cellar in their own "language group," but also as members in their own right of the French Party.

Most of Giovanni's zeal was reserved for the defense of immigrants, who were increasingly the target of assault. He also helped to prepare anti-Fascist propaganda: alongside a bricklayer, another Communist, he churned out tracts on an old manual press.

The police kept close track of political activity among the immigrants and worked tirelessly to suppress it, but Giovanni's recent naturalization spared him deportation. After a while he rose to control a whole group of Communist cells in the neighborhood.

Julien Livi was soon bitten by the same political bug. At the age of fourteen, while working for a few months at the Saint-Louis sugar refinery, he performed his first militant act. The temperature in the warehouse where he handled sugar crates reached as high as 120 degrees. Guzzling down water did no good: he was melting, liquefying. One day a supervisor criticized him for letting sweat drop onto the white granules as they were being prepared for packaging. Shortly afterward, Julien Livi and six comrades handed out a subversive leaflet, "The Red Refiner," denouncing working conditions at the factory. He was immediately fired.

After this, he found himself in a drinking hole in the port, where he got to know the denizens of the waterfront. While his kid brother Ivo stole unripe bananas, Julien teetered on the brink of delinquency. "I know I was close," says Julien. "If I had not already had a sense of political commitment, an attraction for collective struggle, I would have become a punk, a petty gangster. The temptation was just too strong in the port. It wasn't closely guarded or closed off in any way. You saw all kinds of wealth come ashore in sacks—one nick and you helped yourself."

In February 1933, just before his sixteenth birthday, Julien Livi became a member of the Communist Youth Movement. In Germany only a few days earlier, on January 30, Adolf Hitler had been named Chancellor. "It is midnight in the twentieth century," wrote the Communist intellectual Victor Serge. The harshness of the Depression, the revolving-door nature of successive and chronically unstable French governments, ubiquitous corruption, and, of course, the example of the successful Italian and German "models" gave birth to many extreme right-wing associations. Charles Maurras's Action Française movement—monarchist, antiforeign, anti-Semitic, traditionalist—enjoyed spectacular growth. His shock troops, who called themselves *"Les Camelots du Roi"* (The King's Men), were seasoned street fighters who roamed about unopposed. But the real mass movement of the right wing was the Croix de Feu (Cross of Fire), which started out as a league of decorated veterans. Led by Colonel de La Rocque, a former officer on Marshal Foch's staff, the antiparliamentary, nationalistic, violent Croix de Feu numbered one hundred thousand members in 1933. They professed no anti-Semitic beliefs but adopted the techniques of Italian Fascists to clear the streets and hunt down far-left militants.

Opposing these extreme right-wing groups was the main activity of young Communists, and there were clashes with fists and clubs. Julien Livi was one of the first to throw himself into the fray. More than once he returned to the impasse des Mûriers badly battered. It did nothing to cool his zeal. Soon he joined the Communist Party proper, which won him the right to sit in on his father's secret meetings at the café Zitti. At that time the Party imposed on members the ultrasectarian line decreed by the Communist International: "defense of the Socialist fatherland." This simply meant blind support of the Soviet Union and, in France itself, pursuit of the "struggle of class against class." The latter goal held that outside the Communist Party, all political parties were considered the same, all being equally class enemies, and that therefore there was no point in allying with the Socialists. This suicidal policy, which in Germany had hastened Hitler's rise, puzzled the French rank and file. It resulted in an inward-looking French Communist Party and a drying-up of support. Within just a few years, the Party lost half its members; by 1933, it numbered only thirty thousand. But bloody riots on February 6, 1934, forced the Communists out of their isolation: On that night, veterans associations and extreme right-wing groups laid siege to the Palais Bourbon, France's parliament—they were protesting the Stavisky financial scandal, which involved a Russian promoter who had floated a fraudulent bond issue, and which royalists and Fascists believed had reached up into political circles—and the *gardes mobiles* (riot police units) opened fire, killing fifteen and wounding two thousand. The clash did not directly threaten the government, but, more than the event itself, the perception of it on the left set off a chain reaction. Stunned by these developments, Communists and Socialists were pushed by their rank and file into taking a stand. On February 12, in a show of anger at the rebellious right-wingers, the two groups joined forces in Paris amid shouts of "Solidarity!" On that same day, 346 demonstrations were organized nationwide: as in the capital, the opposing brothers, Communists and Socialists, embraced.

In Marseilles too, leftists were swept along on a new tide of solidarity. "The crowds were huge," recalls Julien Livi. "Two processions, Socialist and Communist, met on the Canebière. My comrades were outside the employment exchange on the rue de l'Académie, under orders to defend it. The *gardes mobiles* charged. I remember being hit on the back of my neck. When I came to I was covered with blood. Worse, though, the new pants Mama had made for me were in tatters."

The Fascist peril forced the French Socialists and Communists to re-examine their policies. In June 1934 they held a conference at Ivry: it began with a rehash of the vital importance of the class struggle and ended with a call for unity no matter what. This complete about-face was triggered by a telegram received in midsession from the Comintern in Moscow. "Everything changed in a twinkling," said the future prime minister Léon Blum in *Le Populaire* on July 8. On July 27, the Communist and Socialist parties signed a pact calling for concerted action. This was the beginning of a trend that led to the grouping of left-wing movements known as the Popular Front. This new political direction was immediately beneficial to the French Communist Party, which shook off its siege mentality and in the course of the next year doubled its membership.

Julien, hanging around the port all day, found work on the docks as a casual laborer. Hiring took place at dawn and depended on the jobs going around. But one winter morning, Julien and other longshoremen struck to protest a job they considered too dangerous: the narrow plank ladder up which they were supposed to carry sugar sacks aboard ship was slippery with snow, and their numbed fingers could not handle the bulky bags. Singled out as a ringleader, Julien was never hired again. By the force of events he now became a professional, almost full-time Party worker.

The Popular Front's election victory convinced him that he had made the right choice. Its parliamentary majority in the election of May 1936 was by a mere five hundred thousand votes, but a spontaneous wave of strikes swept through factories and offices before Léon Blum had even had the time to form a government. By June, 2 million workers had put down their tools, primarily in private industry—metallurgy, textiles, and catering. To Julien, it was bliss. He was everywhere at once, addressing crowds of workers. As a delegate for the food-industry unions, he stepped in at every opportunity in breweries, refineries, chocolate factories, and hotels. He worked day and night, sleeping virtually wherever he dropped; he no longer had time to bathe; he walked the soles off his shoes. Ecstatic at this chance to shape history—he was only eighteen—he rarely went back to La Cabucelle.

With his father a neighborhood commissar and his brother a professional agitator, Ivo lived and breathed Communism. In his later years he often said he was born a Communist, born draped in the red banner. To him, his father was the embodiment of generous values, which he instinctively embraced. His father could not be wrong. And Communism singled out the very best, those ready to give their lives for the future happiness of humankind. How could you not want to belong to such an elite?

At the family table, Ivo absorbed half-understood ideas pregnant with mystery and promise: social revolution, the proletariat—notions that became permanent features of his thinking without his ever fully grasping their meaning. He heard talk of Giorgi Dimitrov, who had heaped ridicule on Nazi charges at his Leipzig trial; or of Ernst Thaelmann, secretary-general of the German Communist Party, deported by Hitler to Buchenwald, where he died in 1944. Those two, alongside Thorez and Togliatti, formed part of the pantheon of positive heroes clustered about Stalin, that living god whose name Ivo's father, voice trembling, would sometimes invoke. Communists truly had two countries: their own and the Soviet Union.

And Giovanni gave his own papers to a comrade who had fled Mussolini's Italy so that he and his family could get to the USSR. Telling this story, Lydia commented, "Perhaps he lost his life there in the gulag, still with his Livi identity card. . . ." But for now Giovanni did not ever think that islands of suffering and death—so numerous as to be an archipelago—were scattered across the workers' paradise. He dreamed. In Stalin's homeland, everything was bigger and better. The Soviets were building a finer, eternally braver, world. The proof of this, he told his son, was that they were building roads of steel!

"*Ti rendi conto,* petit, *fanno anche delle strade d'accaio!*"

And his certainties were equally steely.

Ivo was already going to parades as a small boy. Later he would remember one peaceful and good-natured May Day parade, and another, distinctly more violent, where for the first time he saw the *gardes mobiles* charge to disperse the "rabble."

When the Popular Front came to power in France, Ivo was not yet fifteen. Too young to throw himself into the movement, he looked on a little enviously at his brother's brief triumphant returns from meetings and demonstrations. Sentimentally, he was "one of them." He read Communist magazines—*Rouge-Midi* or *L'Avant-Garde.* But when Julien left *Les Cahiers du Bolchevisme* lying around, full of prophetic frescoes and arid concepts, he was lost.

On July 17, 1936, there was a military revolt against the Spanish government (it, too, was called the Popular Front; it, too, had been narrowly elected), and soon General Franco's mutinous forces were locked in civil war against the Republicans. While Blum's government justified a policy of nonintervention by raising the specter of more widespread war, and while the Luftwaffe's Stukas in 1937 brushed aside such scruples and wiped Guernica off the map, Communists everywhere called for volunteers to reinforce the International Brigades fighting alongside the Republicans. Now nearly twenty, Julien Livi burned to join them, but the Party decided he was both too green and too young. When he was turned down, Giuseppina sighed with relief. But the whole family, including Ivo, trembled along with the Albacete and Teruel brigades, the defenders of Madrid. Until Franco's death, Montand carried this Spanish wound within him. It was still gaping thirty years later, when he played the part of Diego, an underground opponent of Franco, in Alain Resnais's *La Guerre est finie,* based on a script by Jorge Semprun.

Ivo Livi never joined the Communist Youth Movement, as many young people from his background did almost automatically. In families close to the Party, joining up early was often the norm: Julien's experience was proof of that. The truth is, the runt of the Livi family shrank from getting too deeply involved in militant activity. He was ready and willing to share hopes and lyrical illusions that wrung the heart and brought tears to the eyes, but he was repelled by ideological squabbles and ritual phrasemaking. He always had a strong distaste for abstract hortatory rhetoric, and the question of his formal membership in the Party never even arose. Besides which, there was the discipline of the militant's life—errands, the distribution of tracts in the early-morning cold, street fights, cell meetings. None of that interested him. Ivo had no vocation for self-sacrifice; he sensed confusedly that his road led elsewhere.

It was enough for him to belong in his heart.

At the end of 1936, Ivo Livi, aged fifteen, took a job at a relatively elegant hair salon called Chez Yvonne et Fernand in the center of Marseilles. Although he now had his diploma, Ivo still had to wash hair and do odd jobs like brushing off towels, as he had done at his sister's salon, to gain experience.

Many of Yvonne and Fernand's customers were prostitutes who plied their trade nearby, around the Opéra, and they needed to have their hair done frequently. Ivo listened to their edifying conversation and filled out his sex education. But he had eyes only for the cleaning woman at the salon, a forty-year-old Greek. One evening he got up the courage to follow her home. He rang the doorbell, but when his beloved opened the door and asked him what he wanted, he stood there speechless, then ran. Ivo was still an innocent, even if the Campanini boys, Toré and Mario, twenty-five-year-old gay blades who rode motorbikes, had once taken him to a brothel near Estèque-Plage.

Close by Yvonne and Fernand's was the headquarters of the Parti Populaire Français, created in June 1936 by Jacques Doriot, a Communist renegade who had shuttled to the far right. A curious blend of revolutionary fervor and worship of order met there alongside the cult of the Leader and a hodgepodge of Fascist-style antiparliamentary thinking. Marseilles was one of the strongholds of the PPF, and its local boss, Simon Sabiani—also an ex-Communist—was undeniably picturesque: standing halfway between politics and organized crime, he ruled a world of street fighters, criminals, and politicians.

As deputy mayor of Marseilles, Sabiani often called on the services of two high-flying lawbreakers, Paul Carbone and François Spirito, whose men ruled the back streets and the underworld. The former had done his military service in the dreaded punitive units known as the Bataillons d'Afrique, in those days the adult-education course for the future elder statesmen of organized crime. After earning the Médaille Militaire at the Battle of Verdun, Carbone had turned sailor and tramped about the Far East, periodically returning with consignments of opium. Marseilles in the 1920s was emerging as a hub of the world drug market and a center for the processing of raw opium. Business boomed for Carbone. He also dabbled in the white-slave trade, in cahoots with Spirito, whose girls, in homage to his elegant air and great height, christened him "Old Buggywhip."

The two cronies, part of Sabiani's bodyguard, had their moment of glory at the time of the Stavisky scandal. On February 20, 1934, after the notorious embezzler's "suicide" had apparently cloaked his ill-doing behind a providential swirl of fog, the papers suddenly had more news: the prosecutor, Albert Prince, a financial expert who had been in charge of the Stavisky case, was found dead on the railroad track near Dijon on the Paris-Marseilles line. A hasty inquiry led to the arrest of Carbone and Spirito. Within hours, thousands of posters went up on the walls of the ancient Greek city: "People of Marseilles, Carbone and Spirito are my friends! I will not allow a hair of their heads to be harmed!" It was signed, "Simon Sabiani, Deputy Mayor." There could have been no more obvious token of the interdependence of politicians and the barons of organized crime. The charges against them dropped, Carbone and Spirito were greeted at the Gare Saint-Charles by hundreds of enthusiastic demonstrators. They resumed their illicit life style and even played at being benefactors of society.

In October 1938, the Radical Socialists held their annual party conference in Marseilles. There, the prime minister, Edouard Daladier—who had taken office in April, ten months after the first Popular Front government had fallen—delivered a speech peppered with such sterling thoughts as, "The road I have chosen is the best one because there is no other." (On September 30, he had signed the Munich Pact, which broke France's commitments to Czechoslovakia and handed that country to Hitler on a plate.) While the Radicals were debating, a fire gutted the Nouvelles Galeries department store on the Canebière, and more than a hundred people died in the flames. What Daladier apparently feared most was that the fire might spread next door to the Hôtel des Nouailles, where he was staying; two women who had escaped the blaze were trapped there on a ledge and screaming for help, one of them a "friend" of his who had come with him to the conference. Who dived into the furnace to save these poor ladies? Carbone and Spirito![7] Criminals, perhaps—but with what panache . . . and what a sure instinct for mythmaking!

Like Sabiani, the strongman of Marseilles, his henchmen Carbone and Spirito were card-carrying PPF members. On his way home from Yvonne and Fernand's, Ivo Livi grew used to the sight of these dons and their bodyguards in their regular barroom hangouts around the Opéra, where most of the city's dope peddling went on. Every so often his boss sent the boy to get him a sandwich at the bar across the street, and the intimidated teenager slowly got to know this shrine of debauchery: the customers in their borsalinos—soft, light-gray felt hats—their silk shirts, and their showy, custom-tailored suits were perfect caricatures of the gangsters so many French writers of the time, including Blaise Cendrars and Henri de Montherlant, sought out in their exotic haunts. Albert Londres ventured into the Marseilles underground and emerged with a picture that must have been close to what Ivo Livi observed. As he wrote in his book on Marseilles: "It is another country. The men wear caps, but fine, costly caps, of light tan and fawn. Their shirts are exquisite; their clothes are brand-new. Judging by their gleaming footwear, none of these gentlemen ever walks. Some sit in the gloom away from the bar. They play cards or converse. Others lean against the bar in deep thought. From time to time

7. Jean Bazal, *Le Clan des marseillais* (Paris, 1974).

some of them actually stroll out onto the sidewalk. . . . This is the underworld's undisputed turf."

Montand, in a book of memoirs composed with a ghostwriter, *Du soleil plein la tête* (*A Head Full of Sunshine*), recalled the revulsion one particular villain aroused in him: "He was fat and of indeterminate age. He looked like a huge toad. The man sent shivers down my spine. Behind his face I saw crime personified, the true worm-eaten face of crime, lurking in the depths of a horrible nightmare." One afternoon, as he worked shampoo into a customer's scalp, the apprentice hairdresser heard a noise in the street outside like a firecracker going off. Across the street a man lay dead on the sidewalk. In a classic settling of accounts, the underworld had just given Ivo Livi his first sight of a human corpse.

By his seventeenth birthday, Ivo had almost reached his full height. At just under six foot one, his lanky silhouette was accentuated by extreme skinniness. His shoulders were narrow, his arms thin; he looked as if he were perched on stilts. In fact, the Italians in his neighborhood called him Gambarina (in Italian, "legs" are *gambe*) because of his resemblance to a stock commedia dell'arte character. Ivo disliked his appearance: he considered himself ugly, with a big nose and a huge mouth that split his face. (Another of his nicknames was *"Mouche,"* or "Mouth.") When he caught sight of himself in the mirrors at the hair salon, his adolescent awkwardness doubled.

So Ivo did his best to be invisible. Appearing in public terrified him. Devoured by shyness, cripplingly timid, he found even the most ordinary gestures an effort. When he took a tram he stayed on the platform instead of sitting inside in order not to meet all those staring eyes. When he finally conquered this imaginary danger, braving the gaze of his fellow travelers and taking a seat, he felt he had won a victory. It was a victory over nameless fears that gnawed at him then and always, no matter how relaxed he seemed on stage.

On one occasion, Ivo went to the Pathé cinema to see an entertainer named Magdaléna, who as a guest artist did imitations of Fred Astaire and Stan Laurel during the intermission. He had saved up for two weeks to treat himself to an eight-franc balcony seat. He wore an overcoat because it was cool, but inside it was baking hot. Throughout the show, Ivo Livi sweltered in his coat, stifling but not wanting to take the coat off for fear he might disturb people or that his long arms would attract attention. One of his heroes, Errol Flynn, was on the screen playing Robin Hood. Ivo knew every frame by heart: he was much better at absorbing the information on the silver screen than he had been at following classes on the blackboard.

For the true—indeed, the only—passion of this teenager in search of himself was the movies.

His first visits were to a theater on the rue de Lyon in La Cabucelle, the Idéal (now a garage). As president of the Cannes Film Festival in 1987, Montand recalled the beginnings of his love affair with the cinema in a nostalgic address: "I fell into movie madness the way you fall in love, just like that, a chance encounter that seemed of no importance at the time. . . . It was in Marseilles in 1930, just before my ninth birthday. On the posters outside was my heart's desire. Her name was Marie Glory."

Many other monarchs of the screen followed Marie Glory into Ivo Livi's heart: Clara Bow, Gloria Swanson, Greta Garbo, Mae West, Joan Crawford. . . . The movies filled his dreams, his spare time, his whole life. He preferred Humphrey Bogart's murderous pallor and light-gray checked suit or the supple gait (which he longed to imitate) of Gary Cooper to the most martial of Maurice Thorez's calls to Communist action or Léon Blum's most eloquent rallying speeches. But his model was Fred Astaire, the man who danced so effortlessly alongside Ginger Rogers in *Roberta* and *Top Hat.* For him, the best movies were musicals.

> I used to go to the two o'clock performance at the Idéal. For a forty-centime copper you got a seat in the bleachers. A couple of francs more and you had a wooden folding chair that made a racket when you got up. The balcony was the place where kids who were going steady went to make out in the dark. You sat through two showings; during the intermission you ate Frigolos—chocolate-coated vanilla ice cream. There I saw most of the classics of the time, as well as cartoons.
>
> When I was working for Yvonne and Fernand, I used to visit a little movie house near the port, the Etoile, on the rue de l'Arbre, where they showed American films in *"version originale,"* meaning undubbed, in their original language. I had no idea what the letters "V.O." meant, but I went there to hear American spoken. It was Hollywood's golden age. What I liked best was the musical comedies. I adored Fred Astaire and Eleanor Powell. Tap-dancing numbers in particular excited me. I even took lessons from an Armenian who taught me that in order to go tap-tap with your feet you have to move your whole body. I wanted to dance like Fred Astaire. And when I saw Gary Cooper, I thought I really was Gary Cooper. I practiced smiling the way he did. It was a dream life.

> And behind this fascination with American movies was the attraction of the United States. It was strange for a kid brought up in a Communist household, but to me America represented democracy, justice, the pursuit of happiness, freedom. It was the Roosevelt era, and the ideals of the New Deal impregnated every American film. My love of movies and my love of America were mutually reinforcing.

In the 1930s, the movies became the major entertainment for every class of society. The advent of talkies, the low cost of tickets, and the physical improvement of theaters and sound systems attracted weekend throngs of ordinary people in search of thrills, hope, and escape. The team of Marcel Carné and Jacques Prévert was especially prolific, turning out *Drôle de drame, Quai des brumes,* and *Le Jour se lève* (the magazine *Pour Vous* published a superb photo of the star of *Quai des brumes* on its cover in May 1938 with the caption "This is Michèle Morgan, one of the hopes of the French cinema, her features exquisitely chiseled and melancholy, her half-veiled gaze hinting at fathomless sadness"). Despite the harshness of the Depression years and the darkening international political climate, French moviemakers from Julien Duvivier to Jean Renoir strove to kindle hopes of a better life and to glorify brotherhood. This "Popular Front" mood, this "comrades first and foremost" spirit, whose atmosphere of riverside dance halls and fairground music was so deftly captured in Duvivier's *La Belle Equipe,* seemed to make little impression on Ivo Livi. No doubt this child of the slums was looking for something more than a mirror, no matter how encouraging that mirror might be. Neither Jean Gabin, France's most popular star, nor the truculent Mediterranean actor Raimu, nor Michel Simon, whom Montand later admired highly, set Ivo on fire. What made his imagination race, what cast him adrift and dreaming for days at a time, were the pictures that came from across the Atlantic.

"He was crazy about the movies," says his sister Lydia. "He would do anything to see a film. One day at Yvonne and Fernand's he heated the curling iron white hot and closed his palm on it. It gave him a blister as big as a pigeon's egg. No question of any more work that day! My mother felt so sorry for him: 'Poor little darling, what terrible luck!' Later he admitted to me that he had deliberately burned himself in order to be able to go to the movies that afternoon."

The young Marseillais tried hard to resemble his gods, or at least to imitate them. He longed to wear Bogart's hats, Clark Gable's suits, the light cashmere jackets Hollywood stars favored. It was the highlight of his seventeenth year when he ordered a tweed jacket at a men's store on the rue de Paradis, High Life Tailleur, which carried the kind of clothes his heroes wore. A whole year's savings vanished at a stroke—but watch out Gary Cooper! Ivo Livi was on his way. Or, rather, as Giuseppina used to shout across the roofs of La Cabucelle:

"Ivo, montaAAAA!"

Chapter 3

Yves Montand was born when Ivo Livi had his seventeenth birthday. By what miracle, though, did this painfully shy teenager, this hairdresser's apprentice fearful of meeting the stares of his prostitutes clients' protectors, this skin-and-bone "Macaroni" who swallowed half his words in a thick, outlandish accent—how did he ever catch fire before the footlights? The story strains the imagination, but this is how it goes.

Once upon a time, on an autumn evening in 1938, Julien and Ivo leaned side by side over a window ledge at number 8, impasse des Mûriers. Encounters between the two brothers were becoming rare. The political militant and union activist devoted his days to the Cause. He rarely returned to La Cabucelle until late at night, and if he sometimes stayed around on Sunday mornings it was for love of a girl he was seeing. Her name was Elvire. She had known the Livis for ages, had played a lot of knucklebone with Ivo in the past, and had entrusted her hair and her secrets to Lydia. She was already almost one of the family.

But Julien was in no mood for fun that night. He had just received his draft papers from the army, and because of his political leanings he had been assigned to a disciplinary regiment near Mulhouse, far north in Alsace, near the German border. From their first-floor windowsill the two boys were looking down at the bowling area in front of the Bar des Mûriers, which, as often happened on a Saturday night, had been turned into an open-air theater. "The stage was perched on trestles and wooden beams used during the week for scaffolding. Sacks and tarpaulins had been hung to create a rough-and-ready backstage, and metal chairs were lined up in front of the café for the spectators, who arrived in little groups, the men wearing undershirts if it was hot, the women clutching kids who tugged to get away." Years later, Montand used these words in his book

Du soleil plein la tête to describe the scene: the picture had been imprinted upon him. An upright piano (out of tune, of course) was hoisted onto the platform. Lights set out on the ground illuminated the efforts of the amateurs, who did their best amid jeers, whistles, and occasional applause. "There we were at the window," says Julien Livi. "Yves was criticizing the kid who was trying to sing. Not very nicely, I said to him, 'Think you could do as well? No! Then shut your mouth!' "

This remark by his big brother, already a man, triggered the decisive move. Do as well? Climb onto that stage? Start singing? However improbable it may seem to us today, knowing what we know, the seventeen-year-old Ivo Livi had never sung, outside a few school choir numbers. No one had ever heard him sing anything. And this totally inexperienced youth, clumsy and beet-red with embarrassment, now approached the organizer of the Saturday-night entertainments.

His name was Francis Trottobas. "I knew him well," Lydia remembers. "I used to do his wife's hair, and sometimes he came to the salon with her. One day I told him about Yves. 'My kid brother annoys me,' I said. 'He doesn't want to be a hairdresser any more. All day long he tries to imitate Fred Astaire; he's even learning to tap-dance. He's getting on my nerves.' And Trottobas said, 'That's just the kind of act I need as an opener . . . someone to warm up the audience.' That's how Yves began." (By Montand's own account, he sought out Trottobas on his own, since he had often seen him bedding down his donkey and cart for the night outside the Bar des Mûriers.)

Trottobas seemed not unduly surprised by this sudden desire for a new vocation.

"So you want to sing? Well, you can start at once."

He took the young man under his wing, gave him the address of a pianist to practice with, and suggested that he choose two or three lively, catchy songs to win over the boisterous Saturday-night crowds. Ivo did not hesitate a moment over his repertory. In that year of 1938, a singer he idolized and longed to imitate had burst upon the scene. Charles Trenet electrified him (as Montand said a thousand times) with a thrilling jolt of dreamy yet intelligent lyrics and a new, different rhythm: *"Je chante, je chante soir et matin. . . ."* Trenet's inspired songs had invaded the French airwaves and the streets and entered the cafés via Vitaphones—the ancestors of the jukebox. In Marseilles, Ivo Livi shut himself in for hours, absorbing his idol's music and words.

So when Trottobas advised him to choose "heartwarming" songs, the budding entertainer was ready. He chose "Boum!" which had won Trenet the Grand Prix du Disque, and "La Vie qui va." On top of this, he had long been cultivating his genuine talent for mimicry with imitations of Donald Duck and Popeye, and he added to these a skit written by the great French comedian Fernandel.

Trottobas sent him to rehearse with a piano player who worked in a dark and dusty apartment on the top floor of a building on the boulevard National, a woman of advanced years whose white hair and spectacles emphasized her severity. She had accompanied enough budding stars to be on intimate terms with the worst croaks and the shakiest false notes, but when she heard Montand she could not believe her ears.

After three songs, her verdict was given: "You sing off-key, you can't keep time, and I don't understand a word you're saying. Do you really want to be a singer?"

Montand was shaken. Seeing him so crestfallen, the pianist softened her tone—well, at least the novice knew all the words, and there was no denying his energy—and gave him a few words of encouragement: "Audiences aren't hard to handle. They want you to be sincere, to put your heart into it. You must learn to carry your heart in your mouth, that's all."

Her "that's all" covered a lot of ground. It meant, Ivo Livi realized, that he must somehow learn to make it all look simple, to mask tireless work and endless rehearsing behind an appearance of facility and total spontaneity.

He emerged from the ordeal determined to fight. Until now a carefree teenager motivated by nothing in particular, Ivo Livi came to espouse a life of dogged, unrelenting discipline that astounded his nearest and dearest. Shut away in the narrow confines of the listening booths in record stores, he listened over and over and over again to Trenet's songs, tirelessly repeating the same lines. This change from idle adolescent to workhorse was marked by a change of name. It was now that Yves Montand shouldered Ivo Livi aside. Trottobas had had little trouble persuading him that his name would not look right on a music-hall program and suggested that he invent a stage name that "sounded good." Trottobas had in mind "Yves Trechenel," a synthesis of TREnet, CHEvalier, and FernaNdEL. But Ivo almost at once hit upon "Montand," in memory of his mother's evening call. Later, he analyzed the genesis of his stage name: "Since I was born in Monsummano, I kind of blended my native village with my mother's Italianized French. It came out as Montand."[1] In any case, the family approved. "Montand is fine! With a name like that, he'll be climbing forever!"

After a few weeks of rehearsal, the big day arrived. Montand had been working on a Chevalier song, "On est comme on est," and had kept the

1. *Candide,* May 22, 1967.

two Trenet titles, enlivening "Boum!" with "jazz" onomatopoeia borrowed—remotely—from Louis Armstrong:

La pendule fait tic tac tic tic
Les oiseaux du lac font pic pic pic pic
Glou glou glou font tous les dindons
Et la jolie cloche fait ding ding dong
Mais . . .
Boum!
Quand notre coeur fait boum . . .

[The grandfather clock goes tick tock tick
The birds on the lake go pick peck pick
Gobble gobble gobble go the turkeytoms
And the church bells go ding ding dong
But . . .
Boom!
Oh when our hearts go boom . . .]

Trottobas had found a small theater with about thirty feet of audience space at the Vallon des Tuves in the Saint-Antoine neighborhood. Once inside the cramped, whitewashed space that served as a dressing room, divided by a threadbare curtain supposed to separate the sexes, the novice was seized by a fit of panic that knocked his legs out from under him and swept everything out of his head. Suddenly he thought he would never make it. He looked at his face in the mirror, drained by terror. He forced himself to focus on details. He checked his stage clothes: a light gray suit, a little tight by now, which he had had to let out; white shirt, blue tie. To hide a steel dental filling he had bought some white mastic at Hollywood Cosmetics, a store on the rue Sainte-Barbe. Would the camouflage work? This minor anxiety, instead of distracting him from his general terror, added to it.

Montand never remembered how he managed to sing, had no recollection of going on stage: all memory of the event until the moment he realized his act was over was gone.

But he had done it. As he collapsed, soaked and exhausted, onto a chair in his dressing room, his memory gradually returned.

Trottobas came in and embraced him. He was voluble and warmhearted: "Wonderful! Don't you worry, I'll stick by you. You'll see, I'll get you to the Alcazar yet."

Montand had not even realized he'd been singing, but the Saint-Antoine audience had—and they had raised the roof. The newcomer had passed his test. He had also earned fifty francs. For many years Montand claimed that it was the fees that kept him going. It seems an unacceptable explanation. That first modest sum—barely enough for a week's worth of cigarettes—could not possibly have forced an introvert like Montand to make such painful public efforts.

> It's really strange. Was it a case of a double identity? Had my body merely been the vehicle for someone else? Who was that guy climbing onto the stage? Was he really the runt of a family of Tuscan peasants? What on earth drove him to play entertainer? I have to watch him from outside, because my whole being, everything I am, recoiled from public exhibition. I have tried all my life long, without success, to analyze this contradiction.
>
> Of course, I had more down-to-earth motives. My imagination set me dreaming of sketches, songs, acts, big hits. I had heard stories of studio electricians and sound men "discovered" by American producers and propelled to stardom in the movies or on Broadway. I, too, wanted out—out of where I came from. Tinsel dreams: champagne, girls, luxurious apartments, glamorous cars . . . And singing looked like a good way of getting ahead by doing what you enjoyed. But nobody had told me about the terrible pain that went with it, churning your bowels, making you nauseated, the panic that dries your throat, makes your legs wobble, paralyzes you. There are no words to convey that pain. And no cure for it.
>
> At the same time, fear is a spur. Because you have to surmount it, work with it—or, rather, in spite of it. It makes you dig deep inside yourself, go beyond your limits. And then suddenly you radiate a strength and conviction that the audience can feel and that you never dreamed you possessed. That's what must have happened that very first night at the Vallon des Tuves. I shot on stage at a hundred miles an hour, full of a ferocious energy generated by the desperate need to surmount my terror.

When you ask Lydia about her baby brother's sudden calling, she invokes the ghosts of bygone Livis. Uncle Giuseppino, who had such a fine voice and who sang in all the villages around Monsummano. Their maternal grandmother, Olimpia, the abandoned child from Florence, surely the offspring of a tribe of wandering entertainers? For Lydia, faithful guardian of the family flame, the heaven-sent gift leapfrogged the generations and settled on Ivo.

Heartened by that momentous September night in 1938 at the Vallon des Tuves, Yves Montand began to appear in small neighborhood halls.

Trottobas put various contracts his way, and Montand gave up hairdressing for good. "When he came home from a performance that had netted him fifty francs," recalls Lydia, "he would pull out his packet of ten-franc bills and slowly spread them on the table, one by one, saying to our mother, 'Look, Mama, another!' And Mama couldn't believe her eyes. Little Ivo bringing home money! Just by singing! And it hadn't been easy for him, because at first our parents thought he was crazy. They didn't believe one little bit in singing. They thought it wasn't serious. But I always backed him."

He was neither rich nor famous. But word spread through the neighborhood, and certain gazes were changing. . . . The inaccessible Bruna of the Bar des Mûriers, who had once treated him so lightly, now yielded to the charms of La Cabucelle's own star.

At Christmas 1938, Montand appeared as a "special attraction" at the Ritz cinema on the rue Saint-Antoine. The posters announced: "A magnificent movie, Clark Gable and Myrna Loy in *Test Pilot,* and during the intermission, by popular demand, Yves Montand, accompanied by Mlle Mado Fancelli." He picked up more experiences of this kind as the winter of 1939 wore on, in movie houses packed to the rafters with the working-class audiences he knew so well, as swift to jeer as to applaud.

With such Saturday-night audiences, out to forget the workweek, Montand's talents as a mimic worked wonders, and his songs were just as well received. But he was not satisfied with easy success. "He had changed completely," recalls his future sister-in-law Elvire. "His self-discipline worried us. It was astonishing. He wasn't the same kid any more."

He never stopped. Whenever he had a free moment he practiced stage movements in front of Lydia's wardrobe mirror. He strove to defeat, or at least to mask, the terrible fear that gnawed at his insides. He was constantly on the alert for models, for guidelines, and the movie screen was his main source of inspiration. He drank in attitudes and expressions. Singing was just a starting point for him, an excuse. What he really wanted was to become an actor. In fact, what he did on stage called more for acting skills than for the talents of a singer pure and simple.

After Montand's maiden performance at the Vallon des Tuves, Trottobas had promised to put him on at the Alcazar—Marseilles's most famous vaudeville shrine. Before he could indulge in such ambitious dreams he had to find new songs to flesh out his repertory. Francis Trottobas sent him around to Charles Humel, a blind composer who lived near the rue Sainte-Barbe. (Humel's wife was one of Lydia's customers, so the young man's burgeoning reputation had already reached the composer's ears.) He invited Montand in and wrote a lively if mindless little song for him:

Je m'en fous je m'en fous
Je m'en contrefiche
Je m'en fous je m'en fous
Moi je tiens le coup . . . Yeah!

[I don't give a damn I don't give a damn
I don't give an everloving damn
I don't give a damn I don't give a damn
'Cause I'm gonna get through . . . Yeah!]

Humel's client was only partly satisfied and asked for something about cowboys and the Wild West. Since the musician was blind and had never seen a Western, Montand talked to him about cowboys sitting around the campfire at night, described the way they dressed. Thus was born—with the help of a songwriter friend of Humel's named Vander—"Les Plaines du Far West," a song that opened doors for the cinema-struck singer and gave voice and expression to his passion for the American myth.

The Alcazar was a Marseilles monument, an institution, the jumping-off point for anyone who wanted to make his name as a singer. Its old-fashioned auditorium—it had opened in 1857—was long and narrow, with sixteen hundred seats in the orchestra and balconies. A massive chandelier threw light on the purple and gold of the colonnades, archways, and wainscoting (its architect had lavishly indulged his taste for the Moorish style). And the centerpiece, dominating the stage, was a weighty allegorical scene embracing the arms of the city, a blue cross against a white background surrounded by monsters, naked women, and angels.

By hallowed tradition, auditions at the Alcazar took place in the afternoon—*and in public.* Facing its ferocious audiences was a fearful ordeal for would-be singers.[2] When he was just starting out, in 1905, the seventeen-year-old Maurice Chevalier underwent the test, without accompaniment and deafened by an irreverent uproar. The atmosphere, he said, "was like a slaughterhouse." But on stage that night, after a plodding start, he turned the situation around. The theater manager, Franck, said excitedly: "Do you realize you'll soon have the whole country eating out of your hand, kid? The Alcazar is the Vatican of vaudeville!"

Once he became nationally famous, Chevalier returned to triumph on the Alcazar stage, as did many others. Alcazar audiences had handed down the heckling tradition from generation to generation. They were made up

2. See André Sallée and Philippe Chauveau, *Music-hall et café-concert* (Paris, 1985).

of a rich social mix. The orchestra was the fortress of the leading Marseilles merchants, owners of the olive-oil and soap-making factories, and often shareholders in the theater, who liked to slip backstage at intermission and ambush young female singers. Up in the balconies, in a state of comfortable disorder and permanent background noise, sat craftsmen, small shopkeepers, and also the menacing forms of bully boys from the Vieux Port. In his memoirs, Chevalier describes "rival gangs firing revolvers at each other from one balcony to the next." One gang leader was actually shot down in the heart of the audience. But the genuine music-hall devotees gathered in the first balcony. These were the true arbiters, the judges who decided whether an act would be a hit or a flop. They strolled from group to group during the show, trading opinions. At intermission they would compare notes on individual performances.[3] Although by the 1930s the Alcazar was converting to the silver screen, it went on offering vaudeville acts. The first half of a show, a succession of magicians, acrobats, and singers, closed with the "special guest star." The second part opened with the "supporting star," before the real star of the evening came on.

Was the Alcazar a launchpad—or a trapdoor to the lower depths? The old theater's formidable reputation (fostered by a thousand anecdotes) and the ferocity of its audiences, who generally arrived armed with automobile horns and sacks of wet plaster, were enough to fuel Montand's worst nightmares. Elvire, then Julien's fiancée, still remembers the chill wind of fear that swept through the house in La Cabucelle: "When we heard he was going to appear at the Alcazar, the whole family shook in its boots. For a beginner, the Alcazar was terrifying." On the big night, a sizable army of neighbors descended on the theater to support its own star. Panic-stricken, Lydia poured cup after cup of herbal tea down Yves's throat to steady his nerves.

The poster for that evening of June 21, 1939, warrants close scrutiny. As it did every year on the first day of summer, the magazine *Artistica* had organized a competition for amateurs. For the first half of the show, the Alcazar, temple of vaudeville, had laid on a dozen amateur "mimics, crooners, song-and-dance artists, and tap dancers" with names like Lyne, Jo Dejean, Princelle, and Henriet Lys. The second half of the show offered the "gracious monologuist Line Cora," the "famous monologuist Jean Denain," "Mitsi Ray the rubber doll," the "intrepid song-and-dance man Sergeot," and, for openers, the "lighthearted mimic and singer Yves Montand." In just a few months, Montand had risen high enough to rate fairly bold type, bigger than the beginners with whom he shared the first half of the act. The star of the show, "direct from Paris," was a young singer

3. See Jean Bazal, *Marseille sur scène* (Marseilles, 1978).

on her way up, Renée Lebas. Fifty years later almost to the day, she wrote to Montand: "A fiftieth anniversary is something to celebrate! I have never forgotten that young man full of fire and budding talent."

Indeed, she had not forgotten, but remembered all the details. "I had been singing for only eight months. I remember that evening at the Alcazar as if it were yesterday. It was a kind of talent competition for amateurs organized by *Artistica* magazine; the second half of the show featured very young professionals. The theater was packed. It was bedlam, for the Marseillais love to yell. There were a lot of celebrities: among others, Alibert and Darcelys were sitting in the front row. The first half was drowned in boos and jeers; the amateurs were heckled and insulted mercilessly. At intermission the performers huddled backstage while the audience gave a thunderous ovation in expectation of its favorite entertainers. They started to stamp and to chant, 'Alibert, Alibert!' and 'Darcelys, Darcelys!' Already paralyzed by stage fright before our turn came around, we were now utterly crippled. The first one on after the intermission was Montand. The master of ceremonies tried to announce his number. But the audience was shouting much too loudly. In despair, he ordered the curtain up and shoved Montand on stage. The yelling went on—and then the miracle happened. Somehow, he managed to put himself across. He was applauded to the skies. Yes, he captured that 'impossible' audience."

With the meticulous care that marked all his performances, Montand had rehearsed his act down to the last detail. He had gotten hold of an acceptable cowboy hat and painted it white. He wore a plaid shirt and a neckerchief. He had hit upon the idea of walking bowlegged, like a man used to spending his life on horseback, and he stayed that way. When he started to sing, the illusion was perfect:

> Dans les plaines du Far West quand vient la nuit
> Les cow-boys près du bivouac sont réunis . . .
>
> [When night falls on the plains where the buffalo roam
> And the cowhands laze in their open-air home . . .]

> Standing bandy-legged through two verses and three choruses was tough, but it worked like a charm. A cowboy on stage—it had never been done. The audience was used to song-and-dance numbers, but with just that little bit of stage setting I had broken the rules. I exited, then came back to take a second bow. The audience yelled for another song, but I had none to offer, and I didn't want to screw up. All I wanted was to be alone with myself and savor that incredible reception. That was the moment when I

said to myself: This is what I want to do. There is no more reason for it not to work. My fear had gone, and it was easier to think straight after the event. My manager, with typical Mediterranean exuberance, was raving. I had "knocked them flat," Trottobas kept saying. "Do you hear me? Knocked them flat!" But I was still worried. Had I really climbed onto that stage and taken on that audience? I couldn't sleep at all that night. I kept wondering if the guy who had sung was really me.

"Once you've sung at the Alcazar, you can sing anywhere." Those words, uttered by Trottobas during a moment of euphoria, were not far from the truth. Indeed, that performance on the first day of the summer of 1939 by a youth not yet eighteen appeared to open all the doors. At Vitrolles on August 6, Yves Montand, billed as "the highly talented song-and-dance mimic," dominated the posters. Tickets cost four francs, with children and the military getting in at half price.

During this summer of 1939, military matters were on everyone's mind. At the start of the year, the war in Spain had ended with the rout of the Republicans. A young man of twenty-four, Artur London, a Czechoslovak Communist who had fought in the International Brigades, crossed the Pyrenees and sought asylum in France; he could not, of course, know that his part in the Spanish civil war would be held against him at his trial in Communist Czechoslovakia after the Second World War. Thirty years later, Montand re-created London on the screen. But what preoccupied the real-life London in 1939 was Germany's annexation of Bohemia. The Western democracies, aware of the extent to which Hitler had hoodwinked them in Munich, were seeking alliances in the East. It was very late. The world was racing toward disaster.

Five days after Montand's appearance at Vitrolles, French and British negotiators arrived in Moscow to discuss a defense agreement with Russia. But Stalin had already entered into secret talks with Hitler: they would lead to the hammer blow of the Nazi-Soviet pact.

At dawn on August 24 in the Kremlin, delighted Soviet and German delegates toasted the pact with champagne. Stalin raised his glass: "I know how the German nation loves its Führer, which is why I have great pleasure in drinking to his health!" The text of the pact was made public that day—but not the secret protocol on the dismemberment of Poland. The world was stunned, horrified: war was now inevitable. On September 1, the German army, its hands now free on the Eastern front, crossed the Polish frontier. On September 3, Great Britain and France went to war. "Talented song-and-dance men" were no longer in fashion.

Montand had vivid memories of that day. He had gone to the movies with a friend, Raymond Saritz, then to the rue d'Aix, where, for the first time in his almost eighteen years, he walked into a brasserie and ordered a pizza. Over the radio the customers heard that France had declared war on Germany. The news troubled everyone, and Montand recalled the pacifist lessons of his kind old teachers Florian and Bondu at elementary school in La Cabucelle. Yet he could not help thinking that unexpected and perhaps exciting things were about to disrupt the present, too-peaceful order of events.

Suddenly sirens howled, and cafés, restaurants, and streets quickly emptied of people. It was a test air-raid alert. The men went home to pack for the journey to their units and to follow the news on the radio. Montand, too, returned to the impasse des Mûriers.

Number 8 was silent and unlit. He called out: "Is anybody here?"

There was no reply. He repeated his question a little more loudly. A whisper came from the depths of his parents' bedroom: "Here we are."

The young man walked into the room and flipped on the light. Giovanni stood by the fireplace, and behind him, trembling with fear, crouched Lydia and his mother. Montand just had time to read the terror in their eyes before they begged him in tremulous voices: *"Spegni, spegni!"* ("Put out the light!") As Communists and Italians, the Livis had every reason to fear the future. All French Communists had been thrown off balance by news of the pact between Hitler's Germany and Soviet Russia, but they had soon recovered and closed ranks behind Stalin's "genius." Their daily paper, *L'Humanité,* briskly announced on August 25, "We joyfully salute this successful Soviet stroke, which fosters the cause of peace." This comment, the prelude to expressions of unreserved official Communist approval in the weeks to come, triggered an explosion of anger in France. Many on both left and right had hoped for an agreement among France, Great Britain, and the Soviet Union. The Soviet reversal had, of course, killed this hope; the whole nation turned indignantly on the Communist Party.[4]

On the afternoon of August 25, the police had closed down *L'Humanité,* and three days later all Communist publications were banned, including *Rouge-Midi,* the paper Montand often read. There were raids on Communist headquarters, information centers, and offices. Drinking holes used for regular meetings of Communist cells were closed.

Nor had the Italian Communist Party in France escaped these repressive measures. On August 26, the government had stopped publication of the paper *Stato Operaio* (*The Worker State*), which was published in Paris

4. See Amilcare Rossi [Angelo Tasca], *Les Communistes français pendant la drôle de guerre* (Paris, 1951).

by the Italian Communist Party and supportive of *L'Humanité*'s Party line. On September 1, Palmiro Togliatti, the head of the Italian Communist Party and one of the leading lights of the Comintern, was arrested in Paris. Other Italian leaders and hundreds of Party workers were interned.

Giovanni Livi was left undisturbed: he had operated so discreetly for so long that a little extra camouflage was all he needed to continue his activities. Still, according to his younger son, he surely experienced moments of torment when the pact was signed. A few years earlier, the great Moscow show trials and the "confessions" of the Old Bolshevik leaders had deeply shaken him. He failed to understand how such heroic figures could have turned traitor. This time he was even more deeply disturbed; the de facto alliance between Hitler and Stalin in the teeth of the Western democracies was shattering to an anti-Fascist like him. He was used to thinking in simple terms: you neither spoke nor dealt with the Devil. Montand would remember his father living through those unbearably tense days in a state of despair, scrabbling in vain for a rational explanation of an event that had cut the ground from under him. For ten days or so, he floundered in depression; then he took hold of himself and clutched at the straws of official justification for the Nazi-Soviet pact: Stalin had been forced to sign it because the Western democracies had been unwilling to join forces with him. It had been a time-saving move. In the end, Giovanni's loyalty to the-party-that-was-always-right (even when it was wrong) swept aside his doubts and reservations. He remained a Communist.

Although he witnessed his father's period of doubt, Montand shared none of his pain. Without question the enemy was Hitler, Franco, or Mussolini—that had been drummed into him often enough at home. But his great passion at the outset of the conflict was still the music-hall stage. His friend and manager Francis Trottobas had been drafted, and Montand visited him at his barracks. While there, he gave a few performances for the troops around Juan-les-Pins, and even posed for an advertisement for Filio shirts. But clearly he could not hope to make a living on the stage under the current conditions.

In the spring of 1940, the French army was collapsing under the sustained German blitzkrieg, spearheaded by tanks; terrified mobs were strung out along country roads in a pathetic exodus. It was against this apocalyptic backdrop that the nineteen-and-a-half-year-old Montand became a factory hand, a metalworker at the Provence shipyards, on the chemin de la Madrague. On May 11, he was given a pass for the port area. On June 15, the day the French government fled Paris for sanctuary in Bordeaux, he was issued a card entitling him to a "worker discount" on the streetcar system. On June 10, Italy had entered the war on the German side, just in time to share the victor's spoils, and the shipyards, as contributors to the French war effort, were bombed by planes from Italy. "Macaronis" living in France had to work even harder to prove their loyalty to the host country.

On June 17, Marshal Pétain, called on by the president of France only the day before to form a new government, addressed the nation over the radio. Montand heard the speech by the "victor of Verdun" on an old wireless set in his sister's bedroom. "It is with an aching heart that I tell you today that we must stop fighting," said the tremulous voice of the octogenarian soldier. At the time, his decision to request an armistice triggered a melancholy sense of relief in the Livi family, in the impasse des Mûriers, and throughout La Cabucelle. That, at least, was how Montand remembered it. After all, the war was going to end; husbands, sons, and brothers would be returning home. Surrender to the Germans (labeled treason by the lonely voice of Charles de Gaulle in London) was considered by the world of draftees as a lesser evil, a way of saving what could still be saved. And the marshal's professed determination to make himself the shield of the suffering French earned him genuine popularity.

As resistance to the enemy collapsed, the army, the state, the government, and the fabric of society all fell apart. France was divided in two, and millions of refugees were cut off below the demarcation line between the occupied North and the "free" South. Terrified by this insecurity, this sudden and frightening void, bombarded by rumors, most citizens clutched for support at the comforting old man who had offered France "the gift of his person."

At the Provence shipyards, Ivo Livi worked in a huge shed amid the din of pneumatic drills, compressors, and hydraulic presses. Blue-clad workers moved about the railroad tracks as giant cranes dipped to hoist heaps of metal sheeting and piles of scrap metal aloft. An unskilled worker, Livi was assistant to a master boilermaker, an aristocrat of the yards free to come and go as he pleased. His job was making buoys to anchor submarine cables designed to block harbor entrances. They were cylinders three feet across and six feet long, sealed at either end with lids that were soldered on white-hot. Montand's precise task was to slither inside the cylinder and, bent double, to hammer the reddened plating into its final oval shape. Flakes of rust flew at each blow, and he swallowed lungfuls of bitter dust. After his first day's work he returned home stunned with fatigue and drunk with the din still ringing in his ears. He had been told to drink milk, lots of milk, to offset the effects of the rust he had taken in. "We kept all the milk for him," Lydia recalls.

The new job was hard, but Montand liked being there. He was happy to be useful, and he relished what he had never before experienced—the warmth and comradeship of the worksite. Later, as a prominent Communist fellow traveler, Montand cited his warm memories of his working-class past. Even at the end of his life, highly irritated though he was by the mythification of the working class (because it fails to reflect the true conditions of working people), he had lost none of his nostalgia for the brotherhood of workers. If Montand was able to put this proletarian past to good use, it was because he had really lived it. And never repudiated it.

In 1987, when Yves Montand was president of the Cannes Film Festival, he received a note reading, "The older workers at the Normed shipyards, which is threatened with closure, want you to meet their delegation. You were once a worker. Only you can understand their problems." Montand was deeply moved that wage earners threatened with unemployment should seek him out. He met the delegates, and they explained their predicament: at the age of fifty they were being discarded, threatened with joblessness and homelessness; the government was turning a deaf ear; and they needed an intermediary. Montand agreed to transmit their grievances to Paris, at the same time warning them that he had no powers, that he could only be a messenger. The workers applauded the former metalworker from the Provence shipyards for rejoining their ranks.

Montand, exploring the working world, realized that it was not the monolithic block of flawless marble that left-wing sycophants loved to invoke. "There are assholes everywhere, even on the job site," he frequently said. Not to speak of real bastards, like the metalworker who liked to crush out his cigarette on the hands of new arrivals. Or the Italian workers who saved money to send to Mussolini. Or those with racist remarks constantly on their lips. Curiously enough, these men, exempted from the military draft because they were working in a defense industry, were only mildly interested in the war and didn't mention it except in passing. What really interested them were wartime shortages and women, about whom they talked crudely and offensively enough to shock and disturb Ivo Livi.

In the evenings, no matter how exhausted he was, and on Sundays, Montand remembered his music-hall world. Alone in his bedroom, he worked at improving his voice and practiced positions and moves. When he came up with a new trick he worked on it tirelessly, made it his own, strove to turn it into a "natural" gesture. He had no idea whether he would ever sing or return to the stage, or feel that terrible but delicious thrill again, but he kept going.

That summer the shipyards laid off part of their work force. France had surrendered, and defense production was no longer an urgent priority.

Three months after signing on, Ivo Livi was jobless. Nor was the overall family situation very bright. Julien, along with 1.85 million leaderless French troops, had been taken prisoner. The last time Yves had seen his brother was during one of Julien's furloughs. He had arrived on May 1, married Elvire on May 4, and left on May 15. He had had time to conceive a child before returning to the front, but he did not learn of the birth of his son Jean-Louis until three months after the event, in his north German POW camp.

Julien's enforced absence through the five years of war—seven years in all, for he had been in the army since 1938—was a trial for the whole family. Mama Giuseppina was constantly worried. Yves was unable to stifle the guilt he felt at being free and living almost without constraints while his brother rotted in a stalag. He was frustrated at being unable to share moments of joy with Julien. And at the same time, the disappearance of the eldest son obliged the younger brother to shoulder his responsibilities within the clan, to give up the ways of the baby free to do as he pleased. He determined to assume those responsibilities as soon as he could.

For the moment, he waited in line to pick up his unemployment insurance. The experience was humiliating to him. He rebelled at having to hold out his palm to an official who settled his fate in utter indifference with a rubber stamp.

Luckily for his wounded self-esteem, this dependence did not last. In the autumn of 1940, he landed a job as a dockworker and warehouseman loading trucks with goods for distribution in the Marseilles area. Very early each morning he left for the avenue Camille-Pelletan, where he had to start up a charcoal-powered truck motor. He cleaned out the furnace and boiler and sorted the charcoal by hand. When the driver arrived, they left for the port to take on their cargo—heavy packages of paper you had to carry on your head, which had the unpleasant habit of folding abruptly in two. It was grueling work. Like Julien before him, Yves learned the knack of distributing loads, walking with legs slightly apart, breathing evenly.

The work developed his shoulders, and he also learned the time-honored gait of the dockworker, a seemingly effortless, fluid, ground-hugging motion. He took careful stock of his body's responses, and later he made rich use of them. "No one moved on a movie set like Montand," Catherine Deneuve says. Montand owed that ease of movement to the dockworker Ivo Livi.

During breaks, the dockworker occasionally remembered that he had been a singer and would sing a few bars. A former classmate from La Cabucelle recalls, "Yves worked alongside my father on the docks. Dad told us it was tough work but that Yves pulled his weight. The dockers got him to sing. It got them through the job, for he already had that strong, warm voice, and his workmates used to say, 'Stay where you are, kid, go on singing!' "[5]

When he took the homebound streetcar at the end of the day, dust-caked, grimy, disheartened, Montand thought back to the young man who had bounded on stage only a year before to face the Alcazar audience. It seemed unlikely that those days would ever return.

As the uprooted government bureaucrats of France settled into commandeered hotels and townhouses in the once-fashionable little health spa of Vichy, the new direction of French policy became unpleasantly clear. The first targets were foreigners, immigrants, and Jews. On July 22, only twelve days after Marshal Pétain had been voted plenary powers, a committee was formed to re-examine naturalization status granted under the Act of 1927, the law that had naturalized the Livis. A new law was enacted, denying all French citizens with a foreign father the right to government jobs. It was Vichy's way of accommodating the tidal wave of xenophobia sweeping the French press. On October 3, without any pressure from the Germans, the Vichy government promulgated a new statute for the Jews—its revenge against the "half-breeds" who had supposedly led France to disaster. "Israelites" were barred from the civil service, from the army (though veterans retained their rights), and from the judiciary. As for non-French Jews, they were dumped into holding camps—which soon turned out to be antechambers to a very different sort of camp.

For the aged Marshal Pétain, nothing was more vital than the need to launch "national recovery" in a country sapped by decades of "permissiveness." The official ideology underpinning the new order—a blend of outdated moralizing, frenzied attacks on parliamentary government and technocratic elitism, and national pride—was to be built upon the ruins of the Republic. "*Liberté, Egalité, Fraternité*" was to be replaced by "*Travail, Famille, Patrie*" ("Work, Family, Fatherland"). The family, society's vital nucleus, was to be promoted to the skies.

In October 1940, Frenchmen who still believed that Pétain was playing a double game with the Germans were shocked when the marshal and Chancellor Hitler shook hands at their meeting in the little town of Montoire. Soon came the October 30 statement by the marshal, which confirmed their worst fears: "A collaboration of our two countries was among the subjects discussed. I accepted the principle. . . . I am this day embarking upon the path of collaboration." But this declaration failed to shake the faith that the vast majority of Frenchmen had in the father of their country.

5. Letter to the authors from M. Di Rocco, October 23, 1977.

Fanned by Vichy propaganda, an insane and sickening cult was now born. In this year of 1940, the most popular song in the country, shouldering aside Chevalier, Trenet, and Fernandel, was "Maréchal, nous voilà" ("Marshal, Here We Are"):

> Maréchal, nous voilà,
> Devant toi, le sauveur de la France
> Nous jurons, nous tes gars
> De servir et de suivre tes pas . . .
>
> [Marshal, here we are
> At your feet, the savior of our country,
> We swear, we your loyal children,
> To serve you and follow in your path . . .]

This idolatry of the head of state was systematically drummed into French youth. Schoolchildren wrote to him, women prayed for him, war veterans revered him.

On December 3 and 4, when the marshal visited Marseilles, a huge, enthusiastic crowd was waiting for him at the decorated and flower-hung Gare Saint-Charles. Every church bell in the city tolled, and when the head of state reached city hall he was acclaimed by thousands of spectators. A crowd estimated by *Marseille-Matin* to be fifteen thousand strong swore loyalty to him as one man, repeating the solemn oath three times.

A military parade had been organized on the Canebière. Two hours ahead of time the famous thoroughfare was packed to overflowing all the way to the Vieux Port. When the parade ended, to thunderous applause, the people of Marseilles surged across the police barriers and mobbed the marshal. Henri Frenay, the future founder of the Resistance group Combat, watched these hysterical scenes of adulation: "Stunned, I saw an old man kiss the marshal's hand. A hefty matriarch, probably a fishwife, knelt and piously kissed the hem of his coat. Never before had I seen such fervor, almost religious in nature. I had never dreamed of such an emotional power."[6]

The youngest Livi made sure that he was not part of the enthusiastic crowd, not even as a bystander. Politics did not yet interest him enough to make him wear out his eyes following the official doctrinal literature. And the Italian immigrant who dwelt within him instinctively mistrusted a government whose first steps had been to eliminate foreigners in France.

Despite the popular fervor that accompanied the marshal on his jour-

6. Henri Frenay, *La Nuit finira* (Paris, 1973).

ney along the Mediterranean coast, Marseilles in 1940 was by no means wholly Pétainist. On the contrary, it seemed to be standing aside from the war, at a safe distance from Vichy's decrees. Thousands of foreign refugees had flocked there, particularly Jews, hoping for passage across the sea to North Africa. The last stopover on the road to freedom, Marseilles was a natural refuge for emigrants—a sanctuary once again, but this time in the other direction: a first whiff of the perfumes of Algiers for those seeking to flee France. It was a special city, living, as it were, between parentheses.

The winter of 1940–41 was unusually harsh, even in the South, and coal shortages left many people helpless against the icy local wind, the mistral. Food was scarce, and getting enough to eat was soon the major national preoccupation. Probably less so in Marseilles than elsewhere, though, for compared with other cities, it was still cheerful and lively. Many artists and writers had moved south to the Mediterranean. Not only that, but Fernandel was playing at the Variétés-Casino in *Hugues,* a musical comedy by Vincent Scotto; Josephine Baker was shimmying at the Opéra in *La Créole;* and Raimu was starring at the Capitole in a review, *C'est tout le Midi,* whipped up by Alibert and featuring a newcomer, called Gérard Oury.[7]

And in early 1941, the cinemas along the Canebière were still showing American films, long since banned in Paris. The people of Marseilles took advantage of this provisional liberty to get out and look for entertainment. It turned out that the dockworker Ivo Livi would be joining forces again with the variety artist Yves Montand sooner than he had dared hope.

Not least because Francis Trottobas, a civilian once again, had returned to his peacetime trade of candy manufacturer—and theatrical impresario.

7. Gérard Oury, *Mémoires d'éléphant* (Paris, 1988).

Chapter 4

Yves Montand's career started up again in the spring of 1941, and it was never to falter. He was not yet twenty. He kept a meticulous record of those beginnings—his real beginnings, not his false start at the Alcazar back in 1939. A photo album with a stiff blue cover, tied with a ribbon of the same color, contains the kind of nuggets biographers dream of: the applause still ringing in his ears, the youthful Montand glued in it press clippings, programs, and photographs of all those formative years. Riffling through this traveler's log, reading the increasingly enthusiastic reviews, seeing Montand's name printed bigger and bolder on the posters provide instant proof of how quickly the singer made his presence felt.

The scrapbook begins with these words, written in a careful hand on the inside cover in the naive style of a twenty-year-old who has just won the lottery and is a relative stranger to grammar and syntax. First, a title: "My Diary, Reviews and Posters." Then, a subtitle: "My Beginnings." Then, a brief entry: "I made my debut one evening at the Vallon des Tuves, in 1938, in Saint-Antoine. What stage fright! But what satisfaction, what delight, that at last I have found my career, my true life! What will it bring me? But what I did not know was that it would be a career of hard work, of struggle, and especially of having to begin all over again every time. . . . My only consolation, after so many obstacles, is that so far I have succeeded. But what lies ahead?" Beneath this note, a signature and the date: April 15, 1941.

The brief self-portrait is squarely on target: hard work, permanent anxiety (despite the author's somewhat premature self-congratulation over his "success," blithely leapfrogging the two years spent in the wilderness of the German invasion and the war). But a clipping from *Le Petit Provençal* of April 22 offers supplementary proof that Montand's career really did begin in the spring of 1941, for it advertises a glittering night at the

Bompard cinema at which the highlight of the evening will be "1941's brightest new young star."

Trottobas had organized a tour of the Marseilles area, with his protégé appearing at Miramas, Aubagne, and Istres. The first time Montand's name appeared in *Artistica*—a sort of guide within show-business circles to entertainment in the Midi—it was spelled with a final *t.* The caption beneath his photo—the singer's hair is carefully plastered down, and he sports a splendid polka-dot tie—called him "a born mimic. Just nineteen, tall, likable, a sharp dresser, energetic and adaptable, this excellent variety artist has a wide range of perfect imitations. One of the best of our tap dancers, Yves Montant is climbing the ladder to stardom with giant strides. . . . Our best wishes to him!"

For his performance at Istres, Montand was scheduled for the first half of the show. Heading the bill that night was a music-hall star, Réda Claire, Egyptian by birth, who gave a throaty crooner's rendition of "Swing, swing, Madame" in languorous tones. He had started out at the Mogador in Paris, performing Russian light opera. His overnight success had shot him to the top of the ladder; there he became the Corsican Tino Rossi's archrival for the loyalty of the *midinettes,* the groupies of the day, who swooned at his amorous sound.

His toupee earned him the nickname "The Girl in Someone Else's Hair," which also alluded to his being homosexual, which he made no attempt to hide—quite the contrary. After the show, Claire kindly offered to drive Montand back to Marseilles, where he lived. The young man hesitated: public transport was a nightmare in those wartime years, but he knew Claire's reputation. He finally accepted, and spent the entire ride removing the hand Claire vainly sought to place on his groin.

One of the enterprising star's big hits was "Si tu reviens, ne me demande pas pardon" ("If You Come Back, Don't Try to Say You're Sorry"). But, in fact, Montand did come back. Despite the lively episode in the car, he attended Claire's final rehearsals for his new show. A few days later, he accepted an invitation to Claire's house. He enjoyed unforgettable, and extremely scarce, pastries in the company of a group of entertaining, cultivated, caustic homosexuals.

Montand was sitting on the terrace of the family home on June 22 when he heard that Germany had invaded the Soviet Union. At long last, his father seemed relieved. Deep inside, the Italian anti-Fascist had never accepted the Nazi-Soviet pact. Did Montand sense that the course of the war had changed? It seems unlikely. He was scheduled to appear on the stage of the Alcazar three days later, and the prospect of facing that ordeal all over again fully occupied him.

In June 1939, when he had brought down the house, the evening had been sponsored by *Artistica,* as its annual championship. War had forced the canceling of the 1940 contest. But the sixteenth championship, in 1941, was going ahead as planned. *Le Petit Provençal* published a full-length photo of "Yves Montant," wearing a pale suit and black-and-white shoes. In a parody of Trenet, his hat is shoved far back on his head, and he is rolling his eyes like his model.

Montand's second test at the Alcazar surpassed his wildest hopes. As *Artistica* said: "Can you imagine how hard it is to imitate universally known stars like Charles Trenet, Fernandel, and Maurice Chevalier? Well, this entertainer brings them to life right before our eyes. And we can assure you that nothing is missing, for Yves Montand catches the smallest gesture, the smallest detail. He was a major hit, particularly with the young, who applauded him to the skies. It was only with great difficulty that this brilliant, up-to-the-minute entertainer took leave of his audience."

This flair for mimicry that the public found so appealing was also attracting the attention of show-business professionals. Less than a week after the Alcazar gala, Montand signed a contract with Audiffred, a Parisian impresario forced, like so many others, to leave the capital for Marseilles. The singer did not remember how they first made contact. Was Audiffred present at the Alcazar? Or did he send an assistant to keep an eye open for promising beginners? However it happened, Audiffred, with his camel's-hair coat and his national reputation as a theatrical manager, impressed the prodigy from La Cabucelle enough to persuade him to desert his local protector, Trottobas. It was not a happy transfer; Trottobas considered the rupture a betrayal, contending that he had discovered and launched Montand only to have the singer abandon him the moment success beckoned.

But Montand did not agree, and he dug in his heels. He saw his opportunity and had no intention of letting the chance slip through his fingers. Henceforth he placed his fortunes in Audiffred's hands. Their first agreement was signed (on pink stationery) on July 1, 1941. It covered two performances on Sunday, July 6, at the Colisée-Plage theater. The singer, referred to as a "variety artist," would receive one hundred francs for the two performances.

Montand recorded the event in his scrapbook with the comment: "Today I signed an exclusive contract with M. Audiffred. So far I have had no reason to complain. But I must not forget that in spite of everything he's a shark. I must be careful, careful, careful." The Colisée-Plage was an open-air music hall; its customers came from the throngs of Sunday strollers. Reviews of that day's performance noted that Fernand Sardou had done an imitation of the actor Raimu, but once again it was Montand who stole the show: "Yves Montand is speeding up the ladder to success; on

Sunday he got the kind of ovation with which audiences crown newborn stars." Clearly pleased with himself, Montand had written in the margin: "Not a bad review, not bad at all."

Everything was going well. After just a few performances the youth who had sweated under bags of semolina only six months earlier was so well known that theater managers vied for his services. On August 13 he reappeared at the Alcazar; *Artistica* reported that "the revelation of 1941 was applauded to the skies." On August 15, 16, and 17, Montand was one of the headliners at the Hyères casino, where, in his own view, he was "a big hit." Then came his consecration: he appeared at the Odéon, a music hall on the Canebière that was the equal of the Alcazar among Marseilles vaudeville theaters and a perfect springboard for an entertainer on his way to Paris. "Today," he told his scrapbook, "my real destiny begins, my journey to . . . ?"

The surprising thing is not that Montand was finally being rewarded by success—after all, he had evident gifts—nor that success had smiled on him after only six months, but that he was determined not to be dazzled by his sudden glory. Although he collected everything written about him with a beginner's pride, he kept a cool head and never forgot that the bubble might burst at any time. The higher he climbed, the more anxious he became. It was a fear that never left him. His only security lay in constant honing of his talents. Throughout his life, he would never relax, never rest on his laurels.

Full of doubts about his voice, his uncertain ear, his shaky judgment, he turned to a pianist, Mme Fancelli, for advice. She was the mother of a very blond, very sweet daughter, Mado, herself a pianist who had worked with Montand—all powerful arguments that persuaded him to practice hard. Three times a week he went for lessons at the young lady's side. We have no information as to whether these private sessions led to any marked musical progress.

Realizing that his strenuous stage exertions demanded a high degree of physical versatility, Montand also decided to take dance lessons. He was given the address of an old teacher on the rue Fortia who was rumored to have been a star of the St. Petersburg ballet before the October Revolution. The fiercely mustachioed old gentleman had indeed dedicated his life to his art, and refused to give his time to casual amateurs. He was hard, even merciless, with his young pupils. More than once Montand overheard cruel exchanges between the master and mothers anxiously inquiring about their daughters' progress: "She is worthless, utterly without talent. Take her away. She was not meant for the dance."

This refusal to compromise appealed to Montand. He attacked his exercises with an energy that more than made up for his lack of experience. The Russian appreciated his pupil's determination and never let up on him. After a few months of torture, the young entertainer had developed elasticity in his joints and flexibility in his limbs; his routines were enriched a hundredfold. The old teacher was pleased with his pupil. He even growled that Montand might have made a good dancer, despite his height.

Montand could readily see what this investment had brought him. He continued to work at the barre all his life, knowing that the painful, exacting discipline drummed into him by the executioner on the rue Fortia made for style, fluency, and sparkle on the stage. When as an established international star he would introduce the hint of a pirouette on a Broadway, Tokyo, or Rio stage, the audience loved it but had no idea what labor lay behind it. And, of course, this was the whole secret of his art: pulling away the scaffolding, going beyond the painstaking construction work, to reveal a simple and harmonious façade.

To round out his theatrical skills, Montand now launched himself with the same furious energy into learning English. He bought a teach-yourself book and began to recite phrases over and over to himself whenever he had a spare moment. It was hard work, and the results were far from impressive. Not only that, but he took a few lessons in reading music. The entertainer had dreams of becoming a jazz trumpeter but soon abandoned them: the laws of music were not, and would never be, his strong point.

Right after Montand's success at the Odéon, Audiffred signed up his protégé for a variety show built around an established music-hall performer, Rina Ketty. Montand was due to appear just before the intermission, after Joe Laurin, "the human seal," and Thot, a ventriloquist. His name appeared in bold type on the program, in letters almost as large as Rina Ketty's. The show opened on September 11, 1941, at the Aix casino, and lasted four days. On September 18, Montand noted in his diary: "Thursday evening: not satisfied at all—audience very cold. Friday night: OK. Saturday: a big hit. Sunday: very happy, a big success. Have decided there's no such thing as a cold audience. They all have a weak point. Finding it is what a good performer has to do right from the start."

Contracts now came thick and fast. Still with Rina Ketty, Montand appeared at the Célestins theater in Lyons for the last four days of September. After his first performance he got lost in the big northern city and wandered about for hours without being able to find his hotel. But it was a warm night, and in the end he slept on a park bench. . . . While in Lyons, Montand performed for the first time on the radio, and congratulated himself on feeling no special stage fright.

Returning to Marseilles, he headed the bill at the National cinema for the first week of October, then was invited to perform at a navy gala at the Opéra in Toulon. France's civil and military dignitaries, including the admiral of the fleet, were in the auditorium. "The show began with a salute to the colors," said a local reporter, "and when the curtain rose to reveal a giant effigy of Marshal Pétain, an unbelievable ovation greeted the head of state." Having that illustrious profile towering behind him did not cramp Montand's singing style. Despite the presence of Jean Nohain, a famed master of ceremonies, as well as Robert Rocca, just beginning his singing career, Toulon's leading critic reported that "the triumph of the evening was Yves Montand," adding: "Remember the name. He reminds us of Chevalier in his early days."

Giovanni Livi, who had accompanied his son to Toulon, stood backstage, eyes shining, at first anxious, later in ecstasy. Retrieving cigarette butts from the floor (tobacco was scarce), he lovingly put together a cigarette to offer his son when he came off stage. There was a charity auction after the show, with frantic bidding for a walking stick that had once belonged to Marshal Pétain. To wind things up, the navy band played a few marches in an appropriate setting: a battleship's gun turret, decorated with a portrait of Admiral Darlan.

Two days later, Yves Montand celebrated his twentieth birthday.

As a seasoned manager, Audiffred now decided that his recruit had sufficiently been put through his paces and had acquired enough honors to warrant top billing. What he had in mind was a major end-of-year show—over three hours' worth of performances, consisting of fifteen acts and sketches—with Yves Montand as the star. He appears on the program cover in baggy trousers with a knife-edge crease, light checked jacket, dark shirt, and white tie. The checked jacket—inspired by Cab Calloway—had been purchased with Montand's very first singing fee at Chez Thierry—"The Chic Man's Store," an upmarket establishment on the Canebière. His right hand is raised in a friendly greeting, his face creased by a toothy smile.

Montand noted his promotion in his scrapbook, writing: "This is *my* show." *Un Soir de folie* (*An Evening of Folly*) ran from October 30 to November 5 at the Casino de la Jetée in Nice, a luxurious establishment built on stilts in the middle of the Baie des Anges. Although Montand and the Philippe Brun quintet provided the musical backbone (Montand was on stage and singing for thirty minutes), the star of the comic turns was Harry Max, one of the glories of the Casino de Paris, currently performing on the Riviera. Montand made friends with him. *An Evening of Folly* was a hit; *Le Petit Niçois* hailed Montand as the "revelation of the season." After

Nice, the show moved down the coast to Monaco, Antibes, and Grasse. Montand was everywhere singled out for praise.

The Riviera, more even than Marseilles, attracted the cream of French arts and letters, and now, with the Germans in Paris, the writers Louis Aragon, Emmanuel Berl, and André Malraux had sought refuge there. Actors like Madeleine Robinson, Michel Simon, and Françoise Rosay glittered in the local theater, while a Cannes hotelier's son named Gérard Philip added an *e* to his name and seized his chance in *Une Grande Fille toute simple.* [1] Ten years later, Philipe and Montand, who might well have passed each other on the Promenade des Anglais, became fast friends.

When, on November 14, *An Evening of Folly* came home to the Odéon in Marseilles, the management decided to give Montand a lavish boost. They put up a huge poster on the Canebière with two profiles of the entertainer. One showed the image from the program cover, with him in a checked jacket and baggy pants; the other, projected like a shadow of the first, in cowboy gear. Just one name, in enormous letters, ran across the top of the poster: YVES MONTAND. They packed the local papers with ads. It worked. *Artistica*'s cavil about the singer's "faulty pronunciation" was the only jarring note in a paean of praise. The box-office take was 184,000 francs.

Then they were off again: to Nîmes, Saint-Rémy-de-Provence, Istres, Sète, Orange, and back to Aix. Every evening the miracle recurred: audiences raved, the act went off without a hitch. His parodies invariably triggered laughter and "Les Plaines du Far West" warm applause. Montand came on stage to a frenzied drumroll of superlatives: "This is what we've been waiting for, ladies and gentlemen," boomed the announcer. "You like Gary Cooper or Maurice Chevalier? Well, tonight we offer you something even better. Tonight we offer you a genuine theater bombshell: Yves Montand!"

The theaters were packed. The French—short of everything, cold and hungry, and unhappy—came out in droves to seek entertainment. Not that Montand himself was in permanent good spirits. Often after a performance he would return to a dingy, unheated hotel room (Audiffred was niggardly with expenses). Travel itself was an ordeal. You had to wait for connections for hours in out-of-the-way train stations, then assault overcrowded trains.

Montand was already thinking like an actor rather than a singer. Although singing was his stock-in-trade, he choreographed every song before putting it on the stage. What he looked for in a lyric was its potential for

1. Gilles and Jean-Robert Ragache, *La Vie quotidienne des écrivains et des artistes sous l'Occupation* (Paris, 1988).

mime, for physical action. Among the musical sketches he dreamed up, "Et il sortit son revolver" ("And He Drew His Gun") had a strong impact on audiences, particularly when the gangster he portrayed really did draw. To him, music hall was still a way of winning his actor's stripes in order to attain his ultimate goal—the movies. He devoured movie magazines, especially the famous Provençal writer-director Marcel Pagnol's *Les Cahiers du Film.* War had not closed the studios where Pagnol worked—he and his companion, Josette Day, lived on the premises—and in the course of 1941 he had made *La Fille du puisatier* (*The Well-Digger's Daughter*), with Raimu and Fernandel. When the movie was released that December, long lines of people waited impatiently along the sidewalk outside the Pathé-Palace.

At the end of 1941, leafing through *Les Cahiers du Film,* Montand came across an ad: Pagnol needed extras for a film he was shooting called *La Prière aux étoiles* (*Prayer to the Stars*), with Josette Day, Pierre Blanchar, Carette, and Pauline Carton. Shooting had begun in August but had stopped when Pagnol ran out of film. Stuffing his stage clothes into a small suitcase, Montand raced round to the Prado studios. They hired him. That day they were reconstructing a fiesta in a suburban café. The two main characters sat chatting at a table. Yves Montand's role was to walk toward them, his back to the camera as it tracked behind him. Just before getting to the table, he turned aside and vanished. The camera went on without him and finished with a closeup of the stars. That was all. A fleeting appearance, barely a few seconds, but Montand was ecstatic. Lights and camera had focused on him. It had felt just right!

"This January 21, 1942," he exulted in his scrapbook, "I took my first steps before the camera under M. Marcel Pagnol's direction. They said the footage was highly successful." Nothing much of it remained after editing, but an assistant who had spotted the "revelation of the season" on the set alerted Pagnol, who asked his extra for a song. Montand at once pulled on his costume and sang four songs in the cramped projection room. The director offered the usual good wishes. A dozen years later, Montand and Pagnol became friends (Simone Signoret and Jacqueline Pagnol had gone to high school together).

Montand's whole life would be made up of overlapping circles of this kind. Nearly half a century later, when he shot *Jean de Florette,* he was astonished to see an old gentleman appear with photos of the young Montand taken on that January day in 1942 as he sang for Pagnol, which *Les Cahiers du Film* had used in its February 1942 number for an article entitled "They Are All Swinging."

By early 1942, "swing" was a hot new craze in France. Launched by the hit song "Je suis swing," recorded by Charles Trenet's former partner Johnny Hess, the new fad had distinctly anti-Vichy overtones—so much so that magazines closely identified with Vichy collaboration sat up and took notice. *La Gerbe* thundered outrage at the "poison of Americanism," at the "insanity of Negro jazz and then swing," at "the contamination of our youth by cocktail parties." A new word was coined to designate the disease: "Americanitis."

Les Cahiers du Film took a different tack, depicting the "folly of the day" as a way of life that expressed itself first and foremost through dress: wide-brimmed hats, narrow neckties, ultralong jackets, trousers cuffed high on the ankle. The magazine lumped Charles Trenet, Django Reinhardt, and, of course, Yves Montand under the "swing" label: "Now we come to a real 'swing' professional, Yves Montand, whose eccentric gifts are on display in many a major theater. Having no partner, he grimaces, writhes, yells, slides, and dislocates himself with enough energy for two. He is 'swing' from head to toe, and since he's well over six feet tall his swing-style shimmying and shaking seem to go on forever." On the national level, the show-business magazine *Vedettes* also devoted an article to "the 'swing' craze," in its March 28 issue: "To be or not to be 'swing,' that is the only question these days. Are you 'swing'? Meaning not are you in the movement (that's old hat), but are you in the rhythm?"

That same month, Montand made the acquaintance of a more regimented rhythm. The meteoric rise of the singer whom the local press was calling the king of swing vocalists was brutally cut short by a summons to the Chantiers de la Jeunesse—the youth labor camps of defeated France.

In its campaign to promote "national recovery," to instill fresh values in a country that had allowed itself to be morally disarmed, the Vichy government focused heavily on the young, a group it was determined to discipline and to drill. The Chantiers de la Jeunesse was one of its most determined efforts. Its founding spirit was the retired General de La Porte du Theil, who at the armistice of June 1940 had been ordered to find useful work for the one hundred thousand youths hastily drafted as France was collapsing; they had not had time to fight and had been dispatched to open-air camps in the countryside. "The results—particularly the physical and moral transformation of this first contingent of young people—were so impressive that the marshal gave the camps permanent legal status on January 18, 1941." This proud judgment was delivered in a special issue of the magazine *Espoir Français* (*French Hope*) in December 1942.

All twenty-year-old males living in the southern, or unoccupied, zone were thus required to go through a form of military service of eight months' duration. Assembling in their home regions, they were sent to the camps and assigned jobs serving the national interest, notably in forestry and agricultural work.

Ordered to report to group 17 at Hyères-Ville, Ivo Livi left on March 13.[2] The spartan Hyères camp was close to the Centurion beach on reclaimed marshland; muddy, reed-fringed ponds were its most visible feature. The recruits slept in unheated wooden huts infested with fleas and bedbugs. As soon as he arrived, Montand, whose reputation had filtered through to the career officers who ran the camp, was assigned to group 8, the entertainment section, whose job it was to enliven evenings around the campfire.

Military-style discipline was the order of the day. Every morning the uniformed recruits assembled to salute the flag and sing the "Marseillaise." Working gear—shorts and a battle-dress tunic—was forest green. The off-duty uniform consisted of a dark brown leather jacket and tan leather shorts. Berets were also forest green. Judging from photos, Montand, a head taller than most of his companions, looked a bit ridiculous in this getup. His beret pushed way back on his head, he has a pleasantly bemused look, and in a group shot he is the only one waving (whether from genuine pleasure or, more likely, to play the clown). In another picture he wears scout-style shorts, boots, thick socks pulled up to the knees, and a tightly knotted dark tie. All in all, rather grotesque—and Montand does not seem to be fooled by it, for his lower jaw is sagging, village-idiot style.

The young men in the camp learned marching and close-order drill. There was a heavy emphasis on physical exercise. Another series of photos shows Montand with a group of youths doing pushups. He is standing slightly to one side, arms folded, watching the show.

Every so often they were lined up in front of an enormous cardboard *francisque* to extol the virtues of Vichy's "national revolution" (the *francisque* was the double-headed ax that Vichy ideologues, on dubious authority, claimed to have been the weapon of the ancient Gauls; Vichy adopted it as a national emblem along the lines of the Nazi swastika and Mussolini's fasces). A camp official would deliver an energetic speech punctuated by quotations from the marshal's more edifying thoughts: France had weakened itself by wallowing in "permissiveness" and "self-gratification," and the hearts and bodies of its sons must now be toughened all over again. With spades and pickaxes, the Hyères youth corps dug trenches, weeded fields, drained swamps. Apparently, Montand threw himself into these manly tasks as halfheartedly as he dared.

2. Recollections of R. Pizzo, secretary of the Association of Former Youth Camp Members, Provence regional delegation, June 20, 1989.

He made friends with two of his hutmates, Mourchou, a farmer's son from Carqueiranne, and Derdérian, an Armenian truck driver and an active member of the large Catholic youth movement Jeunesse Ouvrière Chrétienne. Like them, Montand was dying of boredom, fretting in this swamp in the middle of nowhere, far from the footlights. The actor-dancer, the singer-mime, the stage "bombshell" endured the endless tedium as best he could. He avenged himself by dreaming up pranks and stupid practical jokes with his comrades.

Apart from the sense of serving absolutely no purpose—a sense reinforced by the stupidity of some of their leaders—what troubled Montand most was hunger. The food doled out to the youngsters in those days of acute shortage was uncomfortably reminiscent of Ivo Livi's childhood: watery soups, boiled vegetables, stews of inscrutable origin. Everyone got by as best he could, some with the help of parcels sent by their families. Mourchou in particular was a godsend to his friends, thanks to the produce of the family farm. Nevertheless, the chief obsession of Montand and his chum Derdérian, known as "Der," was finding food. Until they found kindhearted allies.

"One day," Derdérian remembers, "we happened to walk by the kitchens as we strolled round the camp. The cook was tossing pieces of bread to a dog. We went up to the window and saw chunks of stale bread piled up on the kitchen table. Montand poked me in the ribs.

" 'Ask him for a chunk.'

" 'Not me.'

"But he insisted, and I took the plunge: 'Could we have a piece of bread, cook?'

" 'What for? It's stale.'

" 'We're hungry.'

" 'You're hungry?'

"He turned to his assistant: 'They're hungry!'

"He couldn't get over it. He told us to come in, and he shut the kitchen window. He had made a casserole that morning, and he helped us to several ladlefuls. From then on he gave us 'bread' on a regular basis."

This story, with liberal embellishments, was later presented in books and magazine articles as an intrepid midnight raid to force open the kitchen doors.

Apart from hunger pains, the recruits dreaded the assaults of the swamp's thriving armies of vermin. Fleas and bedbugs swarmed from every nook and cranny. At night, you had to fall asleep in your "meat sack" (linen was changed every two weeks) before the itching began; the next day, you would assess the nocturnal damage. Tired of being preyed upon, the little group to which Montand belonged decided on a major counter-offensive. The youths nailed their bedsteads together, burned out with a candle the tiniest crevices in the planks, and set the legs of the beds in pots full of water. Cleansed and quarantined, their sleeping platforms became islands of tranquillity: no night-crawling insect could approach them without first learning how to swim.

Although he was in the entertainment section, Montand did little singing at the youth camp beyond the daily "Marseillaise." But during one furlough he and Derdérian went to hear Maurice Chevalier, who was appearing at the Variétés in Marseilles. During the intermission they knocked at the star's door; he received them cordially. From this first contact with the giant of French vaudeville, Montand chiefly remembered, apart from the legendary charm, two details: the grand old man's scarlet complexion and his small white hands (Montand was used to the hardened fists of manual workers). Derdérian recalls that "Maurice" issued some friendly advice: singing was a rough calling that required patience and hard work. But Chevalier was preaching to the converted.

Montand went on more furloughs than he was entitled to. "We had to keep sending telegrams to the camp," recalls his sister Lydia, "announcing that a grandmother had died or an aunt was on her deathbed. He got away every chance he could." During one such pass, on June 13, he sang alongside Fransined, Fernandel's brother, at a concert at the Marseilles Opéra. *Artistica* informed its readers that on the occasion of its annual variety competition, the "likable and talented 'swing' entertainer Yves Montand contributed 300 francs to the prize money," adding: "Our friend's gesture is all the more generous in light of the fact that he is currently serving his time at the Hyères Youth Camp. Yves Montand thus proves that he has not forgotten the beginners."

As the summer of 1942 and the festival of Joan of Arc approached, youth camp members were ordered to participate in a grand patriotic rally in Marseilles. The festivities were to begin with a three-day march to the ancient Greek city on the coast, and the festival itself would take place in the local cycling stadium before a grandstand packed with officials. The recruits, decked out in shorts and tunics, sported arms and legs painted pink or green, depending on whether they were playing Frenchmen or Englishmen in their grandiose re-enactment of the epic of the Maid of Orléans. (The question of driving the English from French soil might soon become relevant again. . . .) The next day, before the uniformed troops standing at attention in the baking sun, a Vichy emissary delivered a windily appropriate address.

On June 22, the first anniversary of the German invasion of the Soviet

Union, Pierre Laval, head of the Vichy government, made a remark that would come back to haunt both him and France: "I hope for a German victory, because without Germany, Bolshevism would spread everywhere." As he spoke, the outcome of the war was being decided in a number of large theaters. In the Battle of the Atlantic, U-boats of the Kriegsmarine were sending hundreds of thousands of tons of Allied shipping and equipment to the bottom of the sea. In North Africa, the Wehrmacht was pushing toward El-Alamein and the road to Cairo. On the plains of the Caucasus, swastika-emblazoned armored divisions were thrusting at Stalingrad. The Russians were falling back along hundreds of miles of front. At Hyères, most of the officers made no secret of their sympathies: "The Red Army's finished," they told their charges. "Swept away. Russia has lost."

Such an opinion—at the time it appeared irrefutable—was unacceptable to Montand/Livi, the child born and raised in Communism. Even when he saw newsreels showing thousands of dead Soviet soldiers or Soviet prisoners of war, he was convinced the scenes were propaganda. Without the slightest knowledge of what was going on in the field, he wagered that the Red Army would win the war. It was not an analytical judgment but an article of faith, taken in with his mother's milk.

The summer slowly dragged on. Practical jokes—such as pinning epaulets to your shoulders and waking the newest recruits for nocturnal forced marches—no longer kept Montand from apathy. The last weeks were the worst: useless, endless. The moment he was freed, in October, he threw away his forest-green beret. He was just twenty-one.

As soon as Montand returned to civilian life, Audiffred took him back under his wing. Montand's stint at the camp had in no way affected his reputation, and his return was triumphant. The Odéon announced that he was back as its star. The contracts Audiffred signed with the young man were dazzling: five hundred francs a day for a tour of the south from December 5 to 15, performing at Perpignan, Béziers, Montpellier, Nîmes, Avignon, and finally Lyons, where his fee went up to eight hundred francs.

The clause headed "Publicity/Billing" stipulated that "Monsieur Montand will be billed as a special guest star on the posters, and his name will be in bigger type than all other artists or attractions advertised, excluding Monsieur Max Regnier, who will have star billing."

Then, in just one evening, December 23, the artist pocketed fifteen hundred francs; the special provisions in his contract for that gig specified that he would receive "star billing on all posters and publicity materials."

His name was to be "printed in type at least three times larger than that of any other name figuring alongside his own on the program."

And from December 29 to January 3, 1943, Montand sang again at the Célestins theater in Lyons for eight hundred francs a day, with guest-star billing. For the times, and for a son of Giovanni Livi, these were highly respectable sums. Ivo's dream had come true, and he had fulfilled his promise to himself: he was earning a living on the stage.

Marseilles's relative tranquillity came to an end in November 1942. Three days after the American landings in North Africa, Hitler informed Pétain that "to his great regret" he had given orders for a "temporary" occupation of the southern zone.[3] Vichy played for time. The French army confined itself obediently to barracks; the navy scuttled the French battle fleet in its Toulon base. Marshal von Rundstedt awarded top marks for good behavior to the losers of 1940: "The French army remains loyal and is helping our troops; the French police are zealous and a fund of goodwill; the attitude of the population is for the most part apathetic, with the exception of the Marseilles and Roanne regions, which are openly hostile."[4] The "French state" was no longer anything but a fiction whose survival depended entirely on Hitler. Marseilles was about to know occupation.

With the arrival of the Germans, the climate changed. Inflatable barrage balloons protected the port against Allied bombardment. And the invaders did not tolerate for very long the Marseillais hostility mentioned by Rundstedt. Indeed, the city paid a disproportionate price for its rebelliousness. On December 2, barely two weeks after the appearance of Germans along the Canebière, two bombs damaged the Hôtel Astoria and the Hôtel de Rome et Saint-Pierre, where one German soldier was killed. On January 3, 1943, it was the turn of the Hôtel Splendide, which had been commandeered by the German staff, where an explosion killed two people. On the same day, a brothel heavily frequented by olive-green uniforms was targeted.

On January 5, Berlin sent General Karl Oberg, chief of German police in France, to Marseilles. Oberg announced his intentions to his opposite number, the head of the Vichy police, and to the municipal authorities: "Marseilles is a blot on Europe's countenance, and Europe will have no peace until Marseilles is cleansed. The bombings of January 3, which killed

3. Jean-Pierre Azéma, *De Munich à la Libération* (Paris, 1979).

4. Quoted in E. Jaeckel, *La France dans l'Europe de Hitler* (Paris, 1968).

military personnel of the Greater Reich, are proof of this. The German authorities have therefore decided to purge the city's older neighborhoods of their undesirable elements and destroy them by mining and shelling."[5] The French officials voiced their understanding of German concerns and obtained permission to carry out the operations themselves.

The targeted area was the Vieux Port, the historic center of Marseilles. Like most of the city's poorer neighborhoods, the Vieux Port was a kind of village—picturesque, overcrowded, a gold mine of clashing tongues and tales. It also had a famous red-light district: the streets around the rue Saint-Laurent had everything a sailor on shore leave could ask for. A local paper deplored the prostitution, depicting the area as an antechamber of hell: "the foulest of cesspools, where the scum of the Mediterranean piles up, to Marseilles's shame and glory, in a state of decrepitude and decay that assaults the eye. Corruption and leprosy seem to eat at its very walls. It is the abode of sin and death."[6]

The Vieux Port's squalid reputation was not the only reason the invader was determined to cleanse it. For in that warren of alleyways and close-packed dwellings lurked Jews, Resistance fighters, illegal aliens, and deserters from the Wehrmacht. It was here that the city's "cosmopolitan" vocation was rooted, here that a mixture of races—odious in German eyes—defied the orders of their new lords.

January 23 saw the launching of an operation comparable in scale to the mass roundup of Paris Jews the previous July. An SS regiment sealed off the quarter and its streets with armored cars and barbed wire. The next day, the French police moved in to evacuate the whole area. Rooted out of their houses with a minimum of belongings, the people of the Vieux Port went through identity checks that lasted two whole days: forty thousand men, women, and children were thus "processed." Almost six thousand people were arrested (although four thousand were released almost immediately), and the rest were packed into requisitioned streetcars. After transportation to a holding camp near Fréjus, many of them were deported to the concentration camps at Buchenwald and Mauthausen. On February 1, German artillery units mined the deserted houses. The German army paper *Signal* described what happened next: "At noon a bugle blast echoed along the wharves, and a helmeted German officer came running out of an alleyway. For a few seconds, all was still. Then came an enormous explosion: at the foot of Notre-Dame-de-la-Garde the bells in the old Gothic church began to chime, set in motion by the displacement of the

5. Quoted in Anne Sportiello, "Le Vieux Port de Marseille à l'heure allemande," *L'Histoire,* October 16, 1979.

6. Louis Gillet, *Marseille,* October 21, 1942.

air. A cloud of white dust billowed upward. Small black dots darted about—the rats were fleeing. A hail of small stones fell from the skies as six houses collapsed upon themselves."[7]

War had come with a vengeance to the Mediterranean shore. But while Nazis were parading over the ruins of the Vieux Port, other Nazis were surrendering in the debris of Stalingrad. On January 30, 1943, General Paulus (to whom Hitler had parachuted a marshal's baton only the day before) capitulated to the Red Army. The Soviet victory at the Battle of Stalingrad, which had lasted six months and cost the death of 147,000 German and 46,700 Russian soldiers, marked the turning point of the war. It indelibly stamped Montand's life with an imprint that explained and determined his later political commitment: henceforth, he would belong to the "Stalingrad generation."

Yves Montand was then still living with his parents. Because of the danger of bombing (La Cabucelle was close to the port) and of concern for little Jean-Louis's safety, the Livi clan rented an apartment in the Notre-Dame-des-Limites area, where they slept every night; during the day, Lydia went on working in her salon in the impasse des Mûriers. Montand thanked his lucky stars, for he could now take his amorous conquests to the family house at night.

> I had no regular girlfriend, no stable relationship. Naturally, I met girls when I was on tour. It was wartime, I was just twenty, I was beginning to enjoy a bit of a reputation, and I took advantage of it. I sang in one club called Maxim's, where I met a wonderful blonde. Another time, in Cannes I remember, there was a gorgeous, warm-hearted lady announcer in fishnet stockings. I was so nervous and so hungry for a woman that although I did battle five or six times in the course of the night, I was unable to satisfy her. Yet she encouraged me in the nicest way. But too much desire often works against you . . . of course, for a macho Latin it was acutely embarrassing.

Despite his name in bold type on the posters, despite his checked jacket and his height, to his family, Montand continued to be little Ivo, who had to be protected. But he was more than a little proud, now that he was making money, to be able to contribute to the family's finances. At the start of the war the Livis had survived thanks to the permanent waves Lydia bartered for meat and olive oil, while Giuseppina Livi baked bread. Even so, soup had all too often consisted of water and bean hulls. Now Yves's

7. *Signal* (special issue of the *Berliner Illustrierte Zeitung*), April 1943.

performances put more substance into the family meals and made it possible to fill out the parcels sent to Julien.

News of his big brother came from time to time on the terse postcards permitted by the German censors. Julien had worked on a big farm near the Baltic, then in a sugar refinery, then he had been transferred to an airplane factory. "One day," Julien Livi recalls, "I received a package containing a photo and a press clipping showing my brother on stage with a very big audience. I had heard he was singing but had no idea what that really meant. When I saw that crowd listening to him, I couldn't get over it. I showed the story to my fellow detainees. 'That's my kid brother,' I told them. 'Can you believe it? The little so-and-so!' I was tickled pink."

The Occupation had not interrupted Giovanni's political activity. His morale bolstered by the Soviet Union's entry into the war, by the Red Army victory at Stalingrad, and by the Allied landings in North Africa, Livi was still part of a network of Italian anti-Fascists. He printed leaflets on a clandestine mimeograph machine and distributed them in the Marseilles region; the impasse des Mûriers became a safe haven and the Livi house a rendezvous, a sanctuary for fugitives, and a mail drop. It made sense: the house had two doors, and since number 8 was also a business address, people could come and go without arousing suspicion. And the Livis still had their first house, at number 7; normally it was unoccupied, but it was easy to put a guest there. As Montand recalled, he went there twice with bread and soup for transient *compagni* sleeping on mattresses on the floor. Of course, he suspected that these tense-looking, wild-eyed men were illegal aliens, but he never asked questions.

According to Julien, who discussed these things with his father after the Liberation, the clandestines sheltered in La Cabucelle were ranking officials of the Italian Communist Party (including, at least once, a personal assistant to Palmiro Togliatti). In any case, Giovanni Livi had acquired a rock-solid cover: an administrative job at the Casa d'Italia, an agency officially empowered, with the full blessings of Mussolini's Italy, to take care of Italians residing in France. As an employee of the agency, he was entitled to that most precious of wartime perks—a pass.

The owner of the Bar des Mûriers—the Piedmontese Garone, Bruna's brother-in-law and the owner of a superb front-wheel-drive Citroën that Ivo coveted—suspected that his neighbor Livi was up to illegal business. He occasionally saw visitors hug the walls as they approached number 8. Garone was an admirer of the Fascists but he said nothing—perhaps out of national solidarity with Livi, perhaps from a sense of neighborhood closeness. When he was attacked for his ideological leanings at the Liberation, Giovanni Livi stepped forward as a character witness in his favor.

Livi was careful not to recruit from within his family. Julien was surprised at this when he returned from prison. "I asked him why not. 'You had a ready-made cell right here in the house,' I told him. 'You, André [Ferroni], Yves. . . .' But he answered, 'You're wrong. It wasn't that simple. In clandestine work you have to keep every link in the chain separate from the others. Starting with your own home.' He was right, of course."

In the summer of 1943, Montand was again starring on the stage of the Odéon, between July 28 and August 2. He was a resounding success.

At the Odéon, he spotted a girl who was often backstage—she was Greek, and beautiful, and apparently mesmerized by him. The "bombshell" did not worry unduly over whether she was attracted by his person or his reputation. They very soon found themselves alone together in a bedroom. When she saw him naked, the Greek beauty gave a scream of fear—which Yves Montand saw as an instinctive tribute to his private parts. After a moment's bewilderment he tried to reassure his partner, but she went on screaming and leapt off the bed.

A few days later, he had a date with the young lady in a Marseilles bar located in a cellar. Through the gloom, he saw his beautiful Greek friend leaning on the bar in the company of the owner and another customer. Moving closer, Montand recognized this third person, a German in civilian clothes who was surely a policeman, and whom he had already seen on two or three occasions in the vicinity of the woman. She introduced them, and they struck up a friendly conversation, the Gestapo man launching into a wide-ranging political discussion. He turned to Montand and held out both fists, clenched tight and pressed against each other.

"This one is Communism." (He nodded toward his left fist.) "This is National Socialism." (He indicated the right one.) "We're close, yet we can't join forces." (He paused for a moment.) "Or else this is what we have to do." (He described a sweeping circle with both hands and brought his palms together.) "But we have a long road to travel before we get there!"

Montand began to feel uneasy. Why was this German talking to him about Communism?

The man smiled slightly and winked. Suddenly, still smiling, he said confidently: "You're Jewish."

Surprised, but not disconcerted, Yves Montand replied simply and naturally: "No, I am not Jewish."

"Do you have your identity card?"

The singer pulled out his papers. The German snatched them from him. Abruptly his expression changed; it became frightening. His smile narrowed into a thin, hate-filled line; his eyes were like two hard bullets.

"Yes, you are Jewish. Your name is Lévy, not Livi. You have changed two letters in your name."

"That's absurd," Montand shot back. "If I had changed anything at all I would have changed the whole thing and called myself Dupont!"

After a few moments the German gave a sarcastic roar of laughter. Montand steeled himself. But the German suddenly relaxed and said, almost genially: "*Natürlich.* How stupid of me."

He turned to face the bar, raised his glass in a toast, and drained it. The Greek woman had not said a word.

It was not the first time Ivo Livi had encountered this reaction. As a boy at La Cabucelle when he had gone away to summer camp—he must have been eight or nine—he was terrified at the idea of being away from his family. As his father's figure on the station platform diminished and then vanished, he burst into tears in the train; and despite the games and the comradeship, he remained sad for the rest of the summer. He barely noticed when the camp organizer in charge of mail distribution read his name out as "Lévy," so overjoyed was he at having news from home, and he did not even bother to correct the mistake. But the incident remained vivid in his memory.

The second time was at the youth camp—and, it being under Vichy, much more was at stake. The incident took place in the spring of 1942, when the Germans had already adopted the final solution and were making ready for the massive deportation of Jews from France. In the southern zone, still under the control of the French state, vast roundups had begun. One day, the recruit Livi was called to the commandant's office with three companions. Behind the desk, an NCO read out a list of Jewish-sounding names. Montand's was the last.

"So you're Lévy?"

"No, not Lévy. Livi."

The officer checked his list and made a note. At the time, Montand did not realize that he had just escaped the worst of fates. When the three Jews summoned with him disappeared from the camp, he had no inkling of the horrors awaiting them. Even in 1943, when he put the Gestapo man to rights over the spelling of his name, he failed to realize that two vowels might have earned him a one-way trip to Auschwitz.

Only much later, when he learned of the scope of the Holocaust, was he seized with an awful retrospective fear. The heedlessness of youth, the ignorance of the horrible truth, and, until the end of 1942, the relative immunity of Jews living on the Mediterranean coast kept Montand—and he was by no means the only one—from realizing that the Jews faced systematic extermination. Later, Montand developed a deep and abiding love for the Jewish people, and feelings of guilt for this collective (and, in his case, involuntary) indifference probably contributed to this.

It took him another thirty-three years to realize the reason for the Greek woman's screams at the sight of his naked body. In 1976, Montand was in Munich with Catherine Deneuve to receive the German Golden Bambi for their performances in *Le Sauvage.* In his hotel that evening a young German girl, a pretty blonde who was traveling alone, pretended to mistake his door for her own. What followed was equally traditional. But the actor was surprised at the insistence with which the young woman examined his penis. Then he realized: she was wondering whether he was circumcised and therefore Jewish. That painful retraction of his foreskin all those years ago, when he had called out for help to Giuseppina, was responsible for the confusion! And then he recalled the Greek woman's reaction in Marseilles.

Naturally, the encounter with the Gestapo man in the bar had been planned: the girl worked for the Nazis and had been assigned to check people's identities "in the field." Montand was convinced that the appetizing blonde who threw herself at him in Munich was also acting on orders. He never knew for sure . . . but he always considered himself an "honorary Jew."

That uneasy exchange in the bar was not Montand's last encounter with the Germans. A letter dated September 1943 informed him that he was subject to compulsory labor service and summoned him to appear before the selection board to discuss his assignment.

The Vichy government had set up this service on February 21, 1943. It required all young men over eighteen to report for work in Germany. Vichy collaborationist propaganda stressed the material advantages that would accrue to the young Frenchmen. In fact, the 650,000 victims sent across the Rhine and herded into camps just like those housing prisoners of war were called on to labor hard and long in conditions of extreme physical hardship.

As might be imagined, Montand had no wish to go to Germany, but he obeyed the summons because he thought it would simply be a first contact to notify him of his assignment. When he got to the Gare Saint-Charles, he found it hopping with Germans. He went to the appropriate office, where a "gray mouse" (a German army woman) began to take down his particulars. Then she gave him a look in which the young man believed he saw a glow of sympathy—or was it his imagination?—and said wearily: "Silesia. Salt mines."

Instead of giving him back his papers, she pointed to a room on her left. There Ivo Livi found himself closeted with a dozen young people his own age, guarded by three relaxed and friendly French policemen. They did their best to cheer up their "prisoners," who were all stunned by the imminence of departure. One of the policemen came over and whispered, his eyes on the door: "Don't try to run for it by getting into the train and jumping out on the other side. The Germans will be there, with orders to shoot. But as soon as the train reaches Dijon, it will slow down. That's when you can jump and get away to join the boys up in the Vercors."

Montand had no idea what was happening in the Vercors region. He and his companions were transferred to a sort of warehouse on the rue Honorat. When her brother failed to come home to the impasse des Mûriers, Lydia was terrified. She knew only one thing: she must at all costs stop him from leaving for Germany. But how? What door should she knock at? First she must get the family's papers together. In 1929, when President Doumergue signed the Livis' naturalization order, Giovanni Livi had been given an official copy of the decree and was warned that duplicates of naturalization certificates were never issued. But ten years later, the Communist militant had forgotten the warning and given the precious document to an Italian comrade leaving for the Soviet Union. The Livi clan could no longer produce proof of French nationality. Lydia confided the problem to one of her customers, who ran a brothel where a police inspector was a regular customer. The man issued her a duplicate of the certificate.

Lydia next obtained permission to see her brother to take him a few belongings. She found Montand determined to follow the policeman's advice and jump off the train outside Dijon. Increasingly worried, Lydia began to make the rounds of people who might be able to help him—particularly local black-market dealers, renowned for their clout. To no avail. Then she thought of a couple she was friends with because she did the wife's hair. The husband, a former waiter, was now working in the censors' department. He suggested giving his own documents to Montand or else procuring false papers for him so that once he had escaped he would not be bothered at checkpoints. Lydia thanked him but was not satisfied. What she wanted was for her brother to stay in Marseilles. Then she remembered another client, who also dabbled in the black market and who lived on the rue d'Italie. She was not at home. Lydia burst into tears on the street.

The sight of this young woman sobbing attracted the attention of a respectable-looking man of about forty, who came up and asked if he could be of help. Exhausted, at the end of her tether, Lydia told the stranger everything: her big brother a prisoner in Germany, her little brother called up for compulsory labor service, her family's hardships. The man uttered some comforting words, said that these were unforgiving times . . . and started walking away. After he had gone a few yards, he stopped and turned back.

What followed was so unbelievable that even a bad scriptwriter would never have the gall to use it. "I haven't told this story before," Lydia says. "But in 1987, Yves called me from America to ask me for a complete account, which I sent him on May 22." In that letter, Lydia revealed how she had saved Montand from labor service in Germany. "A miracle. Wasting no words, the man gave me a note for Sabiani and an address on the rue Pavillon. Out of pity? Because of my youth? I shall never know. I knew it would be unwise to go there (for me, Sabiani was the world's worst Fascist), but I could think only of you." Ever since the outbreak of war, Simon Sabiani had openly thrown in his lot with the Germans and had become one of the pillars of collaboration. But Lydia repressed her feelings of revulsion and went to the rue Pavillon, the headquarters of the Parti Populaire Français. She walked into a lobby full of men in soft hats with conspicuous bulges at their armpits. A receptionist told her that Sabiani was not there. She pulled out the note scribbled by the man she had met in the street—and whose identity would remain forever a mystery. When he saw the signature, the receptionist hesitated. Then he took the note and went to confer with two other men, who stared at Lydia, doubtless assessing the distance between the powerful author of the note and this frightened, anonymous girl. Finally, the receptionist came back and returned the paper to her with a note telling her to call at German military headquarters at nine the following morning.

Lydia was inside the big building on the Canebière, formerly the main offices of a major shipping line, an hour ahead of time. "I still remember what I was wearing: a pleated white skirt and pinstriped blouse. I suppose dressing properly counted for nothing, but when you're young and when you want something from someone . . . well, people are so much nicer."

Lydia was kept waiting all day long. In late afternoon she was taken to see a German officer—the very model of Aryan beauty as defined by Dr. Goebbels—who treated her politely and very coldly. Lydia stated her case. The German, as icy as ever, asked for the family papers. She handed him the duplicate of the naturalization certificate the police inspector had given her, along with a note from him explaining that the original had been lost.

The officer began to read, then broke off: "Livi, Livi . . . Not Livi, Lévy!"

Like the man in the bar, he was suspicious of the vowels and questioned Lydia at length about her family. He seemed to relent a little when he read the recommendations passed along by Sabiani's henchmen. And when Lydia pulled out press clippings about Montand's stage triumphs, his face softened. He took a piece of paper, scribbled a few words, and stamped it.

Lydia heaped him with thanks and raced off to the rue Honorat. "I was drunk with fatigue, fear, and joy, but I had wings on my feet." It was after 6:00 p.m. Yves's train was scheduled to leave next morning. She reached the station clutching the piece of paper. It opened all doors for her, and soon she was hugging her brother. But Yves protested angrily when he learned that he was free. "He wanted to be a Resistance fighter, he wanted to jump the train. He was so romantic, and so young."

When asked, Montand would question this version of the story, or profess to have forgotten it, yet Lydia sticks to her guns: "There I was in that stinking cell, and there you were—disappointed. You were angry, as only you can be angry. You yelled at me. I can still see you now. Anyway, you shook hands with your cellmates and said see you later. Your anger meant nothing to me when I thought how relieved everyone back home would be."

Until now, Lydia's appeal to Sabiani and the *Kommandanteur* have remained taboo family secrets. But was there any dishonor in a Communist anti-Nazi family clutching at straws to save one of their own? In any event, the grace period was brief.

In the fall of 1943, the German and French police stepped up their pursuit of young men attempting to dodge compulsory labor service. Montand went on giving performances, but he sensed that he was unlikely to slip through the net a second time.

One evening in January 1944, the Milice (the Vichy militia) raided 8 impasse des Mûriers. They meant business: they cordoned off the entire neighborhood and were searching several other houses. They appeared to be well informed, since they burst into the Livis' home by both the front door (which gave onto the impasse) and the back (which opened onto the garden and from there to the boulevard des Mûriers). Yet it was this double entryway that saved Montand. When the militiaman kicked open the door to go down to the basement, he covered up a narrow opening that led to a tiny room where the young man lay sleeping. The night callers ferreted through the house in vain. To the intruders' questions, Mama Giuseppina replied with complete presence of mind: "My son's giving a concert somewhere around Toulouse."

A last look around, and the Milice withdrew.

Montand had been lucky. But he knew it could not last. Sooner or later, he would be caught. He had to act.

> A few days after the raid by the Milice, friends quietly dropped by and said, "You have to go to the Maquis." The maquis? What maquis? It was the first time I had heard the word used in that way. For me, "maquis" meant the fragrant wild vegetation of Corsica and the hills it grew on. Taking to the hills for what? So they talked to me about the Resistance, about men who refused to do compulsory labor service and who had taken refuge in the mountains around Saint-Raphaël and formed fighting units. In January 1944 I knew nothing about all that, which must seem amazing, since my father was in the Resistance. But he had never mentioned it to me! The Saint-Raphaël Maquis seemed not all that serious—how wrong I was! I told them, "Listen, I'm an entertainer, and your Maquis sounds like the movies." I had no wish to go and hide in the mountains. I was singing. It was going well, and I wanted to keep on doing it.

At no point did the veteran Communist Giovanni Livi seek to influence his son. He neither brought him into his underground network nor urged him to join the Maquis. As for Montand, though he was enough of an anti-Nazi to want to avoid labor service, he was neither involved nor informed enough to want to fight the Germans. In these troubled times, it would need an accident of fate to force him to shape his destiny. That accident soon occurred.

For months, Audiffred had urged his protégé to go to Paris (*Artistica* had already alluded to the possibility). With Montand fretting over ways to avoid the labor service summons, his manager presented him with a contract for the ABC, Paris's most prestigious music hall. Audiffred's offer was timely, and it solved Montand's problem. He would hide out in broad daylight, on the stage of the ABC. Harry Max, his partner in *An Evening of Folly,* had left him his Paris address, just in case. But Montand still had to persuade his father. There were undeniable risks. He would have to cross the demarcation line into the occupied zone with his real papers, which showed him to be a labor-service dodger. And anything could happen in Paris, so far from his family. Then there was the financial problem. He spent his money as soon as he earned it and had put very little aside. Giovanni, more moved than his appearance suggested, sensed that this leave-taking was a major break: the baby of the family was quitting the nest.

"Listen, son, I give you six months to make it in Paris. If you don't, you'll have to get a factory job like everyone else. There will always be a place for you here." Lydia did not miss a syllable. A few decades later, she reminded Montand of the words in a letter: "We were worried sick. You were going to be on your own, even though you had Audiffred's contract and Harry Max's address. You were wearing that ridiculous suit of yours, and you had barely a penny."

On February 16, 1944, Yves Montand took the Paris train at the Gare Saint-Charles, his brown cardboard suitcase in his hand.

Chapter 5

On the morning of February 17, 1944, wide-eyed and far from home, Yves Montand left the train that had rocked him the whole night long and descended into the Paris Métro at the Gare de Lyon. Harry Max had found him a hotel ("You'll feel right at home—the family is from Marseilles!"), but first of all he had to find Harry, who lived on the rue Fontaine, at the foot of Montmartre. Dazed by the clatter of the yellow subway cars, intimidated by the automatic doors that snapped shut with the ferocity of meat cleavers, the young southerner asked a fellow rider which subway station was closest to the rue Fontaine. "Bonne-Nouvelle!" the man yelled cheerfully. "Bonne-Nouvelle!" Good news? The man did not look like a Quaker or a Baptist or an evangelist. Could it actually be the name of the stop? But when he saw the name appear in blue lettering against the white-tiled station wall, Montand did not move. The good Samaritan was surprised. "This is where you get off!" he said. Still, Montand waited in front of the door. At last the other man understood: since the door had closed all by itself, the young traveler expected it to open in the same way. A pedagogue to the end, the stranger raised the latch that allowed the door to slide open.

Montand stepped out onto the platform. This was just the kind of situation he loathed—not for the ignorance it betrayed, for ignorance in itself is inevitable and rectifiable and mercifully widespread, but for the feeling of clumsiness that the ignorance generated, the humiliating sense of being a dope. As a traveler from one kind of world to a different one, it was the kind of feeling he could no longer accept.

The episode would scarcely be worth relating if it had simply ended there. But that same afternoon, Montand returned to the subway and learned all the routes by heart, going over them again and again, as if reciting a rosary, "Pigalle, Notre-Dame-de-Lorette, Hauvre-Caumartin, Saint-Lazare, Opéra, Concorde," backward and forward and sideways, deliberately losing himself in the endless white tunnels and making a game of finding his way out again. When he returned to the surface four hours later he was seasoned enough to steal the ticket puncher's seat at Les Lilas.

The entertainer in whose name Audiffred had signed an open-ended contract assaulted the stage of the ABC the way he attacked the subway system—determined to make it his own. The same determination drove him ever after, whenever he felt threatened by memory lapses, to go back over the elusive lines again and again while he turned on a radio to blare out music, news, commercials—anything to throw him off and make the exercise a real challenge.

Finally he was there, on the border of Pigalle, a lunch of cold fish under his belt, ringing jovial Harry Max's doorbell. Hugs and backslapping, then off they went to the rue Blanche. The Palace hotel had a fly-by-night look, and its owner, M. Albert, was no more a Marseillais than Montand. He was a friendly Greek, perhaps a pimp. In the hotel restaurant silent men played cards surrounded by motionless women and greeted one another, movie-gangster style, with a finger raised to the brim of their fedoras. M. Albert was impressed that his new client was an artist who, despite his tender years, was going to perform at the ABC. He was ready to do his utmost for such a guest.

He soon got the chance to prove his hospitality. Hardly had Harry Max taken leave, hardly had Montand unpacked his shirts, than there was a hammering at the door.

"German police!"

Two large men stood outside. On their chests was the word "*Feldgendarmerie.*" The mere sight of it flooded you with panic, even before you had time to reflect that you were a labor-service dodger wanted by the police and that these awful men were paid to hunt down people like you. . . . "Your papers?"

Up bobbed M. Albert, jovial, wreathed in smiles, and waving as many arms as a Hindu goddess. "He's my cousin, ha ha, just imagine, my little cousin, up from the country to see the big city, oh my, yes, just to have a good time, *ja?* have some fun, *jawohl!* and he's going to help me out a little around here, he's a good worker, in this business you need all the help you can get, hard work, *ja, viel Arbeit,* he's going to help out a little and have fun in the city, my aunt's son, *ja,* he's tall, *nein?* . . ."[1]

And M. Albert drowned his visitors' zeal in two large glasses of cognac.

The memory chilled Montand to his last days, but he had little inclination to dwell on that adventure at the Palace hotel. What is more important

1. Dialogue as cited by Montand in *Du soleil plein la tête.*

is the story of his debut. Entering Paris at the portals of the ABC, when you were just twenty-three and had so far won only local fame, was like beginning a political career with a cabinet post, or being appointed cardinal after only a few weeks as a seminarian.

The ABC, located at 11 boulevard Poissonnière, and known as the "Comédie-Française of vaudeville," boasted twelve hundred seats, silver columns, a balcony, and blue-green paneling.[2] The program was changed every two weeks, with two performances a day. Its creator and owner, the Rumanian Mitty Goldin (temporarily "out of town" because his real name was Goldenberg), liked to say that working there was an honor, a consecration, even if you were only the opening act, and that a good show gained more than it lost by having several big names together. In April 1938, he had not hesitated to pair Charles Trenet with, among others, Edith Piaf and Marianne Oswald. And it was at the ABC that Charles Trenet, the "singing fool," had scaled the heights of glory, at the ABC that "La Miss"—Mistinguett—had pulled off a triumph in 1937, at the age of sixty-four.

And at the ABC's door Yves Montand came knocking on February 18, 1944. His contract entitled him to neither top billing nor guest-star status: he had to take his place at the very bottom of the list, crushed by the weight of the big attraction of the evening, André Dassary, a crooner whose hit song "Quand les prisonniers reviendront" ("When the Prisoners Come Home") would wring tears from a stone. In those days a good Paris program blended songs, dance, monologues, and circus-style numbers. A run-of-the-mill act hardly ever lasted more than ten minutes; a big-name singer never ran over twenty (about six or seven songs); a beginner sang three or four songs at most.

At rehearsal, Montand found himself with the Gasty Acrobats, the Wrestling Canovas, the Three Dancing Darescos, the Renati Clowns, the comic Roméo Carles, and others, all solid professionals, untroubled by personal rivalry. But the "spellbinding variety artist Betty Spell," who had guest-artist billing, filled him with despair. He liked Betty Spell. With her curls and striped blouse, she was spellbinding indeed, but she intended to close the first half of the program with a song called "Venez, venez dans mon rancho!" which threatened to take all the steam out of his own "Les Plaines du Far West." Granted, "rancho" was not "ranch," and "olé" was not "hello," but Montand had a sinking feeling that he was starting with the dice loaded against him. The program director refused to budge. The lighting technician listened sympathetically. But Montand had met an inflexible law of the theater: those who listen to you can do nothing, while those who can do something won't listen.

2. See André Sallée and Philippe Chauveau, *Music-hall et café-concert* (Paris, 1985).

By late afternoon, the ABC was already packed for the evening show, even though the competition was stiff now that times were lean, and a night on the town was the last available luxury. The Alhambra was offering *Croisière de charme,* with Georges Guétary; Lucienne Boyer had just left the Bobino theater for the Européen, where she was starring alongside Robert Rocca; Lys Gauty had taken over the Casino-Montparnasse. Frothy comedy was king on the boulevards, while Anouilh's *Antigone* had already been a hit for two weeks at the Atelier. At the movies that same week, *Premier de cordée, L'Ange de la nuit* (with Jean-Louis Barrault), and *L'Aventure est au coin de la rue* were the leading hits. Despite rapid program turnover, reviewers worked hard to cover everything, galloping from movie premieres to theater first nights. Montand knew neither their names nor their faces nor the papers where their reviews appeared. He did not know that he would be meeting Françoise Holbane of *Paris-Midi,* Louis Blanquie of *Le Matin,* and France Roche of *L'Echo de la France.* He knew only that judgment day had come.

Escorted by Harry Max, he arrived much too early, paralyzed by stage fright, and resigned to the worst, wearing a splendid tweed suit bought on the rue de Paradis in Marseilles, his hair glossy with brilliantine. Then he exchanged this garb for his stage clothes: maroon pants and shirt, long jacket with faint maroon-and-red checks, yellow polka-dotted tie.

I was nothing, nobody. People called me Jacques Morand, Yves Montana. . . . André Dassary and Betty Spell, on the other hand, were extremely well known. Betty Spell had a kind of Paris-bred comic appeal, very bouncy and peppy, which didn't particularly appeal to me but which worked well. I liked her physically. Dassary was a product of the comic opera. He, André Claveau, and Guétary were the big songsters of the day. Honestly, though, I didn't really like these "straight" singers. I considered them, spitefully perhaps, as spineless. I liked performing singers—Chevalier, Astaire, Armstrong.

I can still hear Dassary: "When they come home, the prisoners, every church bell in Paris will chime," and so on. Then the announcer called out, "And here is Yves Montand." I bounded on stage in my checked jacket, the conductor rose briefly from the orchestra pit to give me the cue, and I launched into *"Je m'en fous, je m'en fous, je m'en contrefiche, je m'en fous, je m'en fous, moi je tiens le coup. . . ."*—Charles Humel's immortal creation. In the gloom I could see that many of the audience were on their feet and heading for the exit. *"Je m'en fous, je m'en fous, pourvu que ça biche, yeah!"* Then a little tap dancing. Was I driving them away? Did everything bore them after Dassary? I left the stage, put on my cowboy hat, and came back on walking bandy-legged. When I sang *"Dans les plaines du Far West quand vient la nuit,"* people stopped in their tracks and sat back down, curious to see more of this gangling, skinny, double-jointed kid (yes, "double-jointed" is the word; later I saw myself on a newsreel singing "Luna Park" and wondered what that lanky asparagus figure was doing up there). Then there was total silence. Some silences are more shattering than a crowd that's booing. It was a benevolent silence (although I didn't yet know it) but at the same time frightening, because there were none of a crowd's subdued murmurs, slight creakings, contained tension. Nothing. No one moved. I had time—endless time—to wonder, to ask myself whether they disliked what they had seen. And then they were off. It was shattering, I swear it. They clapped, and they never stopped clapping.

It wasn't just a success; it was a triumph, a solid triumph. I hadn't realized that the people leaving weren't escaping but were afraid of missing the last Métro. Nor did I realize, in the heat of the moment, that they were applauding not just a singer whose voice they liked but someone singing publicly about America, who said "ranch" and not "rancho." A nuance today, but all-important then.

Audiffred was beside himself with joy. The third song, "Et il sortit son revolver" (still about America, but not the wholesome outdoors) was received as rapturously as the second. Beginners who brought down the house were at a premium: they were fought over from the Folies-Belleville to the Européen, from the Alhambra to the Fête Foraine. After only three songs Montand had not exactly broken the bank, but he had made a serious dent in it. He had won himself a contract for each day of the run. He should have been on cloud nine.

But he wasn't. Montand was not made that way. Even when everything seemed to be going perfectly, when success was there for all to see, he scrutinized the evidence for every flaw, false note, bad move. Even after his incredible 1982 world tour, he kept intact his private slough of despond. For him, the public was always a skeptical, cynical, world-weary organism, leaning back in its seat and saying, "Go ahead, Mr. Entertainer, surprise me—but I'll be very surprised if you do." Even a whole theater in ecstasy, even an entire sports stadium of people on their feet shouting for another encore, weighed less in his mind than the 6 or 8 percent of the audience who would invariably witness the euphoria without sharing it. It was this unconvertible minority that Montand never stopped trying to convert, even though he knew it could never be done. One can never, never rest on one's laurels.

On March 10, André Dassary, Betty Spell, and the others were replaced by Francis Blanche. The press had delivered its verdict in midrun. Yves Montand was submerged by praise and the kind of friendly advice reserved for entertainers whom the critics believe they themselves have invented, even created. Louis Blanquie set the general tone in *Le Matin* on February 26–27: "You have to admire the spunk of this artist who bounces on stage even before his predecessor's applause has died down." The paper predicted "a promising career," on condition that he discipline himself a little. Françoise Holbane, in *Paris-Midi* on February 29, counseled him to "put order into the workings of a still-unfocused imagination." In *L'Echo de la France* a week later, France Roche agreed that the newcomer had "personality" but suggested that he had not yet managed to define it.

Critical enthusiasm had been tempered by the young man's choice of songs. At a time when jazz and other "decadent" musical forms were banned, it was distinctly rash to heap praise upon an act dominated by transatlantic rhythms and stereotypes. Publications strongly committed to collaboration with the German occupation granted Montand the benefit of his tender years but advised him to call a halt. *Le Petit Parisien* on February 26 had come down hard on Betty Spell, and then continued: "A beginner, Yves Montand, who is not without talent, also went in for this doubtful game [of referring to the United States]. . . . He offers us gangsters, cops, chewing gum, electric chairs, and skyscrapers. What about mentioning their bombers instead?"

So nobody at the ABC was surprised when the rash cowboy was summoned to the Propagandastaffel, the censor's bureau, on the Champs-Elysées. It was a routine, legal measure, for everything published, filmed, or sung in Paris had to be approved by the occupying authorities. It was perhaps true that in show business more than in other fields, performers toed the official line, with the tacit complicity of audiences hungry for the mushy fare then in vogue. Thus, the menu for the first quarter of 1944 was unsullied by the smallest hint of subversion, and the taste of the day was for mush. Like it or not, the leading performers obliged.

Montand had fallen quite innocently out of step. He was certainly anti-Nazi, but when he sang "Je vends des hot dogs à Madison" ("I Sell Hot Dogs on Madison Avenue") or hummed Georges Ulmer's "Jolie comme une rose" ("Pretty as a Rose")—a takeoff on Bing Crosby—he neither believed nor wanted to make the public believe that he had opted for heroic dissent. He was quite simply following his adolescent dream, dancing his way to Hollywood; and too bad if his ambitions irritated the masters of the day. He never, then or later, played the part of eleventh-hour Resistance fighter or boasted of performing acts of premeditated courage.

The fact remains that patriotic fervor in those days expressed itself in ways which in hindsight may seem insignificant or trivial. For example, newsreels were never shown in total darkness, and a whistle, a disrespectful gesture, or a boo could lead to arrest by the Milice. On the other hand, excessive enthusiasm was no less suspect. Thus, when the Germans decided to ridicule Yankee culture by showing Louis Armstrong growling out a blues song or a clip from Paul Muni's *Scarface,* their efforts backfired: no one left the theater, and overeager spectators were in danger of attracting the attention of informers.

So the refractory Yves Montand looked sheepish when he called at the censorship bureau. Curiously enough, a Canadian was in charge of the variety section, undeniably pro-Hitler but inclined to moderation.

Allied pressure against the Axis powers had been building constantly since the Sicily landings in 1943. Allied bombers were reaching Berlin, the Soviets were taking the offensive in the Ukraine, the siege of Leningrad had been raised, and the Battle of Monte Cassino was under way. Despite heavy losses in the Dordogne and Jura, the French National Resistance Council was already working out a political program for postwar France. In Africa, Algiers and Brazzaville were at the boiling point, and along the Channel and Atlantic coasts German invasion watchers were straining their eyes. Only fanatics and those with literally nothing more to lose remained untouched by the coming apocalypse. Vast causes, minuscule effects: Montand's interviewer combed through the lyrics of his songs, finding the gangster's character distinctly preferable to the cowboy's ("too likable"), and he encouraged the novice, since he liked America so much, to choose Mexican rhythms and cut back his "Hello boys!" and "Oh baby, oh sweetheart!" But he uttered no dark threats, no hints of excommunication. For the moment.

Innocent rather than intrepid, Montand had sung as he pleased. And Paris theater managers could not have asked for more.

This was a time neither of joblessness nor of enforced idleness. Montand's reputation now preceded him—a wholesome, lighthearted, supple, virile young man from the Midi whose lack of experience was his trump card. The gods of show business were experts at sniffing the new air. They sensed that the public would soon be calling for old heads to roll and looking for other ones to adore. Montand was brand-new—a decided advantage.

Never mind that he had only just landed on the sidewalks of Paris: the most prestigious doors were opening for him. Renée Lebas, who had witnessed Montand's first attempts at the Alcazar in Marseilles, describes Paris's music-hall hierarchy in these terms: "The ABC was the leading song palace. Next came the Européen, on the rue Biot, in the seventeenth arrondissement, very pleasant, with loyal, lively customers from Clichy. The big, haughty Alhambra, on the rue de Malte, had once been a cinema; my friends and I used to put on variety turns there at intermission. The Bobino and the Casino-Montparnasse had Left Bank, working-class images. The Folies-Belleville was a notch lower. And the most prestigious cabarets were the Beaulieu, the Baccara, and the Night-Club, all on or near the Champs-Elysées." Within three or four months, Montand had explored all these locations, and then some. Engagements were very short—normally two weeks; the programs, printed somehow or other on hard-to-get paper, were undated.

We know from the press notices, for example, that Montand left the ABC on March 7, appeared at the Bobino with Blanche Darly, Roland Gerbeau, and Jules Berry (the border between music hall and the legitimate theater was porous, and many seasoned actors like Berry liked to mix their genres) on March 31, and was at the Européen on April 14. In mid-July he bobbed up at the Folies-Belleville with guest-star billing; a week later he was back at the Bobino, alongside Georgette Plana and Jacqueline Cadet. Numbers were brief but plentiful. Often there were two matinees on Sundays as well as an evening performance (set for 7:00 or 7:30, rarely later). Lighting was the directors' major headache. In cabaret basements, anonymous athletes pedaled away to feed a few feeble dynamos. As the days grew longer, theaters that had sliding roofs would open them and function by natural light. No management worthy of the name failed to provide bicycle garages and a list of nearby air-raid shelters. The theaters offered a strange twilight feast, a fleeting truce as the cycle-taxi whisked you briefly away from the silence of your vanished loved ones, from the lies of Radio-Paris, from obsession with butter, from fear of the sirens.

Montand had no idea how to take things easily. Between music-hall engagements he sang at cabarets: at the Beaulieu, the Fête Foraine on the Place Blanche, the Night-Club on the rue Arsène-Houssaye. He often doubled up, racing from one show to the next. He was still without valid papers, but he crossed the city at night from Pigalle, sinister without its streetlights, to the Champs-Elysées, the watering hole for the vanishing species of well-dressed late-nighters: German officers for whom Paris was still a reward to be enjoyed in civilian clothes.

Saint-Germain-des-Prés, the Café Flore, and the world of subversive intellectuals were utterly unknown to Montand. What he got to know in his own universe was the courtesy prevalent among music-hall performers (they addressed one another with the formal *vous*) and the horrible food prevalent in even the most pretentious nightclubs. He had lost none of his native shyness and hated customers to invite him to their table. But there was no doubt that things were going well, performance after performance.

Like a long, skinny night-prowling cat, Montand regularly breached the curfew in the dark, occupied city. Not unlike one of Jacques Prévert's cats—though Prévert did not yet exist for Montand—a cat clutching a small suitcase containing a lovingly folded stage costume, a cat whistling forbidden blues as it flitted down forbidden streets, with no other identification than a baptismal certificate, without an *Ausweis,* an animal so sure of itself as it went its merry whistling way to this place and that, whistling as loud as it could partly to give itself courage and partly because it liked to whistle, so self-confident that no patrol would be so silly as to check on whether the passerby with the suitcase might not be a labor-service dodger—or at least, so self-confident that a curious German patrol would at least ask questions before shooting. From February 17, 1944, the date of his arrival in Paris, until August 24, when General Leclerc's liberating tanks entered the capital much less furtively, Montand did not once sense danger during his forbidden wanderings. The Germans, he thought, had other fish to fry in North Africa, in Italy, and then in Normandy. War surrounded him without ever really taking hold of his life.

Yet the final hours were drawing near, the time when boys from prosperous families lost the protection that had so far spared them trans-Rhine labor service. It smelled of the end, and, as always when it smelled of the end, the smell was bad. "Guns budded," as the Communist poet Louis Aragon later wrote. Four days after Yves Montand left Provence, red posters had been hastily and abundantly plastered on French walls, announcing the execution of the pioneer Resistance fighters Manouchian and his twenty-two fellow immigrants. The photos that accompanied them were intended to shock, but Montand considered them noble, beautiful. Instinctively identifying with their struggle, he took no active part in it.

Was he indifferent to history? Assuredly not. He had grown up among anti-Fascism, and the guilty memory of his brother Julien, still in captivity, never left him. Was he too frivolous to care? No. He was lighthearted, certainly, thrilled to have traveled so far, exhilarated at the gathering speed of his rise. But he was deadly serious—serious as befitted the king of song he wanted one day to become, inwardly absorbed, consumed with effort, tormented and elated by daily success, terrified that this success might have sprung from a mere misunderstanding, a stroke of luck.

> Although I read in the newspapers about the crushing of the Glières Maquis and the beginnings of the Petiot affair,[3] my interest was only relative. Was I indifferent or selfish? In my defense, I would say that it wasn't much of a life back then. Inevitably, in my kind of work, everything revolved around oneself: you were your own material, and you had to keep on polishing that material. Was this bit of business good or bad? What if I opened with "Far West"? I'd have to try. No, no, a mistake. Maybe I should tell the guitarist that his counterpoint is too fast? On my way home from a performance I was a man alone. No car, nothing. And that endless self-examination. . . . Yes, I was horribly alone. Warm-hearted Harry Max had his own problems. Alone in the depths of winter in 1944 with no heat and no friends, constantly vulnerable to a police swoop. I was determined not to work in Germany. It wasn't courage: it was just a fact.

News of his success reached Montand's fellow guests at the Palace hotel. M. Albert—"Bébert," Montand called him—was so impressed that he would offer the young man the favors of one or another of the creatures under his "protection," a generous and kind offer that Montand usually declined. The ladies came and went, appeared and disappeared. If one looked a little "peaky," she was sent off to get some fresh air in the countryside near Besançon. Montand was getting used to living in a place where the small fry of organized crime hung out, often hobnobbing with Gestapo types, getting to know their ways and the rules they lived by.

One of the strictest of those rules was not to mix business and sentiment. People were fond of the artist, really fond of him, but they decided to fleece him anyway. Nicely, because it was business, it was their living, and a living was what Montand was beginning to make. The ABC had brought him sixteen hundred francs a week, and his wages rose as his reputation climbed. His family had already received a first remittance from him as proof that their faith had not been misplaced, that their littlest fledgling had taken wing. Every pay packet was divided in two: half for Marseilles, half for Paris.

But one night he gave way to temptation. Downstairs in the lobby the boys were sitting under the lamp around a table littered with coins and

3. Dr. Petiot was a wartime poisoner who robbed and killed fugitives from the Nazis who sought sanctuary in his supposedly safe house.

bills. For days Montand had behaved himself, been prudent, working away at the art of amusing others without allowing himself any distraction. But he had a few banknotes on him, earned by the sweat of his brow. He decided to risk them—to give himself a little break. And the itch (he had often noted this trait in his father) to make time fly, to get things going. Naturally, he was in luck. He won several thousand francs (thirty-four thousand, he once said, though later he revised the figure downward). Naturally, his luck changed the next day. He ended up owing more than he could immediately pay. Naturally, the boys—all good friends of his—trusted him fully. He could pay them back bit by bit, at his own rate.

Montand repaid them and, for a time, anyway, kept away from card games. But he never lost his love of card playing, one of the few leisure activities that could absorb and therefore relax him.

Once the audience had left, the ABC stage was turned over to entertainers rehearsing for the next show. Montand became fascinated by a very young, soft-eyed brunette, small and frail—so small and pretty you wanted to put your arms around her. Her name was Louise Carletti, and she was a rising star, a child of the music hall, born into a family of trapeze artists. He had admired her in movies like Jacques Feyder's *Les Gens du voyage,* in *Macao, l'enfer du jeu,* with Erich von Stroheim, in *Patricia,* and, more recently, in *Le Carrefour des enfants perdus* (a social melodrama in which a beginner, Serge Reggiani, demonstrated a remarkable talent for playing young hoodlums). The flesh-and-blood Carletti excited Montand no less than the one on the screen. At the ABC she was working on a sketch under the direction of a novice director, Raoul André, a friend of Francis Blanche.

Today, Raoul André shares an apartment with Louise Carletti in the Paris suburb of Boulogne-Billancourt, not far from the studios where he had made so many films. "When there was no matinee we rehearsed. One day I sensed a shadow behind me in that big deserted auditorium. As soon as the act was over it fled. The next day it was back. I asked Félix Vitry, the future head of the Bobino, in those days in charge of publicity at the ABC, 'Who is that guy?' 'Be nice to him,' he said. 'He's just in from Marseilles. He's playing here right now—in fact, you should take a look, he's not bad at all.' We finished the rehearsal, and the shadow approached, very tall, very polite: 'Thank you for letting me watch, Monsieur. I have a deep admiration for Mlle Carletti.' We did go to see him and decided that he did indeed have something. By our next rehearsal he had grown bolder and suggested we all have a drink. Then he asked if he could walk us home. Louise stopped at the rue Copernic. Montand continued on with me to my place at 7 rue Chalgrin, on the other side of the avenue Foch.

By now it was curfew. He spent the night at my place. I found him likable, funny, lost, awkward. Soon he came back with his toothbrush. And a little later, with his suitcase."

Five years his elder, André was the complete opposite of his guest. Physically tiny, from a prosperous family—his father, a Radical Socialist and high-ranking colonial officer, had been governor of Rabat, in Morocco, and had reorganized the Sûreté in Hanoi—André had a generous, or, at least, regular, income (a "student" allowance from his father and an episodic movie director's salary). His library was well stocked, and he talked movies from dawn to dusk—common ground for the two new friends.

A genuine spark passed between them. Montand was moved by so much freely offered hospitality and attracted as well by the rather bohemian atmosphere of André's basement apartment, with its low couches and its souvenirs of North Africa and Indochina. Stage designers and actors regularly dropped by. "Yves was very rough-and-ready," André says. "Talent in the raw. He was naturally lighthearted. He used to sing in the bath well after midnight, which exasperated the concierge. He was embarrassed as soon as he had to write anything, and he would hand me the phone whenever a conversation became too tricky or required a more subtle vocabulary. But he dressed with care and worked incessantly to cover the gaps in his knowledge."

For the first two or three weeks there was something of a misunderstanding. Montand was dazzled by "La Carletti" (he loitered beneath her balcony a couple of times, hoping to attract her attention), the equal of established movie stars such as Danielle Darrieux and Michèle Morgan (both of them in exile from France for the duration of the war). He was slow to realize that she and her favorite director were carrying on a passionate clandestine affair. But once he caught on, he stopped roaming the rue Copernic and became the couple's best friend. "I was playing the lead in *Monsieur et Madame Roméo,* a spoof of *Romeo and Juliet,* at the Saint-Georges theater," says Louise Carletti. "Raoul and Yves cycled over to watch me almost every evening. Then Yves went on to sing at a cabaret, sometimes the Fête Foraine, but more often the Night-Club. Whenever he could, he brought back food from the club kitchens, once or twice even a block of foie gras."

Eating and staying warm: that was all Parisians thought about. In the apartment on the rue Chalgrin, the walls oozed damp, and the gas pressure was so feeble that the occupants removed the regulators and replaced them with perforated metal tubes in hopes of coaxing out a flickering yellow flame.

Never had their sense of insecurity been so sharp, but neither had it ever been linked with such certainty of imminent German defeat. The scales rocked wildly between fear and hope. On April 26, 1944, Pétain was greeted with adulation in the French capital, but by the end of May, Allied bombers were reaching twenty-five major French cities. On June 4, Rome fell, and on June 6, Operation Overlord, the Allied invasion in Normandy, began. But suspected Resistance fighters were being hanged at Tulle, and on June 10 the Germans locked hundreds of men, women, and children into the little church of Oradour-sur-Glane and burned them alive.

Montand went on shuttling between spacious theaters and elegant small cabarets. He was dazzled by the fashionable clientele and glittering women (wives or courtesans? he never knew) at the Beaulieu, on the faubourg Saint-Honoré, and he fell in love when Irène de Trébert sang "Mademoiselle Swing" at the Fête Foraine. Then, from July 14 to 17, he performed as a guest star at the Folies-Belleville—"palace of laughter and swing," as its manager, Robert Dorfeuil, called it—an auditorium with barely five hundred seats and a balcony floating on a forest of slender columns.

The young Marseillais's name had steadily grown larger on programs: his "cowboy" numbers rated capital letters, bold type, heavy underlining. Introduced by the "charming mistress of ceremonies" Yolande Cartis and backed by Georges Courquin's orchestra, he went on stage just before Jean and Georgette Tissier, performing a sketch written by Maurice Donnay of the French Academy. He grew very fond of the concierge's daughter, a girl of about thirteen who seemed highly resourceful (she later confirmed this impression in her career under the pseudonym "Régine"). When there was a brutal German sweep on the rue Belleville, he barely escaped, flattened behind the theater's hastily lowered mesh storefront. Protected behind this steel barrier, he saw everything—and forgot nothing. A *Feldgendarm* swung hard, wide slaps at the man whose papers he was checking. Caen might have been liberated, and the last cabinet meeting ended in Vichy, but Paris still lived in fear.

Montand went on crossing the storm with the certainty that, come what might, fortune would smile on him. It did. As soon as his contract at the Folies-Bellevile ended, he was back at the Bobino. It was the spot he liked best: the audience was varied, the atmosphere was cozy, it was famous, and its program was always well balanced—you never felt overshadowed by a famous rival. Hillios Carletti, Louise's brother, was one of the acts. The greatest favorite of all was Georgette Plana, her pretty legs revealed by the shortest of short red skirts. She was called back again and again to give encores of "Dominico" and "Les Danses espagnoles." Montand, too, was in great demand. Françoise Holbane, the sharp-tongued reviewer of *Paris-*

Midi who had advised him two months earlier to "put order into the workings of a still-unfocused imagination," was full of enthusiasm by July 24: "What endless possibilities—and he has only just begun to scratch the surface—in that elongated silhouette, at once powerful and elastic; that carefree bravado, at once tough and lighthearted. . . . What's more, he has a fine voice, stage sense, presence, and a knack for effective movement. The most promising of our young pretenders."

By and large, all subsequent praise of Montand the singer consisted of variations on this theme. To keep moving forward, he now needed to square off against real opposition, to come up against a barrier of experience. He sensed that his current success was built on perishable goods—the spirit of the times, indulgence toward a provincial newcomer, the fragile immunity young people enjoy. What he feared more than anything was flickering out as quickly as he had caught fire.

Whence the almost manic stringency of his daily stocktaking. He knew his Mediterranean diction was faulty and bothered Paris audiences; he knew he closed his *o*'s—that he said "har*moan*ica," for example—an idiosyncrasy that triggered friendly sarcasm. Friendly for the moment. . . . He knew all this, and fought hard, with a stubborn blend of pride and humility, to improve himself. "His southern accent was a problem," says Louise Carletti. "So was a very slight speech impediment: the tendon beneath his tongue was a bit short; he needed to loosen it, lengthen it, if his diction were not to be slurred. Raoul's place had a small bar with a mirror. He would stand in front of it, stick a pencil in his mouth, and recite or sing his repertory for hours on end."

Faithful Audiffred now mentioned that a new engagement was in the offing, a step that could easily propel Montand higher and further than ever. The Moulin Rouge, Pigalle's most hallowed name—as a famous bar and cabaret, it had symbolized the Paris of the Belle Epoque as unmistakably as the Eiffel Tower—had for some years been just one among many movie houses. It now planned to return to its legendary music-hall beginnings. The inauguration of the new Moulin Rouge was scheduled for Saturday, August 30, and the star of the show would be Edith Piaf. But an eleventh-hour problem arose: the variety artist Roger Dann, who was to have had guest-star billing, dropped out. The theater therefore decided to scrape together an "interim" program with Charpini and Brancato.[4]

4. So late in the day that some newspapers had no time to correct their ads. See *Nouveaux Temps,* July 30, 1944: the "great songstress" was announced "under the auspices of the Moulin Rouge" in company with Roger Dann.

Piaf would not begin until the following week. And who would replace Roger Dann? Yves Montand.

It was an exciting opportunity. Professionally, the feather-light singer Edith Piaf was weighing increasingly heavily on the scales. She had carved out her own distinct niche.[5] The papers had been full of pictures of Piaf and Charles Trenet visiting the prisoners in Stalag III D, whose wartime "godmother" she had become. On July 23, she had given a spectacular concert at the Salle Pleyel, backed by a huge orchestra and chorus. Montand would have been insane not to hitch his wagon to such a star.

Yet both Montand and Audiffred nurtured doubts that they barely confided to each other. The manager was afraid to admit to his protégé how unenthusiastic Mlle Piaf had been at the idea of having a loud, gesticulating Mediterranean singing cowboy songs to open her show. She had balked: the vulgarian from Marseilles, the loudmouth from the Alcazar, the garlic-eating jokester, with a delivery overloaded with those exotic, exuberant "Ya-hoos!" . . . She insisted on personally vetting the "bombshell" from the Midi.

Montand knew Piaf by reputation, but since he had never seen and hardly heard her, he had only the vaguest idea of her talents. To him, Piaf was merely the latest in a long line of singing tragediennes, catnip for audiences but funereal to the tastes of the laughing Ivo Livi. So much for her manner. As for her lyrics, he had heard only a few of them. The "city kid" in the entertainment section at the youth camp had played a record of hers. When Montand believed he had heard the words *"Ça lui entre dans la peau, par le bas, par le haut"* ("It gets into her skin, in and out, out and in"), he had been amazed, almost shocked. The other song of hers that he had heard more or less in passing was "Le Grand Voyage du pauvre nègre" ("The Poor Black Man's Cruise"), about the last moments of a "*nègre maigre*" (meager nigger) who escapes the slave ship's hold but drowns within sight of the coast—*"Ca y est, fini, Monsieur Bon Dieu, adieu pays, tout l'monde adieu, Ohooo! Ohooo!"* ("I'm a goner, Massa God, I no see my home and kids no more, oh! oh! oh!"). In singing it, Piaf milked the pathos to the last harrowing gurgle.

So neither the manager nor his client really said what was on his mind. Edith Piaf would like to know you better, said Audiffred diplomatically. The gig is in the bag; this is just a matter of professional courtesy. Vexed and anxious, Montand knew perfectly well that a "courtesy" audition was still an audition, but he reassured his mentor: the stakes were too high for

5. We would like to thank Georges Martin, an archivist who over the past twenty years has compiled a gold mine of information on Edith Piaf, for the sources and information he generously made available to us.

him to throw a fit of temperament. If Piaf wanted to test him, she could test him. He would show her what he could do. Raoul André clearly remembers the mixed feelings with which his friend approached the coming encounter. "Yves told me he had managed to get billing as guest star alongside Piaf, but that he had had to go through some sort of audition first, even though the contract was apparently a foregone conclusion. He worked harder than ever on his diction. On the big day, he asked me to go with him to the Moulin Rouge. There were very few people there. Yves greeted Piaf and introduced me. I sat down next to her as he disappeared backstage. He began to sing. She talked to herself as she watched him."

It was 10:00 a.m. on a magnificent summer day. Edith Piaf was wearing a light dress, white with blue flowers; her hair was blond.

While the basic story of what happened next remains the same, there are subtle variations in the telling from one witness to another. For some, the audition becomes a rehearsal; for others, weeks separate the episode from the performance day. (The latter version is unconvincing: Montand's contract had been negotiated on an emergency basis after Roger Dann's defection, and everything suggests that the shock of the meeting between the two artists was sudden and devastating.) Montand himself was vague about the chronology and sequence of events. He often placed the couple's encounter in May (subsequent articles perpetuated this inaccuracy), although the Moulin Rouge's conversion was not completed until the end of July, which means that he and Piaf did not sing together until August 5 to 11. In *Du soleil plein la tête,* Montand says that in his "audition" (his own word) he bowled over the judge. But later he maintained that Piaf's enthusiasm became evident only after the first live performance.

As for Piaf, in the only autobiographical work that seems at all reliable, she also uses the word "audition" and says that her enthusiasm was immediate: "Right away, I was conquered. A stunning personality, an aura of strength and solidity, hands that were eloquent, powerful, delicate, a handsome, troubled face, a grave voice, and, amazingly, hardly any Marseilles accent. At the end of his fourth song, I left my seat and went to the edge of the stage. I'll always see myself standing there, tiny, almost crushed by the lofty figure of that tall young man, raising my face more or less to the level of his ankles. I told him that he was 'terrific' and that it was safe to say he was headed for a wonderful career."[6]

Whatever really happened on the empty stage of the Moulin Rouge sometime between July 31 and August 4, Yves Montand—angry and

6. Edith Piaf, *Au bal de la chance* (Paris, 1958). Extracts from the book describing the meeting were reproduced in *Le Parisien Libéré,* May 5, 1958.

perhaps secretly humiliated at having to submit to the scrutiny of this diminutive diva—encountered what he had never before found in a woman: a blend of passion, laughter, discipline, toughness, application, admiration, comradeship, and rivalry. Although he was wearing a derby bearing the legend "Hot Dogs," he did not feel even slightly ridiculous. He was loved and he loved. Almost at first sight.

I didn't find out till later how determined Edith had been not to like me. But Roger Dann had spoken well of me, and Audiffred wasn't going to let me be condemned without a hearing. What may have made a big difference is that in those days people were quick with superlatives. Someone had said to Piaf: "Montand? Are you crazy? Not him, you don't know him. If he goes on before you, he'll kill you!" Exactly what you should never say to Piaf. "Well, let's see this man who's going to kill me!" There was a strong element of challenge at our first meeting. The Moulin Rouge orchestra was big—twelve or fourteen players, I believe. I asked the ABC's pianist-orchestrator to take a look at my arrangements, and off I went.

There she was in her flowered dress, very pretty, very delicate, with that left-hand-side part in her hair. She had a peculiar way of giving you her hand, with the thumb tucked in (Marilyn and Isabelle Adjani did the same thing, I discovered later, turning their hands into fluttering birds). I sang "Les Plaines du Far West," "Je m'en fous," "Je vends des hot dogs à Madison," and she got up. But as I recall, it was only later, after my first performance, that she heaped praise on me. "Well done, bravo, well done!" She looked adorable, beautiful, with that high forehead, those big blue eyes, and that delicately proportioned body—tiny breasts, narrow hips. . . .

The roof of the Moulin Rouge opened up so that we could work by daylight. We sang at a matinee the first time. When it was my turn—I came on after the acrobats—the audience applauded wildly. And Edith Piaf came to see me backstage. First it was compliment after compliment, really nice ones, sincere. Then: "What are you, Canadian or something?" I mumbled an ambiguous reply (my father, I said, was more or less Canadian). I was still attracted to her, but she was beginning to seem less nice. Then she went on the attack: "Let me tell you something. At the moment you're a big hit because everyone is waiting for the Americans. Watch out—it won't last. You don't have any really good French songs. But don't worry, someone will write them for you." She turned away: "Well, I'm on next. Anyway, you were fantastic. Want to meet later? We can get something to eat."

Up until then I had never had anything but praise. No one had ever said to my face, "That's fine, pal, but. . . ." I tensed. I wanted to take the high road, wanted to say, in the lingo of today, "Keep it up, sweetheart, you interest me!" They're terrifying, the women who take you over, who fight you. But thank you, whoever you are, thank you for bringing those terrifying women my way!

I went up to the balcony. No announcement. Claude Normand's musicians were playing beautifully, but they had left the orchestra pit and were playing from the rear of the stage, so that there was no barrier between the singer—she didn't use a mike—and her audience. Edith came on with tiny, tiny steps: she seemed to take a quarter of an hour to cross the stage. Then she planted herself center-stage and sang "De l'autre côté de la rue." She already had that throaty quality. . . . Then "Les Deux Garçons," and I heard in it everything that had ever meant anything to me—rhythm, jazz. I was already vanquished. Her fourth song was "Il riait": "He was a kid whom fortune's hammer landed smack in the slammer and—how he laughed. . . . And then they found him dead, lying stiff on his bed, and—how he laughed." By now I was completely tense, I felt hot tears, I was crying, I was totally seduced. Then came "J'ai dansé avec l'amour." Her songs were extraordinary blues, waltzes or blues, or both. By now I knew I couldn't turn away, I was a goner.

I had fallen in love without even knowing it, I was head over heels in love with Edith's charm, her admiration for me, her loneliness. Back then, there was nothing of the broken woman about her—sick and drug-ridden—none of the terrible, pathetic images that were later associated with her. She was fresh, flirtatious, both funny and cruel, passionately devoted to her profession, ambitious, a salesgirl out on the town, loyal when she loved, wanting to believe in her love but able to break off with astonishing strength—and she sang better when she was falling in or out of love.

We became lovers in the accepted sense of the word after a week. When she woke up on our first morning at her place on the rue Marceau, she put her hand on her forehead as if she were dizzy and said, "What's come over me?" And right after that she began to talk about my repertory: "Here's what you should do. . . . " At breakfast I told her I was working on some songs. In fact, one of them, "Luna Park," was ready. So I sang and danced "Luna Park" for her at the foot of the bed. Just for her. She laughed and clapped her hands: "You're crazy. You must sing it now, tonight." And I believe we handled the arranging at top speed and went on stage with it twenty-four hours later.

I was twenty-three. It was my first true love. Edith was one of those people who made you think you were God, that you were irreplaceable.

The white Moulin Rouge program—not much bigger than an address book, eight pages printed on cheap paper—opened with a photo of Piaf, eyebrows arched, eyes uplifted as if toward some vision of paradise, beneath the delicate nose a suspicion of bitterness in the lips. The box framing her name ran the width of the central double-page spread. "Comic entertainer" Yves Montand was given second typographical place, his name printed a third the size of hers.

On August 5, 1944, after the matinee that had bowled him over, Piaf invited Montand to dinner behind the Moulin de la Galette, in Montmartre. Never—not just in wartime—had he seen such a sumptuous meal. Entrecôte, several cheeses, wine, a series of tablecloths, an array of different knives and forks—it was bewildering! Edith had invited her librettist, Henri Contet, with whom she had been having a semiclandestine affair. Contet, a brilliant reporter for *Paris-Midi,* had been pushed into this unfamiliar showbiz territory by Edith's powerful enthusiasm. For three years now he had been the mastermind behind her new songs: "Y'a pas de printemps," "C'est toujours la même histoire," "Coup de grisou," "Les Deux Garçons," "Il riait," "Celui qui ne savait pas pleurer," "Bravo pour le clown."

Piaf, the "Sparrow," the street child fascinated by hoodlums, the waif unjustly linked to the 1936 murder of Louis Leplée, manager of the first nightclub where she was paid to sing, the girl who had sung for pennies in Menilmontant and glorified the underworld, "La môme Piaf," was no more. She had been replaced by Edith Piaf, a music-hall star whose reputation would very soon cross the Atlantic. And that change of status—or, rather, of stature—had of course been accompanied by a change in men. The period of Raymond Asso, the man who had finally pulled her out of the gutter, was over: "Mon légionnaire," "Browning," "C'est toi le plus fort," "Chacal," "Madeleine qu'avait du coeur," and "Le Grand Voyage du pauvre nègre." The Contet era was her farewell to Pigalle, gunsmoke and melodrama, gangland myth, submissive female sobs. Mlle Piaf still lived on the dark side, but now, thanks to the instincts of her newest protector, she managed to insert a subtle note of romance and humor:

C'est toujours la même histoire
J'ose à peine vous en parler
Moi j'ai fait semblant d'y croire
Faites semblant de m'écouter . . .

[It's the same thing every time
I don't know what to say
I pretended to believe in us
Why not pretend to listen to me? . . .]

Henri Contet clearly recalls that first groundbreaking lunch with Yves Montand and the first picture he formed of him: "He was extraordinarily shy, awkward and constantly fumbling. He struggled for words, upset his glass. Outwardly, he held up pretty well, he was resourceful, a good-looking kid who had worked hard on his woman-pleasing act. And with his long arms and magnificent hands, he was handsome. But I soon realized that apart from singing, Montand knew absolutely nothing when he came to Paris. If you asked him to write four lines on a piece of paper, the result, in terms of spelling and grammar, was quite startling. What struck me most was the speed with which Yves worked to minimize those handicaps and surmounted them."

Contet was, of course, no ordinary observer. He was doubly qualified to witness the beginnings of the Piaf-Montand affair (and he remained magnanimous enough to hold Montand in high esteem and affection). First, he was the primary victim of the instant spark struck between the newcomer and the star. For a few months, the situation remained more or less in limbo. "Edith," he recalls in broken tones, "had an adorable face, a child's mouth, and a way of looking at you when she loved you that knocked you flat on your back. She was full of vitality, excitable, gay, funny. The tormented Piaf that audiences loved was the professional. In life, she wasn't so tormented, and she quickly picked herself up after setbacks, sorrows, breaks. Yves had the courage to tell me the truth about their relationship, in February 1945 in his dressing room at the Etoile. But you would have had to be blind not to notice before. Edith was crazy about him." It is by no means certain that the old gentleman recalling those far-off days is not still a little jealous.

Second, Contet was a privileged observer of the merciless routine Piaf put her partner through. Virtually every morning from the beginning of September 1944, she shut herself in with her pianist and Montand. She left her love outside. It was time for her "pupil" (actually, he was only six years younger than Piaf) to be put through his paces, to endure her criticism, her harshness, her strictness, her certainties. "Yves," says Contet, "never argued with any of Edith's orders ('advice' very quickly became 'orders'). I believe he must have gritted his teeth more than once, swallowed his exhaustion and his pride, told himself that the rewards of the exercise were greater than its torments. He absorbed everything with amazing relish and speed. And she, in turn, marveled at his talent and will to succeed."

By now, Montand's one desire was to fulfill the promise almost every reviewer predicted for him. Contet himself voiced the highest praise, in an article headed "Revelation at the Moulin Rouge" in the *Paris-Midi* of August 8: "Edith Piaf said to me, 'I know, I know, I'm singing at the Moulin Rouge this week, but I've been singing my songs all over Paris, so why don't we stop talking about me for once and give Yves Montand his chance? He's the kind of beginner who comes along once in a blue moon.' So I watched and listened to Yves Montand. . . . It was worth it. He has a great big laugh, arms like windmills, and hands that make you want to sing, the hands of a poet-lumberjack. Extraordinary hands, full of music, hands that dance to rhythm and blues, hands that snatch at trumpet blasts or shred and sweep away the laughter of saxophones. Then you listen to him. He has a voice that makes you close your eyes—as soon as it stops making you laugh."

This was not reviewing; it was conspiracy. It acclaimed and applauded Montand, but also exhorted him to rise to the heights of the praise heaped on him. How? By correcting just a few flaws: "You wave your arms too much. If you swing your arm out too far, all you can do is swing it back, and the effect is ugly. And try not to sprint onto the stage. Come on slowly—the audience will stick around. The more relaxed you are, the longer they'll have to applaud, so calm down." Montand stored it up, grumbled, ruminated, took it or left it, adapted it, worked it over to suit himself.

But what he needed most was a made-to-measure repertory. The youth who had come from Marseilles was merely a mimic; the man who now sought to take Paris by storm had to be a performer in his own right. He agreed with Contet that his talents needed spicier nourishment. He jumped at the two songs offered him by the composer Loulou Gasté and the lyricist Jean Guigo: "Battling Joe," the legend of the exploited boxer, and "Luna Park," the workingman out on a spree. Nor did Piaf hesitate to share her songwriting talents with her new love, offering him two songs—she didn't write them down, the words simply came to her lips—"Mademoiselle Sophie" and "Le Balayeur" ("The Street Sweeper"), whose first verse sparkled with mischief and double meanings. With material like this, Montand now had a small arsenal of lively, popular tunes.

Piaf wanted him to work more methodically to expand the two extremes of his register: to do love songs, and also to amplify his comic musical sketches and his dancing. For the wonderful thing about Montand was that he could switch from the mellowest crooning to visual gags and back again. Except that the crooning could never be truly casual: it had to suggest intense sensuality, barely hinting at it. And the gag could never be stressed: it had to flash by with the speed and slickness of a twenty-four-frame-per-second cartoon. And finally, Piaf realized that young Livi's proletarian origins were a priceless asset in the climate of the time (and the times to come). Better than anyone else, she, too, had managed to put the putative disadvantage of a wretched background to good use, to set herself up as a daughter of the people. Yves, she felt, should do the same.

To his extreme embarrassment, she showered her handsome lover with gifts, gold rings and watches. Above all, though, she gave him song after song, verbal outpourings of hers that the loyal Glanzbergs, Louiguys, Marguerite Monnots, and Paul Durands transcribed and put into presentable shape for her. Some of these songs would stay with Montand for good—"Mais qu'est-ce que j'ai à tant l'aimer?" ("But Why Do I Love Her So Much?") and, above all, "Elle a des yeux" ("She Has Eyes"):

> Elle a des yeux
> C'est merveilleux
> Et puis des mains
> Pour mes matins . . .
>
> [She has eyes
> What a sweet surprise
> And that lingering
> Morning touch . . .]

Piaf made up "Il fait des . . . ," the story of a jazz fanatic whose vocal cords constrict and whose feet freeze as soon as the orchestra strikes up classical or other serious music, but who explodes to the sound of boogie-woogie. And she also dedicated "La Grande Cité," one of the outstanding postwar songs, to her son of the people:

> Je suis née dans la cité
> Qui enfante les usines
> Là où les hommes turbinent
> Toute une vie sans s'arrêter
> Avec leurs hautes cheminées
> Qui s'élancent vers le ciel

Comme pour cracher leur fumée
En des nuages artificiels . . .

[I was born in the city
Where factories are spawned
Where men work their hearts out
All their life long
With their lofty smokestacks
Lofty and black
Smoke belching black
Like man-made clouds . . .]

She knew nothing of musical scales or harmony. Her English tutor was astounded at the progress she made, but every attempt to write was painful to her. Her hand shook (an alcoholic legacy from her father, Louis Gassion), or the pen would suddenly skid and gouge the paper. In fact, what drove her was a kind of untamed grace. She found her words the way she found her gestures, seemingly without seeking, at one go. She never seemed prey to any kind of soul-searching. Her inner discipline was masked by a hundred impulses, pranks, caprices, tyrannies. Montand described how she was approached by a young singer, Marianne Michel, for a song. Suddenly, Piaf said: "Wait, we might try this: *'Quand il me prend dans ses bras, qu'il me parle tout bas, je vois les choses en rose. . . .'* " Then she corrected herself: "No—'la vie *en rose.*' " A moment later, she was starting on the second verse.

Generous and overpowering, Edith Piaf did not stop with her own creations, but also sent other people's work to her lover. When Contet phoned to read her lyrics he had just dreamed up for Maurice Chevalier—*"Ma môme, ma petite gosse, on va faire la noce, je t'emmène en carosse jusqu'à Robinson"* ("My sweet kid, my sweet baby, let's take a coach and paint the town red")—she begged him, "Save it for Yves, save it for Yves!" Montand was drowned with new material. Contet gave him "Gilet rayé" ("Striped Waistcoat"), the acrobatic adventures of a hotel porter in a "striped, striped" waistcoat, in love with the lovely Lola and obliged to climb endless flights of stairs to serve her the champagne she drinks with a man he's jealous of. So jealous that he kills the lady and the most hateful of her fancy men, and then, in jail—in his "striped, striped" prison garb—dreams of thousands of Lolas. It was witty, surreal, unsingable. Yet Montand sang the convoluted tale, pulling out a chair to evoke the night porter's exhaustion, fluttering his fingers to illustrate his climb up flight after flight of stairs, an authentic tragicomedy in three and a half minutes flat, a song you watched without daring to blink.

Montand was an instant success in the unperformable "Gilet rayé." "We were staggered," Contet remembers. "We decided to go one step further with 'Ce monsieur-là' ('The Hotel Guest'). It was even tougher. A man receives an anonymous letter, catches his wife and her lover red-handed, kills the lover with fireplace tongs, and for the rest of his life is on the run from one hotel to the next ('A murderer's life is hell, from hotel to hotel'). Singing 'Ce monsieur-là' at the time of the Liberation was folly, suicide. The song lasted nearly five minutes, and people were horrified by it. But Montand got to work, devised his own staging, and stuck with it even when the audience was obviously fed up. Then one day he cabled me from Toulouse: 'I've done it, I got them with "Ce monsieur-là!" It works, Henri, it works!' "

From challenge to challenge, from strength to strength, the singing cowboy of "Les Plaines du Far West" was digging deep within himself. Piaf did not make him, did not shape him: she mined him in the way you mine a lode, a vein, a deposit. It was an act of love, an act of faith—and also a way of holding on to him, of monopolizing him. Montand was too much in love not to go along. Although forced to accept—more or less gracefully—the shafts loosed by his beloved despot, he was healed by the tenderness she lavished on him. And by her infinite clear-sightedness. Edith had the intelligence to vary her attack. After urging him to venture deeper into mime, gesture, and movement, she encouraged him to go in the opposite direction, too, to pluck a song from the air and sing it motionless, without a single gesture. And Montand complied. Discarding the man who mimicked Fernandel, he sired the showman whose extraordinarily enduring career was due largely to his art in putting together a concert that blended rough with smooth, strident with sober, the popular themes with the avant-garde.

Edith Piaf and Henri Contet judged the transformation complete when they saw their discovery tackle "Ma môme, ma petite gosse." Montand sang it dreamily, standing motionless. He reached the last verse:

Le soleil se baguenaude
Il y a des valses qui rôdent
Sur des airs d'amoureux
J'en ai le coeur qui chavire
On a plus rien à se dire
Viens on va être heureux . . .

[The sun basks in the sky
Waltzes swirl in the air

To the sound of lovers' sighs
My heart soars to the skies
We've nothing more to say
Come, my love, let's fly away . . .]

As he reached the last words he slowly swiveled in a waltz step that turned his back on the audience. A hand—his own, but you could have sworn it was someone else's—curled around the back of his neck and drew him gently off the stage.

Curtain.

It was perfect.

In the weeks following the audition at the Moulin Rouge, Raoul André received unusual phone calls: "Edith Piaf would call very late and ask, 'Does Yves happen to be there?' As it happened, he was there, and he limited himself to very terse replies—'Yes. Yes. Yes.' Then he would say very casually, 'Well, I'm not sure what time I'll be home.' " That month of August saw Montand's forbidden nocturnal prowlings reach their peak. On one of those warm mornings after, just before dawn, as usual, he left Edith Piaf's apartment at 71 avenue Marceau (Edith was still afraid to confess her infidelity to Henri Contet) for his lair at 7 rue Chalgrin. The Place de l'Etoile was utterly deserted when he stumbled upon the corpse of a German soldier, facedown at the corner of the avenue Victor Hugo. Gobbets of brain had splashed from the gaping skull. It was a dangerous place to be. Montand stopped, looked at the dead man's studded boots, dwelt bizarrely on the thought that millions of identical boots must have been made in the Reich, and continued on his way.

On August 15, Piaf and her protégé raised champagne glasses to the imminent meeting of the Allied armies at Argentan, for the Americans and the British were moving in from Le Mans and Alençon to cut off the enemy pocket in western France. That same day, the Paris police voted to strike as a prelude to rising against the invader. And on that same August 15, unknown to the French, who had ears only for their coming liberation, a convoy rumbled toward Germany bearing the last trainload of deportees.

All the usual ingredients of carefully staged endings began at once to give off their ambiguous odor. Heroism, scorn, terror, misunderstanding, farce, death, lies, truth, and vengeance were on every Paris street corner. From August 19, the beginning of the Paris uprising, everyone in that city of hungry people took part in or witnessed scores of bizarre encounters.

First came a shadowy silhouette ringing Raoul André's doorbell after nightfall. Through the wrought-iron grille and unwashed glass, lodger and host could see the all-too-familiar gray uniform. Montand armed himself with a bottle. Clutching its neck, he opened the door. The soldier who came in spoke not a word of French. Perhaps forty-five, he looked lost, exhausted, and out of touch with time; he walked heavily to the rear of the room, his back turned to the two Frenchmen. He told them in gestures that his own people had left him behind. Dragging one foot, this oxlike apparition bore the emblems and arms of the German oppressor, but the grenade on his belt looked curiously out of place and harmless. Under André's disapproving gaze, Montand, without quite knowing why, poured him a glass of cheap cognac he had purchased dearly on the black market. Then they shoved the intruder out. He left regretfully, footsteps dragging.

A week later, they decided that the German had probably been trying to give himself up. They remembered how ostentatiously he had turned his back on them. But by then, a Wehrmacht soldier had become someone you insulted, arrested, disarmed. This one had called too early.

A second tragicomic episode took place a few days later. A friend of André, a producer named Jacques Baudry, more or less affiliated with the Resistance—its ranks were swelling by the minute—arrived at the rue Chalgrin brandishing a weapon, a small 6.35-caliber revolver, not much more than a toy, he said, and, in any case, not loaded. And to show that the magazine was empty he squeezed the trigger: a slug ricocheted off the table and embedded itself in Yves Montand's right thumb. The surprise was so complete—and, with hindsight, the fear so powerful, for the singer's hand had been but a few inches from his face—that the victim sat speechless for a few seconds before giving a yell of fear. They bathed the wound as they waited for a Resistance doctor to remove the bullet.

That evening at the Théâtre Saint-Georges, Louise Carletti was worried when her usual escort did not appear on time. "Finally they came to get me in my dressing room. Yves was pale, and his hand was bandaged. He was supposed to sing right afterward at the Night-Club and insisted on going through with it." He went on stage with his arm in a sling. As he labored through his four songs, he sensed unusual tension in the audience. The applause had risen several notches, and he heard a low murmur, a respectful buzz of voices. One of the phrases he managed to catch was "He's one of the kids from the Bois." He had no inkling as to how he might have earned this mystifying reputation.

The news he heard the next morning explained the mystery and made his ersatz coffee taste even worse than usual: forty-two young Resistance workers, average age seventeen and a half, had fallen into a trap set by a French Gestapo man; thirty-five of them had been shot by the waterfall in the Bois de Boulogne. Someone at the Night-Club had started the rumor that the wounded Montand was one of the martyrs who had miraculously escaped (in fact, only one youth, who was left for dead, survived the massacre). The atmosphere of almost-liberated Paris was strange indeed: the city that had acclaimed the marshal only four months earlier was now manufacturing heroes with suspicious speed.

Yves Montand never claimed any share of that glory. He, too, eventually took up arms—but under circumstances that in later years he described almost with mockery, even though, had things turned out badly, he might not have survived to jest. The Comédie-Française had set up a "security committee" that was ready to turn Molière's old theater into an Alamo. Edith Piaf's friend Madeleine Robinson phoned her to ask for volunteers to man three-hour shifts. Montand left for this battlefront on Tuesday, August 22. After a brief truce, sporadic fighting had broken out across Paris. To get into the Théâtre-Français, home of the Comédie, near the Louvre, you had to knock twice slowly, then four times fast, and then say the password. Only then were you admitted to a headquarters whose entire arsenal consisted of three grenades and a rifle. The star of "And He Drew His Gun" was never required to draw during his tour of duty under Alfred de Musset's marble gaze.

The Liberation proper took place three days later, and Montand watched most of it at Piaf's side. He was at the Place de l'Etoile when General Leclerc's tanks broke into view on the avenue Foch. Around him the crowd went wild, yelling, singing. Bullets whistled over their heads.

"Down! Down, for God's sake!" yelled a sergeant.

The onlookers flattened themselves on the sidewalks, still keeping a tight hold on their bicycles. Montand took cover behind a tree. Nearby, a tank was shelling the roof of a building on the other side of the Champs-Elysées.

"Cut out that shit!" screamed an officer. "You've just killed three of my men!"

The celebrating began even before the fighting was over. But it failed to dispel the obsession that had dogged France all those years: finding something to eat, a grocery or a bar where any kind of food might still be obtainable. With Harry Max, Montand vainly looked under counters and combed the back rooms of food stores. The only thing you could buy, during lulls, was the Communist Resistance paper *Franc-Tireur,* hastily run off on commandeered presses.

The expression "mad with joy" aptly describes the collective jubilation, but it also describes the confusion and pent-up hatred. Looking down from Edith's apartment on the avenue Marceau, Montand saw a line of trucks filled with exhausted Germans, one with a bloodily bandaged knee, about to leave the city and shouted, "Fuck off! *Raus!*" in imitation of the guttural delivery of the *Boches.* He told the story to us with reluctance. Was it just revenge? Legitimate anger? The idea that his voice had been added to the mob's just to insult the vanquished, however briefly, had stayed with him like a ghost of the cowardice buried deep in all of us.

It could easily have been worse. As they watched the motionless line of trucks, packed with yesterday's conquerors, a young man Piaf knew, wearing a Resistance armband, reached for one of the four grenades he had set out on the windowsill. He was about to remove the pin when Edith intervened: "Don't be a fool! They're leaving!"

The warrior froze. The execution of a herd of unarmed men had been averted by a last-second gesture, a split second's vigilance.

In 1944, Yves Montand saw the world in black and white. In the decades after, his opinion of the Third Reich did not change. But every time he would leave his apartment on the Place Dauphine and cross the Pont-Neuf, he wished that the plaque on the parapet of the bridge that commemorates one of the Resistance's "warriors of the shadows" had said the martyr had been "shot by the Nazis" rather than "shot by the Germans." Only a nuance, perhaps, but one that would make the right distinction, he believed, between Hitler's early German opponents—the ones who had the privilege of being first into the Nazi death mills—and the unionized Paris bus drivers without whose cooperation the roundup (code name "Operation Spring Breeze") of thirteen thousand French Jews at the Vélodrome d'Hiver in July 1940 would have been a comparative failure.

But on August 25–26, 1944, there was no time for such subtleties. And in the murky atmosphere of the great purge of collaborators that followed, the revelation of the horrors that had taken place in Nazi Germany seemed to trivialize the thousand and one daily compromises and betrayals that had kept the Vichy regime going. The barbarism across the Rhine had been such that merely reporting on it helped to induce a state of collective amnesia in France, an act of suppression. Suddenly the country was alive with the unlikeliest Resistance fighters ready to hunt down their collaborationist neighbors, their own patriotic credentials as newfound as their sudden courage. The French citizens whose poisonous letters of gossip and accusation had flooded so many official French and German mailboxes during the Occupation were forgotten. The nation now had only patriots. Hell was other people.

As late as mid-August, one still found mutilated corpses of Resistance fighters in the Luxembourg Gardens, the skin flayed from their hands. The situation cried out for vengeance. But once the Germans had been defeated, the purge struck more or less at random. Half-naked women, their heads shaved, were publicly dishonored for "sinning" with enemy soldiers, and the deranged curses that followed them often came from the mouths of people who had made money from the Occupation or had functioned smoothly as cogwheels of collaboration.

In the entertainment world, artists whose careers had prospered during the dark years fell under reasonably legitimate suspicion: their "ambiguities" had been more visible than those of industrialists, black marketeers, or informers. Aragon made Chevalier sing the Communist "Internationale" in public; even Trenet was forced into retirement for nearly a year; André Claveau, particularly eminent at Radio-Paris during the war years, was temporarily barred from working. Piaf herself was criticized for the visits she had made to her "godchildren" in the German prison camps; but after a brief period her good faith and patriotic motives were acknowledged.

For Montand, the big shock came later. Watching a newsreel with Edith early in 1945, Montand saw his first pictures of the death camps, and they came like a blow to his own person—the crematory ovens, the bunk beds crowded with skeletal zombies, babies torn from their mothers, mass graves. As they left the movie house, he turned on Piaf angrily. Piaf had the simple, rock-bottom faith of a rural peasant, a worker, stubborn and strident, unabashed and superstitious, peppered with charms and saints and lucky prayers. She never went to bed without kneeling to say her prayers. ("Can you picture a Jezebel saying her prayers in a nightgown?" asked Montand many years later.)[7] But that night, he jabbed at the little gold cross she wore and exploded: "What about your God now? There's nothing he can do for us. You're welcome to your paradise! How can you believe in a being who tolerates such a horror?"

Edith Piaf's reply forever appalled Montand: "But Yves, how can we know what sins those people may have committed in their former lives?" The hoary old myth of the Jews' "blood debt," of a race of Christ killers, was as deeply rooted, even in Piaf, as the virtues of the Hail Mary.

About all those years of the Occupation—years he floated through absorbed in his own plans and work—Montand came to develop a kind of vertiginous sense: the idea that one can walk along the abyss and yet manage to go on living; that the boundary between needing to know and needing to remain ignorant is tenuous, indeed; that we absolutely must destroy that boundary.

He would carry everywhere with him, deep in an inner pocket, important and cherished photos, like symbolic wardens, a mini–museum-gallery

7. Radio interview, France-Inter, May 20, 1969.

of his loves and his regrets. A picture of a child in the Warsaw ghetto, hands in the air, eyes stunned, was for a long time the centerpiece of this private portable gallery.

Life with Edith Piaf—daily rehearsals, the search for new songs—seriously began right after the liberation of Paris. Montand found a snug hotel room on the rue de Richelieu, where Piaf frequently joined him. They shared the tiny place with a mouse, which Montand fed sardines in the hope that it would leave them alone. Their life was a blend of fantasy and austerity, of discretion and celebration, of privacy and public appearances. From late September to late October, they both appeared in theaters around Paris, performing at concerts for various causes—the Resistance, prisoners' families, American airmen.

Edith was hardly living a glamorous life, but she introduced "her man" to a world he had never known. One night he might meet the actor Michel Simon or the stage designer Christian Bérard, or perhaps the singer Sacha Guitry, now very much out of favor—he had entertained Goering, and used more coal than common mortals ever were allowed—and eager for help from the "Communist" Montand, who did, indeed, intervene in his favor. Piaf was also an enthusiast of Jean Cocteau's, and the refined Paul Meurisse's former flame (she had starred in *Le Bel Indifférent* with him). Overawed but mesmerized, Montand stepped into this new world the way a man coming in from the rain carefully skirts the living-room rug.

"Yves soon shed much of his awkwardness and ignorance," Contet recalls. "Edith and I were sure that he would become a very great star—you could see that at a glance—and we warned him of the exigencies. We told him about the follies of stars who could scarcely sign their name. Piaf would say to him: 'You have to interest both the masses and the likes of Guitry and Cocteau. And for that, you have to know writers and poets.' I lent him a book by Guillaume Apollinaire, but it didn't take. He loved Verlaine, on the other hand. He was determined to better himself, to educate himself. He fought for it; he became obsessed by it. He was happier with poetry than with novels. I'll never forget one day in 1946, when we had arranged to meet on the Pont de l'Alma. I saw him hurrying toward me, brimming over with excitement, arms flung apart, yelling: 'Henri, I understand Prévert, I understand Prévert!' "

The eternal drama of the self-educated person: where to begin? Which ladder to climb? Lacking guidelines of any kind, Montand struck at random. Having overheard the title in a conversation, he bought Henri Bergson's *Le Rire* (*On Laughter*) and sank into it. And one night, at the stroke of eleven, he turned up at Raoul André's: "Forgive me, I'm looking for something. You wouldn't happen to have a book called *In Praise of Folly,* by Erasmus?"

André rubbed his eyes, rummaged through his library, and, to his own astonishment, found that he did possess *In Praise of Folly.* His friend thanked him politely and raced away with the book under his arm.

The mature Montand considered those first literary feelers to be a kind of interrupted, dislocated foreplay. Only after thirty years at the top of the entertainment world did he have time seriously to educate himself; until then he was only nibbling, sniffing, groping. This was not from any lack of desire, but because exercises at the barre, elocution and tap-dancing lessons, voice exercises, rhythm training, vetting scripts and lyrics, putting shows together, regulating the lighting took all his energy.

It was the price every performer pays. Performing artists, particularly variety artists, and most particularly those who specialize in one-man shows, have concentration problems comparable to those that plague Olympic athletes. Montand's youthful years were swallowed up by the demands of his craft. He would neither complain nor boast of it. He simply had no choice.

Chapter 6

Edith Piaf agreed to a tour of southern France from October 25 to December 9, 1944. Edward Chekler was to lead the orchestra, and the first half of the show would be Yves Montand's. Sharing the billing with the woman he loved was manna from heaven. Both of them were immersed in music, in the same dream. Now they were solidly, publicly, enduringly linked.

Montand plunged into the adventure with a light heart. He was no longer a beginner, of course, and he knew that opening for the great Piaf was a serious challenge. But he was optimistic, for his relationship with Edith was by no means a re-enactment of the Pygmalion story, whatever others might say.[1] Although he did suffer through her enlightened criticisms, their relationship was more balanced than most observers reported. Never in his life had Yves Montand felt so admired; thus far his career had been one unbroken success. He packed for the trip with confidence and enthusiasm.

In fact, though, what he was to call his "greatest sorrow" of this period lay just ahead, and his troubles were not all of a professional nature. Henri Contet (still Piaf's "official" lover) went part of the way with them. On some nights, Montand stifled his jealousy in the solitude of a hotel room and thought back to the song that had so overwhelmed him at the Moulin Rouge: "In my little life there are two boys, one tall, one fair-haired, and each one loves me in his own way"—lyrics by Contet. When Piaf said to him one morning, "You know, at dinner last night"—a dinner for three, of course—"I was looking at your hair and wishing I could kiss it," it was naturally painful.

1. For example, Monique Lange, who in a lavishly illustrated book makes the rather breathless claim that Montand "kissed the hem" of a Piaf who was both "tigress" and "Pygmalion" (*Histoire de Piaf* [Paris, 1988]). Claude-Jean Philippe, in *Edith* (Paris, 1988), steers clear of such judgments.

But these private aches were not the worst. It all started in Lyons, at the Salle Rameau on October 25–27, 1944. (The program announced Edith Piaf performing "songs by Henri Contet," while Yves "Montant" was once again the victim of a spelling error.) He was hardly unknown in the city, having already been acclaimed there, relished for his verve and his flair for mimicry. But now here was the cowboy of "Les Plaines du Far West" soberly singing "Mademoiselle Sophie" and "Elle a des yeux." The audience was not hostile, just cool, polite, rather puzzled, applauding halfheartedly. His looks and his height still had the power to please, but to the audience it was both Montand and a stranger on that stage.

Worst of all was Marseilles. Piaf and Montand appeared at the Variétés-Casino, smack in the middle of the Canebière, from November 8 to 21. The theater owner, M. Franck, was also the proprietor of the Alcazar. Edith had insisted to Franck that Montand's name be printed in letters as large as her own on the billboard over the theater entrance—Piaf on top (dark lettering, thoughtful portrait on the left), Montand below (light lettering, cheerful portrait on the right). No doubt about it: equal partners.

> I was coming home after my Paris "triumph"—and sharing top billing with a national star. I was sure no auditorium in the world could be as familiar to me as the Variétés-Casino. I was used to the enthusiasm and the cruelty of Mediterranean audiences. I knew they were just as capable of acclaiming a beginner as of throwing rotten eggs at an established entertainer who wasn't living up to his reputation. Believe me, on the Mediterranean shore you'll always find sun—but not necessarily warmth.
>
> I began "Sophie" in an unaccustomed silence; then I heard a faint tinkling at my feet. They were throwing money at me—small change. That had never happened to me before, and in Marseilles of all places! A total washout. But I didn't respond to the insult; I kept on to the end as if nothing had happened.
>
> Edith was distressed. She suggested I water the wine a little, dust off one or two old successes. "Listen, Yves, give them what they want. You suddenly give them too many new songs, and they feel lost. Go easier on them."
>
> But I was stubborn, too proud to budge. Since I had now built up a repertory of French songs—and had worked so hard at it!—I'd make them swallow it. Edith argued. I insisted. Mainly for her sake, I thought, but also for my own. Then, little by little, as the tour went on, I found my rhythm, my style. People liked "Luna Park," then "Battling Joe," then "Ma môme, ma petite gosse." I

learned how to hold on to the basic elements, the songs you can't drop, and to try out other titles as I went along, fine-tuning the ones that worked, monitoring those that didn't work right away but might one day, and killing those that would never work.

Montand recovered, but it had been a shock. "At the Variétés," said Contet, "it was tragic for him and deadly for the rest of us. This was a program of songs we had discussed and thrashed out together: if the repertory didn't work out, we all had egg on our faces. Yves was furious. The audience shouted things like, 'What are you saying?' and called for 'Les Plaines du Far West' and nothing else. When he came off stage he tried to turn it against us—you know, 'I told you they wouldn't swallow it here!' 'We don't give a damn,' Edith retorted. 'They'll just have to take it here the way they do everywhere else! Screw them!' But when she told him to compromise because she could see he was suffering, he, in turn, pulled in his head. He hurt, but it didn't stop him. And, in the end, those songs were a hit."

Piaf took it all very much to heart. Anxious for Montand—she considered herself largely to blame—she assumed much of the responsibility and suffered wild stage fright when her lover went on stage. Edouard Derdérian, Montand's pal from youth camp, remembers sitting next to her in the Variétés. "When Yves appeared, I began to express myself in my usual expansive way, meaning to yell out a joke or some encouragement. Very seriously, she laid a finger on my lips. It was not the time for joking."

The Marseilles press wove garlands for Piaf and was decent enough to award Montand a consolation prize. "He throws a few words of American slang into his lyrics, to the delight of the Allied soldiers in the audience," admitted *Le Méridional* on November 9. *Le Provençal* conceded on November 11 that he was "applauded—like the other attractions on the program," and *Midi-Soir* on November 10 granted that "Yves Montand, who is beginning to forget cowboys and rolling plains, has found himself a new personality." There was nothing unkind in any of this, but there was none of the old enthusiasm, either.

If anyone was left unworried by such concerns, it was the denizens of the impasse des Mûriers in La Cabucelle. Repertory problems or no, these were days of glory. Montand had long since told them that he would be appearing in Marseilles, and with Edith Piaf at his side! The neighborhood was already delighted by Ivo Livi's fame, but the idea that Edith Piaf, in person, would be crossing the family threshold was stupefying. As they waited for the two celebrities (arriving, of course, by limousine), groups of kids—and, in particular, the young Jean-Louis Livi, Yves Montand's nephew (and later his movie agent)—shuttled back and forth between the alley and the street corner on the road to the slaughterhouses, where the visitors' car was expected to appear.

It was a long wait. It had been arranged that Elvire, Montand's sister-in-law, would sleep in Lydia's bedroom (his brother Julien was not yet back from internment), leaving her own bed for the visitors. When they finally appeared, the heroes—doing their best to hide their own worries—succumbed to the excitement in the air, and soon they were caught up in the clan euphoria. It was fiesta time. The table had been laid in the dining room—an exceptional event. "It was a merry meal," recalls Elvire. "Edith Piaf poured wine for herself. 'Be careful, Pupuce,' Yves said. He knew she had a low tolerance for alcohol and was watching over her. Just one glass made her lightheaded."

There had been no official announcement of their status (Contet had returned to Paris), but Lydia was not fooled, and she melted at the sight of her baby brother so obviously in love. "I read all the variety news in the papers," she says, "and I whispered to Yves, 'Isn't she with her songwriter, Henri Contet?' 'Mind your own business,' he answered, quite sharply. She was his first grown woman. Before, I had seen dozens of girls—young girls who brought flowers, supposedly for me, but of which I was clearly not the intended recipient. Yves used to say in wonder, 'I'm in love, and then suddenly I'm no longer in love. Is there something wrong with me?' With Edith, it was true love. She was a little shaken by our noisy celebration and seemed surprised that we talked so much and so fast. But she was also attracted by our warm family spirit. She loved it. 'And you complain,' she said reproachfully to Yves. 'You complain! With a family like this!' "

Between the Marseilles hairdresser and the Paris star a friendship quickly bloomed that was to outlast the love between Montand and Piaf. Lydia remained Piaf's periodic but discreet and valued confidante until Edith's death in 1963. And Edith herself, long after breaking up with Yves, traveled south with the men in her life and introduced them—particularly Jacques Pills, whom she married in the United States in 1952—to "Papa and Mama Livi." Lydia paints a picture of Piaf very close to the impression Montand had had at the Moulin Rouge: "At first glance she seemed an ugly, skinny little woman. But when you looked closer, everything about her was pretty: small nose, blue eyes, a sensual mouth, pink complexion. I did her hair. She was a brunette, but she had the fair skin of a blonde—angel skin."

In her unauthorized best-selling biography, published in 1969, Simone Berteaut (who called herself Piaf's half-sister but who was merely an old friend from their street days) insisted that Montand was obsessed with marrying Piaf. Montand would say it was Edith who was thinking along those lines. What is certain is that in the eyes of the Livi clan, those forty-eight hours in the bosom of the family, that introduction to the family (it happened all over again with Simone Signoret), amounted to a betrothal. Piaf and Montand returned to their tour not as a duo but as a real couple.

Montand survived the early disappointments, and it ended better than it had begun. "Even when he's out there alone, he makes the stage look tiny!" exclaimed the *Victoire de Toulouse* on November 25. His own instincts nudged him to remedy the excessively Piafesque notes he had slipped into his songs and the overdramatic lighting. Last year he had taken off. Next year he would soar.

So far, he was numbered among the hopefuls of French popular entertainment. But among those hopefuls, of course, were young people whose upward trajectory might just as easily be reversed. The covers of showbiz magazines are a graveyard of vanished hopes. Montand very quickly fought free of such insecurity. In a few months, Paris trendsetters were knocking at his dressing-room door, not because he had already scaled the heights but because they were certain that he would—and were proud of having predicted it. To Piaf, of course, this was all old stuff. The handful of years separating her from her lover had taught her that rumor was the best of allies: nothing was more damaging to an entertainer than a silent press. Better than any agent, she stirred up interest around her discovery, giving the columnists enough to kindle their interest without satisfying their speculation.

On January 15, 1945, Piaf threw a party for a throng of journalists at the cabaret Mayfair, on the boulevard Saint-Michel, with the more or less open intention of promoting Montand. She did not have to hunt for an excuse. The party took place just before they appeared together at the Etoile, on the avenue Wagram, where, from February 9 to March 8, they continued the act they had honed on the southern tour. Paris audiences reacted warmly, and when their contract at the Etoile ran out they went on to the Casino-Montparnasse, where they stayed until March 22. Reviewers were warm to Piaf's supporting act.[2]

For a decade, the Etoile, formerly the Folies-Wagram, would be Yves Montand's "own" theater. Boasting fifteen hundred seats, it was built in

2. See, for example, *France-Libre,* February 17, 1945; *Ordre,* February 18–19, 1945; and *La France au Combat,* February 22, 1945.

1928 to the theater specifications set forth by the nineteenth-century Second Empire architect Farge: arcaded entranceway, color scheme of red and silver, pink marble staircase. Initially specializing in light opera, the theater had zigzagged from category to category (in 1935, Antonin Artaud, Julien Bertheau, and Roger Blin had staged an adaptation of Stendhal there) and had then been taken over by Camille Choisy, the former director of the Grand-Guignol. Under his aegis, starting in July 1937, the theater had put on *The Threepenny Opera* with Renée Saint-Cyr, Yvette Guilbert, Suzy Solidor, and Raymond Rouleau. At the outbreak of war, it had returned to popular song (with Suzanne Flon as its well-loved mistress of ceremonies).

By the time Piaf and her protégé arrived, the Etoile's artistic director, Arnaut (he briefly took over as business manager for Piaf and Montand), was betting that full-scale concerts rather than a succession of singing acts were the wave of the future.[3] He was counting on the drawing power of stars.

It was a period of historical upheaval. At the Yalta conference in early February, Stalin, Churchill, and Roosevelt froze in place spheres of influence that would divide the planet for decades. On February 27, the Red Army liberated Auschwitz. In France, the Communist Party, whose leader, Maurice Thorez, had returned from the USSR at the end of November 1941, was at the peak of its popularity. In the new Fourth Republic, the French National Assembly was merely "consultative," and General de Gaulle was attempting to steer a narrow course among Christian Democrats, Socialists, and Communists, who flaunted the bloodstained banners of their Resistance martyrs at every opportunity.

They were indeed momentous times. But their very gravity, their very gloom, only served to fill the theaters of Paris. The shared sensation of living miraculously on the crest of a wave, of having survived so many shipwrecks, drove the French to seek entertainment and to find salvation there. Until public life functioned anew, until political parties, unions, and factions reorganized, the theaters and nightclubs offered a shared warmth. There was no milk and no meat, but you could go out at night, and availing yourself of that right was another way of embracing victory.

At the Elysée Theater, Piaf once again had the services of her favorite pianist, the Breton Georges Bartholé. Along with Henri Poussigue's orchestra, he accompanied her and Montand. Bartholé was a regular observer of the morning rehearsals, and it was he who set the tone for the

3. In 1947, Félix Vitry, the future owner of the Bobino, and already familiar to Montand from his time at the ABC, became production manager at the Etoile. See André Sallée and Philippe Chauveau, *Music-hall et café-concert* (Paris, 1985).

second provincial tour the couple undertook: it opened on March 30 at Villeurbanne and ended on June 3 at the Roman amphitheater in Bordeaux. From April 19 to 30, the two singers returned to the Variétés in Marseilles. (On the eve of their concert, *La Marseillaise* warned that it was "advisable to book in advance." The huge front-page banner headline that day announced: "Zhukov's Armies Threaten Berlin from the West." A smaller headline lower down read: "Buchenwald—Even Worse than Dante's Inferno.")

This time, the act ran more smoothly. Montand struggled less and less ("La Grande Cité" and "Elle a des yeux," which he was currently working on, were warmly received), but Edith Piaf's lover-associate-friend had fully mastered his repertory, and a fault line was opening that nothing could correct. The couple faced an insurmountable dilemma: either audiences came for Piaf, and Montand was there just to sweep up; or else Montand scored a real success, in which case Piaf was upset.

"Edith was nervous about coming on after him," says Henri Contet. "She was scared. 'It's too much, Henri,' she told me. 'I think it's just too much.' Yves's physical contribution was extraordinary, he was a monster, you couldn't bring the curtain down, audiences wouldn't let him leave." Piaf's biographer Monique Lange reports a similar reaction from Piaf: "On my tours with Yves, he raised the curtain and I closed the show. I had to bear my cross to the very end every night."[4]

In fact, it seems that Edith Piaf, fearful of competition she might not be able to handle, had considered undertaking the tour without her companion. Proof of this is that on the first night, at Villeurbanne, Pierre Malar was the guest artist. But the next day, Saturday, March 31, Edith herself announced a supplement to the program: Yves Montand. He had persuaded her not to strike out on her own, and the posters were hastily changed. From April 2, in Valence, until the end of the tour, his appearance was specifically spelled out each time.

Most commentators ascribe this tension to the rivalry of two stars competing for applause. But, in fact, what triggered their shared distress was that the program had simply become too much for the average audience. Montand plus Piaf was too big a bite to chew. Moreover, they were not evenly matched. Yves Montand, the revelation of the season, could afford to let himself be kicked around a little by a major star, but Piaf, however fervent an admirer of her protégé, had a reputation to defend.

Their relationship did not seem to suffer immediately. Such lethal processes operate slowly. They both agreed that the following autumn, Montand would get top billing at a prestigious Paris location (the Etoile)

4. Lange, *Histoire de Piaf.*

on his own—or almost: Piaf would precede him there. She also took a solemn vow, swearing not to touch a drop of alcohol for six months. She kept her word. Montand, who hated sloppiness and a lack of personal discipline, always prided himself on his ability to get women with self-destructive habits to abandon them—at least temporarily. Piaf stayed sober for love of him. Fifteen years later, Marilyn Monroe gave him a comparable satisfaction—a comparable proof of attachment.

Throughout that half-year, Piaf and Montand continued to hover between the settled existence of any normal couple and the no-man's-land of hotel living. Between major engagements, they sang in nightclubs. New signs winked along the streets of liberated Paris. The clubs that had dominated the scene during the Occupation (with German support, of course) were either lying low or changing direction. It was a time of innovation, experiment, turmoil. The Club des Cinq, on the rue Montmartre, founded by friends of the middleweight boxing champion Marcel Cerdan, quickly became the "in" place; the bandleader was Michel Emer, just back from the United States, and the club boasted a clarinetist as supple as Benny Goodman and a brass section that recalled Glenn Miller's.

For five years, French jazz musicians—deprived of American scores, forced to dabble in solitude or to embroider endlessly on old themes—had disguised themselves as "rhythm" artists and practiced jazz without ever calling it that. But the Club des Cinq had no ambition to be a temple of jazz (there were many other jazz clubs); rather, it wanted to be the place where revitalized variety acts might explore, in words and music, the tone and sound of the postwar world.

Chez Carrère, near the Champs-Elysées, offered a different atmosphere. A luxurious, intimate interior, all in white—curtains, screens, Directoire chairs, piano. Men without neckties had to remain at the bar. First you dined. Then, around midnight, the owner would "notice" that Mlle Piaf was among those present, as well as M. Montand, a Russian cellist, two English tragedians, and Sacha Guitry (who was everywhere). The doors would be closed. And, just as if it had been an impromptu private gathering at which guests with a little talent amused the company, Mlle Piaf, M. Montand, the Russian cellist, the English actors, and the witty Sacha Guitry would succumb to their host's request. He would announce them himself. The stage was tiny, exquisite. M. Carrère's bedroom did service as a dressing room. A feast of reason and a flow of soul. . . .

When Montand agreed to perform at the Club des Cinq, Edith was able to give him the benefit of her own experiences there: "You're big enough now to insist that business stops when it's your turn. No cash register, no cigarette sales." Montand's contract duly stipulated that restaurant service would be halted during his performance.

Inevitably, though, despite such contractual guarantees, there were ugly moments. So much so that Montand found himself contemplating the question that sooner or later faces all tough but peace-loving men: should I hit him or shouldn't I?

One evening that summer of 1945, he was singing at the Club des Cinq in front of a full house of festive diners. Almost at his feet, next to the stage, a customer dining alone had ordered a lobster. An entire lobster seemed a lot for just one fellow. In those hungry days, it seemed too much—in fact, almost a provocation. Standing and gesturing at the mike, Montand, despite his best efforts, felt his gaze drifting toward the shellfish. He even began to feel a bit hungry. Another few lines, and he looked down again: the glutton had finished only half his prey; worse, he was crushing out his cigar against the priceless flesh, mechanically, as if the lobster were an ashtray. Montand felt a wave of elemental, heartfelt emotion flood through him.

Now for "Battling Joe." Careful, the surface of the raised stage was slippery. A glance at his feet: the diner, too, had noticed. He dipped a careless hand into the bucket cooling his champagne and sent ice cubes rolling one after another toward Montand's feet. By now Montand had graduated from class hatred to direct man-to-man dislike. He finished the song and then said, courteously, in even, neutral tones: "If you're not a coward, Monsieur, I'd like you to join me in my dressing room."

The boor duly appeared.

"Why?" said Montand simply.

"Because I felt like it."

The entertainer's fist flew. One for the cubes. One for the lobster. One for the cigar. One for the contempt.

On another occasion, Edith was queen of the night. Leaning on the bar, Montand opened the gold cigarette case his love had given him. Nearby, a customer laughed noisily and derisively. Shh!! said the other spectators. Montand leaned toward the laughter.

"Monsieur, would you mind making less noise? You're disturbing Mlle Piaf."

"What's that?"

"I said, please don't talk so loudly."

"Outside!"

Climbing the stairs to the street ahead of his foe, having no wish to fight, Montand wondered how he was going to extricate himself. He saw only one way to shorten the business: take the initiative, at once and violently. Before he reached the top of the stairs he swung round and gave the creep a terrible slap.

"We keep our mouths shut when Mlle Piaf is singing!"

His victim reeled back, then lunged forward to counterattack; but waiters swarmed in to separate the fighters.

Montand swore to himself that he would get out of nightclubs as soon as he could (it was five years before he reached that goal). He liked the elegant barmen, the gorgeous girls, the fashionable women, the dinner-jacketed men, the warmth of sumptuous dining rooms. But inevitably, he felt, a dose of vulgarity came with the atmosphere: the cackling of drunken partygoers; kitchen smells in the dressing rooms and even on stage. The more he looked forward to those rooms bubbling with expectation, those eager audiences, the more convinced he became that the transaction was impossible without some reasonable distance between the entertainer and those applauding him. Too much familiarity did not bring a showman closer to his fans; it merely cut him down, dissolved his magic.

And Montand was troubled by the wave of energy that ran through him whenever a confrontation arose. The flow was so violent, so uncontrollable, that it triggered distrust, almost fear, within him. That fear of self (plus a good dose of pride) he felt again thirty years later at Saint-Paul-de-Vence after a disastrous game of boules: enraged, he grabbed a stone bench and hoisted it aloft. Was it the sudden release of an overcharge of energy stored up from the stage? Even decades later Montand was no nearer an answer than he was back in 1945.

At all events, such physical explosions convinced him that unless it was absolutely necessary, brutal violence—although he was capable of it, and, in fact, precisely for that reason—was not a solution that agreed with him. Ten years or so after the war, he publicly struck a comic-song artist who had insulted him on the radio. He had sworn before witnesses to do so. Chance had soon brought them face-to-face in a restaurant, and Montand felt obliged to keep his promise. He walked up to his adversary, coldly, dispassionately. But the memory of it troubled him ever since.

He remained throughout his life a man of Homeric rages, of earsplitting outbursts—but not of flying fists.

Edith Piaf starred at the Etoile from September 14 to October 4, 1945. Montand took over from her on October 5 as the lead performer—and he deliberately made this heavy responsibility heavier. He cut the first part of the show down to the bone and allotted himself the lion's share, twelve to fourteen songs—sixteen counting encores. This was a decisive move away from traditional arrangements and in the direction of a real concert. Not quite a one-man show yet, but almost. Apart from Maurice Chevalier, no one had ever exposed himself for so long to the glare of music-hall footlights, and more than one professional colleague considered so much ambition presumptuous.

A year and a half had elapsed since his first sight of Paris, of the Métro, and of the ABC. A short time, indeed, in which to have made so much progress. Needless to say, Montand worked on his repertory around the clock. Of his songs from the past, he kept only one sure favorite: "Et il sortit son revolver." For the rest, his choice veered from the dramatic to the tender and back again: "Elle a des yeux," "La Grande Cité," "Luna Park," "Ma môme, ma petite gosse," "Battling Joe," "Gilet rayé," "Ce monsieur-là," "Le Fanatique du jazz," "Les Grands Boulevards"—in other words, a full yield of twelve months of doubts and groping. There was also a little song Montand loved, a spirited blues written by Norbert Glanzberg: "Moi je m'en fous, je m'en contrefous" (much better and more defiant, in a different way, than Charles Humel's "Je m'en fous," which he had sung at the ABC). He hit upon the idea of singing it nonchalantly, hands clasped behind his neck, tongue in cheek, swaying from one foot to the other. It was pleasant and mildly provocative. But Montand had now gone beyond mere provocation. This particular "Je m'en fous" was not a hymn to happy-go-lucky heedlessness. Rather, it was an antidote to the somber note of "La Grande Cité." A reminder of your right to fun and leisure, no matter how dark the horizon.

Montand never even considered choosing between lighthearted fantasy and serious, social themes. He went all out for both ends of the spectrum and bracketed them on stage, to the occasional puzzlement of audiences unaccustomed to mixed messages. Traditionally, one entertainer specialized in love songs, another in dramatic themes, and the third, the house comedian, laughed no matter what. But Montand refused to be pigeonholed into just one role. He instinctively saw the entertainer as an expert switch-hitter. If the audience expected a solemn moral message, he would serve up a mischievous sketch. Instead of a sophisticated melody, he gave them "Battling Joe." And when the audience was geared for tap dancing or a flight of lyric fantasy, he stood dead still in a single spotlight and whispered a poem barely borne aloft on the air his lungs expelled. Part of his purpose, of course, was to build a repertory full of surprises, beginning gently, giving the spectator time to breathe, then suddenly taking his breath away. But it was also because Montand was determined to be many beings, never the prisoner—of either a hit or a flop, of either an image or a habit.

The world's first atomic bomb had devastated Hiroshima on August

6. Marshal Pétain had been condemned to death—with indecent haste—by the High Court of Justice on August 11. Pierre Laval had received the same sentence and was executed shortly afterward. The Communist Party's Twentieth Congress pretended to "extend a hand" to the Socialists and the Catholics. Jean-Paul Sartre had created his magazine *Les Temps Modernes.* Montand was by no means indifferent to current events (although he lost no sleep over the wildfire spread of existentialism). On stage, though, he presented both characters who preferred the footlights and those who were troubled by the events of the day. This, perhaps, was why he appealed not just to one but to several highly differentiated audiences.

The formula worked so well that on November 30, after seven weeks of the Etoile being packed every night, he pulled up stakes and took his act to the Alhambra. Reviews were enthusiastic. "Beyond a doubt, Yves Montand is the strongest personality to have emerged in music hall since Charles Trenet's now-distant beginnings," wrote Max Favalelli in *La Dépêche de Paris* on October 28–29. But a questioning note intruded here and there: Who was this singer who forgot he was just a singer? Some reviewers voiced their surprise at the intensity and the pessimism of songs he sandwiched between jokes and dance sketches. Véra Volmane, for example, in *Concorde* on New Year's Eve said that the performance "left a vague anxiety, an indefinable malaise in the depths of the heart." In *Opéra* on December 26, Jean Barreyre analyzed this malaise, claiming that "this disconcerting young singer is the doorkeeper to a new world. He offers not just his own highly personal interpretation of the songs of the 'hot,' 'swing' generation . . . but also the voice of youth, a youth that life—and the philosophers—have weighted down with thorny problems and challenges." Montand, he concluded, was the "singer of a generation forced to look beyond the frontiers of home and homeland."

This was not a reproach. Merely a discovery—that the "minor" art of music-hall entertainment could treat serious themes lightly and at the same time convey, through the voice and gestures of a solitary standard-bearer, the fears, thirsts, and angers of a group, of a part of society united by ideology, age, and way of life. The genuine popular strain embodied by Maurice Chevalier, the modern tempo and dreamlike freedom of Charles Trenet had undoubtedly expressed collective surges that passed through each of them. But Montand, emerging suddenly from the war with a unique blend of craftsmanlike rigor and physical energy, seemed a member of an unknown species. To reviewers, who were struck as much by his social and his tragic sense as by his dancer's poise and expressive hands, Montand seemed, if not avant-garde, then at least an innovator worth following.

But no study of the reviews would be complete without mentioning the renewed complaints about his excessive perfectionism. "He is a young man who has studied, studied hard, studied too hard," wrote François Grousseau in *Paroles Françaises* on December 22, going on to criticize his "automatonlike moves." Montand had to get used to these criticisms: review after review—until well into the 1960s—lauded his timing and the finished quality of his self-choreographed sketches, praised his uncanny ability to fill space, but added that the effect was marred by a whiff of the midnight oil, of excessive study.

> If I went into a dance step, even briefly, just the hint of a step, I wanted it to be perfect, relaxed, natural seeming. You can achieve that only by rehearsing for days. And, as I said, even for the briefest of steps. Talent (forgive me for using big words) is emphatically *not* showing an audience everything you can do—it is giving the audience the impression that it hasn't seen everything, that it has merely been offered a glimpse of what the artist is capable of.
>
> But I have to admit that these reviews irritated me. Too mechanical, they said, too perfect. I've given it a lot of thought, because if a remark comes up again and again, it must mean something. I think the reason my act gave that impression was its running order, the way I methodically switched from strong to weak and back again ("Battling Joe" followed by, say, "Mirettes"). When I say "weak" I don't mean the quality of the song but its rhythm. Today, with lasers and so on, the lighting technician is almost as important as the singer. With singers who explode into shouts, or with violent vibes, you can go beyond the classical norms, you can afford eight or sixteen instrumental bars—more, if the audience goes along—before hitching up the wagon, closing the circle by returning to the opening chorus. But if you want to offer a subtle blend of genres—and that's both my specialty and my great love—you have to follow a carefully laid-out plan of operation, if only for the lighting director's sake.
>
> Artifice will never hold an audience's loyalty for long, but personality and charisma will. Look at Piaf or Brel, to mention only those who are gone.
>
> Within that context, though, whether the beat is strong or weak, you must give audiences total truth, total instinct—particularly instinct—total freshness. If I hadn't, I wouldn't have lasted, I wouldn't have fooled anyone.
>
> And there are two other points. First, I am exclusively a performer. I have never written a single song and never wanted to.

(That isn't just a matter of education: I simply didn't possess the gift of a Georges Brassens or a Trenet.) My great joy—inseparable from fear—is rediscovering on stage, every evening, the pleasure that made me choose a song in the first place. That freedom of choice is all-important to me. That is why I give of myself: to return the pleasure I myself have received. You can't cheat about that. You can't feign it.

The second point is my Italian origins. None of my repertory of gestures is learned. Of course, I studied dance steps, twirling a cane, tipping a hat in front of the mirror; but not a single one of my hand movements is learned, not a single physical expression. That's how we Latins talk: we emphasize what's already self-evident, even before the words come out, for gestures speak much faster than words. What's hard is to express deep feelings, to capture and reinvent them at just the right moment. Bad nights happen when the reinvention doesn't come off . . . sort of a semierection.

In 1945 reviewers seemed very impressed by my big hands, their size enhanced by the dark brown of the sleeves they emerged from. That was natural. It was that same Latin excess, which sometimes irritates me in some of my movies. I wish that what I think of as British manners, a kind of reticence, had been drummed into me as a kid. But on the screen, directors have tended to accentuate my "working-class origins"—which sometimes annoys people, and it annoys me, too, when it's exaggerated or poorly handled.

Lastly, I should say that when I go on stage for "Gilet rayé," dragging a chair to simulate the night watchman who sits down to tell about his hopeless love, it's straight cartoon stuff. Mainly Tex Avery. Disney. Grimault. I'm a member of the cartoon generation.

On the night of his first performance at the Etoile, Montand received a delegation from his family. Lydia and Julien (back from Germany at the beginning of summer—the two brothers had not seen each other for five years) had come up from Marseilles to cheer Yves on.

Lydia was already a committed fan, but Julien was in a state of mild shock. He had returned to a wife he had had to marry all over again, psychologically speaking, and to an unknown son. Now here was his kid brother, apparently well known to everyone in the world but him. And Montand was torn between contradictory feelings, too. He had often felt intimidated by this tough, sturdy older brother, this proletarian militant, and he also felt guilty at having survived the war without serious harm. But this did not curb his pleasure at showing Julien that his adolescent dreams had been something more than the fantasies of youth.

The reunion was therefore touchy, tender, complex, intricate, ambiguous. Which was the big brother, which the little? Which the protector, which the protected? Which the strong, which the weak?

Edith Piaf made the two emissaries from Marseilles sit in her box. She let it be known that it was partly her doing, this recital that was Yves's first solo flight. She also insisted on organizing the sumptuous supper afterward as a "consecration"—Lydia wrote it in her own hand on the menu, which she kept and which Piaf very affectionately dedicated to her—of Yves Montand. Consommé Madrilene, poached eggs Valençay, supremes of chicken in champagne sauce, salade gauloise, cheeses, délices de São Paulo, fruit. Not to mention the Meursault-Charmes 1941, Corton 1929, and Veuve-Clicquot brut 1934.

Never in her life had Lydia seen such abundance. But she remained astute enough to notice a touch of embarrassment in the hero of the hour. Edith insisted imperiously on paying the bill, and Yves, while undeniably overjoyed at his success, could not hide his fleeting exasperation. "Piaf," Julien Livi says today, "seemed very watchful." Brother and sister put these surface disturbances down to the solemnity of the moment and to the strong personalities of the two singers. Lydia thought that Edith was no less in love than she had been on her visit to La Cabucelle, but that Yves's first venture on his own represented both a triumph and a test for his mistress. From this day, October 5, 1945, on, Piaf and Montand operated as independent units. Considering that they were people whose professional lives and private passions were intricately intertwined, it is not surprising that this step was a danger to them. But the next day, when Edith left on a Belgian tour, the climate was more relaxed.

Did Montand feel the wind change? He was wholly absorbed by his concert. He had buried the cowboy persona of his early beginnings. With Piaf's help, he was reaching toward a kind of total music hall (as people would one day talk of total theater) in which each title was a self-contained drama or a comedy in miniature, and he was engulfed in choreographic problems. He might have been content with a career as a crooner—his full voice and his liking for what he called the "coaxing" vein would have made this easy—but he was committed to a much more complex challenge. Responding to the slightest shift in audience response, he strove to regulate a thousand and one details—lighting, movement, rhythm—to give his act exactly the right color, the necessary rhythm.

One small detail escaped him. "Battling Joe" was doing fine, but Montand the singer was strolling straight into a devastating knockout punch.

It was early spring, 1946. Edith was just back from Greece, and I found her a bit . . . distant. She left for Alsace and Germany while I awaited her return in the apartment she had just leased at 26 rue de Berri. It was 2:00 p.m. Then three. Then four. I called her secretary, Mme Bigeard, and learned that Edith was with her, that she didn't want to come over. "Because she doesn't want to see you," said the secretary. I took this badly. I said that wasn't good enough, and that I was leaving. I packed and took a room in the Surène-d'Aguesseau hotel near the Madeleine. I was dying to go over and question Edith, demand an explanation. My father had taught me that when a woman hurts you, you have to stand your ground. . . . So leaving like that was probably the very thing I should not have done. It put me on an irreversible downward slope. My father had been right.

In her book on Piaf, Simone Berteaut depicts a Montand beside himself with rage (which was likely), yelling out his pain, hammering on his heartless lover's door (which he denied).

Unhappy, yes; wanting to weep, yes. But I didn't glue myself to her doorbell. I stayed put for a week, not moving, not yielding an inch. A long time. Then I picked up the phone, I called her. Edith seemed overjoyed. We arranged to meet that very evening at the "general's" place.

The "general" wasn't a soldier but the owner of our favorite restaurant, not far from the rue de Richelieu. Edith called him that because he wore a little military goatee and bossed the customers around. His restaurant had barely a dozen tables. If he didn't like your looks he would say, "We're full, Monsieur, but may I recommend such and such an address." It was our family dining room. It was there I first had the pleasure of drinking Burgundy from a snifter. And the "general" glowed whenever he saw Piaf.

That night, a storm broke over Paris, a monster storm. I cooled my heels at the restaurant. Edith had warned me she was having trouble finding transportation. All the taxis were taken, even the carriages she liked so much that still plied the Champs-Elysées. It was awful. We missed each other. But that mishap gave Piaf the courage to get hold of herself, to put distance between us again. She was brave and clearheaded enough to break clean, to get clear away.

One morning three weeks later I went around to the rue de Berri to see her. Looking very nonchalant, one pal visiting another.

She said: "I'm busy, but I have a wonderful song for you, take it!" And there I was, out on the sidewalk again, with the score of "La Légende du boogie-woogie" in my hand, a mediocre little number I nevertheless tried out at the Club des Cinq. About a train jumping the rails . . . but I was the one who jumped the rails for the next three years. A real void, a black hole, protracted sorrow.

The word is that I was "launched" by Piaf. You can't do much about rumors like that. There's no point saying, "Well, but . . ." or talking about love. People don't even hear you. It's not a legend I object to. When a youngster showed talent, Piaf would go over and sit beside him, and the "Piaf spotlight" would pick the kid out. She applauded, went to see him backstage, and the next day a photo of her latest discovery would appear in the papers. And then she would move away, the spotlight would move away, and she would find someone else . . . and so on.

Professionally I owe a lot to Edith Piaf. But she didn't create me. She helped me—thank you, Edith—and, above all, she loved me, she stood by me. And then she hurt me, with such honesty, such laughter and grace, that I took several years to heal.

Why this suddenness, this brutality? Because Edith Piaf was like that, say those who knew her. And because she felt threatened.

Accounts and recollections of those close to the couple agree. Contet believes that ambition and passion lethally interacted in Piaf: "In matters of love and jealousy, Edith was unconscionable." (The speaker knew from experience.) "It was one of her major faults. Montand suffered cruelly. He was very reserved about it, yet from what he told me I gathered he suffered a blow that went far beyond pride. He loved Edith, and Edith adored him. But professional rivalry most assuredly affected their relationship. What mattered first and foremost with Piaf was her art. The public couldn't get enough of her love affairs, but the truth is, singing came before anything else. She could never allow her lover to steal even a part of her success. It didn't lead to quarrels; Edith simply shut herself off. And when she did that. . . ."

When she did that, it meant she was with someone else. Montand soon learned she had formed a fleeting attachment to a friend on the tour, Luc Barney. Then that her interest in the Compagnons de la Chanson was far from platonic—that her latest beau was Jean-Louis Jaubert, its lead singer, and that she was now directing her magic spotlight toward him.

Sometime after her break with Montand, Piaf confided in Lydia. "You should never wait for a love to die," she said. "That's too horrible. You have to have the guts to separate while you're still in love. Otherwise you hate each other, or you cling to each other out of pity. You should always leave. That's my revenge on beautiful women." Julien adds: "I believe that as Yves's reputation grew, Piaf felt increasingly stifled. It wasn't simple jealousy—more that she was afraid of becoming a prisoner."

Did Montand still hope, after four or five weeks, that his loved one would return? No. She was too violent and too wholehearted to weaken. As a good Mediterranean, Ivo Livi had grown up to see men as strong and women as powerful. He would have been inclined to compromise, to negotiate; he had no leanings toward tragedy and at bottom would have liked to settle things. But in his eyes the infinite tenderness of the so-called weaker sex came with a capacity for determination, decisive action, gallantry in the teeth of the irreparable, a readiness to die. He clenched his fists and swore never again to fall in love.

What did he really owe Piaf, apart from the tears he stifled? Everything, according to the legend: his first steps on a major stage, a balanced repertory, daily self-criticism, the idea of taking the orchestra out of the pit, movement, motionlessness. The legend spread so rapidly (and Edith worked so hard to feed it) that he neither dared nor wanted to deny it, perhaps fearing that any correction might look like thoughtless ingratitude or the churlishness of an abandoned lover. Since he had no choice, he straddled and rode the legend, and made it his own. During an interview in the fall of 1946, for example, he stated: "With Edith Piaf I worked like a madman. I owe her almost everything I know."[5]

But a few decades later, Montand no longer hid the sense that he had been trapped by the legend, a legend so established, so impervious to the slightest correction, that it seemed almost incongruous to assert the obvious truth: one way or another, Montand would assuredly have become Montand. Choosing his words carefully, he argued that Edith helped him to rise quickly—but that she did not invent him. In fact, Piaf had said the same thing to Lydia: "You know, all I did was help your brother save two or three years."

But Piaf's contribution—if it can be judged at all—should be measured not simply in terms of time won or lost. Simone Signoret explained it: "The day she no longer wanted him was the day he became her professional equal. In the beginning, he had been someone to teach. She didn't teach him everything he knew, because there are things no one can teach anyone. One has them or one doesn't. But as soon as he started flying with his own wings, and choosing his own songs, or refusing those she wanted him to sing, Edith left him."[6]

5. *Paris-Matin,* October 8, 1946.

6. Simone Signoret, *Nostalgia Isn't What It Used to Be* (New York, 1978).

* * *

Just as their relationship collapsed, Montand and Piaf appeared together again on a poster—a movie poster this time. It became an unintended separation present, tossed by the singer to the man she still loved—and avoided. "Tossed" is the right word: Piaf, who had already worked on the stage, and acquitted herself well, decided to try movies because the idea amused her, and also because the movies were a magnificent advertising medium, the best way of guaranteeing universal recognition. But her only true passion was the stage, the show, being there in the flesh, immediate acclaim. When Montand confessed to her that the music hall was just an interim phase for him, a stepping-stone to the movies, she had been downright indignant. Give up all that warmth, the public's adoring gaze, its encores? With a talent like his? The arguments grew ugly; sometimes they drove her wild with anger.

But out of love, and mindful of the boyhood dream that had driven the kid from La Cabucelle, Edith decided to help him. In the spring of 1945, Montand had taken part for the first time in a real shoot. In a film called *Silence . . . antenne* (*You're on the Air!*), the filmmaker René Lucot reconstructed a day in the life of a radio station, with announcers, newsreaders, reporters, comedians, singers, and musicians succeeding one another at the microphone. Montand was hired to sing "Luna Park" and "Les Plaines du Far West." His role was not a role: he was simply filmed doing what he usually did elsewhere.

Piaf had better to offer him. In 1942, she had made friends with a reporter who was also a movie fanatic, Marcel Blistène. A Jew and a refugee in the unoccupied zone, he had lived for a while in the home of Piaf's secretary, Andrée Bigeard.[7] Edith had promised him that if he wrote a screenplay for her, she would take the part and fight to have the movie made. She kept her word. In 1945, the script was ready. It was called *Etoile sans lumière* (*Star Without Light*). The plot drew from a well at which every good director had already drunk: a harsh-voiced silent-movie star is dubbed, once talkies come along, by an unknown girl with a melodious voice. One fine day the secret comes out, and the unknown becomes a star (the leitmotif just a few years later of *Singin' in the Rain*). The producers thought the director was too inexperienced, but Piaf stood up for him.

So Blistène was heavily in Edith's debt. The Piaf "clan" virtually monopolized the credits (Guy Luypaerts wrote the music and Marguerite Monnot the lyrics), and once they were ready to shoot—filming began on July 30, 1945, and ended on October 5—Edith asked the director to write

7. See Marcel Blistène, *Au revoir, Edith* (Paris, 1963).

in a small part for "a friend." Thus was born the character of Pierre, assigned to Yves Montand. (Blistène had already met him, for it was Blistène who had organized Piaf's party at the Mayfair.) Pierre, an auto mechanic, is the heroine's awkward, provincial fiancé. She eventually returns to him after her seduction by the dubious world of the movie-star makers, symbolized by the elegant and cynical Parisian Gaston Lansac (the irreproachably nasty Serge Reggiani).

All audiences saw of Piaf and Montand was an attractive shot of them in a car, with Edith's head resting against his shoulder as she sings, smiling, free, a happy glimpse of two young people very much in love. But the experience was neither exciting nor inspiring for Montand. He wandered about among the lights, tripped over cables, tried to hide his embarrassment, obeyed orders, made an effort to decipher film-crew slang, discovered the eternal hidden conflict between crew and sound engineers. "I saw a lot of him on the set," reports Blistène, "much more than his minor role warranted. He followed Edith around; she dominated him totally. I remember him as a model of docility and zeal; he seemed in permanent awe of the mechanics of filming."[8]

The movie came out in April 1946 to more or less condescending reviews about the "naive," "simplistic," even "rustic" young director[9] (although it launched his career, for he and Jacques Feyder went on to shoot *Macadam* [*Back Streets of Paris*] with Simone Signoret). Piaf was praised for the dramatic bitterness she projected; Reggiani's performance was acclaimed; and as for Montand, his brief appearance was called "encouraging"[10] and, inevitably, "likable."[11] These reactions neither delighted nor hurt him. By the time *Etoile sans lumière* began its general run in the major Paris theaters, his thoughts were elsewhere. First of all, the idyll that had linked him to the film was no more. And other, more onerous movie matters now weighed on him. He had just been tapped for a suicide mission. And went for it hell for leather.

They met in late January 1946. Montand was singing at the Club des Cinq, where he now performed regularly. When his act was over, he was told that two gentlemen urgently requested an interview. They introduced themselves as Marcel Carné and Jacques Prévert. Montand had not yet

8. Quoted in Richard Cannavo and Henri Quiquéré, *Montand: Le Chant d'un homme* (Paris, 1981).

9. Jean Néry, *L'Ecran Français,* April 10, 1946.

10. Ibid.

11. Jacques Natanson, *Ordre,* April 12, 1946.

recovered from his success at the Etoile and the Alhambra. News of the outside world filtered through only intermittently. Charles de Gaulle had just resigned as president of France's provisional government, a United Nations assembly had been held in London, the Paris press was on strike. . . . All that Montand knew—he had a radio. But his inner clock drove him, not the dance of the planets. And he knew very little about his two visitors. He knew that Jacques Prévert was the author of a volume of poetry, *Paroles,* published the preceding December. He had leafed through it and had liked it at once. He knew that Carné (with Prévert, in fact) had made *Les Visiteurs du soir,* a film he had seen and enjoyed. And he knew that the pair were one of the best-known teams in contemporary French cinema. To him, *Drôle de drame, Quai des brumes, Le Jour se lève,* and *Les Enfants du paradis* existed only as posters; but he had heard that they carried considerable weight. Carné was thirty-seven; Prévert, forty-six. They were neither novices nor over the hill. All the big studios wanted them.

And they wanted Montand. Urgently. A part that had to be filled. Would he risk a test? Awed and intimidated, Montand did not hesitate: this was the chance of a lifetime, the assignment he had never dared dream of.

The assignment had a long history. In the beginning was a ballet, *Le Rendez-Vous,* with a libretto by Jacques Prévert, choreographed by Roland Petit, a backdrop by Picasso and photographs by Brassaï, and performed at the Théâtre Sarah-Bernhardt by Roland Petit's company to music by Joseph Kosma. Prévert went to the premiere with Carné, Jean Gabin, and Marlene Dietrich, the last two just back from a five-year exile in the United States. Gabin was looking for a vehicle for a triumphant return; Carné and his producer Raymond Borderie (from the Pathé studios) were eager to supply it. And the evening at the ballet set things in motion.

It told the story of a man assured by Destiny that he will meet "the most beautiful woman in the world" and stay with her for the duration of one night. He does meet her—and loses her in the morning. A slender story line, but Gabin was willing. Moreover, he suggested including *"La Grande"*—the great Marlene—in the cast. A few days later, the pact was sealed in the bar at Claridge's, and the artists set to work. Contracts were drawn up (Dietrich was promised $30,000), the screenplay was written, Kosma was signed on to do the music. One evening, he and Prévert met with Gabin, Dietrich, Brassaï, and Carné at a quiet bistro on the rue Dauphine. In a back room was a piano, at which Kosma played the theme song of the movie which he and Prévert had written: "Les Feuilles mortes" ("Autumn Leaves").

Prévert holed up in the south to write. Kosma and Alexandre Trauner, the inventive set designer who had created the ambience of so many of Carné's films, were his neighbors. Prévert was moving in the direction of *film noir,* a development that required courage—and bothered Gabin. René Clément had scored a huge success by portraying a rebellious, heroic, stubborn France in *La Bataille du rail,* a documentary reconstruction of the resistance waged by France's railway workers against the Occupation. But Prévert took the opposite tack. He set his romantic drama about an impossible love in a world of cowards, informers, collaborators, liars, profiteers. Dark was the night, dark the city, dark those postwar hours when honest people's joy masked and submerged shameful memories. There would, of course, be a dance of desire, an innocent pas de deux between lines of white statues. But in *Les Portes de la nuit* (its final title), only the statues would be white, not human virtue.

Then everything began to go wrong. Financial problems. Scheduling problems. Gabin owned a movie property he believed in with all his heart, *Martin Roumagnac:* he insisted that *Les Portes* be finished in time for him to meet his second deadline. Studios, still few and far between, were unavailable. And then *"La Grande"* threw her own wrench into the works. Her contract gave her the right of approval over the script, and the script left her cold. "This film," she decided, "will be a bad advertisement for me abroad."[12] Prévert was running late and had neither the time nor inclination to recast his screenplay. It was the final straw.

Jean Gabin himself was beginning to cool. To no one in particular he uttered the kind of honeyed, ambiguous comment of which he was a master: "It's a story of intellectual masturbators, something straight out of the Café Flore." When Carné suggested replacing Dietrich with a very young actress, Gabin objected in the same spirit: "What does that mean? They want me to act opposite a nymphet? A kid . . . at my age!" (He was forty-one.) "I have to have a woman of between thirty and thirty-five."

By January 1946, Carné was shooting the exteriors without waiting for the conflict to be settled. With Prévert, he wandered the dark, deserted streets of the Barbès and La Villette neighborhoods of Paris, noting wooden fencing plastered with torn posters and faded window shutters. They intended to make lavish use of the transparency process, in which images filmed in advance are projected onto two-way mirrors before which the actors work. People living along the banks of the Canal de l'Ourcq and night walkers crossing the Pont de Crimée in the small hours were surprised to see batteries of lights, technicians drying the paving stones, intrepid onlookers awaiting the actors. The press had promised Gabin and Dietrich. Where were they?

By mid-January, Marlene Dietrich's defection was a certainty and

12. See Pierre Laroche, "L'Histoire d'un film," *L'Ecran Français,* February 6, 1946, and André Brunelin, *Gabin* (Paris, 1987).

Gabin was setting increasingly unacceptable conditions. Despite the good offices of none other than André Malraux, negotiations bogged down. In the final analysis, completing the movie to suit the deadline of *Martin Roumagnac* seemed impossible. They sent the young Serge Reggiani over to Claridge's for one last try. But Dietrich was inflexible: now she refused to countenance collaborators appearing in one of her movies. She withdrew; it was a bitter break, with legal complications. And then Prévert and Carné knocked at the door of Yves Montand.

Blistène served as go-between. "Carné was shattered by the defection of Jean Gabin and Marlene Dietrich," he recalls. "He phoned me to ask about the man making his debut in my film. I was full of praise and arranged for him to see footage of scenes in which Montand appeared. Carné was won over at once, and after a few minutes he decided to hire him."[13]

Carné himself is less sure that his decison was so sudden. But the crisis was serious enough for him and Prévert to think they had to gamble. The cast they had assembled around Gabin and Dietrich was dazzling: Pierre Brasseur (the heroine's husband, a businessman fattened on the Occupation), Serge Reggiani (an evil militiaman), Jean Vilar (a newcomer to the screen, playing the role of Destiny), and many other wonderful actors. Who would dare, in such company, to take on roles originally tailored for two giant stars? The only solution was to risk the total surprise of two unknowns (on the screen, at least). "The most beautiful woman in the world" would be Nathalie Nattier, about whom no one knew anything except that she was pretty. And Diego, the warm-hearted working-class Resistance veteran, would be Montand.

Carné hesitated, then took the plunge: "Since the scene we planned for the tests was a sequence played by the two leading actors, I started to put together couples. After a moment's thought, I paired Montand with Nattier. Physically, they complemented each other, but to say that their test was remarkable would be untrue. Unfortunately, my instinct had been right—the other candidates were even worse. . . . In any case, everyone agreed they were the best. Jacques, who found them 'wonderful,' urged me to hire them. But still I hesitated. From the Alsina hotel, on the avenue Junot, where she was living, Piaf kept on sending ever more urgent appeals." That same day, the director gave a positive response.

The plot was an uneasy blend of hard-edged realism and the wildest fantasy. Montand soon realized that he was expected to play the decent kid,

13. Quoted in Cannavo and Quiquéré, *Montand.*

honest, brave, doomed to endure human wickedness and fate's awful cruelty. Acting opposite Reggiani, playing the loathsome little swine, he felt a certain balance. But the brief amorous encounter, ending at dawn with a suicide and a murder, was still spiced with undeniably sloppy poetic license: for example, Montand-Diego and Nattier-Malou are supposed to have carved their names long ago on a stone on Easter Island. The idea might have worked for a visibly traveled man like Gabin, but the twenty-five-year-old Montand would have trouble projecting such a complex past with any conviction.

Alexandre Trauner had reconstructed the Barbès-Rochechouart Métro station in a hangar vast enough to house a zeppelin. Stretches of the canal de l'Ourcq, of busy streets complete with bakeries, tobacco stores, billboards, and newspaper kiosks, had been built in trompe l'oeil by squads of craftsmen.

"I don't recall that it was a very difficult shoot," says Carné. "Trying, yes, but not really harrowing." Montand's recollections were the same. Trying. You had to move within carefully prescribed spatial limits, be sure your hand did not wander outside the frame, break off the moment emotions surfaced. He was willing to do anything. He wanted to learn; he asked for advice and criticism. But when a take was completed all he heard was a clinical voice saying "Okay! Good for me!" The set, under its glaring lights, seemed cold to him, quite unlike a stage. Where were Fred Astaire and the cowboys of his dreams? He was like a sleepwalker moving in hostile, unmarked territory.

What he needed was approval, but that was not Carné's style. He directed actors by insulating himself from them. He expected them to act, not to be. And he was in the habit of fighting them until they gave up. This was not just a question of character, method, or period. He was used to handling larger-than-life personalities like Gabin and Arletty, who easily put pressure on directors. Montand, both in the role demanded of him and in the way he was ordered around, felt stripped of his feelings, treated like a life-sized mannequin who was shifted from place to place but whom nobody cared about.

With Serge Reggiani he struck up a wary friendship, touchy on both sides, fellowship warring with rivalry. ("He's not an Italian," said the Emilian Reggiani of the Tuscan Livi, "he's a Marseillais.") Reggiani was an alert and amused witness of Montand's hesitant beginnings: "We had already run into each other in *Etoile sans lumière.* But here things were more serious. Yves was truly a beginner—in movies, I mean. As a great stage professional he was used to working alone, and he was uneasy in the middle of our crowd. Back then he had a habit of sticking his elbows out to give himself courage, which irritated Carné and some of the rest of us.

Little by little he got it under control. But there were still his hand movements. And speaking of hands . . . I think of the series of slaps he was supposed to flatten me with. Well, with Montand it was for keeps, with those huge paddles and those wrestler's forearms!"

Montand never told his old friend that Carné had quietly told him: "Don't worry, hit him hard, we'll only shoot this scene once!" On the other hand, it was enormously difficult for him to spit in Reggiani's face when he had been joking with him on the set only moments before.

A further source of anxiety was the decision to bank everything on the two newcomers. Since the original stars had defected, the producers stressed the freshness and spontaneity of the young recruits and hinted at the revelation to come. During the shooting, they saturated the press with tidbits and portraits of Yves Montand and Nathalie Nattier. "A tall kid eager to be accepted for what he is, with a pleasant face, a very young smile, and natural hair"—such were the comments accompanying pictures of Montand. Translation: charming, well built, and a bit awkward. "The most beautiful woman in the world" made the front pages of the movie magazines, her profile standing in for her missing professional experience.[14]

But when Montand answered reporters' questions, he betrayed his fears. He adopted what we would today call a low profile—unassuming, conciliatory, suppressing the rough edges of his personality, accepting the stereotype of honest, small-town kid unable to believe his good luck. "In music hall I achieved a success I didn't expect," he confided to Michèle Nicolaï. "And then, out of the blue, the man I considered our finest director offered me a part. I've always wanted to fly higher and wider, but the movies scared me. . . . At first I floundered. Influenced by Gabin, I wanted to stress my dark side. Marcel Carné told me: 'Be yourself—a big smiling kid.' So I'm the guy who loved life. But life didn't return the compliment—not in the movies, anyway."[15]

And this time, life did not return the compliment in life, either. All the time he was locked into this lighthearted and falsely transparent character, his heart was shattered. He missed Piaf. He was alone—all the more so because the public viewed him as a sort of social phenomenon. He was climbing so fast, so high, that no one would understand a complaint, a serious misgiving. He was talented and successful and lucky (hadn't Carné

14. *L'Ecran Français,* February 27 and May 8, 1946.

15. *La France au Combat,* March 14, 1946.

hired him on Friday the thirteenth, his birthday?), so he had everything he could wish for.

When at last there was a break in the shooting, in early summer, he rediscovered the stage and Edith Piaf at a concert she organized on July 11 at the Club des Cinq, with the receipts going to pay for vacations for the children of prisoners. Luc Barney and the Compagnons de la Chanson were on the program; Edith performed extracts from *Le Bel Indifférent*—not with Paul Meurisse, as scheduled, but with Gérard Landry; and Montand came on in the last half. He was disturbed at being around Piaf as a "pal" (and doubtless somewhat irritated by a cast that clustered her former lovers around their successor), but he was happy to be treading the boards again, put a good face on it, and was applauded. His wounds were not healed, but as long as he was singing, at least he knew who he was.

On August 21, Montand was the subject of a portrait by "Le Minotaure," the pseudonym behind which the editors of *L'Ecran Français* lined up thumbnail sketches of artists in the news. "In profile," it said, "Montand looks like Louis Jouvet. Only younger. A 'swing' Louis Jouvet, a Doctor Knock in love with boogie-woogie and pin-up girls. . . . We'll be seeing his tall form prowling in the shadows of the rue de l'Evangile. He speaks Jacques Prévert's dialogue, and Marcel Carné directs him below the elevated Métro line that makes the dingy houses shake around the porte de la Chapelle. When M. Yves Montand meets Destiny, in this gloom alive with the little people of the night, he has to focus on his role so he won't embrace Jean Vilar and dance around him—because so far Destiny has been kind to him. Enough said. No complaints. . . . He knows he's expected, but he goes to every rendezvous that Chance arranges for him, wild with stage fright and his conscience clear. We shall see!"

Between shooting the last sequences and the premiere (scheduled for December 4), Montand came back to terra firma for about a month. From September 15 to October 9, he returned to the Etoile, with his basic repertory unchanged. (Edith Piaf replaced him there, accompanied by Francis Blanche and the Compagnons de la Chanson.) He longed to do the two songs written by Prévert and Kosma for *Les Portes de la nuit,* "Les Feuilles mortes" and "Les Enfants qui s'aiment," but Prévert had originally wanted Gabin and Dietrich to hum them, and after the withdrawal of the two stars it occurred to nobody that Montand was ideal to sing them—even though they had hired him on the strength of his music-hall prowess. (Irène Joachim and Fabien Loris finally sang them off screen at the end of the film, as Diego-Montand, alone and in despair, plods toward Trauner's fabulous Métro station.)

His stage reviews a year earlier had been warm. This time he received wild acclaim. "We were looking for Chevalier's heir, and we've found him," said *Libération-Soir* on September 19. "A music-hall power," said *Le Front National* on September 21. "No other entertainer has ever shared his joy in rhythm the way he does" (*La France au Combat* on September 19). "He has managed to avoid the pitfalls of banality and superficiality into which his gifts might so easily have lured him" (*Paris-Soir* on September 17). And this, which speaks for all the others, by Jean Barreyre in *Opéra* on September 17: "An audience acclaimed its champion. I can convey the enthusiasm of the public for a young singer asserting his gifts and talent only by alluding to the kind of roar that greets an athletic exploit!"

When the applause died down, Montand assessed it all soberly, at a distance. He thought of a phrase he had heard to the effect that songs are "often the piercing scream of current events." Looking back on the evolution of his work, he said in an interview: "After seven years of war and major upheavals, the public no longer reacted as it had in 1939. Its receptive faculties had unwittingly been dulled by an avalanche of catastrophes. To entertain or to move it, you sometimes have to use shock therapy. Whence the harshness of some of my numbers. This harshness allows one to express certain shades of meaning more clearly, to give full weight to silences and mimed scenes."[16] His choice of words is suspiciously refined—his interviewer may have "adapted" Montand's language—but the remarks capture the conception of song that Montand strove to illustrate.

The little world of film experts is almost invariably sharp-toothed, but the response of the average moviegoer usually mitigates the ferocity of Paris critics. For the premiere of *Les Portes de la nuit,* even that humble solace was denied the film's promoters. The experts were at best skeptical, at worst homicidal; and the audience whistled its frank derision: at the Marignan cinema there were stormy scenes and loud protests against "Les Portes de l'ennui" ("The Doors of Boredom").

Yet the premiere had been a sumptuous occasion. Edith Piaf turned out to support Montand. Photographers swamped the couple, with Edith attentive and smiling, Yves tense and elegant in a tuxedo. The pomp backfired. The size of the budget (100 million francs) and the gargantuan sets were denounced as indecent waste at a time when French stomachs were still hollow. The advance drumbeating and relentless publicity boomeranged. By shouting "masterpiece" ahead of time, by fanning expectations, the promoters had generated a commensurate disappointment.

Everyone suffered torments on the critical pillory. Prévert was harshly

16. *Paris-Matin,* October 8, 1946.

reproached for his self-important verbiage, Carné for his inability to give rhythm to his endless and pretentious scenes. In short, the packaging was divine, the lighting perfect, the atmosphere effective; but it was deadly dull. Even Kosma's music failed to appease the angry scribes. The overall verdict was summed up succinctly by *Paris-Matin* on December 5: "*Les Portes de la nuit* marks the end of Prévert-Carné as a productive team."

The weakness of the lead roles was also heavily criticized. Brasseur, Raymond Bussières, Carette, and Saturnin Fabre were thought to have acquitted themselves more than honorably; Serge Reggiani was lauded. But Yves Montand and Nathalie Nattier were shot down in flames. Even *L'Ecran Français,* a fervent supporter of Prévert and Carné, crushed the young singer whose prospects it had shouted from the rooftops: "Montand is at his ease when he dances, croons, or says nothing" (December 10).

Show-business people are accustomed to ups and downs—torn to shreds one evening, acclaimed the next—but for Montand, this was the most violent of shocks. Until then, he had snatched success from the jaws of failure. Without a musical education, without any kind of education, without a real stage apprenticeship, he had broken through remarkably quickly—and by way of the front door—to the forefront of the music-hall world. With talent, energy, high spirits, and unremitting hard work he had exerted a powerful and instant magic on audiences all over France. Setbacks had been merely technical. There had seemed no reason to think it would not be the same in front of the cameras—his overriding goal, it should be remembered.

Obviously, it had been hard to serve up Prévert's dialogue and to take over a role designed for Jean Gabin. But Montand was above seeking comfort in such excuses. A failure was a failure. And failure was as devastating to him as success had been. "It wasn't a matter of knowing whether I was good or bad," he confessed. "I was nothing. I understood neither what I was saying nor what I was doing. . . . Ever since then I have considered it dangerous to overpraise a newcomer. It can kill him."[17]

The older Montand vacillated between two conflicting reactions to his film debut. One was self-flagellation: "To have Carné as director and Prévert as scriptwriter and then act like a turkey took some doing!" The other, which he would quickly retreat from, was to plead not guilty (or not very) on account of extenuating circumstances. Carné himself takes this tack in his memoirs, seeking to absolve himself for his failure to recognize a future star: "[Montand] was handicapped by his physique, a bit flabby back then, and by his curious accent, which made it sound as if his mouth was half-full when he spoke. But my mistake lay elsewhere. My mistake

17. Quoted in Alain Rémond, *Montand* (Paris, 1977), an excellent filmography.

was to cast him in a role that was not his, and to fail to recognize from his stage performances that he was made for comedy, not drama."

> At that time I was amazed that directors as famous as Carné, Clouzot, and Jacques Becker could be fascinated by music hall and by music-hall performers. Whereas I felt so out of place on a movie set! Suddenly I was confronted with my physical appearance—disastrously, for in the rushes I thought I looked like a big bird—and with a voice that wasn't mine. I worked without any kind of pleasure; I had no way of knowing that the director's aggressiveness wasn't just a question of character but of the responsibilities weighing on him.
>
> The failure of *Les Portes de la nuit* had a deep and abiding effect on me. It hurt all over. Worse, reviewers believed they were punishing me for being overambitious, when in reality I simply had taken orders from Carné, who was determined to dominate his actors and who prided himself on getting them to do his bidding. (As a result, I understood nothing of what he wanted, apart from obedience.) I came out of it crushed. Yet I was still convinced that I could express things, even though I had no idea why they weren't coming out. "Don't worry," said Prévert, "we've made a good job of it." Hervé, the reviewer for *Action,* solemnly wrote: "The Communist Party, and Yves Montand, will one day break down the gates of night." Apart from that, it was a bloodbath!

The cure is well known. With love dead and dreams shattered, all you can do is sing. On January 4, 1947, Yves Montand headed the bill at the ABC, preceded by Robert Rocca and Betty Spell (the same Betty Spell whose "rancho" had driven him to despair almost three years earlier). And back on the boards, as usual, the miracle took place. Mitty Goldin had to turn people away, the auditorium was packed, encore followed encore. Montand had reworked the prelude to "Gilet rayé," added two songs by Michel Emer, and elaborated a new move for "La Grande Cité" which struck a chord with audiences: as he began the third verse he stretched his arms and legs as if he were a crucified form floating above the human inferno.

So things were not so bad. But Yves Montand was still in search of his character. Or, rather, he was embodying it, but unwittingly. At the last general elections, the Communists had won nearly 29 percent of the vote. Their adversaries, the Christian Democrats of the Mouvement Républicain Populaire, were themselves stressing the word "popular" in their name. To quote a later remark, "France worshiped at the feet of a worker-

God."[18] The insurgent workingman, the workingman rebuilding the country, the irreverent, fun-loving workingman looking for amusement at Luna Park. The man of factory and fairground, the man who "rolled up his sleeves" (as Maurice Thorez, now a cabinet minister, put it) and dug coal, the man who gave much and received little. The man of pleasure and of toil, the simple man, the accessible man, the warm-hearted man. The workingman.

Montand was not yet a star. California was far away. But France had found her *"prolo chantant,"* her singing prole.

18. Lucien Roux, in *Le Nouvel Observateur,* January 11, 1967.

Chapter 7

Not until the 1950s did Montand clearly understand the positive social image designed around him as the lyric star of the proletariat, and when he did it was with distinct discomfort, a sense of being locked into a convenient stereotype, playing a predictable role. He did not want to deny his social origins or family ties, but he had set forth on a solo adventure, on his own and without baggage. He didn't want to have his success as a singer attributed to his class. He saw himself as the product of his own labors and his own imagination, not as anyone's spokesman—not even his family's. In order to become himself he had been obliged, like everyone who challenges art and fate, to break away from his own kind. As he saw it, the crucified figure in "La Grande Cité" was a stage discovery, not the embodiment of a social grievance; the singer in "Luna Park" was as much a music lover as a workingman staking his claim to leisure time.

To be a son of the poor, to be of working-class background, was a source of great pride, particularly when messianic fervor ignited the people (or "masses," to use a word Montand did not like, even on his father's lips). It was a source of even greater pride to rise without forgetting one's origins. No one could persuade Montand that a bourgeois education—not the hypocritical conventions of middle-class propriety, of course, but the art of dressing well, of cultivating oneself, of manners—was a negligible matter. Himself a product of the gutter, he hated vulgarity more than anything else. A "prole," for him, was not a paunchy steelworker directing coarse jokes at the prim and proper readers of *Le Figaro;* he was the founder of trade-union centers, the son of the "wretched of the earth" who sees political demonstrations as demonstrations for dignity, the man who put on a clean shirt on May Day before singing the "Internationale."

Montand read the papers and listened to the radio. The year 1947 was one of open schisms, furious eruptions, slowly cooling lava flows. Europe was divided by what Winston Churchill called the "Iron Curtain." In May, the French Communists left the government in order to foment or steer strikes that often bordered on insurrection. Just in time, in carefully regulated doses, the Marshall Plan scattered its bounty. A Soviet bureaucrat, Viktor Kravchenko, sought asylum in the West, asserting, to the derision of the crusading left, that he had "chosen freedom." It was difficult in the black-and-white mood of the day to add even a touch of gray to the label they stuck on you. It was difficult, shackled as you were into the regulation blue coveralls of the authentic workingman, to pursue your own Long March to the Promised Land of California.

Montand was more than ever aware of the distance separating him from Hollywood. He was still bruised by the pummeling he had received for the fiasco of *Les Portes de la nuit;* it was taking a long time to get up off the canvas. He blamed himself for losing his head and accepting an impossible part, for making a hasty decision. He felt he had confused the stage, where you can legitimately aspire to explode before an audience, with the screen, whose audiences see only your ghost, only a reflection of work long since completed, an unchangeable copy of yourself. What was the good of trying to think things through when life itself made a sudden mockery of your best intentions, your most stringent self-criticism? It was in the midst of this examination of his conscience, of this growing determination to master his naive impulses, that the novice actor was once again confronted with the unthinkable.

Tuesday, January 14, 1947, was a red-letter day in Yves Montand's life. First, he refused to go on stage at the ABC. For three whole days the piano had been out of tune and he had been urgently requesting the services of a tuner, in vain. Montand questioned the stage manager early in the afternoon:

"Has the piano been tuned?" (The tone is honeyed.)

"We'll tune it between the matinee and the evening performance."

"Fine. I won't sing till tonight." (Tone still honeyed.)

The stage manager thought it was a joke, but after Montand was routinely announced at the matinee, the stage remained empty. The audience demanded its money back. Mitty Goldin, in person, had to calm the crowd. The singer's contract was at once canceled, with Lys Gauty stepping in at the last minute to rescue the show. *France-Soir* on January 18 found it deplorable that an artist who had "made it" should be "so wanting in respect" to an audience that had paid to see him perform. Precisely, Montand shot back: "respect" for the public meant that all the conditions necessary for a quality performance should be met. And since he had indeed made it, he was in a position to put his foot down and reject compromise when necessary. End of discussion.

But this dispute was not the main reason why Tuesday, January 14, was a date to remember. That evening, instead of giving his concert, Yves Montand concluded an agreement with Jack Warner.

Flashback: at the lower end of the Canebière in Marseilles, the young Montand had often strolled past the windows of an agency that distributed movies made by the big American studios: Fox, MGM, Columbia, Paramount, Warner Bros. . . . Gazing at those cabalistic names, Ivo Livi daydreamed, his thoughts on those airy powers, those mythological deities that had given birth on some distant Olympus to Gary Cooper, Frank Capra, and Fred Astaire. He even imagined that future stars were hired right there, in those Marseilles offices.

But a real man of flesh and blood climbed the three flights of stairs to Yves Montand's dressing room on January 14. Mr. Warner did not beat around the bush. "I'm taking you to Hollywood," he said. "I'm offering you a seven-year contract at a minimum of two hundred dollars a week." What would be expected of him? "To remain at the studio's disposal. With a talent like yours, we're going to be using you a lot. After eighteen months you have the option of taking a six-month vacation in Europe." Then Warner set about flattering Montand: this was the first time since 1928 (when he had hired Al Jolson) that he would be signing a contract in person, and Montand was only the second French music-hall entertainer (after Maurice Chevalier) that America had ever wanted to shanghai.

"Okay, Yves?"

Okay? You bet it was okay! He had heard only one word: Hollywood. The woman he loved, Edith Piaf, had left him, and he was finding scant consolation with his lady friends. He lived in a hotel room. French reviewers had greeted his film debut with kicks and blows. What did he have to lose? At regular intervals, he thought, he could return to France to give concerts. Over there, he would be with the cream of the profession. And over there, when they filmed an actor, they made him look good, they dressed him and lit him to perfection.

It was agreed. They would reserve him a cabin on an ocean liner for July 16. First class. Over there, when they wanted someone, they did not quibble over expenses. By the end of January, the trade press had revealed that Yves Montand would shortly be leaving for Hollywood.[1]

He was twenty-six.

Montand had requested the delay so that he could honor a previous commitment. The director Alexandre Esway—not a giant of the profession but

1. *L'Ecran Français,* January 28, 1947.

a man who had carved out a degree of popular success with action movies, the last a war story about parachutists—had offered him a part that would be less of a change of pace for Montand and his fans: the role of a boxer—a "Battling Joe" from the swampy Landes region, along France's Atlantic coastline—whose manager propels him to the world championship through a series of rigged fights. Discovering the shady deal at the last minute, he decides to fight regardless, on principle, to the last, bloody gasp. The plot, based on a novel by Louis Hemon, was not exactly intricate, but it offered a healthy chance to exploit the image and temperament of the hero of Etoile audiences. No more dark canals and tortuous dialogue, but a simple, hard-hitting intrigue smelling of sweat and sawdust. It was called *L'Idole* (*The Idol*).

Montand naturally took the challenge of the part seriously. While continuing to sing at cabarets and theaters, he went every day to the Mansart gym in Montmartre, undergoing all the tortures the professionals endured: heavy bag, speed bag, weights, jump rope, and so on. His opponent for the world championship—the terrible final fight scene was scripted to last for twenty minutes—was Stefan Olek, an authentic heavyweight bruiser. And his screen sparring partner, Robert Inagarao, well known in rings and wrestling arenas, had been named the leading man of French sport by *Paris-Cinéma.* However ingenious the camera work and special effects, Montand would have to look the part, and the best way of looking the part was not to cut any corners.

The world of the sweet science was not wholly unknown to him. As one of the regulars at the Club des Cinq, he had become friends with the man to whom the club owed its existence: the greatest of French boxers, Marcel Cerdan. A real friendship, regularly kept up. In Cerdan, Montand sensed a kind of innocence as well as complexity born of conflicting drives. A powerhouse of physical strength, Cerdan hated taking a punch. It was no legend: he did everything in his power to avoid being hit, despising the primitive slugger who charged straight at his opponent. And this formidable King Kong had a child's laugh.

Shooting was to begin in May. All through March and April, the apprentice fighter spent hours working on his muscles and sharpening his boxing technique. Harry Max (small, bald, and out of place in this setting) came along to provide moral support, and Cerdan encouraged him. It was an exhausting exercise in discipline, but he had the solid satisfaction of acquiring a physique to fit his frame. And he was conditioning himself not only for Alexandre Esway but for Jack Warner as well.

When they began rehearsing for the final scene, the crowd, apart from a handful of extras, was represented by a painted backcloth, and thick clouds of phony tobacco smoke were emitted by a blower (they were working on a tight budget), but the actors treated it like the real thing. Olek, once one of Europe's leading heavyweights, opened cautiously, as intended. But his opposite number had trained so well that the fight quickly turned serious. As the two men slugged away, the director ran around the ring yelling at the top of his voice. Montand noticed, and dropped his guard. A fatal mistake: an uppercut to the base of his nose sent him to the canvas, where he lay senseless for twenty minutes.

Yves Montand never liked the word "playacting."

He made friends with the director—a genial man, warm and reassuring. When he heard about the Hollywood contract, Esway warned him: "You're making a mistake. You think you'll get a big part right away, but that's bull. They'll keep you shut up in a hotel with other guys who've signed the same piece of paper. One day they'll ask you to do a little test footage, really short, and if that goes well, another test, a bit longer. But they have hundreds of young men and women standing by: you'll be a part of their livestock, the pool they fish in every now and then. Believe me, it's a mistake."

His words caught Montand off guard, and they worried him. In his head, he was already on the boat. But, wanting to be sure of things, he took a step that might better have been taken before rather than after signing the contract: he asked for a detailed translation into French of the pages to which he had appended his signature.

The document has a distinct sociological value. It stipulated that the budding star would not be consulted on the choice of scripts; would accept the screen name given him by the studio public-relations department; would be replaced or not by an understudy during dangerous scenes, depending on the decision of the producer; would keep his evenings at the studio's disposal in order to appear, if necessary, at such and such a location, in company with such and such a person (a clause that would not be modified if he should marry); and would allow his name to be used for publicity purposes for every kind of product—toothpaste, shoes, razor blades, etc.

In other words, trussed like a turkey.

In a cable to Los Angeles, Montand demanded clarifications and amendments. The studio replied that these standard clauses were accepted by all artists on first being signed, and that matters could amicably be worked out in Hollywood.

Distrust leapt into his heart as swiftly as blind trust had earlier guided his pen. Perhaps he should go anyway. Perhaps all that restrictive ritual was a rite of passage that it would be wrong to exaggerate. But nothing would be worse than to come close to victory and then be bitterly frustrated, consigned to the second team, shut out near the gates of paradise.

Torn between pride and lingering gullibility, Montand decided that if he were ever to enter Hollywood, it would be along the royal way—and certainly not in the near-anonymous ranks hastily assembled by transatlantic producers in search of fresh meat. He composed a long and costly telegram politely explaining that it would be best to forget the whole misunderstanding and tear the contract to pieces.

He now discovered American stubbornness in business dealings. He had signed with his eyes open, without any kind of pressure. The studio went to court. A one-sided contract, pleaded Montand's lawyer, Lévy-Oulmann, who demanded one franc in symbolic damages and interest. Breach of a formal commitment, pleaded Suzanne Blum, who represented Warner and who demanded no less than 20,000 francs per day for as long as Montand remained in breach of said contract.

Speeches, demands, appeals. The dispute dragged on. It was the Cold War that saved Montand. Visas granted by the U.S. Immigration and Naturalization Service, even for temporary work, were becoming rarer by the month. When requested for people known for their Communist sympathies, they soon were to be refused outright. From 1948 on, the case dropped out of sight and hearing. Yves Montand did not meet Jack Warner again until twelve years later, at the home of Kirk Douglas, when he was guest of honor.

In Hollywood.

Things were going from bad to worse. The shooting of *L'Idole* went ahead as planned, but that was not enough to pacify an abandoned lover, a would-be traveler who had missed the boat, a film fanatic whose reputation had nosedived. Montand was beginning to learn one of the fundamental truths of his life: music hall was not just a temporary activity; it was the very foundation of his craft, the precious lode without which he was unable to invest elsewhere. He had returned to singing after *Les Portes de la nuit;* he returned to it again after his break with Jack Warner.

In 1946, the Odéon record company had shown interest in recording some of his hits. Although he gladly accepted the extra (handsome) income this brought in, Montand saw it only as a complement to his real work on the stage. And by the late spring of 1947, with America fading into the mist, he was trying to find his feet again. There was no lack of opportunities for performing along the coast that summer. The classic full-length tour began at Le Touquet and ended at Beaulieu, below Monte Carlo, via Deauville, La Baule, Arcachon, Biarritz, Cannes, and so on. Singers and musicians hopped from casino to casino every two or three days. In a setting of elegant merrymaking, they enlivened the evenings of the rich visitors at the big hotels with views of the sea. The performers were put up in rooms at the back, sometimes joined there by ladies of leisure.

Montand got an offer from Les Ambassadeurs in Deauville. Very chic, very expensive. But he had no pianist. Maurice Bua—the pianist whose instrument had been out of tune at the ABC in January—was still on Mitty Goldin's payroll. Jean Marion, who had been an inspired accompanist on several occasions, wanted to move in the direction of composing film scores. Montand sought an all-purpose musician: a rehearsal partner, orchestrator, stage partner. Marion advised him to talk to a certain Bob Castella, whom Montand had not met.

Castella was better known in jazz circles, at the Boeuf sur le Toit and Jimmy's Bar, than in music halls (he had heard Montand only once, at the Club des Cinq), and was a respected figure. Oscillating—swinging would be a better word—between pure jazz and popular music, he was a performer in the tradition of Ray Ventura and Aimé Barelli. At the age of fifteen he had started out, like many others, performing at evenings organized in private homes. Then he had formed his own group. Later, when the war came, he had played wherever he could—particularly at the Salle Pleyel—and with the very best. Pioneer aficionados of "Negro music," readers who fought over articles written by Charles Delaunay, Hugues Panassié, Frank Tenot, and Boris Vian in their impassioned post-Liberation monthly, *Jazz Hot,* even remember seeing Castella's photo in one of the very first issues: a true mark of preeminence.[2]

From his window in the Surène-d'Aguesseau hotel, Montand watched a superb Renault convertible draw up (in late May 1947, Paris was blessed with magnificent weather, and the roof was down). Red upholstery, luxurious and ostentatious. Castella looked small, dapper—cravat and pocket handkerchief, carefully brilliantined hair parted on the left—and wary: when they met he scanned the singer from head to toe, slowly, as if measuring him from a great height. And Montand did not like being studied from a great height—particularly when the examiner was much shorter than he was.

"It was a residential hotel," Castella recalls. "Montand had a kind of mini-suite: a cramped study near the entrance, a bedroom, and a living room where he had set up a grand piano." There was not a single picture hung on the flower-papered walls. The bedroom—a marble-topped bedside table, a pink quilt, a white lampshade—was equally unadorned. Only his book collection made any kind of dent in the conventionality of the setting. On the shelves, somewhat defiantly, were Bergson's *On Laughter,* Gide's *Thésée,* Malraux's *La Condition humaine,* Murphy's *Stalin,* and Sar-

2. *Jazz Hot: Revue du Hot Club de France,* no. 10 (December 1946).

tre's *L'Existentialisme est un humanisme.* There was also an *English Without Tears,* for which the need had abruptly receded. The secretary at Montand's side was called Jean-Claude, the Spanish cleaning woman was Mercedes, and the cat answered to Figaro.

Stung at being placed under a microscope, Montand struck first: "Why don't you play me something?"

"I picked out a few fragments from *Rhapsody in Blue,*" Castella recalls. "Then some jazz. He stopped me. And that's how our story began."

A lifetime story. Maurice-François Castella (Robert is his baptismal name), of Neapolitan origin on his father's side (born in France) and Rumanian on his mother's (who immigrated to France as a child), never left Ivo Livi, a dozen years his junior. He became and remained his metronome, counselor, whipping boy, accountant, major domo, disciple, critic, therapist, crutch, and friend. "Leporello or Sganarelle," says Pierre Boutillier, a friend of both.

Little by little, "Bob" became "Bobby," a name variously uttered in a rush of genuine affection, a roar of ungovernable rage, an air of teasing connivance, or a burst of impatience. Bobby knew everything and revealed nothing. Bobby managed scores and signed checks. Bobby sent flowers, even though he might not always receive them. Bobby let the thunderstorms roll over him and went on saying what he had to say in his flutelike voice, unflappable, deceptively accommodating, truly indispensable. In the midst of earsplitting invective, punctuated by expressions of extreme affection, Bobby, an oak in a reed's clothing, was probably the less fragile component in the partnership he formed with the man who was never his boss.

According to Charley Marouani, Montand's agent, the pair's backstage behavior was the "best vaudeville act" in Paris. And Jorge Semprun, who witnessed them at it for two decades, agrees: "When Montand—with the sovereign dishonesty which only a bond as indestructible as theirs could justify—decides to put the blame for such and such a mistake, failure, or misunderstanding on Bob Castella . . . Bobby accepts it with a smile (a discreet smile, admittedly, for Montand must not get away with thinking Bob is unaffected by his diatribe), which is not the smile of resignation but of unfailing tenderness."

The singer and the pianist got to know each other before reaching Deauville for the start of the tour. Every morning Castella called at Montand's and opened the piano. Together they worked through new songs and revised old ones.

"Technically, there were no problems," says Castella. "Both in his movements and in his stagecraft, he was uniquely himself. He had no need of anyone. Montand's only failing was tempo. He had never had time to study musical notation properly. He was a man who worked on instinct, on enthusiasm. Borne along in the heat of action, he sometimes didn't realize he was missing a beat. My predecessor had warned me: 'Don't try to correct Montand. If he makes a mistake, just make the mistake along with him!' I considered this dishonest and set out to correct him. But Montand would lose his temper quickly; once he got going and you interrupted him, he'd be furious. To tolerate him you had to love him, you had to watch for the right moment, to know that his rages were necessary stages of creation. A good thing I'm patient."

In Deauville, the two associates were soon at loggerheads. Montand sneered when Bob firmly entered his profession in the hotel register as "orchestra leader." He accused Bob of not handling the local staff with sufficient authority, protested that the imbecile drummers or bass players seemed to have some relentless ratcheted windup mechanism, some mathematician's folly, anchored in their brains. And Castella, without undue excitement, discovered that accompaniment—the experience was new to him—did not frustrate him at all, that it did not hurt his feelings to take second place, to give up the chance of shining on his own, so long as the performer he was helping gained from his support.

There were frictions, ruffled pride, defections (at one point, Bob went off to work for Georges Ulmer, before returning to Montand). In the end, though, the pair fell into step. "I became his shadow," says the pianist some forty-five years later, with a subtle blend of humility and pride, "and affection pushed our differences aside. Since then, I don't recall a single night that was a failure—just places where we were more or less comfortable working together."

The partnership soon began to pay off. On October 18, Montand returned to the Etoile, where it was (almost) no coincidence that Edith Piaf and the Compagnons de la Chanson had once again preceded him. For the first half, in addition to Irène de Trébert, she had hired two beginners, France Roche and Charles Aznavour. Big crowd-pullers were scarce, and autumn was the season of great artistic and financial revivals. Paris theater managers could count on four or five performers for sellouts, so until his former love left France for the United States, Montand regularly ran into her.

The year had been too eventful, too full of ups and downs, for Montand to have had time to perfect a concert repertory, a real one-man show, which always presupposed a good number of songs, especially new ones. Apart from two or three discoveries ("Taxi" and "Un Petit Bock"), he made do with the available arsenal and accepted the usual sharing of billing. Eight acts opened the evening; a rising young performer, Line Renaud, was the guest artist, and Montand, coming on after intermission, rarely sang more than twelve or fourteen numbers. A routine performance? It would be tempting to think so, but the reviews and audience reaction indicate otherwise.

"A success that sometimes approached delirium," said one review. "His popularity continues to soar," said another. The stereotype of the "singing prole" was dragged out to do service. "No more tuxedos or boaters! The tall young man wears the neutral hues of the workplace, almost a factory uniform. . . . He steps before us as the representative of democracy." "Yves Montand always looks like the kid next door who has just slipped off his jacket." And *L'Aurore,* with a sniff of disapproval: "They applaud him as soon as he comes whistling on stage, with his gangling gait, his shirt half-open, and his workingman's pants."[3]

Another much-used metaphor was that of the accomplished athlete, with several reviewers likening Montand's style and attack to Marcel Cerdan's. Montand—whose supporters had recently reproached him with courting publicity, with creating too much noise (the story of the ABC piano had not been helpful, and people said it showed him in a fit of pique), with being in too much of a hurry, with believing he was already in Beverly Hills—was definitely back in favor.

One reviewer stood out from the herd. Yves Gibeau, of *Combat,* had followed Montand for a long time, applauding him in Marseilles as far back as 1942. He had been impressed at the speed with which Montand had dropped his Yankee themes for a more personal image, at once both tough and sensitive. But he thought Montand had stopped developing, and that this was a pity. On October 28, he wrote: "The public will probably reject this point of view, but I believe that it is time for Yves Montand, his songwriters, and his musicians to give the matter their full attention."

Gibeau had hit the nail on the head. Montand's current success was a confirmation rather than a promise. He had verified the loyalty of his fans and the durability of his talent, but the cardinal rule of his profession was to worry when everything went too well, to see disappointments in advance. Every night he got curtain calls. If he wanted them to go on, he needed new words, a new sound. The Yves Montand–Bob Castella duo had so far been content to manage what they already had. It was time to reinvest, before their capital ran out.

* * *

3. *La Bataille,* October 22, 1947; *Paris-Presse,* October 29, 1947; *Opéra,* October 15, 1947; *Libération,* October 14, 1947; *L'Aurore,* October 14, 1947.

For Montand, 1948 was a year of transition. The premiere of *L'Idole* on February 13 was neither a triumph nor a disaster. The movie was pronounced honest and unassuming, and the climactic fight earned him a fair amount of praise. After the beating he had taken fourteen months earlier, it was a win on points.

On the other hand, Montand suffered what professionals call a minor flop. In mid-October he agreed to take the plunge in *Le Chevalier Bayard,* a spectacularly staged, slightly batty operetta with a libretto by Bruno Coquatrix and André Hornez and music by Paul Misraki, staged by the Lido's Miss Bluebell. The limitless technical resources of the Alhambra theater provided the means to crank up a stroll through the centuries in fourteen tableaux. Playing a test pilot (the modern knight), Montand finds himself wearing the mail of Bayard, medieval dispenser of justice, after a spiritualist séance. He celebrates the cause of the orphan and the widow:

Sans peur et sans reproche
C'est ma gloire et c'est ma loi
Tout s'éclaire à mon approche
Car j'ai le droit pour moi . . .

[With neither fear nor blemish
'Tis my joy and my decree
When I appear the dragons vanish
For virtue rides with me . . .]

So unabashed were its anachronisms, so unassuming its humor, so noble its sentiments, so timely its satirical shafts that ridicule was averted. Montand and his partners—Félix Oudart, Ludmilla Tchérina, and Henri Salvador—had a great time performing; audiences died laughing, and so did reviewers. All the ingredients for a long and happy run seemed to be in place. Yet bookings tailed off, and after a month the show closed. Nonsense was not yet (or was no longer) in fashion.

Between the movie and the operetta, Montand's life went on. Cabarets, recordings, concerts. Loveless love. Montand was not the kind of man who could live without women: in him, sensuality and insecurity combined to make his periods of sexual famine both rare and painful. He willingly spoke of it, always with gratitude toward his partners, never depicting them as conquests that a man who has done some living displays as trophies of his manhood. But he was haunted by the fear that speaking of his luck might one day consign him to the company of those screen idols who, at the approach of old age, rattle on with suspicious loquacity about their amorous exploits. He admitted he couldn't say no to a pretty woman, but he made a clear distinction between attraction and love.

For the moment, he was determined not to fall in love. Piaf had hurt him too much. No more of that. No more obsessive, weaponless suffering. He entered a down-to-earth relationship with the beautiful Gisèle Pascal and periodically enjoyed intimacy with one of the stars of the moment. At a time when illicit loves were expected to remain hidden, the entertainment world was a less rigid environment than some. And show-business people, once they are well known, fascinate the outside world. One sweet mistress, well ahead of Montand in years and education, urged him between assignations to discover Thomas Mann and Bertolt Brecht.

Despite such fleeting kindnesses, and although he wanted them to remain fleeting, he was lonely. Bob Castella was as yet only a partner, not a friend. Professionally, no new offer had come along to jolt his life out of its rut. Between the lines of his statements to interviewers, a certain confusion shows through. "I'm the same as everyone else," he claimed, as if to convince himself. "I hope to raise a family one day, because I really like children. I hope to have five or six. . . . Like my father, like my brother, I don't think of myself as anything but a skilled worker. Only the trade is different." He boasted a little of cultural matters: "I like Bach, Beethoven, and Tchaikovsky. I love reading, but I have very little time for it. Besides Rabelais, my favorite authors are Prévert, Anouilh, Steinbeck, and Hemingway."

As for the movies, he was probably both telling the truth and launching an appeal when he said: "One day I hope to have a screenplay written just for me. But if people think I'm no good in a movie with an excellent script, I'll cut short my movie career right there. I have too much admiration for Gérard Philipe, Henry Fonda, and one or two others to allow myself to do anything mediocre on their turf."[4]

But a chance encounter was about to restore his sense of direction. Chance and Jacques Prévert, author of *Paroles,* put the man of Montand's life in his path.

> It was thanks to Henri Crolla that I came up for air. He was a gypsy from Naples. Before the war, he played the guitar in the streets. Paul Grimault and Jacques Prévert had taken him in and considered him their adopted son. One fine day he came to see me on Prévert's recommendation, this moonlike character who played by ear like an angel. He wanted to work with me. We got on right

4. All these quotations are from an interview in *L'Ecran Français,* May 25, 1948.

> away. He made me roar with laughter. He was like Chico Marx, small and curly-haired. Musically, he was the equal of his friend Django Reinhardt—the best jazz musicians are blacks, gypsies, Jews, Italians. . . . And with other people he was a wonderful blend of tact, modesty, and a unique sense of humor, unending mirth. When cars were stopped bumper-to-bumper on the Champs-Elysées and he wanted to cross, he would open a rear door, walk through the vehicle apologizing profusely, and calmly get out on the other side. We became chums, then much more than that. I could go on forever about him.

No doubt Montand could have. When he recalled Crolla (who died in 1960 at the age of forty) he would become animated, describe a few of their endless escapades, then suddenly stop in midsentence, undone. It was not the heavy silence of manly grief. It went deeper. Between the singer and his guitar player a playful passion flowered—a passion that Crolla's cancer failed to wither. "With Crolla," says Bob Castella, "it's a little bit like with Simone [Signoret]: he's not around, but he isn't dead." In her autobiography, Signoret said of Crolla: "He is the only dead person I know who can make people laugh till they cry from wherever he is today, and his friends gather to remember him in tears."

Not surprisingly, the immigrant Livi and the immigrant Crolla (who acquired French nationality only in 1946) found that they had much in common. Henri's prolific family—fourteen children were born, six survived—had also left Naples to escape from Fascism. The father and mother were mandolin players, a brother played the violin, another the banjo (Crolla's first instrument, before the guitar), the daughters sang. Once in Paris, the tribe turned itself into a band and played for pennies on street corners. They lived in a tenement in the slums around the well-named Porte d'Italie.

To rise above his background, Montand had met Trottobas and worked his own way up. Crolla was lucky enough to have the best neighbor in the world: a certain Django.

Not far from the "Macaronis" were the "Romanys." Django Reinhardt, born in Flemish Brabant, ten years older than Crolla, shared a trailer with his mother, "Négrosse," his brother Joseph, or "Nin-Nin," and a shifting contingent of relatives: one of many cousins was called "Camembert." Django could neither read nor write, but he had learned the violin and the guitar.

"At fourteen," says the biographical note published by the magazine *Jazz Hot* at the time of the Liberation, Django "was already playing the banjo at outdoor dances on the rue Monge or the rue de la Huchette, and in the course of his wanderings he heard, from the street, Billy Arnold's orchestra playing at the Abbaye de Thélème."[5] Despite a damaged left hand—two fingers had been mutilated by a fire that gutted the trailer—Django forged ahead, performing in front of cafés, particularly the Can-Can on the rue Pigalle, and in Russian nightclubs. At long last, the door he sought swung open: at the Boeuf sur le Toit, where Cocteau applauded him (they later put together an "opera," *Le Manoir de mes rêves,* which never saw the light of day) and record producers noticed him. In 1934, the young Hot Club de France acquired a quintet featuring Django, "Nin-Nin," Louis Vola, Roger Chaput, and Stéphane Grappelly (who had changed the final *i* of his name to *y* in order to seem more American), with whom Django had performed in various cellars and brasseries. The first public performance of the quintet, on December 2, at the Ecole Normale de Musique, shocked the audience. Odéon, which had intended to record it, finally rejected its too "modern" sound. Ultraphone stepped in: Messrs. Reinhardt and Grappelly received a lump payment of 50 francs per side.

Such was the idol of Henri Crolla (who was then about fifteen and known as "Riton"); he was dazzled on the evenings when an employer's Hispano Royale would come to fetch Django from his trailer.

The years 1932–36, the beginnings of France's left-wing Popular Front coalition government, were the heyday of the October Group, which brought together actors, writers, painters, and musicians eager to take art to the streets, to arouse people through poetry, mime, and song. This amazingly gifted crowd often rehearsed together in Jean-Louis Barrault's loft (Picasso's future studio on the rue des Grands-Augustins). There, among others, one would find Yves Allégret, Maurice Baquet, Sylvia Bataille, Roger Blin, Raymond Bussières, Marcel Duhamel, Joseph Kosma, Jean-Paul Le Chanois, Max Morise, the Prévert brothers (Pierre the movie director, Jacques the writer) and their crony Paul Grimault (the virtually undisputed master of French animated cartoons).

This buoyant group—in fact, the cream of their generation—was influenced by Surrealism but rejected its aura of sectarian orthodoxy. And it was close to the far left, being primarily populist and anarchist. "The group was pretty basic," Grimault says today. "We wanted to attack the generals and the priests. We wanted to avenge Sacco and Vanzetti. We watched the rise of Fascism. Until the Nazi-Soviet pact, which threw us all for a loop, we thought the world was relatively simple: it was just a question of mobilizing the armies of justice and progress against the forces of order, of the warmongers, of the profiteers."

The October Group was the second family that took in Henri Crolla.

5. Pierre Bonneau, *Jazz Hot,* no. 2 (December 1945).

His partner Mouloudji, whose family attended its meetings, was already a member. "Riton"—a rough-hewn genius, sensitive, inventive, light-hearted—struck an immediate chord in Prévert and Grimault, and soon Grimault invited him to live in his home on the avenue Soeur-Rosalie (almost next door to the Porte d'Italie), lent him his own guitar, and suggested that he learn the rudiments of musical notation. The young prodigy was gifted with such agility in his left hand that they called him "Millipede." And Millipede happily formed lasting attachments to these lively and affectionate protectors.

Crolla harbored not a trace of resentment about his poverty, and now—housed, fed, clothed, taught by friends with no thought but his welfare—he went on irreverently skirting social conventions, giving away what and when he could, whenever his income came into line with his talent. A respected musician and family man, he often came home at night without his jacket or coat, having just encountered some Crolla down on his luck along the way.

This attitude probably also owed much to the personality of Paul Grimault, his host. From 1930 to 1936, before becoming the most independent of animators, an artist and a craftsman to the tip of his brush, Grimault had been the idea man in a leading Paris advertising agency, Damour, where his office mates were Jean Aurenche (who was to write the scripts for a good half of his films) and Jean Anouilh. It was there that a certain Jacques Prévert came looking for a job. He was given some test copy to write. Half a century later, Grimault still roars with laughter at the memory. "He was asked to promote the qualities of a kitchen salt, Le Sauveur. [The word means both "preserver" and "savior."] Prévert dreamed up a picture of Lazarus emerging from the tomb. Above, a disembodied hand sprinkled him with a saltshaker. I'll never forget the caption: 'Always pink and fresh, thanks to Le Sauveur.' He failed the test, but Jacques and I have been inseparable ever since."

Grimault and his friends founded their own business, making publicity and advertising films, called Les Gémeaux (Gemini), but soon they were branching off into nonbusiness movies: *Go chez les oiseaux* (1939), *Le Marchand de notes* (1942), *L'Epouvantail* (1943). Not since 1917 had a single animated cartoon appeared in France, but *Le Voleur de paratonnerres* took a first prize at Venice in 1945. Beginning in 1947 with *Le Petit Soldat,* Prévert became his friend Paul's chief scriptwriter.

On the avenue Soeur-Rosalie, Crolla received a liberal education that later nourished his relationship with Montand. People's importance, their worth, had nothing to do with their place on the social ladder. That was how it was under Grimault's roof: "My house was packed with gypsies. Django brought his mother, his brother, his wife, who was called 'Naguine,' and his son, 'Bibak.' Henri was proud and delighted to be a part of the group. But Erich von Stroheim and Albert Lewin also came around. I've seen Django dirt-poor, and I've also seen him pull up outside my house in a big American car, pure white, scandalous. 'The most expensive one I could find,' he told me proudly just before he headed south, without a driver's license."

At the outbreak of the war, Crolla, an Italian citizen, was called back across the Alps. He left with his guitar and then deserted with his guitar, on foot, without ever touching a weapon. Back in Paris, he and Django played separately and together during the Occupation. They performed in deluxe establishments like the Schéhérazade and Monseigneur. Once jazz was tolerated again, Crolla earned his living in a cabaret on the rue Delambre, together with Henri Salvador, and above all at the Schubert, a real fanatics club in the depths of a tiny cellar on the boulevard du Montparnasse, close to the Closerie des Lilas.

By the time his path crossed Montand's, Crolla was a well-known musician. In the parallel, underground universe that is the world of jazz, he did not have the stature of Django Reinhardt or Stéphane Grappelly, who spent the war years in London and came back to acclaim in Paris. Crolla was considered a notch below them. But he was seen as a soloist who would undoubtedly prove his worth. "The day is not far off," asserted *Jazz Hot* in May–June 1946, "when those who now underestimate Henri Crolla because he is unassuming, shy, simple, affectionate, and cannot read music will be obliged to recognize his sterling worth."

Montand and his latest recruit now entered what Colette Crolla, the guitar player's wife, called "quasi-married life." She added: "After breaking up with Piaf, Yves had led a fairly solitary existence. He hadn't yet found his connections, his family. He had acquaintances—for example, the Bretons, the song publishers—but not a family. It was with Crolla that he built that family."

The threesome settled into a new apartment Montand rented at the chic address of 80 rue de Longchamp, in Neuilly (its owner, André Dewavrin, was better known by his Resistance *nom de guerre,* Colonel Passy). Bob Castella might have jealously guarded his prerogatives, but he was lavish with his friendship, and he found the invasion of Henri Crolla—whose professional skills were well known to him—highly stimulating. More than most, jazz performers are accustomed to collective invention, to fertile improvisation. And, of course, all three men were of Italian origin. United by common goals and the pure pleasure of discovery, they struck gold almost every day.

There were differences, though. When Montand lost patience or flew into a rage, Bob adopted ostrich tactics, hunching his shoulders over the keyboard, drawing his head in, making himself small and round, as though this streamlined configuration would harmlessly deflect the whizzing decibels. Crolla was more likely to strike back. "He didn't hesitate to point out Yves's faults," says Colette Crolla. "And Yves thought twice about yelling at him, although he yelled to his heart's content at Bob." Grimault says the same thing: "Sometimes Henri grumbled at Montand, getting angry and siding with poor Bob, who hardly ever fought back. But everyone calmed down quickly. Annoyance melted into mischief."

Montand had found more than good friends and good advisers. His friends went along with him, but they also helped him find his own direction. A natural division of labor developed. Bob was the architect; Henri, the decorator. One probed, corrected, buttressed while the other embellished and illuminated (although they were always likely to swap functions). Moreover, Crolla composed—Castella, too, but more rarely. It took him eight months to dream up music to fit Prévert's nimble poem "Le Petit Cireur de souliers de Broadway" ("The Little Shoeshine Boy of Broadway"). On the other hand, suppler, more seductive songs, like "J'aime t'embrasser" and "Car je t'aime" (for which he also wrote the lyrics), burst forth almost spontaneously. Montand owed him the superb sensual blues rhythm of "Sanguine," which remained in his repertory, as well as the music to "Dis-moi, Joe," "Du soleil plein la tête," "Donne-moi des sous," "Saint-Paul-de-Vence," "Monsieur p'tit Louis," and "Calcutti-Calcutta."

Piaf had helped Montand jettison the dynamic but somewhat simplistic songs of his beginnings. To his working-class base, his intuitive feel for minidramas, and his talent for sketches both funny and heartbreaking, Castella and Crolla now added an original sound that had never been really heard in the music hall. For many years, what French critics called "rhythm" had been a part of variety music. Trenet had been the first to exploit it. Now there was another frontier to cross: little by little, Yves Montand began to create an authentic jazz band.

New players were hired over the next decade, but on important occasions the core attracted the participation of the very best: the bass player Emmanuel Soudieux, a crony of Django and Grappelly who had played with Crolla at the Schubert; the accordionists Freddy Balta and Marcel Azzola, who were good enough to play their way from Pigalle to Buenos Aires by way of New York; the drummer Roger Paraboschi ("Para" to his close friends); and the clarinetist and composer Hubert Rostaing, an old friend of Castella's, who after years of concerts became responsible for the group's orchestrations. "Bob came first," he recalls. "He and Montand were a couple—their shouting matches were just a joke. And I was the arranger—in every sense of the word."

The son of a Lyons tailor who had "gone out to the colonies," Hubert Rostaing first encountered music listening to military bands in Algiers. He learned it so well that in 1941, Django asked him to drop the saxophone for the clarinet and help rebuild his quintet, which had been scattered by the war. Rostaing remembers some incredible tours in wartime Belgium: in Brussels, just because the nights were so beautiful, Django would hire several horse-drawn carriages. By the Liberation, Rostaing was beyond a doubt the greatest clarinetist in France—perfectly controlled wind, a restrained, poetic attack. Boris Vian praised "his incredible ability to pick up a tenor sax after not playing for four or five years and play better than the very best, sliding through the virtuoso passages without forgetting to detach a single note, and so lightly that you only noticed it afterward."[6]

Rostaing says of Crolla: "We were fated to meet." And it could be said that Montand, after joining forces with Castella and Crolla, was fated to make the "Django sound" his own—without ever leaving the music hall.

> The piano wove in and out of everything. The brass heated the atmosphere. The drums dominated all the highly visual scenes, demarcating and accentuating the performer's moves. The accordion provided the nostalgic note—Paris, or Panama. And the bass was the foundation, all-important, everything rested on it. I have always been told that the "grandmother," the giant double bass that gives its players such huge backsides—nowadays they use electronic instruments—has the same powerful sonority as a cow's moo: nothing piercing about it, but you hear it a half-mile away. You hear it without hearing it. And if you take it away, everything collapses.

The family Yves Montand was building—or beginning to fit into—extended far beyond this musical group. Crolla's professional connections were the Paris jazz mafia, but his guardian angels—more angels than guardians—were still the October Group, to all intents and purposes Prévert's huge gang of friends and fellow writers. In 1948, Montand had, strictly speaking, no idea what an intellectual was, other than that he was a remote being belonging to a different species. In fact, the only representative of that strange tribe he had ever approached was Jacques Prévert.

6. In *Jazz Hot,* no. 2 (December 1945). Rostaing made the cover of issue 12. A mainstay of the magazine, he gave subscribers real clarinet lessons by correspondence. Some of the recordings he made with Django Reinhardt are still available.

Despite the harrowing fate of *Les Portes de la nuit,* Montand had lost none of his admiration for Prévert; nor had Prévert's loyalty ever wavered. He told everyone that Montand had honorably fulfilled his obligations. "Art is easy," he would add with a grin, "but reviews are tough." So they respected each other, but they were not close. Montand needed a *passeur* to help him across this minefield, and he found one in the person of Henri Crolla. Not that Crolla was an intellectual. That was the whole point: like Ivo Livi, "Millipede" had learned everything as he went along. He was no less timid or touchy—a touchiness on permanent alert—than the emigrant from La Cabucelle. But the company of erudite and creative spirits, painters, people from the world of literature and theater, was an everyday matter to him. He did not see them solemnly draped in learning, as Montand—like many another autodidact—tended to. He saw them sitting at the Flore or the Deux Magots, relaxed, joking, devious or open, drawn to alcohol or not, at once special and ordinary.

In May 1948, Crolla took Montand with him to Saint-Paul-de-Vence, in Provence. For years, the Cannes and Nice hinterland, the foothills ringing the Côte d'Azur, had been a sanctuary for artists in quest of peace, beauty, light, fragrance . . . and a social life as rich as in Paris. Braque, Matisse, and Giacometti were not much farther away from one another there than in Montmartre or Montparnasse. Saint-Paul, a fortified village set dramatically on a steep spike of a mountain, had been discovered by Prévert when he sought refuge in the South in 1940 with his friends Kosma and Trauner. Much of *Les Visiteurs du soir,* directed two years later by Marcel Carné, was shot in this region.

"Let's visit Jacques," said Crolla. Seized by stage fright, Montand hung back. "Come on, it's up here!" And the two men climbed up to the "dentist's house," a barrel-vaulted dwelling built into a corner of the chapel and so named because it had once sheltered the local dentist; Prévert had held on to his dining table, and even his immense armchair. After dinner, Picasso used to draw lyrical arabesques in crayon or chalk on the roughcast walls outside; they were soon covered by dust and faded by rain. Photos plastered the walls within: Prévert with his wife, Janine; with Carné, Trauner, Jean Gabin.

In Yves Montand's vacation house at Autheuil, in Normandy, a large photograph of Jacques Prévert hung to the left of the high mantelpiece in the living room, beneath a painting of a stagecoach and above a white chest that did service as a bar. Prévert—barefoot, wearing a striped, short-sleeved shirt—is lying in a wicker armchair, reading the newspaper with quiet concentration; his profile is sharply drawn in the excellent black-and-white contrast of the print. There were a few works of art (a Picasso plate) and many memorabilia (his first Gold Record, cut for Montand by Odéon after the millionth sale of "Les Feuilles mortes" in 1954, and the three British Film Academy awards won by Simone Signoret), but only one portrait really counted—that of Jacques Prévert.

But true intimacy never really developed between the creator of "Les Feuilles mortes" and its greatest performer. "He was happy to know Jacques the way Jacques was happy to know Picasso," said Grimault. "It was a solid friendship, but Jacques was a monument, he intimidated Yves," says Colette Crolla. They approached each other gradually, the singer awed by the man of letters, but the man of letters equally struck by the entertainer.

The shyness between the two men was unfathomable and often insuperable, but the poet's writing struck the singer with instant and irresistible force. Montand was at first unaware that the black-and-red cover of *Paroles* symbolized the banner of anarchy—not until later did such coded messages lose their mystery for him—but everything in Prévert's work seemed immediately within his reach. He marveled (even though he was a man who filled his notebook day and night with aphorisms, by others or of his own creation) at how apparently inoffensive words could be put together in combinations that triggered such sudden, devastating explosions. So that was culture: this ability to sift through "the terrifying seeds of reality," to say things and say what underlay those things, to complete a sentence by leaving it hanging.

Three years after that first visit in Saint-Paul, in Prévert's generous and lucid poem "Spectacle," he saluted

> ce grand garçon vivant ingénu et lucide
> viril tendre et marrant
>
> [this tall young man alive ingenuous clear-eyed
> tough tender and funny]

Two lines from another long poem were given pride of place in the program handed out by the usherettes at the Etoile:

> A peine est-il en scène
> qu'il est déjà dans la salle
> au beau milieu des spectateurs
> A peine est-il dans la salle
> qu'il fait danser la romance
> et qu'ils sont tout de suite ailleurs
> et la romance et lui
> et tous les spectateurs . . .

[No sooner is he on stage
than he is among us out here
out in the audience
No sooner out here
than he gives wings to our dreams
and all take flight together
he and our dreams
and all of us out here . . .]

Theoretically, Montand needed no help in getting to know Prévert better: the poet-scriptwriter already knew all about him. But would he have advanced so far without a go-between as close as Henri Crolla? It was one thing to receive literary celebrities, as a matter of courtesy, in your dressing room. It was quite another to be accepted as an equal in intellectual society, to be not just known but respected. Montand had never dreamed that was possible. Chance—and his friends—decreed that the people he met there were gentle with him. They showed respect to, even esteem for, a man whose personality had been formed by the school of his own intelligence.

It turned out that this new family possessed a communal residence, a headquarters: an inn called the Colombe d'Or, on the central square of Saint-Paul. Ocher walls, a main building that would have done honor to Florence but still felt local, a welter of subsidiary buildings so jumbled that their tile roofs made a jigsaw down the mountainside to a terrace that gazed out over the valley amid cypresses and fig trees. The proprietor, Paul Roux, and his beautiful wife, "Titine" (a "foreigner" whom Roux had carried away from La Colle, a village that was a good three miles away and therefore on another planet), took care not to turn their house into just any luxury hotel. Their guests never lost the feeling that the owners were making a special exception when they put them up for a few nights in the guest bedrooms. The atmosphere was neither come-as-you-are nor aloof hauteur; the Roux couple sustained a nicely distant tone, warm and discreet, efficient and seemingly impromptu. "It's the only four-star hotel I know where the bar is still the village café," Simone Signoret wrote later.

It had started out as an unassuming establishment called Robinson, a pleasant open-air café with four pavilions—sporting the aces of hearts, spades, diamonds, and clubs—at the corners of a terrace where people danced. Then stone had been imported, vines climbed the battlements, and an "Italian garden" was laid out down the slope. Seven or eight rooms, hardly ever more, each different, with Provençal furniture, were made available for guests. Roux in person cooked his artichokes *farigoule.* And success arrived—not in droves, but in small groups of distinguished guests. Before the war, Winston Churchill and Charlie Chaplin had liked staying there. When Montand spent his first night at the Colombe d'Or, it was a rite of initiation (just as his first visit to Prévert had been).

He got to know Eugène, the jack-of-all-trades who looked after the cash register and answered the phone, and Mme Blanche, who had served so many breakfasts to so many illustrious couples that her memoirs would fill every gossip column in the world. He met other, equally important people: Picasso and Braque, between whom he sensed a palpable ill will, stiffness, jealousy; Aimé, Marguerite, and Adrien Maeght, who dreamed of keeping their Paris gallery going forever as an artistic foundation; Joan Miró; and Marc Chagall. Roux also prided himself as being a painter and had done some very attractive canvases—two fish, a vase with a knife, flowers—that earned him the sincere encouragement of his legendary guests. Francis, the owners' son, commissioned a work from Fernand Léger for the terrace, and when they installed a swimming pool behind the hotel he decorated it with a Calder mobile and a ceramic by Braque.

The atmosphere was neither tourist-Montmartre nor picturesque-bohemian; there were no scrawny budding geniuses, no outlandish figures for visitors to gawk at. Saint-Paul-de-Vence was in every sense a shrine: in those early years (alas, long gone), anything fake was taboo. Montand suspected the good innkeeper of shaving the bills of those who might have difficulty paying and of making up the difference at the expense of those who experienced no hardships. Crowned heads of state, stars, and sightseeing name-droppers unwittingly subsidized Roux's spellbinding literary guests.

But the delightful annex where lovers or writers holed up (Raymond Queneau gave birth to his celebrated novel *Zazie dans le Métro* there), at the far end of the grounds, was never an annex of the political left. Grimault, dropping south to put the finishing touches on a project he was working on with his pal Prévert (*La Bergère et le ramoneur*), felt somewhat uneasy there, for he was a man happiest in his own neighborhood, in modest bistros with rough red wine and mugs of beer, more at ease in the big city than in this most delightful of oases. "Jacques felt at home at La Colombe," he says. "During my first stay, Marcel Pagnol was there working on a film with Tino Rossi. The atmosphere was exquisite, but it just wasn't my world."

Saint-Paul and La Colombe were certainly not everybody's world, but they were Prévert's, and after he suffered a serious accident (a fall from the National Radio building on the Champs-Elysées, followed by a long coma), he decided to move there for good. To a place where people worried if he didn't come out onto the terrace all day. Where Henri Crolla was married in 1949. His two witnesses signed in their usual way, Prévert with a flower and Grimault with a mischievous cat; the guitar player appended a sun to his signature. "My little sun from the Porte d'Italie," Prévert said fondly.

Yves Montand was instantly seduced by the luxury of the place and the aura of discreet harmony. Simple luxury, exceptional enough to relish but understated, unintimidating. He warmed himself in this sun—the sun of friendship, of the clan, of Provence, of poetry.

> Prévert was a sun, with his round face, round nose, round eyes, blue clown's eyes, and that round hat always pushed back on his head. He could also be a daisy—a daisy with a cigarette permanently in the corner of its mouth. Faultlessly dressed no matter what, English-style, but colorful: a black suit, for instance, set off by a yellow shirt and pocket handkerchief. He walked around with his little dog, Dragon, who yapped. I hate people who walk around with little dogs. But Prévert I admired, and later I loved him.
>
> I admired him, as I continue to admire people who can write, people who possess great knowledge or who are more intelligent than I am. I admire the kind of intelligence that comes from the heart, subtle and forceful, unaffected, funny. And, above all, not cold: education is something that should make you feel good, not something to cultivate at all costs for the sake of cultivation, turning a priceless resource into a pain in the ass. I admire his way of telling stories, so wordily you have trouble following them. A bit like Chris Marker, another one I love: where I would use eight words, he uses fifteen, and it's interesting. Taxing, but interesting.
>
> When he was in top form, Jacques was a delight. He'd point out to us even while eating and drinking with great gusto and scraping the rind off his cheese (never cut off the rind!) that learning foreign languages was a waste of time, and that some Czech shepherds he met had fully understood him, with them speaking Czech and him speaking French. The proof? He had pointed at a priest and said "gangster," "crook," and the shepherds had nodded in agreement. . . .
>
> My encounter with Prévert—I mean, its consequences—was more decisive than my encounter with Piaf. I was twenty-eight. I wanted to be around people like Jacques and Picasso not because they were famous but because to me, even though they were older, they represented the youth I had never had, another kind of

> youth. At the time of my first contacts with Prévert, I was like raw material. I did not grasp what Prévert told me, quietly and unemphatically, about the Soviet regime, but I immediately understood his "children who love each other kiss standing up against the gates of the night." His poems, his "songs that are like us"—and that I was to have so much trouble staging—seemed to me not just accessible but crystal-clear. What surprised me most was that such distinguished elders could show such respect for show-business people.

Momentous events were taking place—the Prague coup that delivered Czechoslovakia over to the Communists, the blockade of Berlin, the birth of the state of Israel, the break between Stalin and Tito—and ordinary mortals had to turn inward for strength. Traditional sources of moral authority had emerged battered from the war. You did not have to be fanatically anticlerical to cast a suspicious eye at good Pope Pius XII, guilty of a pronounced preference for Germany and a deafening silence about the Final Solution. You did not need to have drunk antimilitarism with your mother's milk to distrust an army that had believed the Maginot Line was impregnable. You did not need cast-iron ideological beliefs to be surprised that no one in mainland France had protested the massacre of thousands of Algerians in the Aurès region.

Montand was not distressed by the Stalin-Tito rupture or by other events that disturbed the veterans of the October Group. He was politically too gullible, too rough-hewn, to be troubled by these big issues. He preferred to apply irony, salutary laughter, and "holy ferocity" to the vicissitudes of everyday life. And in this domain Henri Crolla was an ideal disciple. Together they pushed the art of the practical joke to new frontiers.

Of course, it was a taste for japes and shared farce that drove them. But their underlying intention was subtler, more poetic—and here again we find Prévert: practical jokes as a form of resistance against the world's stupidity, an individually crafted escape from banality, a nose aristocratically thumbed, all the better when no one understood the reasons for them. One example from among thousands that Montand always related with delight: Henri Crolla knew Marcel Duhamel, one of the leading figures of the Prévert group, translator of Hemingway, Steinbeck, and Peter Cheney, and father of the "Série Noire" thriller collection that Gallimard had begun to publish in 1947, and had got hold of a blank book jacketed with the famous black cover and yellow type. In the evenings, when he was going home, standing on the rear platform of a bus, he would open the book, pore over the virgin pages, burst out laughing, nod, and smile—apparently indifferent to the growing astonishment around him. Or he would sit in a subway car and take notes on a pad without ever removing his attentive, inquiring gaze from the eyes of the man or woman unlucky enough to be seated across from him. And who would finally flee.

Practical jokes are a pleasant way of confirming our sense of ourselves. Often Montand indulged in them as a kind of health measure, a private way of reassuring himself that he was not fooled by the times, by words, by masks. Once, shooting a movie in Rome, he dreamed up a gratuitous game he was the only one to enjoy (had he shared it, all pleasure would have evaporated). Next to his hotel was a well-manicured park where, every afternoon, elegant ladies aired their offspring in luxurious baby carriages. Dressing with great care in a well-cut but sober suit, Montand entered the park a few minutes ahead of the strolling mothers. In a small wastebasket hanging from a lamppost at the end of a path he dropped an apple wrapped in clean paper. Then, timing himself carefully, he waited.

Two ladies appeared, fragrant, respectable. Approaching them, they saw an equally respectable man in a dark suit and well-made shoes. Six feet from the worthy women of Rome, the dignified gentleman thrust his hand into a wastebasket, rummaged inside in sudden frenzy, and pulled out an apple. Eyes alight with pleasure and disbelief, he bit into it greedily, his whole demeanor crazed, overjoyed, and deeply disturbing. Absorbed in his feast, he hastened past the ladies and hurried away, darting eyes alert for anyone who might try to steal his windfall.

Curtain. Montand thought of this little scenario as the "wastebasket-apple" caper. He played it for himself alone—and for his pal Crolla, who would have enjoyed it if he had been there. He played it almost for no reason at all. For the infinite satisfaction of confounding appearances. Forty years later, the "political" Montand—the man speaking out tirelessly on economic topics or East-West relations—would tell himself the waste-basket-apple joke all over again whenever his friends suspected he was becoming too serious.

When he was with Crolla, the game went on nonstop. The spirit of Pierre Dac and the Marx Brothers took over. And Grimault had been a wonderful teacher. When they were on tour, Montand and Crolla would pull off quite spectacular stunts. The core of the hoax was invariably a mental aberration or sudden physical ailment afflicting the musician. He might abruptly turn deaf, or dumb, or insane, and be obliged to leave the stage, sometimes feet first, sometimes surrounded by frantic friends. At table, where his manners were usually impeccable, he might suddenly jettison his fork and stuff handfuls of string beans down his throat. Many a hotelkeeper sincerely believed that this peculiar guest's condition required the most curious therapeutic measures, such as a song before he went to bed. Many a stagehand innocently agreed to remove his jacket and wave it under the nose of the guitar player, who claimed that he could not perform without a symbolic raising of the curtain.

Sometimes the conspirators would strike a little harder than they had intended. The liveliest episode occurred at the Colombe d'Or. Montand liked to take a breather at Saint-Paul-de-Vence between engagements. He took advantage of every concert he gave in the Midi to drop in on the "family." On arrival, he would buy fireworks to set off on the terrace with Francis Roux and Adrien Maeght. One morning he arrived to find the hotel in an uproar. King Farouk of Egypt had reserved the entire restaurant for lunch, and his security men were checking the grounds to prevent any risk of an attack. So painstaking were their precautions that a perverse idea overcame Montand and Francis. They still had two thunderflashes, enormous firecrackers that exploded spectacularly but harmlessly.

Lunchtime came around. The king sat enthroned under a fig tree. His entourage filled the remaining tables. Montand and Francis were concealed in a room under the eaves. Roux selected a high-caliber thunderflash, lit it, and handed it to his accomplice to toss into the garden that lay beyond the terrace. But Montand misjudged his throw: the bomb, meant to fly well clear of the guests, landed smack on the royal table. One of Farouk's bodyguards was alert enough to hurl it out over the valley, where echoes amplified the explosion. Stupefaction, then to the battle stations! Huge revolvers appeared, and a room-by-room search of the building was launched. Sheepish but nonchalant, the guilty pair strolled downstairs to ask what the upheaval was all about.

Clearly, the dark days were drawing to an end. Laughter had brought light, and friends had dispelled Montand's isolation. And work once again consoled and stimulated him. Besides provincial cabarets and concerts, a comeback at the Etoile was scheduled for the fall of 1949. Montand, Castella, and Crolla reworked all of his former repertory. Sure winners ("Battling Joe," "Luna Park," "La Grande Cité") remained sure winners, but they set about exploring fresh terrain. First, there were his friend Prévert's songs. Montand was now determined to claim the two marvels stolen from him during the shooting of *Les Portes de la nuit.* But, to his surprise, test runs at selected performances were disappointing. "Les Enfants qui s'aiment" put the audience to sleep, and "Les Feuilles mortes" met with icy silence. Not "swing" enough, too convoluted, was the invariable objection.

Montand persisted. His literary education might be close to zero, but his stage experience was solid. In five years as a national star he had learned one thing above all others: "Respect the audience" is a golden rule in a trade where nothing durable can be achieved without sincerity, but respect does not mean obedient self-imitation just to flatter the instinctive conservatism of loyal fans whose natural reflex is to keep alive nostalgia for past emotions. You cannot truly love people without shaking them up a little. So Montand stayed on course. He slipped "Les Feuilles mortes" in between "Luna Park" and "Les Grands Boulevards" to counterbalance and boost its light theme with the two strong ones. After all, the Marseilles audience had whistled at the Variétés back in 1944 but had finally accepted the new repertory. He was reluctant to keep Prevért's picturesque "Plombier zingueur," not because he disliked it, but because he hadn't hit on the right mood or hand movements; still, he was sure that one day a natural sequence of weak and strong themes would evolve. Intuition whispered to him that "Les Feuilles mortes," in particular, had the kind of "roundness" and simplicity that propel good songs across borders and touch audiences even if they only understand the theme and the chorus ("La Vie en rose" was like this). Intuition was not infallible, but generally it was right.

Other writers and composers turned up, beginning with a prolific newcomer whose lyrics seemed unprecedented: Léo Ferré. Piaf sent him around (he had given her "Les Amants de Paris"). At the Surène-d'Aguesseau hotel and later on the rue de Longchamp, Montand regularly received calls from this strange, tormented figure, for he liked him, and Ferré always brought something interesting: "Le Scaphandrier" (which Philippe Clay would sing), "La Chambre," "Flamenco de Paris" (in homage to the unquenchable spirit of Franco's opponents). They had their ups and downs, for the Communist Party loyalist was more than a little irritated by an anarchist who burst with bombastic professions of faith and liked to bait his interlocutors. Then, once Ferré started performing his own works, a degree of rivalry emerged, and Montand's occasional rejections strained their relations ("Monsieur Williams," which Montand just didn't get, was an apple of discord). No matter: from "Paris canaille" to "L'Etrangère" (based on a poem by Louis Aragon), Ferré's work helped enormously to establish a literary tone for Montand's work—very welcome at chic cabarets like the Rose Rouge and on the Left Bank, if not for his audiences at the Etoile or the Olympia.

The most fertile encounter of his life had a rather less sophisticated tone. Francis Lemarque was a songwriter who gave Montand—the singer he admired above all others—the ideal counterbalance to his recent artistic advances. He gave him the greatest imaginable value in popular music: a perfectly cadenced melody along with lyrics that were finely crafted but truly heartfelt, and therefore instantly accessible.

To check the authenticity of that heart, we have only to glance at the life of the man who wrote "A Paris," "Je vais à pied," "Toi tu ne ressembles à personne," "Vieux Canal," and two or three hundred other postwar music-hall gems. No scriptwriter would dare dream up a life like his. The room where Francis Lemarque was born, 51 rue de Lappe, was just above a dance hall, the Bal des Trois Colonnes. His real name, he says, was Nathan Korb, and he was the "son of stateless persons from Poland or Lithuania. A strange family, a family without papers or family photos. I spoke Yiddish until I was three and didn't learn French until I went to school. The neighborhood was bursting with music. On my street were about twenty dance halls, cheek by jowl. I loved to listen to the little bands that played in the bistros in the Place de la Bastille. When I came home, around midnight, the dancers were still going full swing. My parents sang, workers sang, in those days. Singing was part of life."

Once again, it was Jacques Prévert who introduced Lemarque to Montand. Young Nathan (born in 1917, the revolutionary year par excellence) had met Prévert early on, and in a predictable way. As a kid he had sung ballads on the streets to make money and escape the discipline of school. As a teenager, he and his elder brother had joined a section of the Federation of French Worker Theaters (the March Group, which never became as famous as the October Group but chalked up some small successes all the same), and the two "Marque Brothers" came to be in great demand. (Their model was another duo, Gilles and Julien, whose repertory they pillaged.) Inevitably, one evening the March Group and the October Group played together, at the Gymnase Japy. Prévert came over to congratulate the high-spirited boys, who at once asked him for two or three poems, receiving "La Chasse à l'enfant," "Familiale," and "Le Petit Cheval" in return. During the Popular Front, accompanied at the piano by the then-unknown Joseph Kosma, they performed with huge success for striking workers.

But Francis Lemarque had not yet reached safe harbor. The war broke up partnerships and ruined careers. Lemarque's remarkable wartime experiences included cabaret work in the unoccupied zone, a stint with a picturesque cooperative that made candy from dates and almonds, and Resistance efforts with the Maquis group in the Castres region led by Dunoyer de Segonzac.

At the Liberation, Lemarque returned to the stage and to nightclubs. Then it hit him: "I had reached thirty and felt I was heading for total failure. I used to drop in on married friends at mealtimes; I was becoming a sponger. One evening I walked into the Club des Cinq, in Montmartre.

Mado Robin was performing, and a singer I didn't know, Yves Montand. I left in despair, whipped, jealous, defeated. That guy was succeeding at what I had been attempting to do for years. Right off, I liked his looks, his unaffected air, at a time when singers brilliantined their hair and tried to look like models. And his hands. And his repertory. He beat me to the finish. Soon my jealousy gave way to a fierce wish to meet him. I told myself he surely needed songs."

Lemarque had never thought of writing songs. "How do you go about it?" he had asked Prévert, curious and awed. The master replied, "Bah! The main thing is not to lose heart."[7]

"I didn't lose heart. I shut myself up for nearly a month in a little room a friend lent me on the boulevard Saint-Germain. I copied out staves and drew spaces over them—I knew nothing about musical notation. I said to myself: 'You have to write a song. You have to be part of what he does. You mustn't be just a passing face he'll never see again.' I wrote 'Ma douce vallée,' 'Le Tueur affamé,' 'Bal, petit bal,' and made a start on 'A Paris.' For six or seven months I believed my songs were atrocious. At that time I was working as a messenger boy at Editions de Minuit [a Paris publisher], and I was thinking of taking a job with some cousins who ran a store on the Champs-Elysées. But before I threw it all in I decided to ask Prévert's advice. I took my guitar along and played my songs. 'I like them a lot,' said Prévert, 'but you're a friend. Better ask someone who really knows the business.' That someone was Montand. He called him then and there. Prévert had no idea that in my mind those songs had always been intended for Montand."

"Send him over right away!" said Montand. Lemarque raced to Neuilly. Montand, wearing a bathrobe, let him in. And he launched into "Ma douce vallée," then the first verse of "Bal, petit bal." Lemarque has never forgotten the exchange that followed, which transformed his life.

"Suddenly he interrupted me. 'Do you have many others like these?'

" 'As many as you want to sing.' "

Overnight, the visitor's fortunes changed. Without a moment's delay, Yves Montand recorded "Ma douce vallée." At once, the "Lemarque sound" caught the ear of disc jockeys. At work the messenger boy sensed the change in attitude: his songs were played on the radio five and six times a day, he was getting royalties, people looked at him differently. Modest to a fault, he was surprised by this. Music-hall managers encouraged him; the best cabarets, particularly the Rose Rouge, were after him. Dance bands played his songs. At the Clairon and the Tambour, on the Place de

7. Quoted in Richard Cannavo and Henri Quiquéré, *Montand: Le Chant d'un homme* (Paris, 1981).

la Bastille, the neighborhood where he had grown up, and which he still loved, his were the tunes you heard.

Montand intimidated him—when two shy people meet, it is inevitable—but Lemarque had realized his dream: he was now a part of the singer's entourage. Contact was direct and affectionate, and they were soon on familiar terms. The Tuscan and the Ashkenazi came from basically very similar backgrounds. They shared the same ideas—like Montand, Lemarque was close to the Party—and they drew their ideas from the same sources: the France of little people proud of their littleness and working to build the foundations of a great future, a future for republican and egalitarian France, the easygoing France of Sunday cafés, of sidewalks and canal barges, of lovers on riverbanks, of accordions and cherry blossoms. Francis was always a welcome visitor. He would arrive on a wave of mirth, his guitar in his hand and songs in his pocket. In all, Montand owed him sixteen great songs; several of them have survived forty years of fickle audiences and changes in style, sound, instruments, and mood—and they are still golden properties.

"Yves Montand was the first one to give concerts without anyone getting tired of them," says the ever-admiring Francis Lemarque today. In 1981, learning that Montand had rented the Olympia for a new show, he dropped round, he phoned. Nothing. M. Montand was unavailable. Hurt, he hesitated before accepting an invitation that arrived in the mail. Finally, he went to the last dress rehearsal. The atmosphere was tense, rigid: Montand had not sung for ten years, and the critics were circling expectantly.

Moi je suis venu à pied
  Doucement sans me presser
J'ai marché à pied, à pied
  J'étais sûr de vous trouver
Je ne me suis donc pas pressé
  En marchant à pied, à pied
Dans la rue il faisait bon
  Je me fredonnais une chanson
Avec le dessous de mes talons . . .

[I came here on my two feet
  Tapping out a gentle beat
With my two hip-happy feet
  And I knew that we would meet
So my heart skipped not a beat
  As I followed my floating feet

Down streets both short and long
Tapping out a merry song
As I whistled my way along . . .]

Montand had chosen that tune to open his act in the spring of 1949, for he loved its carefree mood, its rocking rhythm, which permitted him, as he stood there, tapping in place, to introduce himself gently into his audience's world, to effect the transition from outside to inside, from life to theater. An evening's singing should not begin full-blast, all guns blazing, but gently, suggestively, in a half-dream. There were tears in Lemarque's eyes. He could not help it: whenever Montand sang, he wept.

Luckily, tears came easily to him. For the song that closed the show was the one he was proudest of, "A Paris." It was Bob Castella's favorite. New Yorkers knew it; so did the Japanese, Australians, Mexicans, and Russians:

Des ennuis
Il n'y en a pas qu'à Paris
Il y en a dans le monde entier
Oui mais dans le monde entier
Il n'y a pas partout Paris
Voilà l'ennui . . .

[Trouble
Isn't a Paris monopoly
There's trouble all over the world
Yes but in the rest of the world
Paris isn't there all the time
That's just the trouble . . .]

Now Montand raised the volume to maximum, emptied his lungs:

Depuis qu'à Paris on a pris la Bastille
Dans chaque faubourg et chaque carrefour
Il y a des gars et il y a des filles
Qui sans arrêt sur les pavés nuit et jour
Font des tours et des tours
A Paris

[Since they stormed the Bastille in Paris
There are girls and there are boys
On every street, on every corner
Building towers
Night and day, never stopping
In Paris]

Lemarque, eyes still damp, went backstage and knocked on Montand's dressing-room door. Wrapped in a white bathrobe, his companion of old opened up, a glint of mockery in his eyes. "So you thought we'd forgotten you?" he said.

By May 1949, Montand was almost out of the wilderness; it was Piaf who was floundering. She had signed a seven-week contract at the ABC with the Compagnons de la Chanson, but at the last minute her voice let her down. She asked Montand to replace her, and he quickly agreed. From May 6 to 19, every night was a success, but his revised repertory was not put to the test until November 18, on the stage of the Etoile.

While he was appearing there, French National Radio asked Montand to record an adaptation of John Steinbeck's *Grapes of Wrath.* It was a stimulating experience for the singer. He had heard himself on records. He had heard himself on film soundtracks. Never, though, had he had a chance to study his diction methodically. There was no doubt: he still had the hint of a Marseilles accent, still stressed his *e*'s and *o*'s too heavily. If he wasn't careful, rivals and mimics would eat him alive. *The Grapes of Wrath,* fascinating though he found both writing and plot, was a long, patient, passionate, self-imposed lesson for Montand.

He was singing at the Club des Champs-Elysées when his agent passed along to him another unusual offer. On May 28, Prince Ali Khan, son of the Aga Khan, was marrying Rita Hayworth in his villa at Vallauris: Would M. Montand agree to entertain the happy couple and their guests? It was an amusing offer. Until now, the "singing prole" had not spent much time with royalty. The show-business press buzzed with the news. Montand's curiosity was aroused—and the fee was a generous one. But how could he honor his evening contract at the nightclub? No problem: a special airplane would take off from Le Bourget in the morning with the artist and his accompanists and return that night in time for the show.

Touchdown at Cannes (Bob Castella and Henri Crolla were naturally with him), limousine to the Château de l'Horizon, warm welcome from the prince, introduction to the Aga Khan, luncheon with General Catroux, the begum, and the Hollywood gossip columnist Louella Parsons. Then seven songs performed in a reception room transformed into an intimate cabaret. Rita, in a pale-blue dress, and Ali, who beat time with his foot, were a heartwarming sight. Montand dedicated "Elle a des yeux" to them, singing the chorus in phonetically learned English, as well as "Mais qu'est-ce que j'ai à tant l'aimer?" And back he went at 4:00 p.m., deeply satisfied, a little dazed.

Total luxury, in stark contrast to the potluck character of concert tours.

In an interview with *France-Soir* on May 29–30, Montand did not conceal how flattered he was—and how surprised by the people he had moved among during his intermission. "Very simple, yes, yes, very simple," he said on his return. "A charming couple, nothing aloof about them at all. Almost a village wedding: I was Cousin Victor singing for the family after the feast."

Montand the music-hall entertainer was on cloud nine. Montand the man would soon join him there.

Giovanni and Giuseppina Livi in 1921

Ivo Livi in 1933

ABOVE: The rue Edgar Quinet in Les Crottes. The house in which the Livi family lived from 1927 to 1929 is the first one on the right.

LEFT: During the years in Les Crottes: Giuseppina, Ivo (seated), Julien, and Lydia

ABOVE: Julien, Lydia, and Ivo in 1931

RIGHT: The impasse des Mûriers. The Livis' house is the first one on the right. Before the war, the shop Coiffeuse Jacky was called Salon Lydia, and was actually a small unused garage.

Ivo Livi at the age of seventeen

At the Chantiers de la Jeunesse: Montand (standing, fourth from the right), Derdérian (standing, far right), Mourchou (on Montand's right)

Berlingot and Mlle Fancelli

Montand in his performing debuts, imitating Chevalier (LEFT) and Trenet

Montand and Piaf

During the Liberation (LEFT) . . .
and fifteen years later

Montand in Antibes, 1949

Montand singing in Vence, accompanied by Henri Crolla on the guitar, 1950

The meeting of Simone Signoret and Montand at La Colombe d'Or, August 1949

The wedding luncheon at La Colombe, December 21, 1951. Around Montand and Signoret are Prévert, Pagnol, Paul Roux . . . and, of course, *les colombes*—the doves.

New Year's Eve at Saint-Paul

Lunch at La Colombe with Gérard Philipe

Montand and Bob Castella rehearse at Autheuil for the American tour, summer 1959.

Rehearsing for an Etoile concert, 1958

Shooting *The Wages of Fear,* 1952: Simone Signoret, Montand, and Charles Vanel

Montand and Vanel on screen

Montand in action at the pool of La Colombe, in front of a ceramic by Georges Braque

The house at Autheuil, 1955

In the living room at Autheuil during the 1950s.
TOP, Simone and Yves; BOTTOM, Julien and Elvire,
Simone and Yves, Lydia

Chapter 8

Legend has it that on August 14, 1949, dropping in at La Colombe during a tour of the Côte d'Azur, Yves Montand fell in love at first sight with Simone Signoret. He himself confirmed and validated the legend, and she never denied it. Three years later, in his ghosted memoirs, Montand offered an "official version" composed in a pleasantly inflated style: "There, in the middle of the courtyard, surrounded by cooing doves, was a young woman wearing jeans and an open-necked shirt. She smiled like a girl in an old Italian painting. I knew that her name was Simone Signoret, I had seen none of her movies, I did not know her, but I knew I was going to walk toward her and try not to send the doves flying."

The date is right. The setting is right, if not the clothing. And his reason for being there is right. Montand had to sing in Nice on August 20 and in Cannes on August 21. Simone Signoret owned a little house in the village, bought for "the price of a crust of bread"—10,000 francs, her fee for Leopold Lindtberg's *Four Days Leave.* She was in Provence with her daughter, Catherine, who was four, and her fourteen-year-old stepson, Gilles. Her husband, the film director Yves Allégret, was joining her in a few days. It is also correct that Montand did not know even these bare facts. He did not know that Simone Signoret was the same age as himself, twenty-eight. He knew only that she was an established star whose photograph had appeared on the covers of dozens of movie magazines. Yes, all that was authentic. All the rest needs considerable retouching.

> The scene of our meeting—"I saw Simone standing amid the doves and we walked toward each other," and so on—is a kind of icon. For the sake of good press relations we never denied it. There is, indeed, a photo of Simone on her knees feeding the doves and looking steadily at someone—me, maybe—off camera, as if to validate the legend. But the truth was simpler and sweeter.

I arrived at the Rouxes' after lunch. Bob Castella and Henri Crolla were with me. I was travel-weary. I went up to rest in my room in the annex and didn't come down until dinner. I was at my table in the dining room with Bob and Henri when Jacques Prévert came in with a woman. She was barefoot and dressed gypsy-style, with a rustling flowered skirt and a blouse knotted around her waist. She was outrageously made up, the way women made themselves up in those days, with far too much lipstick; I thought it was a pity to paint such a mouth. They came over. She and Crolla had been friends for years. He introduced us.

In those days the salon at the Colombe had a piano. The atmosphere was very cheerful and relaxed. Bob sat down at the piano and sketched out "Ma solitude," which he played like an angel. Then I was asked to sing one of Jacques's songs.

As I sang I stared—but not too obviously—at that woman, and I saw that she was not indifferent to me, either. And suddenly a memory, an aural image, came back to me from when I was at Carrère with Henri and heard a distinctive voice calling out, "Bravo Riton!" I had wondered what the owner of that unforgettable voice looked like. I'd been so curious that I asked Crolla when we got backstage, and he simply said, "She's a friend of mine, Simone Signoret, the actress with Yves Allégret." When the show was over, Simone and Allégret came to congratulate Henri and pay me the usual compliments: we've followed you for years, we saw you at the ABC, we like you very much, and so on. I had seen her on one other occasion, in the Tuileries gardens at a benefit for veterans of the Second Armored Division [the formation commanded by General Leclerc that liberated Paris in 1944]. She asked for white wine—*"un coup de blanc"* was what she said—and that surprised me, even shocked me a little. Not that she drank wine, but that she ordered it street-style.

So all these rather hazy memories were racing through my head. I finished the song. Then everyone started chatting. I exchanged banal remarks with Signoret—and entered the seemingly careless game in which your eyes hesitate to meet, in which you are excited and troubled by feelings of you don't know what. The kind of troubled excitement that feeds on the excitement of the other person.

The next morning, I went down to Nice to rehearse, but I returned to La Colombe for lunch. Simone, Crolla, Prévert, and I ate together on the terrace. I was wearing a kind of T-shirt, espadrilles, and shorts, which I loathe, but they're sensible when you're driving in a Citroën on the hot dusty roads of the Côte d'Azur. We reached the end of the meal. Henri and Jacques left. She stayed.

We drank white wine. Looked at one another. Picked up the nonconversation of the day before. I "carelessly" took hold of her arm: "You have very slender wrists."

I could have said anything to her, she would have taken it as a compliment, but it was true. We talked about it for years afterward, her "very slender wrists."

She smiled and mumbled a few words I didn't catch. She drank her coffee, I lit a cigarette. It was past two. I cleared my throat and felt obliged to explain.

"Simone"—it was the first time I had called her Simone—"I'm sorry, but I'm on tonight at the Verdure in Nice. I have to rest for at least half an hour."

"You can rest at my place if you like. I have a little house in the village."

As always, it was she, the woman, who took the initiative, and as always, I was surprised. Only later did I discover how deep was her sense of propriety. She showed me around her house, and I found it very pleasant, indeed. We had our siesta together, and we stayed together. Simone came down to Nice to listen to me, and I brought her back. Everyone at La Colombe knew about it—everyone had seen her coming out of the annex.

It wasn't rumors or her reputation that worried her. She saw that there was no turning back from what we were going through, and she worried about the pain it would cause her husband. She wasn't the kind of woman to gloat or to take pleasure in inflicting pain in a love relationship. As soon as I left, she went to Yves Allégret, whom she loved most tenderly. She told him everything, so that he wouldn't suddenly find himself at the center of a soap opera. In a first flash of anger he slapped her twice, hard, but from then on he behaved with extraordinary delicacy.

Four days later I had to leave: the tour was going on to Dax and Biarritz.

In the big front-wheel-drive Citroën, sitting next to Bob at the wheel, I just felt stunned. The break with Edith had been so traumatic that I had sworn I would never again expose myself to that kind of shock. But I had stuck a photo of Simone on the windshield, and however many times I said, "Be careful! Watch out!" and however hard I tried to protect myself, I missed her. At Dax we went back to work, but I felt her looking over my shoulder. Late that night she called me and spoke with all the passion she was capable of, and of course I melted with joy, I was happy. Back in Paris, I had to admit to myself that I had fallen deeply in love. You don't go looking for that kind of thing—it hits you right in the heart.

Their meeting was not just one of those romantic coincidences dear to the readers of movie magazines. So many friendships revolved around this meeting that the series of coincidences is almost alarming.

In December 1951, Jacques Prévert was Simone Signoret's witness at her marriage to Yves Montand at Saint-Paul-de-Vence. Nothing more logical, if such a term can be applied to a love story, for he had been the unwitting architect of their romance.

In the early 1930s, Paul Grimault, Henri Crolla's benefactor, had worked at an advertising agency owned by a man named Etienne Damour, who was also the employer of Simone's father, M. Kaminker, who worked on Damour's magazine *Vendre.* Grimault was fond of the little girl from fashionable Neuilly, who lived on the rue Jacques-Dulud, took piano and English lessons, periodically visited her Uncle Marcel and Aunt Irène (both rich, Jewish, and wholly assimilated—the latter attributes, but not the first, applying equally to Simone's father), wasn't allowed on the scenic railway and other proletarian temptations at Luna Park—in short, the very model of the nice, middle-class girl with a retiring father and a flamboyant mother.

During the Occupation, Simone Kaminker (a risky name) grew up, got her diploma, and supported her family. Her father had gone to London, two younger brothers had been taken in by other families, and the apartment on the rue Jacques-Dulud had been stripped of its furniture. She found a job as an assistant secretary on a collaborationist newspaper, *Les Nouveaux Temps,* whose chairman, Jean Luchaire (he was shot after the Liberation), protected her despite the divergence of political views. She escaped from this job with the help of a movie-loving Communist friend, Claude Jaeger, who took her to explore the other side of the Seine and brought her to safe harbor on the Left Bank in Saint-Germain-des-Prés. At the Café Flore she was dazzled by her illustrious table companions—Soutine and Picasso, Simone de Beauvoir and Jean-Paul Sartre—and surrounded by friends from the fabulous world of entertainment: Roger Blin, Raymond Bussières, Fabien Loris, Mouloudji. And Crolla—"Millipede." But Jacques Prévert was their common denominator.

In an interview in *Look* magazine on August 30, 1960, shortly after winning the Oscar for *Room at the Top,* Simone Signoret said: "The Café Flore was our club. Neither the Germans nor the cops went there, because there were no prostitutes and no black-market alcohol, nor even forbidden music, just coffee sweetened with saccharine and people who talked and talked and talked. It was there that I met many of the people who have shaped my life." The interviewer quotes the following description by Jacques Prévert of the newcomer to Saint-Germain-des-Prés: "A wonderful girl who knew she wanted something but didn't know what it was."

"Simone's loyalty to the group was remarkable," says Paul Grimault. "Often irritatingly so; she could sound like its guiding spirit, its Pasionaria." A thumbnail sketch by "Le Minotaure" in *L'Ecran Français* (its writer must certainly have seen her from very close up) just as her career took off described the Café Flore and its Pasionaria in the following terms: "It is there that people starve with a maximum of wit. To live, to feed herself on horse meat, she gave English lessons and typed manuscripts. She borrowed her male friends' shirts, refused to have her hair done, and discovered a world in which everyone had genius but not the wherewithal to purchase the latest edition of Lautréamont; in which the spice of good conversation helped you to forget, even in the most loathsome of restaurants, that you were drinking acorn coffee and that your feet were cold. . . . She has the go-to-hell tone of girls used to taking care of themselves, the serious voice of women who pass for intellectuals, an intermittent lisp that suits her, and the coarse language that is de rigueur in literary cafés. She has gotten into the habit of admiration. She admires, she loves, she adores her friends, the new Italian movies, Raymond Radiguet, Scotch plaids, naive Sunday painters, the actors she makes movies with, and everyone else."[1]

But before the columnists became interested in her, the renegade from Neuilly had a war to go through and an apprenticeship to endure. What do you dream of when you are twenty and live among artists? Of being like your friends—and, if possible, of being different from them, too. Simone Kaminker, alias Signoret, was soon working in movies, even though her Jewish parentage disqualified her from holding an actor's certification. Playing bit parts here and there, she was soon promoted to the status of speaking extra. On the recommendation of a Saint-Germain regular, Marcel Carné hired her for *Les Visiteurs du soir,* in which in quick succession she portrayed a lady in a bonnet, a bareheaded peasant girl, and a kitchen maid. With the rank and file in the movie, she stayed at a pension in Saint-Paul-de-Vence but dared not cross the threshold of La Colombe. She knew Sussex, in England, where she had stayed in 1937 to polish her English. She knew Brittany, where her family had spent the summers

1. *L'Ecran Français,* December 9, 1947. Signoret was on the cover of the issue, on the occasion of the premiere of *Dedée d'Anvers.*

before the war. She did not yet know the Midi and would make its acquaintance—inevitably—through Carné and Prévert.

It was, of course, at the Café Flore in Paris that she met Yves Allégret, whose brother Marc was an established movie director (*Lac aux dames, Gribouille, Entrée des artistes*). Yves carried a faint whiff of danger from a flirtation with the Surrealists, from sorting Leon Trotsky's mail while the founder of the Red Army was living in Barbizon, from campaigning for the October Group. At the outbreak of the war, he was still an assistant director (to Jean Renoir, among others). When the Occupation authorities sought him for compulsory labor service in Germany, he went into hiding in the countryside of the Haute-Marne, where he remained until the Liberation—a bucolic interlude that found Simone Signoret and Allégret in excellent company: Serge Reggiani, Janine Darcy, Danièle Delorme, and Claude Dauphin shared their spartan retreat.

The actress's breakthrough role was a fruit of this love and coincided with Allégret's beginnings as a director in his own right. *Les Démons de l'aube,* in 1945, made both their names. This first true role for Simone was followed by a big break: the part of Gisèle, a prostitute, in *Macadam* (*Back Streets of Paris*) (released in 1946), codirected by Marcel Blistène and Jacques Feyder. And then a starring role, in *Dedée d'Anvers* in 1947, directed by Allégret. Of her husband and mentor she said: "I was in love with him, flattered that a mature man should pay attention to me. But with him our profession came first. We threw ourselves into work to achieve success. Now, an actress who never stops working can turn into a monster. You live night and day with your part. Nothing outside of it counts."[2]

A lightning career, but fraught with peril. Signoret never had an ingénue stage, never was asked to play the adorable girl for whose caresses a Cooper or a Gable would compete, against a background of pink clouds and celestial violins. No, she played prostitutes—sometimes calculating, at best enigmatic, but more often venomous. This was perilous, indeed.

As it happened, Montand had missed Signoret's key appearances. If he had seen her as the girl in *Les Démons de l'aube* (perverse enough to kiss a man tied to a tree in order to make him weaken and talk), or as the dark soul of *Manèges,* Allégret's latest, due for a fall release, he might have formed an entirely different impression of her.

From November 18 to New Year's Eve 1949, Montand was once again enthroned at the Etoile. And once again, something new was happening. Maurice Chevalier, as well as Pierre Blanchar, Erich von Stroheim, and

2. Quoted in *Look,* August 30, 1960.

other giants, attended the premiere. Many observers said outright that the great Maurice's title was vacant and that Montand was the likeliest contender. Paris arbiters of taste no longer viewed the likable young workingman from Marseilles with quite the same amused condescension as before: he was now a "superstar."[3] Francis Lemarque's songs (for the first time, "A Paris" conquered a big Paris audience) became overnight classics, and so did the new working-class ones. The Prévert selections were still hard to put across; the few that Montand had already performed in the provinces, in cabarets, or in suburban movie houses met with the same reception on the avenue de Wagram—distinctly cool—and only left-wing and intellectual reviewers urged Montand to continue them. The others applauded politely and suggested that if these songs worked it was only "because of the performer's talent and magnetism."[4] Nonetheless, the basic format of Montand's future concerts was now solidly established.

All this work failed to resolve the other dilemma Montand faced. Ever since his return to Paris he was living a passion that simultaneously enchanted and frightened him. He and Simone sincerely tried to sew up the wound they had opened in Saint-Paul-de-Vence, but in vain. When they saw each other, it was blinding love all over again, every moment too brief. They were happy together and wretched apart, consumed, ecstatic, frustrated.

Simone Signoret could not bring herself to leave a perfect husband and a stepson whom she had grown to love, or to disrupt the life of her young daughter. Professionally, she had left everything in limbo. At about this time she was scheduled to go to Hollywood, since after the success (on both sides of the Atlantic) of *Dedée d'Anvers,* she, too, like Montand, had been approached by talent scouts from the major American studios. Unlike Montand, she could read a contract in a foreign language and had turned down the customary seven years' serfdom. But an agent dispatched by Howard Hughes had proved more persuasive, offering a nonexclusive contract for four movies of her choice. She was supposed to leave on a reconnaissance trip.

She stayed. (Throughout her life, Signoret, who was most assuredly not without ambition and proved it in her remarkably rapid rise to the top, retained this capacity to interrupt her career with apparent casualness and then, still more unusually, resume it with great success.) You needed extraordinary confidence in your professional worth, and equally extraordinary determination in private life, to take the risk of living with a man like Montand. Show-business couples do not fill magazine and newspaper

3. *Le Parisien Libéré,* November 21, 1949.

4. *Ce Soir,* November 26, 1947.

space simply because they represent a two-for-the-price-of-one celebrity package. Subject by definition to constant pressure and ferocious rivalries, they magnify a hundredfold the storm centers that exist for every couple. They offer an unending pageant of ruptures and brutal conflict.

With Montand, the risks were even greater. All artists are egocentric. Actors more than others. Music-hall entertainers more than actors. And the three or four genuine exponents of the one-man show—the man who sang "Les Feuilles mortes" is the father of them all—are the most selfish of music-hall people. Their lives are versions, in more or less relaxed, more or less febrile, form, of their uninterrupted attention to their work. Running the most dangerous risks, the most absolute of dangers—that of "dying" in public—for them seems to validate the extreme narcissism of which they are both the guilty perpetrators and the unhappy victims.

In the first faltering steps of their relationship, Simone Signoret realized that with Montand in particular the rules of the game would be even more stringent, the room for maneuvering narrower than usual. This neither angered nor frustrated her. "People have said that I was 'sacrificing my career,' " she wrote. "I was sacrificing nothing. I was simply clever enough not to sacrifice my life."[5] The doubts that assailed her were different. She was afraid of inflicting suffering on her loved ones. What may have convinced her to take the plunge was the certainty that Montand himself was in a dangerous position, that he had no other choice but to break with her or insist that she decide.

As she reported it: "Montand gave me an ultimatum. He explained to me that he had had enough of those ladies who filled his afternoons; I'd better pack my bags and come live with him or else there wasn't any point in even telephoning." But to hear Montand tell it later, it was his back that was against the wall.

> It was intense, violent, a joy, a celebration. And then, at seven, she would go "home"—in other words, to someone else's home. Perhaps it would have worked for a year, or even two. I don't know, I just don't know; it was already unbearable. I asked my agent to set up a tour for me right away. He suggested Casablanca, Algiers, and Tunis. So Casa, Algiers, and Tunis it was. I told Simone, who was still dithering, that I was leaving for a couple of weeks and that if she hadn't made up her mind by the time I got back, I would break off for good. She cried. I felt sick myself. I was sure it was over. On the day of my departure, I ran into a

5. Simone Signoret, *Nostalgia Isn't What It Used to Be* (New York, 1978). All subsequent quotations from Signoret not footnoted are from this source.

reporter friend who was very close to Crolla and Grimault. I told her that our position was unbearable, impossible, that we had no future. She disagreed angrily and bawled me out: "You don't have the right to turn tail and run this way, to flush such an experience down the toilet. Happiness takes time. It's too easy to break up without having tried."

It was precisely what I was afraid to admit to myself—and what in my heart I wanted to hear. Her words ran through my mind the whole time I was away. From Casa I mailed a gloomy letter to Pierrot Prévert, to whom I had confided my unhappiness.

Pierrot old friend:

Well, things aren't too good, know what I mean? Shit. My imagination must be working overtime but in the wrong direction. I tell myself that I have my work and she has her kid. And then I see her—and nothing else, just her. Makes no sense. You know, we spent four wonderful days together. And you know, it's true, for four wonderful days she was relaxed, sweet. Everything.

She was at the station when I arrived, which made me very happy. I had expected her to wait outside in the car because of the people. But she didn't. There she was on the platform, in her raincoat, with no makeup. We wanted to kiss—and we couldn't, because there was this huge crowd of idiots from the festival on the same train . . . but we didn't leave each other. We held hands and went off to have breakfast at the Place Dauphine with Henri, his wife, and Bob.

I'd better stop now, I don't want to bore you. Sorry, but I've gone on about this so much to Henri, and I felt the need to chat with you.

A big hug, Pierrot old friend, and for everyone else as well,

YVES

I won't ask about the job, because it would just be politeness . . .

As soon as I reached Algiers, I wrote to Simone. She answered, but the mails were too unreliable for us to have a real correspondence. By now I was dying to get back, to finish the jc and get back to her. The tour I had asked for seemed endless. (Between Algiers and Tunis, a sandstorm forced our plane back the airport, and we had to land again and sleep in the plane unt the storm ended.)

> After that, things moved swiftly. I got back to Paris. A week later, Simone moved in with me on the rue de Longchamp. Allégret agreed to let her take Catherine and begin divorce proceedings herself. We started to live together. For life. For good.

A divorcée in 1950 was far from being a rarity, but Signoret could certainly seem a contradiction in a country that was Catholic and birthrate-conscious, where matrimonial stability was seen as a key to the reconstruction of France. Even the Communists preached this message. Divorce, yes; but only if you were the injured party, not the unfaithful one. Nevertheless, and despite the "scandal," Simone Signoret became a symbol in the eyes of many of her fellow citizens, particularly women. She was beautiful, well educated, a mother, a wife; she was a towering figure in her profession, but she had refused to sacrifice her private happiness on the altar of success.

For the next thirty-five years, no couple's opinion was sought after by the French press and public opinion more than Montand-Signoret's. From the right-wing *Le Pèlerin* to the Communist *L'Humanité,* they were asked about passion and reason, about fidelity and freedom of choice, about jealousy, money, and aging, about professional obligations and parental responsibility, about public commitment and private life. They gave detailed, honest answers, probably flattered at the questions, irritated when the inquiries became indiscreet, and always fully aware of the chasm separating the general and the particular, the tension between personal intimacy and public solidarity.

Their ups and downs only made them more popular. People liked them for loving each other right up to the end, through all their travails. People liked them for continuing to put up with each other despite their differences. People liked them so much that after Simone Signoret's "departure" (which is what their friends called it), Montand felt almost obliged to apologize for going on living, when people didn't realize how much he continued to live with her in the years after she was gone.

A model couple? Definitely not. But decidedly emblematic. Their mishaps, their errors, offer a privileged view of the nature and the underside of a myth.

Catherine Allégret is the first and best witness (and product) of the communal life that now began. "I feel as if I have always known Montand," she says. "I have no childhood memories predating my mother's meeting with him. If I told a psychiatrist that my childhood trauma stemmed from the intrusion of this man into my mother's life, it would be a lie. He must have been extremely nice to me from the start. He has made me laugh more than anyone else in the world. And he's the person I have feared most. I was frightened of his rages—the man should have been baptized Heavy Metal. But the Mama-Montand connection was a natural."

Less natural was the home where the singer and actress began their life as a couple. Like every home, the little apartment on the rue de Longchamp had a memory, and even a record keeper. Montand's housekeeper did not take well to the intrusion of a rival, and she avenged herself by announcing in Simone Signoret's presence that "Mlle Ghislaine" or "Mlle Chantal" had called. "If one is beginning something," the recipient of these shafts soon concluded, "one really should start from scratch." The neighborhood, Neuilly Saint-James, was one of the nicest, but a new love adapts more readily in a new nest.

Even if you were well off (without being rich, without having amassed capital, Montand and Signoret were by now insulated from unexpected difficulties), finding an apartment in Paris in the 1950s was a challenge. Once again, their connections came to the rescue. "My husband and I lived at the Hotel Henri IV on the Place Dauphine," says Colette Crolla. "I was pregnant to the eyeballs, and we urgently needed bigger quarters. One evening someone told us a bookshop was for rent next door to the hotel. We looked at it; it was magnificent but too expensive for us. So we passed the word along to Yves and Simone."

Thus was born the "trailer," a narrow, delightful space running from the quai des Orfèvres to the Place Dauphine, which André Breton, in *Nadja,* calls "one of Paris's shyest neighborhoods." A real square with real trees, where the employees of the national Mint, in blue coveralls, played boules during their noon break, and whose proudly regional restaurants dispensed authentic *andouillette* and Beaujolais Nouveau to the magistrates from the Palais de Justice. Through the workings of love and friendship, Simone was realizing in life a dream, and also a challenge. During her Café Flore days, broke, just starting to do bit parts, she had stood across from the Ile de la Cité between Roger Blin and Fabien Loris, had counted the sixteen buildings bristling on the bow of the island, and told her companions, "One day I'll live there." That day had come.

Only two inches separated the top of Montand's head from the ceiling; the bookshop's tiny office area, on the Place Dauphine side, meant that Catherine would have to make do with a folding bed. The storefront, on the quai side, became a living room with a picture window protected by a few bars (a concession to fame). An upstairs room made a delectable bedroom with a little window overlooking the Seine. Only the cellar was spacious. But to Montand, who had known nothing but furnished rooms and hotels, and whose real-estate ambitions were (and always remained) the least of his cares, it was precisely the close-confined warmth of the place that appealed. They just had room to squeeze the piano through the door to the living room, just had room to fit chairs around a dining table, just had room to separate the working and eating area from the living-room section, with its gray-beige armchairs by the window. But that was what he liked about it.

There was no architect and no decorator. Simone ferreted around, matched furniture, bought pictures by amateurs—it was their freshness she loved—rather than by "name" artists. Even later, the "trailer's" charm stemmed from its lack of a master plan, from the fact that it grew out of progressive layers of sediment rather than from a deliberate design. And from layers of life itself. Gradually, sweet and not-so-sweet memories found their way onto its walls—a kiss at La Colombe, Casque d'Or in all her glory, the defeated, pathetic Madame Rosa, Montand receiving ovations in the Soviet Union or in New York, or else with a noose biting into his neck during the shooting of *The Confession:* images, friendships, regrets, jokes, laughter, the ghostly piled-up bric-a-brac of family life.

It was luxury without ostentation, elegance without pretension, mahogany and fine books without posturing. It was the perfect reflection of the most basic tastes of the Montands for unaffected simplicity, and of the guilty relationship they would always have toward money.

And it was a family circle again. Ivo Livi had grown up with the unity of the clan as an ultimate barrier against poverty, insecurity, and hunger—a unity symbolized by the nightly gathering around the family table. "For Yves," says his brother Julien, "mealtimes were always Marseilles, the family back together again. You left your problems behind when you sat down at the table. It was time, however briefly, for good food and laughter before returning to everyday life."

Simone Kaminker had not inherited this tradition. With her it was fine if lunch was an apple, and the hour was a matter of indifference. But the intensity of her social life gave her a healing substitute for what she had never known in Neuilly: her circle of friends was like a clan at least as strong as her own family. She liked her home to look crowded; she liked people having to squeeze in. Two upper rooms and part of an attic became free and she grabbed them—not in order to have more room to move around in, but to be able to squeeze in more people. Snugly. "Mama had made up her mind to live there, and she was on the lookout for even the smallest cranny to expand into," is how Catherine Allégret sums it up.

Simone Signoret was a sorry housewife but a wonderful hostess. In almost thirty-four years of married life she only once—*once*—cooked dinner for Yves Montand: overdone spaghetti (a rash choice). But she loved entertaining. There had been little enough solidarity in her own home, even though her younger brothers were very dear to her (one of them, Jean-Pierre, lived for a time with his two children on the upper floors at the Place Dauphine). She sensed how much such a feeling of belonging meant to her man, and now she also made ready, in a mood both curious and somewhat intimidated, to be introduced to his family.

Knowing that his sister needed a break, Montand took advantage of a stay at La Colombe to invite her over, and there Lydia and Simone met. Signoret adopted her sister-in-law so readily, and was so eager to become an adoptive member of the family, that she and Lydia joined forces to look for a house that Montand wanted to give his parents. Together they combed the real-estate ads and visited agencies. Finally they found the right place: a modest, comfortable bungalow at La Pounche, in the commune of Allauch. With its peaceful and unassuming setting, it would satisfy the Livis without disrupting their lives.

But the decisive test was meeting the Marseilles clan in force and on its home ground. "Ever since the Flore," admitted Simone Signoret, "I had been living in a leftist milieu and feeling very much at home there, but I had never had any contact with what is called the working class. I really knew it only through what I had read and what people had told me. I was absolutely typical of what is called a leftist intellectual, with all that includes of the ridiculous, but also of the generous. Oddly enough, my first meeting with Montand was also my first incursion into the workingman's world, the proletariat, if not the subproletariat."

Now she was discovering a universe regimented by the gas-factory siren, becoming aware of the smell of the slaughterhouses, savoring the flirtatiousness of Papa Livi and the family's determination to put a good face on things—which was not (or not wholly) affectation so much as a way of asserting the self-respect of the poor. "When Montand took me there, it was the first time in my life that I had sat down at a table among people who had all worked in factories."

Julien did not stay long after lunch that day. Since returning from Germany, he had resumed life as a Party worker. He had quickly risen through the ranks of the Communist-run food-industry union, becoming a permanent member for the Marseilles region, then assistant secretary general. The promotion meant that he had to move permanently to Paris in the summer of 1950. Julien's wife, Elvire, not at all happy at the prospect of leaving the Midi, watched Signoret: "How happy my mother-in-law looked to have this pretty lady at her table, eating her chicken with her little finger in the air! She was so appealing! She hid her shyness under an incredible curiosity; she got as much fun out of listening as talking. When somebody started telling her about himself, she knew everything about him in a couple of hours. If she was embarrassed it didn't show; she asked so many questions, she talked her shyness away, and other people's embarrassment as well."

It was Simone, again, who suggested bringing Elvire and Julien to the Place Dauphine. They were in an unenviable position. Promoted to the national executive of his union, Julien Livi, whose salary as a permanent Party worker was extremely low, found himself hard-pressed to provide for himself what he demanded for the members of his union. "First we lived in an awful hotel at La Grange-aux-Belles," reports Elvire. "Then we managed to trade our Marseilles lodgings for a tiny apartment in Saint-Maur, without utilities, without even a shower. Yves and Simone visited us there after a few months. They were shaken. 'You can't stay here!' said Simone. And that's how we ended up on the sixth floor at the Place Dauphine, in a big room divided in two, with a kitchen, a bathroom, and a view all the way to the Panthéon."

It was not just a temporary rescue. The cell the family now formed would endure for fifteen years. Jean-Louis came to live with his parents (he was five years older than his cousin Catherine, with whom he shared the attic-studio at the very top of the building; when she was a little older, the girl went back downstairs to repossess the microscopic "blue room" at the bottom of the "trailer"). Julien and Elvire left early in the morning, he to union headquarters, she to the offices of the SNECMA aircraft-engine corporation. Jean-Louis attended the Lycée Charlemagne; Catherine, the neighborhood public school. And at dinnertime, as was only fitting, everyone took his place at the family table: Montand at the head, Jean-Louis on his left, Elvire on his right, Simone next to Jean-Louis and opposite Julien. Catherine—until she was old enough to hold her own with the grown-ups—ate in the kitchen with the woman you never, never called the "maid."

The household was run in hit-or-miss fashion. The talents of the cook, Marcelle Mirtilon (she received supplies direct from her husband, Georges, a porter at Les Halles), made every visit worthwhile. But the schedules, temperaments, and professional constraints of the adults made it difficult to organize the children's lives. Signoret tried hiring a nanny, who turned out to be low on zeal, feeding Catherine canned sardines and leaving her out in the rain at the entrance to the Palais de Justice. Three years went by in this way. Then the actress went upstairs to see her sister-in-law. "You have to run my house," she said.

Elvire Livi—whom Catherine called "Auntie" and whom Signoret herself had appointed the girl's second mother—thought for a while, then left SNECMA and took on the management of the "kibbutz." She handled the household budget, changed the flowers every Tuesday, sorted the mail and answered fan mail (as well as insulting letters), took phone messages, looked after Catherine whenever a tour, a shoot, or a concert came up (in other words, all the time), and watched like a hawk over Montand's diet whenever he was in training for a new commitment.

Much laughter, much love, much work. The ark on the island seemed safe, warm, and sturdy.

For thirty months after Signoret's decision to share Yves Montand's life, her movie career experienced a marked lull. Apart from two short but dazzling appearances in Max Ophuls's *La Ronde* (with Serge Reggiani in the opening sketch and Gérard Philipe in the final scene, in which she played . . . a prostitute), she made only second-rate movies (*Le Traqué, Ombre et lumière*). Yet no one had ever suspected her of lacking professional drive. The truth is, her new role as a Montand "groupie" (the television director Jean-Christophe Averty called her this later, using a then-fashionable label) took up almost all her time.

It was only half true to ascribe the temporary lack of ambition to passion. She went everywhere with Montand because she loved him madly, but also because she was utterly fascinated by his work. Like many actors who had worked only on movie sets, she was awed by the immediacy and fragility of the relationship between a music-hall entertainer and his audience. Other kinds of fears and enthusiasms are born on movie sets, but that straight shot to the heart, that physical embrace, that unique self-exposure are without equivalent, except perhaps during sex. From their first meeting at Saint-Paul-de-Vence, from that first evening at the Verdure theater in Nice, Signoret entered the dream world of all who have shared, however superficially, the appalling stage fright of the performer who goes on without a safety net.

Simone Signoret possessed one most unusual characteristic: she derived as much satisfaction from admiring as from being admired—a state of mind that was not without aristocratic overtones (after all, they were an elite) and that endured. Even in nightclubs, where the exercise was notably less spectacular than in the music hall, she fulfilled her groupie role with unfailing radiance. Everything amused her, everything alarmed her.

She adopted a respectful tone to describe the ritual that preceded Montand's going on stage: the slow detachment from reality, then the period of concentration, the essential parenthesis inserted between real time and performance time. In Japanese Noh theater, by early morning actors are in the space where they will perform that night. Montand would have been happy to emulate them. "If the curtain goes up at nine, he gets [to the theater] at seven," said Simone Signoret. "But already at six, wherever he may be, he isn't where he is. He's somewhere else, and he's alone. At first that was quite hard to understand. It was as though he had suddenly left me. He was there, but he had left me. It took a little while before I realized that from six o'clock on, I wasn't supposed to talk. I was supposed to be available, invisible, and especially I wasn't supposed to be elsewhere."

Then came what she likened to the moment before a bullfight when the picadors visit the torero: the moment when the musicians came to salute their "boss." At this juncture he was a solitary species doomed to lead them out with "nothing in my hands, nothing in my pockets" (the refrain of a new song), and weather the shock of the first contact with the audience. They joked fleetingly, briefly, unemphatically. Montand warmed up his voice with Crolla: before the curtain rose, the guitarist-friend was much more than a brilliant technician; he was a talisman whose presence meant that everything would be fine. Never did Montand go out to meet the crowd without first quickly patting Crolla's head in a near-superstitious gesture.

Simone knew she had to keep away, staying within reach but at a distance. So as to leave the experts in peace, of course. But also for another, more complex reason: Montand had by now reached the point where he was no longer one person but someone obsessed by the bizarre cohabitation within him of "I" and "he." Three decades later, Jorge Semprun, following Montand at the Olympia, and then on his international tour, made the same observation: "Sometimes he would speak directly to himself, addressing himself in the third person: '*He* slipped up there,' or '*He* jumped the gun there.' Or any other critical comment on his own performance of the night before. But invariably, it would be in the third person. As if, upon becoming himself again—'I,' Montand—the only part of himself he could grasp was this third person, removed both emotionally and in time. *He* comes in from here, *he* stops there, *he* moves over to the right."[6] A music-hall artist—or, in any case, Montand the artist, the entertainer who stages his own scenes—no longer belongs to himself. Or, more accurately, he can retain control over who he is only by splitting off from himself.

A few newsreel sequences (notably a Soviet documentary made in 1956) show Simone Signoret kissing her husband a split second before the curtain rises or watching him from the wings—touching but inaccurate images. As a rule, once the show was in progress, Montand preferred his friends to leave the backstage area and join the audience. In fact, those close to him noticed that just as he took the plunge, he would make a

6. Jorge Semprun, *Montand: La Vie continue* (Paris, 1983).

sideways gesture of farewell that was addressed to nobody in particular, neither the technicians nor the dresser, but which probably helped him tear himself away, to pivot and face the waiting monster. Knowing there were friendly faces out there—their exact locations were unimportant—had a beneficial effect on his perception of the monster, not taming it, perhaps, but reducing it to manageable proportions. The barrier of the footlights is so stark that this reassurance was only an inward one: all Montand ever noticed in the auditorium were tiny, untoward events: an usherette opening a door in the rear, an irritating cougher. But if he were to tame the beast—and he was there to do just that—the support of his invisible allies was an enormous asset.

When the encores ended, the "groupie's" job was still not done. Her idol relaxed, drew a deep breath, luxuriated in the softness of his bathrobe after the stiffness of his stage clothes. But he still had to return slowly, by stages, to dry land.

Signoret recalled questioning Jacques Brel on this point. She and Montand both loved Brel. He had often visited the Place Dauphine in the days when the Paris glitterati mocked his Belgian accent and his rumpled, choirboy look; Montand had to work hard to champion a fine Brel song, "Voir." (In a letter to his wife, Brel attested to Montand's considerable influence upon him: "No one else will ever be able to put over a song the way he does. . . . It convinced me to write some poems and recite them without a guitar."[7] "Le Grand Jacques," who went on to conquer audiences three hundred nights a year, defined the ideal stage companion: "She should be there before he goes on stage, but she shouldn't be visible; she should be in the audience during the performance, and she should be there at the end, but she should disappear the moment people start arriving in the dressing room; she should go home very quickly and prepare dinner, and be on the threshold when her guy arrives, saying 'Bravo, bravo! You were even better than you were yesterday!' " Brel addded that no such woman existed. Simone Signoret agreed but thought she came "halfway" to being that woman. Her husband considered that she had come all the way.

Being behind the scenes in music hall was a whole adventure for Simone. She had never been on a theatrical tour and found it fun and exciting to dash from city to city, rebuilding one's nest every night. You land in a nondescript hotel room with a flowered bedspread, one bedside light not working, the plumbing in the tiny bathroom gurgling all night. You pull out your toiletries and

7. Quoted in Olivier Todd, *Jacques Brel: Une Vie* (Paris, 1984).

bathrobe right away just to make the place your own, to make this particular city be the city you'll be singing in. You have dinner in an unfamiliar bistro. Not until after the show have you really conquered the place. Then you know that your toothbrush is waiting for you back at the hotel. Tours are tiring, but when you're young—and we were—they're fun.

What was wonderful at night was that I no longer returned to an empty nest. It took me by surprise each time—surprise at the joy of being with someone who laughed with me and cried with me. Because I made her cry, too; I used to bawl out Simone terribly, asking for a yes or a no, and like all performers I was cruel, given to unjust fits of anger that helped me get rid of my anxiety.

I don't remember who said, "Women are loving, men are solitary: together they rob each other of both love and solitude." That yearning for solitude initially pushed me away from Simone, even though I was in love. I believe it was an unconscious wish to hold on to the sadness that tears me down but perhaps also helps me to sing.

And then I saw that happiness gives you strength, that it was wonderful to sing a song she liked, to feel, as I sang, what she was feeling as she listened. I kept telling her I wanted to succeed in movies. She told me I was wrong, that in the theater I was dependent on no one but myself and my audience, that I needed neither director nor scriptwriter, and that *that* was what was fabulous. I dug my heels in; so did she. We squabbled about it for hours, for days.

She didn't stay backstage when I was singing. I don't like people who are close to me to stand in the wings. It bothers me. The stage is a ship that belongs to the show, the audience; there shouldn't be anyone weighing it down. At the start of every performance I took off my wedding ring. But knowing Simone was in the audience was total joy—a joy that bore me aloft.

The conflicting pulls of solitude and happiness yielded the most bountiful of harvests. Starting on Monday, March 5, 1951, Yves Montand booked the Etoile for his first completely one-man show. No more jugglers or acrobats, no announcers or guest artists. With a repertory of twenty-two songs and two poems, he shouldered all the risks himself.

He was alone on the billing, and he had evolved a way of being more alone on stage than he had ever been before. He remembered the way Piaf, back in the summer of 1945 at the Moulin Rouge, had moved Claude

Normand's orchestra behind her so that there would be no sound wall between her and the audience. Montand used the same technique but added another touch: between himself and his quintet he hung a sea-green scrim that left the players free to accompany him flawlessly but without a single visible move to distract the audience. Some complained that he was hiding his colleagues (whom he always announced by name). But Montand, with Castella's backing, resisted all pressure: his show was as much a visual as an aural one; the new setup increased its effectiveness. And since then, the use of such screens has become widespread.

"I believe I've perfected the formula, at least for me," Montand told a reporter from *France-Soir* on March 1, just before the final dress rehearsal. "What is that?" he was asked. "No more blahblahblah. Songs." More than a hundred performances later, on June 29, just before the final curtain, he put it this way to a reporter from *Ce Soir:* "It's the words that interest me most in a song. It's the words I work hardest on." The press noted that when he decided to end the run, the box office was still under siege, with seventeen hundred people packing themselves in for each performance. On June 27, fans mobbed the box office for a last chance at applauding the hero of the season.

Montand's concert was a success from the very first night. Every major name in theater, movies, and music hall was there: Georges Auric, Jacques Becker, Bernard Blier, Martine Carol, Marie Daems, Henri Decoin, Suzy Delair, Danièle Delorme, Jean Gabin, Odette Joyeux, Paul Meurisse, François Périer, Madeleine Sologne, Erich von Stroheim. As Montand would remember, these fashionable appearances, these marks of encouragement, many of them insincere, both moved and embarrassed him. Of course, he was flattered at the recognition, touched that his friends had taken the trouble to come: he was moved to see Edith Piaf in the third row between Eddie Constantine and Charles Aznavour. But he hated having to begin. What he was greedily looking forward to was the inner signal that would come through after five or six performances, telling him that fear was on the retreat, that the show was holding up, that he would now be able to liberate his own real pleasure in performing.

As usual, he scanned the reviews like a hawk, alert for criticism that might trigger some new approach or rectify a fault. But this time there was a wall-to-wall red carpet, showerings of bouquets. He was unanimously hailed as "number one among popular singers," "modern," "human," "athletic," "serious," and "funny" all at the same time. Too serious, said some. The few reservations harped on this point, and were not without ideological motives. "Unfortunately," complained *L'Aurore* on March 13, "the amusing Montand is also the deadly enemy of the Montand who sometimes takes himself too seriously as he trots out his boring message."

"A pity we don't occasionally glimpse a patch of blue sky above these dark streets, a pity the entertainer too often gives himself the airs of a false messiah," declared *La Croix* three days later.

Such thrusts were aimed at the "red" Ivo Livi and reflected the irritation among some Frenchmen at the growing influence of left-wingers in the country's cultural pastures. This was the year that Gérard Philipe played *Le Cid* at the Avignon festival, Jean Vilar was named director of the Théâtre National Populaire, Hubert Beuve-Méry, founder of the newspaper *Le Monde,* defeated his right-wing adversaries on the paper's board, and Sartre brought out *Le Diable et le bon dieu.*

Nevertheless, the complaints were not unfounded. Just as he switched from light to strong songs, Yves Montand blended genres and moods. The format of the one-man show freed him to go further into the pink register and further into the black one. Along with Kosma's "Dis-moi, Joe" (music by Henri Crolla), Francis Lemarque's "Le Cornet de frites," next to "Clémentine" and "her well-behaved little breasts," he ran the alarming "Actualités" ("Newsflash"), by Albert Vidalie and Stéphane Goldmann: "One hundred miners groan beneath a continent, above them a regiment is on the march, there will be ten survivors. . . ."

The Prévert gamble was already won. "Les Feuilles mortes," "Les Enfants qui s'aiment," and "Le Petit Cireur de souliers de Broadway" were requested every evening. This was one more reason, Montand believed, for exploiting victory. The previous year, "Barbara" had won the Grand Prix du Disque and cemented the popularity of the Prévert-Kosma duo. Little by little, other singers—Marianne Oswald, Yves Robert (at the Rose Rouge), Cora Vaucaire, Juliette Gréco, Les Frères Jacques—as well as Montand were attuning the public's ear to these unrhyming rhymes and arhythmic rhythms.

But, typically, Montand sought a new way of interpreting "Barbara," now that it was an undisputed hit. He began to feel that the poem was too softened by Kosma's music. He decided simply to recite it, without a single note of accompaniment. He also recited "Le Peintre, la pomme et Picasso," a drama in miniature. The practice was common in cabarets and nightclubs, but unheard-of before thousands of people in a music hall.

Montand made no attempt to hide what determined his choice of songs. In interviews (in *Le Figaro,* and particularly in *L'Humanité* on December 16, 1951) he delivered a simple message: a good song, a popular song, can and should pull in the whole audience, whatever the listeners' different origins. The mistake was to draw a border between the two banks of the Seine, to establish a poetic pecking order, to address this or that song to different sections of the audience—Prévert to the orchestra and "C'est si bon" to the balcony. Even though he shared the just cause of the wretched of the earth with his Communist, trade-union brother and acknowledged the need for violent emancipation, the "singing prole" instinctively maintained a standard of beauty that transcended class. The beautiful was neither "bourgeois" nor "petty bourgeois" nor "proletarian." The beautiful was subversive because it was beautiful; it belonged to everyone, provided it was offered for the judgment of everyone.

The 1951 show was a milestone in Montand's career, and not just because it ushered in an illustrious series of standing room–only concerts. For the first time, Montand the singer was completely himself. He had discovered the right distance. He never again performed as part of a show. He had put together a group of musicians who played jazz the way he liked it. He had built an extended repertory, thanks to his collaborators' and his own talent at shifting from one category to another. He fed on outside influences, then weaned himself of them. He had everything. What more could he want?

Chapter 9

Montand still dreamed of breaking into the movies. But having made his mark behind the footlights, he was determined never again to endure the humiliation of being treated like a clumsy novice. Simone Signoret helped him to understand why he found it so difficult to switch from one medium to the other. First, in the legitimate theater and before the cameras, you never get inside a role: it's the character you are playing who takes you over, steals your body, your brain, your worries; it's the role that gets inside you. Being a music-hall artist, she told him, is the opposite: it means being yourself, coming on stage in your own special costume, singing your own songs, backed by musicians you know and trust, and having your own lighting technician. Having the guts to entertain, to move and win over an audience that is there to see you being *you.*

Montand had taken no risks in the movie world since meeting Simone. He had accepted a couple of singing appearances in low-budget movies (*Paris chante toujours* and *Paris sera toujours Paris*) and had acquitted himself well in a sketch in a harmless little film, *Souvenirs perdus,* made in 1950 by Christian-Jaque, the director of *Les Disparus de Saint-Agil* and *Fanfan la Tulipe.* Playing a street singer who supplants Bernard Blier in the affections of an amorous widow, and accompanied by Crolla, he sang "Tournesol," a charming song by Jacques Prévert. It had been fun. Christian-Jaque congratulated himself on acquiring "this actor nobody wanted" for his movie. "Where did directors get the idea that a man who can do what Montand does on stage would be bad on screen? He was splendid in the sketch I gave him. I'm convinced that the first people who directed him simply went about it the wrong way."

This was good to hear, but not good enough to negate the bad memories of earlier experiences. Then Montand was approached by Henri-Georges Clouzot. Just back from Latin America, Clouzot wanted to adapt for the screen a novel by Georges Arnaud, *Le Salaire de la peur* (*The Wages of Fear*), about a quartet of down-and-outs, half hoodlum, half bum, stranded and broke in an imaginary Guatemala. Beaten down by poverty and tropical heat, they agree to drive two trucks loaded with nitroglycerine to a blazing oil gusher; the nitroglycerine is meant to extinguish the flames with its blast—unless it extinguishes the truck drivers first. Clouzot was eager for Montand—the muscular, physical Montand, the man who had once hammered sheet metal at the Provence shipyards—to play Mario, the youngest of the four drivers.

Montand turned him down flat. He knew Clouzot's reputation: a tough director who bullied his actors, a right-winger, a close friend of Pierre Fresnay, a professional with impressive credentials (*L'Assassin habite au 21* and *Le Corbeau*) but a tyrant on the set. Montand explained his refusal as honestly as he could, saying that he was not yet ready to take on such a heavy responsibility, that he could not accept a commitment sight unseen and run the risk of appearing mediocre or inconsistent.

Clouzot had anticipated this refusal. Buttressed by his wife, the irritating, capricious, but persuasive Brazilian actress Vera, also a leading player in the movie, he laid siege to the "trailer." To Montand he stressed the power of the story, the violence of the social climate it portrayed, the tautness of the script. Montand and Signoret had visited Rio and seen its teeming hillside slums called *favelas,* and soon Montand began to weaken, resisting with dwindling energy, and finally admitting what was paralyzing him: he was afraid of *The Wages of Fear,* afraid of acting poorly, afraid of having to banish his stage persona, afraid he would be unable to achieve the split personality that theater people talked about so much.

Clouzot stuck to his guns. Why not make a test, he suggested. He sensed that Montand was now hungry for the role and that a satisfactory test would win him over. Montand was in the middle of an engagement at the Etoile. The Clouzots and the Montands moved out to an inn owned by Montand's friend Carrère at La Moutière, not far from Paris, and the singer steeled himself for an expected ordeal of daily auditions. Wisely, Clouzot handed him a script as far removed as possible from what came naturally to him—Anouilh's *Le Rendezvous de Senlis*—and asked him to work on it, like any first-year student at drama school. Montand floundered but dug in. His moods swung wildly; he considered giving up. And then, suddenly, it clicked—"it" being the ability to move, think, and speak like someone else. Once this barrier was crossed, the two men settled down to a painstaking technical examination of speech problems, timing, blocking. For Montand, this was unprecedented: he was back at school of his own free will and putting his trust in someone other than himself.

After Montand's final performance at the Etoile, Clouzot never left his side. He followed his pupil to Saint-Paul-de-Vence and became a regular at the Colombe d'Or, all the while continuing to work out the final arrangements for his movie.

"We'll shoot it in Spain," he told Montand.

"In Spain? Not a chance! Count me out."

"Just who do you think you are, so high and mighty?" bellowed Clouzot.

Signoret came to the rescue: as long as Franco was alive, neither she nor her husband would cross the Pyrenees, she explained. Clouzot cursed, sighed, tried every tactic he could think of. He knew that ever since the crushing of the Spanish Popular Front, every left-wing intellectual had a reproduction of *Guernica* in his living room and believed that a stubbornly maintained boycott would eventually undermine Western Europe's last surviving Fascist dictatorship. And with his own wife lined up against him, Clouzot had no choice but to yield. "You win, *compañero,* you win," he said with a sigh a few days later.

So it was finally in France—near Saint-Gilles, in the Camargue—that they built from scratch the village of San Piedras: a hodgepodge of ramshackle huts huddled around a dingy church and graveyard, a factory, and a café. Only the mosquitoes were real. With the help of a little concrete and whitewash, some metallic cutouts designed to replicate Guatemalan vegetation, and sun-browned extras hired in Marseilles, the set designer, René Roux, managed to create a convincing Central American no-man's-land. The proximity of Nîmes, sixteen miles away, made it easier to house the crew, and it was planned to film the sequences showing the trucks moving through the mountains on roads in the Cévennes, near Anduze (where the local attraction turned out, providentially, to be an exotic grove of authentic giant bamboos).

The down-and-outs in *The Wages of Fear* might have hailed from anywhere. In casting them, Clouzot was determined to blur their national origins so that moviegoers would be as confused as the characters themselves about where they came from. Mario, Corsican for the purposes of the script, would be driving one of the trucks with Jo, a gangster godfather who initially impresses and intimidates him but who falls apart as the drive wears on. The drivers of the second truck were a German (played by Peter Van Eyck) and an Italian (the rotund and expressive Folco Lulli). Clouzot had asked Jean Gabin to play Jo, but he refused: Gabin was reluctant to take on the part of an aging fraud, a pathetic old coward—it was not positive enough, not macho enough. After a few tests, the part was offered to Charles Vanel, who was delighted with the windfall: the antihero role interested him far more than an umpteenth resurrection of the stock adventure parts he had played during his incredible thirty-year career. Vanel, who was over sixty, had first appeared on the screen in 1912, in a silent short called *Jim Crow.* He was still in demand, but it had been years since he had been seen in an above-average movie, and his career had been in decline for a decade.

Often, movie actors cannot or will not discuss exactly how they do their work. It is at once too dislocated, too confusing (only during editing does the jigsaw begin to yield its secrets), too emotional, and too firmly situated in a time frame that is ephemeral and meaningless to an outsider. To help promote a film, everyone will say that everything has been "wonderful" and that everyone owes everything to everyone else. Two or three carefully rehearsed anecdotes add spice to the account. Montand always loathed this whole charade.

Nevertheless, the story of the filming of *The Wages of Fear* deserves to be retold, because it was truly colorful, and because, for the first time, Montand felt like one of a group—a member in good standing of a substantial, going concern. The budget for *Les Portes de la nuit* had undoubtedly been just as big, but Carné had lacked the time and perhaps even the desire to explore the terrain beforehand with actors hired at the last minute. As a result, Montand had been lost from the start. "With *Wages,*" he said, when the movie was released, "things were completely different. First of all—and this was obviously of the greatest importance—I didn't feel as if I were suffocating within my role. And then, I had had the time and the opportunity to think about acting for the screen."[1]

Judging by the account in Signoret's memoirs, the first phase of operations, which opened on August 27, 1951, was a healthy, good-natured romp, and the atmosphere was festive: evenings at the Hôtel du Midi in Nîmes (she rechristened it the Hôtel Toto, after the name of its owner) were lively from the first night. To amuse himself, Clouzot decided to provoke Signoret by launching into a long and tearful panegyric of what he called the "poet and martyr" René Brasillach, a notorious right-wing collaborationist. The Pasionaria of the Café Flore immediately struck back, and then, to Clouzot's huge delight, voices steadily rose. Vanel and Montand, feigning a drunken quarrel, suddenly exploded.

"I've made a hundred movies, and I have no intention of taking advice from a song-and-dance man!" yelled the veteran.

"And I can't stand the sight of silent-movie stars!" the hoofer roared back.

Under the appalled eyes of the innkeeper, who believed his own

1. Interview with José Zendel, *Les Lettres Françaises,* February 26, 1953.

dinnerware was being destroyed, they rose and shattered a dozen plates (bought in the market that morning), the crash of crockery punctuating the angry shouts.

Later, Montand was overcome by an urge to do mischief at the sight of a flock of pilgrims on their way to Lourdes, Nîmes being the last stop on their journey before reaching the sacred grotto. The heady aura of sanctity they gave off awoke the prankster who was never far below the surface, and one evening he succumbed. Wearing a beret and a pair of extra-short shorts, carrying a small bucket and a spade, he went down to the lobby and began to scrape among the potted plants, digging here and watering there and mumbling snatches of threats and obscenities—the living image not of a peaceful simpleton but of one of those truly alarming village idiots, at the sight of whom the most charitable of souls crosses the road in sheepish retreat.

Vanel has described another instance of Montand's penchant for playing practical jokes on a shoot: "One day, he started to shiver and rave. . . . At once, the rumor spread that he was suffering from sunstroke or had swamp fever. 'But we're not in Guatemala here!' said Clouzot. 'This is the south of France!' Everything quickly gained enormous momentum: Montand capered through our poor little movie-set village like a madman, firing shots into the air. Dario Marino rushed in, blood all over his hand, yelling, 'He shot me, he'll kill us all!' And I said to Clouzot, 'We can't go on filming with this guy, he's crazy!' "[2] Only when Marino washed off the "blood" he had borrowed from the makeup crew did Clouzot realize that the set was not doomed to instant destruction.

But making *The Wages of Fear* was, in fact, a painful experience. The first problems lay in the directorial methods dear to Clouzot. His reputation had not been exaggerated: he was a martinet, a relentless taskmaster, an exquisite torturer. According to legend, he once slapped the face of Bernard Blier to "liberate" his anger, to provoke the reaction he was after.

On the very first day, Vanel, no greenhorn, saw which way the wind was blowing and confronted him: "Listen, Clouzot, you might as well find a replacement. We're not going to get along!"

"You want to leave? Fuck off, then!"[3]

Vanel was battle-hardened enough to be able to put his contract on the line, but Montand, on frailer foundations, was in a more dangerous position. He was likely to crack Clouzot's skull if the director insulted him, but professionally speaking, he was on shaky ground. Fortune had decreed that the two major challenges he had met in his efforts to become a movie star

2. Jacqueline Cartier, *Monsieur Vanel* (Paris, 1989).

3. Ibid.

were with two notorious tyrants—exactly the kind of people he would never bow to. What kept him going was the preparation he and Clouzot had lived through together, the personal link they had forged. This relative intimacy helped him to develop defenses: whenever Clouzot roared, which was often, Montand gave him a warm, trusting smile and waited for the storm to pass. A truly creative performance!

Another factor that helped was his growing understanding of the maestro's technique and objectives. Just when everything looked right on paper, it would fall apart on the set. An actor was required to play the scene with his back to the camera? Result: the mood evaporated—all you saw was a nondescript man climbing out of a nondescript truck. So the props department would add a sheet-metal palm tree in the distance. "Okay by me," said the cameraman. But when they showed the rushes (Clouzot insisted on bringing the hotelkeeper along as an unwitting guinea pig), the picture was flat and dull: the camera had erased all the distances. Disaster. Clouzot had planned that in the scene with the out-of-control gusher, the blowers would belch flames fifty yards in the air; but they broke down. Disaster. Fascinated, burning with curiosity, respectful of this tyrant, at the mercy of every passing cloudburst, Montand, stifling his urge to rebel and moving far beyond what was required of him professionally, explored the colossal but fragile machinery of moviemaking.

Vanel and Montand were subjected to the most awful circumstances. Submerged in a pool of crude oil and exposed to gas fumes, they contracted conjunctivitis. But oil was not their greatest enemy. Worse was inundation of the purest kind: a deluge of rainwater. The Nîmes area had been chosen for its vegetation and rock formations, as well as because it supposedly offered the best chances for prolonged sunshine. But 1951 proved to be an exceptional year. For nearly a scriptural forty days and forty nights, it rained, the wind moaned, sun and moon remained hidden, the sets sagged and their colors ran, vehicles bogged down, cranes toppled. Extras, actors, and crew huddled in the hotel scanning the skies for a break in the weather.

They had planned to shoot for nine weeks, until the end of October. November came, and the key sequences showing the trucks on their trip were still to be tackled. Week after week, the production floundered—and was postponed. The budget was in ruins. Vera Clouzot fell ill. The director himself broke his ankle. By the end of November, the situation was catastrophic: the days were now disastrously short, it had not stopped raining, and the movie was 50 million francs in the red. There was nothing to do but to give up and have everyone go their separate ways. Six months later, they started up production again under more beneficent skies. The second half of the script, trucking the nitroglycerine into the oil field, shot in the

Gardon valley, took the whole summer of 1952. "Over budget" was an understatement. Everything had doubled: costs, deadline, blood and sweat.

And yet . . . at the 1953 Cannes Film Festival, *The Wages of Fear* won the Grand Prix, Vanel carried off the award for best actor; the movie played to packed houses; foreign audiences were enthusiastic. Some reviewers reproached Clouzot for spinning out the story (the movie lasts 155 minutes), for his almost sadistic assault on moviegoers' nerves, for his deliberate stress on evil. But floods of praise and tributes to the effectiveness of his direction washed such reservations aside. Vanel, it was said, had been given the best role of his career and Montand his first real part.

On this last point, the critics were unanimous. "Difficult though it is to accept Charles Vanel as the weakling and Yves Montand as the strong partner, the director's touch is so masterly that he manages to put every paradox across," wrote Georges Charensol in *Les Nouvelles Littéraires* on April 30. André Bazin, writing in *Le Parisien Libéré* on May 4, felt that Clouzot had "failed to define the character" of Mario as sharply as that of Jo, the phony godfather. But most observers agreed with the critic of the *Franc-Tireur,* that the movie was "unsqueamish, unadorned, unsentimental," and that Montand had managed to transpose to the screen some of the exceptional presence he generated behind the footlights.

Was *The Wages of Fear* the "very great movie" that Simone Signoret called it in her memoirs? (Signoret, incidentally, would join forces with Vanel under Clouzot's direction for *Les Diaboliques.*) In retrospect, its virtues endure and its faults leap out. Though the suspense has lost none of its bite, visually and verbally it is heavily dated. The role of the brawny truck driver Mario undoubtedly lacks human depth: once again, Montand had been locked into the stereotype of the brave and impulsive workingman. It is hardly surprising that Montand would later insist his real movie career did not begin until *Compartiment tueurs* (*The Sleeping Car Murders*) in 1965. But he acknowledged a heavy debt to Clouzot. Thanks to him, Montand was now identified with an international hit that opened both studio doors and moviegoers' hearts, and he had taken his first practical steps into an exploration of the real meaning of acting.

In September 1951, at the "Hôtel Toto," Montand and Signoret experienced an ordeal that seemed tragicomic at the time but was pregnant with consequences. Simone had earlier agreed to play alongside her friends Serge Reggiani, Claude Dauphin, Loleh Bellon, and Raymond Bussières in the film that her friend Jacques Becker was making, *Casque d'Or,* and the hour had now come for her to join all these friends. A sleeping berth awaited her aboard the train taking her north from Nîmes to Annet-sur-Marne, where the exteriors were being shot. Just as she was boarding the train, she begged off. It took all Becker's subtlety ("You're right, love is something that has to be tended like a plant, we'll just replace you . . . ") for pride to win out over passion—and that only after thirty-six hours of hesitation. Rather than lose the man she loved, Simone Signoret almost abandoned the role that she herself and countless movie lovers were to consider the best of her career—that of Marie, the fatal seductress of Manda, played by Reggiani.

This separation, the first in two years, was viewed by Montand and Signoret as an unkind shaft of fate, of the harsh rules of their profession. Each weekend, from Saturday night to Monday morning, they would rush into each other's arms—with such haste that they once missed each other, crossing paths, with him in a car and her on a train, each hoping to surprise the other at journey's end.

Serge Reggiani recalls that Signoret, while flawlessly behaved on the set, forgot absolutely everything off it: "For the opening and closing sequences of *Casque d'Or* we were supposed to waltz, but Simone couldn't waltz. Instead of learning, which would have been relatively easy, she would rush off to see Montand and come back just as clumsy as when she had left. I finally had to carry her—her long dress hid her feet—through the shooting."

Signoret and Montand were inseparable, and the passion that tied them seemed strong enough to need no social sanction. They considered marriage rather "bourgeois," and had it not been for Catherine, who would otherwise have found herself in an uncomfortable position, they would have left things as they were.

But since they were doing it, they might as well do it in style. At the stroke of 11:00 a.m. on December 21, 1951, Ivo Livi and Simone Kaminker exchanged the ritual vows at the Saint-Paul-de-Vence town hall, in the basement of the fortress. Mayor Marius Issert graced the ceremony with a brief address (under the enamel plaque created by the painter Borsi, also among the guests): "I thank you," he said, "for the honor you do our little village." Never had the cramped citadel, squeezed in between the smithy and the graveyard on the rocky spine overlooking the Mal-Vent valley, played host to such battalions of reporters and photographers.

The atmosphere was festive. Simone Signoret wore an old cream silk Balmain suit under a mink coat; she pinned up her blond hair under a black hat and wore a gold-and-diamond collar. Montand had chosen a blue serge suit. The tambourine players were late; so were Marcel and Jacqueline Pagnol; but the procession moved off in time in the direction of the Colombe d'Or, where the table had been set up in the bar. The two witnesses, Jacques Prévert for the bride (a poppy in his buttonhole), Paul Roux for the groom, followed the couple out under a shower of rose petals and a blunderbuss salvo from the local hunters federation.

The reporter from the regional Communist daily, *La Marseillaise,* in the issue of December 23, sounded a lyrical note: "It was the great friend of the workingman who walked with springy stride down the narrow streets of Saint-Paul-de-Vence. A wholesome couple marching into the future. I could almost hear Yves saying once again to the woman who was about to become his wife, 'I shall try to relive through my songs the road already traveled by the people from whom I spring!' "

True to their natures, Signoret and Montand had managed to combine chic with modest sobriety. The guests were not really just anybody: apart from those already mentioned, the actress Deanna Durbin and the poet André Verdet were in the party, there as "neighbors." It was also as "a neighbor" that Pablo Picasso sent the newlyweds one of his ceramics and a good-luck message drawn with instruments then unknown in France, felt-tip pens. The menu (*pissaladière,* chicken with tomatoes, plus flambéed snipe shot the day before by Montand) was robust and rustic; the wedding cake was "sculpted" by Paul Roux himself.

It was a lovely day—a dove flew in through the dining-room window and settled above Simone's head, wings folded like Picasso's famous dove of peace—but it changed nothing. After two weeks' vacation, Montand left on a tour. He performed in suburban Paris in February, then went on to Switzerland and Belgium, Signoret in tow.

In Brussels they went together to the press preview of *Casque d'Or,* on the Place de Brouckère. Montand had never seen Simone look so beautiful on the screen. He was proud of her—proud that this woman was his. Alas, the audience was clearly bored. After four days, the movie was withdrawn from the theaters. And the Brussels test turned out to be premonitory, for the Paris reception was no less cool. Signoret was given relatively mild treatment by the reviewers, but they assassinated Becker, pronouncing him guilty of a frivolous story line and hamfisted direction (*Les Cahiers du Cinéma* led the pack), and they buried Reggiani.

There is not a movie lover alive today who would not declare *Casque d'Or* a masterpiece. If anyone still believes that judicial error is less implacable in the world of the arts than in the law courts, he would do well to remember that after this film, Serge Reggiani didn't get a movie job for five years. He caught up with his theater work while in the film studios the rumor spread that he was "jinxed." One is unlikely to understand much about the strangeness of artists if one does not take into account the kinds of false death to which they are sometimes consigned.

Although Becker's movie enjoyed a different fate in Germany, and then in Italy (and the English valued it to the point of giving Reggiani the British Film Academy award), the infamy was more than Signoret could swallow. She announced to the press that she was leaving the screen.

The news of her departure gripped France. How fine, how noble! A star, one of the best of the best, renouncing the false glitter of fame for the quiet life of a "normal" spouse, and declaring herself happy to do so! Thoroughly modern Simone, so much the mistress of her movie roles, preferring to be her husband's mistress! The chorus of approval was deafening. And the heroine briefly reveled in the giddy intoxication of making a dramatic break.

It was not the spirit of sacrifice that intoxicated her. First of all, she truly, naturally, and unaffectedly relished the peace of retirement: knitting, chatting with friends, the warmth of evenings spent with Montand. And she liked being perceived as a model, she liked their marriage to be the object of attention and emulation, she liked the meaning of their deeds to be commented on—as long as their meaning was clear to her as well.

Signoret was thus the most effective shaper of her own legend. "I'm convinced that we are all fashioned by one another," she wrote. "Even the opinions we decide on throughout our existence are always caused by someone else; a chance encounter, or perhaps because you'd like to be esteemed by certain people." Not only was the actress Signoret conscious of the gaze of others, but the private Signoret felt the need and the duty to move under a gaze infinitely sharper than those of Saturday-night audiences. Simone needed a public: although she had deprived herself of one, she knew that another would not be lacking.

Montand was deeply in love, but he was a little startled by his wife's ability to throw off her commitments overnight. He was incapable of going three months without an engagement. After the wedding, he treated himself to only a two-week break before going off on tour; he took another ten-day breather, finished *The Wages of Fear,* took off another week, left on another tour, worked on his next concert, accepted a small part between two long-term appearances, raced down to Cannes, and so on. He abhorred a vacuum. Not until 1989 would he live through months on end without any real deadlines, letting himself drift, giving himself time to live, as Signoret had done. And even during this "vacation," he fought against the pleasure of having no burdens.

So the period in which the heroine of *Casque d'Or* decided to go on leave was highly instructive for Montand. It revealed the outright conflicts between them, the diametric oppositions that sparked countless altercations, rages, jousts, quarrels. They loved each other passionately, but this had little effect on their shouting matches.

A close look allows us to see through some apparent contradictions.

While he was happy to have Simone as a groupie, Montand was not a strong advocate of keeping a woman at home and would have been angry if she had sold short a talent so far above the ordinary. And, in fact, it was he who shoved Simone back in front of the cameras. She explained it in good humor: "Montand is always super in a major crisis. If there's a fire, it's Montand who finds the water. If you're losing blood, it's Montand who knows how to make a tourniquet. He's a man to cope with major occasions. But let's say that for the routine stuff he can at times be a trifle difficult—that is, when he's not downright impossible. On that particular day I was knitting, as a devoted, unobtrusive, and happy wife likes to knit." Whereupon the singer—in the middle of a rehearsal—flew into a rage, bellowed out that a score was missing, wildly waved his arms at his horrified musicians, and finally turned to the knitter and shouted: "What are you doing sitting there knitting?"

"I'm here because I want to be here. If I weren't here, I'd be working."

"Easy to say! To work, someone's got to offer you a part!"

Stung, Signoret immediately called the Hakim brothers, the producers of *Casque d'Or,* who just before she made her dramatic farewell to film had offered her the role of Thérèse Raquin in Marcel Carné's next film. She did not know whether the part had been filled. She knew that the usual rule was never to seem to be asking. But the Hakim brothers bore no grudges, and Carné was more relieved than angry: Simone would be Thérèse; the contract was in the mail.

"See!" she said to her husband as she hung up.

Filmed in the winter of 1953, the adaptation of Zola's novel was shown that fall at the Venice Film Festival. "I was back from afar," admitted Simone.

Another Signoret stereotype was simple and more widely held, not just among certain of Simone's friends, people of wide knowledge and ready speech, but all over the Left Bank. According to this legend, there was on the one hand Simone the intellectual, known in the best bookstores, speaking several languages, quick with apt and erudite quotations, a spectacular social lioness with a writer's ear for trenchant language, a sharp wit that rarely misjudged a target and never missed it, on easy terms with musicians (not a group known for its erudition) but capable of standing up to Sartre, hiding her shyness behind a foursquare personality and an agile tongue. On the other hand there was Montand the intuitive fellow, scarcely educated, having learned things in bits and pieces, trawling in empirical knowledge, culture, and ideas and digesting everything with the obsessive slowness of a cow chewing its cud. A man whose strength was a formidable energy and a capacity for herculean labor that made up for the absence of natural grace. Of course, a man with a certain flair, perhaps even a startling and mysterious flair, but a man who seemed in permanent need of proving himself, as if he were some vessel of which he was the more or less accidental resident. Montand had something, said the mischievous, but Signoret was the brains.

Many things can be said to debunk this brutally Manichean view of the two. It is true that Montand, like many autodidacts (sometimes the word agreed with him, at other times it made him wince), prowled around ideas, hesitant, aligning and comparing them in his notebook or on his chalkboard without daring to take full possession of them, awed by the confidence and aplomb of people who could compare them, reject them, condense them, expand them. It is also true that the give-and-take of social interchange was not his strong point. Moreover, his gaze sometimes betrayed a kind of dreamy remove, a turning-in upon himself—what his teachers had once called his "inattention"—that was disconcerting to those talking with him. Seeing him so obviously elsewhere, they wondered if he was anywhere at all.

And it is true that Montand's attempts to acquire conventional cultural polish were not always entirely successful. Around Signoret you read, you read a lot, you read naturally, and the echoes of that reading were all around you. One day, Roger Pigaut, a close friend of Simone's and an avid consumer of books (which is certainly untrue of the many actors who quote and even recite Musset and Claudel for show, having barely skimmed the texts), might speak passionately of *La Condition humaine,* and the next, behind his back, Montand would conscientiously plow through Malraux's pages. The next time around, the talk would be of *Les Thibault* and of Maupassant. Montand would go on plowing, but *Les Thibault* was so long. . . .

In whom could he confide his embarrassing doubts? Which confessor would agree to hear of this sin that was not a sin? After an appendix operation, Montand talked to his surgeon, Dr. Lébovici: "Tell me why I have such trouble concentrating on a book, either unable to keep going or creeping along line by line! You'll probably say I'm not wasting my time, and I suppose you're right. But I can't help it: to me it seems like lost time, wasted time."

"You mustn't think of it simply as a problem of education, or training," said the doctor. "The mind cannot be everywhere at once. In your head, you never take a break, you never stop thinking of the show, of the running order of a concert, of new characters, of lighting problems. So you really don't have leisure to read. What's blocking you is your art."

Nearly forty years later, Montand reported this conversation with gratitude. Because the doctor had heard him out like a brother, because he had broken through the silence that always blankets complexes, because he had supplied him with a plausible explanation of his difficulty. It was no easier to devote yourself to the Etoile or to the philosopher Montaigne than to work in a kitchen or a bakery. Especially if no guidelines and no priorities had been laid down for you in your childhood.

Signoret was always extremely careful to balance the scales. She constantly sought the approval and the authority of the man she loved, whose practical intelligence she savored. It was a constantly surprising intelligence, sometimes circling, sometimes going straight to the target, leapfrogging the usual hurdles faced by conventionally educated minds.

What is certain is that throughout the thirty-six years they lived together, they both tried to preserve a common front, a way of saying, "No, this woman is not simply a left-wing intellectual whose mind and senses were sent spinning by a pleasant, handsome, talented, and rough-hewn male; no, this man is not simply a son of the people whose head was turned by a Saint-Germain-des-Prés intellectual who also happened to be a star." Signoret was too subtle not to sense Montand's ambivalent reaction to this sudden contact with people whose language, references, and discourse attracted, irritated, and destabilized him—his fear that he might not be giving true education its due, his fear of being duped by fancy talkers and parlor theoreticians. When he consulted her on his choice of songs, she gave her honest opinion. She was his first audience, and she maintained stricter standards of honesty with Montand (whom she called "Montand" because "Yves" was Allégret) than with any other. But she made sure that all criticism between them was a two-way affair, that no difference of opinion ever led to real misunderstanding. However lively their exchanges, solidarity was the basic marital code.

Elvire and Julien Livi witnessed this delicate game close up. "In a public figure like an actor," says Montand's brother, "the timidity of the self-taught man and the need to compensate for his lack of education are heavy burdens: speech, choice of words, even the way you move can be dangerous traps. Yves had to learn to get over his complexes; he had to realize that what lay behind his terrible shyness was often not so much character as culture. Simone helped a lot. Thanks to her, especially, he developed his capacity to seize ideas in midflight, in midconversation, even though he is a man who has always had an uneasy relationship with the written word." And Elvire adds a qualification: "Complexes with regard to education, writing, certainly. But none toward Simone."

Jean-Louis Livi, the son of Julien and Elvire, grew up in the shadow of Montand and Signoret. For many years he was one of Paris's biggest film agents. He makes the same point: "Montand had the confidence of the man who is himself, who feels he is himself, the man who sings better than the others, who is well-built, who respects Proust to the skies but believes there is more to life than Proust, who has fun. And however intellectually superior Simone might have been, she was impressed, she was thrilled by this guy, who had certainly read less than she had but who was capable of the most extraordinary flashes."

And as he came into contact with minds more cultivated than his own, Montand was able to verify something he had long suspected: one idea, however close it might seem to the truth, always hid another. But in the early 1950s, he pursued the thought no further; in those days, the "right" ideas seemed clearly signposted. For Montand, becoming intelligent, becoming educated, did not imply stifling his own terms of reference. It meant the gradual realization, over the passage of two decades, that convictions were not necessarily supported by fact. He was also emboldened to resist the false imperative of adopted tastes or ideas considered to be the natural baggage of a cultivated man. It was years before he could admit that classical music (Mozart excepted) lulled him more than it galvanized him, that he preferred jazz and rock, and that he sometimes yawned at chamber music.

In mid-1953, Yves Montand and his wife were again separated, for a month and a half. The somber, dark-haired Thérèse Raquin had slid under the skin of the blond, vivacious Simone Signoret. Montand went to Rome and Florence to shoot a film—a series of sketches with Danièle Delorme entitled *Tempi nostri,* directed by Alessandro Blasetti. Not exactly a landmark in film history, it was more a pretext for a semivacation in the sun and a return between takes to his roots in Monsummano Alto.

It was the first time Ivo Livi had made the pilgrimage to his village birthplace. He went without any strong feelings: he carried no picture of it within him, and he knew of the pain that had attended Giovanni Livi's expulsion. His homecoming did not, of course, go unnoticed. A drove of cousins, many times removed, turned out to demonstrate overflowing emotion. So the visit was a hurried one. Proud though he was of his peasant, Tuscan, and anti-Fascist origins, Montand felt no great need to manufacture late-blooming, artificial roots for himself.

Danièle Delorme went along with him. They laughed a lot together, admired the hills and farmland, sampled the new wine. For Montand, at least, there was an unsettling quality to their companionship. But Simone had laid down the rules of the game: she had agreed to tolerate adventures that might develop during a separation provided they did nothing to damage the fabric of their marriage. Montand had agreed. But she was adamant on one point: she did not want her own female friendships to be marred by hypocritical silences or suppressed anger, to be damaged by vicious gossip that, sooner or later, thanks to some well-meaning spy, would reach the "victim's" ears. She had even pronounced to her husband the names of two friends who were to be considered taboo: Danièle Delorme and Jeanne Moreau. True friends—so close that she never wanted to associate them with the smallest hint of unpleasantness.

So Montand respected the rules. Compliance was not easy: it was summer, and the women were beautiful. As soon as he was left to himself, temptation gnawed at him. Not the temptation of major infidelity, but of flirtatious escapades with no strings attached and no expectations. Would he have accepted such behavior on his wife's part? In the comfortably theoretical context of a dining-room conversation, yes. How could you deny the person you loved the pleasure you desired for yourself? he would have argued. But theory made no allowances for the vigilance of the Tuscan male, capable of considering, in serene and oddly detached tones, that his companion might, like himself, be swept away by fleeting passions, but this required a heroic suppression of hot-blooded instincts. "Montand was always very jealous," says Catherine Allégret. "And Mama was a very Mediterranean wife. She immediately cut off all her old contacts when Montand entered her life and only gradually refilled the void with friendships and bonds of affection. But the basis of their relationship was a very powerful intimacy between them, usually with him working and her standing by him."

Simone Signoret returned exhausted by *Thérèse Raquin.* The adaptation, by Charles Spaak and Marcel Carné, had deepened the gloom of Zola's story. Although a controversial piece, it won the Silver Lion at the Venice Film Festival. But it was not the demands of the role that had undermined Signoret. In mid-August, she lost the baby she was carrying. She and Montand had been hoping for this birth. She had two more miscarriages (each time after a testing role, and each time very late in the pregnancy). This was a subject that gossip columnists were never allowed to probe. Neither of them ever spoke, except to the closest of friends, of the pain and the irreparable loss.

With Simone convalescing in a clinic, Yves Montand returned to his traditional vacation duties (other people's vacations, of course). He was due to appear at the Etoile on October 5. With only a few more weeks left for fine-tuning his act, he embarked on a true battle campaign: Knokke-le-Zoute, Deauville, Les Sables-d'Olonne, Arcachon, Biarritz, Cannes, Menton, Nice, Juan-les-Pins, Vichy, Royat, Aix, Chamonix, Evian. . . . In addition to his daily phone call, he sent Catherine and Simone audiotapes in which he spoke of his love and his sorrow at being away. Mother and daughter would listen together as the tape slid through the big recorder, until the moment when Montand's voice would say to Catherine, "And now, Mademoiselle, I'd like you to leave the room so that I can be alone with Simone. I have things to tell her in private."

Nerves were taut at the Place Dauphine as Monday, October 5, approached.

"He paced up and down the living room," says Elvire Livi. "He didn't notice you were there. He was rehearsing the words of a song. When the musicians were there, voices rose angrily the moment a wrong note was sounded. He had planned each day's meals far in advance, in a menu he had written in his own hand and pinned up in the kitchen: calf's liver, ground beef, chicken, fish. Just so many grams, not fifty too many! Not a drop of hard liquor, just a little wine, cigarettes rationed. The barre was in the cellar, and he practiced at it every morning. And bad-tempered! Simone made herself scarce. Even after the premiere, you had to wait a few days for him to relax. It was no fun, no fun at all!"

Julien: "I'd just call out, 'Hello, everyone!' and go straight on up to the sixth floor. There'd be lots of time later to discuss the war in Indochina."

Jean-Louis: "His physical workout consisted mainly of standing at the edge of the cellar stairs and touching the first step down with his fingertips, well below his toes. Knees absolutely straight. Between five and six, he'd go to bed and fall asleep immediately; my mother would wake him after half an hour."

That was the "domestic" approach to the big night.

And then there was the night itself. Christine de Rivoyre, assigned by *Le Monde* to capture the premiere, described the auditorium in the following words: "Simone Signoret, once the dazzling blond Casque d'Or, now with hair dark as the wing of Thérèse Raquin's raven, stood at the prow of the boxes on the right. With her in the same vessel was Danièle Delorme, tirelessly greeting people; Gérard Philipe, a loyal friend; and the breakaway faction of the Comédie-Française, represented by Marie Bell and Jean Chévrier. Farther back, Erich von Stroheim, a gold bracelet on his wrist. Across from them, Edwige Feuillère, wrapped like Snow White in cloudlike furs. And a fiercely mustachioed Serge Reggiani; Renée Faure, looking like a fair-haired Shakespearean page; Madeleine Robinson, 'a tall simple lass in a beret'; Simone Simon, pink and ecstatic, signing autographs at intermission. And Pierre Prévert, Maurice Druon, Becker, Cayatte, Autant-Lara, Max Ophuls, and Pierre Brasseur, once again wearing Goetz's beard [from his role in Sartre's *Le Diable et le bon dieu*]; Aragon, of course, and Elsa, her eulogized eyes alight with pleasure. All these fine people behaved admirably, almost as well as the fans perched higher up watching out for their man in his regulation dark brown suit." The critic for *Le Figaro,* Pierre Macaigne, clearly eager to drop a note of vitriol into the ocean of acclaim drowning "Comrade" Montand, thundered in vain against this cult of personality—the flow was irresistible. Montand's twenty-third and last song was "A Paris." He waved farewell. His distinguished audience (everyone had paid, on principle, for his or her own seat, which was more unusual than one might think) called him back. Stock-still, very quietly, he gave them "Les Feuilles mortes." Silence. The emotion was palpable. For a second, the spectators were transfixed. Then bedlam. "En-core, en-core, en-core!"

Montand feared encores as much as he relished them. He preferred them to silence, of course, but was afraid that tacking on more songs might erode and unravel the close of the show. When it was over, you should end it at full steam, in top form. You shouldn't let yourself be nibbled away, drained by the need to prolong what had to be ended, and should end on a high note.

But he surrendered, and the song he selected for his surrender was like a confession: "C'est si bon." Curtain. Wave. Curtain. Wave. Curtain. Wave. Curtain. They would not let him go. Montand looked at Signoret, who had come to join him backstage after "Barbara"—theoretically the second-to-last song—with a mixture of triumph and apprehension. He walked to the footlights, arched his back, arms outstretched toward the distant balcony, then bowed to the audience below, showing that every spectator was entitled to respect, no matter what his seat had cost. Then he left. No more surrender. On the other side of the curtain, the noise of a swelling ocean, of waves breaking over the auditorium. En-core! They were still there, refusing to go. People began to whistle. The balcony was torn between ovation and demonstration. "Yves Montand was booed because he refused to go on singing," trumpeted the popular press (for example, *Paris-Presse* and *L'Intransigeant*).

Officially, Montand was scheduled to perform for three weeks. In fact, there were more than two hundred performances, from October 5, 1953, to April 4, 1954. Six whole months, nearly two hundred thousand tickets sold, gross receipts of 200 million francs. Plus the huge success of the live recording of the show. Plus a Gold Record (one million copies sold) for "Les Feuilles mortes." An all-time record. They came from all over France, in chartered buses. They came from abroad. The capital's most illustrious guests made a point of being seen in Montand's dressing room. On October 31, for instance, Signoret and he were photographed by a *Paris-Match* staffer with Maurice Chevalier, Kirk Douglas, and Gary Cooper. Of the star's dressing room, Signoret said that it became "the famous ship's cabin in the Marx Brothers' movie" every night, with friends and colleagues piling in once their own commitments were over.

From an artistic and musical standpoint, this 1953 concert was perhaps no better than those of 1951, 1958, 1968, or 1981. But it burns with a special flame in the memory of the faithful. "A high-water mark," said Paul Grimault. "What I would most like to relive," said Colette Crolla, "is one of those evenings at the Etoile." "The fear Montand felt," added Serge Reggiani, "was so violent that to crush it required an added burst of energy that allowed him to embrace the audience with unparalleled warmth."

The litany is endless: "I well remember," says Catherine Allégret, "the first time Mama got all the kids at the Place Dauphine together to go and see Montand sing." The parents were paralyzed with stage fright (Julien: "I was in agony. At least Yves could get it all out, but we cringed for him at every note, at every toe tap, at every announcement. We left the theater wiped out"). But for the children it was a party.

Jean-Louis: "Simone sat us right up at the top next to the man who controlled the lighting. He had a big card in front of him with the instructions written on it. For example, he had to cut everything the second Montand raised his arms in 'Les Routiers.' For us it was magic—and it *was* magic. I've been lucky enough in my job to attend hundreds of shows, and I still do. Today I have a better idea of how miraculous that 1953 show was. You weren't entering a theater. You were entering a cathedral—a warm cathedral, full of goodwill, where everyone was taking communion. You didn't even have to think, people were enjoying themselves so much: between 'Quand un soldat' and 'Les Saltimbanques,' Montand slipped in 'Une Demoiselle sur une balançoire.' Between 'Flamenco de Paris' and 'Le Peintre, la pomme et Picasso,' he did the tap-dance routine of 'Il fait des . . .' When we went to see him at the end of the show he still hadn't come back down to earth, he was still in his own world. He called over the musicians: something hadn't gone right, they had to fix it right away. Right away! He was quite capable of rehearsing after the show, in his white bathrobe. Only later did he turn back into the person we knew."

The extraordinary reception extended to the star of the Etoile owed a great deal to the composition of the show. Montand had divided it in four: one-quarter on popular themes (Paris opened the evening, and Paris closed it); one-quarter pure poetry (Prévert mostly, but some Apollinaire as well); one-quarter comic sketches (of which "Le Chef d'orchestre est amoureux" was the main innovation); and one-quarter more-or-less political songs ("Quand un soldat," "Flamenco de Paris," "Le Chemin des oliviers," "C'est à l'aube").

This meant a very wide register, from the casual fantasy of "Dis-moi Joe" to the unforeseeable love of "Il a fallu" and the social realism of "C'est à l'aube."

Always a nimble, amusing entertainer, Yves Montand had become the spokesman for the best of the French, for those who loved and made France, who had little respect for the tottering institutions of the Fourth Republic, who condemned France's colonial adventures. Montand was at the apex of his popularity in every sense of the word. In a short but incisive biography of Montand (publication coincided with the opening at the Etoile), the critic and novelist Christian Mégret wrote that Montand embodied "the man of the masses, the man of today, aware of the evils of the age." It was no accident that he was politically committed, if not in his art, then in his life.

> That concert of 1953–54 was one of the most complete I ever gave. It rested on the values of the people of my generation and the next, values that then appeared unassailable—the demarcation line between good and evil seemed clear. My repertory wasn't political, but it drew on that shared warmth, absorbed it, and gave it back. It happened that most of the lyrics were free of the often whining note of the left, that a breath of realism blew through them. In those days I thought I believed in a simplified form of Marxism, but in my view, "Sanguine" was as much the herald of a "glorious future" as "C'est à l'aube." I always hark back to a particular image when I try to recall the atmosphere at the Etoile: the Paris transport system was on strike, but the audience came along just the same, and the lobby was packed with hundreds of bicycles! And a particular feeling: it was terribly cold that winter, even in the theater—the boilers were out of order for five days—but the audience wore coats and mittens, and we all got warm together. People understood right away. When I announced "Barbara," a song "by Jacques Prévert and by . . . Jacques Prévert only," they laughed at once. For only then did they realize I would be reciting the poem.

Montand would know other and perhaps more spectacular glories. He was to triumph in the United States and in Japan. But he probably never again encountered that sense of fusion, for it came as much from the climate of the times as from the atmosphere of the show. Nor would he experience the perfect coincidence of public love—the nightly embrace with thousands of people—and private love. An interview with Montand

and Signoret in *Comoedia* on December 2, 1953, a venerable magazine for show-business amateurs and professionals, sounds almost like a lyrical duet:

> SIGNORET: I'm only an actress. He isn't a performer; he's a director. The audience doesn't come to see one story, but twenty-five stories, which have meaning only through what he brings to them. For nine weeks I haven't seen a single movie straight through. His concert schedule allows me to see only the beginning or the end.
>
> MONTAND: When I married my wife, she was an artist. I wasn't about to ask her to give up a profession she loves. That would have been a terrible loss! But obviously, no matter what you say, you're not going to like it when you know your wife is playing a love scene with someone else! I knew she would give up the movies if I asked her, but I also knew that she would eventually suffer for it. I, too, could give up singing for a year for her sake—
>
> SIGNORET: I'm not asking it of you.
>
> MONTAND: How long can it last, a love like this? Two years, five years, ten years? For life, I hope. . . .
>
> SIGNORET: I refuse to act in the theater for a very simple reason: I don't want to leave home at eight every evening. I absolutely don't want us to end up meeting in corridors.
>
> MONTAND: We could act together, but we'd need a play in which we were already husband and wife.
>
> SIGNORET: Meanwhile, I'm happy to be second fiddle while he's filming. And I don't get involved in his songs.
>
> MONTAND: Don't say that! Your judgment is surefire. . . .

A "love like this" needed more than a nest (the nest was the "trailer"): it needed a bigger space in which to take refuge, to unfold, to give of itself. A place for its most trusted witnesses to gather. For the first time in his life, Montand had earned a real fortune, and for the first (and last) time in his life, he wanted a house. He was torn between peasant caution and dreams of châteaux with rolling lawns, turrets, and statues. But his incapacity for intelligent management of the capital so suddenly amassed by a sworn enemy of capitalism militated against delusions of grandeur.

After combing the countryside, Montand and Signoret finally found a house in the Eure, at Autheuil-Authouillet (between Pacy-sur-Eure and

Louviers), which offered a rural compromise like the urban "trailer" on the Ile de la Cité. It was a house without turrets or a hall of mirrors, a white cube soberly topped by gray slate, with well-proportioned windows overlooking a meadow and an avenue lined with tall trees. From outside, it was majestically simple. Inside, it was warm and light, with old tile floors, hospitable fireplaces, a broad staircase, and a mansard roof. Slender columns broke up the vast living space. The dining room was both spacious and cozy. Fifty-five miles from Paris, it was conveniently located yet deep in the country.

The property included a small farm boasting some ten cows. Rather optimistically, Montand hoped that its produce would cover the costs of its upkeep. Simone and Yves then presented their find to their future caretakers, Georges and Marcelle Mirtilon, the cook from the Place Dauphine and her husband, the porter at Les Halles. Both of Norman origin, they leapt at the chance to replant their roots there. Adding fifteen sheep to the ten cows, they enthusiastically agreed to become stewards for the Montands. Some observers sourly pointed out that the sheep were marked with a large *M* (which is what the Mirtilons had always done in their home village) and judged it to be the sign of sudden megalomania on the part of the "prole"-turned-squire. "We didn't look for people to take care of the house after we bought it," retorted Signoret. "We loved people who loved the country, and on our second inspection of Autheuil, before we actually purchased it, we took along Georges and Marcelle. They liked it. We bought it."

Montand and Signoret adopted the same approach with their friends. Autheuil would be communal or nothing. "Yves and Simone took us there," François Périer recalls, "Reggiani, Pigaut, José Artur, Brasseur—the whole gang—and asked our opinion. Soon we had all adopted Autheuil as a place to rest, to write, to rehearse, to get together. Simone and Yves frowned on any infidelity to this commitment. At Autheuil we were at home. When a few of us began to earn a little more and organize our lives more independently, when we ourselves bought country homes, it was almost as if we had committed adultery. 'But you have Autheuil!' Simone would object."

Signoret, as usual, took the matter of decoration into her own hands: white walls, objects chosen as much for what they recalled as for their intrinsic value (two bays in the big living room were filled with trinkets and curios brought back from a thousand trips), furniture "that isn't 'fine furniture' but that is fine," paintings that wouldn't raise an auctioneer's temperature but that had been cadged from clever dealers (there were also Picasso's ceramic, a Lurçat tapestry, a Giacometti painting, and two "compressions" by their friend César).

In theory, at least, the owners reserved most of the main floor for themselves. The rest was given over to visitors, particularly the third-floor garrets, which had curtains made by Signoret herself. Her fee for *Les Diaboliques* was converted into a swimming pool with a special children's area that was open to the village children one or two days a week in summer. In the Norman backcountry, this was an unheard-of innovation. Montand converted a barn into a small theater, complete with film projectors, a growing collection of priceless movies, and a miniature stage, where he sharpened his acts. The meadow behind the house was supposed to be a lawn but remained a meadow.

Loves were born and died at Autheuil (Jacques Becker married Françoise Fabian there in 1959). Books were conceived there. Film scripts—by Becker, Costa-Gavras, Resnais, Corneau, Dabadie-Sautet, Semprun—were hammered out, their dialogue sharpened there. Chris Marker worked there with camera and pen. Luis Buñuel practiced marksmanship at dawn to relax.

Simone Signoret died there.

And yet, if nostalgia inhabited the house, it was a nostalgia for constant, uninhibited high spirits, nostalgia for the best kind of laughter—the laughter that feeds friendship. "It was a house where if it rained cats and dogs it did so outside," said José Artur, "where the future belonged to those who went to bed late." (After the publication of his book *Micro de nuit* in 1974, Artur was elected official historian of life at Autheuil.) "On New Year's Eve," he said, "we'd wish each other the year we deserved, nothing more. If the house had been robbed, memories rather than articles of value would have been lost. It was the kind of house where 'no one was against the marriage of priests provided they loved one another.' It was wisest to leave your pretensions at the front door."

By the summer of 1954, the tone of the place was established. "For several years," says Catherine Allégret, "Autheuil was wonderful, ebullient. Bernard Blier, Pierre Brasseur, José Artur, and Pierre Mondy played ghosts and sloshed buckets of water over each other like kids. Marcel Achard would mislay his glasses and bathing trunks—always with dignity—on the edge of the pool. For once in my life, at least, I saw my parents have the time of their lives. And you know, to see Montand relaxed you have to be up early." Jean-Louis Livi speaks with the same enthusiasm: "Yes, strange as it may seem, our relatives were actually relaxed. And beautiful. They were in their thirties, their careers were going full steam, they could talk, tell stories, mime." His mother, Elvire, was often there: "Pierre Brasseur cheated; Serge Reggiani and Raymond Rouleau squabbled with their girlfriends and made up the next day; Becker, Pigaut, and Blier spent the weekend. Games of ambassador and poker went on until dawn." "Don't try to make me confess that we had momentous ideological discussions," says Serge Reggiani. "With Montand in those days, I chiefly recall laughing my head off."

All in all, Simone Signoret created at Autheuil a group as picturesque, talented, and friendly as the one that had illuminated her twenties. Invitations were issued mainly by her, and it was she who called the social tune. Not that Montand shrank from fun, but between two rounds of poker and a well-deployed practical joke, he often felt the need for a respite—a walk across the fields, a moment on his own in the little theater. Sometimes Simone made skillful use of their friends to drive home a criticism she felt with regard to a song or an accompaniment. She launched the *banderilla,* then stood back and let the chorus, as if by accident, confirm her first impression. Montand was not fooled, but he pretended he was, and his wife knew he knew.

Some practical jokes have endured in the memories of those who witnessed them as perfect symbols of the spirit of Autheuil. Once they selected as victim Montand's agent (let us call him "Monsieur B"), a gullible, lisping man who swallowed stories as eagerly as he swallowed percentages. A wave of jubilation rolled across the household when Monsieur B was announced. Those who excelled at short improvised scenes—and they were many and highly qualified—opened fire. The result was more or less as follows:

Act One. Montand greets Monsieur B and immediately starts singing the praises of certain flowers, particularly certain gladioli whose bulbs, imported from Asia, are extremely rare and expensive. But his talk quickly veers toward less pleasant subjects. I can't stand it, he suddenly confesses, I live among spongers, false friends who abuse my hospitality.

Act Two. Everyone is at table. Serge Reggiani mumbles Neapolitan proverbs. Looking tense, Signoret keeps a hawk's eye on the guests. Pierre Brasseur has clearly been hitting the aperitifs too hard. François Périer suddenly races out of the house, first dropping a mound of dirty laundry in Simone's lap.

Her eyes cloud with tears.

"I'm off to Paris. Can you do these by tomorrow? Ciao!" And he is gone. Montand moans into Monsieur B's ear: "Did you see that, did you see that?"

Act Three. Enter José Artur, looking gleeful that he has arrived before dinner is over. His arms are full of flowers from the garden—the gladioli, the priceless gladioli, not just cut but uprooted, complete with bulbs.

Act Four. A few glasses later, Artur breaks down and sobs. His friend (it is clear he is referring to a male) has walked out on him.

"He'th homothecthual?" lisps Monsieur B. "I thought he wath married. Thith ith terrible!"

Glaring murderously at Monsieur B, Montand growls that, yes, Artur is married, but it is all very complicated, homosexuals are secretive people, which does not mean they don't have feelings like everybody else, does it?

Act Five. On the feeblest of excuses, Monsieur B makes his getaway before the coffee arrives. Nobody bids him goodbye.

Chapter 10

Every year, the mayor of Stockholm holds a reception in the Hall of Golden Mosaics, in the town hall, in honor of Nobel Prize winners. But on March 19, 1950, the Socialist mayor of Stockholm was greeting not famous writers or renowned scientists but delegates from the World Committee in Support of Peace. They had reached swift agreement on the text of a speech composed in a tavern basement by the Russian writer Ilya Ehrenburg: "We demand an absolute ban on the atomic bomb, a weapon of terror and mass extermination of populations. . . . We consider that the first government to use atomic weapons against any other country would be committing a crime against humanity and should be treated as a war criminal. We call upon people of goodwill the world over to sign this appeal."

With this profession of faith, the Stockholm Appeal, one of the biggest public-opinion operations ever launched on the world by Communism, was under way. For behind the universally acceptable pacifist and humanitarian message lay a vast campaign of political manipulation masterminded by the Soviet Union. While this seems fairly obvious today, at the time millions of people signed the appeal in good faith. They truly feared a new world war—a nuclear war—between the United States and the Soviet Union.

Within just two years of the surrender of Germany and Japan, the Allies, so recently united against Fascism, were squaring off in Europe and Asia. On the chessboard of Eastern European countries liberated by the Red Army, the Soviets had swiftly deployed their pawns: through rigged elections, physical threats, and "mobilization of the masses," non-Marxist parties were thrust aside and then eliminated. As early as March 1946, in his famous speech at Fulton, Missouri, Winston Churchill had denounced the "police regimes" imposing their law on Eastern Europe. Communist parties seized power in Warsaw, Budapest, and Prague. Within a few months, two antagonistic blocs had frozen in place, one led by the United States, the other under Soviet domination.

Everyone had his own theory about how the Cold War had come about. In March 1947, the U.S. president presented to Congress what would be known as the Truman Doctrine: "It must be the policy of the United States to support free peoples who are resisting attempted subjugation by armed minorities or by outside pressures." A few months later, Marshal Aleksandr Zhdanov, the official ideologist of the Soviet regime, retorted: "Two camps have formed in the world: on one side, the imperialist and antidemocratic camp, whose essential aim is the establishment of world domination by American imperialism and the crushing of democracy; and on the other side, the anti-imperialist and democratic camp, whose essential aim is to weaken imperialism." Behind the routine language, the intentions of both sides were clearly set forth. The Berlin blockade, the partitioning of Germany, and Mao Zedong's victory in China further accentuated the division of the world.

On April 4, 1949, in Washington, D.C., twelve Western foreign ministers signed the document that brought into being the North Atlantic Treaty Organization, an agreement whereby each member was to consider an armed attack upon any one of them as an attack upon them all. The USSR reacted as if *it* had been attacked. Henceforth its most skillful propagandists depicted the Americans as warmongers and the Soviet Union as the champion of peace. Denunciation of the atomic bomb was a powerful weapon in this ideological battle: lovers of peace were against the bomb; the bomb was American; therefore, lovers of peace were against the United States.

To help in this crusade, the Soviet Union mobilized Communist parties under its control in the West, but the Soviet leaders were astute enough to enlist the support of the West's progressive, humanist, pacifist intellectuals as well. Whence the idea of organizing, from behind the scenes, huge rallies designed to attract and recruit the Western intelligentsia.

At Wroclaw, in Poland, where the World Congress of Intellectuals for Peace was held in August 1948, the peace movement was launched. In April 1949, in Paris, the World Congress of the Partisans for Peace held its first meeting. Picasso produced a lithograph, *The Dove of Peace,* for the occasion. The Nobel Prize–winning physicist Frédéric Joliot-Curie, a Communist since 1944 and chairman of the French atomic energy commission since 1946 (a post from which he was removed in 1950), opened the proceedings before two thousand delegates from seventy-two countries. He portrayed the NATO pact (which France had signed) as an act of surrender to American capitalism. For five days, a hundred delegates held the floor, singing the peace-loving virtues of the USSR and denouncing

America's warlike intentions. In deep, solemn tones, the black singer Paul Robeson declared: "Not until I went to the Soviet Union did I feel that I was a human being."[1]

The peace movement strove to take on the aura of a pacifist International. Its main objective was to have the Stockholm Appeal signed everywhere by illustrious persons—artists, intellectuals, the clergy. Every day, every week, the Communist press published the names of distinguished signatories: Jorge Amado, Louis Aragon, Pierre Benoît, Dmitri Shostakovich, Ilya Ehrenburg, Duke Ellington, Thomas Mann, Pablo Neruda. As well as the painters Chagall, Gromaire, Matisse, Pignon. And in show business, Marcel Carné, Noël-Noël, Michel Simon. . . .

On May 2, 1950, *L'Humanité* told its readers that "the popular singer Yves Montand has signed the Stockholm Appeal," adding that he had appended this sentence: "I sign so that I may continue to sing for a long time." From that day on, Montand's name was on the Communist mailing list for petitions and propaganda. On May 25, under the headline "They All Signed to Outlaw the Atomic Bomb," *L'Humanité* published a drawing depicting Jean Stock (the French middleweight boxing champion), Serge Reggiani, Simone Signoret, Gérard Philipe, and Pierre Brasseur dancing in a circle with joined hands. Even the great Maurice Chevalier himself said in *Lettres Françaises,* "I'd like to see the list of those refusing to sign! They are people who support suicide without having to commit suicide themselves." Shortly afterward, he rather ostentatiously withdrew this statement.

Within a few months, according to the organizers, the Stockholm Appeal had garnered 12 million signatures in France. The Communist press was quick to point out that the figure far exceeded the number of regular supporters of the Communist Party (which had won 5 million votes in the general elections of 1951). It stressed the diversity of the people who had chosen to march with the Communists. Churches, the object of particularly sedulous wooing, were heavily represented in the peace movement. One of the most visible clerics was the Abbé Boulier, a mainstay of the Jeunesse Ouvrière Chrétienne; he likened the Communists to unwitting worshipers of Christ: "I wager for the Church, for the Gospel, for life itself, against death and hideous slaughter. You call that playing the Communist game? You could find no higher praise for them!"[2]

This policy of reaching out to Catholics soon bore fruit. Questioned

1. Quoted in Bernard Legendre, "When the Intellectuals Went Off to the Cold War," *Historia,* April 1979.

2. "Trois lettres sur le mouvement de la paix," Paris, 1953, in Bernard Legendre, *Qui a dit quoi?* (Paris, 1980).

by *Le Figaro,* the actor François Périer claimed that his faith had motivated him to sign: "You tell me that this text was composed by Communists. That's something I never thought about. I am a Christian, and I would have preferred that it had come from the Vatican. Unfortunately, it was not the Vatican that asked me to sign." Like many progressive Christians, he considered the Communists of the 1950s as the new Christians of the age. Périer laughs about it today. "Simone asked me to sign the appeal," he says. "I agreed but said I'd have to find a good reason. Right after my statement she phoned me: 'You dirty rat, you were perfect playing the believer.' I said, 'Not at all. I was perfectly sincere. The appeal is a great Christian text: it is paved with good intentions.' "

Moreover, since the Liberation, a considerable sector of the French intelligentsia had been living under the influence of the "Stalingrad effect," for the Red Army's triumphant victory in 1943 had created an aura of glory for the Soviet regime and its leader. Many young intellectuals who had found political commitment in the ranks of the Resistance belonged to the "Party of the Martyrs." The French Communist Party, with hundreds of thousands of members, multiple labor-union connections, and a network of allied organizations, claimed all credit for the achievements of the Resistance and proclaimed itself the sole spokesman of the working class. And French intellectuals, ever ready to canonize the proletariat, the only revolutionary class recognized in the Marxist gospel, identified the Communist Party with the workers. Allied to the prestige of Hitler's conquerors, this class complex increased Communist influence in France tenfold.

Beyond the small but noisy inner circle of card-carrying intellectuals, Communism exercised its attraction on fellow travelers, both better known and more numerous. Outside a handful of borderline signers who speedily regretted their gesture, the great majority of supporters of the Stockholm Appeal belonged in this category. They were not Party members, but in most essentials they toed the Party line. The writer Julien Benda, author of *Le Trahison des clercs,* commented on this choice: "Make no mistake: the two blocs currently facing off in France are *class* blocs, each with its own Internationale. . . . The French must choose between these two class blocs and what they represent on French soil."[3] And Benda lashed out at sensitive souls like Léon Blum, who rejected a dictatorship of either the right or the left. For fellow travelers, the Soviet Union embodied the hope for a new society based on equality. This quest for a better future erased the ephemeral mistakes and the inevitable imperfections that cropped up on the immense construction site where Socialism was being built.

3. Julien Benda, *Europe,* March 1948.

This Manichean logic about a war between Good and Evil, Day and Night, dominated the postwar generation of intellectuals in France. For them, it was unthinkable to turn against a Russian people who had sacrificed themselves in battle against the Nazis. Anti-Fascism *was* Moscow, whereas across the Atlantic, warmongers who had already proved their willingness to use nuclear weapons were plotting a preventive nuclear strike against Russia. Much later, writing her memoirs, Signoret stressed the power of this argument, then widely believed: "It was massive refusal of the atomic bomb. When people refused to sign [the petition], the usual question asked them was: 'So you're *for* the atomic bomb?' . . . It would have been hard to say, 'Oh, yes, I like it very much,' after you had seen photographs of Hiroshima."

A considerable minority of the French people feared a major conflict. The outbreak of the Korean war, a month after Montand signed the appeal, bolstered that fear. On June 25, 1950, well-equipped North Korean troops crossed the 38th parallel, which had marked off the respective American and Soviet zones of influence in Korea since the Japanese surrender; under the auspices of the United Nations, whose forces were led by General Douglas MacArthur, the United States came to the assistance of South Korea. Here, too, Communist propaganda managed to present America as responsible for the war, adding somewhat to the success of the peace movement.

In December 1952, Yves Montand took part in the deliberations of a Congress of Peoples held at the Vélodrome d'Hiver in Paris. Behind the stand, where he sat with a row of Communist leaders (Jacques Duclos, Benoît Frachon, Waldeck Rochet) between Sartre and Michel Leiris, was a huge poster of Picasso's *Dove.* Thirty years later, Montand chaired a television program, *La Guerre en face,* calling for sustained Western vigilance toward the Soviet military threat. Many took the opportunity to remind him of his former pacifist commitments.

> We were manipulated, but I don't regret signing the Stockholm Appeal. In the context of the time, of the Cold War and the threat of war, fighting for peace seemed all-important. I remember a big meeting at the Vélodrome d'Hiver where Duclos was overwhelming. In our innocence we were completely won over by him. We're not asking you to be Communists, he said, or even to sympathize with the Communists; we simply ask you to fight alongside us for peace. Let us preserve peace, or else we won't even be around to discuss our political differences. It was persuasive because people were genuinely fearful. Simone's father had said to her, "We have to leave Europe; there'll be war

> between the Americans and Russians at any time." We went along wholeheartedly: who could be against peace? It wasn't until much later that we realized the whole campaign was intended to gain time until the Russians, too, acquired the bomb. When that happened, the peace movement and the rallies and parades came to an end.

From the day they signed the Stockholm Appeal and appeared at peace movement meetings, Montand and Signoret were classified as fellow travelers of the Communist Party. For Montand, this commitment coincided with his coming together with Signoret. Does this mean that the Left Bank middle-class intellectual lured the singing prole onto the Communist path? The facts indicate otherwise: Montand had been committed from birth, a Communist at heart by both heritage and upbringing. The lyrics of some of his songs already put him in the ranks of the mobilized. Before living with Simone Signoret, he had performed two or three times at militant functions, particularly in support of striking miners. Since 1948, he had attended the annual book sale organized by the Communist-influenced National Writers Committee. He was one of the family. Signing the appeal merely confirmed his sympathies. It was the first time he had been asked to sign a public statement. It was also the first time the Communists had employed massive petitioning as a form of political action.

After that, the two stars were active together in the peace movement, which in Montand's mind was distinct from the Party. When people told the Montands that this was not the case, they angrily cited the long list of supporters who packed the rostrums but were not Party members. Today the distinction seems artificial, but it appeared very real then.

The Korean war supplied friends of Communism with their first chance of defending positions on an international scale. Not for a moment did Montand doubt that the real aggressor was American imperialism. When General MacArthur, after retaking South Korea, moved to invade North Korea, the singer saw it as a confirmation of his belief. He was not alone. The left-wing intelligentsia took up the North Korean cause. The Communist press overflowed with accounts of napalm bombing of peaceable villages. Picasso painted a picture, *Massacre in Korea,* in which robot soldiers fire on a group of naked women and children. Roger Vaillant wrote a hard-hitting play, *Le Colonel Forster plaidera coupable* (*Colonel Forster Pleads Guilty*). General Matthew Ridgway, MacArthur's successor, was accused of using bacterial weapons, which earned him the nickname in France of "Black Death" Ridgway.

When, in May 1952, Ridgway was posted to Paris as commander in chief of NATO forces, the Communist Party organized a street demonstration that degenerated into a riot, with violent clashes all night long. Montand's sister-in-law, Elvire, escaped with a badly bruised leg. André Stil, editor in chief of *L'Humanité,* and Party leader Jacques Duclos were arrested. For several days, leading Communist figures lay low; the controller of the Marseilles region, Politburo member François Billoux, hid in Giovanni Livi's house—the one Montand had bought for his parents at La Pounche.

The second line of attack for para-Communist organizations was the struggle against the French war in Indochina. The peace movement came out in support of dockers who refused to load war matériel and of Raymonde Dien, a demonstrator who had thrown herself on a railroad track to prevent a munitions train from leaving. In Toulon, Henri Martin was sentenced to five years in prison for giving sailors leaflets criticizing the dispatch of an expeditionary force to Indochina. He became the prototype of the revolutionary hero. Communist artists and intellectuals chose him as a model; Eluard and Aragon dedicated poems to him; realistic portraits of Martin in his cell were published; and Sartre himself wrote *L'Affaire Henri Martin,* a blend of case history and accusation that had vast influence.

It was at this time, in February 1952, that Francis Lemarque brought Montand the first lines of an antimilitary song:

Fleur au fusil
Tambour battant
Il va
Il a vingt ans
Un coeur d'amant
Qui bat
Un adjudant pour surveiller ses pas
Et son barda contre son flanc
Qui bat . . .

[With a flower in his barrel
And a beating of the drums
He goes
Twenty summers old
And a lover's heart
Which beats
A noncom behind him
His knapsack beside him
Which beats . . .]

Montand was impressed. "When I stopped singing," Lemarque remembers, "he said, 'Finish it as quickly as you can and bring it over.' The next day it was done. The song ended with the words 'When the guns fall silent forever.' He was against this ending, which he considered too dogmatic, and he was right. He liked the song so much that he sang it two or three days later at a fund raiser, the text in his hand—he hadn't had time to learn it." Singing "Quand un soldat" in the middle of the Indochina war amounted to a militant gesture. The government banned the song from the airwaves.

Montand was now exposed to reprisals. He received death threats in the mail. On several occasions hostile groups tried to disrupt his act. In Lyons, activists threw stink bombs in the auditorium just before a performance, and firefighters had to turn on the blowers to ventilate the theater. That same night, pamphlets were stuck to the fender of the truck carrying his equipment, and the police commissioner warned Montand that his safety as he left the theater could not be guaranteed. But when the show was over, Montand walked out the front with his head high through the hostile crowd outside. Nobody made a move.

At Mantes-la-Jolie, posters announcing a Montand concert were smeared with tar. Another evening, during the big show at the Etoile in late 1953, a squad led by Jean-Baptiste Biaggi, an extreme right-wing lawyer, took over the front row, their feet right at the edge of the orchestra pit. As soon as the curtain went up they unfolded copies of *L'Humanité* in order to disrupt the show and block the audience's view. Montand hesitated. If he broke off and addressed the interlopers, things were likely to turn ugly. He decided to keep a close watch on them and go on singing. But the moment the curtain went down for the first time, he rushed backstage and grabbed the *brigadier*—the big, bludgeonlike staff used to strike the three loud blows that herald the beginning of a stage performance in France. He kept it close by him until the finale. "He warned us," said Paraboschi, the drummer, " 'I'll beat the brains out of the first one to come up on stage.' " Bob Castella remembers hostile but low-key demonstrations at the Etoile: "When the song was over, one spectator yelled from the audience, 'Montand to Indochina!' He answered, 'No thanks, not for me,' and the whole auditorium applauded."

Montand passed up no chance of performing the controversial manifesto song. During an official fund raiser at the Comédie-Française, where the French president, Vincent Auriol, was expected, the organizers discreetly asked him not to perform it, but Montand disregarded the request and treated the celebrities to his antiwar message.

But even as he sang—

> Quand un soldat s'en va-t-en guerre il a
> Des tas de chansons et des fleurs sous ses pas

Quand un soldat revient de guerre il a
Simplement eu de la veine et puis voilà . . .

[When a soldier goes off to war he has
Songs and flowers at his feet
When a soldier returns from war he has
Had mere luck and that's all . . .]

—he became somehow uneasy: suddenly the gesture felt like a too-easy provocation.

In the early 1950s, Montand gave unvarnished expression to his beliefs, both in life and on stage. Interviewed in *L'Avant-Garde,* the Communist Youth paper, on April 4, 1950, Montand himself confirmed this: "The role of a singer is to reflect the life of all workers without exception." In 1952 he sang for workers at the Renault factory in Billancourt and held a gala for Secours Populaire Français (French Aid) at the Mutualité hall. At a peace movement rally at the Porte de Vincennes he sang "Quand un soldat," while Gérard Philipe recited Eluard's poem "Liberté" and Signoret read a statement of her own. (Montand and Philipe often worked together on such occasions. Bringing the king of French music hall together with the leading movie box-office draw guaranteed the Party a huge turnout.)

Under the left-wing direction of Jean Vilar, the Théâtre National Populaire was drawing audiences very similar to those who came to see Montand. The TNP was a presiding spirit, almost a priesthood, with a passionate, talented, ferociously egalitarian troupe (each of whom, whatever the role, received the same wages), from which had risen the "gemlike flame" of Gérard Philipe. Montand went to sing at Suresnes, at a weekend rally organized by the TNP. "Our cause was the defense of peace," as Anne Philipe, the wife of Gérard, has explained. "World war seemed imminent, and to us the Communist Party represented the only guarantee of peace."

As already mentioned, Montand also took part in the annual book sale organized by the National Writers Committee. The committee advocated "battles of books": writers close to, or already members of, the Party were mobilized to champion progressive culture against the "literature of decadence." In Paris, the annual sale had become a major social-political event of the autumn season, and it attracted the great names of letters and entertainment. In 1952 it was held at the Vélodrome d'Hiver, which could handle thirty thousand people. Writers were flanked by artists; in the stands were Bernard Blier, Alain Cuny, Danièle Delorme, Juliette Gréco, Jean Marais, Noël-Noël, Micheline Presle, and Jacques Tati. Montand and Signoret stood in for Eluard, who was ill and dying. "The two stars were mobbed repeatedly," reported *Les Lettres Françaises* on November 27, alongside a photo of the embattled couple.

So many celebrities were proof of the Communist Party's drawing power. Yves Montand sacrificed himself in the ritual of book signing, autographing copies of his ghostwritten autobiography *Du soleil plein la tête,* based on conversations edited by Jean Denys. Curiously, though, Montand, although invited, never performed at the yearly Fête de *L'Humanité,* which drew large composite throngs more numerous than the Party's actual membership: he feared that if he appeared in an overtly Party setting, he would lose a part of his public. He accepted invitations that went with his status as a fellow traveler, but he was careful not to be seen as an official Party artist. Still, the press, particularly on the right, persistently labeled him a Communist, although he was never a member of the Party.

Once, at least, Montand seriously considered taking the leap. Most artists and intellectuals who joined the Communist Party did so because they saw it as the party of the working class. Generally of wealthy or middle-class backgrounds, they were ashamed of the social infamy of their origins, and they sought to wash away the stain by immersing themselves in the proletariat. But Ivo Livi's roots absolved him from sharing the sense of guilt that drove so many intelligent people to grovel before workers-turned-apparatchiks.

An inverse form of guilt tormented Montand. Born into poverty and lucky enough to emerge from it into fame and fortune, he blamed himself for not sharing the real life of the militants—those who distributed pamphlets, stuck up posters at night, sold *L'Humanité* door to door. The former metalworker was embarrassed at being a silk-shirt militant, a figurehead at meetings, an excuse for petitions, taking no real risks himself. After the anti-Ridgway demonstration and the arrest of Duclos and Stil, the Party seemed threatened with repression: at this juncture, Montand briefly thought of joining.

Communist leaders or journalists sometimes dropped by to chat in the "trailer." The writer Claude Roy also called, more as a neighbor and friend than as a Party member. But the Communist who wielded the most influence over Montand at this time was his own brother, and it was to Julien that Yves broached the question of joining. "During this difficult time for the Party," says Julien, "my brother wanted to stress his solidarity by joining openly. I believe he had also been asked to do so by people at the head of the Party. I was against it. Our father had always said, 'You don't approach the Party as if you were going to the theater. If you don't like a play, you can walk out. If you join the Party, you accept everything.' Leaving the Party was a major strike against you, particularly if you were well known. My brother was under all kinds of pressure from social circles whose convictions were not rock-solid. For all these reasons I advised him to stay outside. He objected that emissaries from the Party had insisted. So I went to the top. There were some lively discussions. But it ended there."

The fellow-traveling Montand might not pay membership dues, but he opened his pocketbook. In response to one collection drive sponsored by *L'Humanité,* he personally delivered a million francs in bills wrapped in newspaper to the daily's headquarters. Another time, following a phone call from her brother-in-law, then in Italy, Elvire Livi took 600,000 francs to the Party offices.

Everyone except the Party leaders eventually believed that Montand and Signoret were Party members, and France's most famous fellow travelers did nothing to correct the misapprehension. "We didn't think it was wrong to be a Communist," wrote Simone Signoret. Indeed, they considered themselves Communists at heart and were proud that people believed they really were; to them, holding a membership card was a mere formality. Besides, they "agreed with them on most things."

What held them back from total commitment was the Party's ideas on art and literature and the role the Party assigned to intellectuals. Laurent Casanova, watchdog of the intelligentsia, issued strict instructions to the faithful: "Accept every one of the working class's political and ideological positions; defend every Party position in all circumstances and with utmost resolution; cultivate love of the Party in its most conscious form: Party spirit."[4]

As if the Party fetters were not yet tight enough, some intellectuals even hailed the Party as the sole source of their genius. André Stil, awarded a Stalin Prize for his socialist-realist endeavors, knelt in deep humility before the godlike Party: "This is why we must so insistently reiterate that when we manage to write good things, it is to our Party that we owe them. This is why—even if it embarrasses or amuses some of you—I wish to say again today that it is not only as a militant but as a writer that I owe everything to the Party."[5]

This subordination of talent to dogma led artists and writers to a utilitarian conception of art that the Party leader Maurice Thorez had set

4. Speech at the Salle Wagram, February 28, 1949.

5. Speech at the Ivry city hall, April 11, 1952.

out in uncompromising terms: "Against the decadent works of bourgeois esthetes, partisans of art for art's sake, against the deep-rooted pessimism and backward-looking obscurantism of the existentialist philosophers, we raise the banner of an art drawing its inspiration from socialist realism and comprehensible to the working class, an art that will help the working class in its fight for freedom."[6] Let the scientists fight bourgeois science with proletarian science; let the artists vanquish bourgeois culture with proletarian culture.

Required to glorify the virtues of Communism, the apostles of socialist realism were drowning in an insane personality cult. The former Surrealist Paul Eluard wove the following garland for the brilliant "Guide of the World Proletariat":

> Et Staline pour nous est présent pour demain
> Et Staline dissipe aujourd'hui le malheur
> La confiance est le fruit de son cerveau d'amour . . .
>
> [And Stalin for us stands firm for tomorrow
> And Stalin for us clears today of fears
> Our trust is the fruit of his great love . . .][7]

Official painters favored trowels over paintbrushes in order to portray larger-than-life miners or metalworkers.

Montand was not wholly convinced by this proletarian modishness. When he and Signoret watched a Soviet film in which bright-eyed peasant girls harvested wheat while singing odes to Stalin, he acknowledged that the photography was acceptable, but nothing more. Politically speaking, the eager neophyte was prepared to swallow a lot, but in his own field, where he judged according to his own standards, he could not swallow such a reductive concept of creation.

And Montand was himself the object of careful surveillance by guardians of the temple. The "comrades" observed that in "Luna Park," the worker from Puteaux, looking for fun as soon as he had an idle moment, did not present a sufficiently militant profile. Montand replied that proles also had a right to amuse themselves. Of course, of course, they said; but it would distract them from the revolutionary struggle. The worker would no longer be thinking of fighting; he would be strengthening himself to the advantage of his capitalist exploiters.

6. Speech at the Strasbourg Congress, 1947.

7. Paul Eluard, *Les Cahiers du Communisme,* January 1950.

Similar pressures were put on him to drop "Une Demoiselle sur une balançoire" ("A Girl on a Swing"), which was much too frothy for the men of steel. The singer refused, but he provisionally agreed to retire "C'est si bon" from his repertory. He liked the tune and the seeming frivolity of its theme:

> C'est si bon
> De se dire des mots doux
> Des petits rien du tout
> Mais qui en disent long

It was distinctly too "American" for the temple guardians. In vain, Montand protested that the song and the rhythm had been invented by American blacks, that Louis Armstrong had transformed "C'est si bon" into an international success. He had to back down. It was the only time he did so, but it was once too many. Florimond Bonté, a Communist leader, even pressed him to sing a song he himself had written about Paris. Montand flatly refused.

But the main thrust was directed at Prévert's poem "Sanguine," whose open eroticism offended the alleged modesty of the masses:

> Oh sanguine joli fruit
> La pointe de ton sein
> A tracé tendrement
> La ligne de ma chance
> Dans le creux de ma main
> Sanguine joli fruit
> Soleil de nuit!
>
> [Sweet blood-orange
> Your nipple
> Tenderly traces
> My lifeline
> In my palm
> Sweet blood-orange
> Night sun!]

To the killjoys, Montand retorted that workers, too, sometimes made love. He went on singing "Sanguine"—but with intermittent spasms of doubt. Perhaps the Party was right to preach "revolutionary morality"?

In fact, Stalinist puritanism was based on a radical critique of "bourgeois morality," which was held to be heavy with active or incipient putrefaction. Communist intellectuals constantly championed the ethic of the New Man, the disciplined rigor of the militant, against the craven lies of a decaying society. The model was the "positive hero," the virtuous worker who embodied optimism in the form of unswerving confidence in the future, a sharp contrast to the neurotic flounderings of the enemy camp. The proletarian press of the day bristled with bayonets. Annie Besse, for example—who was later better known by her pen name, Annie Kriegel—attacked the author of *Le Noeud de vipères* (*The Vipers' Nest*) in the following terms: "M. Mauriac can rest assured that no Soviet man will ever seek to wrest from him the bloated, lying suppuration that is his inner life."[8]

The Communist ideologue Jean Kanapa was shocked by the extent of public obscenity. "One particular week in 1952 was the last straw," he wrote. "There was *Sensuality,* a Swedish movie, and also *Sensualità,* an Italian film. There was *Susana la perverse* and *Les Surprises d'une nuit de noce.* . . . At the theater *Une Femme nue dans le Métro* was playing: there were even colored posters to illustrate it, in the Métro, of course."[9] That at such a time of moral fence-building the Party's favorite singer could celebrate *"l'orage heureux de ton corps amoureux"* ("the happy storm sweeping your amorous body") looked like provocation, even irresponsibility. But with the significant exception of "C'est si bon," Montand persevered, rejecting a "proletarian" line that would have yielded only inane and insipid songs. Even at the height of his enthusiasm for the Party, he was unable to make politics and esthetics rhyme.

By refusing to conflate singing with resolutions adopted at Party congresses and to accept the need for immediate "relevance" in entertainment, Montand excluded himself from the category of "integrated" artists, whose work directly educated the workers and raised the "consciousness of the masses." Here the line between militant and mere sympathizer was clearly drawn. On the other hand, his fame, as well as that of Signoret and other fellow travelers, reflected glory on the Party—the more so since this distinction between "comrades" and "friends" permitted the Communists to widen their nets and appeal to a broader constituency. "What is more precious than friends," asked Signoret, "especially when they don't go around proclaiming that they are not comrades?"

So the Party proudly exhibited its "friends" Montand, Signoret, and Philipe, knowing it would be tactless to impose overly strict rules on them. Theirs was privileged treatment and relative freedom, granted in return for the publicity they brought in. In a sense, they were more valuable to

8. Annie Besse, *La Nouvelle Critique,* April 1953.

9. Jean Kanapa, *Situation de l'intellectuel: Critique de la culture* (Paris, 1957).

the Party on the outside, considering the return expected of them. Throughout the 1950s, when Montand and Signoret were "betrothed to the Party," the Communists used him at least as much as he used them. Sometimes they did not even ask his opinion. In June 1951, a pamphlet issued by the Communist section of the sixth arrondissement tampered with a series of quoted remarks by Montand and Gérard Philipe, making it seem that they were calling for support for the Communist leader André Marty in the forthcoming elections. Outraged that his name had been exploited without his permission, Montand raised the roof. His brother carried his complaint to the top, where they ascribed the blame to a rash "local initiative."

And, of course, Montand's name was constantly solicited for petitions. According to a careful count done by *L'Humanité* of the period from January 1951 to June 1953, his signature appeared beneath sixteen appeals. It put him among the country's leading signers.

And yet the Communist Party was simultaneously drawing in upon itself and becoming a beleaguered fortress. Young people who had embraced Communism at the Liberation, borne on the romantic wings of the Resistance, began to ask themselves questions when Tito turned overnight from hero into traitor. The Central Committee hacks in Moscow were now declaring that the maverick Yugoslav marshal used Gestapo tactics and ran American spy networks inside the "people's democracies." In December 1949, a Communist official, Georges Cogniot, asserted that Yugoslavia was as sadistic and police-ridden as Hitler's Germany.

It was for "Titoism" that Lazlo Rajk, the Hungarian minister of the interior, was tried and executed in the first in a long series of trials in Eastern Europe—trials that were strongly backed by France's Stalinists. When André Breton asked Paul Eluard, his former companion in the Surrealist movement, to help in Rajk's defense, Eluard responded with this unforgettable formula: "I have too much to do with the innocent proclaiming their innocence to spend time on the guilty asserting their guilt." Party theorists talked of "aggravation of the class struggle," saying it was logical that traitors were trying to sabotage the building of Socialism. When Montand read that Secretary of State John Foster Dulles had urged investing millions of dollars in efforts to destabilize the East European nations, he did not doubt the truth of the charges, particularly when those on trial in Eastern Europe began to confess.

Although he did not let it show, Montand was shaken in November 1949 by the revelations of the historian David Rousset, who called for a committee of inquiry into Soviet prison camps, of which he himself had been an inmate. At once, Pierre Daix shot back in the Communist *Lettres*

Françaises: "Why is David Rousset inventing Soviet camps?" Rousset sued the paper, but survivors of Hitler's camps came forward to support Daix and his followers. Sartre and Maurice Merleau-Ponty entered the debate with an article in *Les Temps Modernes* in which they estimated the number of prisoners in the Soviet Union at 10 to 15 million. Daix, again in *Les Lettres Françaises,* asked the two philosophers whether they were "with the Soviet people or with its enemies."

Like the vast majority of fellow travelers, Montand could not accept the idea that favoring the Soviet camp also meant tolerating Soviet concentration camps. This was too monstrous to be credible. When an atom or two of suspicion intruded every now and then, it was wisest to dispel it before it compromised the stability and coherence of the system as a whole. Faith did not tolerate the slightest uncertainty; otherwise, it collapsed. So Montand was careful not to read through the report of Rousset's committee of inquiry or the comments on the case in *Le Figaro.* Reading your enemies was already treason. Listening to the other side's point of view was outright surrender. At a dinner party one evening, a guest hazarded a joke about the Soviet camps. Signoret and her husband at once left the table. Better lies about the truth than the truth about lies.

Montand's attitude during the Slansky trial exemplified this schizophrenia. In November 1952, Rudolf Slansky, the secretary general of the Czechoslovak Communist Party, was tried for crimes of "Titoism and Zionism." The correspondent for *L'Humanité* in Prague reported that after interrogation, the accused confessed that he "had planned to become the Czechoslovak Tito," his goal being to force his country "into the imperialist camp." Recalling his father's unease at the time of the Moscow show trials before the war, Montand reflected that the list of turncoats was growing suspiciously long. He was still groping for an explanation when a reporter from *Le Figaro* called to ask his opinion of the Slansky trial. Montand—and this was a sign of his doubts—asked for time to think and phoned his friend Claude Jaeger. He advised Montand to reply in the same terms Eluard had used. Montand therefore said that he was too busy with the innocent asserting their innocence to concern himself with the guilty asserting their guilt.

Among the fourteen defendants charged along with Slansky in Prague was Artur London, the deputy foreign minister. One cannot fathom the expiatory rage with which Montand approached the task of playing London in a film seventeen years later unless one recalls that earlier zealot's remark. At the time, he did not imagine for a moment that the trials were rigged. He never forgave those who knew for deceiving him. He never forgave himself for believing them.

How could we have swallowed such horrors? It must seem strange indeed to the youth of today.

How could eminent scientists have believed in "proletarian science"? How could brilliant writers and superior minds have given their blessing to such a system? If all those people with intelligence and knowledge were led astray in this way, how could I—uneducated, a product of La Cabucelle—have had doubts?

If I wavered for a moment, I thought of the heroes of Stalingrad, of the 20 million Soviet citizens killed in the war against Hitlerism, of a country devastated by war. If I had known about the gulag during the war I would have been horrified, but I still would have been on the side of the Red Army. That kind of loyalty may be incomprehensible to those who have not lived through war, but for my generation it was an article of faith.

Yet it was in the name of that loyalty that we accepted the unacceptable. The Party spirit canceled out questions and criticism. Fear of giving ammunition to the enemy pushed aside all doubt. There were examples in my own family. One evening, Julien came home shaken to the core. In an unsteady voice he told us that the Party wanted to expel him. We were stunned. They wanted to expel him because he had not escaped from the POW camp during the war. The thing was finally cleared up, but what was horrible about the whole business was that not one of us dreamed of questioning the Party's actions. On the contrary. I said to myself, "The Party can't be making a mistake, Julien must have fouled up somewhere." Our conditioned reflex, in little things as well as in grand causes, was that the Party could not be wrong.

In fact, this blindness was love. Try telling a man that his fiancée or his wife is cheating on him. If he loves her he'll refuse to accept it; he'll deny the evidence even if you have written proof; he won't leave her. We were in a state of emotional dependency in which arguments were of no avail.

Throughout this period Julien, a card-carrying Communist, perpetuated Papa Livi's militant tradition: as a trade-union official he defended the workers, and when his professional duties took him to the Soviet Union he sent back postcards brimming with his happiness at being in paradise. "From Kharkov, 65 percent destroyed and now totally rebuilt," he wrote in 1952, "affectionate greetings from an enthusiastic traveler." As an apparatchik close to Party ruling circles, he was the voice of the Party at the Place Dauphine. When arguments among friends in the "trailer" grew too noisy, Montand called his brother to the rescue. But in private, the family compasses did not point to exactly the same north. Although Signoret backed the Party to the hilt in public, within the family circle she voiced objections that nettled Julien Livi. "It isn't true that Simone helped push my brother toward commitment," Julien says firmly. "If anything, she pushed him in the other direction. She was critical of the Party. I had endless arguments with her—about the Spanish civil war, for instance, in which she championed the anarchists. We clashed often, and violently."

Julien swallowed the Party line whole, including its declarations about literature, while Simone was warier. She exploded when her brother-in-law argued that Hemingway could be better occupied than writing empty tales like *The Old Man and the Sea,* or when he repeated the Stalinist comment on André Gide's death: "He isn't dead; he was dead already." (Since his skeptical book *Retour d'URSS* [*Return from the USSR*], Gide had been a favorite target of Communist mudslingers.)

Julien feared the influence on his brother of Signoret and her Trotskyite connections. His fears were pointless, for deep inside, Montand already agreed with the essentials of her criticisms (even though in the heat of discussion he disputed them violently). Moreover, Montand provided his clever Left Bank wife with a sure anchor in the working world, and there was nothing more precious to a progressive intellectual—however irritated she might be by "proletarian orthodoxy." Thus, the almost imperceptible seeds of dissension had already been sown, though the hour for the final break had not yet struck.

For years, the Communist Party called the faithful back to the fold by warning them that going public with their doubts would be playing into the enemy's hands. Sartre had said that it was vital not to take hope away from the masses, and France's red intelligentsia, already bogged down in class guilt, was particularly sensitive to this bludgeon of an argument. Like their friends, Montand and Signoret were subject to this blackmail, and frequent attacks on them from the right seemed to confirm the thesis that there was no neutral terrain.

"Periodically I would be portrayed 'selling *L'Humanité-Dimanche* in a mink coat,' or, worse, 'sending out the maid to sell *L'Humanité-Dimanche* while watching from a distance to make sure she does it well,' " joked Signoret. The commonest form of attack addressed the fatal dichotomy between the Montands' life style and political opinions. In February 1952, on the day of a public transport strike, a "bourgeois" daily published a photo of Montand beside his car, a superb Bentley, with the caption: "No bus today? Yves Montand had his Bentley!"

There was a story behind that Bentley. As soon as he started to earn real money, Montand recalled the dreams of the urchin who had admiringly stroked the gleaming chrome of the café owner Garone's front-wheel-drive Citroën. First he bought himself a Citroën. Then, in order to be able to ferry his musicians and their instruments on tour, he acquired an enormous black American Packard. One day he stopped at a red light on the boulevard Saint-Michel, and a student whistled through his teeth, calling out contemptuously, "Plutocrat!"

Montand decided that for someone known for singing "Je vais à pied" ("I Go on Foot"), the Packard was not a model of tact. He looked for another car, as powerful but less ostentatious. A few years earlier, when he had been going around with Gisèle Pascal, he had run into Prince Rainier of Monaco. Rainier had seemed interested in the actress, and Montand had fallen in love with the prince's Bentley. When he heard it was for sale, he at once sank all his savings into buying it. Fortunately, the press never learned that Montand's Bentley had belonged to the man who inherited the Rock!

Just before the Etoile concert in 1953, the daily *Combat* prominently displayed a new article sneering at the contrast between Montand's songs and his way of life. The story triggered an avalanche of letters, which *Combat* published under the headline "The Montand Affair." Most readers vigorously defended the singer, and these marks of support, proving the extent to which Montand's popularity went way beyond the circle of Communist sympathizers, were music to his ears. Montand was ready to take responsibility for his stand as a politically committed singer, but not to be imprisoned within the bounds of an "official" singer. Diversity of audience was important to him, and workers' blue coveralls had never been required wear for his Etoile concerts. He considered it out of the question to sacrifice his stage career to his presence on official Communist hustings. Between the Etoile and the Party, between Crolla and Thorez, Montand had made up his mind from the start. Friends from that period insist that politics was far from dominating his life. "Yves and Simone were close to the Party," recalls Serge Reggiani, "even a bit Stalinist around the edges, but it was mainly words. They didn't actually *do* much. They hardly ever joined street demonstrations. Basically, I had the feeling that neither Montand nor Simone was truly committed, in the sense of that commitment shaping their lives." Paul Grimault recalls a Montand who didn't take himself too seriously and didn't meditate constantly on the fate of humankind. "Prévert and I did not consider him a Stalinist," he adds.

Montand found it difficult to back the Party's ideas on one by-no-means-minor point: its reflexive anti-Americanism. It went against the grain of the kid from La Cabucelle who had dreamed of New York, the movie-infatuated boy who adored American musical comedies, American democracy, the American New Deal.

But in France in the early 1950s, criticism of the United States had turned into phobia. The sentiment was not new. Since the Wall Street crash and the Depression, many commentators on both the right and the left had railed against North American civilization, which they saw as inhuman, production-obsessed, machinelike, soulless. The postwar global spread of American influence further offended the nationalist in every Frenchman.[10] Onto these longstanding feelings, which the Party efficiently exploited, was grafted the East-West confrontation.

Yankee imperialism was military, it was said, aiming to dominate the planet, and it lit fires wherever its interests were threatened. Communist propagandists worked this vein to remarkable effect during the Korean war. GIs were portrayed as the new SS, and General Ridgway (despite the fact that he had parachuted into France at the head of the 82nd Airborne Division after the Normandy landings) was a "Nazi." Since U.S. forces were based on French soil as part of NATO, it became a high-priority Communist goal to demand their departure. "U.S. Go Home" graffiti flowered on French walls. To many, the equation of Americans and Nazis seemed hard to refute: the Yanks had simply taken the place of the Nazi Occupation forces. In May 1951, *L'Humanité* even ran a survey on what it called "The American Occupation in France." As early as January 1948, *Les Lettres Françaises* published a cartoon showing Dr. Goebbels handing out anti-Soviet pamphlets to a gratified Uncle Sam.

United States hegemony was also economic, exercised through the Marshall Plan. Communist thinkers could not find words strong enough to denounce this "colonization" of Europe, this stranglehold by the Wall Street "trusts." Montand never managed to suppress a smile when he heard the word "trust." As a child at the family table, he had often heard the grownups discuss the awful "trusts" and the no-less-awful Trotsky. For a long time, the similarity of the two words led him to believe that Trotsky himself ran the trusts.

Although he and Signoret were prepared to accept denunciations of American military and economic imperialism, they balked when the criticism spilled over into American culture. Ever since the Communist Party had discovered Joan of Arc and the French flag, its house intellectuals had postured as the guardians of tradition, the true heirs of the nation's literary and artistic heritage. The people who went into ecstasies over mediocre Soviet theatrical productions or lauded the "positive" heroes of socialist-

10. See Michel Winock, "L'Antiaméricanisme français," *Histoire,* November 1982.

realist movies strenuously rejected all transatlantic imports. Aragon was dismayed at Faulkner's influence. Ilya Ehrenburg said sneeringly of the Americans, "The dollar has gone to their heads. They seriously believe that Broadway movies [sic] are more beautiful than the Acropolis and that *Reader's Digest* is better than Tolstoy."[11]

The French-language edition of *Reader's Digest,* with its naive, simplistic enthusiasm for the American way of life, was an easy target. But despite the violence of the assault, the magazine's circulation of 1.2 million was among the highest in France. Coca-Cola, that disturbing beverage concocted by a "racist trust," was also thrown into the mixer. "Soon they'll be saying 'Coca-Cola *über alles*' the way they used to say '*Deutschland über alles.*' But what is Coca-Cola? One characteristic of this drink is that it creates a dependency, like narcotics."[12] To this dark picture of Yankee domination must be added the incursion of Camel cigarettes, which had dethroned the native Gauloises; the proliferation of comic books; and the invasion of Hollywood movies.

Montand did not go along with the ritual diatribes on the last two points. He had signed a petition protesting a 1946 Franco-American agreement that allowed American films to flood the French market. But he was too fond—and had been fond for too long—of transatlantic films, actors, and directors ever to approve a blanket denunciation of Billy Wilder or Frank Capra movies, most particularly because they reflected New World ideas of justice and freedom. Here again, he kept his objections to himself. Anti-Americanism was inseparable from the Party.

This Satanization of America reached a paroxysm with the Rosenberg case. This time, Montand and Signoret really were inclined to believe that the seeds of Fascism were growing in the United States. Arrested in 1950, Julius and Ethel Rosenberg were tried for treason the following year, charged with building a spy network for the Soviet Union and, in particular, with handing over secrets about the atomic bomb. The trial left an aftertaste of doubt: how could a lowly engineer have transferred such important information on a piece of paper? But the issue was contested in an international climate favorable to paranoid imaginings: Cold War in Europe, hot war in Korea, Communist victory in China. The Rosenbergs proclaimed their innocence. The jury found them guilty, and the judge condemned them to death. There then began a worldwide campaign in favor of the accused spies—a campaign whose participants came from fields far beyond Communist spheres of influence. In their calls for clemency, Pope Pius XII, French president Vincent Auriol, and Bertrand Russell all

11. Ilya Ehrenburg, *Action,* December 15, 1949, in Legendre, *Qui a dit quoi?*
12. Ibid.

asked that the pair be granted the benefit of the doubt. The French intelligentsia took up arms as if faced with a new Dreyfus affair.

> We were stupid and we were dangerous. I've said it before and I stand by it. If you were a member of the Party in those days and you worked in an "interesting" area of French industry, you regarded it as your duty, should the Party request it, to find out how this or that item was manufactured. I would have done it myself. I did not see it as a form of treason at all. On the contrary: it was for the good of the working class, of mankind. We still don't know whether the Rosenbergs were guilty or not, but if they did hand over secrets, it would have been in this same spirit—to serve the cause of peace.

At dawn, in Sing-Sing prison, on June 19, 1953, the Rosenbergs went to the electric chair. A wave of indignation followed, and the whole of America, held to be guilty of officially sanctioned murder, was heaped with opprobrium. Two days before the accused were executed, thousands of construction workers had paraded through East Berlin calling for higher wages and the promise of free elections; Soviet tanks intervened, firing into the crowd and killing more than a hundred people. *L'Humanité* resurrected the thesis that this was a "Fascist putsch" concocted by former Nazis. Not one fellow traveler—not Montand or anyone else—protested at the crackdown. Years later, Signoret said she felt she had been manipulated to attend to the defense of the Rosenbergs: "While the whole world and I were fighting for the Rosenbergs," she said in an interview in *L'Express* in 1970, "there were heaps and heaps of Rosenbergs in the USSR. And those who orchestrated the anti-American witch hunt here knew perfectly well what was going on in Soviet Russia."

Thus the revulsion triggered by the Rosenberg executions effectively masked the crimes committed on the other side of the Iron Curtain. What made things look worse was that the Rosenberg drama unfolded against the background of Senator Joseph McCarthy's witch hunts. On March 21, 1951, the very day the "Communist spy" trial had ended in New York, hearings before the House Committee on Un-American Activities (HUAC) began in Washington, and subversion in Hollywood was on the agenda.

Created by the House of Representatives in 1938 to fight Nazi and Communist influence in the United States, the committee had focused on the latter since the war. In 1947, it began looking into the movie world, in which the American Communist Party had acquired real, if limited, influence in the 1930s. By subpoenaing famous Hollywood figures, the committee was, of course, guaranteed welcome publicity. Gary Cooper assured them that he turned down any script that contained even a whiff of Communist ideas, and Actors Equity president Ronald Reagan assured them that they could count on his vigilance. Walt Disney testified that attempts to subvert Mickey Mouse had failed.

By the end of its inquiry, the committee had garnered ten names, among them some of Hollywood's greatest scriptwriters, including Albert Maltz and Dalton Trumbo, as well as the director Edward Dmytryk. Called to Washington, the so-called Hollywood Ten invoked the Fifth Amendment and refused to say whether they were Communists. They were sentenced to prison terms for contempt of Congress, despite the support of some members of their profession (including Lauren Bacall and Humphrey Bogart). The heads of the major studios conferred, then announced the suspension of the ten and promised that no Communist would ever work in Hollywood again.

When HUAC resumed its activities in 1951, the climate had changed. The inquisition that followed took place against a background of collective madness that had seized a fearful America. For a year, an obscure senator from Wisconsin had been the star of American politics. On February 9, 1950, addressing the Republican Ladies Club in Wheeling, West Virginia, Joseph McCarthy had brandished a list of 205 names of supposed Communists who, he claimed, had infiltrated the State Department. The crusade to purge America was under way, and the cartoonist Herblock popularized the word for this attitude, which left a stain on American history: "McCarthyism." As the crusade gathered momentum, no sector of politics, business, or entertainment escaped suspicion. Blacklists of people who were not to be given jobs were circulated; "graylists" fingered more doubtful cases. Aragon's magazine, *Les Lettres Françaises,* published a "McCarthy list" of authors whose works were "banned, destroyed, or burned." According to the weekly, Einstein, Freud, Gorky, Dashiel Hammett, Hemingway, Thomas Mann, Maupassant, Sartre, Steinbeck, and Zola—among many others—were condemned. Under the headline "Book Burners in the United States," the magazine reproduced several articles from the American press describing the autos-da-fé—and inevitably invoked dark parallels with Nazi Germany. Had Thomas Mann not figured on the "Otto List" in 1941?

With growing anger, Yves Montand and Simone Signoret watched the pestilence attack the world dear to them. How could they continue to speak up for American movies when the industry was banning humanitarians and progressives? Charlie Chaplin, a resident of the United States for more than forty years, returned to Europe; Jules Dassin, John Berry, and Joseph Losey left. Montand and Signoret's anger rose another notch when they saw directors or actors they admired cooperating with HUAC. It looked as if the American democracy that Montand had always worshiped—even as a Communist sympathizer—were about to go under. Blackmail at the workplace had brought everyone face-to-face with his conscience.

For this time, several witnesses—out of conviction or fear for their jobs—agreed to cooperate. Lee J. Cobb, who had created the title role in *Death of a Salesman,* gave in after two years of uninterrupted pressure. Dmytryk, who had kept silent in 1947, divulged twenty-six names in 1951, then explained his action in a long article in the *Saturday Evening Post.* Elia Kazan took out an ad in the *New York Times* to justify his "betrayal" (he had belonged to the Communist Party from 1934 to 1936): "My personal experience of dictatorships and of their coercing of minds had left me with an unwavering hatred of them. An unwavering hatred of Communist philosophy and methods, as well as the conviction that we must never stop resisting them."

Just before testifying, Kazan talked with the playwright Arthur Miller. They had often worked together; Kazan had directed the first productions of two of his friend's plays, *All My Sons* and *Death of a Salesman.* Kazan told Miller he intended to talk, arguing that he was not going to sacrifice his career for a cause he had rejected. Miller tried to dissuade him. The next day, Kazan testified in Washington, and Miller left for the little Massachusetts town of Salem.

For some time, Miller had been seeking an idea for a play that would address this inquisitorial mood. "What I sought," he wrote, "was a metaphor, an image that would spring out of the heart, all-inclusive, full of light, a sonorous instrument whose reverberations would penetrate to the center of this miasma."[13] Now Miller came across a book by Marion Starkey, *The Devil in Massachusetts,* describing the Salem witchcraft trials of 1692. In the court records, Miller examined the interrogation that had taken John Proctor to the gallows for entering into a pact with the Devil.

Driving back to New York, Miller listened to the account of Kazan's testimony on the radio. Across three centuries a parallel between the two situations emerged, even though, as supporters of the committee pointed out, there had never been any witches, while the Communists were most assuredly real. But for Miller, the connecting thread was the ritual of interrogation that demanded confession. Thanks to the FBI, the committee knew everything about the American Communist Party and its affiliates.

13. Arthur Miller, *Timebends* (New York, 1987).

What it was determined to get were confessions, names of accomplices, public exorcism. "What was manifestly parallel was the guilt, two centuries apart, of holding illicit, suppressed feelings of alienation and hostility toward standard, daylight society as defined by its most orthodox proponents."[14]

In the intolerant climate of the time, Arthur Miller denied that he had written a play about McCarthyism; however, some of its lines sounded too contemporary to fool anyone in 1953: "But you must understand, sir, that a person is either with this court or he must be counted against it, there be no road between. This is a sharp time, now, a precise time—we live no longer in the dusky afternoon when evil mixed itself with good and befuddled the world. Now, by God's grace, the shining sun is up, and them that fear not light will surely praise it." In the climate of the day, his play, *The Crucible,* met with only modest success in New York.

In late 1953, a friend sent Montand and his wife a translation of *The Crucible,* which their friend John Berry had enthusiastically praised. They read the play in bed, passing the pages to each other one by one through the night. Neither had even heard of Arthur Miller, who was unknown in France at the time, but when dawn came they were determined to perform the play in Paris. Montand wanted the text to be adapted for French audiences by Sartre—their first choice—or by Marcel Aymé. According to Signoret, the philosopher let them know through his secretary, Jean Cau, that he was declining the honor—without having read the text. Only later, when he attended rehearsals, did he regret his peremptory refusal.

Marcel Aymé also turned them down at first. But for love of an actress who was hoping for a part (she failed to get it), he finally accepted. The only condition set by Montand and Signoret before tackling the operation was that Raymond Rouleau direct. Once Jacques Becker's favorite performer, Rouleau had made himself a towering name as a theater director since the war. He was also a hard taskmaster, reputedly so inflexible that many actors hesitated to put themselves under his command. Rouleau had met Miller in New York and knew the play. He eagerly accepted when M. Julien, manager of the Théâtre Sarah-Bernhardt, asked him to direct it.

For both Montand and Signoret, appearing in a stage play was an adventure. Simone was a screen star; she feared the stage and worried that her voice would not carry. Montand—apart from the "Chevalier Bayard" caper—knew nothing about the legitimate theater. But he had mastered the art of having a direct relationship with an audience, and had learned to control his fear.

14. Ibid.

He still had to absorb the essential: acting on stage. Rouleau was meticulous, a perfectionist—qualities his pupil appreciated. The director put Montand to work at a pace he was always equal to; long afterward, Rouleau still remembered it. "Montand," he said, "was a model student. . . . He knew nothing of the theater. Not a thing. I had the privilege of watching the whole of his development from within the work we did together. I know how unremittingly he works; I've seen it with my own eyes. He learned. He never stopped wanting to learn. . . . He experimented, he sought, he labored."[15]

Montand also enlisted the help of some of his actor friends: José Artur and Serge Reggiani put him through classical passages from Racine and Molière. And to bring the mechanisms of intolerance and inquisition into clearer relief, Rouleau constantly sought French analogies in the play. He spoke of the yellow star worn by Jews during the war, of the "special" French courts that had prosecuted Communists and Jews during the Occupation, of the wartime letters in which neighbor had denounced neighbor. When the cast heard that Arthur Miller would not be able to attend the final dress rehearsal because his passport had been withdrawn, the parallels between McCarthyism and the seventeenth-century witch hunt convinced the least committed of the performers.

Miller had conceived *The Crucible* before the Rosenbergs' execution, but for Montand and Signoret the Proctor and Rosenberg dramas overlapped. Signoret has acknowledged how much her reading of Ethel Rosenberg's prison letters helped her achieve the emotional level she sought. Everyone noticed that the final farewell scene, in which Proctor embraces his wife with his fettered hands, closely resembled the photo, seen all over the world, of the Rosenbergs before their execution.

Signoret also added that her identification with the martyred couple who refused to confess would have been lessened had she been aware that others, in Prague, were swinging from gallows after confessing to imaginary crimes in Communist courts. Guilty or innocent (no one, even today, can say for sure), the Rosenbergs were the only people condemned to death during the American witch hunt; on the Communist side, the victims numbered in the millions. And for them, there had generally been no hearing. Montand never regretted defending the Rosenbergs, but he became obsessed by this imbalance when he played Artur London in *The Confession* many years later.

Les Sorcières de Salem (*The Witches of Salem*) was a triumph. The critics hailed both the play and its French adaptation, and applauded the perform-

15. Quoted in Richard Cannavo and Henri Quiquéré, *Montand: Le Chant d'un homme* (Paris, 1981).

ances. Apart from the satirical *Le Canard Enchaîné,* which brought out the heavy artillery ("A fence post would have performed better than the wooden M. Montand"), the press heaped Montand with laurels. Most lyrical of all was his friend Claude Roy in *L'Humanité-Dimanche* (December 19, 1954), who wrote: "As for Yves Montand, he was overwhelming. . . . He did not become a greater actor this week just because he is built like a sports star, has made huge strides in diction, is intelligent, and was admirably directed by Raymond Rouleau. He is a great actor because he has thrown onto the scales his pound of flesh, his heart, along with his conviction and his convictions. We were expecting an actor. We were given a man."

The play was so successful that it ran through all of 1955. Montand took advantage of the summer recess to shoot a film by Claude Autant-Lara, *Marguerite de la nuit,* a variant on the Faust myth, set in Montparnasse in the 1920s. It was savaged by the reviewers. The budding critic François Truffaut pulled no punches: "*Marguerite de la nuit* is a dead film, a strange spectacle that arouses only painful feelings—including the sense that we had not been invited along." But Montand, acting opposite Michèle Morgan, came off relatively well; several critics compared him to the great Louis Jouvet.

With summer over, *Les Sorcières* resumed; but the company was obliged to break off at Christmas 1955. With a movie in Italy coming up, Montand had other commitments. The year 1956 was at hand.

The year of vast upheavals.

Chapter 11

At the beginning of 1956, barely out of John Proctor's shoes, Montand left for Italy to shoot *Uomini e lupi* (*Men and Wolves*). The director, Giuseppe de Santis, creator of *Bitter Rice,* was one of the founders of the Italian neorealist school, whose practitioners invariably laid a thick layer of social meaning on their films. Montand had nothing against this. He was delighted to be playing opposite Silvana Mangano in a story in which romantic intrigue was a pretext for describing the harsh living conditions in the villages of the Abruzzi. Much later, he criticized the film as "very Manichean, very simplistic, very much in the style of what was done at that time, and I have to admit that I approved."[1]

Signoret accompanied her husband, but in March she had to leave for Mexico, where Luis Buñuel was expecting her for the filming of *La Mort en ce jardin.* She could not make up her mind to go, could not bear leaving Montand, invented a thousand excuses, and finally tore herself away in floods of tears. This three-month separation—the longest they had known—was painful for both of them.

Most of those connected with *Uomini e lupi* were Communists or Communist sympathizers; in the evenings the crew, the director, and the scriptwriter, Tony Guerra (later to collaborate with Fellini and Antonioni), discussed politics with all the volubility and passion that Italians bring to the subject. Toward the end of March, the name of *Compagno* Khrushchev began to leap again and again into their talk. Montand heard the exchanges grow livelier and angrier. One evening, a comrade exploded: "So that's it. Now I can go to the pope and say, 'You were right. It doesn't matter; we must just accept the truth.' "

Thus echoes of the earthquake that was beginning to shake the Communist world had reached this remote village in the Abruzzi. The leaders

1. Quoted in Alain Rémond, *Montand* (Paris, 1977).

of the Italian Communist Party had decided to relay to the faithful the substance of the speech Khrushchev had delivered to the Twentieth Congress of the Soviet Communist Party. On the night of February 24–25, behind locked doors, General Secretary Khrushchev had delivered his denunciation of the cult of Stalin's personality. That same night, a single copy of his speech was delivered to the foreign delegations in Moscow, with orders to return it the next morning without making a single note. Despite these precautions, fragments of Khrushchev's address soon filtered out via the American embassy. The whisper arose that the general secretary had denounced Stalin's "crimes," backing the charges with an impressive list of details, figures, and even case histories.

On his return to Italy, Palmiro Togliatti, the leader of the Italian Communist Party, gave Central Committee members a preliminary exegesis of Stalin's "errors." This was how Montand, thanks to the *compagni* around him, was so quickly informed of the existence and the content of Khrushchev's speech.

When he got back to France, Montand realized that the French Communist Party was not as ready as its Italian counterpart to denounce the abuses of the "cult of personality." On his return to Paris from Moscow, French Communist Party leader Jacques Duclos, although fully informed, had invoked the name of Stalin to wild applause from Party members gathered in the Salle Wagram. And when, on June 6, *Le Monde* published the famous document, the Party's Stalinist leadership objected that the text had merely been "attributed" to Comrade Khrushchev; since the known source of the leak was the U.S. State Department, it was easy for them to challenge its authenticity. Montand was more than disturbed: he did not doubt the report for an instant. He talked it over with Simone, back from Mexico, for hours. They were appalled at the extent of the "violations of Socialist legality" outlined by Khrushchev; at one swoop they saw that what they had been trying to refute for years—what Kravchenko, Camus, and David Rousset had been saying—was tragically true. But at the same time, Montand decided that a system capable of such self-criticism retained validity. He deplored the crimes and errors set in motion by Stalin's bloodthirsty madness, yet he hoped that the machine would prove able to correct itself. He looked foward to a reformation of Communism; to him, a renovated, de-Stalinized Marxism continued to represent the best hope for the future. His family helped nudge him in this direction.

Julien Livi, his union-leader brother, at first questioned the veracity of Khrushchev's speech. Then he took the document published by *Le Monde* and studied it for several hours. He rose from his reading bewildered, convinced that Communism had been disfigured under Stalin. "I wept over it," he said. "To learn that Stalin was a criminal was a fearful shock to me. When I was a prisoner in Germany it was Stalin who gave me, and millions of others, the courage to live and to hope."

Early that summer, Montand and Signoret went to East Germany to shoot the movie version of *Les Sorcières de Salem.* Raymond Rouleau again directed, but this time the adaptation was by Sartre. The shooting, on the shores of the Baltic, took longer than planned, and it was not until September that the crew returned to Paris to finish the interior scenes.

Days went by, and they fell further and further behind schedule. Montand began to worry, for at the beginning of the year he had signed a contract for a tour of the Soviet Union and Eastern Europe to begin in November. Montand owed his popularity in the Soviet Union to Sergei Obraztsov, director of the Moscow Marionette Theater. During a stay in Paris in 1954, Obraztsov had attended the Etoile concert. An instant convert, he had bought every Montand recording he could lay his hands on. Thanks to the radio, the strains of "A Paris" and "Les Feuilles mortes" were now familiar to millions of Soviet citizens. The fact that he was a fellow traveler obviously bolstered his attractiveness to audiences in the East, of which there were a thousand tangible signs. In 1955, the Soviet magazine *Literaturnaya Gazeta* had asked Montand to contribute an article; in 1956, about a hundred young people from Leningrad wrote him a group letter—naive, but an index of his reputation in Russia; it asked for the words to a song for a festival they were having. In short, Montand seemed to be Soviet youth's foreign idol, and when he was asked to sing in the "homeland of Socialism," he did not hesitate. The promoter of the tour was Georges Soria, a novelist and former Spanish civil war correspondent, a man of unshakable orthodoxy. (In 1949, he had published a manual entitled *How the Russians Live,* in which, among other pearls, he explained why there were no strikes in the Soviet Union: "Since there are no capitalists in the Soviet Union, workers and employees who went on strike under a Socialist regime would be striking against themselves.")

By mid-October, the shooting of *Les Sorcières* was so far behind schedule that Montand realized he would never be able to leave on November 6 as planned. He therefore warned Soria that the tour would have to be postponed for at least a week. Soria got the Russians to agree to a new schedule, starting on November 12. Montand, reassured, could therefore concentrate on the intimate scenes between John Proctor and his wife without worrying about the time. But then he began to fret: he had not been on a music-hall stage for more than two years and needed to get the machine back into working order. Every morning he put himself through grueling physical workouts. At night, after a day in front of the cameras, he and Bob Castella rehearsed his one-man show.

* * *

In the so-called people's democracies, the Khrushchev speech had generated shock waves. Poland was one of the first nations to put it to good use. Victims of the early Party purges there were rehabilitated, particularly Gomulka, the Party leader who had been shunted aside in 1948 and now became the popular figurehead of renewal. But the de-Stalinization process seemed too slow to most Poles. In June, tens of thousands of workers demonstrated on the streets of Poznan, demanding bread and free elections. The army opened fire; fifty people died. Agitation continued in the fall and spread. Under pressure from the streets, Gomulka was readmitted to the Politburo. Diehard Stalinists were alarmed. As the conflict between old and new intensified, workers mobilized in the factories, and Soviet troops surrounded Warsaw. With armed conflict seemingly inevitable, Khrushchev arrived unexpectedly (he had invited himself to the decisive Central Committee meeting held on the night of October 19–20), accentuating the mood of crisis. No one slept in Warsaw that night. Finally, the Russians backed down, agreeing to allow Gomulka to experiment with "national" Communism.

For two days, Montand and Signoret were glued to the news from Poland. Then professional commitments reasserted themselves.

But even as calm was returning to the banks of the Vistula, events on the Danube were taking the strangest of turns. As in Poland, the first signs of liberalization in Hungary took the form of rehabilitation measures. On October 6, Lazlo Rajk, executed in 1949, was accorded the full honors of a national funeral. Marching beside his widow and her son at the head of a procession of more than three hundred thousand people was Imre Nagy, twice removed from power for having called for a reform of the system. Like Gomulka, Nagy, who had long studied in the "homeland of Socialism," was a symbol of hope for the vast throng braving the biting wind.

In July, the old Stalinist apparatchik Rakosi—known affectionately to the Hungarians as the "bald assassin"—had stepped down in favor of another Stalinist, Erno Gero. This switch had done nothing to appease the liberalizing zeal of intellectual circles. A week after Rajk's funeral, Nagy was readmitted to the Party. In the tense days that saw Poland's fate played out, a wild ferment overtook Budapest. The Hungarians hung on the decisions of the Soviet Union. Gomulka's Polish victory, on the morning of October 21, seemed to signal a new era. The Polish example and Moscow's tactical retreat appeared to herald Hungary's own destiny.

The intellectuals of the liberalization movement drew up a ten-point program proposing nothing less than the reform of Hungary's Communist system from within. Even more radical, the students demanded evacuation of Soviet troops, freedom of opinion and the press, and general elections. They also called for a huge demonstration of solidarity with Poland for October 23. Initially forbidden, at the last moment the gathering was permitted, and all Budapest spilled out into the streets. Good-natured crowds of workers flocked in from the suburbs to shouts of "Long live Poland! Long live Nagy!"

A group of demonstrators headed for a statue of Stalin towering twenty-five feet above the edge of a public park. A few bold spirits tossed ropes, which were at once seized by hundreds of hands. Someone even brought up a truck, but its engine raced in vain: the tyrant would not fall. Then metalworkers with blowtorches appeared and set to work on the colossal legs. The huge bronze figure swayed, then toppled, and in its fall the dictator's head rolled loose. Yet another symbol.

Gero had underestimated the scope of the movement. In a radio message, he threatened "enemies of the people" and extolled the virtues of the Soviet Union. The demonstrators saw his words as a deliberate provocation. A raging group of young people attempted to storm the radio building, which was guarded by three companies of the political police. Shots were fired, but the attackers, reinforced by soldiers who had come over to their cause, fought back: the doors were smashed in, and the building was torched. The good-natured demonstration had turned into insurrection.

In a session that went on all night, the Central Committee decided to place Nagy at the head of the government; a little later, it requested the Soviet garrison to restore order. Throughout the day, the number of clashes increased. Kadar stepped in for Gero. But no move now could halt the democratic revolution in its tracks. The insurrection spread beyond Budapest. Military units, headed by the insurgent colonel Pal Maleter, joined forces with the protesters, who now demanded free elections, abolition of the political police, and the establishment of a multiparty system.

Because Soviet tanks had withdrawn from around Budapest, the Hungarians believed they had repulsed the Red Army. Nagy, realizing that the regime no longer enjoyed popular support, hesitated at first, then endorsed the demonstrators' boldest demands. On October 30, he promised a return to a multiparty system. The next day, he denounced Hungary's membership in the Warsaw Pact and proclaimed the country's neutrality. The uprising was becoming steadily more anti-Communist. Members of the political police, who were guilty of brutal excesses, and Party dignitaries were hunted down and executed, often in ugly circumstances.

For the Russians, the line had been crossed. The Kremlin, convinced that a neutral and independent Hungary would trigger a chain reaction throughout the Eastern bloc, decided to counterattack. The international situation favored them—for the English and French had just launched the Suez expedition.

On the evening of November 1, Yves Montand and Simone Signoret were in the studios on the rue Francoeur shooting one of the trickier scenes from *Les Sorcières.* Simone-Elisabeth confides for the first time in Yves-John, confessing her burning passion for her husband, the "best of men." Montand-Proctor explodes.

"The best? Then the whole human race must be slaughtered!"

Mercilessly, Rouleau ran the scene through thirteen takes, until Simone wept real tears and Montand's eyes glowed with real hatred. The thirteenth satisfied him; it gave Montand a moment to answer a reporter from *L'Humanité,* who wanted to know his feelings before he left for the USSR. "I don't have any. I can't say anything. I'll say a lot once I'm in the Soviet Union, and even more when I get back."

At dawn the next day, the second Soviet intervention in Hungary began. Tanks that had regrouped around Budapest opened fire; Nagy called for resistance on the radio, but Kadar was simultaneously announcing the formation of a "revolutionary worker-peasant government" requesting help from the Soviet troops, already in action. Nagy sought sanctuary in the Yugoslav embassy. From then on, the Hungarian insurgents waged a savage but desperate fight. Tanks fired at anything that moved. There were thousands of victims. It was mainly the workers who fought (they made up 80 percent of the thirteen thousand people treated in hospitals).

Pictures of the fighting aroused intense feelings in the West, where public opinion was solidly behind the martyred Hungarians. The French Communist Party was alone in applauding the Soviet intervention: "Barring the way in a supreme burst of energy to Hitler's former henchmen and to the reactionaries and representatives of the Vatican elevated to power by the traitor Nagy, the Hungarian working class has formed a worker-peasant government and taken conduct of the nation's affairs into its own hands," said *L'Humanité* on November 5.

On the rue Francoeur, Montand was still wrestling with John Proctor, whose torments now seemed petty indeed compared to the agony of Hungary. The shadow of Budapest hung over the set. Gérard Philipe, just back from a tour of Poland, where he had already lost many of his illusions, ate dinner with Simone and Yves at a bistro as a television screen showed the Soviet intervention. Leaning on the counter, the three fellow travelers wordlessly watched the gutted buildings, insurgents running through gunfire, corpses, victorious tanks. Philipe, in the middle, suddenly grabbed Montand and Simone by the backs of their necks and said in a low voice: "You're going to enjoy the Soviet Union, really enjoy it! It'll be like this. . . ." And he pretended to strangle them and then to beat them over the head.

On Tuesday, November 6, Sartre dropped in at the studio after shooting was over and had a drink at the bar with Montand. He lashed out at the Russians and expressed total support for the insurgents. Montand listened, defeated, tired, demoralized. Could he really go off and sing in the country that had sent tanks against a people demanding its rights? Sartre was careful not to offer advice, but he knew Montand had to make up his mind. He foresaw that the Budapest rising would fan flames of anti-Communism reaching everyone whose lives revolved around the Communist Party. But he had no inkling of the virulent anger for which Montand would become a symbolic target.

On the evening of November 7, 1956, a crowd gathered at the Arc de Triomphe to protest the Soviet aggression in Hungary. When the meeting was over, three thousand youths led by far-right groups marched down the Champs-Elysées in the direction of Communist Party headquarters, yelling, "Thorez to the gallows!" A clash with Communist militants defending the headquarters turned into a pitched battle. The attackers smashed down the doors and shoved their way up fiercely defended stairways. Soon fire broke out on the ground floor. The same struggle took place at *L'Humanité,* where typesetters defended their workplace with lead slugs and ink bottles. Clashes shook the neighborhood all night long.

Throughout these days, with the whole world, from Budapest to the Suez Canal, going mad, Montand faltered. Family and friends gave him different and sometimes conflicting advice. The beginnings of de-Stalinization had assuaged some of his doubts and apparently confirmed his confidence in the system's potential for self-renewal. But the rejection of Communist power in Hungary had revealed such hatred, so many errors! On November 12, he again confirmed the date of his departure, in an interview published in *Le Figaro:* "I made this commitment eight months ago, and as a professional I must honor my contract. I therefore leave on Monday."

It seemed astonishing, not to say frivolous, for the press to take sides in the matter of Montand's departure in the midst of the Hungarian drama, with thousands of refugees fleeing death or captivity. Yet hatred and loathing crystallized around the name of this popular singer and fellow traveler; Montand's attitude was seen as a barometer of left-wing feeling. And he went on hesitating, changing his mind almost hourly. His professional conscience urged him to go: tens of thousands of Soviet citizens had paid for their seats four months in advance, he had signed contracts, he had to honor them. Simone wept. She wanted him to cancel the whole thing.

Elvire Livi witnessed her anguish: " 'If you go,' she told him, 'you'll be finished. You'll never sing in France again.' " Julien Livi adds: "The pressure from his wife was terrible at that time. I said to Simone, 'Aren't you ashamed? Can't you see what you're doing to your husband?' " He urged his brother in the opposite direction, of course. Julien supported the Party line on the Hungarian "counterrevolution" and pleaded with Montand to resist the pressure.

Montand went through every imaginable frame of mind. He was not impervious to Julien's reasoning: in the teeth of the enemy, you had to close ranks behind the Party, whatever its mistakes, simply to avoid replenishing your adversary's arsenal. And his sense of belonging influenced him strongly: he was not yet ripe for a political and emotional break. He remained in the bosom of the "family" because it was "his" family. His attachment to his father was still the cardinal value, the cornerstone of his life. The tanks in Budapest bore the same red stars as the tanks at Stalingrad. At the same time, he refused to voice approval of the bloody repression.

Montand consulted his musicians. They were not overly enthusiastic about going. One mentioned family problems; another had political reservations. Freddy Balta, the accordionist, declined to give an opinion. Most of them expressed apprehension but left it up to him. Simone Signoret remained ferociously opposed.

By November 11, street clashes in Budapest were rarer, but all Hungary was in the grip of a general strike. Montand issued a statement he had worked on with his wife: "My orchestra and I have jointly decided to postpone our tour of the USSR and the people's democracies. World events, and France's internal situation, make it impossible for us at this time to leave our wives and families and travel to any country whatsoever." It was a postponement rather than a cancellation. The singer had bought himself a few weeks' breathing space—time for feelings to cool.

In late November, Gérard Philipe invited Montand and Signoret to lunch. Around the table were his wife, Anne, Claude Roy, and the widow of Paul Eluard.

> It was a beautiful day. We were all sad and extremely concerned. Gérard began by talking about Poland. He told us what he'd seen, the mistakes, the poverty. What he said hurt me, badly. Because not for a second could I question the words of this man, who was honesty itself. He had entered the fight for peace on the side of the Communist Party because he sincerely believed in the ideals of democracy and freedom. And in Poland he had realized he was wrong. What made it even harder to bear was that he

spoke with great sadness, with alarm, and without anger. Everyone began to talk, freely and spontaneously. Everyone said what he was really feeling, and all of us condemned the Party's position.

Simone said nothing. She was listening extremely attentively, but she never once commented on what was being said. I kept quiet, too. I was torn by contradictory feelings. Unhappy feelings.

That conversation cut me like a knife. I felt, I knew, that my friends were saying fair and true things, but at the same time I didn't want to hear them, I didn't want to accept them. It wasn't clear in my mind—it took me years to get to the bottom of my hesitations, to understand that accepting their remarks meant rejecting my father's ideas, the ideas of the world I was born into. I still equated the Communist Party with the workers; I couldn't budge from that point. It was terrible: I knew Gérard Philipe was telling the truth, but I couldn't listen to him.

The more upset I became, the deeper I retreated into my shell. Inside I was boiling. I got angrier and angrier at the gibes of my friend Claude Roy. When, still talking about the Soviet intervention, he began to make digs about "proletarian internationalism," I went off like a bomb.

"Stop! I don't want to hear any more. None of you sitting around this table can hope to understand the Russian Revolution; it wasn't made for people like you. It was made for the workers and peasants. It isn't our revolution. It's theirs."

I was yelling, and all the angrier because I knew even as I spoke that my argument was falling flat, which just made me sadder. My words were like a cold shower. People stopped talking. They looked at me, and I could see a gleam of pity in their eyes: poor Montand, he's such a fanatic he's not worth talking to! And yet when lunch was over, Roy came up to me and said in a friendly voice, "Let's meet again soon, okay?" He knew just how torn I was.

On November 7, along with the Communists Roger Vailland and Claude Morgan, with Sartre and Simone de Beauvoir, with Vercors and Prévert, Claude Roy had signed a letter denouncing the use of artillery and tanks to smash the revolt of the Hungarian people. For a long time now, Roy, a man Montand liked and respected, had been chafing at the Party bit. A few days after the lunch with Gérard Philipe, he came to Autheuil. Their conversation impressed Montand enough to leave him with a very precise memory of it: Roy knew that the singer's attachment to the Party, no less emotional than political, lay in his identification of Communism with the working class. Roy therefore told Montand that his many journeys to the countries of the East had left him with the absolute conviction that living conditions for workers and peasants there were disastrous. It was fantasy to believe that the region's Communist regimes served the proletariat. He went on to recall the censorship "temporarily" established in 1918 by Lenin—for a week!—that had never been lifted. Finally, he told Montand that in the USSR the sons of Abraham had to write the word "Jew" on their identity cards (just as Georgians or Ukrainians specified their origin—except that there was no Jewish republic within the union). Montand took it all in without a word.

Officially, during November Montand neither condemned nor condoned the Russian intervention in Hungary. He was split down the middle, but he concealed it; in his public behavior he remained true to the image of a faithful fellow traveler.

"I was only fifteen," says Jean-Louis Livi, "but I have a clear memory of that time. My uncle shifted through contradictory moods. One day he would sneer at Imre Nagy. The next moment he would swing to the other side of the fence and have a shouting match with my father. I even had to hold my father back, because they nearly started swinging. Then Montand would be off in the other direction again. One afternoon I went with him and Catherine to see *Rio Bravo.* The newsreel before the movie showed a parade in Red Square. The audience began to protest, and someone hollered: 'Death to the Commies!'

"Montand stood up in the dark and yelled at the top of his voice: 'Stalingrad!' "

Montand confirmed the story years later: in his anger, he had reached back to the solid old values of anti-Fascism.

On November 22, after tortuous negotiations between Belgrade and Budapest, Nagy and his friends left the Yugoslav embassy, where they had sought asylum. But despite the assurances he had received, despite Yugoslav protests, he was arrested and whisked off to Rumania.

This violation of a promise shocked Montand and Signoret even further; they spoke of it to Claude Roy. "They were really shaken," says Julien Livi, "but what shocked them most during those endless days was Stil's article in *L'Humanité.* They couldn't get over it." *L'Humanité*'s special correspondent in Hungary, André Stil, had cabled on November 20: "Budapest begins to smile again through its wounds." Yet all over Hungary, acts of repression against those who had taken part in the uprising were intensifying; arrests multiplied. According to official figures, nearly three thousand people had died during the street fighting; the real tally was probably much higher.

* * *

At the end of November, with the Communists back in control in Budapest, the first secretary of the Soviet embassy traveled to Autheuil. He told Montand that he understood his concerns and accepted his reasons for postponing the tour until this difficult period was over. He suggested, however, that perhaps it was now time to look at the matter afresh. Deftly, the diplomat reached for the singer's soft spot: "You know, when we were surrounded at Stalingrad we had no hope left, but we went on fighting. Even at the darkest moments we must refuse to lay down our arms."

Once again, Montand was thrust into agonies of indecision, tormented by the dilemma that Sartre had cruelly summed up for him: "If you go, you stand surety for the Russians; if you stay, you stand surety for the reactionaries." On the morning of December 3, alone, he came to a decision. It was a whim, or, more accurately perhaps, a fit of rage. That morning he received a call from the German producer Deutschmeister. Montand had signed a contract with him to make a film in early 1957 on the life of the painter Modigliani. The producer was blunt: if Montand left to sing in the East he could not shoot the film, for distributors and theater owners would refuse a movie whose star had compromised himself with the butchers of Budapest. Montand listened, then, without raising his voice, said: "I did not think I would go. Now it's all clearer. I'm leaving."

That same day, with Signoret's help, Montand wrote a letter to the director of the Moscow Marionette Theater:

My dear Obraztsov:

You and your troupe and the Moiseyev Ballet of Moscow are among those who have contributed most to a cultural rapprochement between our two countries, and consequently to a détente, if for no other reason than the success you had in Paris.

As far as I personally am concerned, you have made it possible for the Soviet audience to know my work, and if today people hum my songs in the streets, it is thanks to your godfatherly help.

This is why I chose to send this letter to you.

I would like to tell you today about the profound distress felt by a great number of French people because of the Hungarian drama. I mean most particularly the members of the peace movement, the only organization within which I am active. A great many French people resisted the enormous and monstrous anti-Soviet propaganda machine, and they proved it by not associating themselves in any way with this propaganda in public. Nevertheless, they wondered about certain things, and they continue to do so.

I am one of those people.

Today there was an extraordinary meeting of the national council of the French peace movement. There is a wide divergence of opinion among the militants on a possible interpretation of the events that have taken place in Hungary, while there is absolute unanimity against the French pursuit of the Algerian war and against the Suez adventure. But we are all in agreement, all militants for peace, whatever our political opinions . . . whether we are intellectuals or manual workers: we all firmly resolve to try to prevent by any means we can a return to the Cold War, and consequently the possibility of a hot war. And this is why, as far as I personally am concerned, I am happy to ask you to tell Soviet audiences that I shall arrive in the near future, in hopes that I will thus be able to help a little in the maintenance and development of those cultural exchanges which are a contribution to the consolidation of peace.

So, *à bientôt,* my dear Obraztsov

With kind regards,
YVES MONTAND

This strikingly moderate letter was published the next day in *L'Humanité, Libération,* and *France-Soir.* Clearly Montand was not breaking with his Communist family, nor was he distancing himself from the peace movement. In denouncing the "monstrous anti-Soviet propaganda machine" he did not shrink from using Stalinist jargon. What was more, he conferred on his tour a political meaning that went beyond his artistic vocation, presenting himself as a messenger of peace. For the Hungarians, as it happened, a Soviet peace.

Not surprisingly, this somewhat labored letter provoked violent responses, both in the press and in the hundreds of threatening and insulting letters that arrived at the Place Dauphine. Angry strollers yelled recriminations at the ground-floor windows. Elvire remembers the ordeal: "People rapped on the windows. If you left them just a little bit open, they threw things inside or spat out insults. Montand got a lot of anonymous phone calls. The days before his departure were very hard."

Three days before that departure, now scheduled for December 16, Montand was dealt a fresh insult. Every Wednesday evening the radio station Europe 1 ran a live broadcast, "Musicorama," from the Olympia music hall. On December 13, Montand agreed to appear on the program in a last rehearsal before Moscow. As usual, the station announced its schedule thirty-six hours in advance. Anonymous letter writers at once warned that they would prevent Montand from singing. The threats were so numerous and so detailed that the producers and Bruno Coquatrix, manager of the Olympia, decided it would be wise to cancel.

Waiting for the train to the airport on the morning of December 16, Simone was still unwilling to leave. Wearing a mink coat and holding an armful of red roses, she put on a show of happiness for the photographers, but she was close to tears. Montand forced himself to smile, teeth clenched. When the time for farewells came, Simone whispered to many of those present: "I'll never forget you came today."

It was long past nightfall when the Ilyushin 22 touched down at Vnukovo Airport, about fifteen miles from Moscow, but a huge crowd was waiting. As soon as the plane came to a standstill the fans overran the snow-covered airstrip and besieged the passenger stairs. The Russian press reported:

"The aircraft door opened. Simone Signoret appeared at the top of the stairs, and behind her a smiling Yves Montand. He raised his hand and said: *'Bonjour les amis!'*

" 'My friend from far away,' said Sergei Obraztsov."[2]

The heroes of the day were mobbed by photographers. As a French paper put it, "Happy shouts went up. People wheeled out fragments of French: *'C'est si bon, Montand!' 'Bravo d'être venu!'* "[3]

Montand and Signoret had left Paris amid insults and sneers, almost like a pair of felons; they arrived in the Soviet Union as heroes. Montand fought his way to the waiting microphones and said a few words: "I am deeply moved. I am not a politician; I am only an artist. I have come here at a time when cultural exchanges are more important than ever, because they serve the cause of peace among peoples."[4]

He had little time to rest from the flight. His opening night was scheduled for December 19 at the Tchaikovsky Concert Center. People had fought for tickets. "For days in advance," reported the special correspondent for *France-Soir* on December 21, "a large crowd stood in line for tickets. There were ladies complete with chauffeur and limousine and astrakhan furs, the sons and daughters of the elite taking temporary leave of their institutes of higher learning, flocks of young female fans, old ladies,

2. *Sovietskaia Kultura,* December 18, 1956.

3. *Libération,* December 18, 1956.

4. *Sovietskaia Rossiya,* December 18, 1956.

suffragettes of a century ago, squads of soldiers, young men and women from the factories. People kept all-night vigils. Grandmothers—patient *babushkas*—were dragooned into service to save their grandchildren's place in line."

On that first night, the auditorium was packed with officials and the Moscow social set—the foreign minister, the minister of culture, foreign ambassadors and their wives (with the conspicuous exception of the representative of France); the approved crème de la crème of arts and letters; gold-braided officers. But it took some time for them to warm to the occasion. Few spectators understood the words, and it was not until the sixth song that Montand, petrified by stage fright, began to emit that mysterious magic called presence. But he was reassured by the seemingly endless final ovation, the bouquets, and the bravos.

The Soviets were certainly applauding the man who sang "A Paris," but they were also playing host to a "messenger of peace," acclaiming a man who had braved the storm and come to them at a time of extreme international tension, a time when East-West exchanges were dead in the water, when even the Moiseyev Ballet no longer performed on the other side of the Iron Curtain for fear of triggering hostile demonstrations. The Soviet press systematically emphasized the symbolic importance of Montand's journey, and Montand soon had proof that the men in the Kremlin attached a definite price to his presence.

As his fourth performance opened, he noticed that the box downstage right, normally closed, was crowded with the leading figures of the regime—Nikita Khrushchev at their head, as protocol dictated. That same evening, Montand had been bothered by something that happened just before the curtain went up. An Armenian had managed to slip through every barrier and reach his dressing room, where he asked the star to help him flee the Soviet Union. "Life is impossible in this country," he said. Montand, trying to concentrate before going on stage, led him to the door ("Do you think it's easy everywhere else?"), but he could not forget the frantic young man's eyes and words.

After the show, an official told the entertainer that Politburo comrades wanted to meet him.

"Why don't they come to my dressing room?" retorted the actor. Like all entertainers, he assumed that if you wanted to congratulate a performer, you called on him, even if you were royalty.

The official insisted: supper had been prepared, but the comrades did not want to disturb him; they would wait as long as was necessary. Montand and Signoret exchanged unbelieving looks; they sensed that they were about to go through an out-of-the-ordinary experience.

And, indeed, Khrushchev, Molotov, Bulganin, and Malenkov were awaiting them in a small salon converted for the occasion into a dining room.

"I feel as if I'm in a newsreel," Simone whispered to Montand at the sight of the dignitaries lined up as if on parade.

They all introduced themselves, then sat down around a narrow table, with the two French visitors on one side and Mikoyan, Molotov, Khrushchev, Bulganin, Malenkov—in that order—facing them. The interpreter, Nadia Nechayeva, was seated at one end. "I was told at the last moment that I would be translating," she said. "I was shaking with fright. It was virtually simultaneous interpretation."

Right away, "Comrade" Nikita congratulated the singer on his performance; he had particularly liked "C'est à l'aube," he said. Montand thanked him. Mikoyan proposed a toast to the Livi family, reeling off all their names, beginning with Giovanni. The guest of honor was staggered. And as the borscht was served, Mikoyan opened fire: "So, M. Montand, the Fascists allowed you to leave?"

For a second the singer was at a loss, then he replied: "It wasn't the Fascists who delayed me; it was what happened in Budapest. The Fascists were very happy about what happened in Budapest."

Nadia finishes the story: "Yves said, 'Budapest was unspeakable, we were stunned, how could you have done it? What happened? Really, we don't understand.' Khrushchev made a joke of it: 'We pulled the Hungarians back into line, we restored order, and now we'll send them all the advisers they want us to!' "

Montand and Signoret told their table companions, who seemed not to know, about what had happened in Paris in November: the distress of the Party faithful, Sartre's anger ("The party of the executed must not become the party of the executioners"), the demonstrations and counter-demonstrations, the schisms within the peace movement, the deep concern of Claude Roy and fellow travelers such as Vercors, Roger Vailland, and Gérard Philipe—all friends of the Soviet Union who refused to countenance the victors of Stalingrad becoming the butchers of Budapest. Khrushchev listened attentively to the flood of words, translated at top speed by young Nadia. He was astonished. So it was not just the Fascists who had spoken out against the Soviet intervention?

"No, Mr. Khrushchev, the Communists, too, were troubled."

The round, jovial little man began to bounce in his chair.

"To understand what happened in Hungary," he said, "you have to go back to Stalin."

And Khrushchev launched into a violent attack on the "Little Father of All the Peoples." He recalled his report to the Twentieth Congress, adding details and commentary, telling how Stalin had liquidated the

Polish Communist Party, describing the trials, the deportations, the millions of deaths. He pounded on the table with his fist to emphasize his words.

> I stared at him, horrified, frightened. He was looking me straight in the eye and talking about Stalin's crimes. So it was true! Words poured out of him, he played whole scenes, he mimicked famous people. He was a fantastic actor, but I sensed the accents of truth. He seemed relieved to talk, to justify, to explain before his colleagues. At times he was funny, at other times moving. His character seduced me. He told us how the veterans of the International Brigades who had fled Spain for Moscow were liquidated. I had known part of the story ever since learning about his report, back in the Abruzzi, but hearing it from Khrushchev's mouth was absolutely overwhelming.

"The whole time Khrushchev was talking," said Nadia, "Yves kept his eyes on his face. Suddenly Khrushchev broke off: 'Why are you staring at me like that? You're thinking, And what were you doing all that time, Mr. Khrushchev?'

"He smiled. Yves went on staring. Khrushchev continued, more seriously: 'Nothing. I did nothing.'

" 'Why not?'

" 'Because we were afraid, M. Montand. Stalin had changed a lot. He was no longer the same man. When you went to see him toward the end, you never knew if you would come out alive.' "

Without notes or tapes, it is impossible to reconstruct those four hours of conversation. We have to rely on what the few witnesses recall of its high points. Their recollections conform without being exactly similar. What emerges from their memories of that extraordinary evening are highlights, reflections of the general mood and each guest's state of mind. The tone was cordial, often warm, but Montand—who had good reasons for saying more than Simone—did not back off. He was outspoken with the masters of the Kremlin, just as he had been a faithful fellow traveler with his Paris friends. Politely but firmly, he interrupted the only man—the other dignitaries having fallen silent—addressing him.

"Excuse me, Mr. Khrushchev, but doesn't that add up to a great many mistakes? The Poznan riots, boom! Budapest, boom!" (At each "boom!" he struck himself on the head with the flat of his hand.) "Before that, there was Tito. That went boom boom!" (Two blows to his skull.) "You can't go on saying they were counterrevolutionaries, or traitors, or deviationists!"

Montand decided it was time to stress that his presence in the USSR should not be interpreted as approval of the repression in Hungary, even if his decision had been so interpreted in France. Khrushchev smiled and thanked him for his frankness. Relaxing, he adopted a teasing tone: "Decidedly, my friends, you are too sentimental."

"If we are here," retorted Montand, "it is very much for sentimental reasons. If people from the West like us, whose lives are comfortable—if we turn toward Communism, it is indeed for sentimental reasons."

The child of La Cabucelle explained to Khrushchev that he had no complaints about his life in the West. He had everything he needed—a fine house in the country, the freedom to sing what he wanted. Simone pointed to her bracelets and the high-fashion clothes she was wearing. Really, she insisted, their sympathy for Communism sprang from "an emotion unaffected by self-interest."

"It's precisely because we are sentimental people," she said, "and not political activists that the pictures out of Budapest shocked us. You cannot ask us to be sentimental when it's a question of defending the Soviet Union and reproach us for our sentimentality when we're talking about Hungary."

With that, the tension cleared; Mikoyan proposed more toasts, and the conversation turned to cultural matters. It was late, and the end of the evening was approaching. Raising his glass of Armenian brandy, Khrushchev proclaimed his delight at encountering divergent opinions in such a friendly setting. He was beaming, blooming, rubicund.

Montand rose to reply.

"I'm no expert at toasts. I would just like to thank you for letting my wife and me tell you things we would never have said in public. I was doubtful about coming to the Soviet Union, but I now know that I was right to come, for I have had the privilege of being able to speak freely with you. I was not completely convinced by your arguments. I hope our own have taught you something. Thank you for coming to hear me sing. I raise my glass to the Soviet people and to peace."

Well past midnight, Montand and his wife took their leave. Before drifting off to sleep, the singer gave a sigh of satisfaction: "Now nobody likes us. But don't we feel good about ourselves!"

By morning, all Moscow—reporters, diplomats, artists, and members of the *nomenklatura*—was rustling with rumors of that summit supper. The couple was bombarded with invitations to orphanages, dance schools, factories. On the morning of December 30, Montand and Signoret visited the Likhachov automobile plant. With the flatbeds of four parked trucks making a stage, Montand sang "Les Routiers" and "Un Gamin de Paris" to eight thousand workers. To the special correspondent of *L'Humanité,* this miraculous encounter between the "singing prole" and his natural public was too good to pass up: "Once again," he raved, "it was dreamlike, inspiring: sixteen thousand hands applauded their sympathetic idol. Eyes bright with emotion, he waved a bunch of flowers over his head as he bade them farewell."[5]

The Soviet Union seemed in the grip of Montand mania. On Gorky Street, the day after their arrival, a girl presented them with a huge bunch of flowers in the name of the employees of the Botanical Gardens.[6] In front of the monument dedicated to Moscow's founder, people stood in line for an autograph (a good opportunity for the Parisian to learn the word *"otchered,"* or line, one of the most frequently used words in Russian). Their visit to the famed Metro, with its marble walls, was cut drastically short because of the mobs that gathered. Hundreds of letters, greetings, gifts, and poems reached Montand and Signoret at their hotel. "When children were born in the farthest reaches of Siberia," said Simone, "we received telegrams announcing that they had been baptized 'Yves-montand.' " Technicians and engineers aboard the North Pole 6, a floating research station, sent greetings to Yves Montand "from the ice-covered Central Arctic wastes, from the heart of the dark polar night." The newspapers were full of similar messages, their degree of spontaneity impossible to determine—quite forced, probably, when *Sovietskaia Kultura* published a message from young workers declaring that "we love your songs, but we love you even more for your life as a simple French worker."

After five performances at the Tchaikovsky Concert Center, Montand moved on to Uljniki Stadium, a huge indoor sports arena with eighteen thousand seats. It was the first time he had performed before such a large crowd. From the back rows, Montand was a tiny outline. He was strongly tempted to belt out the songs to reach those distant onlookers, even at the risk of marring the harmony and disrupting the intimate rapport with the audience he so prized. After the second number he found the solution: he decided to sing just for himself, without raising his voice, as if he were alone. It worked. The sense of intimacy spread backward from row to row. He would remember the experiment twenty-six years later when he faced the massed spectators at Maracanazhino Stadium in Rio.

The audience at Uljniki Stadium was humbler and less glittering than the one at the Tchaikovsky (seats were cheaper, and the temperature higher). In fact, there was pandemonium. His performances in that vast stadium included some of the great moments in Montand's professional life. Contrary to his custom, and despite his weariness, Montand yielded

5. *L'Humanité,* January 1, 1957.

6. *Moskovsky Komsomolets,* December 20, 1956.

to encores, giving three renderings of "Les Grands Boulevards," "C'est à l'aube," and "Les Feuilles mortes."

I was rather irritated by the little throng of people who stuck to us like glue, people who apparently lived very well. Simone and I weren't fooled: they were part of the *nomenklatura,* privileged members of the regime; they were a screen between the Russians and us. But the quarantine zone they established didn't prevent us from seeing women of all ages sweeping the streets in the snow, clearing snow at minus twenty-five degrees centigrade, or doing heavy work in the factories. We sensed quite clearly that Party members were a separate breed. The first time I got into a car I was alarmed at the way the chauffeur drove. He went straight at people: a Party official always had the right of way. I called him on it, and he gave me to understand that pedestrians were supposed to get out of the way when they saw an official limousine. The top people had all the rights, including the right to run people over.

Almost by accident one day, looking for Ehrenburg's house, we discovered the reality of everyday Soviet life that our escorts had been trying to hide. We had strayed into an outer suburb of miserable wooden shacks, housing several families apiece. It all shocked me. Simone and I talked about it constantly. But a funny thing happened: I was shaken, I could see that it clearly wasn't paradise, and yet the old reflexes were still operating. Simone hammered away at the things that depressed me—lines outside stores, different categories of restaurant—and I instantly bit her head off, because what she said sounded true and I didn't want to accept it. I would say: "Just wait, Simone, give them time. Khrushchev had the courage to tell us: they've made mistakes, okay, but give them time to recover. We can't junk it all now."

This game lasted almost the whole trip. I remember an extremely violent argument at the Hôtel d'Angleterre in Leningrad. I was in a strange mood: all I wanted was to believe, and yet I couldn't. I could see it didn't work, I felt it in my guts, but I didn't want Simone to keep irritating the exposed nerve. That night I was really whimpering over my lost illusions. Then I grabbed Simone, who must have made a particularly shrewd observation, and shook her, yelling that she would never understand anything at all. I know today that my anger was a form of despair.

We had a close relationship with our interpreters, especially Nadia. We talked with her a lot. She told us a Russian proverb

> that deeply impressed me: Russia is a mother to foreigners and a wicked stepmother to her own sons. . . . Despite everything I saw and didn't want to see, I was bowled over by the Russians, by the people, by the guys who came to clean out my dressing room, by the cleaning woman with her slop bucket. It was difficult to be anti-Soviet when you aren't anti-Russian.

Simone Signoret was not the only one who had to endure the wrath of a Montand torn between faith and disenchantment. "I had picked up some Russian during the four years I played in a White Russian band in Paris," said Marcel Azzola, "and I talked to the other musicians. They told me stories about life in Moscow. I quickly understood that it was no fun. Once or twice I tried to talk to Montand about it. He cut me short: 'Don't worry about all that, Marcel. You don't understand.' "

On New Year's Eve 1956, Montand, Signoret, and the whole troupe were invited to the Kremlin for a reception attended by nearly three thousand guests in St. George's Hall. At midnight Khrushchev kissed Signoret on the mouth, Russian-style. Montand had to be content with a two-fisted handshake. A few toasts later Comrade Nikita took to the dance floor. Watching him, Montand came close to thinking that a leader who could dance on his heels like a Ukrainian peasant could not be all bad.

The next stages of the tour provide two pictures that neatly sum up what was going on in the singer's mind. In Leningrad, he was overwhelmed by the sight of the vast forest, stretching to the horizon, planted at the border the Germans never managed to cross. Each tree represented one victim of the 900-day siege of the city—a reminder of the heroism of a people to whom the Frenchman felt indissolubly linked. And in the Kiev region, whose brightly painted houses (or at least those spared destruction) enchanted him, he was taken with Simone to a *kolkhoz.* There, quite by chance of course, peasant girls in white blouses were rehearsing for a performance and—again by chance—propaganda cameras stood ready to film them diving into the feast that awaited them. . . .

"*Kolkhoz* schmolkhoz," grumbled Crolla.

It was an icy departure. The Moscow air was so cold that Nadia's copious tears almost froze into stalactites. And their reception in Warsaw on this January 18, 1957, was cool, but not just because of the wintry temperature. Montand, Simone, and the musicians had not been unduly surprised to be flying in an aircraft reserved for them, with a cabin refitted as a saloon and a charming samovar corner. When they arrived, the Poles informed them that the craft belonged to the leadership of the Soviet Communist Party.

A thoughtful gesture by Comrade Nikita. But to arrive in Poland as an ambassador of the Kremlin was not the most tactful beginning.

After a few hours, Montand's interpreter decided to explain the reason for further coolness. There was a rumor in Warsaw that this French friend of the Russians had insisted on being paid—very generously—in dollars, which would explain the exorbitant price of tickets. Furious, Montand set things straight at a press conference the next morning, where he read a statement he had scribbled on envelopes from the Hotel Bristol, where the troupe was staying.

"A rumor is afoot in Warsaw," he read, "which I insist you refute in your newspapers, for it is false and affects me personally. It is said that I am being paid in dollars. This is untrue. I have made special arrangements, knowing Poland's difficult economic situation. I pay my musicians in francs—this part of my fee is in hard cash—and my own share is in zlotys."

(Back in Paris, Montand got a letter from a Polish friend that explained it all: "The pathetic lie about the dollar was entirely the fault of the Estrada agency, which organized the concerts and failed to explain the high prices. They wanted to cover past deficits and combat illegal ticket sales, but they were wrong not to say so in the press.")

Though this unpleasantness cast a shadow over his Polish stay, Montand enjoyed the same triumph as he had had in the Soviet Union. On opening night, the thirty-five hundred spectators in the Hall of Congresses of the Palace of Culture were still on their feet yelling "encore" fifteen minutes after the curtain had gone down. Four extra performances were added, the last two broadcast on television, to meet some of the demand.

Montand also sang for workers in the automobile plant at Zeran and gave a special benefit gala for students. The official press was full of weighty dissertations on this artist who "sings of the pain and the joy of everyday life, of striving and toil, of the beauty of the world, the goodness of men, the greatness of struggle and sacrifice."[7] And as in Moscow, Montand received an avalanche of letters and cards from female admirers. One stood out for its note of humor: "Your show on January 25 was very nice, but it's a pity you forgot to bring the proper clothes with you. We in Poland expect entertainers to wear tuxedos."

In that winter of 1957, Polish intellectuals and artists still believed that Gomulka would usher in a "human Communism" that respected freedom and artistic creation. They were soon disappointed by the tightening of the government's grip, the return of censorship, and removal of the right to strike. But the men and women who met Montand and Signoret still talked

7. *Przeglad Kulturalny,* February 14, 1957.

of the enduring nature of the "Polish October." They talked and talked, almost nonstop, so that the singer had to clear his dressing room a few minutes before each show. "During that week in Warsaw," said Signoret, "singing for Montand came to mean a kind of intermission between conversations. I have no idea how he lasted through it."

There is no doubt that Montand was making strides in his understanding of "Socialism in action." He said as much just before leaving: "I am glad to tell you that this second leg of my tour of the countries of Eastern Europe has been a major personal step in my search for the truth. That search was one of my reasons for making this long trip." He was not yet ready to face his discoveries—but the tour was a step that led him away from Communism.

After Poland, Montand performed in what was then the German Democratic Republic, followed by Czechoslovakia, Rumania, Bulgaria, Yugoslavia, and Hungary. In Eastern Europe as everywhere else, a tour is an exhausting slog, a succession of hotels, theaters, lighting problems, late dinners, lightning visits. Also official receptions, endless toasts, talks with comrades, interview after interview, unexpected visitors, unanswerable questions, unplanned benefits.

An unbelievable success. A marathon. Immense fatigue.

In Prague they saw nothing except the route taken by his limousine between the huge Hall of Congresses, where he sang, and the Hotel Alkron, where he stayed and received visitors—Lise London, for one, whose husband, Artur, convicted alongside Slansky, had been released from prison only a year earlier. "I went with a delegation to his hotel," she remembers. "I had already met him in Paris in 1948, and that day in Prague we brought a bouquet for Simone Signoret. Montand, who did not know I was London's wife, told me about his talk with Khrushchev, but I sensed that he was most disturbed by the Hungarian events. He needed to talk; he was a man in pain."

Simone was getting impatient. She reminded her man of the time. "Montand," she said, "come on, we'll be late."

Had she known the identity of the visitor—she would play her on the screen twelve years later—she undoubtedly would have acted differently. Only a few days before, she had sent temperatures soaring with an undiplomatic question about Rudolf Slansky's widow.

By the time their plane was headed for Sofia or Bucharest, the French group's favorite game was to spot the local "Moscow University" from the air—in other words, the copy faithfully and unfailingly reproduced by local architects, right down to the narrow windows designed to combat harsh winters. But more than architectural standards were bequeathed by the Soviet big brother. What little Montand and Signoret glimpsed of Rumania and Bulgaria groaned beneath the weight of Soviet influences.

Things were different when the travelers reached Belgrade on March 4. The air seemed lighter, as if Tito's rebellion had spared Yugoslav Communism the dull conformity of the Eastern satellites. Three performances had been planned, and a fourth was added. Here as elsewhere, their success surpassed all expectation. Two days after they arrived, a call came for Montand and Signoret. A voice informed them that Marshal Tito had invited them for tea. A large and slightly battered American car picked them up at their hotel.

> In front were two guys in civilian clothes who didn't speak a word of French. Who didn't speak at all, in fact. The car left Belgrade and drove quite a distance. Suddenly, as we drove through a thick forest, everything about the ride seemed bizarre: the phone call, the car, these two rogues.
>
> I asked Simone: "Where are we going? And who are these guys?"
>
> We were tired, and through a sort of self-hypnosis we began to panic. The hoodlums up front were as mute as ever, answering our questions with vague gestures. We already saw ourselves as kidnap victims. I muttered to Simone: "If anything happens, if the car stops, open the door and run."
>
> Finally, after about three-quarters of an hour, the car turned off into handsome grounds and stopped in front of some steps. Tito and his wife were waiting for us; he was immaculately turned out, with a pearl in his white tie. Communication was at once easy, direct, warm. He was delighted to be seeing entertainers. As soon as we met, he said: "I feel as if I'm at the movies."
>
> But he was also pleased to be talking to French people. He was not overly fond of the French Communists, and he remembered the Party's campaigns against "Titoist traitors." My conscience wasn't too clean, because like everyone else I had gone along with that denunciation. One day in Saint-Paul, I don't know what we were talking about, but I had said, "That's Titoist propaganda." Prévert gently put me in my place: "What's that word 'Titoist'? What does it mean?"
>
> Now here I was, face-to-face with the "traitor." The man who

had been right, despite all the other Communist parties. He was amusing and full of charm. He told us stories of the days in the 1930s when he was on the run in France. The first rule, he said, was to be very well dressed at all times. It had been a time when the way you dressed said what class you belonged to. Workers wore blue coveralls and cloth caps, and the middle class wore suits and hats; Tito—who didn't call himself Tito then—was always immaculate, dressed to the nines. He even walked a little dog on a leash. Who would have suspected a well-dressed gentleman, his dog at his side, of being a secret revolutionary and Comintern member? Tito was still laughing about it.

But not everything was funny in the Marshal's Socialist Yugoslavia. Even as Montand and Signoret smiled at their host's jokes, Milovan Djilas, an old friend of Tito's who had advocated democratization ahead of anyone else, was meditating on his fate in Stremska Mitrovitza Prison, where foreign publication of his book *The New Class* had landed him.

On the tour, the French party occasionally phoned family or friends in Paris for news of home. Francis Lemarque recalls one call from Simone, who was in Sofia at the time: he lacked the heart to tell her that the anti-Montand press campaign was still in full swing. Biaggi, the right-wing lawyer who had disrupted performances at the Etoile in 1953 and triggered the cancellation of the broadcast from the Olympia, warned that if Montand performed in Budapest, he would never again sing in France. In fact, the singer himself had already worried about the timeliness of the visit. He announced that his whole fee would be turned over to the Hungarian Red Cross and even specified that his visit not be interpreted as a gesture of support for Kadar.

Four months after the crushing of the revolt, Budapest still bore visible marks of the savagery of the fighting, even though Montand and Signoret's guides claimed that the gutted, bullet-pocked buildings dated from the war. But they were surprised to see signs of relative material prosperity compared with the other Communist countries. Stores were better stocked, people better dressed. Yet the leaders of the 1956 insurrection, intellectuals, even "liberal" Communists were in prison. During an interview with the minister of culture, Montand asked him why Communist intellectuals were being jailed.

The minister did not know who he was talking about. . . .

Budapest was in a state of shock. As an official guest of the authorities, Montand was presented by them, whether he liked it or not, as a proof of normalization. Yet not long before his arrival, leaflets had been discreetly circulated calling for a boycott of the show: "A good Hungarian will not attend Yves Montand's concert. Think of the young October heroes! No true Hungarian will be at the show."[8]

So as soon as he reached Budapest the singer asked to make a statement. On the stationery of the Grand Hotel Margitszigeti Nagyszallo, he penciled the following words:

> I have hesitated about coming to sing in Budapest. Only an article warning me that Maître Biaggi had threatened me with tear-gas bombs if I sang in Budapest crystallized my decision. There are certain kinds of threats that act as a spur.
>
> If Hungarians were in a mood to laugh, they would probably laugh heartily at the idea that they owe my arrival in part to M. Biaggi. Alas, Hungarians are in no laughing mood. It has been a long time since they felt like laughing. Neither the Germans, nor Horthy, nor the failure of Socialism have made them feel like laughing. Nor have the recent months. But they can tell the difference between the sugary taste of crocodile tears and the bitter salt tang of their own. Crocodiles don't help much when they weep from far away. I preferred to come and see them, speak to them, listen to them, and sing them my songs.
>
> As the son of an Italian anti-Fascist (and proud of it), now a naturalized Frenchman (and proud of it), I venture to claim that I bring more warmth, friendship, and love to their bruised hearts than M. Biaggi's tear gas will ever bring them.
>
> And although none of their problems has been solved, although their wounds still bleed, although the hopes of their October have collapsed, at least for the two hours they spend with me they will feel the urge to laugh again, because I shall have performed my task, which is to take people out of themselves for an hour or two.

The words breathed sadness and disillusionment. Montand was no readier to laugh than the Hungarians. But despite suspicion, ambiguity, and the hostile leaflets, his success in Budapest, as everywhere, was phenomenal.

> I saw the most sublime girls in Budapest, twenty-year-olds, girls you could die for. And yet, not a single one. . . .

Simone was watching like a hawk. Her vigilant gaze had registered the sudden temptation: "They were beautiful, and they seemed to have a great

8. *Le Figaro,* March 14, 1957.

deal of freedom. I am speaking of the female groupies of that week in Budapest. Unfortunately for them, and perhaps for him, the ancestor of all groupies was also there, right in his dressing room."

Friends were waiting at Le Bourget to welcome the travelers back from the cold. Julien Livi was there, surrounded by union workers he had brought along after an office meeting, in case the "Fascists" had dirty tricks up their sleeves. He was asking questions the second he got a chance: "Well, what was it like? What did you think of the Soviet Union?"

" 'An unforgettable reception. At times it was fantastic, but at the same time there were things you couldn't accept.' "

The tour had removed the scales from Montand's eyes. The Montand who had come back from the Socialist paradise was a different man.

> Today, with hindsight, I have no regrets, even though I know I played the Party's game and upset a lot of people. This is a selfish point of view, for I was its chief beneficiary. It opened my eyes. I learned, on the spot, many things they didn't know in Paris. I had believed in the possibility of a better world and had met fine men and women with the same dream. For me it was a true and fundamental belief. In the name of that belief I condoned crimes and horrors through my own ignorance. What that tour of 1957 allowed me to do was to reclaim myself. I stopped being a faithful follower. From that point on, I formed my own judgment of things. I never again said a cat was black when it was gray. The events of 1956 and 1957 meant the loss of faith for me. I began a long march within myself. I continued to hope; I ceased to believe.

In 1957, Montand distanced himself from Stalinist Communism; he did not make a complete break. In London that August, for the release of *Les Sorcières de Salem,* he said, "Everyone capable of thinking for himself has reshuffled his political opinions in the course of the past few months."[9] In February 1958, he confided to a reporter: "I've finally realized that my profession does not allow me to take a political position. I publicly acknowledge that in real life, a man who thinks the opposite of what I do is not necessarily my enemy." The reporter, who had known Montand for twenty years, had never seen him so emotional, nervous, tense. He warned the singer that he intended to publish these startling admissions.

But Montand went on: "It was largely out of respect for my father that

9. Quoted in *L'Aurore,* August 28, 1957.

I've done what I have. But today I feel all too clearly that I've been exploited, used to advertise an idea, just like a shampoo or a drink. I still believe in goodness, in brotherhood, but it's no longer a one-way street." *Paris-Presse* ran these declarations on its front page, and *Le Figaro,* once so scathing, conceded that "his sincerity and motives have never been in doubt. . . . Now at the peak of his popularity, Montand has nothing to gain from his stance. It is a matter of conscience. And of courage. For the Communists will not forgive their former comrade for lifting the Iron Curtain."[10]

Montand had not yet paid his dues to Communism, however. On February 16, 1957, Imre Nagy and his companions were hanged after a mockery of a trial. For the first time Montand publicly rebelled, condemning this murder. His brother criticized him, saying that his statement gave ammunition to the enemy. The resulting shouting match was unusually violent.

The fellow traveler was becoming a doubter.

10. *Le Figaro,* February 27, 1958.

Chapter 12

"I shall not be singing in the United States."

It was not a refusal but a statement of fact. More than ever, Montand longed to explore Broadway. He had visited New York a thousand times in his dreams, exploring the piers running snaggle-toothed up the Hudson and strolling along the East River from the Williamsburg to the Queensboro Bridge. He had celebrated a hundred triumphs at Sardi's. He had walked down blind alleys with Capra, danced along the sidewalks with Gene Kelly, dueled with Fred Astaire for Cyd Charisse in Central Park. In movie after movie.

But he would never sing there, he told reporters at Saint-Paul-de-Vence on February 18, 1958, for a simple if not a satisfactory reason: the U.S. government had refused him a visa. What stood between him and his transatlantic dreams was the question every visa applicant was required to answer: "Are you or have you ever been a member of the Communist Party or an organization affiliated with or having common activities with the Communist Party?" The answer to the second part of the question was, of course, yes, and that yes automatically got a no from the U.S. Immigration and Naturalization Service.

Despite his legal skirmishes with Jack Warner (they had fitfully flared again when *The Wages of Fear* was released), Montand had been approached on several occasions by Gene Kelly about movie work. He had also received offers to sing at New York nightclubs. He would willingly have accepted these had he not been declared persona non grata by the American authorities, but each enticing project came up only to nosedive. Montand consoled himself by flying off on March 4 to a film festival in Punta del Este, Uruguay, where he introduced *Les Sorcières de Salem* as a noncompetitive entry. At Orly he found himself in the pleasant company of Magali Noël and Estella Blain. Jeanne Moreau also went along, to promote *Ascenseur pour l'échafaud* (*Frantic*). He and Moreau returned via

Rome—his wife's veto obliging the actor-singer to suppress the feelings his charming companion aroused in him.

Signoret was herself wrestling with multiple difficulties. With the East European trip over, her career was at a standstill. It was not just a matter of ideology. Actresses approaching the age of forty, whatever their track record, suddenly learn they are on a fatal trajectory to a kind of Bermuda triangle: the product no longer sells, the phone stops ringing. And in the late 1950s, your fortieth birthday seemed particularly demoralizing—perhaps it always does. Although Signoret had never played young, lissome, inviolate characters, movie producers were fiercely alert to signs of aging in a woman they had once claimed to adore.

So when the British producer Peter Glenville offered her work in Hollywood, it seemed an invitation straight from heaven. Alas, Glenville's American associate, Bill Goetz, had to turn down the "witch" from Paris in a long and embarrassed cable: the McCarthyite difficulties were not over. Glenville refused to drop her in favor of a politically acceptable alternative, and he finally shot *Room at the Top* in England, with Jack Clayton directing. The movie takes place in England's industrial North, where an ambitious young man setting out to crash the bourgeois establishment falls in love with Alice Aisgill, an older woman who is intelligent, adulterous, and wise in the ways of love. Montand and her daughter Catherine saw Signoret off at the Gare du Nord, where the Golden Arrow boat train would take her to London. As she said goodbye to her loved ones, Signoret had no idea that this stopgap assignment would give her what the movie world was to regard as her greatest role—and an Oscar for best actress.

During the few weeks of separation, Montand honored a commitment to the American film director Jules Dassin. Denounced in 1951 by his colleague Edward Dmytryk (director of *The Caine Mutiny*) before HUAC, Dassin had had to flee to Europe. The Cannes Film Festival had awarded a prize to his *Rififi* as a consolation for the injustice done him, but the brilliant creator of *Night and the City* remained an exile, an outlaw. Seeing that Montand was not exactly shrouded in sanctity since his tour of Eastern Europe, Dassin thought he'd be ideal in the role of Matteo Brigante in *La Legge* (*Where the Hot Wind Blows*), the scarred and mustachioed godfather in an Apulian village, and Marcello Mastroianni's rival for the affections of Gina Lollobrigida.

La Legge is not a masterpiece, but Montand came out of it unscathed, with reviewers who savaged the film praising him warmly. He was no longer a beginner. *The Wages of Fear* had been a major advancement, and the early jinx had been exorcised. Still, his career on screen was not really taking off: he had respectable titles to his credit (such as Luis Saslavsky's

Premier Mai, a pleasant melodrama completed in the winter of 1958, in which he played alongside Maurice Bireaud and Nicole Berger); he had succeeded, although without the unanimous approval he was accustomed to on stage, in putting across powerful characters (notably John Proctor); he was making money. But he was not yet headed for movie greatness. And that was what he wanted more than anything else.

Montand resolved not to let his dissatisfaction fester. That autumn he once again laid siege to the Elysée music hall. Was he sure of victory? Yes and no. Apart from extremists, almost everyone had liked the Montand of 1953–54; and even those who were lukewarm about his politically committed persona had still laughed along with him when he sang his entertainments. But in the four years since then, Montand's position had become more ambiguous, riskier. Forewarned, the Communists now saw him through less rose-colored glasses, and others—not just on the right—were not ready to forgive the comrade who had done a song-and-dance routine on the ruins of Budapest.

These were turbulent times. The few Frenchmen who bothered to stay informed—which required a conscious effort, for the press was vigilantly censored—could no longer ignore the fact that the authorities in Algeria were routinely using torture against captured opponents of the French colonial regime, and rebels of the Algerian National Liberation Front, though not winning on the battlefield, were gaining a hearing at the United Nations and in other influential foreign forums. Charles de Gaulle, back in power after a murky *coup de force,* was busily building a foundation of legitimacy for his new regime, a task completed—and the Fourth Republic buried—on September 28, 1958, when eight voters out of ten approved the new constitution he offered them. Not since the Liberation had the Communist Party fallen so low. Fully discredited, the Socialist left was fragmented.

Montand, as was his habit, opted to surprise the public. People expected him to inject a deeper note of gravity into his repertory, to color it with the somber hues of the day. He did just the opposite.

As he rehearsed for his concert at Autheuil, his concerns were everything but political. He planned to convey to audiences the message that he was a hoofer and only a hoofer—by no means politically deaf or blind, but certainly not the bearer of a redemptive or revolutionary message. He dropped "C'est à l'aube" (an archetypally symbolic number), the herald of radiant dawns that had so pleased Khrushchev, and replaced it with a song that describes the whimsical notions of a young ticket puncher on a bus (the composer Philippe Gérard, coauthor of "C'est à l'aube," had come upon the old song and adapted it).

"Le Chat de la voisine" ("My Neighbor's Cat") opens in speedy and lightweight fashion, like so many other songs that achieved instant popularity in the 1930s:

> Le chat de la voisine
> Qui mange la bonne cuisine
> Et fait ses gros ronrons . . .
>
> [My neighbor's cat
> She eats and grows fat
> She's sleepy and purry
> Soft, warm, and furry . . .]

At a perfectly whimsical moment several verses into this sexy froufrou, it is brutally interrupted by a dark *sprechstimme* aside:

> Je ne dessinerai pas l'homme et son agonie, l'enfant des premiers pas qui gèle dans son nid, je ne parlerai pas du soldat qui a peur d'échanger une jambe contre une croix d'honneur, du vieillard rejeté aux poubelles de la faim, je n'en parlerai pas, mieux vaut ce petit refrain. . . .
>
> [I cannot dwell on man and his death, on freezing infants, I'm not going to talk about the soldier who fears trading the loss of a leg for military honors, or the old man picking the sidewalks for food, which is why I sing along in this mood. . . .]

And then back to the entertainment with the cat. It was a perfect way to signal that he wasn't taken in, that the professional entertainer had limits. Yves Montand liked singers with a message no better than he liked vapid "singer-singers." Having already come perilously close to that abyss in which an artist compromises his freedom and renounces the emotional ambiguity that is the very stuff of art, he now gave the scales a tip in the other direction and hit the balance between the two extremes he disliked.

Twenty-four songs, sixteen new titles, with romance, merriment, and tenderness setting the tone. There was Panama and its "Grands Boulevards," and Montand even wheeled out Piaf's old gift, "Mais qu'est-ce que j'ai à tant l'aimer?" But the worker was still present—as the strolling pleasure seeker of "Luna Park" or, if one of society's victims, in an exotic place, for example, a peasant planting coffee beneath a murderous sun (here the beam of a single spotlight picked out the motionless Montand, standing as if he himself were planted, his face hidden under a tattered sombrero). Individual men and women, each with his or her own dream.

Ivo Livi no longer believed in a glorious Marxist future. Without repudiating his past or his adolescent dreams, he was determined to put this across. The overall result was a show of great gaiety and charm in which social distinctions were blurred beneath a cloak of farce. It welcomed the audience with open arms—"Good evening, friends, pals, how are you tonight, the show is on . . . "—and each half ended with a caper and a clatter of tap-dance steps ("Un Garçon dansait" and "Le Fanatique du Jazz").

Not surprisingly, Montand's preparations for this comeback took on marathon dimensions, and he poured even more of himself into the work than ever before, if that was possible. First he had a transition to make, a proper note to strike; and, like the political climate, the music-hall world had changed. Georges Brassens, Jacques Brel, René-Louis Lafforgue, and many other outstandingly talented writer-singers were revolutionizing popular song. Montand sensed that he seemed out-of-date, so he worked harder than ever to stress the different nature of his muse. And he proved to his own satisfaction that this refusal to conform allowed him to perfect his technique and to keep varying his register.

His orchestra also needed rearranging. Bob Castella, Emmanuel Soudieux, Roger Paraboschi, and Freddy Balta stood loyally by. So did his sublime clarinetist, Hubert Rostaing, who also contributed new arrangements. Montand and Rostaing also decided to recruit a new trombonist, Claude Gousset. But Montand's old friend Crolla was unavailable. His reputation was now so exalted that he had been lured away to compose movie scores. (He began by writing for one-reelers by Georges Franju and Jacques-Yves Cousteau.) Didi Duprat replaced Crolla on guitar, but without stepping into the mascot role that had fallen to Crolla in the course of a passionate, hilarious friendship.

The group camped at Autheuil for most of the month of August. The little theater was busy ten hours a day, with Montand, as usual, wearing his colleagues down. While the most athletic or the weariest relaxed in the pool, Rostaing composed waltzes, which he dedicated to Catherine Allégret.

As a last precaution, Montand afforded himself the luxury of a full dress rehearsal before an invited audience. On September 9, on the night off of the Ballets Vargas, then appearing at the Etoile, Montand invited eight hundred guinea pigs, most of them workers and engineers at Philips, which was now his recording company. Signoret scanned the auditorium, took notes, and swapped impressions with Castella and Rostaing. Even this was not enough. The out-of-town previews were as arduous as rehearsals: from September 20 on, they ironed out the last wrinkles and fine-tuned the transitions in Melun, Grenoble, Switzerland, Annecy, Lyons. . . .

Then came the Paris premiere. Once again, the "flower of arts and letters" was out in full force. And once again, the press raved: "A Triumphal Arch for Yves Montand" was the headline above Claude Sarraute's review in *Le Monde* on October 8. The run did not end until March 8, 1959. In five months and 160 performances, two hundred thousand tickets had been sold.

These were five months in which Montand progressively mastered his fear. And five months in which Signoret knew enormous joy and bottomless grief. *Room at the Top,* released in London in November, enjoyed an outstanding success in English-speaking countries (although France seemed unimpressed) and won for her a second British Film Academy award and the Palme d'Or at Cannes. But Signoret's brother, Alain Kaminker, a young and talented filmmaker, was drowned on December 10 off the Ile de Sein, where he was filming fishermen. His death, Simone Signoret said reticently, "marked a frontier" in her life.

This harrowing frontier, while the most painful of all, was but one of many Montand and his wife were soon to cross—geographical, professional, private.

Early in December 1958, an American agent, Norman Granz, called on Montand in his dressing room at the Etoile. Granz, who numbered Oscar Peterson and Ella Fitzgerald among his clients, was the promoter of "Jazz at the Philharmonic" and the owner of Verve Records. He was a serious man, a man in a hurry, stubborn, a gourmet. He wanted to invite Montand to Broadway—not to a nightclub (however famous) but to a theater, where he would perform the whole of his show in French. And it would work, said Granz. So what if Americans knew him only from *The Wages of Fear* and as the singer of "Autumn Leaves"? It would work anyway: Montand would take them by storm. Was it not rash to stray onto turf belonging to Frank Sinatra, Ray Charles, Frankie Lane, Eddie Fisher, Doris Day, and Sammy Davis, Jr.? wondered Montand. Not rash at all, insisted Granz: the States hadn't had a real look at a Frenchman since Chevalier. When? Next September. A visa? The climate was getting warmer; a visa was no longer a problem.

On this last point Granz was overly optimistic. The applications the Livis sent to the United States embassy met with a refusal accompanied by sincere regrets, delivered to them in the "trailer" by two regretful diplomats. Eisenhower and Khrushchev might be engaged in a hectic, thorny correspondence on the subject of reducing the threat of thermonuclear war, but suspects were still suspects. Granz took the blow as a personal insult; he moved heaven and earth, agencies and consulates. At the end of January 1959, the two entertainers' passports were adorned with the requisite stamps, together with the comment "One Entry." A bare-minimum visa, valid from July 15 to December 15—just enough time for a temporary work contract.

Montand's terror, which had been fading, came galloping back. Just as he was beginning to regain confidence, to enjoy audiences shouting their enthusiasm each night as the curtain fell (Simone Signoret, herself buried under telegrams confirming the triumph of *Room at the Top,* remarked ironically of her star husband, "He didn't realize it was Greta Garbo handing him his towel every evening"), here he was courting the disequilibrium and terror of a dangerous venture all over again. "I wanted to enter America through the front door," he admitted on his return from the great endeavor. "When our friends heard about the offer, they all warned me that I'd fall on my face. Everything was against me: my reputation as an Iron Curtain star, my alleged political beliefs, my total ignorance of the English language, and the impression I gave of wanting everything without having to pay for it."[1]

After the Etoile show, there were other commitments to be honored before New York. Montand was grateful that his physical conditioning program had been so stringent, because he needed to be in good shape for the ordeal ahead. "An Evening with Yves Montand" (the title dreamed up by Granz and Montand's new agent, Jacques Canetti) was amended, cleansed, and decanted more obsessionally than ever. As soon as the curtain fell on the last Etoile performance, Montand launched into a previously planned tour of London, Israel, the French provinces, Brussels, Holland, Sweden, and northern Germany. After three weeks at La Colombe, he was off again: Nice-Deauville via Biarritz, La Baule, Saint-Malo, and all the usual stops. In Biarritz, Lauren Bacall, recently widowed, dined with Yves and Simone. In earlier days she and Humphrey Bogart had shared supper at Maxim's with the Montands, and she and her husband had courageously come to the defense of the Hollywood Ten. Now she offered her good wishes and encouragement to the Proctors and promised to see them in New York.

In Moscow in 1956, the Montands had received a welcome worthy of heads of state (friendly states, to boot). On Thursday, September 10, 1959,

1. Interview with Francis Rico in *Candide,* July 1962.

when they landed in New York, M. and Mme Livi, their presence on American soil only briefly to be officially tolerated, lined up like everyone else at the glass cages where immigration officers sat enthroned. Bob Castella and Hubert Rostaing were their only escorts: the American Federation of Musicians was ferociously protectionist about foreign competition. As for Catherine Allégret—just turned fourteen—it had been agreed that she would cross the Atlantic only if the show crossed a respectable box-office threshold; Montand's contract stipulated that the tour would last as long as more than half the theater's one thousand seats were sold.

Four days earlier, a large advertisement had announced to readers of the *New York Times* that Yves Montand, "France's most popular entertainer," would be presenting a one-man show of twenty-four songs beginning Tuesday, September 22, at Henry Miller's Theater on West Forty-third Street. The designer had skillfully retouched Montand's image, disciplining the wavy hair and reinforcing the Latin note; the lines on his face were subtly enhanced, expressive, virile. "Mail orders now!" the theater advised. But this routine exhortation had no connection to the public's actual intentions. It was impossible to determine in advance what kind of audience would come. Of course, Montand was known to fellow professionals; some had already applauded him in Paris. Of course, recordings of some of his songs, like "C'est si bon," had been played on American radio. And the worldwide success of *The Wages of Fear* had brought him the beginnings of movie fame in New York. But his stage reputation would have to be built from scratch. And it was Signoret's features that were familiar to Americans: *Room at the Top* filled hundreds of movie theaters every night. A customs officer had already identified the actress at the airport. Simone scented the danger—not the danger of overshadowing her man and wounding him, but of heightening his vulnerability at the very moment that he had to make the effort of his life. "In Paris, Montand is Montand, and I am myself, and we are man and wife. In Moscow, I was Montand's wife. In New York . . . my greatest worry was that they would see Montand as an actress's husband."

Montand scarcely had time to relish the bizarre sense of déjà vu that overcame him as they drove through Manhattan with Norman Granz: all these streets, avenues, buildings, signs, and people were the streets, avenues, buildings, signs, and people of his favorite movies. Granz always put up his guests at the Algonquin Hotel, on West Forty-fourth Street. Twenty years earlier, its lobby cluttered with mahogany furniture had been a shrine for the intellectuals who gathered at its famous round table. Now the bar overflowed mainly after the theater, but the hotel's small and rather shabby rooms still possessed a family charm.

Signoret was delighted, but Montand was heading into a deep, dark tunnel: he had just ten days to get to know a group of new musicians, and he spoke barely a word of English. All that survived of his early efforts to learn the language back in Marseilles was a fistful of disjointed phrases. In Moscow there had been no problem: he had had his own troupe around him, and audiences were used to foreign entertainers' ignorance of their language. In the United States, even with the world's best interpreter and adviser at his side, he was running a very different professional risk. In Eastern Europe, coming from the outside had been a plus. For Americans, whatever their relish for European exoticism, it was different.

Bob Castella was hardly further advanced in speaking English than his employer. Both of them went to Berlitz three times a week throughout their stay in New York. The two first words Yves Montand picked up were "tooth" and "rehearsal," "tooth" because a wisdom tooth was torturing him and he had to see a dentist early each morning, and "rehearsal" because that was where most of his energy went. There were rehearsals every afternoon, and they began with a disappointment: Hubert Rostaing, whose participation had been painstakingly negotiated, was at the last moment barred from playing. "The musicians union wouldn't budge," he says. "I wasn't even allowed to unpack my clarinet. I was disappointed, of course, but I stayed for a month anyway, listening to the arrangements, to keep Yves comfortable." A pleasant surprise, though, was the outstanding ability of the artists recruited by Norman Granz. Jimmy Giuffre, who replaced Rostaing, was reputed to be America's finest clarinetist. Nick Perito (accordion), Al Hall (bass), Billy Byers (trombone), and Jim Hall (guitar) were all topflight musicians. The black drummer Charles Persip quickly replicated the tempo of "Le Carrosse." Bob Castella and Montand never did master English, but at rehearsals the universal idiom of their profession obviated the need for words.

Granz's reputation in the jazz world was richly deserved. At first, the six American musicians he had hired were puzzled by the extreme care with which they were expected to follow Montand's movements: they had never seen a singer move that way, telling a story in song. But then they entered into the spirit of the thing and followed Bob and Rostaing. Real pros. Good ones.

The daily rehearsals aside, Montand had to find a way across the language barrier and somehow convey to the potential American audiences what he was all about. By definition, a one-man show meant that the artist was alone on stage. It was out of the question to have an announcer delivering wooden translations of the songs as they came up. What Montand—and Montand alone—had to do was to give the audience a twenty-second summary of each new number, a feel for its mood. Since he couldn't really learn English in time, he would have to learn the words phonetically, and the introductions had to be clear, amusing, striking—not nearly as simple a task as it might seem.

The chief author of the summaries, recruited by Granz with the Montands' blessing, was in every way exceptional. Then forty-five years old, Michael Wilson was a considerable Hollywood figure whose career had been ruined by McCarthy and his followers. A philosophy graduate, he had worked as a scriptwriter in the early 1940s, served brilliantly in the Pacific as a Marine lieutenant, then returned to writing screenplays. (He had written, among others, *Five Fingers,* directed by Joseph L. Mankiewicz.) When hauled before HUAC and asked to confess his left-wing beliefs and denounce his friends, he refused—and was blacklisted. Like many of his fellow unfortunates, he moved into the black market, turning out scripts whose authorship others would claim (with or without his permission). The best—or worst—illustration of the hypocrisy then pervading Hollywood came in 1957, when Pierre Boulle was awarded the Oscar for best screenplay for *The Bridge on the River Kwai,* whose real authors were Carl Foreman (also on the blacklist) and Michael Wilson.[2] When Montand asked Wilson for his help in 1959, he was working on the script of a movie that would triumph three years later: *Lawrence of Arabia.* He did not operate above-ground again until 1965.

This talented wizard set to work condensing the plot and action of each song—not summarizing, but simply suggesting what it was about. Helping him was a friend of Hungarian origin, Laslo Benedek (he had directed the movie version of Arthur Miller's *Death of a Salesman* in 1951 and *The Wild One,* with Marlon Brando, in 1954), who was as fascinated as he by the challenge of this assignment. Delighted with the final result, Signoret helped her husband learn the perfectly crafted vignettes syllable by syllable. Montand regretted his inability to appreciate the rare delicacy of the phrases he monotonously and obsessively memorized. "If you could have seen me," he later said, "spending nights learning English sentences by heart, listening to tapes until my ears hurt, following my teachers' instructions in front of the mirror. . . . I was like a deaf person unable to hear his own voice."[3]

A few days after Montand's arrival, Norman Granz took him to the Apollo Theater in Harlem to hear Ella Fitzgerald sing. Montand was dazzled, but he was otherwise not really available to be entertained or to see the sights of the New World. What little free time he had was carefully devoted to promoting the show. One by one, New York's entertainment reporters trooped into his suite at the Algonquin. The interviews were all

2. See Victor Navasky, *Naming Names* (New York, 1980).

3. Interview with Rico in *Candide.*

more or less the same: the singer was asked to define himself, and his charming wife—discreetly translating questions and answers—offered appropriate comments on the married life of entertainers. One result was a page in *Newsweek* titillatingly entitled "Explosive Frenchman." Montand: "In America if you have a good voice you sing Gershwin and Cole Porter. To become a star in France you have to find your own songs. Talent helps. But there's Chevalier, Trenet, or Piaf. To that talent you have to add your personality." Signoret: "We have conflicts, more violent perhaps than in other households. We fight and then we get over it. All that is very Latin. When I'm really mad I sit in the back of the theater and think, 'What a bastard! But my God, how good he is!' "[4]

The closeness of Montand and Signoret attracted the sympathy and curiosity of an American public used to the spectacle of stars mutually devouring one another. A New York *Post* reporter, Helen Dudar, raved about the actress's modesty: "Even though she is better known in the United States through her movies, Miss Signoret thought of delaying her arrival a week so as not to deprive her husband of the smallest scrap of attention."[5] Several notches higher, *The New York Times Magazine* sent a very young reporter, P. E. Schneider, to write a profile of Montand. This time, none of the customary anecdotes, just serious talk, with the reporter stressing the seriousness of Montand's staging and use of props.[6] In return, the French couple decided to confide in this resourceful and polite young man. They asked him to stay to lunch and talked to him off-the-record about their difficulties with American officialdom: "Your country has finally granted us visas, but it's not we who have changed, it's you," they told him. Drawing courage from their companion's apparent openness and honesty, they described their mingled doubts and convictions about their host country. Readers of *The New York Times Magazine* never learned of this setting straight of the record, but at least Montand and Signoret had done it.

All this verbal foreplay was the least of the Montands' worries. No matter how well the show was promoted, it was on stage that the battle would be fought. Basically, the test lying ahead of Montand was like the one he had faced at the ABC in 1944, except that the stakes were higher and the symbols heavier. Ivo Livi, who had dreamed of Manhattan on the docks of Marseilles, was getting ready to conquer America. Or to lose it.

4. Quoted in *Newsweek,* September 28, 1959.

5. Helen Dudar, New York *Post,* September 20, 1959. The article called Montand "The Man in the Open-Neck Shirt."

6. P. E. Schneider, *The New York Times Magazine,* September 13, 1959.

"What do you need?" When you rent a theater in the United States all you get is a bare auditorium. Nothing: no batten, no footlights, no piano, no curtain, no lights—nothing, nothing, nothing. Seats, with a coating of dust. And then, pleasant and businesslike, they ask you: "What do you need?" The cleaning squad drowns the place in shampoo. White trucks roll up with cranes and the curtains are hung (afterward, two guys will ask you for fifty dollars every week just to check that it goes up and down). Then more trucks come in, with the batten and the footlights. They offer you a piano—white, gray, green, yellow. Then it's the painters' turn: they always repaint the stage, it's a tradition. I wanted it gray, with two yellow stripes at the foot. New lighting is installed in the foyer.

And the place is yours to do what you want with!

On Monday, September 21, 1959, it was the same old miracle all over again. But this time the miracle came not from his own kind, not from the faithful Etoile audiences, but from Marilyn Monroe and her beau of the evening, Montgomery Clift, from Lauren Bacall, Ingrid Bergman, Sidney Chaplin, Marlene Dietrich, Kitty and Kurt Frings, Martin Gabel, Paulette Goddard, Adolph Green, Frank Loesser, Sidney Lumet, and many others he had briefly met in the gloom of European cabarets. His publicity man, Richard Maney, a veteran of forty years on Broadway (known as "the most eloquent communicator since Saint Paul"), had done his work well. But in the end, the person for what the gossip columns later heralded as an unequaled Broadway opening was Yves Montand. And despite Simone's support, he had rarely been so alone.

Even afterward, sponging himself down in the little cement-walled dressing room in the basement, or popping champagne at the Algonquin among talkative admirers, he remained alone. He was waiting for the newspapers, for the judgment of the experts, the six or seven reviewers from the leading New York dailies whose word would decide the longevity of his venture. Maney passed on a highly excited comment from Marilyn Monroe: "He's so wonderful, he sings with his body!" Hubert Rostaing (who had been sitting next to Monroe and was surprised to find her round, almost plump) told him he had felt real warmth from the audience—not simply curiosity about the visitor from Paris but something Montand had won with his own efforts. He was touched, it was nice; but it did nothing to calm his fears. He did not want to hear the praise but to read it in black and white.

In the middle of the night, Maney's assistant, who had gone round to all the newspaper offices, returned with his arms full of the hoped-for and dreaded pages.

Not a single harsh word. Approval so total and so impressive that we must record it faithfully. Richard Watts, Jr., writing in the New York *Post:* "All I can do for Montand is dust off and use an old adjective: superb. . . . Let's call it charm, a pure and almost animal magnetism. But there's more. M. Montand possesses the happy and very unusual knack of conveying to us ordinary and envious men why he fascinates women. And this is not all. The fact is that he sings well and distinctly (so distinctly that you almost question the usefulness of the mike), that he acts with extreme ease, that he displays a sharp sense of humor and irony, and that he uses his limited English without playing coquettishly to the gallery. . . . All our singers, including the great Mr. Sinatra, could sit at his feet and take a lesson from him."

John McClain, in the *Journal American,* also accorded Montand comparable stature to Sinatra's, adding that his voice and his talent set him apart from the "lover-boys," the sugary crooners who reigned in most of the major New York nightclubs. In similar tones, the reviewer for the *New York Times,* Kenneth Campbell, stressed the depth and breadth of the singer's repertory: "He has the art, the personality and the talent to offer his audience a whole series of works in which he celebrates the daily life of the average Frenchman. He is subtle and funny, and once in a while serious or sad." And Walter Kerr, writing in the New York *Herald Tribune,* declared: "It is not enough to single out his bright talent. More than anything else, Yves Montand is captivating."

It was an unprecedented evening, said the reviewers. "The intensity of the applause," wrote Robert Coleman in the New York *Mirror,* "was worthy of a promising opening at the Met." Frank Aston in the *World Telegram and Sun* raved as enthusiastically as the audience he described: "At the end of the performance the crowd was wild with enthusiasm. It would gladly have heard him until breakfast time. Which would have been only justice: it was much too good for just one evening."

In plain language, the echoes of approval meant that the show would last—and play to packed houses. In just one hundred minutes, Montand had moved into a new dimension and had filled Norman Granz's cup to overflowing. He became the man not to miss. At the end of three weeks, with the Henry Miller booked for another show, the singer moved his concert to the nearby Longacre Theater. Forty-two performances in all. And when Montand stopped after a month and a half, it was not because the demand had dried up: the cautious Granz had planned a standby tour, in case the New York venture ended badly, that would take him to Montreal, Toronto, Los Angeles, and San Francisco. From there he would leave the United States for Japan.

Those six New York weeks were weeks of glory. In a series of interviews that formed the bedrock of her autobiography *Nostalgia Isn't What It Used to Be*—the title came from a graffito seen in New York—Simone Signoret admitted: "We were quite simply royalty. We looked at New York and thought, 'We didn't have to sell out a thing to reach this point.' It was both pride and joy."[7]

Did Yves Montand relax once he had crossed the barrier? Did he surrender wholeheartedly to "pride and joy"? Not really. For him it was not enough to have triumphed: he needed to analyze that triumph. So he combed the weekly press, the reviews and the magazines that soon picked up where the dailies had left off. They were no less enthusiastic. On October 5, *Time* hailed "the most brilliant music-hall artist to have made his presence felt on stage since the Second World War." *Commonweal* on October 16 called Montand "a pal" and stuck four labels on him: sophisticated, adorable, sweet, and sure. *The Reporter* on October 29 said: "His work points up the spectacular drop in quality of mass entertainment in our country these past few years. . . . Very few Americans—perhaps only Frank Sinatra and Sammy Davis, Jr.—could stay on stage for a whole evening without sounding like a jukebox. Even Sinatra and Davis are limited by their repertory to a two-dimensional register. They are unable to project the illusion that they can surpass their capacities." And *Vogue,* in its November issue, purred, "He produces at will a full, sexy, infinitely seductive sound."

Similar points cropped up from one magazine to the next. First, the deceptive simplicity of set, props, and costumes ("He looks," said *The New Yorker,* "as if he drives a taxi during the day"). Second, the breadth and range of his repertory, the ordinary-guy vein, free of vulgarity, the attention paid to life's "little nothings." Finally, the show's immaculate finish. Not one American critic voiced the reproach of excessive perfectionism so monotonously leveled in France. On the contrary: the extreme precision of Montand's every move, and the laborious preparation it implied, were all to his credit. Reviewers especially noted his instinctive elegance in the transitions, his passage from strong to light themes: "Like a good lover," said Henry Hewes in *Saturday Review* on October 10, "he takes care not to let anything happen too suddenly."

While all this pleased Montand, one aspect of his press—patiently

7. From an unpublished interview. Our thanks to Dominique Miollan, who participated in and deciphered these conversations, for supplying us with the original recorded tapes.

translated and classified by Signoret—intrigued him. "Attractive, sexy, exciting": he was unused to seeing these adjectives linked to his name, and he hovered between pleasure and bewilderment. As a young man, with his long nose and big mouth, he had considered himself impossibly ugly; and he had hated the sight of his lean profile in the rushes of his early movies. Yet now he was being presented as a sex symbol. Flattering, of course, but he knew the glamorous reputation of Latin lovers, the romantic aura of Paris, and even the volatile perfume released by certain French words (*bonsoir, bistro, chéri*) had helped to nourish this virile image. But he was in New York to seduce, not to be stereotyped as a Latin lover.

The other touchy point concerned his English. As he memorized the brief introductions preceding each song, he had striven to avoid typically French errors of diction, the kind Chevalier had deliberately stressed for their appeal. Manhattanites in the know had warned Montand that the days of the "ooh-là-là" Frenchman were numbered. So he was grateful to the *Post*'s Richard Watts for pointing out that he did not try to wear his French accent on his sleeve.

The dressing room at the Henry Miller, and then the Longacre, was never empty after the show. A procession of New York actors knocked at Montand's door: "You don't know me, but. . . ." Montand did not know them, but as the heroes of all his favorite films trooped in one after the other, beaming, accepting him as an eminent member of their family, he recognized each one of them. Montand and Signoret, awed foreigners who at first had hesitated to enter the portals of Sardi's, on West Forty-fourth Street, were now fought-over guests of honor at evenings there. On one unforgettable night, a tall, elegant gentleman came up to their table and introduced himself with careful tact, wholly unnecessarily, as Henry Fonda. The Montands were a little surprised by the relaxed way in which show-business people in New York let their hair down. In France it was the rule to keep your talents to yourself as soon as the footlights went out. Here, on the contrary, you were expected to abandon yourself to the wildest improvisations once you were in private. If you had a gift for mimicry, you kept your companions in fits; if you were a singer, you tried out a new song; if you were a comedian, you rolled out your latest joke. Yves and Simone (it was finally and firmly established that Yves—not to be confused with Eve—was a male first name) enjoyed this trouper conviviality, in which everyone opened his bag of tricks before the best, or the worst, of audiences.

But another encounter overshadowed all others. Arthur Miller, working desperately to finish a screenplay, had been unable to attend Montand's opening night (where Montgomery Clift had replaced him, as we have seen, as his wife Marilyn Monroe's escort), but he came the next evening with Marilyn—who was seeing the show for the second time in a row—to salute Montand's success and renew acquaintance with his own *Les Sorcières de Salem* stars.

Miller and Montand had briefly crossed paths in Paris in mid-November 1956, five months after Miller's marriage to Marilyn Monroe. Miller had sought permission to leave the United States before then, but HUAC's watchdogs had denied him a passport and therefore the pleasure of witnessing his play's success at the Théâtre Sarah-Bernhardt. But things were easing up; he had taken advantage of a trip to London, where Monroe was making a movie with Laurence Olivier, to visit Paris, get to know the Montands, and encourage Raymond Rouleau on the set of *Les Sorcières de Salem.* His Paris hosts had found him attractive and warm, if somewhat solemn. Now, in 1959, the air was clearing somewhat—Miller remembers the "cooling of the anti-Communist fever"—and he was at the peak of his fame, a hero of the American left, an unchallengeable moral symbol, who to artists and thinkers all over the country embodied courage, loyalty, and unshakable liberalism.

Montand and his wife were doubly drawn to the man who invited them to dinner at his home. He was not only a playwright of the first rank but the finest American example of what in Paris was known as a committed intellectual, a symbol of resistance to intolerance. In the Millers' handsome white apartment at 444 East 57th Street, the talk was initially lighthearted. Bob Castella was surprised by Marilyn's simplicity. He was expecting someone affected, sophisticated, manufactured; but the "sex bomb" of Hollywood publicity releases, purring huskily into a microphone, lashes fluttering, all milk-white curves and platinum glitter, the star of whom it was whispered that she was sometimes sewn into her dresses without anything much on underneath, was for the moment a pleasant, unaffected, blue-eyed woman who called her husband "Poppy" and clearly loved being a hostess. She gave Montand friendly smiles and admiring looks (the language barrier was decidedly forbidding). But the true star of the evening was Miller, with whom Signoret launched into a passionate discussion whose main points she periodically passed on to the other French guests.

"I believe," says Miller, "that they both felt very uncertain as to the legality of their presence on American soil, and I personally have no doubt that quite a few members of the administration would happily have expelled them for any reason at all." Yet Montand had included only one political song in his repertory, Léo Ferré's "Flamenco de Paris," about a Spanish Republican exile, and the press had generally avoided political labels. But in the times they were living through, Miller told Signoret, the heritage of the Cold War was heavy, even though there were now palpable signs of improvement. Asked about their visit to the USSR and the "people's democracies," the Montands made no secret of their reservations and disappointments, and took a position with which Miller himself was in sympathy. Very quickly a thread of sympathy and understanding was woven between the visitors from Paris and their distinguished New York host. And it was not just an evening of unbroken ideological politics, for they also enjoyed themselves, drinking Italian wine and eating the wonderful food prepared by Lena Pepitone, Marilyn's maid (in her memoirs, she said that Montand looked like her employer's former husband, the great baseball player Joe DiMaggio).[8] In short, Yves and Simone were able to do some catching up on business that had been interrupted by the Cold War. They were at last finding what, in the United States as elsewhere, was the real nourishment in their existence: partners, comrades, colleagues, friends.

And an audience.

In Montreal, French to the core, Montand felt entirely at home. And he felt at home in Toronto, too, seemingly so American. It was Los Angeles, in between, that threw him. He and Signoret arrived on Wednesday, November 4, with his premiere at the vast and venerable Huntington Hartford Theater scheduled for the following Monday. Four days for rehearsals was cutting it very close, especially when only the clarinetist and the guitarist remained of the musicians who had joined him in New York. In fact, there was scarcely time to say "So this is Hollywood," to realize that only the two blocks west of Vine Street stood between him and Paramount, that Columbia Pictures was only just a bit farther north past Santa Monica Boulevard—and that the routine was suffocating him: nothing but work, work, work. Work and fear.

And yet there had been that thrill when he and his wife looked down from the airplane and saw those huge brash capital letters spread out along the crest of the hills: HOLLYWOOD. "I'm always sorry," wrote Simone Signoret, "for the people who reject gifts their adolescent memories may offer. As that plane circled down I was eating one of Proust's memory madeleines, as big as a doughnut." And as she said in an unpublished interview: "To get there owing them nothing for what we had achieved—that was the height of luxury. You had to have your head screwed on not to go completely crazy in Hollywood. I can imagine what it might do to

8. Lena Pepitone, William Stadiem, and Maurice Hakim, *The Secret Marilyn.* Such "as-told-to" recollections are not always reliable.

twenty-five-year-olds. You could have become fatuously pretentious. If you didn't know that there were other things in the world, if you didn't have thousands of years of civilization behind you, plus four years of German Occupation, there would be no reason not to swallow it all as absolutely normal and turn into a zombie. If I had gone there in 1949, either I would have turned right around again and left, or else I would just have flopped down into that sugary, wonderful world."

If they had accepted those earlier offers from Jack Warner and Howard Hughes, the ultimate revenge would have been much less sweet.

Their revenge began even before the show opened. Anne Douglas, Kirk's wife, who was French, had phoned the Montands when they were in New York, inviting them to celebrate their first days on the West Coast at the Douglas home. It turned out to be something more than a simple little dinner among almost-compatriots. Hollywood was not Greenwich Village. Montand was the most illustrious of recently imported artists, a revelation if ever there was one, and Mlle Signoret was the only Paris actress whose latest movie had gone over better in the States than in France. It was therefore one of those fabled California gatherings that awaited the Montands at the Douglas home on Saturday, November 7.

"Spectacular." It was not just anybody who called it that; it was the ample and terrifying Louella Parsons, who along with Hedda Hopper reigned over the gossip, scandals, contracts, loves, breakups, heart attacks, and court cases so beloved and so familiar to the newspaper territory they patrolled. "What a rush from party to party Saturday night!" she panted in the Los Angeles *Examiner* on November 9. "First the party thrown by Anne and Kirk in honor of Simone Signoret and Yves Montand: the whole world hurried there. Then the party for California's favorite son, Vice-President Nixon, at the side of his ravishing Pat." Parsons had excellent reasons for mentioning the probable Republican candidate in the upcoming presidential election: like him, she had lashed out at "misguided" Americans of all kinds when the witch hunt was on.

In truth, the Douglas party somewhat eclipsed the campaign celebration intended to promote Richard Nixon. Hollywood's bigwigs had to give precedence to Nixon, but before going home they all made a quick side trip to view the competition. Jack Warner—the very symbol of his breed—had every possible legal and political reason for boycotting the man he had once tried to kidnap from the ABC. Nevertheless, he came over to shake the hand of "that son of a bitch." It should be remembered that the two French stars were still in principle reds, armed with very temporary visas. But that Saturday night they were the center of a throng that included Gary Cooper, George Cukor, Judy Garland, Henry Hathaway, Gene Kelly, Dean Martin, Kim Novak, and Gregory Peck. Not forgetting the French consul in Los Angeles, the novelist Romain Gary, who apologized to them for his lugubrious expression ("Don't think I'm bored; I'm always like this, it's my nature"). The fact that Hollywood was rolling out the red carpet reflected both the professional stardom they had acquired and the changing times ahead.

When Montand was introduced to Walt Disney, it was especially significant. At the age of thirteen he had written to him from La Cabucelle to say how he adored cartoons and had begged him for an autograph. How could Mr. Disney even begin to understand how, by inventing Donald Duck, he had virtually imprinted Yves Montand on Ivo Livi's retina?

Two days later, as Montand prepared for action in the dressing room of the Huntington Hartford, celebrities were gathering for a gala dinner at the Brown Derby, just opposite. Afterward, they had only to cross the street to attend the show. Cobina Wright, the gossip columnist of the Los Angeles *Herald Express,* and fighting to keep pace with her two big competitors, carefully recorded the guest list: Lucille Ball, Richard Burton, Gene Kelly, Dorothy Malone, Lloyd Nolan, Bob Osborne, Gregory Peck, Frank Powell, Shelley Winters, and a hundred others. Nobody—friend, foe, or neutral—wanted to miss the fun.

Los Angeles reviewers, influenced by their Broadway colleagues but invariably delighted to be able to differ from them, were obliged to parody, almost word for word, what had already been written or said around Times Square. "Memorable," shouted the *Valley Times.* "Montand fascinated his audience," stated the Los Angeles *Examiner.* The Beverly Hills *Citizen* added Montand's name to the very short list of artists capable of holding a show together single-handed: Al Jolson, Maurice Chevalier, Victor Borge. Once again, American critics applauded Montand's technical perfection. "Impressive work, M. Montand," approved Harrison Carroll in the *Herald Express.*

He sang at night—and in the daytime, too. No question of strolling through the Farmer's Market or along the Walk of Fame, where bronze plaques recalled the illustrious feet that had trodden these sidewalks, or of suppressing a chuckle at the sight of Grauman's unbelievable Chinese Theater. No. Throughout his stay in California, Montand rehearsed. And this Sunday, November 15, he starred in one of America's top television variety programs, the "Dinah Shore Show." He could not have chosen a more popular or more sought-after forum.

At the beginning of 1959, the United States boasted 36 million television sets. The figure grew monthly; by 1961, 85 million homes had a television. It was no accident that the televised debate preceding John F. Kennedy's extremely narrow victory (the margin was only six hundred thousand votes) over Richard Nixon was considered by most experts to have been the decisive factor in the Democratic candidate's triumph. Understandably enough, the decline of the great movie studios coincided with the rise of television. Throughout the 1950s the studios had tried everything to ward off the danger: Cinerama, CinemaScope, 3-D, VistaVision, Panavision—any discovery that promised to enhance the glamour of the silver screen and ridicule the small screens flickering in American living rooms. They had produced *The Robe, Samson and Delilah, The Greatest Show on Earth, The Ten Commandments, Ben Hur.* To no avail: the exhausted movie industry was drifting toward available markets and jettisoning the rest.

Montand appreciated the care that Dinah Shore brought to the preparation of her program. She was a well-made-up fortysomething, with auburn hair, a flashing smile, and pearls—the look of the average American woman who had ceased to be average thanks to the trust so many average Americans had invested in her—and she choreographed everything as meticulously as a musical comedy, down to the smallest detail, the smallest exchange, the smallest note. It was agreed that Montand would sing two songs from his show, "A Paris" and "Un Garçon dansait." (The latter told the story of a café waiter and music-hall fanatic who dreams of becoming Fred Astaire. It had won every heart in Manhattan and Los Angeles, with audiences marveling at Montand's virtuosity and the intelligence of the story line. The waiter turns out to be no Fred Astaire: the moment his dancing attempts to imitate his great model's, he falls on his face. Montand danced the story in such a way as to suggest convincingly that he possessed enormous resources, but through a deliberately bungled pirouette he sidestepped pretentiousness and parody.) It was also planned for him to chat with Dinah and then sing and dance with her in a duet.

On Sunday, Dinah Shore smiled at the cameras (and at her 40 or 50 million viewers) for the third time that day: "I wish I had time to read you some of these notices of a show that has just finished its run on Broadway and is now touring the country. . . ." Entering to applause, Montand polished off the two songs and embarked on a meticulously memorized conversation with Dinah, dealing chiefly with the pitfalls of the English language. Then came their duet:

Ev'ry morning
Ev'ry evening
Ain't we got fun

No money
But honey
Ain't we got fun . . .

The very next morning, Montand was off to San Francisco to sing for a week at the Gary Theater, beginning on November 16. This was to be the end of his American tour. Then he was supposed to return to France to spend Christmas with his family before flying to Tokyo. Huge Japanese theaters had been booked: the Shoshika Central and the Shinjuku Koma in Tokyo each boasted three thousand seats, he had been told. One concert, in Osaka, would be in an Olympic stadium capable of holding fifty thousand spectators. Japanese agents reported that scalper ticket prices had already escalated, jumping in three days from three to nine thousand yen.

The week in San Francisco ended in triumph. In full command of his powers, riding on a glowing advance reputation, Montand now knew exactly where he was headed. Reviews were ecstatic; he was buried in praise. Dinah Shore called from Los Angeles to tell him that his television appearance had triggered an avalanche of enthusiastic mail.

Everything was wonderful. Everything suddenly seemed easy. Was this the end of the tunnel?

Apparently not. Either fate supplied the fuel to rekindle his inborn fears or else he himself went out in search of them, relentlessly seeking out the terror that drove him on. Fear of the void was always stronger in him than fear of abundance.

That autumn, Simone Signoret had been first and foremost her husband's escort, and she had missed no opportunity to say so. Yet her own star had never been higher, and she received offers from every quarter. William Holden wanted to direct her in an adaptation of Joseph Kessel's *The Lion* in Kenya. Paramount wanted her to partner Bing Crosby. Elia Kazan apparently approached her about doing a version of Colette's *Chéri,* but Kazan was on Simone's blacklist, and she refused to meet him. Signoret's agent was a busy man, indeed, particularly now that people were mentioning her in connection with the Oscars that would be handed out the following spring.

But the phone call Simone now answered in San Francisco was not directly intended for her: "You and Yves have to come back to Hollywood. Fox wants your husband to be Marilyn Monroe's leading man in her next movie."

On your left as you come in from the sea, the Beverly Hills Hotel, at 9641 Sunset Boulevard, flaunts a yellow-pink Mediterranean Revival façade more or less derived from Andalusia. Thirty or so bungalows lie scattered amid palm trees and bright patios across ten acres of tropical grounds. Each bungalow is divided into three or four apartments. The Montands were given the key to number 20, on the second floor. The walls of their suite were decorated with crocuses and other huge flowers; the green-carpeted living room had a "French-style" fireplace (with gas-fired logs); there were lots of couches, the armchairs were soft and deep; the engravings were Venetian and hackneyed; and the kitchenette was as modern as it was superfluous: a phone call brought room service. Around the bed stood low tables to dump scripts on—for the guests were all in the same profession.

Spyros Skouras, the Greek immigrant who since 1942 had been the tyrannical president of 20th Century–Fox, lived by a golden rule of the industry: there is no good contract without ballyhoo.

Signing this particular contract had become a matter of great urgency. The screenplay of *Let's Make Love,* written by Norman Krasna, a noted name at the time, was originally meant to have been directed by Billy Wilder; but Wilder had backed out, and Fox had hired George Cukor. Then a game of musical chairs had begun: the search for a leading man who could play opposite Marilyn Monroe. Cary Grant had begged off: the character of a half-naive, half-arrogant millionaire bowled over by a blooming chorus girl was not what his fans expected of him. Rock Hudson would have accepted, but he was tied up elsewhere. For Charlton Heston, the money was not enough. Gregory Peck had been tempted, hesitated, then pulled back, deciding that any partner of Marilyn Monroe's would have to play second fiddle.[9]

So Montand was not inheriting a tranquil estate. But assuming his limited English could allow him to detect any traps in the contract offered him, he saw little reason to hesitate. Highly excited, Simone urged him to accept: a musical comedy had never killed anyone, she said, and this was an unheard-of chance to be involved with a cast that would be a powerful draw. Thirty years later, Arthur Miller reached a similar conclusion: "I am sure [Montand] accepted for one good reason: it meant he was breaking into American movies as the leading man opposite Marilyn Monroe."

Indeed, only the slightest of delays occurred between the call summoning the Montands back to Hollywood and their affirmative response to Skouras. Simone Signoret read the script at top speed to make sure it contained nothing vulgar or untoward (she even laughed occasionally, which comforted Montand). But their deliberations were brief and to the point: there are some opportunities you do not brood over. In 1973, the French journalist Pierre Desgraupes asked Montand at what point he felt

9. See the account of this episode in *Look,* July 5, 1960.

he had become an international star. Although objecting to the term "star," which he despised, Montand answered like a shot: "The minute they said to me, 'Monsieur, do you want to make a movie with Marilyn Monroe?' Can you imagine, this *babi* from Marseilles and Les Crottes ending up in the Hollywood he'd been dreaming about all his life? When you're a kid you say to yourself, 'I'm going to sing, and then I'll become king of Marseilles, and after that I'll go to Paris and knock them all flat, and then I'll go to New York, and after that it's Hollywood, and after that—SPLASH!' "[10]

Giovanni Livi's youngest son was convinced that he had scaled a peak. Of course, he had almost no idea of what lay ahead, though he knew that he would be working alongside the likes of Gene Kelly, Bing Crosby, and Frank Sinatra for one of those giant Hollywood corporations whose logos—drums beating and trumpets blaring—preceded the projection of the wonder of wonders on the screen of the Idéal, hard by the oil factory at La Cabucelle.

The all-powerful Screen Actors Guild sent an official to help Montand negotiate with the agents of Jerry Wald, the producer designated by Fox. The sparring between experts—they pretended to be fighting one another but showed a suspicious degree of mutual understanding—began, punctuated by simulated threats to drop everything, as the actor whose fate was being decided looked on, appalled:

FOX'S AGENT: Is your client okay?

MONTAND'S AGENT: He's okay. What are you offering?

FOX'S AGENT: Fifty thousand dollars.

MONTAND'S AGENT: You're joking.

FOX'S AGENT (indignant): Well, forget it! (He hangs up.)

Montand protested that it wasn't important. Fifty thousand dollars was fine, it was plenty. "Don't worry," his agent said confidently. "He'll call back. Leave it to me, leave it to me." Sure enough, after a decent interval the phone rang again.

"Yes?"

"Well, we thought maybe, maybe, we can go up to seventy-five thousand."

"Forget it!"

Montand turned crimson: just for the thrill of wheeling and dealing,

10. Quoted in *Le Point,* February 19, 1973.

this creature was threatening to kill his dream. He tried to light a cigarette, but his hands were shaking. He pulled Signoret aside and said in consternation: "These Americans are crazy!"

Another ring.

"Okay, it's a deal. One hundred thousand."

No need for Signoret to translate. They broke out the champagne, they danced. Bungalow number 20 celebrated.

But the Montands' enthusiasm was quickly dampened by the immediate consequences of the agreement. First, there was Catherine in New York, who would have to be sent home. Then there were the Japanese in Tokyo, who received the good news with open anger. In vain Montand promised nine concerts for them in mid-March of 1960. In vain he sent his apologies, offering to deposit a sum roughly equivalent to his fee for *Let's Make Love* in case he defaulted. The Japanese press trumpeted its outrage. "M. Montand, You Are Not a Respectable Artist," said one headline. French dailies reported the protests but could not conceal how deeply flattering this American breakthrough was to their own national pride.

Montand also contracted for three films after *Let's Make Love.* Their timing would be jointly agreed upon, and the fee for each would be not less than one hundred thousand dollars. Since the tax rate in California at the time was only 5 percent, he would clearly pocket a fortune, or at least the beginnings of one. From this point on, his enhanced professional stature would go hand in hand with a social transformation: he became wealthy, wealthy enough to enjoy a regular income regardless of whether he did any further work. This was a new security, in which, for the moment, he saw only the advantages.

Apart from the Japanese objections—which caused him genuine remorse—the year 1959 ended in euphoria for Yves Montand. Spyros Skouras celebrated with a monster reception in the Fox dining room on Pico Boulevard. And he and Simone saw the New Year in at Romanoff's with the greatest practitioners of the movie art. Three years earlier, they had been celebrating in the Kremlin.

> The celebrations were short-lived. Once everything was signed and sealed I said to Simone, "Well, now I have to make this movie!" I dived right in; it was sink or swim, so I swam. The old fears returned. We plastered the rooms of the bungalow with scraps of dialogue; I learned them phonetically. Fox gave me a teacher—an old lady, Miss Gertrude Faukler, who tutored me every morning at her home, not far from where my friend Gene Kelly lived. The man I was to play in *Let's Make Love,* the

millionaire Jean-Marc Clément, naturally spoke with a French accent. But he was also supposed to express himself like a product of the best British schools, elegant and stiff. I struggled to get out words like "I shouldn't, I couldn't." They came out something like "I shouduhuh." I felt as if I were back in *Les Portes de la nuit* all over again.

It was an amazing feeling when the Fox limousine drove me through the studio gates for the first time. After that? After that I did my job—the same job as before, but in an unknown language, and therefore with heightened fear. A Hollywood set is a set, just another set, maybe a bit bigger, a bit better equipped—but not always. Still, for the kid from La Cabucelle, it was the most fabulous of dreams come true.

"It would have been crazy to say no to Cukor. It was also crazy to have said yes. Montand was crazy. But he was right," wrote Simone Signoret in *Nostalgia.* During the interviews on which her book was based, she added—but did not include the point in her book—that *Let's Make Love* was a "premonitory title." And, indeed, Montand's Hollywood stay did not, except symbolically, represent the major professional stride his singing tour had been. But it was a far-reaching transformation of his life as a man—because of a next-door neighbor.

Chapter 13

We have reached the point where legend takes over, where storytellers jump the tracks, where witnesses conflict. In the course of endless press commentary, in an avalanche of books as lightweight as they are prolific, the Yves Montand–Marilyn Monroe affair has been scrutinized from every angle and in every light. Sugary romance for some, Greek tragedy for others. One observer depicts Montand as a cynic who deliberately seduced the tender star and abandoned her to the Nevada desert and to barbiturates. Another swears that during their springtime romance they considered marriage. Signoret is sometimes described as jealous and calculating, sometimes as heroic and serene.

This confusion is not just the product of the voyeuristic tittle-tattle and prurient fact twisting that columnists and scandal sheets so shamelessly indulged in. It stems from a much simpler cause: the truth has never been officially established; no one has told the whole story. In his memoirs, *Timebends,* Arthur Miller sidestepped the episode, perhaps from tact, modesty, or pride, perhaps from reluctance to send one more wave washing over the wreckage of his second marriage. And perhaps he was unwilling to rekindle the quarrel that pitted him against several of Monroe's friends—including Signoret—when, following Marilyn's suicide, his play *After the Fall* revealed some of the most intimate workings of a relationship in which cruelty warred against powerlessness. Montand, too, kept his silence to the end, apart from a handful of interviews that focused on Monroe herself rather than on their relationship.[1] As for Simone Signoret, she kept to herself feelings that must have been extraordinarily complex, recounting in her memoirs only what she saw with her own eyes, and her own warm friendship with Marilyn.

1. See *Elle,* October 30, 1972; a radio interview with Charles Villeneuve over *Europe 1,* November 25, 1974; and a 1974 television broadcast.

Montand at first hesitated to talk to us about Marilyn, wary of seeming to indulge in indiscreet revelations. He decided to do so, he told us, to give balance to his story, and because by that time he was able to talk about it without hurting anybody. The story was dear to him, and telling it seemed the best way of both shedding light on a woman who was often betrayed, manipulated, caricatured, and abused, and highlighting the bizarre circumstances of public figures whose inner conflicts and secret drives are brutally extracted by the media and then crushed out of recognizable shape.

For a long time there was nothing but neighborliness and work on the joint project between the leading man and woman of *Let's Make Love.* In early January 1960, Arthur Miller and his wife came to live in Los Angeles. They were assigned bungalow number 21, the twin of the one occupied by Yves and Simone. Skouras's minions naturally knew that the Montands had performed in a play by Miller and that the four had been friendly in Manhattan. And better than anyone, they knew how hard Marilyn had fought to ensure that the new Broadway star—despite Cukor's worries about Montand's linguistic shortcomings—be given the leading male role in *Let's Make Love.*

Fox knew everything, foresaw everything, took care of everything. Jerry Wald was terrified of the eccentricities Marilyn was famous for. Although she had been, and still was, a cast-iron box-office draw—since 1953 she had been ranked as one of the top ten money-making stars—she had a terrible reputation for her latenesses, panic attacks, moods, absences, and insomnia. So it is understandable that Wald, eager to have Marilyn and at the same time to limit the damage she invariably caused, was very pleased that she was pleased with the choice of Yves Montand. His men in New York told him that as soon as the contract was signed, Marilyn—who had not danced seriously since Howard Hawks's *Gentlemen Prefer Blondes* in 1953—had returned to dance classes, enthusiastically and with discipline. So in Fox's view, Montand's contract did not simply mean that a new talent had been signed up, but that the movie had been saved, or at least given the green light. The providential Frenchman was coddled and spoiled. His Japanese debt was wiped out (Skouras handled the tab in return for the promise of one more movie). His work permit was taken care of: red or not, Montand and Signoret had their visas extended. "I recall," says Arthur Miller, "that Simone in particular was worried that the State Department might get its hooks into her and send her home, which was a possibility, but in my view unlikely given Fox's influence."

The tenants of bungalows 20 and 21 settled in. Marilyn regularly attended dance class and began to study the theme song of *Let's Make Love,*

Cole Porter's "My Heart Belongs to Daddy." Montand "said his English prayers," as his wife put it, deep into the night. And Simone led a life of semi-leisure, lunching in excellent company in the hotel's Polo Lounge, trying out her anthropological skills among the teeming and brightly hued tribes of Hollywood, window-shopping for antiques, enjoying luxury and relaxation with that natural talent for killing time so foreign to her husband.

"The Millers" and "the Montands." Mrs. Miller startled Mme Montand just a little when she confessed, apropos of nothing in particular, that working in movies did not fulfill her; when she required two or three hours to paint herself and dress up for one of her rare excursions; when she complained of her knobby knees. And she touched, seduced, and amused Signoret in her moments of rare abandon when the two of them invaded the redundant kitchenette to prepare pasta, or had their hair bleached on Saturdays by an old lady, formerly with Metro-Goldwyn-Mayer, who had once exercised her talents on Jean Harlow's platinum locks.

Throughout this period, Montand was not in the least fascinated by his future partner. He thought her friendly, gay, and more talkative than her husband, but it was Miller who really interested him, who aroused his admiration, respect, curiosity, and soon a kind of tenderness. When they came up for air, one from his pages of typing, the other from his bundles of phonetically transcribed dialogue, they would stroll together around Beverly Hills. They were the only pedestrians on these roads where nobody ever succumbed to the crazed notion of going on foot—roads that served only as asphalt bridges from one enclosed and manicured property to another. One day a motorcycle cop even stopped to ask the suspects where they lived, and seemed surprised that the denizens of their hotel would choose to wear out costly shoe leather in such a senseless fashion.

Curiously, Montand understood Miller's English. Was it the writer's careful diction? Was it a mutual will to communicate that swept linguistic barriers aside? The playwright scoffed disapprovingly at the pure air breathed by the privileged residents of the neighborhood (long before the environmental movement began, Hollywood residents who could afford it fled polluted Los Angeles to take refuge in their Palm Springs haciendas or seaside villas): "You can't call this place a city. It doesn't smell like anything. In Europe you can smell everything—cooking, garlic . . ." Remembering the smells of La Cabucelle, Ivo Livi thought with the faintest of inner smiles that his life had been liberally perfumed with the odors of garlic and sardines. And he was touched that such a successful man should try to distance himself from the sanitized symbols of his own success.

In a somewhat suspect biography of Marilyn Monroe (its theme might be summarized as: "But why did she make love with anyone but me?"),

Norman Mailer argues that Montand could not have failed to impress his companion: "Montand, in fact, is part of the perfect prescription for Miller's noble worker, since he comes from peasant stock in Italy, and his father has been a political activist who hated Mussolini enough to emigrate."[2] No doubt Miller, pre-eminent spokesman of the American left, was susceptible to Montand's proletarian origins, but this is not enough to explain the growing understanding between them. Normally taciturn by choice, Miller talked a great deal to Montand—of Dreyfus and of Pierre Mendès-France, of an idea he had for a script, of how his grandfather, in his eighties and on his deathbed, had mustered the strength to sit up and give him his watch. And Montand listened, as he always liked to listen to people whose raw materials were words and whose beliefs were the foundations of their lives.

Soon Montand knew absolutely everything about Jean-Marc Clément, the fabulously wealthy French businessman who is landed by chance in the world of show business. Learning that an acting company has made him (along with Maria Callas, Elvis Presley, and several others) its whipping boy in a planned musical comedy, he decides to investigate, incognito. Hired as his own double, he falls in love with the delectable star Amanda, who refuses right up to the last scene to believe that he really is Jean-Marc Clément and not an unsophisticated down-and-out imposter. In the interim, the industrialist pays for private song and dance lessons from Bing Crosby and Gene Kelly. But he is, and remains, "only" a millionaire.

Montand soon realized that the script was no masterpiece and that all its redeeming virtues had been allotted to Marilyn. He, a singer-dancer-mime hailed by critics across the United States for his sure and supple touch and timing, had been sidelined into the role of a stiff and lumpish young man whose only spectacular number was a sketch that lampooned his clumsiness. So he had just fifty skimpy seconds of real-life Montand, in the scene where his character dreams he can outdance Astaire. In other words, he was a foil. American producers whose female stars feared strong competition loved to pair them with a Continental, a Latin lover who exuded a torrid mythic aura without threatening the status of the fragile star. Montand accepted this unequal share—he saw it as his entrance fee to the Hollywood club—but the nature of the role he had inherited kept him in agonies of anxiety. How could he master a script that called for an Ox-

2. Norman Mailer, *Marilyn* (New York, 1975). The narrative is as inconsistent as the accompanying photos are beautiful—perhaps the most beautiful photos of Monroe ever brought together in a single volume.

bridge accent covering his native French tones? How could he twirl the umbrella of hereditary arrogance when his legs were jelly? If Montand's job had been to move and to sing, everything else would have followed. He was required to do exactly the opposite!

He had no idea that Marilyn Monroe was going through similar agonies, though for opposite reasons. The weight of the movie rested on her—as she wished—but she found the responsibility terrifying rather than flattering. She had suffered cruelly in the past through clashes with antagonist associates, most recently Laurence Olivier and the transvestite duo in *Some Like It Hot,* and the recent success of the latter had neither reassured nor comforted her. She felt that she was not a "real" actress tackling a "real" role, despite regular attendance at the Actors Studio in New York alongside Marlon Brando, Montgomery Clift, and Paul Newman, and coaching by the resident guru, Lee Strasberg. Appalled by the gap she perceived between the star the studio exhibited in the glass case of its meat department and the actress she longed to become—a member of the cast of *The Brothers Karamazov,* not a pinup whose lingerie set small-town pulses racing—she approached anything resembling light comedy in a trance of total frustration.

Monroe's distress was so obvious that Arthur Miller broke off from the screenplay he was writing for John Huston, *The Misfits,* and came running to perform last-minute tinkering on *Let's Make Love.* He injected a few notes of humor, flattened out anything that might have thrown a shadow on Amanda's character, pocketed a check from Spyros Skouras, and resented himself for prostituting his art in this way, even though it had been for love. Inevitably, artificial constraints of this kind introduced a fatal disequilibrium into their marriage. Miller began to feel that he was turning into Mr. Monroe.

Some thirty years later, he gave a bitter account of this passage in his memoirs: "I had all but given up any hope of writing; I had decided to devote myself to giving [Marilyn] the kind of emotional support that would convince her she was no longer alone in the world—the heart of the problem, I assumed. I went so far as to do some rewriting on *Let's Make Love* to try to save her from a complete catastrophe, work I despised on a script not worth the paper it was typed on. It was a bad miscalculation, bringing us no closer to each other."[3] He later confided that in his opinion, Montand acquitted himself more than honorably in a role fraught with risk: "He managed to lend the appearance of charm to an empty and synthetic character."

Neither Simone Signoret nor Yves Montand guessed the seriousness

3. Arthur Miller, *Timebends* (New York, 1987).

of the situation. In truth, Montand knew nothing of Monroe's career or personality. He had seen all of John Ford, all of Capra, all of Kazan, but he had not seen Billy Wilder's *Seven Year Itch* (1955), which had propelled Monroe to the heights of stardom, or Joshua Logan's *Bus Stop* (1956). He was hardly even aware that little Norma Jean Mortenson, daughter of Gladys Baker, a film editor with chronic mental problems, and of an unknown father, had spent her childhood being shuttled between foster homes and orphanages. Nor did he know that she had fought tooth and nail to join the thousands of girls for sale in Hollywood, aspiring stars gravitating around the California moguls, and then fought again, once inside the palace of mirages, to rise from the ranks of the harem.

Elia Kazan was more than merely friends with Marilyn Monroe in the days before the actress became a myth and married first Joe DiMaggio (a marriage that lasted only a year of highly publicized ups and downs) and then Arthur Miller. In his bitter memoirs, Kazan looks back with a horrified tenderness at the starlet's sincere tears over the death of her protector, the talent agent Johnny Hyde, whose wealth she spurned and whose memory she honored. "Relieve your mind now of the images you have of this person. When I met her, she was a simple, eager young woman who rode a bike to the classes she was taking, a decent-hearted kid whom Hollywood brought down, legs parted. She had a thin skin and a soul that hungered for acceptance by people she might look up to. Like many girls out of that kind of experience, she sought her self-respect through the men she was able to attract."[4]

Montand also knew nothing of Marilyn's fight to get free of the control of Darryl Zanuck and the other princes of the big studios, founding Marilyn Monroe Productions with the help of a loyal friend, the New York photographer Milton Greene. The endeavor did not survive past Olivier's *The Prince and the Showgirl* (1957), but it enabled her, when she rejoined Fox (Zanuck was no longer chief of production), to demand greater authority over scripts, directors, and even cameramen. It was a limited victory. Marilyn wanted Hollywood to take her seriously, and Hollywood considered her an exciting little doll (she was thirty-three) who would quickly lose her enormous sex appeal if she persisted in listening to woolly Manhattan intellectuals and taking herself for a budding Sarah Bernhardt.

These were the reefs that still lay hidden between Montand and his neighbor when shooting began in mid-February. At 5:30 every morning, a sleepy Marilyn rolled herself into a ball in the back of the red Ford that took her to makeup (a *Life* story showed no fewer than seven experts slowly reconstructing the illusion of the previous day: two hairdressers; a

4. Elia Kazan, *A Life* (New York, 1988).

wigmaker; specialists in false eyelashes, powder, and pancake; and the artist who lined her lower lids, making sure they looked pale—a sign of youth—and guaranteeing a bright gaze. Montand, spared these female torments, enjoyed a further two hours' sleep before a second Ford (his was gray) stopped at the hotel for him.

George Cukor was a gentle, cultivated, patient man, witty and biting. In *A Star Is Born* (1954), he had painted a candid picture of the majestic and carnivorous rites of Hollywood life, a faithful comment on the business by one of its own; Cukor, approaching his sixtieth year, knew it all by heart. He was one of those homosexuals in whose company women sought haven; he was known for his ability to work smoothly with even the most difficult of them—Greta Garbo, Ava Gardner, Katharine Hepburn, Jean Harlow, Judy Holliday, Sophia Loren, Lana Turner, among others, all said so. He greeted Montand warmly, reeling off dozens of stories and pretending not to notice that his listener, cautiously sporting an accommodating if baffled smile, did not understand a word he was saying. Little by little, still obsessed by his "English prayers," Montand began to relax.

At first Marilyn was absorbed by the musical numbers. One Saturday afternoon, before they started work together, Montand watched her go through a final rehearsal. Black background. Long, plump legs made to look slender with black silk. A too-long Irish sweater. Artificially tousled blond hair. A wink from the full pink face:

My name is Lolita and uh
I'm not supposed to play
With boys. Moi? Uh uh
Mon coeur est à papa
You know le propriétaire
Ba da ba da ba da ba da
bee a ba da ba da bee a ba da

As a seasoned practitioner of this demanding art, Montand honestly felt that his partner did not move all that well. There was a persistent stiffness of which Monroe was well aware, and on her own she asked the choreographer, Jack Cole, to run her through the exercise again. "She is not a great dancer and she knows it," Cole told *Life* reporters who recounted it to American readers on August 15. "She is a great star short on the basics, on experience. But her fear of doing badly motivates her unbelievably. She wants it, she wants to do the number better than anyone else could. She is such a perfectionist that she always wants a little more time, just one more rehearsal."

This perfectionism, minus the perfection, won over her privileged audience. No doubt Marilyn was not and never would be a star dancer. But when she sang "bee-do bee-do bee-do wah" in her breathless little-girl voice and wiggled her exquisite curves, she seemed to Montand fresher and funnier than all the Pavlovas in the world.

A watchful shadow hovered in the background. Paula Strasberg, wife of Lee, high priest of the Actors Studio, did not let her pupil out of her sight for a moment. Eternally draped in a black sack dress, her thin hair pulled back, her only jewelry a watch on a chain around her neck, her lips disapprovingly pursed, Mrs. Strasberg was Marilyn's coach. In her youth, at the dawn of the Roosevelt era, she had been a member of the Group Theatre, an ebullient and iconoclastic gathering of talents who wanted to revolutionize the American stage. (Its leading lights were Lee Strasberg, Harold Clurman, and Cheryl Crawford, and its chief supplier of scripts was Clifford Odets.) Paula Strasberg had belonged to the same cell as Elia Kazan in the days when joining the Communist Party was an indispensable part of an antiestablishment stance. Then, with her husband, she had become a pillar of the Actors Studio, a school that taught not technique but an ethos, an in-depth exploration of the self, a way of breathing.

Consulted by her charge on every line, every gesture, she shadowed Marilyn from set to set. Billy Wilder, Olivier, and most other directors who worked with Monroe had nightmare experiences of this dual-control operation. Miller knew Paula Strasberg well, both professionally and personally, and he, too, had few kind words for her. But Monroe insisted on Paula's monitoring presence.

In a sense, Montand was lucky to have been so wholly preoccupied by the need to master his own lines. (Years later, viewing the movie, he would still wonder what throat that voice speaking English could have come from. The English language finally became familiar to him, and he grew to like strewing his conversation with Americanisms, but the brutal initiation never lost its mystery for him.) If he had had time for a closer scrutiny of the trap he had so cheerfully walked into, he would have run for his life. But the very innocence he brought to the assignment served him far better than he could have imagined.

> I was a million miles from thinking that anything whatsoever could happen between Marilyn and me. A million miles. If I was thinking of falling in love with anything, it was the English language. All around me people were eating, talking, living. All I could do was think of my script. Because it wasn't sinking in, it wasn't becoming part of me. It was the hardest time I've ever had in my acting career. Imagine a lawyer or a professor or a politician

having to learn a hundred-page speech in a foreign language *by heart* in three weeks! I had to express myself with facility, and to that I had to add a certain controlled hauteur. I was so frightened, I hardly noticed Marilyn or anyone else. I found her plump and pretty, and thought that my friend Arthur had a very beautiful wife. But I had only one thought in my head: the script, the script, the script. And I was in love with Simone, period.

The first day of shooting, fear paralyzed me. The reader will understand nothing of this if he subscribes to the old notion of actors screwing all day long, wearing sequins, driving wonderful cars, living in luxury hotels—all of which happens, of course. In the beginning, Marilyn and I had only one thing in common: our obsession with our work. She worked, worked, worked. She, too, needed to win.

We shot the movie chronologically, beginning with the first meeting. Marilyn-Amanda speaks first.

"You're really French, aren't you?"

"Yes. Very much so."

"Been here long?"

"I go back and forth. My family is rather transatlantic. . . ."

Oh, the "th" in that "forth"! I had worked on it by saying "FifTH Avenue, FifTH Avenue," over and over again. And I was trying to be as stiff-necked and British as I could.

In the end, it didn't go too badly. But something happened a little earlier to bring us closer. I was waiting for her so that we could start the scene. She was late. (I knew almost nothing about her, but her reputation for tardiness had certainly reached me.) At last she arrived and apologized: "You're going to see what it means to shoot with the worst actress in the world!"

When she said "with," her tongue peeped out between her teeth. It was enchanting. I sought the right words to answer her gently: "So you're scared. . . . Think of me a little bit. I'm lost."

And that admission suddenly liberated her. She couldn't get over it. The Continental playing opposite her, the man of whom she had formed a forbidding image (shades of *The Wages of Fear* and *Les Sorcières de Salem,* the success on television, the applause on Broadway from people like Marlene Dietrich and Ingrid Bergman, and so forth)—well, the Continental was shaking in his boots and not hiding it. That was a real shock for a woman whose relations with other performers were complex-ridden, who considered herself, not without reason, more or less despised by Hollywood. It was the first time that a leading man—a man supposed to keep his end up, with whom she, too, had to hold her own—had ever taken her into his confidence simply because he shared her fear.

She never complained to me about her earlier conflicts. Of Tony Curtis in *Some Like It Hot,* she simply said, "It wasn't easy." But from that moment on, she knew that I knew, that I had seen into her (as Elia Kazan most certainly had done before me). Arthur Miller probably did not fathom the true nature of that kind of panic: he wasn't an actor. He had a perfect understanding of what actors and actresses do, but you have to be an actor yourself to guess at the inner chemistry. And even then . . . !

A little later, a second episode confirmed my impression. We had gone to dinner in town, the four of us, and were driving back to the hotel. Simone was talking to Arthur. Marilyn said quietly into my ear: "You know, Cukor is not a very great director."

I scraped together my fractured English to protest: "Sorry, don't say that. Is not true. . . . Cukor great director, and he loves the actresses. You look beautiful, but I think you're afraid of acting. You need rehearsals."

After a pause, she said: "Yes, you're right. I think maybe we need rehearsals."

And that is how, seeking to calm our respective fears, we began to work together. I would knock at her door, or she would come to me. "How are you?" "Fine." "Let's get to work." We would sit facing each other and rehearse. She corrected my English, and I did my best to get her to trust herself. The image that comes back to me is of Marilyn in plaid jeans, a shirt open at the neck (but with absolutely no intent to allure), and those incredibly blue eyes that maintained the clarity other women's only rarely possess. Was it the special light of those winter days in California? I don't know.

There was no doubt that Montand was a good influence. At first, Monroe was her old self: not exactly temperamental, but constantly hesitating before taking the plunge. The slightest excuse sufficed for her to put off the moment they said "Action!"—a drop of sweat, a platinum strand that refused to lie flat, the "My Heart Belongs to Daddy" sweater going baggy from so many rehearsals. She was not wasting her time; indeed, from her point of view she was gaining time. She ran to take shelter with Paula Strasberg, biting her nails as she listened, then she disappeared, walking her stage fright far and wide in the vain hope of exhausting it, of putting it to sleep. And Montand waited, sometimes patiently, sometimes not, sensing that he was becoming an object, a thing parked in the corner until it was time to start. "I'm not a car," he would quip ruefully, preferring to joke rather than explode in anger, as Tony Curtis had done.

As Signoret told the story, one morning at ten her husband called from the studio in distress: Marilyn had not appeared, and the crew was idle on the set. Miller was away from Hollywood at the time, having gone to Ireland to finish off the script of *The Misfits* with John Huston. Simone knocked at the apartment next door, shouted, thumped. Nothing. Montand returned to the bungalow, scribbled a note, and slid it under his neighbor's door. It ended with the words, "Don't leave me to work for hours on end on a scene you've already decided not to do the next day. I'm not the enemy, I'm your pal. And capricious little girls have never amused me." The message was slowly pulled inside, but there was no response—until that night, when Miller called from Dublin: Marilyn, he told them, was too ashamed to come out. So the Montands went over to rescue a weeping child who beat herself on the breast and said, "I'm bad, I'm bad, I'm bad, I won't do it again. . . ."

Montand's use of the word "capricious" had probably struck home. Slowly, Monroe found her footing again. With more and more rehearsals, she mastered herself, respecting schedules and the rules of the profession no better and no worse than any other actress. It was such an unexpected switch that Cukor, Miller, and Jerry Wald thanked Montand profusely and drew deep sighs of relief. It had been four years since Monroe had behaved in near-normal fashion.

Was it the miracle of burgeoning love? That is, of course, the version championed by many commentators. Norman Mailer duly worked this lode: Montand, he wrote, bragged to friends, " 'She's got so she'll do whatever I ask her to do on the set. Everyone is amazed at her cooperation, and she's constantly looking to me for approval!' " This was true, Mailer concedes, and then somewhat perfidiously questions the results of the phenomenon: "She has never made a movie where she is so agreeable to a director. She has also never made a movie where she is so ordinary. A sad truth is before us again. Art and sex are no more compatible than they care to be."

"I've skimmed Mailer's book," Montand said when it came out. "It reads to me a bit like the rich man's *France-Dimanche*" (a tabloid-style sensation sheet). Stressing the degree to which stereotypes contaminate even the best of novelists, he added, "Marilyn was no more a vamp than any department-store clerk." (Chance decreed that a quarter-century after the release of *Let's Make Love,* Montand, presiding over the jury at the Cannes Film Festival, had to confer with the author of *An American Dream* and *The Prisoner of Sex.* He tried, briefly, to tell Mailer that he had been on the wrong trail, but Mailer, whether conciliatory or evasive, merely cut him short: "Come on, forget it, forget it.")

In fact, Marilyn's change of attitude came well before the idyll that was about to unfold. Nor, Montand would insist, was this just a question of chronology. Of course he had been flattered to hear during negotiations over the contract for *Let's Make Love* that Marilyn had told the press, "Next to my husband, and along with Marlon Brando, I think Yves Montand is the most attractive man I've ever met," but in 1960 he was convinced (and he remained so always) that the soothing effect that seemed to produce such spectacular results was the product not of sudden passion but of a possibly even more secret kinship: the same constitutional anguish, the same acute fear of derision. Whether the vehicle was a masterpiece or not, a brilliant script or a laborious piece of hackwork, they threw themselves body and soul into their movie work, with few illusions about the results.

Just as surely as Montand knew he was judged in music hall for what he was, he experienced the unjust but sovereign law in the collective adventure of moviemaking that says you are almost never blamed or praised for what you really are. The Hollywood star Marilyn Monroe was a perfect victim of this infernal machine. For Montand, who had fought fifteen years for recognition, it wasn't hard to sense her obsessive will to succeed. That, he says, was the first secret of his power over Marilyn.

> What contributed enormously to bringing us together was, first, that we both came from poor backgrounds and, second, Marilyn's behavior during the witch hunt, when she wholeheartedly supported Miller, to the fury of the studios. But there was also something deeper. My affection for her grew once I realized her vulnerability, her lucidity, her true sadness at not being given a real part to play in our movie. (She thought she had had that chance in *Bus Stop,* although I would have thought *Don't Bother to Knock* was a better example.) She would have given anything to have people in the business ask each other, "Did you see Monroe in such-and-such?" But she knew the score very well, she wasn't fooled for a moment by her star disguise. And even though I adored her "boop-boop-ee-dos" as much as everyone else, I drew certain parallels between us. When I began in movies I wasn't very good. After a while I believe I chalked up two or three honorable performances, but with a few false starts as well, and with performances leaning too heavily toward the ordinary nice guy. At the time of *Let's Make Love,* my breakthrough couldn't be taken for granted. And I wasn't fooled, either.

Two events now transformed the climate and set the clock racing. Toward the end of March 1960, the nominations for Oscars, awarded in April, were announced. And in that era, the Oscar was very rarely given to anyone who was not an English speaker, not from the United States, not from Hollywood. But the five nominations for best actress were Katharine Hepburn and Elizabeth Taylor (*Suddenly Last Summer*), Audrey Hepburn (*The Nun's Story*), Doris Day (*Pillow Talk*), and Simone Signoret (*Room at the Top*).

No matter what the final outcome, this was already an event. To have a French actress in a modest British production among the finalists was a break with the past. And since Signoret was regarded as a near-Communist and had long been persona non grata on American soil, it was quite simply astounding (so much so that the venomous Hedda Hopper "forgot" to mention her name among the nominees).

Marilyn, too, was forgotten. The star of *Some Like It Hot* was *a priori* left on the sidelines, excluded from the ranks of the great. It is inconceivable that she did not feel a stab of jealousy at the realization that her apparently self-confident friend Simone, so lucid and quick with words, had imposed her almost matronly self on the movie world with such authority. The contrast between them—or, at least, the contrast between their public images—was glaring. In her mid-thirties, Monroe doggedly cultivated the persona she had been stuck with a decade earlier, a persona she both hated and used as a safety net. Signoret had caught Americans, especially American women, off guard with her assertion that age was not such a terrible peril, that being a Hollywood goddess did not tempt her. "I feel no desire to become a real star," she had told Laura Bergquist in an article in *Look* on January 19. "It would be a crushing burden, and I am too lazy to let myself be contaminated by obligations that do not amuse me. I know a great European actress who watches her face, her body and her bank balance twenty-four hours a day. I would bet that even her delightful husband has to make an appointment to make love. What kind of life is that? At the moment lots of people like my work, and it is wonderful to be liked. But next year a new face will push mine aside." You needed iron self-assurance to air such beliefs to Californians.

The second event was no less unexpected. From early March to mid-April, under orders from their powerful union, every actor in Hollywood joined in a strike for the right to a share in residual royalties paid by the television networks for broadcasting films produced by the movie studios. The clash was a symbolic commentary on the disintegrating industry. For weeks, sets were deserted, and all shooting stopped. It would have been foolhardy not to heed the union's call. Yves Montand and Marilyn Monroe were on strike.

As the conflict dragged on, Miller decided to take advantage of the lull to breathe some New York air and finish *The Misfits*—the "great part" he intended for Marilyn, which would turn out to be his parting gift. The couple left bungalow number 21. The Montands waved farewell from their balcony.

"Good luck! I know you're going to get it!" the star shouted up to the antistar in her soft, high-pitched voice.

She meant the Oscar, of course. And, of course, Simone got it.

On the April evening when Hollywood ecstatically abandons itself to its traditional narcissistic orgy, all eyes were riveted on the procession of limousines, the black and white of the tuxedos, the bare shoulders and the long-considered gowns (Simone's was black dotted swiss). She had stage fright, as did Montand—he was to be one of the evening's performers, for Vincente Minnelli had asked him to perform two songs. Two cases of stage fright, and then stage fright for each other.

When Montand's turn came, Bob Hope, the master of ceremonies, called on Fred Astaire. And it was Fred Astaire who announced, "I have the great honor, the great pleasure to present to you a French singer called Yves Montand. . . ." Whereupon Montand launched into "Un Garçon dansait," his imitation of none other than Fred Astaire, and after that "A Paris." Memories of many stages, of many emotions. He bowed and then rejoined Minnelli backstage. Minnelli suggested he return to his seat in the auditorium. "No, no," said Montand, "the next Oscar is for best actress, and my wife is going to get it." As this short exchange took place, Rock Hudson was unsealing the envelope.

A *Life* photographer caught Signoret at the precise moment her name was read out. She has clapped her hands to her chest and is exhaling with such energy that her breast thrusts forward as she half rises. Joy can strike you with the same violent shock as disaster. And that is what her eyes and body are saying.

Afterward came unbridled jubilation. Along with the *Ben Hur* team (which had carried off no fewer than ten trophies), Simone presided over a banquet at the Beverly Wilshire Hotel. Her personal victory also represented a victory of Hollywood over itself: by voting for Signoret, it had finally exorcised its witches. Many of the evening's most wildly applauded winners were refugees from the blacklist.

Montand had confused memories of the evening: an avalanche of congratulations heaped on them by unknowns, endless offers from producers (who later invited Montand to poolside or to a game of liar's poker, where Henry Fonda was his partner), the insistent question, "Are you all right, sweetheart?" from a Simone determined that her husband would not start to feel like M. Signoret.

No, he assured her, he was not jealous at all. Just proud and admiring.

Meanwhile, Marilyn *was* jealous. Not only was the professional respect she yearned for disappearing over the horizon, but the counterweight to that bitterness, her union with Miller, was crumbling. All the elements were in place for an intrigue that would leave scars of a quite different kind.

Negotiations between the actors union and the studios came to an end. The studios came back to life, work on *Let's Make Love* was scheduled to resume, and in bungalow 20 at the Beverly Hills Hotel, the coveted golden statuette sat next to a photo of the house at Autheuil. But the strike had compromised the couple's careful plans and thrown off Montand's schedule by two months. Now he was obliged to cancel his Japanese make-up tour, and Signoret was due to fly to Italy. They would meet again in Paris at the beginning of August; never, except for the shooting of Buñuel's *La Mort en ce jardin,* which had taken Simone to Mexico in 1956, had they been far apart for so long. And at just this point, the Millers returned to Hollywood so that Marilyn could resume work. But the playwright then immediately left, claiming commitments to the children of his first marriage and the need to get together yet again with John Huston.

Montand did not hold the keys that might have helped him decode several signs; only later did their meaning become clear. Monroe, one weekend before leaving for Reno to check on the location for *The Misfits,* whispered affectionately to Montand: "I'll miss you." He noted down the words and later asked a friend what they meant. Nice, he thought, when the phrase was translated; he was touched and thought no more of it. And as he was saying goodbye, Miller muttered, "What will happen will happen." Or was his halting English playing tricks on Montand?

> I had Marilyn all to myself and didn't know it. It was as a partner and a friend that I called on her to rehearse with. (After her weekend in Reno, the apartment next door had been given to someone else, and her bungalow was now farther away.) I didn't dissociate her from her husband. The first time I really saw Marilyn was on a Sunday . . . and we had been around each other a good long time. But nothing, strictly nothing. However, in our profession it can happen that after a difficult scene you experience a kind of euphoria, a sudden unwinding that can lead to a burst of tenderness.
>
> Every night after getting back from the studio we worked for an hour or two. When we got up after it was over, we were both still living in the tension of the rehearsal, I'd be smoking cigarette after cigarette, and then she'd smile and say: "Okay, now we'll

eat." Then I looked at her, and I thought she was amazingly beautiful, healthy, desirable—but I didn't desire her, I was somewhere else entirely. It seems strange, almost stupid; all I felt was this powerful radiation, the impact of this amazing charisma. I was proud of her hard work, her concentration. I perceived the warmth as the warmth of friendship.

One day she was really wiped out, much too tired to rehearse. And I had a tricky scene the next day. I was getting ready to leave the studio and go work on my own at home when I bumped into Mrs. Strasberg. "Go and say goodnight to Marilyn," she said. "It'll make her feel better. It's bothering her that she can't rehearse." I went. I remember that the living room was all white—white chairs, white curtains—with the exception of a black table. There was caviar and, as usual, a bottle of pink champagne. I sat on the side of the bed and patted her hand. "Do you have a fever?" "A little, but it'll be okay. I'm glad to see you." "So am I, I'm glad to see you." "How was your day?" "Good, good." The dullest exchange you can imagine. I still had a half-page to work on for the next day. I bent down to put a goodnight kiss on her cheek. And her head turned, and my lips went wild. It was a wonderful, tender kiss. I was half stunned, stammering, I straightened up, already flooded with guilt, wondering what was happening to me. I didn't wonder for long.

The next day it seemed at first that things were back under control. We worked. But it was a forest fire, a hurricane, I didn't even try to calm myself down. On the set it was total symbiosis. Marilyn was confident, laughing—and Marilyn's laugh was something. Back at the hotel that night she used every wile in the book to sneak by the back way into my bungalow.

Marilyn, they say—and lots of people will tell you this in good faith, based on their information—was an unbalanced woman sapped by drugs. But the woman I knew for three months was not that woman. On the outside she played at being Marilyn. Inside I encountered a woman who was strong, full of good sense, with the vitality of a peasant standing foursquare, solid, a German peasant: Marlene Dietrich at her very beginnings, in her very first photos, before *The Blue Angel*. . . . Marilyn often came to my apartment very early in the morning and we'd have breakfast together. Breakfast with Marilyn was gigantic, gargantuan: two fried eggs, little sausages, cream cheese and smoked fish, milk, fruit juice (to be fair, lunch on the set was minimal). But what an appetite! Or, rather—and excuse me if it's not the usual connotation—what health!

In Marilyn there was without any doubt a constant and obsessive awareness of her limitations, the conviction that she was not the great actress she longed to be. But she had an immense character, an extremely strong nature—even though, in life as on the screen, she had that little-girl voice. The fascination she exercised and her seductive power were present almost without her knowing it, whether she used them or not. She had no need to check the seam of her stocking to give you ideas: when she talked about the rain or the fine weather or the cafeteria menu, she had the same power. She had a kind of innocence; and the less she tried, the more attractive she was. Marilyn was a being apart, in the sense that it was her own inner light that drove her into the spotlight. If you believed in God you'd say that God alone could generate such a light—a light beyond the control of those it burns in. Marilyn suffered at not being a recognized actress, but she was not really an actress at all: she existed somewhere far beyond mere play, mere enactment.

Yves Montand did not control or fully understand what was happening to him. It was the first time he had "cheated" on his wife, as he understood that term: it was the first time he had been "involved" elsewhere. For he realized well enough that what was starting with Marilyn Monroe was not a simple pleasure trip or the extension of a movie-lot extramarital friendship of the kind common in their working environment.

A number of premonitory symptoms had already warned him that a fortieth birthday is not just another milestone. Married or unmarried, he had often felt a throb of desire on meeting this or that person—like everyone else, but perhaps with a little more violence and emotion in this essentially impetuous man. Nevertheless, on two or three occasions (and particularly since the start of his United States tour) he had been thrown off stride by a less commonplace feeling: the frustrating, delectable, and unpredictable urge to love and be loved, to be the object of tenderness and to reciprocate without restraint. Once it was an anonymous form encountered one morning in New York on his way to the Berlitz School (he turned to race after the unknown woman who had excited him and watched her vanish into the crowd). Another time it was the cool beauty of Jane Fonda sitting quietly in the lobby of the Algonquin (mentally, he felt ready for all manner of "treason"). Or, in Los Angeles, the freckled, peaches-and-cream complexion of a Hollywood actress like Shirley Mac-

Laine. So shaken was he by these lyrical gusts that he passed the information along, candidly and without adornment, to Simone—who was understandably unenthusiastic.

Monroe and Montand hid their love affair as well as they could, which is to say not very well. Cukor knew. Although there was nothing odd about a series of comings and goings between the dressing rooms of the leading male and female actors, he was too clever and too well placed not to detect and decipher the half-executed gestures and fleeting looks. At the hotel, the problem of slipping from one bungalow to the other was adolescent; inevitably, someone noticed. One fine morning in June, a cleaning woman was startled to find herself nose to nose with Monroe as she left by the back door of Montand's apartment. Sooner or later all the gossip columnists, with paid informers on every street corner, were including the leads of *Let's Make Love* in their daily inventory of reported nocturnal spottings.

Seeing danger ahead, Montand stepped up his precautions. He and Marilyn most often dined out together with Paula Strasberg as chaperone. According to their new schedule, the last takes of *Let's Make Love* would be over before the end of June. As summer approached, Montand hovered between intoxication and panic. Even his happiness, his guilty happiness, disturbed him. Worse: there were unmistakable signs that in his companion's eyes such unalloyed joy seemed to be made to last. Monroe clung to him. He was both delighted and devastated by this, neither able nor willing to hurt her, but obsessed by the inevitable consequences of his indecision. Introduced to Milan Kundera a quarter-century later, he plunged into his writings and meditated long and hard over certain passages. One he frequently quoted says: "Seducing a woman is within any fool's power, but knowing how to break is a whole art form."

> The public and many of my friends thought I was mainly flattered by the relationship. I was certainly flattered. But to a much greater degree, I was touched. Touched because it was beautiful and because it was impossible. Not for a moment did I think of breaking with my wife, not for a moment; but if she had slammed the door on me, I would probably have made my life with Marilyn. Or tried to. That was the direction we were moving in. Maybe it would have lasted only two or three years. I didn't have too many illusions. Still, what years they would have been!
>
> But the way that Simone chose to behave meant that the question never arose.

June drew to an end. So did Marilyn's part in shooting *Let's Make Love.* She left for New York, while Montand stayed on in Hollywood. Cukor wanted him to dub a handful of scenes in which his diction had been faulty. During those ten days on his own he underwent all the pangs of tormented conscience.

From Rome, Signoret was showing signs of life. The Italian scandal sheets gave her a first inkling, when the headline "*Schiaffi a Hollywood*" ("Slaps in Hollywood") caught her eye on a newsstand. Amused, she looked closer and learned that the injured party was named Simone Signoret, who had received a couple of energetic slaps from her husband to cool her morbid jealousy! She was no longer laughing, but she went on smiling. Soon, though, despite the exquisite sweetness of the Roman spring and a close circle of friends, she no longer smiled. The Los Angeles columnist Dorothy Kilgallen had fired the first shot, announcing that "an actress whose name came up at this year's Oscars is currently having marital problems." After that, it was a feeding frenzy. The actress of the year (known in the Italian tabloids as *la pantera rossa,* the red panther) was urged to defend her honor, to counterattack.

Signoret wrote Montand a painful letter, its tone deliberately neutral, in which she tried hard to understand, to explain. She enclosed a handful of press clippings but was careful to add not a whisper of her own to the torrent of gossip. This contained approach was infinitely more effective than anything in the "How could you do this to us?" vein.

Its recipient, constitutionally inclined to guilt, did not know where to turn. He feared that Monroe might aggravate matters by making a public statement, that she might issue ambiguous denials that would merely feed suspicion. And the hypocritical gossipmongers, under cover of their preaching, were throwing her a lifeline. In an open letter, Hedda Hopper told her: "You have still to prove that you are a great actress. Your success is due only to publicity. I beseech you, Marilyn, stop this self-destruction."

It is also likely that the Fox publicity people became involved. *Let's Make Love* had gone way over budget (not to mention the effects of the actors strike), it was a lightweight script, and there was concern over how well it would do: it might, therefore, be good business to spice its public launching with this providential and titillating windfall. The studio went to work.

The tabloids were stuffed with breathless tidbits: some reported that the star turned up at bungalow 20 naked beneath her coat, and that Arthur Miller, leaving his pipe behind in the hotel, had surprised the lovers in bed. More reputable publications dished up superb photo reports. That summer, *Life* published an article with a subtly equivocal message: "Yves Montand uses his Latin charm to become Marilyn's screen lover. . . ." Everyone, from local rags to nationwide publications, trained his sights on the affair.

On June 30, Montand changed planes in New York on his way back to Paris. Monroe had planned a surprise for him. She was waiting for him at the airport with her press secretary, hoping to turn his brief stopover into a tender interlude. She had even booked a room in a nearby hotel—under an assumed name—complete with flowers and champagne on ice. Montand came down the stairs into a pack of insistent, even aggressive reporters; Marilyn's emissary pushed through the mob to tell him he was expected.

What happened next belongs only in trashy novels: a bomb scare delayed his flight to Paris, and it was announced that some time would elapse before aircraft and baggage could be cleared. Montand played a tight hand. He turned down the hotel but accepted the champagne. He and Marilyn said farewell in a rented Cadillac limousine, slumped for three or four hours in the back of the heavy, air-conditioned vehicle, nibbling caviar and sipping champagne. Montand kissed Marilyn and told her gently that he had no intention of leaving Simone. He said that he had been happy with Marilyn and hoped that he had occasionally made her happy, too.

The things one usually says on such occasions.

> When the first reports about us came out ("seen together at So-and-So's, at the theater," et cetera), I sent an embarrassed and convoluted cable to Rome, which Simone answered with silence. She had the strength to wait until the situation was clearer before reacting.
>
> On my return, of course we had a fight, but just one, and we didn't mention it again for three months. At first our feelings were terrifying, violent; then things calmed down, peace returned—or seemed to. She said, "Tell me everything, and I'll understand everything." I told her everything, or everything I could tell her without kindling the retrospective jealousy that is the worst of all. It was at Autheuil. There she was—beaten, sad, wounded at the thought that the fantastic ten years we had shared had been tarnished in this way. I was sorry to have inflicted pain on her. That was what I was sorry for—only that. Wherever I went and however I lived, she would be there. And I didn't want to drive her away. When I tried, when I succeeded a little, it was because I, too, was fighting to survive.
>
> After my confession, she fended off the gutter press with an amazing burst of pride and intelligence. The following week a British television crew was scheduled to come and interview her, supposedly about her Oscar. When the inevitable question came up

(across the Channel and the Atlantic, the feminist leagues were shouting "Kill him!"), she quietly said, "Do you know many men who would sit still with Marilyn Monroe in their arms?"

That sublime retort was doubly subtle: it partially exonerated me (even though it was very hard—harder, perhaps, than an open declaration of war); and it punctured the absurdity of the situation. It was rather like the Jewish joke of the businessman who confesses to his wife that for prestige purposes he has been keeping a dancer. Later, when they see the dancer at the local casino, the wife whispers, "Ours is the best-looking one." Okay, Simone's man had cheated on her, but with the most beautiful girl in the world.

Our life started up again—wobbly at first, but it started up. We were able to get the engine going. And Simone made a mighty effort not to use the episode to fuel her anger during those husband-and-wife arguments in which everything just comes tumbling out. She behaved like a real grownup. Which I was not, and still am not.

The next year, 1961, for my birthday, she gave me a watch—I still have it—with a dedication on the back. This time it didn't say "I love you" but just "For another October 13—1961."

Fully one hundred photographers and as many reporters were waiting for Montand when he landed at Orly on July 1, 1960. Jostled, peppered with questions, he made two or three remarks of general interest: "The United States is twenty years ahead of the rest of us. . . . It's all movement, a naive and optimistic young nation. . . . California is Marseilles ten times over." The reporters and cameramen could not have cared less. What interested them was Marilyn and Simone, and the look of the prodigal spouse returning to the wife he had "sullied."

Alas for them—Simone was not there. There would be neither public comedy nor public tragedy. There would be nothing for them to see. She had mapped out the operation with the meticulousness of a presidential secretary and asked her husband to respect it down to the last detail. After talking to close friends, she was convinced that the worst mistake of all would be to be seen awaiting the traitor, pink with pleasure at the thought of bestowing on him the victor's kiss. She had therefore decided, first, that she would stay in Italy, detained by her professional commitments and the need to rest for several days after they were over; second, that Montand would go to Normandy until her return; and third, that he would leave Autheuil only to fetch his wife from the airport. Did this mean that everything would begin again as before? It would not be so fast, or so easy.

More than ever before, the Montands would have liked to be treated like an ordinary couple. An impossible desire. Says Catherine Allégret: "I was on the beach at Saint-Jean-de-Luz with a classmate who had invited me down there for summer vacation. A vendor went by, selling *Ici-Paris* or *France-Dimanche,* I don't remember which. . . . He was yelling, 'Read about Montand and Marilyn! Read about Montand and Marilyn!' If I could have dug a hole in the sand and buried myself alive I would have done so. A few hours later, I received a cable from Montand: 'Don't believe the papers. I love you, I love you. Montand.' That night I had a raging fever, although the doctor could find nothing wrong with me."

The popular magazines and dailies fell upon this model couple suddenly convulsed by debauchery, upon this irreproachable pair of stars who had now been dragged back into the common fold. A whiff of vengefulness hung over the pack. This was the couple who had been so fond of preaching sermons, awarding points for virtue, dictating what was right, beautiful, and true. Now it was time to deflate them—in the name of healthy morality, and in the most compassionate of veins.

"[Simone] wanted to look beautiful for his return. . . . 'Marilyn is a wonderful girl but . . . I love Simone,' " shrieked *Ici-Paris* on July 6, deprived of tears at Orly. "She bites well and claws even better," the same weekly later added, in tribute to Signoret's fighting spirit. And a few months later: "Three fiery women in Yves Montand's life: Edith Piaf, Sagittarius; Simone Signoret, Aries; Marilyn Monroe, Leo." *France-Dimanche* condemned the "homewrecker" Marilyn, voiced pity for Simone's "tortured nerves," praised Arthur Miller's heroic silence. The headlines were black and bold, the photos suggestive, the captions blunt.

"The Montands have survived Hurricane Marilyn," said *Paris-Match* on July 16, only to revive the hurricane in its very next issue: "Things are serious. They have been fighting for the last twenty-four hours. Yves wants to return to New York, without Simone. Yesterday he reserved a single seat on Air France. Simone immediately called to reserve the seat next to it. Yves at once decided to cancel his. The game went on through four phone calls. Finally Simone surrendered. Yves wants to leave alone, because what he wants more than anything else is to get to Hollywood alone."

It was all pure invention. Montand had to return to the States after Bastille Day because he had to start filming on *Sanctuary,* adapted from Faulkner's novel of that name and from the play the author had extracted from his *Requiem for a Nun.* Fox had offered to free Montand of further obligations if he agreed to move at speed from one production to the next. On paper, the work schedule was relentlessly dense and somber. On the set, the young British director Tony Richardson found himself hopelessly torn between Zanuck and Faulkner; almost with one voice, the press warned that such a union could produce only conflict and confusion.

Signoret decided not to go with Montand. She was already under unremitting siege in France; the phone rang unceasingly and mail poured in, all of the "My husband also deserted me for a blonde" variety. With no desire to take on the New York and California media as well, she decided to let both time and ink flow before joining her husband in Hollywood.

From New York, Marilyn Monroe's agent issued a statement by the actress that was tailored to burst all speculative balloons: "Most of my partners have said unpleasant things about me after we have worked together. Yves Montand is the only exception to that rule. But is that any reason for me to marry him?" It seemed uncluttered, unequivocal.

Reality, for Marilyn, was much less so. She arrived in Reno on July 20 to start work on *The Misfits,* happy as a child to be teamed with Clark Gable, but sharing with Montgomery Clift, another cast member, a constitutional angst of the kind that never goes away. Miller slaved over the script, closeted himself with Huston, rewrote dialogue just before it was filmed, lived and slept with his typewriter. But not with his wife.

At the very moment when Marilyn had finally landed a real part in a real film, she was living through and hastening the dissolution of the marriage that had made it possible. It was poignantly ironic that Miller, while staying in Nevada, with its quick-divorce laws, eager to free himself from the ties of an earlier marriage, had dreamed up the short story on which the screenplay was based, and that it was here he witnessed the death throes of his love.

The nightmare began all over again for Marilyn. The morning latenesses, the nights of insomnia, the strains on the crew. On several weekends she fled the heat of the desert and went to Los Angeles. She tried to contact Montand, who remained unyielding (he did not know how disturbed she was, and was resolved to follow the line of conduct he had laid out for himself, however painful). He received affectionate and charming letters from her in which she called him Monsieur, and a dog-eared postcard saying "I love you." He went on burying himself in work and lining up contracts, as if to ensure that no pause or respite would leave him free to be on his own. As soon as he finished *Sanctuary,* he began work under Anatole Litvak on *Goodbye Again,* an adaptation of Françoise Sagan's novel *Aimez-vous Brahms?* with Ingrid Bergman and Anthony Perkins. Then, at the very beginning of 1961, he partnered Shirley MacLaine in an American-

Japanese coproduction, *My Geisha.* Four movies in a single year: an overdose.

By mid-August 1960, Signoret was back with him in Hollywood. Just for two weeks, she explained. Assailed by the press, she tried to pour oil on the waters by assuming an almost bantering tone. In a long interview with *Look* on August 30, she quipped: "I must be pretty rash to abandon Yves first to Marilyn and then to Ingrid!"

It was clever, but it wasn't enough. Everything was a trap. That summer's showbiz periodicals were one endless soap opera. The Fox promotion people stoked the fire whenever it seemed to be dying, and Marilyn never stopped making headlines. She was hospitalized for ten days, suffering from drug abuse and depression, and this brought the snail-like progress of *The Misfits* to a halt. While there, she vainly tried to reach Montand by phone. People were saying that the Millers were on the point of separating—and, indeed, their divorce was announced on November 11, as soon as shooting was over.

The second wave of publicity was perhaps even higher and more overwhelming than the first. The big debate of the day was not the one pitting Richard Nixon against the very promising John F. Kennedy, but the question of just how much Montand was to blame for Marilyn Monroe's divorce.

Watching like hawks, Hollywood's columnists turned the simplest acts into portents, the most casual remarks into confessions. When Simone Signoret returned to Paris at the end of August a few days before her husband, it was clear she was "fleeing." And when Montand left Paris for Los Angeles in the last week of November, he was clearly "flying to join Marilyn" (the real reason was to wind up work on *Goodbye Again,* to dub *Sanctuary,* and to do the groundwork for *My Geisha*). The cruelest shaft was appropriately loosed by Hedda Hopper, who claimed that Montand had dismissed Marilyn's feelings for him as a "schoolgirl crush." The expression was unworthy of the lowest of boors; not only that, but its use implied a mastery of English quite beyond Montand in those days; even decades later he had difficulty pronouncing the words. Nevertheless, many authors have quoted the phrase without consulting its supposed author.

French gossip columnists even pored over the cables that overwhelmed the postmistress at Saint-Paul-de-Vence. All of France learned that Yves Montand had cabled his wife from Hollywood: "It's disgusting. I am with you with all my heart and I love you, my love, I love you." *France-Dimanche* went in for progressive escalation with banner headlines. November 9: "Yves Montand Says 'It's No Fault of Mine' but Things Look Bad Between Marilyn and Her Husband." November 16: "Montand the Reason for Marilyn Monroe's Divorce." And on December 6, "from our special New York correspondent Gerard de Villiers," "Marilyn wants to marry Yves Montand, she only likes winners, she tries to contact him daily. . . ." And so on, as fall turned into winter.

At the Paris premiere of *Let's Make Love,* at the Palais de Chaillot on October 3, Jean de Baroncelli noted in *Le Monde,* "Yves Montand wore a somewhat weary smile." The reaction to the movie in the United States had been somewhat chilly, and *Time* on September 19 had observed that Montand had "suffered the conflicting constraints of a role in which he was supposed to be ignorant of song and dance." Britain had been a little warmer, with every paper from the *Daily Express* to the *Times* claiming that Montand had saved the film. In France the critics were polite but lukewarm.

With hindsight, Montand judged the movie severely: "It was a part that could have shot me down in flames for the rest of my career . . . a part that just didn't hold up." He added, perhaps remembering his insane dream of conquering Hollywood, and the insane reality of conquering Marilyn: "It hammered me into the ground. There are movies where you need to be Einstein, but you're only a human being."[5] And, indeed, the actor's "weary" look as 1960 came to an end was surely due to his feeling "hammered"—by life, by the press, by fear of the present and the future, by himself.

The moral jury before which he stood accused was heavily stacked. It was only too true that he had committed adultery, but he disputed the other charges. No, he had not cynically seduced and abandoned a woman: he had underestimated how greatly he would be implicated and his own desire to go beyond a sweet, ephemeral liaison. No, he had not shattered the harmony of his friends' marriage: the flaw was already there, and so deep that what had happened was in all likelihood the effect rather than the cause. But how could he put such subtleties across when everything delicate, fresh, complex, and heartbreaking about the brief affair was being crushed beneath mountains of vulgar headlines?

Among all the inanities flooding into the Place Dauphine, one piece of information was accurate: Marilyn tried tirelessly to contact him. By mail, by telegram, by telephone. She clung, she was alone, she was sad. She invited him to Manhattan; she threatened to come to Paris.

Just before Christmas, she learned that he would be stopping off in New York on his way to Tokyo. She stepped up the pressure. The tormented Montand was further troubled by knowing how fragile Marilyn was and having no wish to aggravate her distress by rebuffing her too brutally. To scotch any possibility of ambiguity, he put off his departure

5. Interview with Paul Giannoli, *Candide,* May 22, 1967.

and spent Christmas and the New Year with his family—a development immediately picked up by the scandal sheets.

It was probably a less joyful New Year's Eve than the last one, spent at Romanoff's in Hollywood, where Simone had been enchanted to dance with Gary Cooper. But it was a chance for them to reaffirm their joint wish to continue their life together. "The crisis had been deadly serious," says Catherine Allégret. "I remember Montand shutting himself into the theater at Autheuil and Mama hammering on the door and yelling, 'I know you're in there!' The fact is, though, Montand came back because he wanted to. It certainly wasn't his first slip. (It's not his fault—he can't help paying court to women, he doesn't know how to form friendships with them.) But Mama always stayed his wife, as he wanted."

A letter Signoret wrote to her husband from Hollywood two years later shows how the couple had progressed. Though she notes that the Beverly Hills Hotel brought back memories of the days when she was "the victim of bungalow 21," she calls him "my very dear love."

What a strange year! Until his Broadway triumph and recognition in Hollywood, Montand had been following a straight, upward path, its driving force the dream of a young man fulfilling step by step the promise he had made to himself. It was the same in his private life: the young man had met and married a young woman; shoulder to shoulder, the two of them had worked at fulfilling their shared ambition, moving ever higher, marital harmony offsetting professional stress.

The Marilyn episode had revealed a fault line—or, at the very least, a turning point. Real change had come about without Montand's noticing it. He had encountered time.

In 1960, too, Henri Crolla died of cancer. Crolla was a friend in the passionate sense Montand gave to the word—the sort of friendship that comes close to love, simulating its rages, its jealousies, its joys. "When we buried Henri at Saint-Cloud," says Paul Grimault, "Yves began to weep. He was shattered. He wept and wept and wept. It wasn't for the spectators: there weren't any. Even though I was half destroyed myself, I remember thinking that such violence of feeling was somehow abnormal."

Montand had encountered age—and, worse, the injustice of age. Working alongside actresses, witnessing their moments of panic, patiently waiting while a partner rid herself of a wrinkle or summoned the hairdresser, he should have been—and, in a certain way, he was—aware of this. But he had never stopped to think that this inevitable visitor would call on him. If Simone had put on weight, he argued, it was because she refused to be obsessed by calories, and good for her! But, of course, it was not so simple: Simone was putting on weight because it was terrible to have been the dazzling Casque d'Or and to realize that age was eroding you. This was the dawn of the 1960s. The baby-boom generation was making its presence felt in entertainment, sports, the consumer world—inventing its identity, its status symbols, its market, its clothes, its dances, its films, its slogans. Never before had there been such a massive and assertive invasion by the young.

It was now that Yves Montand realized he was no longer young. He was forty. His wife, scarcely older chronologically, was more mature—in obedience to the pitiless law that sends women out to hold the front-line trenches of age. Together they were to succeed again—not in sticking the pieces of an earlier life back together again but in prolonging their association and their affection under new rules. Seeking each other out, they strove to move together to a new beat, despite the growing disparity between their inner rhythms.

The so-called 121 affair showed how hard it was for Signoret and her husband to be on the same wavelength, even in political matters. She was no sooner back from California, leaving Montand behind to dub *Sanctuary,* than the film director Claude Lanzmann appeared on her doorstep brandishing a petition whose original author was the writer Maurice Blanchot. "We respect and consider justified the refusal to take up arms against the Algerians," it said. It ended with a declaration of faith: "The cause of the Algerian people, who are making a decisive contribution to the destruction of the colonial system, is the cause of all free men." To those in power, the words were the height of provocation at a time when many young draftees were searching their consciences, and when the "suitcase bearers"—the network of militants under Francis Jeanson who had decided to help the Algerian rebels—were being tried by a military court in the old Cherche-Midi prison.[6]

No time to dither, said Lanzmann. Signoret didn't dither. Already feeling guilty at having followed the Algerian drama from such a distance—an understatement!—the Oscar-winning Frenchwoman, the queen of Hollywood, dived into the fray. She signed. With one hundred twenty other "delinquents," all intellectuals or artists (from Simone de Beauvoir to Pierre Boulez, from André Breton to Alain Resnais, from Roger Blin to Claude Sautet, from Marguerite Duras to Florence Malraux), she went onto the government blacklist, banned from appearing on radio and television, in government-funded theater, and so forth. The cream of dissident

6. See Hervé Hamon and Patrick Rotman, *Les Porteurs de valises* (Paris, 1981).

Paris was on the index. Outflanked on its left, the Communist Party gave grudging support. The government dug in but was embarrassed. There was an angry international reaction.

Signoret signed alone, for the phone wasn't working too well between Paris and Los Angeles. Unable to contact her husband, she decided not to commit him to the struggle without consulting him. In theory, irreproachable conduct; in actuality, Montand resented that she had not presumed he would go along. Once back in Paris, without assuming the martyr's crown, he voluntarily shared the fate of the blacklisted, refusing to appear in end-of-the-year broadcasts and declaring that he would stay out of show business until the charges against all the signatories were dropped. One of the couple's friends said maliciously, "Easy to be that kind of left-winger. She signs with the 121 and he makes money in Hollywood."

He held his peace. Yet this was only the beginning. For while his own escapades had cost him what public-relations people call a loss of image, Signoret was harvesting the fruits of her courage, dignity, and intelligence. Her popularity soared. Henceforth she would be one of France's untouchables. Montand's true punishment for his adventure with Monroe was not a violent quarrel followed by a period of mandatory reparations; it was the unredeemable debt he had contracted toward a "perfect" spouse. There were few men, and even fewer women, who would see things as Catherine Deneuve saw them: "Signoret didn't just flaunt the scratches she had sustained from life's minor tussles. She bore Marilyn etched on her face like a permanent scar. It was too much—at once too big and too petty."

> Gradually we traded the fire of our first ten years for a bond that was calmer but just as strong. Every couple has to walk through a no-man's-land. One day, Simone said to me, "I love you, but I am no longer in love with you." That was after fifteen years. It was a time when we were happy to see one another, but without the thrill of desire. She was strong for both of us.
>
> I made use of her, too—of her tyrannical sense of ownership. It's true, I allowed myself to be taken over. But what I couldn't bear (and still can't bear) were the jealous, snide comments. We had made it, our marriage had held up, we were left-wingers—all unforgivable. So people said she had settled for a man who was beneath her. It was insulting—to her. Why would a woman of her strength, who refused to bend for anyone, obstinately remain with such a man for thirty-seven years?
>
> Let's tell the whole truth of this story. When I left for Japan in mid-January 1961 to shoot *My Geisha,* my head was like a

punching bag. Simone was in terrible shape. Marilyn, after trying to come to Paris, kept cabling that she would be landing in Tokyo. I was completely adrift, and I did a lot of stupid things all over again (just like a man when his wife is giving birth, at the very moment when he's supposed to behave well and be responsible).

One night in Japan, I saw Simone on a television program about *Les Mauvais Coups,* which she was shooting. Sad, so sad. I wanted to fly back to Paris for the weekend. We wrote every day. I was lost.

When I returned from Tokyo, Simone told me I was still distracted, still elsewhere.

My Geisha (its scriptwriter, Norman Krasna, had also written *Let's Make Love*) helped Montand to clear the air with his Japanese fans and gave him the great pleasure of working alongside Edward G. Robinson and being Shirley MacLaine's leading man. He had admired her in Hitchcock's big 1954 hit *The Trouble with Harry* and had met her on the Hollywood set where she was shooting Billy Wilder's *The Apartment.* She was the American woman he had imagined in his childhood. He found her witty; they laughed a lot together. Before work started she warned him: "No monkey business."

Back in Paris, Montand attempted to take honest stock of his credits and debits, to draw up the balance of the past eighteen months.

The singer's record in the United States was well in the black: he had definitely arrived. When he returned to perform on Broadway for six weeks, beginning on October 24, 1961, a huge "Sold Out" sign went up outside the Golden Theater, on West Forty-fifth Street, on the very first day. It was 1959 all over again. The *Post,* the *Herald Tribune,* the *Times,* and the rest of the papers were unanimously approving. Montand, said *Time,* "has a seducer's voice in a truck driver's body. . . . He is one of the most effective love potions ever poured across the footlights." And *Newsweek,* in the same vein, evoked his "madly virile Latin charm."

The Americans had not forgotten that he sang and danced like an angel. Signoret rediscovered all the old familiar pleasures: sharing standing ovations with her husband, the bridal suite at the Algonquin. During the first quarter of 1962 they toured Japan and England. Montand was most assuredly the best-known French music-hall performer in the world. The only artist who in the space of four years had conquered both Moscow and New York.

The movie inventory was less positive. While *Let's Make Love* enjoyed a solid run despite reviewer reservations, *Sanctuary* was a flop. *Goodbye*

Again, ignored by French critics, fared much better across the Atlantic. And moviegoers saw *My Geisha* as at best a pleasant romp, at worst a dreary melodrama.

Internationally, on the stage, Montand had arrived, in spectacular and undeniable style. But he had not achieved a parallel breakthrough on the screen. Moreover, his continent-hopping had somewhat obscured his tracks, blurring the personality that had once been so clearly defined (too much so for his own taste). In Japan they called him "the American." And in Paris they came close to calling him the same thing—but grudgingly rather than affectionately. "Yves Montand has left us" almost became "Yves Montand has abandoned us." In other words, he had grown too big for France, too big for the world of the humble worker. He had been tempted by distant shores, returning richer and less approachable, and trailing clouds of scandal.

No one actually accused him of treason, but the idea was there. It was a contradiction that pursued him for years. The public expected him to be both a symbol of social success and the simple kid from La Cabucelle. It liked him to shine on foreign stages yet remain truly French, to taste success yet spurn its profits, to be an international star yet continue to embody the boy next door.

He studied the balance sheet closely, weighing what could be salvaged and what could not, and decided that the time had come for him to return home. To the Etoile.

While Signoret returned to French cinema, with René Clément directing her in *Le Jour et l'heure,* Montand announced his Paris comeback for November 1962. He prepared with especially meticulous care.

The political air was stifling. While talks with the Algerian National Liberation Front moved slowly (the Evian agreement, the last stop in a war that former prime minister Guy Mollet had called "foolish and endless," was signed on March 18, 1962), the OAS (Organisation de l'Armée Secrète, or Secret Army Organization), a ragtag, covert, and bellicose group of diehard French opponents of decolonization, stepped up its campaign of intimidation and violence. At the Charenton Métro station, on February 8, nine demonstrators—all Communists protesting the "Fascist threat"—were trampled or crushed to death in a police charge. The major left-wing parties, whose attitude throughout the Algerian conflict had been less than clear-cut (the Socialists had dishonored themselves by arguing in favor of the war effort; the Communists had supported the Algerians only with extreme prudence), solemnly buried their martyrs. This helped people to forget that very few Frenchmen had protested when hundreds of Algerians in Paris had been the victims of bloody immigrant-baiting forays during 1961, particularly on October 17.

Montand followed the events very closely. As a citizen, he demonstrated (after Charenton, for example) and petitioned. As an artist, he agreed to narrate the commentary and sing the theme song of *Le Joli Mai,* a powerful film by Chris Marker that evoked all the convulsions of this critical year for France. And he thought long and hard about the composition and function of his concert in this context. The old brand of automatic, self-righteous commitment now horrified him more than ever: it was so convenient, so easy to settle into the warm nest of a just cause. Yet the violence of the times had somehow to be addressed.

And there were newer challenges to be faced. Not only was Montand no longer alone on the French stage—there were Brel, Bécaud, Salvador, Brassens, Ferré—but the new babies, the blaring, shrieking new wave, Johnny Hallyday and the rest, were twisting, rocking, rolling, and yelling "Death to the old!"

Montand concocted his prescription drop by drop. He carefully avoided the urge to hop on the youth bandwagon. He even brought his postwar classics out of retirement, including "Les Grands Boulevards." And he reflected back the somber hues of the times. In 1958 he had dropped "C'est à l'aube," deciding that after his tour of the East the song might smack too heavily of socialist realism. In 1962, when he was more likely to be suspected of favoring American imperialism, he reintroduced the song, closing the show with it. (It depicts the dawn awakening of condemned Algerian inmates, executed amid indifference at the Maison-Carrée prison, or tortured by army interrogators in the cellars of the Villa Sesini.) As for the rest, he followed his heart, singing "L'Etrangère" (Aragon-Ferré) and his friend Prévert's "Dans ma maison."

It worked. The Etoile was packed right up to the end of the year and into 1963. Despite the rock stars, the Hollywood detours, the moral confrontations, Montand, who had just encountered time, also found that he could overcome it.

But some critics voiced reservations. They said that the artist had not changed enough and reiterated the old charge of his excessive perfectionism. On the left, reviewers decided he was no longer what he had been. As Claude Gault wrote in *Témoignage Chrétien* on November 9, "I thought back to the old Montand, in the days when you felt you were on one side of the barricades with those who considered him their troubadour. . . . You have become another character, doubtless far superior to the one you once were. But your place in the family is empty now. And it's hard to think who might fill it, unless it be Yves Montand."

Montand did not take this criticism lying down, and he answered it pointedly. "There is no such thing as 'commitment,' " he told an interviewer in the same left-wing Catholic paper on November 23. "It's an invention. The way the expression 'he practices in front of the mirror' is an invention. Or 'he rehearses until he achieves perfection.' Or 'he times every hand movement to the split second.' Words. Hot air. But people go on using them. They understand absolutely nothing about music hall. There are no music-hall critics, there are just nice people who see the fruit of long labor in a perfectly spontaneous gesture. . . . Everything has changed in the last twenty years. I will always be on the side of the oppressed. But I'm not going to be anyone's standard-bearer. I don't deny my origins; neither do I give them an aura they don't possess, or no longer possess. Old-style working-class solidarity is over. And if you're looking for who's to blame, just glance back over the last fifteen years. No, I was never the standard-bearer of a youth movement. Let's say rather that I reflected a period that was very harsh, very violent."

While getting ready for the show, Montand heard that Marilyn Monroe had been found dead on the night of August 5, 1962. He at once phoned his wife, shooting in Toulouse with René Clément, with the news. He never revealed exactly what he felt.

Yves Montand's American period—he would often return to the United States thereafter, but it was never the same—ended with another death.

His concert at the Etoile was going full swing when he received an unusual invitation: John F. Kennedy and the leaders of the Democratic party would appreciate it if the Frenchman would agree to perform at the president's Inaugural Anniversary Salute in January 1963. Montand accepted at once. For him, Kennedy was the heir of Roosevelt's generous and forward-looking tradition. Kennedy, Khrushchev, Pope John XXIII: these men of goodwill seemed to be attempting to reinvigorate the domains under their command despite the naysayers, the dogmatists, the nuclear missiles, and the past. So Montand broke off his Paris engagement just long enough for a round-trip transatlantic flight. In Washington he plunged into the democratic America he loved, with trumpet blasts and political stickers and music-hall acts interspersed with the speechmaking. (A celebrity from every friendly country had been invited; Montand's three songs were sandwiched between a German and a Spaniard.)

That evening, January 17, Vice President Lyndon Johnson invited the most famous of the visiting performers to dinner. Montand sat at the main table next to Jacqueline Kennedy. After dessert they brought in a piano and rolled back the carpets. Kennedy sang an Irish ballad. Kirk Douglas danced, then Gene Kelly. Montand—inevitably—was asked to sing "Les Feuilles mortes."

On his return to Paris, Montand received a personal letter from President Kennedy. It would later hang framed in the living room at Autheuil, together with a similar letter from Martin Luther King, Jr., and the medal, bearing Montand's profile, commemorating the first transatlantic satellite broadcast.

On November 22 of that year, Montand left a rehearsal of *A Thousand Clowns* and walked home from the theater chewing over his lines. Suddenly he saw black headlines plastered all over the newsstands announcing the Dallas assassination. "It was a bereavement," he said. "Deep, real grief."

Chapter 14

During the shooting of *Let's Make Love,* Montand learned that a young American of only twenty-three, Herb Gardner, whose experiences as a peanut vendor had made him an expert on theater audiences, had written a play with him in mind as the leading man. *A Thousand Clowns* was the story of a maker of children's movies who grows weary of his life and drops everything to live poor but happy with his nephew, a twelve-year-old boy. At the end, the character abandons the outcast life and returns to the system, to the anonymous ranks of middle America's thousand clowns. When Montand read it, he was won over.

His return to the stage in this play, directed by Raymond Rouleau, was almost unanimously hailed by the press. But meanwhile, he kept busy in the movies, too. While performing at night at the Gymnase theater, Montand began shooting *Compartiment tueurs* (*The Sleeping Car Murders*), a first movie by a relatively unknown young director named Constantin Costa-Gavras. Simone Signoret had drawn "Costa" into her orbit when he was René Clément's assistant on *Le Jour et l'heure* in 1962. Like all the Montands' important encounters, this one seemed preordained.

Costa-Gavras's politically committed career as a filmmaker was firmly rooted in his own past. He had been only a boy when the Germans occupied Greece. During the winter of 1941, people were starving in Athens. Every morning, eight-year-old Konstantinos watched the carts go by, heavy with the night's dead, their arms and legs jerking to the motion of the wagon. His civil-servant father went into the Greek resistance under the banner of the Communist-controlled National Liberation Front and sent his family to the countryside; during the civil war that followed, he was sometimes interned and sometimes kept under house arrest. As the son of a Communist sympathizer, Costa-Gavras was denied the right to a higher education; he left for Paris in 1953 and entered the Sorbonne. Coming as he did from a country where Communism was outlawed, he couldn't get over the fact that on French soil you could read *L'Humanité* in broad daylight.

Then he learned of the existence of the Institut des Hautes Etudes Cinématographiques, the Paris school of cinematography. "I discovered the true cinema in Paris," he said. "The first movie I saw was Stroheim's *Greed.* I remember that when the lights came on I sat still for a while; I hadn't dreamed such a thing was possible. Soon I was going to the movies every day. I realized that film was not just an entertainment but a way of saying something." Students were expected to write a paper on a film of their choice to complete their course. Costa opted for *Les Sorcières de Salem,* though he never finished his report.

The young Greek began in the profession as an assistant on *L'Ambitieuse* (1959), directed by Yves Allégret, Signoret's first husband—another portent. Next he was hired by Jacques Demy for *La Baie des anges* (1963), and then by René Clair. Eventually he was assigned by René Clément to handle preshooting costume continuity before the shooting began on *Le Jour et l'heure,* in the course of which task he called on Signoret at the Place Dauphine with sketches of the costumes intended for her. During the first week of shooting, Montand spent an afternoon watching as his wife played a scene in the church of Saint-Eustache. Costa remembers someone whispering, "There's Montand." He turned and made out a tall figure seated in the shadows.

Once the take was over, Signoret said to him, "Come along, I'll introduce you to another immigrant."

Like all assistants, Costa dreamed of bringing his own vision to the screen. For a time he thought of adapting Aragon's *Les Beaux Quartiers*—one of Signoret's favorite novels—but he finally opted for a thriller by Sébastien Japrisot, *Compartiment tueurs.* He gave his screenplay to a secretary to type; without telling him, she passed it along to Julien Dérode, director of the Boulogne studios, outside Paris. One day, Costa received a cable from Dérode, who was abroad at the time: "Screenplay most interesting. We must meet."

Back in Paris, Dérode summoned Costa and questioned him: "Who were you thinking of for the cast?"

"I see only one: Catherine, Simone Signoret's daughter."

"Does Simone agree?" asked Dérode.

"I'll have to ask her."

What followed demonstrates the fallibility of secondhand reporting, the great difficulty of reconstructing the true course of events.

This is Costa's version.

"So I went down to the Colombe d'Or and gave Simone the screenplay to read. And I asked her about Catherine.

" 'She has to take her baccalaureate exam first. But I could play the old actress.'

"I was stunned. Having Simone in the movie! I was jubilant. Then Montand appeared.

" 'Say, Costa, apparently you've written a good screenplay. Anything in it for me?'

"I was dreaming: Yves and Simone for your first movie!

" 'Read the script,' I stammered. 'If a part appeals to you, take it.'

"He was tempted by the character of Cabaud, a sexually disturbed introvert wrongly suspected of the murder. He asked me what I thought. But I had other ideas: 'If it would amuse you to play Inspector Grazziani . . . it's a more interesting part, especially with a Marseilles accent.'

" 'With an accent? Oh, absolutely not.'

"Simone was nodding hard at me to insist. I insisted. And he played him."

Montand's version was markedly different.

According to him, Costa-Gavras was having trouble finding backing for the film, and he showed the screenplay to Signoret and him. At Auteuil the couple eventually suggested that they put the production together as a cooperative venture, with their fees drawn from the film's profits. From the start it was agreed that Montand would play Inspector Grazziani, and only later, at the Place Dauphine, did he hit upon the idea of giving his character the accent of La Cabucelle. As for Catherine Allégret, she was given the part of Bambi much later.

These small disparities are of more than anecdotal interest. If there is a dispute over the parenthood of this honest small-town cop with a Canebière accent, it is because he became a landmark in Montand's development. For the first time in his screen career, Montand felt completely at ease. Was it because this was a family enterprise? Not only were Simone and Catherine involved, but the other cast members were friends. Autheuil regulars accepted minor parts because Yves and Simone headed the billing. Montand's sense of ease also stemmed from his relationship with the director: Costa was much younger, it was his first film, and he was a close friend. A far cry from tyrants like Carné and Clouzot, whose imperious eye and ready bellow terrified everyone.

He could relax, have fun putting his character together, mix in dozens of fresh ingredients for authenticity—such as Inspector Grazziani's constant head cold, which keeps his nose more or less permanently in his handkerchief. At long last, Montand, who in the music hall could create a character with only one or two gestures, was free to exercise his kind of mastery. For the first time on a movie set he did not cringe upon hearing the word "Action!"

Rehearsing with Raymond Rouleau for *Les Sorcières de Salem,* 1956

A visit with Arthur Miller on the set

Arriving in Moscow, December 1956. At lower left are Obraztsov and Simone; right of Montand, the interpreter, Nadia Nechayeva.

Back in Moscow for the Russian premiere of *The Confession,* June 1990. In Red Square with Costa-Gavras

The March 8, 1957, meeting with Tito, who inscribed the photograph

In the Saint George room of the Kremlin

Montand and Signoret at the opening of a new show at the Lido, 1958

One hour before going on stage, New York, September 1959

On Broadway, Montand imitates
Fred Astaire, in "Un Garçon
dansait."

Arthur Miller, Signoret, Montand, Marilyn Monroe, and Frankie Vaughan meet the press before the shooting of *Let's Make Love.*

ABOVE: Marilyn and Montand studying the script

RIGHT: Rehearsal

ABOVE: Laughing with Cukor between takes

RIGHT: *Let's Make Love*

BELOW: Cukor directs a scene.

Lunch with Reggiani at La Colombe d'Or, 1965

Montand between mother and daughter

Costa-Gavras and Montand during the shooting of *The Confession*

With Václav Havel in Prague, January 1990

With Jorge Semprun

In Israel with Shimon Peres and Natan (Anatoly) Sharansky, June 1986

After the fall of the "colonels," the trio of *Z* in Athens, 1974

In Hollywood, 1968: front row, left to right, Lee Marvin, Robert Evans (producer at Paramount), Barbra Streisand, unidentified, and Clint Eastwood; back row, Rock Hudson, John Wayne, and Montand

Shooting *Manon of the Spring* with Daniel Auteuil and Claude Berri, 1985

At the Cannes Film Festival, May 1987. It was the first public appearance of Carole Amiel with Montand.

The christening of little Valentin, in the arms of his mother, with Jean-Louis Livi (the godfather), Christine Ockrent (the godmother), and Montand, January 1989

ABOVE: With granddaughter Clémentine

RIGHT: In cowboy duds for Jacques Demy's *Trois places pour le 26* (1988)

Montand and Valentin, June 1990

"He was totally liberated," says Costa-Gavras. "I was not a superstar, so he felt safe. For a beginner like me, getting started was half the battle. In the first scene we filmed, Yves's character calls on Simone's and says: 'Are you aware of the purpose of this visit?' (It later became a game with us. For years we said to each other: 'Are you aware of the purpose of this visit?') Then Simone tells the inspector about a man she has seen on the train: 'He was kind of ordinary, his clothes were a little tight, a bit like someone behind a desk.' Meanwhile, Montand, his gaze lifeless, is giving a perfect imitation of the character she is struggling to describe. When we saw the rushes that night, everyone roared with laughter. And we were off."

The Sleeping Car Murders was a tight, fast-paced thriller. It was a minor movie, yet Montand dates his real breakthrough as a movie actor from it, as if the seventeen films he had made before did not exist. Thanks to Costa, thanks to the freedom Montand was allowed, thanks to the rediscovered accents and odors of his own childhood, he found he could play comedy naturally and with relish, that he could let a character settle inside his skin and draw on his own history, his own temperament, his own words to express that role. He discovered he could transpose his famous stage presence, a blend of self-abandon and fidelity to self, to the screen. Since *Les Portes de la nuit* he had been both convincing and unconvincing, depending on whether he himself had been convinced or not. He had sometimes been awkward, sounded false. All that was over.

With his vocation as an actor at last confirmed, Montand returned only twice in the next thirty years, in 1968 and in 1981–82, to the one-man show. From now on his priorities were reversed, and film became his main field of endeavor.

This transformation, which took place when he was on the threshold of his forties, became apparent in his appearance. Gone was the beanpole silhouette of the past, replaced by a man with heavier shoulders and with more depth to his face, greater gravity in his eyes. Montand had matured. He was ready to take the screen by storm.

Good things never come singly. Just as Yves was making the acquaintance of Montand the actor, his path crossed that of the Spanish activist Jorge Semprun, whom Signoret had met a few years earlier. The encounter changed his life.

> It was almost love at first sight between us. We met at the Colombe d'Or. He was sitting at our table, with Simone and his wife, Colette, and he was in my chair against the wall. I came in

and thought, Who is this guy who's taken my seat? I gave him a dirty look. Simone introduced us. For half an hour I was curt with him, and then we found we had an amazing amount in common.

It was a love story. He was a man I loved the way you love a woman. I truly loved him—without the slightest ambiguity—and he loved me back, even though in background he was more reserved than me and showed his feelings less.

There were strange affinities between the poor child from La Cabucelle and the offspring of Castilian gentry, between the self-taught entertainer fighting the eternal handicap of a prematurely curtailed education and the highly educated esthete. But these two men had shared the hopes and disappointments of a whole generation. Semprun's life was a virtual synopsis of contemporary history. To Montand he seemed a modern hero, a survivor of the century's tragedies, an emblem of the revolutionary myths that he himself had embraced.

The Spanish civil war overtook the Semprun family in the Basque country. His father, the former civil governor of Toledo, went into exile with his seven children, who were raised by strict German governesses. The elder Semprun represented the Spanish Republican government at The Hague, where young Jorge combed the museums and read Baudelaire. In 1941, by now a student at the Henri IV *lycée* in Paris, he carried off second prize in the national philosophy competition. At another time, Semprun would have been marked for a brilliant academic career, but he preferred learning how to strip a Sten gun, and in 1942, at the age of eighteen, he joined the French Resistance and the Communist Party. The following year he was assigned to picking up weapon and supply drops with the Jean-Marie Action network in Burgundy. During an operation in September he was arrested by the Gestapo. Deported to Buchenwald at the age of twenty, he found a place in the camp administration thanks to the covert Communist organization and his fluent German—his governesses had done their work well. In this strategic, protected post, he was supposed to help in deciding the fate of deportees—who would live and who would die. A most unliterary way of experiencing good and evil, of crossing and recrossing the blurred frontiers between the two.

After taking part in the liberation of Buchenwald by the inmates themselves, Semprun returned to Paris on May 1, 1945, an activist member of the Spanish Communist Party. He lived by translating, and for a time he worked at UNESCO. He was an intellectual devotee of Stalin and wrote poems to the glory of La Pasionaria.

In 1954, the Party leadership sent Semprun to Spain on his first secret mission. At thirty, he became a traveling salesman of revolution, carrying out illegal activities against Franco's regime under a series of assumed names. As a member first of the Central Committee and then, in 1956, of the Politburo, he became (under the name Federico Sanchez) a leader of clandestine operations. But by the time he met Montand, early in the summer of 1963, Semprun had resumed legal existence in France, for he had argued with the leadership of the Spanish Communist Party and moved into the ranks of the dissidents—although Montand did not at first know this.

Surmounting their first instinctive mistrust, the two men warmed to each other, one fascinated by the glorious militant he himself might have been, the other attracted by the artist he himself had never ceased to be beneath his militant's armor. "It worked," said Semprun, "not because there was an intellectual giving lessons on one side and a singer on the other. Not at all. I loved what he did on stage, and, what's more, I considered it important. He sensed that I felt no condescension toward a 'minor art.' "

But the roots of the friendship between Montand and Semprun went much deeper than politics. By 1963, they had reached more or less the same ideological point: they were both skeptical Communists who had lost their illusions but not their hopes.

During this summer of 1963, Montand attended a film festival in Moscow with Signoret. He noted with pleasure that Khrushchev had loosened Stalin's grip, permitting publication of Alexander Solzhenitsyn's novel *One Day in the Life of Ivan Denisovich* and promising that by 1980 the Communist system would reach perfection. Hell, thought Montand, who still believed in Kremlin predictions, these poor Russians who have suffered so much still have seventeen years to wait. One year later, Khrushchev and his rosy forecasts were brutally shoved into early retirement.

As for Semprun, the first months of his friendship with Montand were taken up by ideological skirmishes with the Spanish Communist Party leadership. Nevertheless, even during a period of painful revisionism when he was charged with the grossest deviations, Semprun did not break with the Communist ideal. "In the fall of 1964 I was still caught up in senseless illusions: the illusion that I could maintain and advance Communist values despite the Party or even in opposition to it, the illusion that the consequences of Stalinism could be wiped out through revolution. . . . I still didn't know that world revolution was a historical myth."[1]

Henceforth, in the last stages of their quest for a vanishing hope, the two men evolved together, from criticism of Communism to outright rejection. Semprun's influence became ever more decisive as Montand fell

1. Jorge Semprun, *Quel beau dimanche* (Paris, 1980).

prey to doubts and questions. Just as his brother Julien had been his Communist conscience during the Cold War years, Semprun emerged as his anti-Stalinist conscience during the years of thaw.

At the time of his expulsion from the Spanish Communist Party, Semprun was working with Alain Resnais on the screenplay of *La Guerre est finie* (*The War Is Over*). Resnais had been playing for a long time with the idea of depicting the daily life of a professional revolutionary. "No question of doing a film on Spain," he told Semprun, "because it's too close to you, and I know nothing about it. What interests me is your experience as a militant."[2] At length, Semprun proposed a story that begins with the burial in France of a Spanish refugee. Little by little, around a central thread of Spain and exile, they built the story of Diego, who was and was not Jorge, who was *almost* Jorge. It took three versions before they came up with a final script.

"You never wrote a story for Resnais to turn into pictures," says Semprun. "You wrote for him and with him, which sometimes also meant against him and against yourself. . . . It's well known that Resnais never writes a word or a line of a screenplay he intends to shoot, yet there's never a word or a line that is not marked with his touch, his vision of the project. . . . You didn't just eliminate an adjective, you rewrote the whole scene, as many times as was necessary. . . . And suddenly, after a roundabout series of approaches that seemed like blind groping, after successive rewrites, his original intentions became explicit, and for better or worse you found yourself writing what he had decided you'd write."

Semprun knew intimately the world of the Spanish Republican exiles, veteran fighters of a lost war still in its endless death throes a quarter-century later, retired secret agents mouthing hazy slogans, mechanically predicting general strikes that were now only expatriate fantasies. For while Franco's dictatorship was murdering people, everyone else—including the French who voted for the Communist Party—was on the beaches of the Costa del Sol.

Semprun approached his analysis as if the story lay on a psychiatrist's couch, and by a miracle the wrinkles of his memory corresponded exactly to Montand's new face. Montand incarnated his new friend's crucial passage from a militant to an everyday life—a professional, artistic, legal, "normal" life. He helped Semprun to leave his old life for a fresh one: it was an act of midwifery that lay at the bedrock of their friendship. Semprun acknowledges it: "With *La Guerre est finie* I aged three years overnight. It was my purge. Because of that movie I was able to move quickly through

2. Quoted in *CinémAction,* November 1985.

the pain facing every militant who tears himself away from the Party. Montand made the break easy for me."

The role of professional agitator had not actually been conceived with Montand in mind: he was on the list between Paul Newman and Vittorio Gassman. Resnais decided to evaluate their respective potentials sequence by sequence, and sequence by sequence he graded the actors in his mind. In the end, Montand came out far ahead. Resnais then asked Costa-Gavras for a working copy of *The Sleeping Car Murders* (the young Greek was at the editing stage) and viewed it with Semprun. He emerged convinced that Montand would make the best Diego.

The producers were more cautious, questioning the choice of Montand on commercial grounds. But Resnais sensed that Montand's innate stage effectiveness would transfer to the screen, and he thought, too, that Montand's political pilgrimage had predestined him for the part.

> The romance of the Spanish civil war, an unclouded concept of commitment, and the life of a professional agitator all interested me enormously. Diego's loyalty to an ideal despite his doubts about what he was doing coincided with my thinking at the time. My personal history gave Diego credibility: I identified with him.
>
> I can never thank Alain Resnais enough for giving me this part. He is a director who knows the actor's trade from the inside out; he knows how an actor is put together. The way he works is remarkable, very precise. Before he shoots a scene, he seems not to know how he's going to proceed. Some directors write down every detail and know exactly where they're going to place the camera, exactly what movement the actor will make; you have to fit into the prepared mold. With Resnais it's completely different. He takes the time to explore every possible line of attack. For example, if I am to enter a room, he weighs the whole sequence: Should I sit down at once? Should I unpack my bag first, read the mail, lie down? This may take a half hour, an hour, but the scene is always tighter, more finished. He gets what he wants not in spite of but because of the actor, and for an actor this is fantastic. After *La Guerre est finie* I said to myself, even if I never make another movie it won't matter: I'd had my revenge on the cinema, I've really made a film.

Montand tackled Diego with the seriousness he brought to every professional challenge. For hours, he and Semprun ran his Spanish lines through a tape recorder. Semprun was staggered, overwhelmed, at the first screening of the film. He had invested so much in it, bidding farewell to twenty years of his life, and this performance by a close friend was like looking into a mirror: "He *was* Diego, and that helped me to be myself. To be myself once again." So, too, Montand, by letting a friend's character invade him, had sought and found himself. *The Sleeping Car Murders* had freed him; *La Guerre est finie* confirmed his freedom. "When I met him," says Semprun, "he had decided he would no longer be an actor, that it was over, that he had failed in that field. Diego changed everything."

The press realized it. Montand's performance was praised to the skies—"Proof at last that Montand is one of our two or three great film actors" (*Candide,* May 30, 1966); "Outstanding" (*Le Monde,* May 11, 1966); "An admirable performance of unimpeachable sobriety and conviction" (*Carrefour,* May 25, 1966)—and the film itself drew almost as much praise.

Along with Jacques Rivette's movie based on Diderot's novel *La Religieuse* (*The Nun*) and Claude Lelouch's *Un Homme et une femme* (*A Man and a Woman*), *La Guerre est finie* was chosen to represent France at the Cannes Film Festival. But it was a strange choice for an era obsessed by law and order: the state secretary for information banned *La Religieuse,* and the festival committee turned down *La Guerre est finie* so as not to offend the Spanish government. (Lelouch, remaining in competition, carried off the Palme d'Or.) But Resnais's film was shown in a Cannes theater, and Spanish newspapermen covering the festival awarded it a "Luis Buñuel prize" created especially for the occasion. It went on to garner other awards: the Louis Deluc prize, the New York Film Critics prize for best film of the year, and Best Foreign Film prize from the Association of American Film Distributors. After thunderous denunciations from Franco, the movie was excoriated by the Spanish Communist Party; at the Party's request it was withdrawn from the Karlovy Vary festival in Czechoslovakia in 1967, where Resnais and Semprun had gone to present it.

In the world at large, the 1960s marked a resurgence of revolutionary ideals. Guerrilla movements flourished in Latin America, Castro's Havana appealed to students as the new revolutionary Mecca; tropical storm zones were spreading in Africa and Asia, while in Beijing youthful Red Guards proclaimed that Mao the Great Helmsman had reinvented democracy. A strange fever ravaged campuses from Berkeley to Berlin. It was a time of fiery slogans, raised-fist salutes, and fevered interpretations of the Marxist creed. Against this swirling romantic background, the subtle questions asked by *La Guerre est finie* seem astonishingly level-headed. Because it was the product of a generation already infected by doubt, the film highlighted the absurdity inherent in political commitment (precisely because commitment insists on being absolute, life-and-death), as well as the weariness that came from so many years of clandestine living.

Only two years earlier, Yves Montand had been wondering whether it was worth pursuing a film career. Now he had played the lead in eight movies. In *Is Paris Burning?,* a French-American blockbuster production with a galaxy of international stars, Montand played a sergeant in the fabled Second Armored Division of the French army. For the Paris premiere the producers had planned a military parade and fireworks. But rain canceled everything—except for Montand, who sang "Le Chant des partisans," the Resistance anthem, from the first floor of the Eiffel Tower to a vast throng of umbrellas.

Racing cars had fascinated Montand since childhood, and he next agreed to play a racing driver in John Frankenheimer's *Grand Prix.* Professional racers like Graham Hill actually drove the cars, but the actors had to give credibility to the closeups. Montand took lessons from a former champion, Jim Russell, to help him through the racing scenes, learning how to skid, negotiate high-speed turns, downshift in a split second. In the excitement of shooting Montand, carried away by his part, failed to weigh all the risks involved. On the first day, at Monte Carlo, his car was thrown off balance by the camera that was mounted on its nose; it went into a spin and crashed into a wall. Gasoline spurted from its ruptured tank and drenched the driver. Luckily, the car did not catch fire. Later on, at the Spa track in Belgium, the race sequences were shot in driving rain; Montand, hunched over the wheel and speeding along with visibility down to zero, told himself over and over again that he was crazy to be risking his neck in this way. He wasn't the only one to think so. The people from Lloyd's canceled the life-insurance policy of fellow actor James Garner.

Then, in 1967, riding the fabulous success of *A Man and a Woman,* Claude Lelouch began work on *Vivre pour Vivre* (*Live for Life*)—this time the story of a man and two women. Montand played a weather-beaten star reporter who takes his world-weariness and lust for women all over the world, from Kenya to Vietnam. It was a stock character, but the critics praised both the director and Montand. Then, determined not to be stereotyped, and looking to surprise his admirers—a golden rule on stage—Montand followed up Lelouch's crowd pleaser with the difficult (and skimpy) *Un soir, un train,* by the Belgian director André Delvaux.

Montand the self-taught man from La Cabucelle liked the idea of entering the complex world of a university professor obsessed with controversies in linguistics, a man who discovers the frailty of certainties, the depth of unexpected changes beneath the surface of things. Once again, reviewers praised Montand for his precise portrayal of an intellectual adrift, a man who thinks he knows everything but finds he is ignorant of the most important truths. "I shuddered when I heard that Montand was going to play a university professor," wrote Jean-Louis Bory in *Le Nouvel Observateur,* "but I was wrong: he was exactly the man Delvaux sought to create, because Delvaux reduces him to the essential: a physical presence, a physical weight, and a face you can read like an open book."

Delvaux believed he discerned the signs of inner evolution in Montand's work. "For three years Montand had been negotiating an all-important turn," he says. "He was detaching himself from his familiar persona to become a profoundly truthful actor, idiosyncratic, gifted with exceptional insights." Henceforth critics discovered this "new" Montand and hailed the birth of a great actor with every subsequent film.

In the spring of 1968, Montand suddenly interrupted this series of dramatic roles and ventured into comedy. That, too, was a revelation. But in the spring, another comedy dominated the stage, abroad as well as in France.

For a man who had been the prototype of the committed singer in the 1950s, Montand went through the crisis of 1968 almost nonchalantly. He felt sympathy for the revolt of the students, of course, and even a certain admiration for the demonstrators' courage. (He had always detested crowds and felt real fear at the prospect of being swallowed up in a procession.) But he was now approaching fifty, and he shrank from the absurdity of chasing along with a youth movement; the May revolution was not his, though he welcomed, without too much faith, the possibility of change. Fiercely opposed to rabble-rousing tactics, he could not see himself crying "We are all German Jews!" up and down the Paris boulevards—even though the slogan touched him and he found the agitator in chief, Daniel Cohn-Bendit, appealing.

Semprun, who saw the uprising above all as a revolt against Stalinism, threw his sympathies behind those who were questioning the established order—and on the left that happened to be the Communist order. But Montand did not perceive the anti-Communist dimension of May 1968 until later. At the time he stood by, interested but not implicated, convinced that a man of his generation should not hitch a ride with twenty-year-olds. When he was asked to sing on Sunday, May 20, outside the Renault factory on the Place Nationale, he declined, explaining that "it would be arrogant and demagogic, and the fact that it would be so much elegant self-advertisement would make it even more shameful."[3]

3. Quoted in *L'Express,* June 10, 1968.

Throughout *"les événements,"* Montand was alone in Paris. Simone, marooned in Saint-Paul by a transport strike, telephoned often; from a distance, and given the media distortion, it seemed as if Paris had been taken over by crazed hordes, but Montand dispelled her fears. He was ideally placed to observe developments from the sixth floor at the Place Dauphine, where he had a peerless view of the Place Saint-Michel, the heart of the disturbance, and could follow the close-quarter fighting, his eyes smarting from the tear-gas fumes drifting up to his balcony.

By the end of May, the situation in Paris had gotten out of hand, and the government was panicked by a situation that had gone far beyond its control. Several million strikers expected that their demands would be met, and when the minimum industrial wage was raised 35 percent in one stroke during the Grenelle negotiations among unions, management, and the government, this expectation seemed to be confirmed. But on the morning of May 27, the Grenelle agreements were rejected by the rank and file at the Renault plant. A rally of all protesters was planned for that evening at the Charléty stadium, and the prime minister, Georges Pompidou, in a threatening mood, forbade any demonstrations. Former prime minister Pierre Mendès-France responded that he would go to Charléty himself, making it clear that he feared deliberately provocative action by the authorities. Montand telephoned Signoret to read her Mendès-France's statement: he was their neighbor in Normandy and had met them two or three times, and they admired his integrity. Basically, their reaction was the same as his: a surge of protective emotion for the boiling student movement.

After the return to normalcy, with repression following hard on the heels of dissent, Montand and Signoret emerged from their silence to protest the government's proposal to expel aliens. In a press statement, they said: "Our age and situation did not incite us to play a part in the events of May 1968. But the minister of the interior has clearly threatened to expel 'undesirable' aliens, and we would be ashamed of being French if we didn't immediately protest these moves, for which we would be tacit complicitors if we pretended we had not heard of them."[4]

Early in August 1968, Montand flew to join his friend Costa-Gavras in Algiers for the filming of *Z.* Like many Greeks, Costa was familiar with the story of Gregorios Lambrakis, the physician and Democratic Left member of Parliament who had been run over by a pickup truck in Salonica on May 22, 1963, as he emerged from a meeting where he had protested

4. Quoted in *Le Monde,* June 30–July 1, 1968.

against the stationing of Polaris nuclear missiles in Greece. He died four days later, without having regained consciousness. An inquiry had determined that it was a premeditated murder organized by an extreme right-wing group. The Greek writer Vassili Vassilikos, who obtained the investigating magistrate's records, rendered this story faithfully in a novel.

Costa-Gavras had been thrilled when he read it in 1966, just before the colonels launched their putsch, and he immediately began planning to translate it to the screen. He naturally offered the task of adaptation to his friend Semprun. "Jorge was in the Midi. I called him; he knew of the Lambrakis affair. He said, 'I'm on my way.' The book had not yet been published in France, and I read it to him, translating as I went. At the end he said, 'If you're in, so am I!' "[5] Obviously, sentimental considerations were at play in Semprun's enthusiasm, but it was also the old anti-Fascist reflex: the dictatorship the colonels were setting up under the Athens sun was not unlike Franco's, and Semprun had long mourned the Greek resistance that had been crushed—with Stalin's blessing—by the British army in 1944.

Costa obtained an advance of 1 million francs from Darryl Zanuck's United Artists and shut himself in with Semprun to create the screenplay. The first readers were Simone Signoret and Yves Montand, who at once accepted the role of Lambrakis. But the producers, alarmed at the political hue of the story, were no longer so keen. Costa-Gavras was about to give up when Jacques Perrin, an actor whom he had already cast, improvised as a producer and unearthed partners in Algeria, while the leading players helped lighten the budget by agreeing to work practically on spec. Interrupting rehearsals for a comeback one-man show at the Olympia, Montand went to Algiers to shoot the handful of scenes in which he appeared. In all, he is on screen for only twelve minutes, but his presence haunts the entire two hours of the movie.

Released in February 1969, *Z* weathered a few uncertain days (only 22,660 viewers turned out the first week) before taking off like a rocket, with an eventual 1.5 million tickets sold. In the heated post-'68 atmosphere, this political film in thriller's disguise, remorseless in its unbaring of the facts, relentlessly paced, ran for thirty-six continuous weeks in Paris. "France's first great political movie," ran a headline in *L'Express* on March 3, 1969, adding: "Effectiveness without compromise, instructiveness without pedantry: the rarest of balances between action and thoughtfulness, between ideas and entertainment."

At the Cannes Film Festival, *Z* won the jury's special prize, then triumphed in the United States, where it won two Oscars. But reviewers

5. Quoted in Semprun, *Quel beau dimanche.*

on the extreme left objected to the movie. At a time when the intellectual's credo was still to "go to the people," these militant moviemakers saw in *Z* all the old flaws. Financed and filmed like any other bourgeois movie, they argued, it ignored the working class. Worst of all, the filmmakers had invoked the primacy of the law as symbolized by the honest magistrate in the story; they had set themselves up as defenders of "bourgeois freedoms" that, in the eyes of leftist critics, were a mockery. The post–May 1968 left spurned the idea of a state based on law, and pontificated instead about "participatory" or "proletarian" democracy. Yet if the Greek colonels had needed to destroy a "bourgeois democracy," it surely meant that democracy possessed some virtue in its protection of individual rights—including those of subversive individuals. At a time when the intelligentsia was denouncing "formal liberties," which it considered outdated, Costa-Gavras's plea for the rights of man was a decade ahead of its time.

While Montand was in Algiers, Warsaw Pact troops invaded Czechoslovakia to quash the increasingly liberal government there. Like so many others, Montand had been watching eagerly, with hope in his heart, as the Czech president, Alexander Dubček, fought to give his country "Socialism with a human face."

> I was knocked flat on my back. Since 1956, Hungary, and my visit to Eastern Europe, I had kept my distance, but I had stayed within the family circle. This was the last straw. I was disappointed, disgusted, nauseated. The Russian tanks in Prague were the *coup de grâce,* the end of the illusion that Communism could reform itself, could be reformed. My reaction was instant, primal: I closed the Communist chapter of my life.

Alone and thinking dark thoughts, Montand at first said nothing on the subject of Czechoslovakia. Political debate in Algiers centered more on the previous year's Six-Day War between Israel and Egypt and the continuing Arab-Israeli conflict. One evening, Arab students criticized Montand's "Zionism" (a term whose exact meaning he did not understand), and he defended Israel tooth and nail.

On his return to Paris at the end of August, he was absorbed by work on his comeback to the stage for the first time in five years. As usual, he was terrified. As usual, he was both right and wrong to be—right, because he was better when he was afraid; wrong, because Parisians were now indissolubly attached to him. Thirty-three evening performances, 2 million francs in sales, tens of thousands of frustrated spectators complaining that the show closed too soon. He was, and he remained, the king of music hall.

Was it a victory won in advance? Montand was insulted at the suggestion. The trend among performers in all fields in the autumn of 1968 was to let it all hang out, to pick up the crumbs of that springtime on the barricades. It was the easiest of temptations. Montand was sympathetic to the May movement, but he detested both those who exploited it for their own ends and the eleventh-hour converts who arrived late on the barricades (the line between the two groups was not always clearly drawn). So Montand refused to sing the "Internationale" just because it was in fashion and because the young technocrats in France's elite universities had brought Marxism back into favor. Recovering from the disease of being a fellow traveler had been harrowing; he had no intention of relapsing.

So his show offered no revolutionary message, no conniving nudges to rebellion. He simply sang the songs he loved—"L'Etrangère," "Coucher avec elle," "Planter café"—whether or not they toed the Party line. He resurrected oldies that were dear to him to quash any doubts about the generation he belonged to (including, almost defiantly, "Les Plaines du Far West"), and the new numbers, such as Pierre Barouh's "La Bicyclette," tended to be about love and butterflies rather than the Vietnam war. He dusted off "Bella ciao" (how many in his audience realized that Italian anti-Fascists had marched to the tune of this seeming love ditty?). He sought out Utopia in the work of Nazim Hikmet, not of Mao or Marcuse, celebrating neither a Messiah nor a Messianic class.

There was a little grumbling in the back rooms. Here and there his concert was judged noncommittal, detached. But on this point he was never again to yield. Claude Sarraute, covering the premiere for *Le Monde,* took the measure of the road he had traveled: "In the public mind Yves Montand used to be the 'prole,' the militant, the Renault worker, the truck driver, Saturday night on the town, the hard-boiled egg broken on the countertop. . . . That Montand is no more. The former worker has turned not respectable but intellectual. The machine operator's smock has become the reporter's jacket, the bicycle of distant childhood vacations has replaced the bikes threading through the factory gates in the gray dawn light. Yes, Montand has changed. Along with the times. He interprets in his own way the last barricades, and all on his own he embodies the doctrine that the road to real power leads through knowledge rather than money."

When his six weeks were over, Montand announced that this was it, that he would give no more concerts. That he was leaving the young Yves Montand behind him. That the star of the Etoile had died a natural death.

Chapter 15

In September 1968, Montand agreed one evening to serve as guest editor on a Radio-Luxembourg program. And for the very first time he spoke his mind about the events of the past spring in Paris and in Prague. His rumbling anger at the Communists, so long suppressed, burst out with a new violence. The Soviet intervention in Czechoslovakia? "Already there had been Budapest, which was difficult to swallow, but which I swallowed anyway when I went to Moscow. But the kick in the teeth last August without a word of explanation—never again! When things stink we have to say so. When people go on lying and killing and—what is even more disgusting—informing, then that damns a whole political system." Questioned about his refusal to sing outside the Renault factory in May, Montand replied coolly: "A strike isn't a garden party." (*La Vie Ouvrière,* the newspaper of the Communist labor unions, reported this on October 9 in the following terms: "Nine million strikers now know, thanks to Yves Montand, that their strike has been nothing but one long social whirl." This was exactly the opposite of what he had said and did little to quell his anger at the Party.)

A double break now lay ahead for Montand: with his political family and with some of his real family. He had just returned to the Place Dauphine when his brother Julien burst in, beside himself with rage. The scene that followed saw an explosion of passion and anger the likes of which the family had not yet known.

"I was at union headquarters," recalls Julien Livi, "where I had spent almost all of May working night and day to keep the Paris region supplied with food. A comrade came and told me that Yves had attacked [Communist trade-union boss Georges] Séguy on the radio. I called home. Elvire confirmed the news and asked me to come right away.

"I arrived. I'll remember the scene all my life. I must have looked madder than hell, because he said: 'Calm down, have a beer. Let me play the whole tape for you.'

"I listened, and when it was over I exploded: 'That's despicable. How could you say such things in public?' I was furious, ready to punch him. I managed to hold myself back, but then everything came rushing out. I yelled at him, and he yelled back. The whole neighborhood must have heard. He tried to argue with me, and quoted Semprun, which only made me madder: 'Semprun is a liar,' I said. 'He may be able to take you for an asshole, but not me.'

"That made him even angrier. He was shouting at the top of his lungs. I left, slamming the door. I was in such a state that when I got back to my office my secretary had to go out and get me a new shirt, my own was so wet. As far as I was concerned, we were through."

With this explosion of anger, this release of thoughts too long suppressed, Montand weaned himself, at the age of forty-seven, from an ideological tutelage that went back to his childhood—throwing out not only Julien's orthodox instruction but his guilt at having escaped from his background. The taboo he had broken over the air at Radio-Luxembourg was the self-censorship that forbade clan members from voicing open criticism of the clan. Henceforth, Montand not only thought for himself (he had done so since 1956) but also spoke without fear of giving ammunition to the enemy. For the enemy had changed: it was now Communist ideology itself. Montand suffered through this reversal of values. At the moment of desertion, all heretics go through such rites of passage, in which anger wars with defunct faith. That the separation went hand in hand with a break between brothers only heightened the anguish.

The four years separating the brothers meant that Yves and Julien had never enjoyed a day-by-day closeness as children. When Ivo entered his teens, Julien was already busy at political work that kept him away from home. When Yves was seventeen, Julien left for the army, and it was seven years before he saw his brother again. Yet Julien had remained very present in Yves's mind during those years of separation—as a model, and sometimes as a source of guilt. In the impasse des Mûriers, a photo of Julien in prison uniform hung on his bedroom mirror—a permanent reminder of the proper code of conduct. And after the war, despite his stardom, the kid brother still needed his elder's protection, sometimes without knowing it.

In the 1950s, the circle of friends who gathered around Montand and Signoret took on greater importance, but Julien and Elvire were emphatically included in the circle, their left-wing connections an additional bond. Still, the first clashes between the brothers were born of political disagreement. When Montand returned from Eastern Europe in 1957, Julien had reproached him for behaving badly in the "people's democracies." Montand rebelled. But these bursts of anger had soon faded. A much greater threat was the arrival of Jorge Semprun, and it was no accident that Julien lashed out at him during the big quarrel. Elvire Livi has expressed it exactly: "Jorge Semprun was Montand's spiritual brother. From the moment they met, he completely ignored his real brother. And for that I will never forgive him."

That day, the day of the broadcast, Montand yelled so loud that he lost his voice. The doctor diagnosed blistered vocal cords.

"You could have destroyed your voice for good," he warned Montand. "Please, please, don't utter a word for the next forty-eight hours."

That night the audience at the Olympia was surprised to see the singer come to the front of the stage. With great difficulty, he managed to whisper a barely audible "Ladies and gentlemen" that brought an "Oh!" of disappointment from his listeners.

"I am very sorry . . ."

The sounds seemed to be emerging from a cheese grater.

Having taken the first public leap into doubt, Montand went still further. He gave an interview to *Témoignage Chrétien* on September 26 in which he continued along the road of heresy: "Things are not so simple as people tried to make us believe, with the bad guys on one side and the good guys on the other. That's ridiculous, absurd. . . . I certainly continue to believe in a better future, but not in a Socialist heaven. I have no hesitation in condemning them, in saying no."

This continuation of the fraternal quarrel meant a total separation at the Place Dauphine. Julien never came down to the "trailer" any more; he remained blockaded in his sixth-floor apartment. Both of them too rigid and too proud to take the first conciliatory step, the brothers avoided each other. And at this very moment of their quarrel, the father they both loved died, on October 7, in his house at Allauch. Giovanni Livi was seventy-six years old; he had been half paralyzed since suffering a stroke five years earlier and had needed full-time care (arranged by the devoted Lydia and paid for, as usual, by Montand). To the end, Livi was the person whose unspoken approval Montand always sought, the supreme source of authority, the voice of his origins. For a long time, he had identified loyalty to Communism with loyalty to his father: breaking with one meant an unconscious break with the other. Does this mean, though, as Semprun put it, that "this private bereavement facilitated the process of political bereavement," or that "despite all the pain it brought him, his father's death facilitated the break with the 'Holy Family' "?[1] The chronology of events

1. Jorge Semprun, *Montand: La Vie continue* (Paris, 1983).

seems to support this theory. Yet Montand's public sally against the Communists on Radio-Luxembourg and his clash with Julien took place two weeks before Giovanni's death. Montand had cast off the moorings while his father was still alive, under his father's gaze. He was already an orphan of the Party before he became a real orphan.

> I did not discuss politics with my father in the years before his death. He had grown much weaker and no longer read the papers. And then I was never really on such terms with him. It was Julien who talked politics with him, because Julien had become what he is, a professional militant, out of admiration for our father. In a way, he carried the torch. I used to kid around with my father. As far as practical jokes, funny stories, laughing, and having a good time were concerned, we were on the same wavelength. Unlike Julien, who wasn't there at the time of the Nazi-Soviet pact, I had seen my father full of doubt, pulled in two directions. I don't want to extrapolate from that, it wouldn't be fair; but I think that basically he would have agreed with me. My father was an Italian Communist, while Julien is a French Communist.
>
> It wasn't his death that freed me to speak. I had already reached a point where I could no longer keep silent. But I'm convinced that in condemning the horrors of the Communist system, I have remained loyal to my father.

Behind the political quarrel an increasingly venomous second conflict was emerging—the brothers' fight over their father's inheritance. Which one spoke for Giovanni's memory? Long after his death, Papa Livi continued to serve as both trophy and yardstick. For years, Montand would "speak" to his father in dreams and even in a waking state. Semprun frequently witnessed this "dialogue," and once reported the following bizarre exchange: "One day Montand said to me, 'I don't talk to my father anymore. He told me to push off. He said, "You're old enough now; it's time you took care of yourself!" ' "

We can only guess at Montand's distress over Giovanni's death. Reserved as ever, he never publicly uttered those inadequate formulas that heal only superficial wounds. He did not go to Marseilles for the funeral, because he had to sing at the Olympia that evening, as he did every evening. The law of the stage makes this kind of split inevitable, but his absence at the graveside added fuel to the family quarrel.

Indeed, with the patriarch gone, the family cell disintegrated. "The break was terrible to live through," says Jean-Louis Livi. "Everyone suffered. Everyone took it on the chin: Montand, Simone, my father, my mother, Catherine, and me." Catherine Allégret: "I hate politics. Politics destroyed my family—because the 'sixth floor' was my family, too. I called Elvire 'Auntie.' She was my second mother. She was the one who raised me. I saw terrible things done because of politics. They tore each other's guts out: Montand's hatred of Stalin was as violent as my uncle's primitive Communism. There was no room for anything in between." A few months later, Julien and Elvire Livi left the Place Dauphine. Montand and his brother virtually never met again.

Immediately after closing at the Olympia, in November, Montand flew to Hollywood to begin *On a Clear Day You Can See Forever* (his fourth film of the year!), with Barbra Streisand. Just before the New Year, Costa-Gavras called him in his Beverly Hills Hotel bungalow to offer him the part of Artur London in *The Confession.* "On Christmas Eve," he says, "Claude Lanzmann told me about a wonderful book that had just come out, Artur London's *The Confession.* I raced to a bookstore and gobbled it up. Right away I wanted to turn it into pictures. I talked to Jorge about it. He knew London and knew his story. He said: 'To play London? Montand.' I agreed immediately: for me, there was no one else. I wanted to work only with Montand. So we called Los Angeles. Yves's answer came at once: 'If you and Jorge want to go ahead, count me in!' "

Although he had accepted his friends' proposal, Montand had misgivings. Artur London's tragedy was not unfamiliar to him. He knew that the Czechoslovak Communist, a veteran of the International Brigades in Spain, chief of the secret immigrant labor organization during World War II, had been deported to Mauthausen and then, in 1949, appointed deputy foreign minister of his country. In the early 1950s, London had been tortured physically and psychologically for twenty-six months by the henchmen of his own party. Although London had stood up to the Nazis, he had slowly cracked at the hands of his Communist torturers and signed the most lurid confessions. Montand knew that a story of such power, transferred to the screen, would deal a devastating blow to Stalinist Communism.

But the old paralyzing doubts returned. Would he not be giving ammunition to the enemy? At a time when Vietnamese peasants were being napalmed and Latin Americans were groaning under right-wing military dictatorships, often with the connivance of Washington, this screen denunciation of the Communist system might look like indirect support for the imperialist camp. His hesitation reflects the state of mind of an age in which the Soviet empire continued to exert effective ideological sway, despite its inhuman face. But—and this was a sign of an irreversible change—Montand took his doubts no further. The truth was the truth, and it was right to speak it, even if it hurt both speaker and listener.

He was due to return to Paris in April. Meanwhile, Costa-Gavras and

Semprun went to see Artur and Lise London. The two men wisely wanted the film to be associated with the book and had no wish to commit themselves to anything without the Londons' approval.

London had wanted to write his story ever since his release from prison in 1956; in a way, he had already begun it while in there. After his trial he smuggled out of prison two texts written in a microscopic hand on onionskin paper, four pages one time, three pages the next, in which he described the methods that had been used to extract confessions from him. Typed, they came to sixty-five pages. Later he had drawn up two reports, of one hundred fifty and two hundred pages, for the rehabilitation commission. Together, these documents were his starting point. "Gérard waited until the time was ripe," recalled Lise London. (Gérard was Artur London's alias as a secret agent and Resistance fighter. His friends and family continued to call him that.) "He was afraid that he wouldn't be believed, that he would be treated as another Kravchenko. He wanted to write first and foremost for Communists. When the Prague spring came, he was decided. He completed the book in four or five months."

The arrival of the Soviet tanks in Prague never fully re-established Stalinist order in Czechoslovakia. During the short months preceding "normalization," passive resistance generated a climate in which political differences were blurred and a degree of tolerance reigned. In April 1969 an explosion of joy hailed the Czechoslovak ice-hockey victory over the USSR. At that same time, *The Confession* was published in Prague: the first printing of thirty thousand copies was immediately sold out.

Costa-Gavras wanted to start filming on the spot. In Czechoslovakia, he and Semprun met one Podleniak, the bureaucrat who headed the Czechoslovak movie industry, and he seemed highly enthusiastic. They met again at Cannes, where *Z* was a triumph, and signed a joint-production agreement. But that summer, the totalitarian noose began to tighten around Prague again, and an ideological purge was under way. Podleniak told Costa by phone that it would no longer be possible to shoot the movie in Czechoslovakia. Shortly thereafter, he was replaced and "reduced to the ranks."

Nevertheless, Costa-Gavras sent his chief assistant, Alain Corneau, to Prague. "Costa wanted me to check things on the spot," said Corneau, "to keep an eye open for possible locations. I got there around the first anniversary of the Soviet intervention. There were tanks everywhere and kids hanging around waiting for God knows what. I went to the studios; they were deserted. A man there told me that everything was booked and we couldn't use the equipment. He also asked me to meet him in a bar that night. There he said to me, 'Don't you realize what's happening here? Get out, quick!' But I took a look around the city, which was later helpful in our search for another site. Then I came home."

With shooting scheduled for September, they launched a quick search for a new location. Corneau noticed that the houses in Prague looked very like those in old Lille.

The adaptation of London's book was ready. Stripping down a complex story, spread over several years, and reducing it to a two-hour time span comprehensible to audiences without diluting it, had presented thorny problems. And Costa and Semprun had refused, for "moral reasons," to "exploit . . . suspense and character identification."[2] In other words, they were determined not to use simple dramatic sleight of hand of the kind that traditionally keeps the viewer on the edge of his seat: Will the hero be equal to the ordeal that lies ahead? Will he survive it? Early on in the script they inserted "flashforwards": in the midst of an interrogation we are shown Artur London several years later, recounting his adventure on a terrace beneath a Mediterranean sun. These sunlit interludes undercut the raw emotion of the plot, obliging audiences to distance themselves, to absorb the historical background, to remember that this was not a thriller. Semprun and Costa were aiming for a cerebral rather than a visceral effect.

Semprun insisted on assuming sole authorship of the dialogue and the adaptation. His reasons, he said, were political—as if the London case presented him with a chance to settle, or to pay, accounts. It did. When Costa had first mentioned *The Confession* to Semprun, he hadn't been surprised to learn that he and London knew each other, but he had no idea how well.

It turned out that when Semprun joined the French Resistance he had been given the same *nom de guerre,* Gérard, as London—not by accident, as he later learned, but in tribute to a legendary leader. The senior Gérard had fought in Spain with the International Brigades, which inevitably forged a link between him and Semprun. Then he had been deported to Mauthausen; and for a survivor of Buchenwald, no tie could be more binding than the inmate's tattoo. And it was precisely because of Buchenwald that London's tragedy had imprinted itself upon Semprun's conscience: on three occasions and in three different books, Semprun had tackled the node at which the horror of the Nazi camp system became entangled with monstrous Communist totalitarianism.

During the 1952 Slansky trial, at which London was also accused, one of the fourteen men in the dock was Josef Frank, assistant secretary general

2. Ibid.

of the Czechoslovak Communist Party, who was accused of having been a Gestapo agent while an inmate at Buchenwald. Frank confessed. Now, Frank had been a companion of Semprun's in that camp, where both had belonged to the same clandestine Communist organization. Semprun therefore knew that Frank could not have been a Nazi agent. "You knew Frank was innocent," Semprun's fictional hero Federico Sanchez would tell himself accusingly. "You knew right away that both the charge brought against him and his confession were false; through a kind of sickening vertigo you saw all the implications of Frank's innocence. It was like a drop of acid that began to eat away at all your certainties."

It was ten years before the acid etched a deep enough hole. In 1952, the militant Spanish Communist Jorge Semprun had kept silent, hugging his secret to himself, even though he was sure the trials had been rigged; in 1969, writing the screenplay for *The Confession,* the silence of 1952 bled from every line. The scene in which faceless policemen scatter the hanged men's ashes in the snow is of frightening power. All that remained of Josef Frank, who had escaped the Buchenwald crematorium, was one of those handfuls of ashes.

Like his friend Semprun, Montand dragged around with him like a ball and chain the memory of his own conduct during the Slansky trial. He remembered repeating Paul Eluard's words over the phone to the reporter from *Le Figaro:* "I have too much to do with the innocent proclaiming their innocence to spend time on the guilty asserting their guilt." The "innocents" had also been the Rosenbergs: at the Théâtre Sarah-Bernhardt in 1954, Montand and Signoret had identified with them when they played the Proctors in *Les Sorcières de Salem.* Reading Artur London, Montand realized again that the innocents proclaiming their innocence might have been guilty, while the guilty asserting their guilt might have been innocent.

It was precisely because the Montands had been the soul of *Les Sorcières de Salem* that Costa-Gavras wanted Simone to play Lise London, whose militant road had been no less heroic than that of her husband. The daughter of a Spanish Communist, she had started working for the Party at the age of fourteen; she spent the two years between 1934 and 1936 in Moscow, where she met and married London; by 1936, at the age of twenty, she was working with the International Brigades. An anti-Nazi Resistance worker from the start, she was arrested and condemned to death early in the war, but was spared by the birth in prison of her son, Gérard. In May 1944, she was transported to Ravensbrück, and until she left for Czechoslovakia in 1949 she held important posts within the French Communist Party apparatus.

One day, long after her husband had been arrested—she had no news of his whereabouts or fate—reading a paper over someone's shoulder, she saw his name on a list of those about to be brought to trial. Lise was convinced that Artur would deny the charges leveled against him. When she heard her husband's voice over the radio confessing his crimes, she did not hesitate for a moment between the Party and her husband: she at once wrote a letter and repudiated the latter. It was this act that made Simone Signoret hesitate to accept the role. "For her," said Lise London, "it was unthinkable for a wife to act toward her husband in that way. Whatever he had done, you remained loyal to him. To persuade her, Chris Marker organized a showing of an Italian documentary about *The Confession* in which I explained why I had written that letter. After that, she accepted."

Even so, those who have never experienced such perverse turns of faith will find Lise London's act hard to understand. In the depths of his prison, crushed by despair, London continued to share the same faith as his wife. He knew what her reaction would be and was not surprised by it: "I just continued to trust my Party. . . . I know such feelings are incomprehensible to those who have no idea what a Communist is, but I was expecting a letter calling for my punishment."[3]

So powerful were the ties between Signoret and Montand that she could not bear the idea of betraying him even by proxy. "Simone was bothered," said Costa-Gavras. "She kept saying, 'I can't use those words, they aren't me.' It was painful for her to embody a character whom she despised ethically, and we crossed swords several times during shooting. Her reticence reflected a more general unease she felt toward the whole enterprise. Basically she went along out of loyalty, particularly to Montand."

Shooting began on September 22, 1969, in Lille, where the houses, cobbled streets, and swaying streetcars did indeed fairly reflect Prague. The crew even managed to get hold of some Czech automobiles, whose body work was virtually impossible to replicate. (An assistant stumbled across one by chance, parked on the rue Ponthieu. He waited for the driver, a Czech tourist, to turn up, and the Czech immediately lent the vehicle and gave Corneau the name of a friend, also in France, who owned a more recent model.) For the interior scenes, Corneau found a hospice, an enormous eighteenth-century building whose cellars presented endless visual opportunities. The sinister location enhanced the psychological gloom of the story, inescapably claustrophobic, insecure, threatening. Every week an elderly patient died. One part of the building, which the hospital director asked his guests to avoid, housed mentally ill patients; one

3. Quoted in *Démocratie Nouvelle,* July 1956.

day, while the crew was filming a scene in the yard, heads appeared at the windows above them and began to chant with waves and grimaces: "Montand! Montand!"

"You're popular here, too," said Costa.

Costa-Gavras was a meticulous director. For the courtroom sequences, the set exactly replicated the original, taken from a document in the Prague archives. He chose the welder's goggles Montand is made to wear—soon to become famous through posters plastered around the world—with the same care. From a dozen different pairs, he picked out one with the glasses linked by a strange-looking iron bar: in his mind, they echoed the fetters on London-Montand's wrists. (Ten years later, Montand learned from the revelations of Sandor Kopasci, the Budapest police chief who had joined the uprising in 1956, that when Imre Nagy was brought back in handcuffs from Rumania to be executed, he had been made to wear such goggles.)

Montand had no intention merely of playacting against a painstakingly reconstructed background. His whole life had prepared him psychologically for the role of London, and he was determined that audiences see the victim's physical suffering. London had lost about thirty pounds during the interrogations between his arrest and trial. So Montand went on a savage diet that stripped thirty pounds off him in six weeks. To avoid temptation while the crew was tucking into its hearty evening meal in the communal kitchen, he came in through a back door and went to a little room, where he wolfed down his five ounces of grilled meat and a few green beans. Sometimes, out of the corner of his eye, he saw dishes being carried in for his friends; he quickly turned away and ate even faster.

"Occasionally he came in during lunch," said Costa-Gavras, "and walked between the tables insulting us. 'Bunch of bastards, still eating!' And he'd leave. Then he'd be back to swallow a spoonful of spinach and three mouthfuls of meat. Just enough to keep him alive. And even then. . . . " As the weeks went by, Montand melted away, obsessed by his weight, periodically tortured by temptation.

> I committed sacrilege. One afternoon, we were shooting a scene in which a great pig of a guard—beautifully acted by Gérard Darrieu—eats a big sausage sandwich while interrogating me. He ate in front of me, drank beer in front of me, belched in front of me. In the room next door were several identical sandwiches in case we had to do a number of takes. I walked past the room. I scolded myself: hang on, hang on, you mustn't! Then suddenly I cracked, I hurled myself on a sandwich like a madman and gobbled it down as if someone were trying to snatch it away. For a few seconds I forgot I was Montand. I was London, and I was terrified

that the soldiers were going to beat me. And then I was horribly guilty. All those days of effort only to give up! But the slip didn't add an ounce to my weight. The unbearable lightness of being. . . .

Montand's overheated identification with his role was not limited to the crash diet. He asked to have his hands cuffed behind his back, which caused shooting pains in his shoulders. He chose cuffs that bit into the wrists, even keeping them on between takes so that they bruised his flesh and the pain he felt was genuine (a month after the shooting was over he still bore the stigmata). In one scene the jailers throw a bucket of water over London to revive him as he lies unconscious in his cell. Montand insisted that the water they used be ice-cold. The scene required twenty-one takes.

During breaks, Montand forced himself to walk round and round his cell without stopping, at one point fainting from fatigue. Before shooting began, Montand, Costa, and Semprun had agreed not to shoot the harshest scenes of physical torture, but they retained sequences in which London is punched around by his guards. Montand asked the actors not to treat him gently, but to throw him violently against the walls. "Costa appreciated this concern for truth," recalls Alain Corneau. "He wasn't above roughing up the actors to rattle them. One day he collared a happy-go-lucky guy who couldn't wipe the blissful look off his face, and shoved him around in earnest. It was to make him angry and really go for Montand's guts."

In their hotel, Montand disregarded the star suite reserved for him and took a small, spartan room overlooking the courtyard. He covered the window with a black curtain to cut himself off from the world. He holed up in this solitary retreat after his skimpy evening meal, seeking through this act of deliberate isolation to come closer to the prisoner he was playing. Often he slept on the floor in his prisoner's uniform, shivering with cold. One night he had a nightmare: he was locked in his cell, and the walls crept inward while the ceiling sank down to crush him. He shouted and woke up. Signoret and Costa-Gavras came running: they found Montand looking haggard, drenched in sweat. He had the same nightmare the next night, and the night after that. The guests grew accustomed to the yells that occasionally broke the silence of the night. When Artur London called to see how the film was coming along, Montand told him of the recurring nightmare. Gérard stared at him, amazed: "That's the very same dream that haunted me in my cell in Prague!"

After a few weeks of this routine, Costa was so worried about Montand's physical and psychological condition that he proposed—unsuccessfully—they take a break. Montand's body was so thin that his ribs stuck out. His gaunt, unshaven face and dark-ringed eyes indicated general debility and fever. A privileged witness of this deliberate act of penance, Semprun analyzes it today with the advantage of hindsight: "He paid obstinately and heavily for his past ignorance, for his blind faith, for his smart-ass remarks . . . but he paid, too, for all of us. He paid our debts and set us free. He purchased a new life for all of us with the passion he brought to his work."[4]

Everyone who witnessed Montand's hand-to-hand struggle with his past was staggered by his physical transformation, his urge to punish himself, to atone. "He took personal identification as far as possible," said Alain Corneau. "He must have been drawing heavily on intimate dramas, on personal conflicts. Sometimes he seemed utterly drained; it could last for days." Costa-Gavras used almost the same terms: "He was completely sunk in his character. He lived it. He suffered night and day. I believe it's the furthest an actor has ever ventured into his part. I believe he must have dug deep within and come up with very personal issues to feed on." And Semprun said, "Identification carried to that extreme is almost dangerous. It had a Christological quality to it."

Lise London accompanied her husband to Lille and watched a few takes. "We were shattered when we saw how wholly he had put on Gérard's skin," she said. "It was extraordinary. Gérard couldn't believe his eyes. It wasn't Montand he was seeing but himself."

> It was easy to get inside that part. It came along at the right time, at a time when I wanted to tell subsequent generations how insane we had been. For me, *The Confession* was my farewell to the generous sentimentality of the left—a left that had been blind to its own crimes and had cultivated a Messianic pose, proposing to bring happiness to human beings even if it meant slaughtering them. Since I, too, had believed in it, there was naturally an element of penance in what I was doing. An internal cleansing. Through physical suffering. But let's keep things in proportion: it wasn't Siberia! Anyone can bring off a physical feat for the purposes of acting a part. What I went through was child's play compared with what London had endured. Comparisons would be grotesque. I remember what he said to me on the set: "You look exhausted; you must be feeling terrible." From him it was a great compliment, but really. . . .
>
> And, of course, to play a part well, really to "be" your character, you have to maintain a little distance. It's better to be sober when you have to play a drunk. My face had to show

4. Semprun, *Montand.*

fatigue, but I still had to conserve enough energy to work eight hours a day. Sometimes I played poker all night. It was an escape, but I did it with a clear conscience, because the next day I looked more wiped out than ever.

Through those six weeks of fasting, Montand dreamed of the last day of shooting and the banquet he would enjoy. That night he ordered every course, but he could manage only a few mouthfuls and a half-glass of wine. His body was no longer used to plenitude. It took him several months to put back on those lost pounds, and he missed the sense of weightlessness his fasting had brought him. Drained, wrung out, he rested at the Colombe d'Or and waited for the movie to be edited.

As soon as it was over, Costa-Gavras announced a showing for the actors and crew, at the end of April 1970. "The Londons sat in front," said Costa-Gavras. "We were a couple of rows behind them, with Yves and Simone. When the lights came back on, Gérard sat dead still for perhaps ten minutes. Montand whispered to me, 'He didn't like it, it's no good.' Gérard seemed to be in a state of total collapse. He couldn't speak. Then we went to the bar, and finally he got it out: 'It was unbelievable!' " Lise London also recalled the viewing: "Gérard was stunned, absolutely overwhelmed at living through his own story all over again. Even seventeen years later he still had nightmares, still couldn't wear anything on his wrists that reminded him of handcuffs. And now to be pitched right back into it. . . . As for me, I was convinced I was seeing my Gérard on the screen; I had to force myself to say, 'That's not Gérard, that's Montand.' "

When *The Confession* was released, on April 29, 1970, the press unanimously hailed the burning rage that drove the actor. "Montand does not just incarnate Artur London. His identification is so complete, so painfully absolute, that one would be ashamed to call it an acting performance," wrote Jacqueline Michel in *Télé 7 Jours*. "Hats off to Montand," said Jean Cau in *Paris-Match*. "He inhabits the body of his character with such passion that the bones truly jut through the skin." Reviewers praised the tautness of the screenplay, the nightmarishly claustrophobic vision of a machine that ground men to powder and hammered individuals with humiliation and renunciation. Jean-Pierre Melville (with whom Montand was about to make *Le Cercle rouge*) summed it up with this delicate compliment to Costa-Gavras: "Last year, with *Z*, you brought glory to our profession; this year you bring honor." Despite the film's difficult subject and oppressive mood, audiences voted en masse in favor of the makers of *The Confession:* 450,000 viewers in Paris, more than 2 million in France, and ninth box-office position for 1970. As with *Z*, its reception abroad surpassed all expectations.

The movie's impact and popularity forced the French Communists to react. They had tolerated London's book when "normalization" in Czechoslovakia was not yet complete, but in 1970 the wind from the East was blowing cold again. Georges Marchais had replaced Waldeck Rochet at the head of the French Communist Party and was pushing it back into hard-line positions. The Party could not admit the movie's explosive denunciation of the Stalinist system. The Communist leaders, among the first to see *The Confession* at a private viewing at the Boulogne studios, shouted with indignation at the end, the projectionist told Costa-Gavras.

L'Humanité on April 29 accused the director of transforming a deliberately Communist book into an "anti-Communist film." But Artur London himself crisply outflanked this maneuver in an interview in *Le Monde* on May 20. "Costa-Gavras and Jorge Semprun have respected the spirit of my book," he said. "The screen images do not betray the written word. . . . The movie is faithful to the spirit of the book; from this it follows that if you are against the film and deplore its release, you admit that you are also against the book and deplore its publication."

Then, on August 5, London was stripped of his Czechoslovak citizenship. Stalinist winter had returned to Prague. Alexander Dubček was expelled from the Communist Party. Rudolf Slansky, son of the man hanged in 1952, lost his factory job, his pink slip stating simply that his dismissal was intended to "improve the quality of the collective leadership of the factory." (Twenty years later, the first decision of President Václav Havel was to name Slansky ambassador to Moscow. The fallen Dubček became president of the National Assembly. And *The Confession* was finally shown in Prague.)

The Party's condemnation of a work in which Montand had given so much of himself merely deepened the chasm between the former fellow traveler and the Party dignitaries. As always in Montand's life, the public quarrel went hand in hand with a family one. Julien no longer lived at the Place Dauphine, but, still faithful to the Party line, he wrote Costa-Gavras a letter in which he rehashed the arguments put forth in *L'Humanité.* "Basically," wrote Julien, "this film could only be, one, an attack on the ideas of Communism in general and the Soviet Union in particular; and two, and most important, a good-conduct medal awarded to capital, to the old society, for the numberless crimes committed since time immemorial against those it crushes and exploits, foremost among them the Communists. It is plain as day that both story and dialogue are designed to deal the heaviest possible blow against the Communists and their past and present struggles." Three pages of these bitter thoughts followed. Montand was angered by Julien's blindness. He would so much have liked to convince him, yet he was banging his head against a brick wall. "He suffered badly through this time," said Artur London, "and it is to his credit that he stuck it out. He suffered particularly badly from his brother's antagonism."[5]

With twenty years' hindsight, Julien Livi has softened his earlier judgment: "That movie hurt. My reaction was certainly too hot-blooded; it stemmed from my own doubts and thoughts, which I turned against the man who had meant so much in my youth. Today I would not condemn my brother for taking part in *The Confession.* Perhaps the film helped speed the course of history."

Two years later, in February 1972, a group of skilled workers at Renault, led by Maoist comrades, questioned the authority of their supervisors and roughed up some executives. The ringleaders were fired. To force management to rehire them, they went on a hunger strike—to widespread indifference. Simone Signoret's help was now solicited: she was asked to support the hunger strikers to show that they were not alone. At first reluctant to play the role of a lady of charity, she finally agreed. Sartre, Costa-Gavras, and Chris Marker also visited the hunger strikers. But on February 20, a young Maoist worker, Pierre Overney, was gunned down by a security guard at the factory gates. At his funeral the actress joined the huge crowd paying its last respects to "Pierrot." His photo still hangs among the many pictures on the wall at the Place Dauphine.

But Montand was attending another funeral. His mother had died at the age of seventy-nine in Marseilles. The whole family was there. Lydia had lost the letter in which Giuseppina had dictated her last wishes, and wondered whether they should have a religious ceremony. She finally decided to ask a priest to officiate.

> I hate funerals, ceremony, cemeteries. I looked at my mother's body, already stiff, and at her face, forever inanimate. . . . It wasn't my mother. It was something alien. I kissed her, and I'll remember to the end that feeling of burning cold.

A winter sun warmed the terrace of the house at Allauch where the Livi clan awaited the funeral. Montand, expressionless, wrapped in a trenchcoat, paced up and down; a few feet away sat Julien: the two men had not really spoken for more than three years. Julien beckoned his son Jean-Louis over and whispered to him: "Go and cheer him up. He looks like a big bewildered bird."

5. Quoted in Richard Cannavo and Henri Quiquéré, *Montand: Le Chant d'un homme* (Paris, 1981).

The two brothers sat side by side in the car following the hearse. "I had a three-quarter view of my father and Montand," said Jean-Louis. "It was a sad sight. My father's face was stony, and Montand was weeping silently, eyes wide open and staring straight ahead." Just a few weeks earlier, at Christmas, the Livi brothers had exchanged greetings one last time for Giuseppina's benefit. "My mother had sensed something," says Lydia. "She said, 'Don't those two get along any more?' But her suspicions were allayed, because when Yves arrived he was fantastic: he kissed Elvire and Julien as if nothing had happened. My mother was happy. She died two months later."

Montand spent a good part of 1972 in Chile, where he had played the hero in Costa-Gavras's latest film, *State of Siege,* the third part of a trilogy: after the films attacking Greek colonels and Stalinist interrogators, Costa-Gavras attacked the methods used by the United States to consolidate its hold over Latin America. Armed with his unrelenting camera, he was smiting oppression worldwide, whether Fascist, Communist, or imperialist. In this story, every detail of which was authentic, Montand plays an official of the Agency for International Development who is kidnapped and then executed by urban guerrillas: he has been a CIA agent, an "adviser" to the political police, not a hero but a swine who is sure he is right; as well as being a good father and husband, Mitrione is convinced he is defending American values. The story was directly inspired by the Tupamaros' kidnapping and execution of an American citizen in Uruguay, Dan Mitrione. With the scriptwriter Franco Solinas, Costa-Gavras had done extensive research, and he reconstructed the case with his usual precision. He had even gotten hold of recordings of conversations between the guerrillas and their prisoner.

Montand went through the looking glass. The shooting gave him a chance to discover the Chile of Salvador Allende, who had been in power for two years, and whose government was already stumbling under contradictions and threats.

One night, Montand and Costa were invited to dinner at Allende's country home. The Chilean president made no secret of the economic and other difficulties facing him. When he was overthrown the following year in a coup led by General Pinochet, Montand felt the need to do something to demonstrate his feelings. He hit on the idea of returning to the stage for a single benefit gala, its proceeds to go to the Chilean refugees. In *La Solitude du chanteur de fond* (*The Loneliness of the Long-Distance Singer*), Chris Marker's camera catches what this eight-day marathon must have meant for a man who had not performed on stage for more than six years (anyone interested in Montand's stage work will find in it the subtlest and most complete of portraits). In particular, it catches the tiny tear in the singer's eye when he sings the wartime anthem "Le Chant des partisans."

A tear, when all is said and done, for the left.

Chapter 16

Sixteen films in ten years. For Yves Montand, the 1970s were the decade in which he brought together everything he had to offer, deployed the whole spectrum of his strength and vulnerabilities. The most popular French actor of his generation now successfully stormed screens on five continents, rounding it off with an ovation at New York's Metropolitan Opera House.

Jean-Louis Livi began acting as his uncle's movie agent at the start of this prodigious decade. "All those years," he recalls, "Montand was France's leading actor. There was Jean-Paul Belmondo, who was his own inimitable self. And there was Montand, in the prime of life, acting in the most beautiful films of the time, with fantastic directors who were then also making their mark."

Not all the films were resounding victories. Pierre Granier-Deferre's *Le Fils* (1973) was a flop, though Montand liked the story and the director. *Le Hasard et la violence* (1974), an effort by Philippe Labro to escape from the "efficient" style that had made his name, bogged down in the twists and turns of a convoluted script. Claude Pinoteau's *Le Grand Escogriffe* (1976), a slapstick comedy about a sensitive subject—the kidnapping of a child—was badly received. Joseph Losey's *Les Routes du sud* (1978) suffered from outright schisms among director, scriptwriter (Semprun), and star: Montand said bluntly that Losey thought "like a 1950s Stalinist."

Montand occasionally accepted a role for sentimental reasons—out of friendship, respect, or simply because he liked one particular sequence (the very beginning of *Les Routes du sud,* for example, in which a German Communist soldier deserts to warn Stalin that the Wehrmacht is about to attack, and ends up being shot as a provocateur). But weighing on the other side of the scales were an unbelievable number of fine films: the comedy of *Le Diable par la queue* (1969) and *La Folie des grandeurs* (1971), the bittersweet humanity of *César et Rosalie* (1972) and *Vincent, François,*

Paul and the Others (1975), the stark austerity of *Le Cercle rouge* (1971), the throat-catching suspense of *Police Python 357* (1976) and *La Menace* (1977) . . . and many others.

The clearest sign of how much Montand had been released and liberated in the 1960s was the breadth of territory he now covered. In 1967–68, he had gone from the highly showbiz *Vivre pour vivre* to the complex, meditative mood of *Un soir, un train.* He had become the symbol of a new political cinema. He was stretching himself, mixing styles. Less than three weeks after the Paris release of *Z,* in February 1968, he shared top billing in Philippe de Broca's comedy *Le Diable par la queue,* in which he played a phony baron and genuine thief, gambler, braggart, and seducer. The reviewers rubbed their eyes: Could this really be the same man, tap-dancing for Broca one minute and symbolizing trampled democracy for Costa-Gavras the next?

He enjoyed taking the risk of muddying his image by mixing tears with laughter. French audiences accommodated easily and loved both sides of him. In the United States, on the other hand, the admiration was mixed with puzzlement. The greatest American directors—Elia Kazan, for example—had hailed the Montand of *La Guerre est finie,* seeing him as an actor who carried on in the politically committed artistic tradition of Albert Camus. Now he was playing a commedia dell'arte role! In truth, though, the fans of Montand the singer were not surprised: ever since the Etoile, ever since he had produced his own shows, Montand had always blended humor and gravity, "Sir Godfrey" and "C'est à l'aube." Now he had transferred to the screen what he had always done on the stage.

In 1970, after *The Confession,* he made *Le Cercle rouge,* under the direction of Jean-Pierre Melville. Alongside Alain Delon, François Périer, and Gian-Maria Volonte, he played a fallen policeman, a drink-sodden former sharpshooter (the movie includes a highly realistic delirium tremens sequence). The black and bitter movie and his role were of almost Japanese austerity.

"You are your own material," Montand would often say about his one-man shows. And now he was in a truly comparable situation before the cameras. As César in Claude Sautet's *César et Rosalie,* he walks, talks, weeps, deals cards, and laughs just like Montand. Like Montand, César is both sly and naive, selfish and endearing, brave and fearful, enthusiastic and hot-tempered. It might seem that it is easier to work close to one's own nature. On the contrary: it had been easier for Montand to play Mario in *The Wages of Fear*—muscular, sleek, a bit shallow. What requires true sleight of hand is to devour and then regurgitate yourself, in public, stark naked—and yet at one step removed from yourself. César is *almost* Montand, and the "almost" is what makes his performance such a towering feat.

"A revelation, but hardly a discovery—a great actor is born," wrote Danielle Heymann, who had followed Montand since the Liberation, in *L'Express.* The "great actor" had already had a chance to show his stuff, but his performance in *César et Rosalie* was indeed a revelation. Montand himself would admit it when he said of the director Claude Sautet: "He truly saw right through me, and without my knowing it, if that's possible."[1]

What was so special about this César, this self-made scrap-iron merchant, loudmouthed, generous, kind, manly, vulnerable, who plays a desperate game between Sami Frey and Romy Schneider? César banished forever Montand's boy-next-door persona of the 1950s, as well as the fulfilled, confident man of the following decade. He gave the actor in him precisely what invalidates or compromises the term: a character four-fifths of which was himself.

For both audiences and critics, *César et Rosalie* was the movie of the year in 1972. "Yves Montand plays César with extraordinary delicacy, feeling, and wit. . . . With this performance, he emerges as France's leading actor," wrote Henri Chapier in *Combat* on October 27. "By turns bellowing and pitiful, crafty and blundering, Yves Montand performs with outstanding brio," said *Le Monde* four days later. "He has never been better."

The director Claude Sautet, the medium who had summoned up this spirit, was a man of wide reading and a skilled technician who prepared his shoots with ferocious dedication. Like Montand, he had bounced through the ideological ups and downs that had dominated two political generations (he himself had left the Communist Party in 1948, during Stalin's attack on Tito). Eight years separated the first draft of the script from the final version, completed in collaboration with Jean-Loup Dabadie, which gave Montand top billing.

"At first," says Sautet, "the main characters were the ones played by Romy Schneider and Sami Frey. Then I started to think about a third character, along the lines of Broderick Crawford or Vittorio Gassman. I was still feeling my way when I was pulled into the screenplay of *Le Diable par la queue.* 'I'm going to choose Montand,' Philippe de Broca said to me. Montand? In a comedy? That surprised me. When I saw the film I thought, He's perfect and he's funny. But could he play a totally everyday, ordinary part? My image of him was of a serious, hardworking guy, a singer full of charm, yet the bearer of a serious social message from the left."

As in any worthwhile screenplay, the meeting that so influenced their respective destinies came about by chance. "It was at the Boulogne studios in 1971," says Sautet. "Yves and Simone came out of a screening of *Le Chat,* Granier-Deferre's beautiful movie starring Gabin and Signoret. He

1. Quoted in Alain Rémond, *Montand* (Paris, 1977).

grabbed my arm and said with a kind of childlike enthusiasm, 'Ah, that Simone, no use denying it, I'm jealous!' We talked for about ten minutes in this superficial tone, and I thought, Well, he is funny, he has a sense of humor, and from a source no one seems to have suspected. Why look further? He *is* César. From then on, I stuck to him like glue. I fall passionately in love with my actors, I seek out their vulnerable, hidden zones, I dream of an osmosis between their temperaments and what's in my head. An actor can get into anything, but first it has to pass through him. I can no longer imagine anyone else playing César. If an actor is perfect, the part is his forever."

The commercial success of *César et Rosalie* revealed the enormous sentimental capital on which Montand could henceforth draw. His extraordinarily accessible talent came from the curiosity of the self-taught man who has traveled many roads; from his accent, lined features, and cocky humor; his ready energy and obvious vulnerability; his reticence and anger; his self-mockery and high spirits. The Montand character had acquired maturity, depth, texture, warmth. It gained from straightforward exposure just as it was.

The following year (Montand completed no fewer than four films in 1972!), Sautet and Dabadie did it again. *Vincent, François, Paul and the Others* was a box-office hit from the very start of its release in October 1974. Vincent was Montand, François was Michel Piccoli, Paul was Serge Reggiani. "The others" were the young Gérard Depardieu, and Stéphane Audran, Ludmilla Mikaël, Marie Dubois, and Catherine Allégret. "More of a pack movie than a buddy movie," says its director, "a pack whose common bond is lost illusions and middle-age melancholy."

A small-scale industrialist whose business is in trouble, Vincent is not César but is very much like him—tenser, more threatened, more scrupulous. His relationship with François (Piccoli), a wealthy doctor, and Paul (Reggiani), a failed writer, is painful and equivocal, as are his relationships with women, who have the best—or, at least, the truest—parts, in the movies as in life. Authentic actors' cinema. On October 28, 1974, Jean-Louis Bory in *Le Nouvel Observateur,* who had pilloried Montand on his return from Hollywood ten years earlier, laid down his arms: "Hard to say whom to admire most. But I know: Stéphane Audran and Yves Montand. They have one scene together that quite simply lays bare the workings of the heart on screen." And Gilles Jacob in *L'Express* on September 30 uses the identical term, "workings of the heart," to describe the whole film.

There was a third Sautet-Dabadie-Montand joint effort, in 1983—*Garçon!,* a less finished, patchier work than its predecessors. Montand hesitated about it, for the screenplay seemed lame to him, beginning brilliantly and then tailing off into a recounting of the hero's rather improbable loves. Sautet suspected that Montand found the character a little too colorless, a little too commonplace, for the public, political figure he had by then become.

But the friendship and cooperation continued. When Dabadie was invited to the Place Dauphine one morning and rang the bell at the thick, low-jambed door, Montand opened it, a tray in his right hand, a dish towel over his left arm, his manner that of the perfect servant. It was his way of saying yes to the script of *Garçon!,* accepting the role by donning the costume.

The third field Montand explored during the 1970s was the thriller, the action movie. Nothing very new on such well-traveled ground, perhaps, but things were not that simple. First of all, Montand relished focused stories, unconventional themes, out-of-the-ordinary messages—and *Le Cercle rouge* was the best illustration of this. (*I comme Icare,* a conventionally made movie, harked back to the assassination of John Kennedy and the theory of a decoy marksman.) And the sheer number of films he made that required a heavy physical investment—chases, stunts, weapon handling, and so on—was surely no accident. Montand was testing his fifty-year-old self: the rushes every evening offered a faithful record of where he was speeding up and where he was slowing down, of what his body had believed it was achieving and what it really had achieved. It was both a challenge and a test before the pitiless mirror of the passing years.

In 1974, the young director Alain Corneau, Costa-Gavras's assistant on *The Confession,* made his own way with *France société anonyme,* a work that delighted lovers of great cinema and filled producers with despair. "If I had to do it over again I would still do it," says Corneau. "But it was time for me to give birth to a movie that a few viewers might pay to see. So I thought of trying a genre I loved deeply, *film noir.* I started with the idea of a cop on the skids who finds he is the prime suspect in the case he himself is investigating. That was the basis of the screenplay Daniel Boulanger and I hammered out for *Police Python 357.* Asking Yves seemed a little strange. In spite of *The Sleeping Car Murders* and *Le Cercle rouge,* this honestly didn't seem to be his line. And in 1975, remember, cops-and-robbers movies were suspected of being tarred with the Fascist brush. Yves studied the script for a couple of hours. I waited. It was yes. Without him we couldn't have done it."

Montand liked the story. He also liked Corneau, whom he had come to admire when they were working with Costa-Gavras. A genuinely cultivated man, Corneau was also an accomplished technician, sure of what he wanted but infinitely flexible and patient in his handling of actors. Fairly soon the helping hand Montand was offering the young Corneau (he was thirty-three) became more than that: the movie turned into a family affair. "I would never have dared suggest that Simone Signoret play a supporting role," says Corneau, "although I learned later that professionally speaking, this was not a very bright period for her. To me she was royalty, and Autheuil was the holy of holies. So when Montand suggested we bring her in, and when the two of them later brought in François Périer as well, you can imagine! What amazed me was that when we started out, these great actors, these stars, were more apprehensive than I was: for them every movie was a first time."

For all of them this shoot was a happy event. "My greatest joy in working with Montand," says Corneau, "was in discovering how contradictory his star image is. He mingled the intelligent, fatherly approach with a childish naiveté that was its exact opposite. In my opinion, that is what makes him a successful actor: the big, reassuring guy hiding an extraordinarily feminine fragility."

The murdering police inspector, the paralyzed heiress, a hamadryad mistress, the embattled cop—it all had the look, the tone, and the pace of a classic thriller (Montand, in a clue deliberately planted by Corneau for the delight of true movie lovers, wears the same jacket as Clint Eastwood did in *Dirty Harry*), and it has audiences on the edge of their seats. Despite a tight budget, the crew had the impression they were wallowing in luxury—the excessively rare luxury of the "second degree," in which good guys and bad, violence and silence, panic and plotting are not neatly arrayed on either side of a Manichean dividing line.

The crew was richly rewarded when the film came out in 1976. *La Croix* compared Montand to Humphrey Bogart (a comparison that now occurred with increasing frequency). And Jean-Luc Drouin, in *Télérama* on March 31, saw in Montand "the only actor who stands comparison with the great American stars. . . . Voice, gestures, ideas, he brings the same talent to all of them. He is at once Sinatra, Mitchum, and Fonda."

In other words, what Montand had gone to look for in Hollywood, Paris now gave him.

Alongside the *série rose* (the pink of blood, not of petals) movies of Sautet-Dabadie, a *série noire* was also evolving, with Corneau as its connecting thread. *La Menace* (1977) took Montand to Canada. Twenty-five years after *The Wages of Fear* he was driving a truck again, one of those giant rigs that ply the highways of the New World, a truck that in the end fatally crushes him. The director was aiming for a maximum of abstraction, for an almost machinelike aridity: the scenes between the "heroes" are skeletal; for twenty-five minutes—a world record!—there is no dialogue at all. On the other hand, Corneau invested heavily in a florid profusion of stunts and car chases, all the unspoken tributes to a decadent and outdated cinema. The leading man, more "American" than ever, has a good time. And audiences gobbled it up.

In *Le Choix des armes* (*Choice of Arms*), which closed out these fertile ten years, Corneau tried to restore the atmosphere of a traditional French crime thriller—the rituals and the code of the old-fashioned gangster milieu, in which middle-aged hoodlums, halfway to retirement, are jostled by up-and-coming youngsters. He even wanted to shoot it in black and white, then decided this would be forcing the joke. But he eagerly collected the clichés of the genre and stamped them with his own personal mark. Montand, Catherine Deneuve, and Michel Galabru, the veterans of the party, have the luck to cross swords with a Depardieu on his way up and to shepherd a couple of eye-catching neophytes, Richard Anconina and Gérard Lanvin. Montand, playing a carpet-slippered former hood obliged to bring his gun back into service, was hailed as a physical actor comparable to late-vintage John Wayne, at once powerful and scarred.

It is impossible to separate the professional Montand from the civilian. The two pictures merge. Unlike his wife, Montand was virtually without an alter ego capable of functioning at a relaxed pace, of stopping to take a deep breath. When he was a singer, he lived on the stage; when he was a movie actor, he lived on the set. And he felt more support, more security in movies than in one-man shows: you could depend on a film unit—with all the constraints and compromises such a dependence implies—and you were not left alone on your ice floe.

Montand no longer knew—or had never known, since he had never taken one—what a real vacation was. For him, travel meant inspecting a location or leaving for a shoot; it meant one more airport, one more hotel. As soon as his plane landed he raced to inspect the theater, before unpacking his bag and taking a quick look at the houses and streets. It was phantom traveling, with everything glimpsed, skimmed over. "He doesn't know what it means to sit still," said Catherine Allégret. "He devours himself."

To him, a film was a time and a place you looked at, you entered, you settled into. Even when working in Paris, he sometimes stayed at the Concorde-Lafayette hotel rather than return to the Place Dauphine and his family: it would have meant leaving the cinematic circle, abandoning the crew. Like many actors, he needed to make his costumes and props his own. Perhaps the outstanding example of this is the Police Python 357, a monster of a handgun weighing two pounds, with a kick that would break a beginner's wrist, which he wore in the movie of that name. He carried it constantly, polished its holster, took advice from an expert (the man who developed the splayed-legs instinctive-firing posture), who taught him to draw with feet pointing parallel and the pocket of his jacket weighted with keys or coins to make it swing at the right moment. He practiced alongside special police units. In short, he became a cop.

His directors and screen partners were impressed by this determination to achieve identification. "The way he lived the ups and downs of his character in *César et Rosalie* was wonderful," says Claude Sautet. "If César was in a good mood in the script, Montand was in a good mood. But if the plot suddenly turned against him, he would turn gloomy." During the shooting of *Vincent, François, Paul and the Others,* the script called for Montand's character to have a heart attack. He put so much heart (so to speak) and apprehension into it that he suffered palpitations and had to consult a specialist, who spoke to him of the "black eagle," the suffocating feeling that grips your chest during a coronary. On the day of the filming, he succumbed to the attack with such abandon that no one dared shout "Cut!" once the scene was over: admiringly, and a little afraid, the director, cameraman, and crew gazed in silence at the figure on the floor.

His roles could be vectors of these all-but-real feelings. In 1975 he worked with Catherine Deneuve in Jean-Paul Rappeneau's *Le Sauvage.* It is the story of an artistically inclined perfume manufacturer, a crusty misanthrope, who isolates himself on a desert island, where he is pursued by a ravishing young lady.

Montand respected and admired Deneuve. But when they met again in Paris two months later for the continuity scenes, he reflected with a certain amount of remorse and frustration that he had been distant, even harsh toward her, whereas now he would have liked to talk to her, invite her to dinner. In *Choice of Arms,* on the other hand, Deneuve played opposite him in the role of a gentle, supportive, understanding wife. When shooting was over, they all went their different ways. For Montand it was death—a small death. For two weeks he wondered wretchedly, "But why hasn't she called?" She was his wife, wasn't she? It took two or three weeks for a character to take its leave, painfully, shred by shred.

In short, the man during the movie was not the same one as the man in the mirror. And the man after the movie was torn for a while between the two. The end of *Police Python 357* perfectly illustrates this blurring of his internal borders. Montand had grown used to the weapon. He handled it with skill. When his contract was over he missed it (emotionally, that is: he has no liking for death-dealing weaponry). He obtained a permit, walked into a prestigious gunsmith's on the Champs-Elysées, and went down to the basement range to try the weapon out. It was pathetic! His shots seemed to miss the target deliberately. He stopped right there. The adventure was over; he was no longer either a cop or a marksman. All he kept was the regulation blocked-barrel Python he had used in the movie.

Alain Corneau has said that Montand became "strung-out" on a role. In his early movie days he used to prowl around the cables and booms, seeking to understand the rules of the game, the workings of the machine. And as a leading man he was equally assiduous, if for different reasons. Three considerations, in strict order, determined his acceptance of a role: the story, the screenplay and his part in it, and the director. He did not see himself simply as a cog, no matter how vital. Long accustomed to creating himself, to directing himself, to selecting his material, he wanted to be a part of the conductor's brain waves, to be able to question, correct, enrich the process.

"There are actors who view the rushes, and there are those who don't," said Corneau. "I can't begin to imagine Yves not doing so. He also watched the editing. He didn't interfere technically, but he watched each successive scaling-down, made comments, checked to see if a scene ended with him or not, voiced agreement or disagreement. If we were stubborn, he gave up; but if he really believed he was right, he dug in his heels. What was very good, what saved the relationship, was that he said what he had to say. To your face."

The negative side of this prodigious availability, this creative tension, was an undeniable tendency to take over the set, to plant himself at the heart of the operation. All showmen are by definition so inclined. But Montand's egocentricity was no less legendary than his extraordinary powers of concentration. "We are all gifted narcissists," François Périer said with a smile, "but Yves is certainly one of the most gifted of us all." Gérard Oury takes a slightly more complex view: "An actor who isn't a bit of a narcissist, a little bit vain, is no longer an actor. If he doesn't contemplate his own navel, if he doesn't hunker down at his own center, he stops being the selfish child determined—and legitimately so—to grab the best part for himself like a toy. But it must be strange to be at once both Stradivarius and violinist."

Narcissism is the need to offer your best profile to the camera (for Montand, it was left three-quarter, the profile heightened in Chris Marker's documentary of the 1974 concert). It was the thousand big and small deals struck with the director over a simple shot or a line. Above all, it was the half-fascinated, half-antagonistic relationship with the other actors—the good ones, the beautiful ones. Claude Sautet knew what risks he was running when he put together the cast of *Vincent, François, Paul and the Others.* All "Macaronis" together, all good friends, of course, forever joking on the set and heaping compliments upon one another after the rushes. Yes, but . . . but Piccoli almost backed out (to be replaced by

Rochefort) when he learned that Montand was making more money than he was . . . but Reggiani found himself clashing with his old friend. Each in his own way had been a child prodigy, and now, much later, their lives were on parallel courses separated by an unspoken question: they admired one another, but did they like one another?

The crafty Sautet put cameras everywhere, so that no one could suspect the others of stealing a scene. He exploited the rivalry without which actors frequently fail to give the best of themselves. As for Montand's special narcissism, Sautet would quietly observe, "The only real difference between him and other actors is that he doesn't hide it. Or hides it so badly, so guilelessly, that no one is fooled. I loved his Latin cunning; it was both annoying and attractive, and you had no need to worry about it."

In this kind of joust, money was above all a sign of status. Montand wanted to make money to prove he had made it, not to amass it. In 1968, Paramount wanted to pair him with Barbra Streisand in a musical comedy, *On a Clear Day You Can See Forever.* They offered $200,000. He respected Barbra Streisand and admired her as a singer, but he had no wish to be anyone's prop or to return to the hackneyed role of the Latin lover. Four hundred thousand, he countered, "just to see what they say." Signoret and Semprun laughed heartily—until the studio accepted. Trapped, he left for New York, had a taste of Barbra Streisand's talents, and at length found that his own musical numbers—except for one superb sequence in which he sang on the roof of the Pan Am building—were ruthlessly pruned.

Often, on the other hand, he agreed to receive a percentage of the gross in order to help a director he was fond of (*Z, The Confession, César et Rosalie,* and *Vincent, François, Paul and the Others* were all in this category). Alain Resnais unfailingly acknowledges that Montand got only 80,000 francs for the months of work that went into *La Guerre est finie.* But if the producer was prosperous (like Gaumont in *La Folie des grandeurs*), if the contract symbolized his ranking in his profession, Montand asked for the maximum and considered it morally right. On principle.

In other words, when fees soared far above normal criteria, money was only a surrogate for the competition that invariably raged among leading performers: it registered your continuing climb, your sustained box-office appeal, or your decline. In the entertainment world as elsewhere, there are greedy or miserly people, but they are the exception, not the rule. At these inflated levels, a sum like 500,000 francs was only secondarily a pocketbook question. It was mainly a question of image—of an image that needed defending, that might lose its luster and fade away. Lots of money was reassuring.

Apart from the Autheuil house, bought for 14 million francs in 1954, Montand had become co-owner of the café on the square at Saint-Paul-de-

Vence; in 1972 his friend Paul Roux, the owner of the Colombe d'Or, had offered to buy it with him, and he had just earned 2.5 million francs for *La Folie des grandeurs* and was happy to invest part of that sum. In this building he fitted out a small three-bedroom apartment where he would stay when he was in the Midi.

Of course, Montand was rich. The money counted for itself, even if he did not count it. "Ex-pauper, not nouveau riche," as the French comic Coluche used to say. Marked by his beginnings, Montand lived within his means. He banked the money he earned. Bob Castella managed the accounts, in which Montand took no active interest. He would call his comfortable nest egg his "security blanket." His golden rule was never to lay hands on it. For him, money was not the impersonal zeroes that pile up on bank statements but a roll of bills you can feel in your pocket. He liked cash; it meant being able to hand out princely tips when you left a restaurant. From the very start, Montand liked to show off his generosity. Naturally, he helped his family. Until the end of their days, his parents lived in the house he had bought them. He helped his sister Lydia. For the Mirtilons, who had looked after Autheuil for so long, he built a house on an adjacent property.

And like many others, he was always being asked for money. And always gave. His files bulged with thank-you letters. In May 1989 he decided to incorporate his talents. He would give half his post-tax earnings to selected charities. He studied records, deserving cases, projects. He was quite aware that he would be doing little to repair the world's injustices. "It's between me and me," he said.

> The hard thing in this profession is that you can only be understood by someone else in the same profession. Otherwise, feelings, reactions, and conflicts that come from deep inside you are seen as superficial whims. Everyone grows old, everyone knows what it means to grow old. But to grow old when your name is Romy Schneider, Simone Signoret, Isabelle Adjani, or Marilyn Monroe—nobody else knows what that's like. (It's easier for men: Paul Newman and Sean Connery have never stopped being handsome.) Everyone knows or thinks he knows that he is secure in his job. But we actors are permanently insecure, and our jobs are our lives. It is inevitable that in a high-living craft like ours everything seems to center on yourself.
>
> For example, my first contacts with Romy Schneider were tricky, and age worried her. We became really close when we began to work for Costa-Gavras. I then saw face-to-face not just the fabulous Romy Schneider the actress, but a real woman who spoke

to me frankly of her real complexes—she admitted to me that she considered herself humorless, a little bit stiff, too Germanic. Her distress touched me deeply.

But don't be deceived by the seeming intimacy you may see in a movie. In *Clair de femme,* for example, we had a very difficult scene, a mutual disrobing (rarely portrayed, because the absurd is always close to the surface in such scenes). Then we lay on top of each other. Maybe that seems erotic to audiences, but when you're shooting there are fifteen people milling around you. A crew member stands on the bed and holds you up with straps, because the camera is perched high behind your shoulder. "Careful, you're hiding her! Pull him, Marcel, pull him toward you!" Mystery and fantasy go up in smoke. You say, "I hope I'm not crushing you, sweetheart?" She shifts her breast a little to the side. A closeup of your hand traveling beneath the sheets. "Lower, bring your hand down! No, higher!" Believe me, if there's an exchange of warmth, affection, desire, it's before or after.

Getting actors to talk about one another can be frustrating. Either they carefully measure out mutual praise, or else they betray incestuous jealousy through some act of treachery. When Catherine Deneuve, a superstar if ever there was one, was brought together with Montand, it was in almost total secrecy (the Bahaman island chosen for *Le Sauvage* was isolated and remote). "At first," she said, "I believe he saw me as an elegant and rather useless blonde, a gold digger. He realized, though, that I'm friendly, very private, that you can trust me with a secret, and that I'm a good listener. Montand is an uncomfortable man to work with because he is totally committed, into it to the hilt. And because he wants to direct or at least codirect. It isn't that he wants to control things, no. It's his one-man-show background: it gives him his own directorial vision. It's exhausting, and it's touching. Still, I didn't feel I was being bossed around. Montand and Depardieu both attack a scene one notch above ground level. What astonished me was that Montand came to watch the rushes even on days he was not in them. He's a crazily realistic actor—fell in love if his character fell in love. He's an Italian, a man of the Mediterranean sun, and a comedian who's taken too seriously sometimes. He's unique in his genre, this terrific mixture of weightiness and lightness. And he has a remarkable sense of space and movement, a grace, something of the dancer in him, which you find in women but not often in men."

Gérard Depardieu agrees. He first met Montand when Sautet directed them both in *Vincent, François, Paul and the Others,* and he joined forces with him again (and with Deneuve) in *Choice of Arms.* There was an instant spark between the two men, like the current that flows between Papet and Daniel Auteuil throughout *Jean de Florette.* As soon as he encountered a talented young performer, Montand melted and took him under his wing. He also shared a certain similarity of origin and experience with Depardieu.

"We are both children of the streets," said Depardieu. "But Montand inherited a strong family structure, while in a way my folks were gypsies. . . . For me he was a kind of protector. He gave me not advice but shelter. I was struck by his fears, his uncertainties. I used to wonder, He's so good, why does he get into such states? Not star behavior at all, but a sort of anguish, combined with peasant cunning. The moment Montand enters a luxury hotel he looks around for the emergency exit. This is a poor man's reflex—the reflex of people used to moving about, to being on the road, to nothing having a fixed place. His way of working, well, you can't call it working; it's living thought, it's fear in action inside a man who is at once a landscape artist (that's the singer) and the wind (that's the actor), inside a man who feeds his fear the way you put logs onto a fire."

Anguish. Pierre Granier-Deferre emphatically agreed. "Anguish, in my opinion, is practically Montand's driving force. Because he ends up doing fantastic things simply by surmounting that anguish. I believe he is afraid of everything. Yes, everything. So he hides behind a barrage of silly, pleasant talk."[2]

This mask of relaxed high spirits—anyone who knows the Mediterranean coast will recognize it—is sometimes the best way of keeping your distance without showing contempt, condescension, or coldness. It was Montand's way. A solid build and irrepressible good humor hid secret reserves, wary mistrust, a bottomless sense of guilt.

> I get it from my mother, and from my Communist upbringing. You have to set an example, you have to be irreproachable, you have to be likable. How I've tried, and at what cost, to be liked at all times! This was the number one rule in music hall when I started out! Despite the gaps in my education and manners, the gods—or the devils or circumstances or fate—have given me this intangible mysterious thing, charisma. And I've spent my life torn between gratitude for receiving the gift and fear of betraying it—see my mother, right up there over my head?—by not using it properly or not enough.
>
> And then there's the myth of the "positive" hero. That's my

2. Quoted in Richard Cannavo and Henri Quiquéré, *Montand: Le Chant d'un homme* (Paris, 1981).

father. When I began to sing and try out steps, he said to me, "If I were you, son, I'd want to be able to dance on top of a bottle. . . ." I understood the metaphor perfectly. And I tried to do it.

If you believed the fan magazines, the guilty insomniac child hidden within Yves Montand should have been enjoying the sleep of the just. He was now popular beyond belief. When he was forty, American women had fallen in love with him; fifteen or twenty years later, he was not only shattering box-office records, but the women of France had voted him their number-one sex symbol. *France-Soir* magazine published an opinion poll in which 30 percent of the respondents said they would rather go on vacation with Montand (who never took a vacation!) than with a drove of illustrious rivals: Philippe Noiret (who polled 21 percent), Jean-Paul Belmondo (16 percent), Bernard Pivot (13 percent), Gérard Depardieu (10 percent), and Alain Delon (9 percent).

If they had only known! If they had known that their ideal French male was split right down the middle. In the glare of the lights he waved, glowed, smiled. But on the home front it was not all roses.

First of all, home had shrunk, and the family's ideological wounds were raw. And second, married life was no longer what it had been. It would be tempting to write that a crack appeared during Montand's forties, which widened to a chasm during his fifties. Chronologically, this might be accurate, but in fact it would be wrong, for "crack" and "chasm" imply an imminent break or rupture, and such a break was never seriously considered. On the contrary, Montand and Signoret rejected the possibility, in both words and deed. Despite their shouting matches—there is no other word for them—they clung fiercely to each other to the very end: not just until the death of one, for when one survives there is no end. If they ran each other ragged, it was not through indifference but through jealousy, dependency, solidarity. Through love.

After the Marilyn Monroe episode, little by little they regained their equilibrium, their sense of themselves. Not the fever of their beginnings, but a firmly anchored union, lit by affection, desire, happy reunions.

The 1970s were very different, and they might well be summed up in lines that Semprun slipped into *Z:*

"How is your wife?"

"She is well. We age differently."

While Montand soared and overflowed, stamping the screen with the image of a man ever more handsome, agile, warm, Signoret swiftly drifted downstream from the sunlit pastures where her course had begun. And because she was intelligent, proud, and courageous, because she was not just any faded star trying to patch up the illusion with pathetic artifices, she dared to take the opposite course: she smashed the mirror; she declined prematurely. Since she was getting old, she would help the process along, accentuating the damage rather than submitting passively or fighting back with no hope of victory.

Between the (almost) superb fifty-year-old of Melville's *L'Armée des ombres* (1969) and the blowsy old heroine of Mizrahi's *Madame Rosa* (1977) there were only eight years—and an abyss into which she not just fell but threw herself. "I've lived, I've aged, I've grown fat, and basically I've tried to make an asset of it," she commented serenely to *Le Monde* on June 12, 1973.

A powerful feminist wave—in France, a major cultural consequence of May '68—was sweeping the West, and although Signoret's attitude was praised and incorporated into the feminist arsenal, her behavior conceded nothing to the spirit of the times. For her it was a private matter. Looking back, Catherine Allégret feels that her mother simply went out to meet the dreaded enemy face-to-face: "Despite her grand declarations about age, I am not sure that deep down inside Mama didn't suffer very badly through it all. It was truly the sin of pride: I am Simone Signoret, and I will work with my wrinkles, my years, and so on."

And she managed it: René Allio's 1973 *Rude journée pour la reine* proved it; so did several television series. But there was a price.

> One evening it hit me. Suddenly I saw Simone with white hair. It had been turning salt and pepper, then suddenly it was white. We were at Autheuil; she was in an armchair—I still have it—wearing glasses and knitting. I looked at her for a long time. I wanted to take her in my arms and hold her (afterward, I was sorry I hadn't). She noticed. She was surprised, but pleased. I was absolutely staggered, I was in love. It was a moment of great tenderness and peace.
>
> It wasn't seeing her get old that I couldn't stand. It was her tendency to self-destruct, the methodical nature of that self-destruction. I told her so. I asked her what had happened to our so-called great love now that she was letting herself go. She smiled and said: "Yes, I'm letting myself go, yes, I find myself ugly, so what? Might as well accelerate as step on the brakes, no?"
>
> It wasn't easy for either of us to go from Casque d'Or to Mme Rosa. To be Casque d'Or's lover was simple, but it took a lot of love to love Mme Rosa. And after those difficult years she had a health problem (benign, but the operation was painful). She pulled herself together and began to take care of her husband again. I had

my old Simone back, in blue with a white collar, very beautiful, less cutting.

If you mention her name today, the picture that jumps to my mind isn't Casque d'Or or the fascinating stranger I met at the Colombe. It's this woman in white who couldn't watch television unless I gently held her hand. When I "feel" Simone, that's what I feel: that warm hand in mine.

In her early years, Signoret had never liked alcohol, although she was fond of champagne. Later, having become something of an honorary Englishwoman (in 1966 she even had the nerve to play Lady Macbeth in London in Shakespeare's native tongue, a disaster she recalled wryly in her memoirs), she had discovered the smoky bite of Scotch, the tang of malt whisky. Not that she was ever drunk or unsteady. It was a long, gentle process—an aperitif, red wine during the meal, Fernet-Branca bitters afterward "to help the digestion." Nothing spectacular. Just a magnificent actress on the road to Mme Rosa. Her intellectual sharpness, her interest in events, her incredible ability to listen, her verbal agility and gift of repartee, her flair for writing, her analytical strength were unimpaired. It was the woman who was damaged, along with the man to whom she was viscerally linked.

Was she seeking to hurt Montand, or herself, or both of them? She could not have chosen a deadlier weapon. Ivo Livi, offspring of a Tuscany in which wine was simply an exhalation of the hillsides, was baffled by this thirst, by this lapse of self-discipline. Piaf and Marilyn had both restrained their destructive tendencies for his sake, if only for the duration of their love. But whether it was for his sake or to hurt him, Simone Signoret was deteriorating, losing her looks, disintegrating. She was deliberately pushing where it hurt both of them most.

It was not just wrinkles, puffy eyes, a spreading waist. What was at stake was the very essence of their relationship, what made it live. It was the drama, both buried and in the open, of two inseparables. "They acted out *Who's Afraid of Virginia Woolf?* twenty-four hours a day," says Catherine Allégret with her usual frankness. At Autheuil, the Place Dauphine, and Saint-Paul-de-Vence, friends were dragged against their will, silent or evasive, into countless quarrels. Because the chimney was smoking. Because Upper Volta had changed governments. Because So-and-So was wrong. Or right. Because Simone intended to float on life like a cork in the ocean and Montand longed to master destiny. They pushed the game to the very limits. They exchanged notes and messages. Montand kept with him a note from Signoret in which she comments on the divorce of friends:

"Did you see this? They're finished. Things aren't going well between us, either, but it's fantastic that there's anything between us at all." On other occasions she warned him: Be careful, if you go on this way I'll divorce you.

What was the real meat of these exchanges, the heart of their antagonism? It is all summed up in this letter from Simone—she slipped it under Montand's door after a fight in 1978—a letter that the actor has recited to himself over and over ever since:

> You like to make me feel guilty because you are not happy. You are not happy because you're built that way. I have seen you enthusiastic, funny, anxious, passionate, jealous, angry. I have never seen you "happy." Happy to while away the time, happy to loaf, happy to listen, happy to share. You are the most selfish person I have ever known. You are the most selfish jealous unhappy and generous person I have ever known. You are the most arrogant, the least grateful toward those who love you, the cruelest toward those who love you. You are the sweetest toward people you do not give a damn for, the most wounding toward people who love you. You loathe yourself for being yoked to this too-old, too-fat "contemporary." Shake off the yoke. I won't love you any the less.

The letter was cruel but not unjust. Montand himself would admit it. In it, reproach, *la mise en demeure,* and false incitement to desertion all mean the opposite of what they say. No need to be an astute reader of minds to guess that "Shake off the yoke" calls out for the opposite. And gets it. As soon as they were together, Montand and Signoret clashed and quarreled. As soon as they were apart, they exchanged cables worthy of lovesick wooers. "I love you," Montand once cabled for no particular reason, because he wanted to, and three hours later came the telegraphed reply, "I love you, too."

No sooner were they together than the knives came out. Time after time at Autheuil, Montand rose from the table, slammed the door, and strode out into the garden to take deep breaths and wait for his anger to ebb. But he always came back. Time after time, with deadly aim, Simone would challenge him over a trifle, a detail. But after reading him his lesson she would praise her man to her friends. Alain Corneau, a privileged observer, insists that "intellectually, it was not at all a one-way street between them, as many people think. Often, Simone told me about great decisions in their life for which Montand had been responsible. She would say, 'You know, he felt it. With me it's not so simple, I have to think. But he reacted instinctively, and he was right. I just followed him.' She was very moving at such times, very little-girl, a groupie to the end." Anne Sinclair, a close friend of the couple, fills out the picture: "Yes, they fought all night long, but they never really sent each other packing. Simone regretted that she did not belong to the people, and Montand belonged to the people because he was endlessly generous. If he wasn't, what would have stopped him from shutting himself comfortably away on some fancy estate? Without him, Simone would have ended up as a Left Bank intellectual. Like everyone, he made mistakes, but he sensed things."

A scene in *Police Python 357* is particularly heartrending to those who know what happened during the shooting. Marc Ferrot, the cop played by Montand, agrees to help Thérèse, played by Simone, to kill herself (an invalid, married to the guilty man, she has decided to end it all). The crew was shooting on the banks of the Loire, and Simone was unable to play the scene. She was in her car, a Mercedes, a revolver in her hand. She was supposed to ask Montand to pull the trigger with her. But the words refused to come out. Corneau insisted, begged her. After a prolonged paralysis she took the plunge, with the desperation of a drowning person, ad-libbing a few words roughly corresponding to the script. It was the only take. Neither she nor her husband nor the director mentioned it again.

Strong characters, strong emotions. And stormy crossings. They did not really reach the far shore until the beginning of the 1980s. Scared by an attack of pancreatitis, she gave up alcohol overnight. She made sure that guests felt no need to abstain in her presence, but she stuck to her decision with the same determination she had brought to her earlier, self-destructive course.

They passed through painful stages on their way to final reconciliation. The point at which they realized that their sex life was fading. The point at which it seemed "more sensible" to have separate bedrooms—at first tearfully, then softened by tender good-nights, warm evenings watching television (Simone never missed an appearance, however fleeting, by any friend or partner, no matter how many years ago they had met).

With a blend of admiration and weariness, Montand observed the startling tribal instincts his wife cultivated and sharpened. On permanent alert, scrupulously checking on working relationships and plotting the course of wobbly ones (if she was wrong or behaved unfairly, she would be just as assiduous in admitting her mistake), Simone was the soul of a clan that served as her family and to which she tirelessly added.

It was a male clan. Although Simone had signed the famous "343 Manifesto," published in *Le Nouvel Observateur* on April 5, 1971, in which 343 women admitted to having had abortions, calling for legalization of what was already a fact of French life, in her heart she was no feminist, nor did she wear a yearning for sisterhood on her sleeve. On the contrary: a cynical observer might almost conclude she was a misogynist, much too conscious of women's power not to surround her nest with a sturdy, crowded circle of males. Little by little, the unwilling star, the actress who refused to manage her career sensibly, transformed herself into a matriarch enthroned in her salon, loquacious and attentive, devouring books, curious about everything and everyone, a great watcher of television, her mind constantly active, and obsessed with writing.

Montand watched this transformation with mixed feelings. Of course, he liked the constant flow of friends, righteous causes hammered out by the fireside, heated arguments. But there was a disequilibrium in the seeming harmony. The friends were Simone's friends. And even when they became his own dearest friends—like Chris Marker and Jorge Semprun—they came to him via Simone. When his wife said, "Better ask the singer about that one!" he could barely hide his irritation: he was, of course, aware of his acknowledged authority in the household, yet while he had methodically struggled through *Salammbô, Les Cloches de Bâle, La Condition humaine,* a lot of Maupassant, and nearly all of Sartre's literary output, he was and would always be the dunce of the class. He did not feel at home at home. He felt he had been dispossessed. This feeling intensified when Signoret, dissatisfied with the rough transcript of interviews she had granted the writer Maurice Pons, decided to write her own memoirs. *Nostalgia Isn't What It Used to Be* was published in 1976. For five or six years before that, Simone scribbled relentlessly, experimenting with small-scale projects—short stories, recollections of her brothers, of Saint-Gildas, in Brittany, where the war caught up with her family—and Montand was the first to see these attempts. Both proud and jealous, he encouraged her. He liked to say that it was largely thanks to him that she ventured onto this new terrain, and he went on loyally encouraging her when she put down not only her own life story but large slices of their shared itinerary.

Nostalgia was a legitimate success. Signoret was not just witty and gifted, with an innate feel for effective narrative, but a real writer. Montand was delighted, yet he could not avoid the disturbing thought that this story that so fascinated readers—and that now belonged to its narrator—was also, and sometimes primarily, his own.

" 'Dispossessed' is the word," says Semprun. "Yves was indeed dispossessed when Simone became the couple's official historian, the exclusive owner of the legend. She tacitly claimed this status for herself. When, in turn, I wrote my own book about them, and showed her the manuscript, she asked me to make certain corrections, and it was obvious to me that she, in her turn, felt dispossessed."

Mutual loyalty, total mutual trust, unbreakable bonds—and continual conflict for ten long years, which did nothing to diminish their need for each other. Montand more or less openly admitted it during a 1972 interview:

> "You've been married twenty years?"
> "Twenty-three."
> " 'When you are old and gray and full of sleep . . .' "
> "A pretty thought. But it's not always a picnic."
> "What isn't a picnic? The fact that you're both actors?"
> "Not at all. But as you get older, well, I believe you feel the need, not for more freedom, because both of us have always been free, and if we decided to stick together it's because we like to be together, but what I'd call the need not to get on each other's nerves. I mean that if she wants to get up at three to write, she gets up at three, and if I want to go to bed at nine, I go to bed at nine."
> "Has respect for each other's freedom forced you to make sacrifices?"
> "No. What we've junked is what people go on calling love, but which is really just a sense of ownership. Once you've taken the machinery apart and realized that it's no longer love with a capital "L" but a kind of habit of tenderness, the relationship becomes much simpler."[3]

Simpler? Up to a point. What Montand did not admit—and what he could barely acknowledge after Signoret's death, so strong was his determination to honor the memory of the woman of his life—is that despite everything, he was suffocating.

"Ah! My oldest one is back. . . ." Beginning around the mid-1960s, Simone Signoret often spoke of her husband as if he were a teenager under her protection, someone whose impatience and lapses she tolerated. It was a maternal way of speaking, a maternal warmth, a maternal indulgence, a maternal stranglehold. Semprun remembers her saying, "Montand? He's like a playboy on the Riviera!" and insists that the words were uttered lightly. The rule the couple now lived by stipulated that each was free in his movements and moods (but, of course, the scales are never equal in such matters), provided neither one exposed the other to publicity or ridicule. It mattered little to Simone that her husband was vulnerable to the charms of Karin Schubert, the queen of Spain in *La Folie des grandeurs.*

3. Interview with Catherine Laporte, *Elle,* October 30, 1972.

But the Livis joined forces to sue *France-Dimanche* after it published a fake interview on May 25, 1971, under the headline, "My Wife Allows Me to Be Unfaithful Sometimes" and ran a topless photo of the German actress alongside one of Simone biting her nails. The magazine was fined 30,000 francs and forced to publish a retraction.

Was this the reaction of a couple turned respectable? Certainly not. It was a question of pride and of love. What had hurt Simone most in the Marilyn Monroe scandal had been not the moral violation but the public humiliation. Montand was therefore careful to keep his escapades private (the *France-Dimanche* incident being the exception that proved the rule), because guilt was as destructive to him as frustration, because it was all-important to him not to hurt Signoret. The playboy was discreet and secretive; he sought no lasting relationship.

But it was also true that Montand, who had had neither the courage nor the time when he was younger, was now feeling his oats. He was breaking loose like a young man—breaking loose from a family routine that fettered him, from a marital bond that had turned bittersweet. He no longer fought temptation: he looked for or grabbed every opportunity with something like a glutton's delight. The summer of his fifty-third year was, he said, a dazzling one, "like an expiring nova."

Was all this just a seven-year itch? Perhaps. But Catherine Deneuve is probably right, too, when she says that Montand had had an excessively somber view of life thrust upon him—by the poverty of his origins, by his ideological upbringing, by his unique talent, by his environment, by the acquired or innate trait that had made him a loner.

Montand's most important safety valve through these complex years was neither furtive pleasures nor exotic escapades. His real secret life was poker. He had always played, of course, for matchsticks or for tiny stakes. But now it became something else. This time he was playing with the grownups, with professionals, or with amateurs who might just as well have been pros.

He entered a fellowship dedicated to a shared passion. There were some figures from the entertainment world, but mostly they were people he would not normally have mingled with: industrialists, executives, the director of a radio station, a publisher. "I was getting into bad company," he explained. Through successive siftings over the years, the group finally came down to six or eight addicts who met three or four times a week, the first session on Tuesday and the last, when they stopped the bank, on Sunday.

As conscientious practitioners, these gentlemen avoided marathon sessions, although they sometimes went on when it might have been cavalier of the loser of the evening to put the cards away too soon. This was Montand's first lesson: a strong player is an ascetic—the absolute opposite of César in Sautet's movie, with feverish, smoke-reddened eyes slitted with fatigue. They would meet in one's or another's apartment toward late afternoon, play for two hours, dine well but lightly, then play again until midnight. The mood at dinner would be jovial. Back at the card table, it was still polite, but there was no more joking. There was no dress code. Appearances were dictated more by individual superstition (a player wearing a certain jacket when he won tended to wear it again the next time) than by convention.

The sums that changed hands each week could be high. But Montand was no Rudolph Valentino or Jules Berry, two legendary movie-star gamblers. He was not a man who would leave his shirt on the casino floor. (Besides, roulette did not interest him; what he liked about poker was that you were responsible for the course of events, the cards being merely a pretext.) He drew on his recording royalties, and on them alone, to gamble.

He learned patiently; in other words, he lost for a long time. He learned that losses are cumulative and follow a geometrical progression, that when things go badly the urge to double, to raise the stakes, is enormous, and fatal nine times out of ten. He saw that something within him—an imperceptible movement of the body, a too-obvious casualness, excessive stiffness—invariably betrayed a lie or a bluff, even when he believed himself to be under perfect control. It cost him months, years, perhaps, and a lot of money. But he learned. "One day," said Jean-Louis Livi, "he said to me, 'That's it, I believe I can play, no more losing for me.' And, indeed, he turned things around. Which was what he had been after." Bob Castella, keeper of the bank, sighs and says, "Yes, in the long run we didn't do too badly." By the end of the 1960s, he was just in the black.

The suspense had been endless. Apart from the sporting challenge, the pleasure of the joust, it is likely that Simone Signoret's husband was glad to be able to allow himself a major thrill. Here, too, Montand the gambler was satisfying his need to break loose. This said, Simone neither opposed nor tried to restrain her husband's poker playing. It was part of the unspoken contract: he'd go off to play, and she, with her guests at Autheuil, would continue the uninterrupted conversation that had become her whole life. Semprun analyzes her position in all this in the following way: "Simone never helped Yves financially; her relationship with money was perverse, at once reckless and guilty. She brought the pessimism of the persecuted to the subject, perhaps remembering the Jewish girl with no papers in occupied Paris. To her, money possessed the irresistible power to corrupt. When my screenplays started to earn me money, she warned me very seriously. I had to explain to her that in my family we had been living with money for generations."

Mingling with people far removed from his usual circle also appealed to Montand. He was surprised (and intrigued) by the casual way in which top industrialists treated politicians, surprised (and curious) to hear, say, that Boussac was finished, that it took half the time to produce a ton of steel in Japan that it did in France. One evening, he was introduced to a newcomer named Wado. Too reserved to use a nickname clearly intended only for close friends, he learned that the man's real name was Edouard-Jean Empain, a baron of industry and the heir of illustrious iron manufacturers, who was then at the head of a colossal and diversified empire that ranged from highway construction to Pluton missiles. Wado was a gentle man, a timid player at first, but he grew bolder. And once the game was over, he, too, issued predictions that the singer-actor heard with interest: "No, Concorde will never be profitable," and so forth. On January 23, 1978, Edouard-Jean Empain was kidnapped from his home. Mutilated, imprisoned under atrocious conditions ("It was *The Confession,*" he later told Montand), he was not released until two months later. He emerged from the ordeal not only in shock—that was natural—but viewing the world with a piercing, disturbing, detached gaze. The public discovered the loneliness, sincerity, and bewilderment of a man in whom the Paris jet set had seen only a fabulously wealthy playboy. Montand was very moved by the horror that had struck Wado (his kidnappers, common criminals, had lopped off one of his forefingers to prove they held him).

As Montand drew closer to Empain, he realized that Wado had no illusions about his birth or his wealth. But the incident had consequences for the baron's poker partners. Logically enough, the police explored every possibility, including that of an unpaid poker debt. Soon the capital buzzed with stories of Montand's nights of debauchery with his capitalist cronies. Irritated, he agreed to be interviewed on television over Europe 1. "This is my private life," he said. "I played with Wado, not Baron Empain. I will not be voting on the right at the next elections, simply because it's sad to live for money alone." He added that his behavior was no more immoral than that of a family man spending part of his budget on the soccer lottery, nor that of the state that grew rich from the lottery. In a magazine interview he was asked, "Do you not consider that your fame, and the fact that you are admired and liked, confer moral responsibilities on you?" "You sound just like Simone," he retorted. "I always tell her that maybe

I do have a certain responsibility—but I also want to live like a man, with my own drives and my own faults."[4]

And more private still were the tears that sometimes rose to his eyes when, as night fell, he left Autheuil, where Simone was leading her own life, and sped toward Paris to drown his sorrows.

> In the second half of the 1970s (about the time of *Madame Rosa*), poker was mainly an escape. I used to leave in sadness, a lump in my throat. It lasted five or ten minutes, sometimes until the moment I sat down to play, and then the game took over, and so did I.
>
> You can't play with people you really like, with a friend who has money difficulties and who is trying to recoup. You can't, it's horrible. And that's what gives poker its cruel and exciting appeal. You have to stay cool. You may want to kill a big winner whose luck is getting on your nerves, you may want to beat him, but you mustn't ever try, you mustn't fight against the big winner. Better to learn how to lose, to lose as little as possible when luck's against you, and to win the jackpot when you're in luck. That's a real poker player. Learning to lose also teaches you how to win without holding big cards, with a low hand. And, contrary to what people believe, with a minimum of bluff. Bluff is a long-term operation based on psychology, attrition, good or bad luck. And last-minute bluff is always suicidal. The essential, main challenge is to diversify your playing, to become relatively unpredictable . . . if that's possible.
>
> I was a player, not a gambler. The two are quite different. A gambler is a sick man, addicted to the game. After a time he no longer knows whether he is winning or losing; what counts for him is the thrill. It's a blend of sadism and masochism. At the point where I'd throw down my cards, the gambler would keep going. He wants an eight, so he goes for it, even if his chances are mathematically slim. Whereas what attracts me is the need to hold yourself back. (I'm speaking of the pure game, not the kind of stag evenings marked by jokes and good food.) The best moment is when it all begins. At that moment, everything can happen. . . .
>
> Poker was more or less compatible with my profession. When I was shooting *Le Cercle rouge,* in which I had to look beaten up, no problem. But for *César et Rosalie,* I felt guilty and played only one night a week.

4. Interview with Gilbert Salachas, *Télérama,* April 30, 1980.

And when I decided to sing again, I stopped altogether. Poker and concerts absolutely do not mix.

Montand had not lost his voice. Thanks to a 1974 benefit for the Chileans, thanks to television appearances, and thanks above all to the loyal, vociferous, smoky, poetic virtuosity of Jean-Christophe Averty, with whom he made four television shows—"Happy New Yves" (January 1, 1965), "Montand chante Prévert" (October 19, 1968), "Montand de mon temps" (March 5, 1974), and "Montand d'aujourd'hui" (May 7, 1980)—Montand stayed before the public eye. ("Averty," he said, "was the great trailblazer, the pioneer. . . . He was sweet, tender, a born sufferer who could not bear to see television go down the tubes.")[5]

Thus he dabbled for a whole decade, when suddenly the music bug bit him again. "It was at Autheuil," says Semprun. "He took a top hat out of a closet. He put it on and strolled around in it. Suddenly, in the mirror on the door separating his bedroom from the bathroom, Montand saw his own reflection. Instinctively, not yet thinking of anything, he did a couple of dance steps. Not much, a step or two, a wave of the arm, a bow, and a sweep of the top hat. He straightened up, his heart racing, and decided to go back to the stage."[6]

With his fiftieth birthday behind him, Montand rediscovered the terror and the joy of facing an audience. He had exorcised Montand the singer with a light heart. But when he had the choice—as a younger man he did not—he backed toward the precipice. He understood Jacques Brel, who vomited every night before the curtain went up. Running across Gilbert Bécaud during a tour in Nîmes, he was baffled by the performer's jubilation at "getting out there" again, and he had been astounded when Maurice Chevalier had visited his dressing room in 1968 and, hopelessly homesick, said over and over again, "How fabulous, how fabulous to be in front of the people again." No, for Montand to take the plunge again, cunning was needed; he had to tame his panic, tell himself yes, then no, then yes again; he had to drag poor Bob through every twist and turn of the cruel labyrinth.

He never did discover what had motivated him. He recorded "Rose de Picardie" almost by accident, then surprised himself whistling it in the bathtub. But viewing the rushes of *Choice of Arms* during a sequence in which his body was supposed to be utterly relaxed, he was shaken by the lag between the energy he thought he had put out and the obvious failure

5. Ibid.

6. Jorge Semprun, *Montand: La Vie continue* (Paris, 1983).

of the machine to keep up with his intentions. Perhaps precisely because of such surprises, he went ahead.

A show is quite different from a screenplay. Everyone has ideas for how movies should begin, but the rest rarely follows, and the beautiful initial image may slip away like so much sand. In putting together a concert, on the other hand, the opening establishes the mood and dictates what follows. Montand could see just how to begin. He even saw a top hat and cane under two spotlights on an empty stage. And he could already hear "Malgré moi," a short poem Prévert had given him fifteen years earlier that he discovered in a vest pocket:

> Embauché malgré moi dans l'usine à idées
> j'ai refusé de pointer.
> Mobilisé de même dans l'armée des idées
> j'ai déserté.
> Je n'ai jamais compris grand-chose
> ni petite chose
> il y a autre chose.
> Autre chose c'est ce que j'aime qui me plaît
> et que je fais.
>
> [Hired against my will by the factory of ideas
> I refused to punch in.
> Drafted against my will in the army of ideas
> I deserted.
> I never understood the big things
> or even little things
> just other things.
> Other things mean that what I like is what I
> like doing
> and what I do.]

Montand's grand return in 1981–82 is impossible to describe, so much did past and present mingle, so strong was the memory it left in France and abroad. From October 7, 1981, to January 3, 1982, the Olympia was under permanent siege. Well before the first night, 180,000 people had fought for and purchased every single seat. And it was the same at every one of the forty-eight out-of-town appearances following the Paris engagement.

Catherine Allégret gave up her own commitments. She designed the program and the record jacket, sorted mail, channeled calls, arranged interviews. Everyone in the clan, the family group, has kept his own talismanic memory of the tour. Montand's agent, Charley Marouani, recalls his anger in Marseilles when he noticed that the bleachers at the back of the huge tent were uncomfortable. Upholster them, he said. But the budget? Damn the budget; he would pay. But it was already May 1, an official French holiday. Damn May 1! Find an upholsterer. Finally, they unearthed an Armenian dealer who put together a crew and agreed to work illegally. The spectators in the back rows were a little more comfortable. A question of respect.

For Bob Castella, the amazement was the delirious welcome Japanese audiences gave in giant auditoriums, watching in inscrutable silence one minute and then erupting in thunderous, hot-blooded emotion the next. For Pierre Boutillier, seated next to Daniel Gélin at the Olympia premiere, the great moment was his neighbor's tears when Montand began "Les Feuilles mortes," or a year later in San Francisco, on October 13, 1982, when the whole theater sang "Happy Birthday" in Montand's honor.

Jorge Semprun began the book he dedicated to his friend with the scene he most vividly recalled from the international tour. In Rio on August 31, 1982, in Maracanazhino Stadium, a covered arena in which twenty thousand spectators were packed, the acoustic specialists had managed to kill the echo by spreading ten thousand empty potato sacks on the concrete stands. Before the Brazilians—of whom not many could have understood French—Montand sang Baudelaire's "Les Bijoux," and the enormous crowd, hanging on every note, every sigh, listened with religious intensity. Catherine Allégret squeezed Jorge's hand and whispered, "The man is crazy!"

But if Montand was asked to pick out one evening (not only from this latest adventure, but also, perhaps, from his entire career), he did not hesitate: on Tuesday, September 8, 1982, New York's Metropolitan Opera House belonged to him. In ninety-eight years the shrine of world opera had never deviated from its classical vocation. Montand was the exception. Clive Barnes, writing in the New York *Post,* justified the breach in the following terms: "He is a classical artist gifted with his own style and an innate grace who has as much right to perform at the Met as Placido Domingo."

Simone Signoret, her eyesight beginning to fail, crossed the Atlantic for the occasion. She waited until the lights dimmed in the vast auditorium (scalped tickets had fetched as much as $120) before threading her way to her place. The ruse did not work. Applause broke out; the audience rose to its feet and applauded Casque d'Or and Alice Aisgill for fully five minutes. Catherine Allégret was overwhelmed, but she spared a thought for Montand waiting in the wings, petrified: "My God, he'll never be able to come on now, how can he. . . ." He came on. And it was astounding.

The standing ovation after the curtain went on and on and on. Later he would swear that when the audience finally let him begin the concert his knees were knocking together and he was terrified that people would see his trouser legs shaking. All the same, no one, not even his musicians, noticed.

What new source of fear could he possibly find now?

Chapter 17

By the mid-1980s, magazines, radio, and television were clamoring for words from Montand the actor, now transformed into Montand the news item. Nothing was more irritating to the public figure he had become than hearing that he had suddenly gone into politics.

"I've been in politics for forty years," he would growl. As this book has shown, such was indeed the case. But it was also true that after some ten years as a Communist fellow traveler, after another decade of silent withdrawal from political involvement, and then after the great family quarrel, his post-1968 political statements had been expressed largely through his movie roles (*Z, The Confession, State of Siege*). In the mid-1970s, however, a new Montand had emerged—the former Communist and fighter for human rights who now excoriated dictatorships on both left and right. The song that symbolized this period was without a doubt "Casse-têtes." This was the era of the Montand who sang for Chilean refugees, who joined a delegation to Madrid in 1975 alongside people like Foucault, Debray, Lacouture, and Costa-Gavras in an attempt to save the lives of eleven condemned men. Henceforth his name would be associated with Argentine torture victims, Turkish labor leaders, Soviet psychiatric-hospital inmates, and Czechoslovak intellectuals.

Since the publication in 1974 of *The Gulag Archipelago,* the "Stalingrad syndrome" that had so long molded Montand's thinking had been supplanted by the "Solzhenitsyn syndrome." At a time when French Communists were denouncing anti-Soviet activities and left-wing intellectuals were attacking the banned author, Montand found in Solzhenitsyn's towering, laborious reconstruction of the gulag tragedy the power of a truth too long masked by state lies. By demonstrating the terror that lay at the heart of the system, Solzhenitsyn kicked away the foundations from under the apologies for Communist evolution. Montand deduced from his reading of *Archipelago* not so much the revelation of its horror as the conviction that Communism could never be amended. The anti-Stalinist became an anti-Communist.

Montand drew nourishment from the antitotalitarian philosophy that prized individual rights above all else, that considered the state based on the rule of law to be the supreme good. He had grown wary of universalist theories, of fine-tuned programs that claimed to be preparing the ground for radiant morrows (always, of course, for future generations). He rejected any political program whose self-declared goal was human happiness, for he knew that such grandiose ambitions (and such a convenient excuse) led straight to the camps of the Kolyma. If Citizen Montand still wanted to believe in a better world, he adopted systematic doubt as his strategy, and these words of F. Scott Fitzgerald as his motto: "We have to understand that things are hopeless, and nevertheless be resolved to change them."

From 1975 on, along with Simone Signoret and Jorge Semprun, he poured most of his political energies into support for the struggle of the dissidents in Eastern Europe (he was, for example, a member of the committee for the release of the Soviet mathematician Leonid Plyutch). And he pulled no punches with the Party. On December 14, 1976, he made the first of a series of angry assaults whose outspoken tone and vehement language were an emphatic break from the patient and professorial tone of most broadcast political debate. That morning, from the studios of Europe 1, he replied to remarks made during a television debate the night before by the Communist leader Jean Kanapa following a screening of *The Confession.*

To mark that occasion, the regulars in the "trailer" had pulled their chairs in a tight circle around the television set. Besides Montand and Signoret, all the usual friends were there: Semprun and Costa-Gavras and their wives, as well as Chris Marker. All of them leapt in their seats when Kanapa "admitted" that *The Confession* was a heartrending work, authentic down to its last frame, and that the Communists themselves should have made the movie. Everyone present remembered the contemptuous review in *L'Humanité* six years earlier. Yet here was the French Communist Party's leading theoretician attempting to put on a benevolent public face, alleging that his party had been ignorant of the horrors perpetrated on the other side of the Iron Curtain.

On the air the next morning, Montand gave free rein to his anger: "It is especially hard for me to hear men of my generation—particularly those who head the Party machine—claim that they did not know. . . . They should come clean and say, Yes, we were stupid; worse, we were dangerous—dangerous and stupid." Was Montand thinking of Sartre's reference to the "cretin" Kanapa ("You need more than one swallow to make a summer, and more than one Kanapa to dishonor a party")?

Montand was determined to let it be known that the London case was not just a matter of history. "In Czechoslovakia today," he said, "there is still institutionalized informing, there are still psychiatric hospitals where hundreds of people are incarcerated and where perfectly healthy human beings are reduced to eating their own excrement."

To his brother Julien (with whom he now communicated only by letter), to his sister, and to the friends who condemned him for lashing out at the Party just as it was seeking a metamorphosis, Montand replied with a letter pulsating with anger, a letter dashed off in one sitting, with no care for grammatical niceties. Dated January 15, 1977, it attests to the exact state of Citizen Montand's feelings:

> What gives you the right to go on preaching to us? What the hell do you mean when you say, more or less, "We made a mistake and we admitted it, so you must go on believing in us"? (What a feat! What guts!) Just who the hell do you think you are?
>
> Whom should we believe? I'll leave that to the believers. . . . Which doesn't automatically make me strong. I am as weak, as weaponless, as ridiculous, and as pitiful as the meanest citizen of this planet, yet I still fight to remain clearheaded and to remember among other things that there is no big daddy in the sky, that there never was, that there never can be. . . . Enough! We swallowed it all in the name of "discipline," of "solidarity," in the name of denying the enemy ammunition. Just carry out orders, they said. And they CARRIED OUT THE ORDERS! And what do you say to that? "So sorry, we didn't know. . . ." Fine! (Forgive me, though, but you had to be extraordinarily blind and deaf, and assholes too, didn't you? But the worst thing is, you didn't *want* to hear! And all the pious roses in the world can't cover your horrible stench!)
>
> Someone had to take a stand. So I did.
>
> And I took that stand against you, my family and friends, and I've taken it for the last twenty years! And for the last twenty years I, along with many others, have committed the crime of being right before it was time. But tell me what my crime really was! And tell me what you have done! Nothing! Oh yes, I'm sorry—more preaching! Taking a stand meant having the courage to make *The Confession* in spite of you and in spite of the ties that bound us. . . . And what was your reaction? "Insulted" yet again by your own

> brother, you reacted with the base instincts of a born follower: you dragged the movie, the director, and the actor along with it through the Stalinist shit heap! Yes, shit heap! Then, five years later, the Party says, "It's right and proper to show this movie: it's faithful to the book." So does that mean we're no longer scum? After an about-face like that don't we have the right to expect (not apologies, I wouldn't dream of asking so much) but perhaps a little humility, a little human warmth, a little shame? Not a chance. . . . You simply preach another sermon!

Montand hurled the words at the page, just the way he spoke: a raging torrent that washed away the memory of a whole life, former noble commitments, dead illusions, trampled hopes. The surprising, startling vehemence of his public utterances welled from this deep personal wound, from the irresistible need to prove to his family that it was not he who had weakened, that, on the contrary, it was he who had maintained fealty to the ideals of justice and freedom. When he apostrophized the Communists, Montand was also addressing one specific Communist: his brother Julien. It was Julien who stuck stubbornly to his course in spite of the historical tide overtaking him and threatening to sweep him away.

The fratricidal duel over their father's spiritual heritage came into the open in the autumn of 1977. Franz-Olivier Giesbert of *Le Nouvel Observateur* asked Montand how he had become a fellow traveler of the Party. "My background," replied the artist. "In a way, I was a Communist from birth." He added, speaking of his father, "Politically, he was really a Socialist, but a unitary Socialist." Although incomplete, the definition was not inaccurate: like all Communists, Giovanni Livi had, indeed, been a Socialist before joining the Communist Party. In the next issue of *Le Nouvel Observateur,* Julien Livi published a clarification, reminding "Monsieur Yves Montand" that "Father was one of those who actively contributed to the foundation of the Italian Communist Party." Then he added a sentence that infuriated Montand: "Until his death, and Yves Montand should at least be decent enough not to conceal it, he remained loyal to the generous ideal that had shaped his whole life."

This public exchange sealed the family break. Henceforth, the passion of their rival claims came close to hatred. Three days after the interview in *Le Nouvel Observateur,* the Union of the Left, the association of left-wing parties cobbled together for election-fighting purposes, blew to bits. By September 22, 1977, the break between France's Socialists and Communists was inevitable. Within this context, to a Party member as orthodox as Julien Livi, the association of Giovanni and the epithet "Socialist" was utterly unacceptable.

The struggle between brothers now led to another consequence, partly personal, partly professional. Jean-Louis Livi, Julien's son and Montand's movie agent, decided to stop representing his uncle. The letter Montand sent him at this time reveals the depth of his pain:

Jean-Louis,

Clearly, caught as you are between an uncle who at the age of fifty-six presumes to express his personal opinion (which nobody has to share) in a magazine, and a father four years older who takes him severely to task in the same magazine, calling him "Monsieur Yves Montand," your position as representative of the said uncle is difficult.

I suppose it always has been, and I admire you for having filled it for so long.

I admire you even more if, as your father claims, you have always shared his opinions concerning me; for in that case you must have suffered indeed in 1969 when conducting negotiations for the shooting of *The Confession,* most of whose participants were clients of your agency.

I had been planning one day to give you a long account of my family memories, but there's no longer any need. Hold on to the memory of your childhood. I'll hold on to mine, to the memory of my teens, my youth, my manhood. Of Papa (whom we never called "Father"), I hold on to the memory I hope many sons will hold of their fathers. And I will continue to consider amazing (as well as ignoble, insulting, and plain stupid) the medal for good filial conduct your father awarded himself in his public clarification—in which he has the nerve to tell me to be decent to a dead man, when that dead man is the man I loved most of all in the world.

It's true, of course, that the term "unitary Socialist" has become obscene since last September. And that it was vital for the PEDIGREE of a hard-line Stalinist to be restored in the columns of the same paper in which his young brother had uttered such a filthy term.

How pathetic.
MONTAND

It was all out. The family rift was permanent. It radically affected Montand's future political course.

* * *

All over the world, Socialist models were crumbling into horror or absurdity. China buried its Great Helmsman beneath a mountain of honeyed tributes, while the victims of his Cultural Revolution numbered in the millions. "Liberated" Saigon was instantly and brutally "normalized." The groans of a martyred people rose from Khmer Rouge Cambodia. The great collapse of Marxism was indeed the collapse of a messianic faith. Hell was no longer only other people. Alongside his friend Semprun, Montand was now fiercely intent on dismantling totalitarianism.

With Graham Greene and Arthur Miller, Montand helped found the International Support Committee for the Czech signers of the charter adopted on January 1, 1977, most of whom were hounded by the police. The three designated spokesmen of Charter 77 were Jan Patocka, Jiri Hajek, and Václav Havel. In October 1978, Montand read a statement by Havel at the Mutualité conference center in Paris: "The present regime in Czechoslovakia, enmeshed in its lies, must continue to falsify to survive. It falsifies past, present, and future. It claims that its omnipresent and all-powerful police apparatus does not exist. . . . Since the regime in fact represses people's very lives, every demonstration of a simple human desire becomes a political act. . . . That is what it means to be a dissident, and I stress the fact that this word, invented in the West, defines our situation only inadequately. It is not a profession, even though one may devote twenty-four hours a day to it. It is quite simply an existential attitude."

> When I went to Prague in January 1990 to hand the Jan Palach prize to the students of the city at the request of the Charter 77 Support Committee, there were many images jostling inside my head. The Russian tanks in Prague in 1968, the filming of *The Confession,* the meetings and rallies to support Václav Havel and his friends. And here I was now with President Havel on that vast square, black with thousands of students! I was truly glad to be saying a few words to them, to be invoking the old dream of a greater Europe, founded on a common cultural heritage of democracy and freedom. Simone had been gone for more than four years, but I felt her at my side. She was still there when I went to put flowers on the grave of the student who burned himself to death to protest the Soviet invasion. What better measure could there be of the way history had reversed itself? A few days earlier, the square had still been called Red Army Square; now it bore Jan Palach's name. I was so moved that Simone's presence at my side was a comfort. I thought of the battles we had waged together; I thought of all those young people arrested and

imprisoned after the Prague spring; I thought of my father and was sure that wherever he was, he would be proud of me.

The actor turned human-rights activist could not be accused of aiming only at targets on the left. He was conspicuous outside the Argentine embassy in March 1980, for example, calling for news of the "disappeared" and for the release of the pianist Estrella, and with Simone Signoret in 1978, demanding a boycott of the World Cup soccer tournament—scheduled, of course, for Argentina. But throughout this period, Montand stayed away from French political debate. For him, the election of Socialist François Mitterrand to the presidency did not automatically represent a passage from darkness to light (though he had voted for him).

At dawn on December 13, 1981, Poland awoke to war. Tanks patrolled the streets of the major cities, the trade union Solidarity was outlawed, activists were rounded up before breakfast, and martial law was decreed. General Jaruszelsky was hoping that his military coup, supported by Russia, could neutralize the open rebellion of civil society against the Party and the state. That Sunday—two months to the day since his return to the Olympia—Montand was giving a matinee performance. For half a year, he had passionately followed the efforts of Lech Walesa and his associates to set up an independent trade union in a Communist country; a few weeks later, he had welcomed the leader of Solidarnosc, accompanied by the French Communist trade-union leader Edmond Maire, in his dressing room after the show. Jaruszelsky's putsch was a blow to his heart.

Many left-wing intellectuals considered the French government's initial reaction a disgrace. Foreign Minister Claude Cheysson put his foot in his mouth with a comment he would later regret: "This is an internal Polish matter. . . . Naturally we will do nothing." Prime Minister Pierre Mauroy confirmed that his government rejected "any interference in Polish affairs." Two distinguished teachers at the Collège de France, Pierre Bourdieu and Michel Foucault, launched a petition denouncing the government's caution. Montand and Signoret at once added their signatures to the statement, beside those of Guy Bedos, Patrice Chéreau, Marguerite Duras, Costa-Gavras, Bernard Kouchner, Claude Mauriac, Claude Sautet, and Jorge Semprun.

On the morning of Wednesday, December 16, Foucault and Montand were invited to explain their move over Europe 1. The actor read out the manifesto written by Bourdieu and Foucault: "By affirming, against the dictates of morality and truth, that the situation in Poland concerns only the Poles, are France's Socialist leaders not granting more importance to their domestic alliances than to the assistance due every nation in danger? Are good relations with the [French] Communist Party of more importance to them than the crushing of a workers' movement beneath a military jackboot?" After Foucault had spoken, the actor expressed his sorrow, and then he exploded, his voice choked with anger: "They have asked for free elections. Free elections! The most elementary of things." Almost more than the event itself, Montand's cry of rage sent shudders through the political establishment. A motorcyclist was dispatched from the Elysée Palace, the President's residence, to pick up a tape of the broadcast. Public opinion was overwhelmingly in favor of Solidarnosc: Socialist headquarters was inundated with hundreds of calls and letters from militants seeking a clarification of the Socialist position.

That same day, after the weekly cabinet meeting, President Mitterrand issued a statement in which he altered his sights and squarely condemned the Polish army's coup. But at the meeting, behind locked doors, Mitterrand vented his anger at the actions taken by these intellectuals, always readier to criticize than to close ranks. He was particularly harsh about Montand: "A right-wing anarchist! Did anyone bother to protest when General Evren's military government imprisoned Turkish democrats and trade unionists? For a lot of people, Poland is a pretext for domestic agitation."[1] The Bourdieu-Foucault petition had become the Montand appeal.

In the days that followed, Minister of Culture Jack Lang (who had called the signatories "clowns") in his turn organized an official evening of protest against Jaruszelsky. The initial blunder was atoned for, but the episode meant that a gap had appeared between the Socialist government and a large section of the Socialist intelligentsia. Montand the entertainer continued to entertain, but he did not forget Poland. At the end of his show at the Olympia every night, a huge banner bearing the word "Solidarnosc" was unfurled over the stage. He wore the insignia of the Polish union in his buttonhole—a tiny gesture, perhaps, but essential if memories were to be kept alive. On December 28 he sent a big check to the Solidarity Coordination Committee. Four days later, on France-Inter radio, he attacked the secretary general of the French Communist Party: "As for M. Marchais, who accuses us of being men of the phony left, he can screw himself!" And in February he proved that his indignation was not selective when he signed a declaration of support for Turkish trade unionists who had been sentenced to death.

With hundreds of congratulatory letters reaching the Place Dauphine, expressions of support coming in from all sides, and an avalanche of favorable press comment, Montand was astounded by the impact of the

1. Quoted in Pierre Favier and Michel Martin-Roland, *La Décennie Mitterrand* (Paris, 1990).

stand he had taken. He was no longer just a face on the screen, a figure on the stage. He was an effective spokesman. Henceforth, it was his own message he intended to disseminate.

The show and the world tour that followed kept Montand out of the public arena until the middle of 1983. During those eighteen months, as "Les Feuilles mortes" winged its way from Rio to Tokyo, French political life took a significant turn. Strangled by the economic constraints it had promised to shake off, the Socialist government had been forced to adopt a policy of austerity. Prices and salaries were temporarily frozen, and an electorate that had voted for a Socialist dawn now had to tighten its belt. President Mitterrand promised effort and still more effort, committing himself to a tough policy of industrial reorganization entailing layoffs and joblessness. Thrown off balance, the militant left found itself bereft of its traditional guidelines. The generous and free-spending Socialism of the past had given place to rigorous, if not exactly cheeseparing, economic management. It was a complete turnabout, effected under emergency conditions—a sudden jettisoning of all the old left-wing beliefs. It ignited Montand, and suddenly he was everywhere.

His return to Paris, following a midyear vacation in 1983, was a Montand festival. "Sneer, snarl, or enjoy it, the facts are undeniable: France's political star this September is a singer-actor who made his name with other people's words but who is still a draw when he decides to speak for himself," said *Le Point* on October 3.

Even before this, in the heat of midsummer, an article in *Libération* signed by Montand with two others had accused the French government of "backing into a military commitment" in the former French territory of Chad, stressing that the Libyan tanks supporting guerrilla dissidents there were Soviet-built, and arguing that Colonel Kaddafi's imperialist thrust must be countered at once. The article amounted to a severe criticism of the left's pro–Third World and noninterventionist traditions. Not long after it appeared, French paratroopers were dropped on N'Djamena.

(Those who remembered Montand's earlier antiwar stands had also been surprised by a Montand interview in *Figaro-Magazine* in April. At that time, *Fig-Mag* was further to the right than most periodicals, and Montand's appearance in its columns startled even those closest to him. "It's suicide!" was Semprun's alarmed reaction, and Signoret disapproved. For her, there were places you didn't show your face as a matter of principle. More sensitive than her husband to the uneasiness such a violation of taboos might arouse among left-wing militants, she feared that tactical errors would distort the substance of his message. Montand rejected this.

"You're being a boy scout! I'm not interested in preaching to the converted. Or haven't we learned anything?"

"Better to be a boy scout than to speak for those bastards!"

"Do you really think two million readers are two million bastards?"

Simone's oversensitivity raised Montand's hackles, and he slammed the door after a memorable squabble. He no longer gave a damn about being exploited by the right. He meant to say what he wanted where he wanted, without kid gloves. Without being impossibly stretched between too-absolute truths.

On Sunday, September 4, the citizens of Dreux, a community with a large immigrant population, went to the polls to elect local leaders, the results of the previous election having been annulled. The first round of voting was a bad setback for the left; more significantly, though, the candidates of the extreme-right National Front grabbed a staggering 17 percent of the vote. Overnight, France was confronted with the issue of immigration and the threat of a racist groundswell. The left gathered its forces for the runoff vote, while the traditional right wing joined hands with the far right. The former mayor of Dreux appealed to Signoret, who started a petition whose signers (from Costa-Gavras to Guy Bedos, Patrice Chéreau to Montand, Depardieu, Minkovski, and Kouchner) declared that "all France is concerned at the recrudescence in Dreux of the racist thinking that leads to civil war and to war itself." Without specifically giving support to either side, the statement implicitly backed the candidates of the left by denouncing the alliance that had formed around the National Front. "Why is this millionaire song-and-dance man sticking his nose in here?" asked the National Front candidate Jean-Pierre Stirbois.

Ivan Levaï, the editorial director of Europe 1 radio, asked Montand his opinion. From the Colombe d'Or, Montand explained why he had signed the petition, reiterating his revulsion at slogans calling on Muslims to return to their North African slums. But when pressed, he readily rounded on his favorite adversaries, "our Stalinist leaders, hand in glove with the informers in Prague and the Pinochets in Warsaw." He added that if he were a voter in Dreux he would abstain rather than associate himself with those who condoned the invasion of Afghanistan and the repression in Poland. And he hammered at the fact that the real enemy was the system that had spawned the gulags. Montand was unaware that their conversation was being recorded. But when Levaï asked his permission to broadcast it, he readily agreed.

Ivo Livi needed sermons about immigration from nobody. In this graduate of La Cabucelle, raised among "Macaronis," Armenians, Spaniards, and Arab kids, dislike of racism was inborn, an article of faith. (He had carefully clipped and kept an article dated 1948, in which France's minister for health and population declared that in order to recover, the country needed to attract 3 million foreign workers.) The ideas of the National Front sickened him, and since—wrongly—he assumed that almost everyone shared this feeling, he preferred to stress what in his eyes was the real danger: global East-West confrontation. The Soviet Union had decided to station its three-thousand-mile-range SS-20 missiles in the East; but in Western Europe a pacifist groundswell had arisen in opposition to a parallel deployment by the United States of its Pershing missiles. West German demonstrators were chanting "Better red than dead!" Here Montand backed the French government position. "Why didn't the pacifists demonstrate when the Soviets deployed their SS-20s?" he asked. "Better red than dead? No! Neither red nor dead! Free!"

The bombshell was still to come. On January 3, 1984, Montand was the lone guest on the influential late-night TV program "Les Dossiers de l'écran."

He prepared alone, and with great care. In big letters and on large sheets of paper he set down key terms ("the principal enemy today" and "red Nazi") and catch phrases ("freedom is the right to tell people what they don't want to hear"), but during the show he had no need of them. His host first asked him questions about his career and his loves; political questions were not broached until shortly before midnight. He mentioned the gulag system, criticized Socialist leaders who extended their hand to the Soviet Union's Stalinist leadership, and poured scorn on Transport Minister Charles Fiterman, who had spoken in 1980 of the "Polish miracle that has generated a 150 percent increase in industrial output." He expressed his hostility to unrestrained capitalism and his support for liberal capitalism. By turns serious, winning, and passionate, Montand put on an outstanding performance. As soon as the broadcast was over he called Simone.

"Wonderful," was all she said.

In fact, the impact was enormous. Nearly 10 million viewers remained glued to their sets until the end. Only at year-end festivities had the French ever stayed up so late and in such numbers before their television screens. As midnight struck, Montand's audience was larger than the president's had been at 8:30 that evening. Thirty-two thousand calls (an all-time record for the broadcast) swamped the switchboard, with 95 percent of the questioners seeking the actor's political views. In the days that followed, there was an unprecedented outpouring of press comment.

The broadcast marked a turning point. "What Montand asks for and speaks for," said Philippe Tesson, "is the best part of ourselves, the generous, fair, innocent part. He sends back our best reflection. His words, his features, even his slips, radiate light, simplicity, humanity, kindling the belief that everything is possible within the public weal." André Frossard wrote in *Le Figaro:* "He did not simply dominate the screen, he set fire to it. The anger of an honest man is a wonderful thing." Under the heading "Political Star Yves Montand," Jean Bothorel asked in another *Le Figaro* story whether he had "become the conscience of millions of Frenchmen. . . . On his side are intelligence, sincere anger, and the taste and talent for a lethal political shorthand. He lands squarely on the truth. Neither to the right nor to the left."

On the left there was astonishment. In the course of a long editorial in *Le Nouvel Observateur,* the magazine's editorial director, Jean Daniel, wrote: "I hope and would like to believe that all politicians, and particularly the current administration, saw Yves Montand fill the screen and sit down face-to-face with France on Tuesday night. . . . What verve! What charm! And what mastery as well! Apart from the closing minutes, when he veered off into money matters, his act was flawless. Was it studied, rehearsed? Yes: for a whole lifetime." Daniel's conclusion summed up the general feeling: "Yes, Monsieur Montand, you are decidedly a phenomenon."

Other commentators sought to explain the phenomenon. Some recalled the artist's past. "The fact that he was so long an effective symbol of commitment to Communism," said *Le Monde,* "seems to be an enduring reason for the hearing Montand has received." There was a similar diagnosis by Philippe Tesson in *Le Quotidien de Paris:* "Montand would not be Montand without his Communist past: he comes from so far back." Indeed, Montand's strength lay in the fact that he spoke with almost a half-century of history behind him, and that the errors and deviations he listed had been so widely shared that confessing to them conferred authenticity on his present statements. "He speaks," said Pierre Billard in *Le Point,* "from the height of his stature as a man of the people, just back from a painful exploration of the land of illusions. The road he has traveled is a reconstruction, almost a caricature, of the odyssey of the conscience of the left."

What this moment really dramatized was the dissolution of the French Communist Party's intellectual dominance. On the political and electoral level, however, the Party had kept a privileged relationship with the Socialist left, and was still officially part of the government. This anomaly, this anachronism, was what Montand denounced. In his vision of imminent cultural change, he was far ahead of the politicians. "The French intellectual establishment, so long a fief of the left, is breaking with its political gurus. M. Montand is to be congratulated for saying aloud what others were muttering to themselves," Flora Lewis sagely noted.[2]

Montand's power also sprang from the iconoclastic bluntness of his language, which rejected political pigeonholes and ideological divisions. To a nation emerging from an era of certainties on both the left and the right, Montand offered the language of doubt. To Frenchmen weary of the left-right divide, he stressed that it was time to end the civil war: the good guys were not all on one side, nor the bad guys on the other.

Montand found the torrent of praise that now submerged him embarrassing rather than intoxicating. But as a professional, he saw better than anyone else how powerful a force television had become. A month later he was back on the small screen, in another starring role.

In November 1983, the television journalist Jean-Claude Guillebaud proposed that Montand serve as narrator on a broadcast about the world economic crisis. After hesitating ("Between you and me, I know nothing about it," he admitted to *Le Nouvel Observateur*), he agreed to go along. A professional to his fingertips, he buried himself in the book on which the program was based, *Le Pari français* (*The French Challenge*), by Michel Albert, a former commissioner of the French Economic Plan. He listened faithfully to the economist Jean Boissonnat over Europe 1, devoured the economic press, consulted businessman and essayist Alain Minc, and declared himself "ninety percent in agreement" with the script they wanted him to read. Recorded at the end of 1983 and aired a month after his appearance on "Les Dossiers de l'écran," the broadcast benefited from the enormous media prestige Montand had now acquired. Rarely had a television show been so eagerly awaited. Members of the administration fought to preview the tape of "Vive la crise" ("Let's Hear It for the Crisis") in order to prepare their comments. Montand appeared on the covers of twelve magazines. On the night of the broadcast, the press reported that President Mitterrand had watched it live and liked it, despite one or two "overdramatized" touches. That night, Montand was invited to watch the broadcast at the home of Jean Daniel of *Le Nouvel Observateur.* Among the guests were Prime Minister Michel Rocard and the Czech novelist Milan Kundera.

There were some sour press comments the next day, but most reviewers heaped praise upon Montand.

The ink flowed abroad as well, and in France the press had to hurry to keep up with the firebrand. Economic Minister Jacques Delors, Social

2. Flora Lewis, *International Herald Tribune,* January 15, 1984.

Affairs Minister Pierre Bérégovoy, and the Communist Trade Union Secretary General Edmond Maire took up their pens to approve or admonish Montand. People more or less forgot that in this broadcast—unlike "Les dossiers de l'écran"—the actor was not speaking his own words but was narrating a script written by others. True, he had asked for changes, and the closing minutes were partly his own invention, so a definite ambiguity lingered: Was it Montand the actor who had convinced viewers, or was it Citizen Montand offering his own learned views?

Apart from its lively, high-relief format (economics narrated like a suspense story), the broadcast's astounding success lay in the message it delivered: the economic crisis then afflicting the industrialized countries, it said, was not an act of fate, an accident, a classic depression. Inflation and rising unemployment, it suggested, were the result of a global distortion, itself triggered by an enormous transformation: the conditions that had guaranteed steady expansion ever since the 1950s had been totally altered by the ups and downs of the monetary system, the emergence of new competitor nations, and the mutation of the raw-materials market. France had to adapt or stagnate. For the French, tightening their belts, awaiting layoffs, keeping an eye on their spending, such explanations—situating their particular cases within a global context—were just what the doctor ordered. And Montand emerged as the great communicator of the economic crisis, at the very moment that President Mitterrand himself embarked on an agonizing change of course. In September 1983, he rehabilitated, amid great fanfare, one of the taboo words of the Socialist left: profit, "providing it is equitably distributed," was henceforth acceptable, even beneficial. In other words, production, modernization, and reorganization had to come before Socialist-style redistribution. It was a creed Montand could wholeheartedly support.

The "Montand phenomenon" that had registered in opinion polls now became a political reality. And the real politicians and journalists began to wonder what use the actor would make of the enormous capital he had amassed in a few short weeks. Would he turn pro and plunge into a political career? Interviewed over Europe 1 by Ivan Levaï the day after "Vive la crise," Montand denied any such ambition, but the conversation betrays real confusion on his part:

> "I am more than ever concerned by public affairs. In my present state of mind I am considering never singing again, never acting. I would feel too uncomfortable."
>
> "What does that mean? No more songs, no more cinema? Just politics?"
>
> "We have to put things in context. I've asked for nothing.

Everyone's getting excited, on the right, on the left. I wonder why. I've done nothing. I've simply turned up for broadcasts. People asked me questions, and I answered the best I could, I hope sensibly. But it isn't something I went looking for."

"Let's be clear. Will you run for the presidency one day? Yes or no?"

"For the nth time, no! Is that clear enough?"

But clear or not, doubts lingered; people speculated. Some polls had 36 percent of the French ready to vote for Montand in the next presidential election. An extravagant figure, indicative of the extent to which public opinion was floundering. Montand had not so far expressed himself as exhaustively and as coherently as voters had a right to expect from a future candidate. His anti-Communism was decidedly on target, but it was no substitute for broad economic and social aims or a clearly defined foreign policy.

For now, he was a useful Jeremiah rather than the potential leader of a troubled nation. After the war, Sartre, Camus, and later Raymond Aron had served as guides to the intelligentsia and the educated public. Now that ideologies were being thrown overboard, it was a sign of the times that a song-and-dance man was energizing the country. Sartre was dead, and the intellectuals were silent.

> In itself, being president didn't interest me: essentially it would have represented the fulfillment of a dream of glory and success, of ambition. All things being equal, I already had those things. But I felt the need to speak out. And to speak and be heard, you have to play the game. I wanted to play politics without becoming a politician. Which is impossible.
>
> I was shocked but very moved when the media propelled me in the space of a few short weeks to the status of a presidential possibility, and when twenty or thirty percent of people questioned told the polls they would vote for me. It terrified me, but it indicated that my words had met some kind of expectation, some kind of demand. It did not go to my head. I had been armor-plated ever since my 1956 trip to Moscow, where they greeted me like a head of state. So I kept my perspective: what worried me was how to channel this unexpected groundswell, how to use this upsurge of feeling. After all, I was just a hoofer, a mouthpiece—a talented one, perhaps—and I told everyone who interviewed me that I had done no research, made no plans, that

the whole wave had broken over me in the course of three broadcasts.

This didn't alter the fact that I was now clearly on a path to an ill-defined destination. I went to bed every night thinking, Well, Montand, what are you going to do now that you've stirred all this up? It was true I felt uncomfortable about singing or playing comic parts: I didn't want my professional work to dilute my political impact. I had always been passionately interested in political questions; but at that precise point in time I felt that I could be useful simply by saying certain things, exploding certain taboos.

But I didn't see myself embarking on a traditional political career, either. It wasn't my job, and I'm not trained for it. Mainly I saw that one of my strengths lay precisely in the fact that I was speaking from outside the political circle. The further I went, the more clearly I saw that it was a cruel, merciless game. In my own life I had always won what I really desired; but this was a series of events that had happened to me, that had been decided without me, against my deepest wishes. And I was alone. Going any further would have meant a team of supporters, a collective project in which I would be the great communicator. But there was no one.

To prepare for "Vive la crise," Montand conferred with Michel Albert and Alain Minc, which effectively brought these two economic "managers" onto what imaginative reporters were already calling the actor's "presidential staff." Montand also listened to a couple of analyses of the international situation by Marie-France Garaud, Georges Pompidou's former adviser. Though she did help him, the press attributed a behind-the-scenes role to her that she never played. The facts were duller. Citizen Montand traveled under his own steam. He tirelessly jotted down thoughts and ideas, or the quotations he liked to slip into conversations (for example, this remark by Jean Rostand: "As long as there are dictatorships I will not have the heart to criticize democracies." Or this by Zola: "The question is, will we ever build happiness with truth?" Or this one: "The left is my country, not my prison, even if it often becomes a tomb for many").

Apart from the faithful Bob, Montand had nothing approaching a secretarial staff. He answered his voluminous mail personally (hundreds of letters whose contents would disturb the calmest of us: various correspondents seeking to create Montand committees; others urging him to declare, saying they were ready to support him).

As for Signoret, she supported her man. A veteran of forty years of petitions, protests, and demonstrations, she was not one to oppose his participation in the national debate. What she feared was that Montand would cut himself off from his ties to the left, but on essentials she approved what her husband was doing. Nevertheless, people tried to split them, even set them against each other. In the fall of 1983, *Le Nouvel Observateur* ran an interview under the heading "Signoret Answers Montand." It angered them both, and Jean Daniel sent an apologetic telegram: "Title given to interview in no way fits its content. Sincerely regretful over mistake counter to my principles." Whatever the tactical disagreements between them (Catherine Allégret reports that they were considerable), Signoret confirmed over the air in 1985 that she was in full agreement with her husband's actions. Adding that she, too, had "crossed the line," she said: "I used to be quite soft on anti-Communism. Now I believe I'm going to join what *L'Humanité* calls the anti-Communist 'clique' or 'lobby.' "

One movie actor who successfully made the conversion to national politics at this very time was, of course, Ronald Reagan, weather-beaten by the sun of Hollywood Westerns and now ensconced in the White House. No sooner had the "Montand phenomenon" emerged than French journalists avidly studied the parallels. Would Montand be the French Reagan? On "Les Dossiers de l'écran," he had deftly sidestepped the issue: "Reagan is a good president, but he was never really a success in show business, which is not my case." Ronald Reagan was not just a mediocre actor who had skillfully forged a political career; he had become a symbol of the 1980s, of unabashed capitalism, and the symbol, too, of a newly victorious America, proud of its flag, able to stare down the pre-perestroika Soviet Union.

Reagan's firmness in the East-West dialogue won Montand's approval, but Montand was sharply criticized for being the apologist of a man whose economic policies had pushed millions of Americans over the socioeconomic edge. Montand invariably countered this objection with the remark that he supported liberal capitalism but not the deregulated variety, and that the excesses of the marketplace had to be corrected by policies of social justice and regulation.

Also, Montand was irked by the condescension French journalists had for the "cowboy president." To them this legitimately elected president, in the White House thanks to the full support of the Republican party, was nothing more than a second-rate actor, an amiable, barely literate figurehead. Montand sensed that his own appearance on the political stage triggered similar responses: to be in politics you had to belong to the harem, be a product of one of the major schools. In case you got too big for your britches.

The American media nonetheless applauded Montand's political emergence. On March 23, 1984, ABC ran a two-and-a-half-minute segment on its evening news program about him; in February, *Paris-Match* had suggested a one-on-one interview with the French actor quizzing the U.S. president. Nothing came of it, but contact had already been established between the two men; on December 5, 1982, Montand was invited to the White House for a reception in honor of Gene Kelly. In 1987, when he went to New York and Washington for the release of *Jean de Florette* (a trip for which, as usual, he had to request a temporary visa—struck with the same old code number, 212-(D) (3)(A) :28—for the Immigration Service had not forgotten the Communist of the Cold War years), he said over and over in interviews, "Don't see me as an unconditional supporter of Reagan's, far from it. But I'm not going to deny that he has done positive things."[3]

And Reagan called Montand at his hotel to find out if all was well: "Are you comfortable there? I hope you have everything you need. I'm very happy you're here."

When he was asked in March 1985 to appear on a new television show, "La Guerre en face" ("War Across the Rhine"), Montand seized the opportunity to satisfy his appetite for strategic questions. He had often said that he was better versed in geopolitics than economics (on which, it will be remembered, he had merely recited a script with which he agreed "ninety percent"). Jean-Claude Guillebaud and Laurent Joffrin based the new program on a fictional premise: a conventional Soviet thrust through Germany comes up against NATO forces in the first few hours and in days breaks through Western defenses. Could Western Europe defend itself by conventional means, or should France use its nuclear weaponry to stop the Soviets? The underlying thesis was that the balance of terror—East-West nuclear parity—that had guaranteed peace in Europe since 1945 was now broken. The creators of "La Guerre en face," backed by a swarm of experts, were seeking to provoke debate on the relevance and limits of France's nuclear deterrent at a time when the Americans were preparing their "Star Wars" defense system.

For Montand in particular, the aim was to promote vigilance over the continuing Soviet threat, to maintain a spirit of readiness at a time when pacifism was gaining ground in Europe. Montand feared a militarily neutralized Germany. (He liked quoting Aristotle to the effect that "Peoples unwilling to defend themselves court disaster. It is always through them,

3. Quoted in *Le Monde,* June 27, 1987.

as if by accident, that invaders rush in.") He mocked the pacifists as "generous, well-meaning lambs who believe wolves are vegetarians."

Controversy also swirled about Montand's person. *Le Matin,* a paper close to the Socialist party, depicted him on its front page wearing a warrior's helmet. *Le Canard Enchaîné* cackled at "Yves 'Montank.' " The Communist Party delivered the heaviest counterattack. "His ideas sound like the click of a rifle bolt," *L'Humanité* wrote after the first of Montand's major television broadcasts in September 1983. "This man does not think, he shoots. At anything red." In a clear indication that the Party leadership took its adversary seriously, the writer dwelt ponderously on Montand's "nightly poker games with Baron Empain," his "colossal wealth." Charles Fiterman added: "A sorry spectacle, I must say—this man attacking his past and his youthful ideals just to curry favor! With whom? It is truly sad. I pity Montand."

As always, the family quarrel burst out anew. In the fall of 1983, the French Communist Party weekly *Révolution* gave four full pages to "The Ballad of Julien," a union worker's account of his childhood and youth in Marseilles. Not until page four did the uninformed reader learn that he was Montand's brother. The end of the article sought to shatter the myth of the "prole" Montand, claiming that he had seldom worked and had cut himself off from his roots.

Now a message appeared in *L'Humanité* among letters from readers shocked by "La Guerre en face": "Deeply disgusted by the broadcast, which dishonors its creators and their tame mouthpiece, I more than ever support those who accept neither the lies nor the rationale of the arms race nor hatred among peoples." Only those in the know realized that the "tame mouthpiece" was the letter writer's brother.

In his turn, Montand pulled no punches in his reply in *Paris-Match:* "When the Party said the [Moscow show] trials were a good thing, the Party was right. When, ten years later, it said they were a bad thing, it was still right, because the Party is always right. . . . I am so sickened, revolted even, that if a certain man over the age of fifty-five and still a MEMBER of the Communist Party were to seek me out to say hello, I would puke all over him. That's how strongly I feel." Inevitably, his words angered former Resistance fighters who had stayed with the Party, particularly when he added: "I have no wish for such a man to speak to me. He is as dangerous to me as an SS man, as any fanatic. I can be patient with a Party member if he is thirty-five, forty, forty-five, or even fifty. But no older than that. Because those guys know." These inflammatory remarks, stripped of all pretense at politeness and intended to remind readers that Stalin had slaughtered more Communists than Hitler, were, of course, directed at

Julien. On April 27, 1985, he counterattacked, writing Montand a long letter that pumped the quarrel up to explosive heights:

> Yves?
> Montand?
> Livi? Up to you.
>
> Not much to add to my short and dignified reply to your hysterical rantings. Except perhaps to say that it's sad to think they were aimed at your brother.
>
> I know, you don't choose your family, but it exists all the same. . . . Believe me: when I see how far you've come I pity you.
>
> But you see, if there is one thing that comforts me when I contemplate the verbal diarrhea you splashed all over *Paris-Match,* it is the thought that our parents never had the sorrow of seeing it.
>
> It occurs to me that one of the warmest admirers of your prose would have been Uncle Gigi.
>
> In fact, I'm sure that that Fascist, the one who ordered them to beat up Papa, the one who rubbed his hands over the fire, who meant to roast us all, would be one of your most fanatical supporters today.
>
> Your threats against the Communists are the same ones Gigi directed at Papa. They are exactly the same as the threats that I and many Communists have endured since the beginning. And only too often they have been followed by crimes and aggression.
>
> I hope for your sake that our grandchildren do not have to curse you one day for your filthy actions.

The letter left Montand ice-cold with fury. The whole saga of the Livi family began with that act of original sin committed by blackshirted Uncle Gigi, the embodiment of absolute evil. Comparing Montand to Gigi was the same as accusing him of betraying his father. It amounted to removing the meaning from his life. But the words Julien flung in his face give us an unintended key to Montand the public man, to his sometimes irrational reactions, his uncontrolled anger, his obsessive anti-Communism. He suffered from not being understood by his own kind, and he hated their blindness. This was not just another squabble, the kind of disagreement every family experiences. The Livi quarrel mirrored a half-century of history, with the fate of both brothers caught up in the larger collective experience of a generation that had believed Communism embodied humankind's highest hopes. One, refusing to acknowledge that blind faith might be the most treacherous mask of all, was determined to remain rooted in the mythic ideal. The other, believing like René Char that "the word 'happiness' is the Trojan Horse of intolerance," was convinced that apparent denial could be a higher form of loyalty.

Early in 1985, the economist Jacques Attali invited Simone Signoret, Yves Montand, and some others to dinner with François Mitterrand. It was the first time either of them had met the president. They had deliberately stood aside from the Socialist administration, and Mitterrand had referred to them as "parlor pinks." Signoret had explained their position in an interview in *Le Nouvel Observateur* on March 27, 1982: "On May 10 [the date of Mitterrand's election to the presidency], like all those who voted the way we did, we were very happy, and if we kept our distance it was to avoid becoming courtiers. . . . True, perhaps we didn't yell 'Bravo!' loud enough to show we were happy, but we were certainly noticed when we shouted 'Watch out!' when we weren't happy. But friends are supposed to say 'Watch out!' Friends, not courtiers."

Since then, the president had acknowledged the actor's mastery on television. But he had not masked the irritation he felt when the shafts aimed at his administration seemed too sharp. Answering a question, a week or so before "Vive la crise," about the Montand phenomenon, Mitterrand had complimented him: "He is an interesting character. A man who deserves respect. And what talent! If every politician in France were as talented, the country would be unrecognizable."

All the guests that evening were in excellent spirits (Claude Durand, Signoret's publisher, was also present). They talked about unemployment and the rise of the dollar. Mitterrand, who had not forgotten Montand's comments about Chad, launched into a vast geostrategic discussion, outlining the technical obstacles that increased the difficulties of military intervention in that country.

Years later, in 1987, as president of the Cannes Film Festival, Montand for the first time accepted an official invitation to the Elysée Palace. François Mitterrand seated Montand across from him, with the wry comment: "Why not? After all, we're both presidents."

The politician Montand was no less split than the actor Montand. Brushed by the dream of courting the highest office in the land, loving the French and loved by them, was he not seeking to exorcise the immigrant child he had once been? All foreigners, all those who come from elsewhere, have felt this need for integration. Costa-Gavras, yet another immigrant, suggests the following possibility: "He had succeeded in absolutely everything: raised in the poorest sections of Marseilles, he had become the master of the one-man show, one of the world's great performers. He was greeted everywhere as a star. Heads of state were flattered to have him at their table. He was a *monstre sacré.* But deep inside him, indestructible, a bit of the immigrant had survived, a part of him he did not deny but which he sought to reabsorb completely so that he could become a Frenchman like everyone else. His 'political breakthrough,' his smash hit in the polls were simply further confirmation that he was at home, that he was accepted."

As Montand forged deeper into politics, the barrier between the power of comedy and the comedy of power grew increasingly blurred. Appropriately, Semprun now set to work, with Costa's help and Montand's approval, on a screenplay that was a kind of allegory on the vanity of all things. *Montand président* tells the story of a famous actor who is elected president because he tells the truth, acknowledging all his convictions and all his difficulties. Once in office, he sees that reality is more complex. Frustrated at every turn, he soon has to plot, cheat, dissemble, playact to achieve his goals. Everything becomes burdensome: his ceremonial duties bore him; receptions, dinners, and speeches put him to sleep. Until one day, alone in front of his mirror, he puts on his top hat and begins to sing and dance—just for himself. . . .

The story never made its way to a movie set. But rarely had life—even imagined life—and the world of entertainment been so intimately mingled.

As Costa-Gavras recalls: "Around the time we were discussing this film, we went for a drive in his jeep. Montand said, 'We could have a scene in which he drives a jeep with music like this.' And he sang to me. It was the showman expressing himself. But then, as I listened, I realized, 'No, in his mind he's already campaigning—for real!' When we got back I said to Jorge:

" 'We've been rehearsing the campaign.'

" 'For the movie?'

" 'No, no, the campaign, the real one.'

" 'You're crazy!'

"But I wasn't crazy: Montand had indeed been feeling out a movie scene, but he was also testing ideas for a possible run at the Elysée. In his mind the two things overlapped."

In 1987, encouraged by the sustained groundswell of public opinion, somewhat bored with a show-business world from which he had little more to expect, Montand settled down to some serious thinking. A number of financiers and politicians had approached him. No one knew whether Mitterrand, locked into an uneasy coalition with a conservative-dominated parliament, would run for office again. For a time Montand was convinced that the political tide was running in his favor and that he could attempt to do in France what Reagan had pulled off across the Atlantic. After all, the road to the Elysée was much shorter than the road he had traveled from La Cabucelle. For a president, the main thing was to be able to communicate, to uphold the overriding national values. There were advisers to help with ideas, plans, portfolios. Someone who could recite Baudelaire to a Brazilian audience could surely assimilate a few notes on inflation.

The vision was more than a little naive. Nevertheless, when people recognized as serious and competent urged you to take the leap, when the press shouted you on, when your standing in the polls soared, when pressure intensified, your head was turned and the scenario became (almost) plausible. "I truly believed he was going to run," says Catherine Allégret. "At one point he slipped from his own reins. He's a man of immense pride who is constantly challenging himself. And this challenge has always helped him to survive." Ivan Levaï agrees: "During this period he was wondering what to do with his life. He had made a success of everything. I'm convinced he was tempted to play the game, to stir things up. Absolutely anyone in his situation would have felt the same urge to translate his fame into action." Reggiani, who rarely saw Montand at the time, says: "He was not playacting. I'm convinced he thought seriously of running. He is charmingly naive." But according to Anne Sinclair, "He was quite clearheaded. He had always believed that he should use his reputation to communicate ideas, but he never considered running. What drove him was altruism, not anything personal." His close friend Semprun is of the same opinion: "He always kept an ironic distance between himself and the situation he had been thrown into. We used to joke about it; he would shoot me a look and whisper, 'What the hell can they be thinking of?' "

In December 1987, Anne Sinclair invited herself and the television cameras to Autheuil to ask the question with which the press was obsessed: Would Yves Montand be a candidate in the May 1988 presidential election? "Montand at Home," broadcast over Télé France 1, was planned as a collage of serious comments on the economy and foreign policy, of childhood memories, and of personal confidences, with a few songs thrown in. Sinclair's principal aim was to offer Saturday-night entertainment to viewers—and, indeed, the broadcast attracted 22 percent of the French audience. After all, cameras had almost never ventured to Autheuil before, and Montand was very big news.

A poll taken a week before the broadcast indicated that 29 percent of French voters felt inclined to vote for Montand.[4] Another poll gave the

4. *Le Journal du Dimanche,* December 6, 1987.

star an impressive approval rating of 78 percent; 65 percent of respondents applauded his intervention on major national issues, 74 percent believed him sincere, 60 percent considered him to be abreast of events, 66 percent thought him equal to the job. A sweeping vote of confidence. Despite his eighteen-month absence from the television screen, the "Montand phenomenon" was still riding high. The political analyst Olivier Duhamel noted that Montand's strength lay in the fact that he occupied no clear position in the traditional opposition of right and left: at a time when "many Frenchmen are bewildered by the great left-right divide, Montand seems to embody a sort of aspiration toward consensus on major, fundamental issues." Nevertheless, he concluded, Montand would never be president: "He lacks the support of a major party and the profile of a statesman. This tidal wave of support is not the equivalent of votes."[5]

Montand agreed. At the very end of Sinclair's broadcast, after a period of contrived and somewhat labored suspense (requested by the producers and agreed to by Montand), he swept aside the idea of his candidacy: "Let's be serious! I have never had such an ambition. I know my limits: I have neither the education nor the experience to be president of France." In short, a denial.

Troubles now flooded in. Ten days later, *Le Canard Enchaîné* informed its readers that Montand had received 800,000 francs for taking part in the broadcast (the fee had already been alluded to on Radio-Télé Luxembourg). Further disaster followed when the press jumped in to savage the man who had demanded payment for delivering his own message. Could one pocket such a hefty sum and at the same time preach austerity? Montand at once responded: "I have nothing to hide, I've stolen nothing, I have no reason to blush." His defense was plain: Télé France 1 was a private station. Scheduling Montand in a prime-time Saturday-night slot had been sound business, netting the station an estimated 3 million francs in advertising revenue.[6] Why, he asked, should he have helped to swell the profits of M. Bouygues, the station owner, a concrete manufacturer? His logic seemed unanswerable: profit-based commercial television had a duty to pay for performances that made profits. Such commonsense arguments might have been irrefutable, except that it had been an ambiguous evening's television, an uneasy blend of politics and entertainment. No one denied Montand's right to a top fee from TF1 for a show. What grated on the public was that the show had dressed itself up as something other than mere entertainment.

5. Olivier Duhamel, *Télérama,* December 9, 1987.

6. *Le Point,* January 4, 1988.

A glance at the origins of the broadcast help explain how the trap had closed around Montand. Charley Marouani, the agent who negotiated the fee, explains things this way:

"When he mentioned the proposed broadcast with Anne Sinclair, I told him at once not to allow commercial breaks. Montand agreed. I had lunch at Fouquet's with Etienne Mougeotte [of TF1]. TF1 was hungry for Montand. I said to Mougeotte: 'You can have Montand for nothing, but only if there are no commercial breaks.'

" 'That's impossible, Charley.'

" 'If there are going to be commercials, then we demand one million francs to change your mind.'

" 'I'll call you.' "

A few days later, after negotiations between the agent and Mougeotte, TF1 agreed to a fee of 800,000 francs.

In the furor that erupted, two charges stood out. The first was that Montand had not publicly acknowledged that he was receiving a fee. If he had ended the broadcast by thanking Bouygues for his handsome gift and announced to viewers that the money would go to good causes, people would have applauded. It did not occur to him, and he was sorry his interviewers had not asked him the question. "When Montand told me he was getting a fee for the broadcast, I told him that was his problem," says Anne Sinclair. "I should have said, Don't do it. I didn't consider the consequences. I tucked the matter away, I buried it, and we didn't mention it again. If I had asked him about the fee during the broadcast, he would, of course, have answered without hiding anything, and would have emerged a big winner."

The other charge concerned the substance of "Montand at Home" and the essential ambiguity of the show. Was it politics or entertainment? Montand the potential presidential candidate could not turn his geopolitical ruminations into profit. The sharpness of the public reaction proved that many viewers were watching the politician that night, not the actor. Accustomed to a moralizing, sincere, message-bearing Montand, they objected to having TF1 serve him up just like any other product. They were offended, too, that the denouncer of evil had let himself be bought. The star's political commitment, his deeply felt anger, and his sincerity had brought him enormous credit. And at one stroke that moral image had been warped. A wave of invective broke over him. All those Montand had angered now went for the chink in his armor. It was open season.

Against this background, spontaneous gestures of support or friendship were of enormous importance to him. They came from Daniel Auteuil, Jean-Paul Belmondo, Jean-Jacques Cousteau, Jean-Luc Godard, Jeanne Moreau, Michel Piccoli, Michel Sardou, and many others. But the most comforting letter came from Dr. Escoffier-Lambiotte, secretary general of the French Medical Research Foundation, which the actor had sponsored and backed:

> At a time when I note that a handful of petty, envious hacks and also-rans have the gall to criticize you, I would simply like you to know that you have my fullest support, as well as that of the very many researchers who have been helped by your efforts and generosity.
>
> Talent is, of course, a gift from heaven. But at the level to which you have raised it, it is the fruit of enormous labor, and I really fail to see in the name of what moral standard it should be loaned out gratis to a commercial operation. . . . Even though no one can be unaware that you have put that talent—without remuneration and on numberless occasions—at the service of totally disinterested causes. . . .

Montand had not just made a mistake; he had done the wrong thing. But he stuck it out to the end, going public with his earnings and seeking, with endearing clumsiness, to show that the check had not been important to him. After taxes and his agent's commission, he received "only" 350,000 francs, which he doled out among various charitable institutions (some gifts, such as the 100,000 he gave to soup kitchens feeding the poor, had already been earmarked before the trouble started). In the end, he was left with just enough of the fee to buy dinner for four at the Tour d'Argent.

> If the public believed after a half-century of living with me that I was a man who secretly filled his pockets, it wasn't worth explaining my behavior. Why should I prove myself innocent of a crime I hadn't committed? My logic was simple: private television can afford to pay. People had wanted a commercial station, and now they had to live with the consequences.
>
> I was naive and even a bit stupid. It's true: today, with hindsight, the objections seem obvious. But back then I didn't see them, and neither did anyone else. No one told me I was walking into a trap; everyone just assumed that a station grown wealthy on advertising revenue should be prepared to pay the piper. People wanted the laws of the marketplace: so be it! That was all I was obeying. I had no intention of hiding anything. I would have blessed God or the Devil or the Grand Rabbi of Paris if Anne Sinclair had thought of asking me about it. It looked to me like excellent business: if I, with all that power going for me, could

make them pay through the nose, all the entertainers who followed me would also be able to ask for substantial fees. I wasn't wary enough, I didn't look at the negative side: I would never have dreamed that people who trusted me would be so offended. That I do regret. But I don't regret making commercial television pay. It seemed right. It was a matter of principle.

In the fall of 1988, General Pinochet, who had held the reins in Chile since 1973, sought to obtain legal confirmation as head of the Chilean state through a referendum. The democratic opposition, calling for a no vote, asked Montand to come and support their campaign. He immediately accepted, certain that he was acting in strict conformity with his earlier commitments, in particular the benefit concert he had given for Chilean refugees fourteen years earlier. For three days he met with human-rights workers, called on Salvador Allende's widow, and took part with half a million Chileans in a "March of Hope." He also visited the house in the Victoria neighborhood, one of the poorest townships in the capital, where the French priest André Jarlan had been shot down in 1984 by a "stray" bullet. Montand meditated for a moment in the tiny seven-by-twelve-foot room, then was led to an open window and handed a microphone. Moved to tears, he uttered a few words for the enthusiastic crowds in the street. On his return, Montand was astonished to learn that the French foreign minister had been scathing about the trip of "the great artist whose name we all know, and who paraded the streets with a loudspeaker."

Three weeks later, Montand was in Israel. Since his first trip there with Signoret in 1959, he had never lost his almost visceral attachment to the Jewish state—which made his concern for the distress of the Palestinians and the future of the West Bank all the sharper. Toward Jews, Montand felt he owed an unredeemable debt: for not having shared their sufferings, for not having reacted, whether through ignorance or thoughtlessness, at sight of the yellow star during the war. He believed firmly in a remark by the philosopher Etiemble: "The moment anyone touches a hair or the honor of a Jew, my life and my freedom as a goy are threatened." He had been shattered by Claude Lanzmann's Holocaust movie *Shoah.* In June 1986 he returned to Israel, after twenty-seven years.

A new friend, Jean Frydman, had organized the trip. A former Resistance fighter, with many contacts in Israel, Frydman had hit upon the idea of asking Montand to perform a symbolic act: reopening the road linking Israel to Jordan through Aqaba. The project foundered on King Hussein's objections, but Montand, as the personal guest of Israeli prime minister Shimon Peres, received a statesman's welcome.

When the Jewish state celebrated its fortieth anniversary two years later, it naturally turned to Montand for a grand ceremony at Masada, the fortress situated on a towering rocky spur of the western bank of the Dead Sea, where beleaguered Jews had held off the Roman legions for three years and then chose to kill themselves rather than surrender. Before the sound of Mahler's Second Symphony boomed out, Montand proclaimed:

Glory, yes glory to the fighters of Masada
Tribute to the martyrs of Masada
So that your children
And your children's children's children
May say after you:
Never again, never again Masada!

For those moments of fervor he would have borne all the injustices on earth.

In the spring of 1989, the Communist leadership in Poland was forced by Solidarity to organize elections that were almost free, an unheard-of event in Eastern Europe. Opposition candidates were permitted to run—even though the quota of seats allotted them was established in advance. Lech Walesa's friends invited Montand to help them campaign. He did not hesitate. Arriving in Warsaw with photocopying equipment, he met university students campaigning for the recognition of their union, took part in several meetings, kneeled at the grave of Father Popieluszko (murdered by Party thugs), embraced Walesa, and sang "Les Feuilles mortes." Before returning to Paris, Montand told the students: "You must force the authorities not to step back from this. What is happening in Poland is a springtime that could turn into summer."

Solidarity's crushing victory forced the Communist Party to negotiate, then to retreat. For the first time since Yalta, a non-Communist government saw the light of day behind the Iron Curtain. It was the beginning of a major tremor: in the space of a few weeks, from Berlin to Prague, from Budapest to Bucharest, the totalitarian system was swept away. The collapse of Communism was a harbinger of the end of the century, a sign that the world had now to be considered in a new light, from a new angle.

Communism had branded Montand's life, just as it had shaped the existence of millions. Whether people had found in it reasons for living or had died for it, whether they had supported or opposed it, Communism had been the axis around which the thoughts, passions, hopes, and anguish of several generations had swirled for more than sixty years. Communism was collapsing, literally under its own weight. But its disappearance created a vacuum. It was now possible to challenge the faithful for lack of faith. The very object of faith had now dissolved. Before humankind could move into a new century, it would have to live in a void.

In June 1990, *Moscow News,* a paper in the vanguard of perestroika, invited the makers of *The Confession* to show their film to the Russian public. In the auditorium of the Moscow Cinema Center, the Soviet capital's leading lights fought after the showing to question Montand, Costa-Gavras, and Semprun. "Khrushchev," said Montand, "tried to save Communism in his country. Gorbachev is trying to save his country from Communism." A very, very old, frail gentleman rose from the audience and said to Montand in a voice that was still strong, "That one there—I want to tell him this: your film speaks to us Soviet citizens as well. The people sitting here all have either a parent or another relative or a close friend who died out there. We have all suffered the way this man in *The Confession* suffered. We watched it as we would have watched our own film. It is our story. It is our film." The old man sat down amid applause: it was Obraztsov, who had welcomed Montand to Moscow in 1956 and had introduced his songs to the Soviet Union.

Later, in a hotel bar with yellowed windows, the quartet (Chris Marker had joined them), in a mood somewhere between hilarity and nostalgia, appended a final period to the cinematographic and political adventure begun twenty years earlier. During those years Montand had often said: "I'll believe in democratization when they show *The Confession* in Moscow." It had just happened; he still felt he was dreaming.

"Do you realize what we've lived through today, men?" Semprun, the former Communist leader, now minister of culture in Spain, was only half joking when he said: "We spent our youth fighting democracy. We'll spend our old age defending it."

They smiled.

Montand, suddenly very serious: "I'm laughing, but I don't feel like laughing."

Around midnight he went for a stroll in Red Square. Illuminated by powerful floodlights, the domes of the church of St. Basil the Blessed looked like huge pastries. The Kremlin walls stood out against the dark sky, and above them the red flag fluttered in a beam of light. Gazing upward, Montand fixed his eyes for a moment on the banner of the October Revolution.

"Even when they've forgotten about Communism, the Russians should hold on to that flag. But without the hammer and sickle. Just for the background."

And turning his back on Lenin's mausoleum, he walked away.

Epilogue

A June morning. Sunlight floods the boulevard des Capucines, in stark contrast to the Olympia's stage door on the rue Caumartin. In daytime, a music hall is a strange place. A scattering of lights, pale and cold, fails to warm the blue of the ceiling or the faded red of the seats. The black curtains sag heavily. Yves Montand—dark suit, pink shirt, black tie—has called for two props, his top hat, in a white box, and Sir Godfrey's weapon, the swordstick that suspicious Japanese customs men almost confiscated in 1982, and which slid from its scabbard one evening on a tour, embedding itself in a seat next to an alarmed spectator.

The musicians unpack their equipment. Montand shrugs off his jacket, approaches the mike, and addresses an invisible technician: "You couldn't add a couple of spots, could you? It's a bit chilly up here."

Warm light at once bathes the island, the no-man's-land in which a dozen of them are busy. In theory, they are rehearsing for an appearance on a Saturday-night television show. But the real stakes are quite different. Montand is treating himself to two days at the Olympia in order to test his sixty-eight-year-old self. The singing bug has bitten him again. Not that his political passions have died; far from it. In the movies, there was his triumphant portrayal of Papet in *Jean de Florette* and *Manon of the Spring,* and the failure, despite critical praise, of *Trois places pour le 26* (*Three Seats for the 26th*). Now it is time to return to song. Montand has therefore resolved to give the engine a run, put his stamina to the test, see what the other Montand, the hoofer, is still capable of. A concert is a ten-thousand-meter race. Well, he is going to tackle the marathon! Between today and tomorrow he is going to put his broadcast together and repeat his 1981–82 show three times in a row. If he survives, it will mean he is indeed alive.

Today's audience is just six people. Never mind. Six or six thousand, Montand has stage fright. A judgment from on high is what he really wants.

A spectator is missing from the center of the eighth row. That had been Simone's place. It was there she used to sit, critical and attentive. Simone Signoret died on September 30, 1985, at the age of sixty-four. She had cancer, and she knew it. At first the doctors hoped that her condition, though painful, was benign. But the first surgical probe revealed that it was widespread and probably incurable. When she awoke—by this time she was almost blind—she clasped her daughter's hand, then her fingers quickly climbed to Catherine's eyelids to feel for tears. And Catherine—breeding will tell—managed to keep dry eyes. Dr. Leon Schwartzenberg never left Signoret's side, even sleeping at Autheuil when needed. She insisted that she was at peace, that she was not afraid, that all she wanted was to be free of pain.

The reporter Jean-François Josselin, one of her last visitors, has described how he came upon her reading: "She moved her hand in recognition and said, 'I'm sorry, but I believe I'm about to go under.' I kissed her cheek. Just as I was leaving her bedroom she stopped me. Her cat's eyes, her sea-green eyes, were looking lovingly at me." Yvette Etiévant, who had begun her stage career alongside Simone, has kept the same picture: "I came to see her one day. That night she called me and said, 'I felt you were sad. I don't want you to be.' It wasn't just words."

The profound crisis, violent and harrowing, that had shaken the woman and the actress in the 1970s had leveled off into a meditative, even serene phase in which, despite her progressive blindness, writing had played an increasing part. First there had been a translation (*Une Saison à Bratislava,* published in 1981), then a novel, *Adieu Volodya.* Four months before her death she was still writing "Music-Hall" scripts for television, but her talent for literary creation, which both frightened and stimulated her, was gaining the upper hand.

On that Monday in September, around seven in the morning, Catherine Allégret found her mother dead. Montand, who had been at Autheuil the day before, had had to leave for the Midi, where he was shooting *Manon of the Spring* (whenever he could, he escaped to get back to his wife). The network moved into action at once, and the news spread. Catherine was briefly worried that Montand might hear about it on the radio before she managed to get through to him; indeed, this is very nearly what happened. He recalled feeling as if he had left time, a feeling as unreal as the birth of a child. He would have preferred not seeing Simone in her coffin, just as he had not seen his dead father. For such images are dead pictures whose meaning lies elsewhere.

There was a big crowd the next day, Tuesday, October 1, at Père Lachaise cemetery in Paris—all her friends and acquaintances, all those she had worked with, as well as the curious, the souvenir hunters. Simone had loathed burials, lofty sentiments, pomp of all kinds, and funeral pomp above all else.

Montand never revisited her grave. Simone was not there. She was in the air, she was all around him, holding him ever in her arms as she had all his adult life. Not simply because a thousand reminders—a sudden recollection on opening a drawer, a particular dish on the menu at La Colombe, the sign pointing to Antibes at a particular crossroads—brought her continually back to life. It was much more than the nudge, the pang of memory. She was a real presence. "The dead are not absent," Montand concluded. "They are invisible."

Mediterraneans talk to their dead, and the dead reply. A close friend describes standing next to Montand before the Wailing Wall during a visit to Jerusalem. They were separated for a few moments. Back in the car, the actor said to him in very casual tones, "I slipped a photo of Simone into a crack in the wall. But she hollered and said she couldn't live there. So I put the photo back in my wallet." And Semprun: "A few Sundays ago we were watching a Formula One race on television. Yves suddenly flipped the remote control for a few seconds. And there was Simone on the screen, looking a little bit forbidding—it was a rerun of *Madame le juge.* Annoyed, Montand said to me, 'She pulls that on me all the time.' And a bit later, thoughtful and admiring, he said, 'Did you see the way she looked at me? Her expression?' "

In his early days as a widower, Montand thought of selling Autheuil. But later he came to feel that the place protected him and that his constant encounters there with the memory of his beloved kept him warm. He maintained the second-floor office, where Simone worked, exactly as it was. The typewriter, lamp, and vest on the back of the chair remained as she left them. He even kept a few of her clothes he loved: a raincoat, a dress. And the slender black shoes Simone wore in New York the first time they visited: the Indian summer had been so hot that the spike heels sank into the streets. He would swear there was no fetishism in this, nothing morbid, that these souvenirs did not take him back. Merely that seeing them made him smile.

He continued to wear the watch she gave him in 1961, the after-Marilyn watch, the one victoriously inscribed "another October 13." Simone herself had enjoyed this emotional relationship with objects, whose value in her eyes lay in their history, not their price. She never forgave herself for losing a small necklace decorated with a heart that Montand had given her in Hollywood. The day he absent-mindedly told her she didn't wear it much she burst into tears.

* * *

A dozen rows back, stage right, Carole Amiel is seated at the end of the row. Valentin, the son she bore to Montand five months earlier, is sleeping in the dressing room (she is keeping an eye on him via walkie-talkie). Carole is a kid from Saint-Paul, or almost. She was born in Epernay, but in the mid-1970s her father, a furniture dealer, decided to move closer to the Côte d'Azur, between mountains and sea. He bought a property near the Maeght foundation at Saint-Paul-de-Vence. So at the age of fourteen, Carole enrolled at the Montaigne school in Vence. The first time she saw Montand was in 1974, as he walked his dogs through the village.

The crew Charley Marouani hired for the 1982 tour needed a multilingual assistant. Carole, then twenty-two, spoke English and Italian fluently and managed German and Spanish very well. They took her on, and she made her first, fascinated acquaintance with the world of entertainment and the man who stood at its center. It began in the French provinces. She was touched to see Montand every afternoon inspect the theater where he would be performing, distressed at the idea that the view from some of the cheaper seats might be obstructed by a pillar. And it went on through Rio, New York, San Francisco, Montreal, Tokyo . . . Between the young woman and the singer a friendship blossomed, slowly and in secret. One of her jobs was to check sound quality, and especially to make sure the cordless microphone Montand used in order to be able to move freely after "Sir Godfrey" was working properly (it was fragile and temperamental). At the end of the song she had to be in the wings to tell him that all had gone well. On opening night at the Met in New York, Montand was horrified: no Carole (she had been unable to fight her way backstage). Returning to face the audience, he hid his anger, holding it in until the end. What a time to leave him in the lurch! After the last curtain he headed for his dressing room, feeling the rage rise within him, crying "CAROLE!"—and then stopped dead: Simone stood there, looking astonished. How on earth could she have left the auditorium so quickly? And now she had misread his shout, which she interpreted as a call of greeting. He tried to explain, became tongue-tied, floundered. Had Simone, who usually forced herself to ignore her spouse's escapades (one day she confided to Bob Castella: "I know very well he isn't always alone, but I don't want to know about it"), sensed that this one was more important than the others? She was jealous. Montand continued to reproach himself for never clearing up the misunderstanding.

For five years his liaison with Carole endured, veiled and sporadic. Strong-willed and a born groupie, at once level-headed and passionate, Carole accepted everything: she remained carefully in the shadows, taking a secondary role. She was available and discreet. Montand—guilty, of course—was disturbed by this daydreaming kid—she talked to rabbits, she got up in the middle of the night to feed a mother donkey—with a solid, practical mind. In 1987, as president of the Cannes Film Festival, he decided it was time to air the secret. Not to wed, but to come in from the cold. In any case, the paparazzi would sooner or later have unmasked them. "You can't make your life over," he said, "you just go on living." The press went wild at the sight of Yves Montand on the steps of the Saint-Paul city hall between Carole Amiel and Catherine Deneuve. "Climbing those stairs in my black dress was like performing at the Metropolitan Opera for me," says Carole.

Montand's companion thought long and hard over the last page of *Nostalgia Isn't What It Used to Be,* in which Signoret speculated that some "beautiful young creature" might one day take her place or follow her, entering her husband's life permanently. "If it were to happen," said Signoret, "I think that cutie would occasionally run into me around the house . . . even if I never went there. It wouldn't be fair to her; not fair to weigh on the present and the future in the name of the past . . . but it would probably be like that." Carole got the message; she understood that Simone was not someone you replace. "The warning she posted at the end of *Nostalgia* seems absolutely credible to me: if you live with Montand, you more or less live with Simone as well. They are inseparable. I can't ask Simone's friends to welcome me with open arms. I make them uneasy, it's inevitable. But time is on my side, and it will blow over. The main thing is for Montand to find some kind of equilibrium."

Paradoxically, just as he was going public with his link to a very young woman, Montand had become the elderly peasant Papet for cinema audiences. The two movies adapted by the director Claude Berri from books by Marcel Pagnol concern water rights disputed among Provençal peasants, a relatively serious theme, light years away from the gentle whimsy usually associated with Pagnol. Montand labored over the physical look of Papet, the antithesis of the card-playing Mediterranean stereotypes he had known in Marseilles: piercing eyes, sober tight-fitting suit, elegant close-clipped mustache. And he was glad to catch up with his real age, and then to overtake it, through a portrayal of a physically handsome character. It was not just the pleasure of working with Gérard Depardieu and Daniel Auteuil again, nor the satisfaction of being associated with a movie that broke the box office. It would not have taken much for him to go on dressing like Papet and holding on to the mustache.

And now—a paradox to end all paradoxes—Papet was a papa! He first had wind of the possibility while shooting *Trois places pour le 26.* Wrong, he both thought and said aloud. Utterly wrong. It was already wrong for a retiring man to appear in restaurants with a woman who might easily be his daughter. And now this unexpected little brother, this fragment of himself—altogether wrong. "He did not want a child," Carole would confess, "but more because of his age than from any deep-seated reluctance. Admittedly I made the decision, not Montand. He didn't like it, but he's happy about it today. It was the only thing I could give him that he had never had before, and also the only way of being with him my whole life long." Shortly after Valentin's birth, on December 31, 1988 (the Saint-Georges clinic in Nice was besieged by photographers), the young mother said right out: "If you're looking for the selfish one, it's me."[1]

Carole Amiel claims that her son was not born on New Year's Eve by accident. "The night before," she says, "they showed *Manon of the Spring* on television. The sight of Papet on his deathbed shattered me. I burst into tears. Did the shock do it? The first contractions came at dawn."

Valentin did not long remain an abstract little baby. As the weeks went by, Montand realized that fatherhood was not a given, not a natural instinct, not a feeling you either have once and for all or don't. It was a love story that made itself up as one went along, that was surprised by itself, by its own power, by the delight it inspired. Although he and Signoret had been childless, Montand had always been at ease with children. And he had always cultivated the child, the blend of fantasy and fragility that had endured deep within him. How many people know that on certain afternoons this very serious gentleman, this revered performer, treated himself all alone on the boulevard de l'Opéra to a smorgasbord of cartoon movies, sitting among the kids and their pretty mamas? The kid who had come along moved him deeply, brought him great joy.

Noting this evolution, Jean-Loup Dabadie wrote a prose poem for Montand, a song to be spoken. For a few weeks the recipient did not react, did not even acknowledge receiving it ("I know him," said Dabadie, smiling. "He needs time to make words his own"). He was right. Montand did not want to say anything to an audience or a camera that did not reflect his own truth. In the background, a rock beat:

> Valentin, cette musique que j'aime n'est pas la mienne,
> et le monde qui vient,
> c'est le nôtre mais c'est le tien.
> Une journée nous sépare,
> tu es le tout petit matin, Valentin.
> Je suis la tombée du jour, mon amour.
> Parce que, tu sais, pendant longtemps
> on sera enfants ensemble.

1. Quoted in *Paris-Match,* January 12, 1989.

Si tu tombes d'un arbre, je compterai tes larmes
et si tu vas au coin, ça sera au coin de moi. . . .

[Valentin, this music I love is not mine,
and the world that's on its way,
is ours but also yours.
There's just a day between us,
you're the tiny little light of dawn, Valentin,
and I'm the evening, my love.
If you fall from a tree, I'll count your tears,
and if you're sent to the corner, I'll be there with you. . . .]

Carole, raised a Catholic, wanted her son to be christened. The ceremony took place far from the cameras. The television anchorwoman Christine Ockrent was the godmother and Jean-Louis Livi the godfather. The choice of his nephew (once again Montand's agent) was symbolic, strategic even. For Jean-Louis stood at the exact intersection of the highways and the fault lines that ran through the clan: between Julien and Yves (they spoke over the phone after Valentin's birth), between Catherine (legally adopted by Montand) and Carole. Jean-Louis Livi, godfather of Valentin Giovanni Jacques Livi, was guaranteeing the continuity of the clan.

"Bobby! Stop, Bobby, stop! STOP, BOBBY, BOBBYYY!!!"

Montand has missed a bar, and Bob Castella is waving accusing fingers in front of his face. The inevitable ensues: the Olympia resounds to angry bellows, shuddering to its foundations, the loudspeakers going mad. Bob goes into the stance he usually adopts to weather such storms—neck pulled in, shoulders aerodynamically rounded. This is nothing. The "big fellow" is warming up, filling his lungs.

Three minutes later, after the last bars of "Le Carrosse," seeing Castella on his feet, he is suddenly worried: (Tenderly) "You're not tired, my old Bobby?" (Imperiously) "A chair for Bobby, a chair, quick!" (Sardonically, to the musicians) "Ninety-three, deaf as a post, and indestructible, what an athlete!" (Professionally) "So, shall we go on? What are you doing there? Stop dragging your feet!"

"Three, four," pipes the aged pianist.

While Montand was still alive we asked Bob Castella why he put up with him; the answer was as ready as it was serene. "Because he's never unfair." Jaw dropped. Not unfair? *Montand?* "No," said the accompanist, "not unfair. Emotional, hot-tempered, quarrelsome in the heat of the discussion, granted. But truly malicious, knowingly unfair, malevolent—certainly not."

And why did Montand lean on a partner so frail, so casual, so dispassionate? "Bob frail? That's a laugh," the singer would counter. "He's perhaps the most amazing man I've ever met. His seeming lack of passion gives him unbelievable strength. The strength and the stubbornness of an ant."

For the second time that day, the artist repeats his 1981 concert repertory on the Olympia stage. The voice is thicker, the physical bulk more impressive. Along the way, Montand is irritated by a memory lapse, and then he relaxes, unwinds, his hands come alive, the shoes start to tap, the shoulders roll, the eyes sparkle. Suddenly the test, the physical exercise, is replaced by pleasure at breaking free, moving, playing on the low notes. He tackles "A Paris" full blast, emptying his lungs. The musicians, too, have regained their form. Arms widespread, Montand holds the last note as long as he can, then stops dead.

"All right, children, let's do it once more!"

And it's "A Paris" all over again, still full volume, but more smiling, more cheerful.

"That's better. Again. . . ."

"He'll kill them all," whispers Marouani.

In the darkness, the "audience" feels that first delightful thrill of mingled awe and pleasure. It is a privilege to sit in on this exploit, to see a man grow fifteen years younger in fifteen seconds. Jean Frydman is silent. Chris Marker jokes, "Montand performs even better when he's tired."

He is right. Montand liked to exhaust himself. It would be so understandable just to bask under the plane trees of Saint-Paul or the hedgerows of Autheuil. He would say it himself: what is sweeter than lunch at the café on the *place* in April, when the first broad beans have come in, the artichokes that melt in your mouth? It is 10:00 or 11:00 a.m. Someone brings bread, another country ham, someone else the Saint-Césaire olives. Everyone has his own wine, his own specialty: oil brought back from Italy, a Roquefort cheese, a salami. It is a hearty lunch, but the fun is clean. Then you play boules with the requisite gravity. . . .

Yes, it would be utterly understandable.

A tape recorder sits on the piano. The musicians stand in a circle around it and around the pianist, Bob. Montand has acquired a new song by Pierre Barouh (who wrote "La Bicyclette"). It is called "Le Cabaret de la dernière chance" ("The Last-Chance Saloon"). He tells them that the chorus must sound "amateur," nostalgic . . . it has to have a whiff of prewar champagne.

"But mainly amateur. The guy's there without being there . . . you understand."

Montand turns to face the auditorium, waits for the accordion to start him off, and then sings, his whole being relaxed:

> Il y a ceux qui rêvent les yeux ouverts
> Et ceux qui vivent les yeux fermés . . .
>
> [Some dream with their eyes wide open
> Some live with their eyes tight shut . . .]

Acknowledgments

Index

Photographic Credits

Acknowledgments

This book would not be complete unless we expressed our personal gratitude to those who so greatly helped us with their hospitality, their advice, and their observations, or with the records, photographs, tapes, movies, and correspondence they kindly made available to us.

First, our thanks to Yves Montand's family. His sister Lydia Ferroni not only granted us long interviews, but was our guide through the Marseilles neighborhoods where the youngest son of Giuseppina and Giovanni Livi grew up. Despite wounds that have not yet healed, his brother and his sister-in-law, Julien and Elvire Livi, as well as his nephew Jean-Louis, agreed to meet with us on several occasions and gave us a better understanding of what held the group together and what divided it. Catherine Allégret paid us the compliment of speaking to us candidly, as is her habit. Bob Castella, impossible to place except within the family circle, violated a long-standing rule of silence to help us.

Carole Amiel emerged from the privacy she cherishes.

Jorge Semprun, despite his government duties in Madrid, made a point of being a part of our investigation.

Several friends from Montand's boyhood and professional beginnings shared with us their recollections. Edouard Derdérian and R. Pizzo (Secretary of the Association of Former Youth Camp Members, Provençal Regional Delegation) were enormously helpful. Raoul André, Louise Carletti, Henri Contet, and Renée Lebas helped us build a picture of Yves Montand's early career.

Georges Martin, who has devoted years to research into Edith Piaf's life, gave us a thousand items of chronological and musicological information.

Colette Crolla, Paul Grimault, and Francis Lemarque fleshed out our picture of Montand singing his way to triumph at the Etoile. Marcel Azzola and Roger Paraboschi put the finishing touches on this portrait of a colleague and a friend.

Movie people can be hard to pin down, being often abroad or else the prisoners of shooting schedules. Our thanks to Catherine Deneuve, Gérard Depardieu, François Périer, and Serge Reggiani for granting us their time. Directors Alain Corneau, Constantin Costa-Gavras, Gérard Oury, and Claude Sautet and his associate Jean-Loup Dabadie were equally generous.

Yvette Etiévant welcomed us to the offices of Artmedia. Charley Marouani gave us a glimpse of an agent's life. Pierre Boutillier, Jean-Claude Guillebaud, Ivan Levaï, Anne Sinclair, and Bernard Kouchner were all helpful and friendly, particularly at Autheuil.

Lise London, whose memory never fails her, re-created Yves Montand's visit to Prague in 1957 for us and shared her recollections of the shooting of *The Confession.*

Nadia Nechayeva, in Moscow, filled in the background of the meeting between Yves Montand and Nikita Khrushchev. From Roxbury, Massachusetts, Arthur Miller was kind enough to reply to certain of our questions.

Jean-Christophe Averty, who knows everything about music hall in general and Montand in particular, dropped everything to check the accuracy of our chronology. Chris Marker gave us many of his own pictures and brought a critical judgment to our manuscript. Stéphane Khémis read it with a historian's vigilant eye.

In the thirty months it took to finish this book, several witnesses have died. Neither Anne Philipe, nor Hubert Rostaing, nor Francis Trottobas knew when they agreed to help us that their time was so near. It is fitting that our last lines should salute their memory.

Index

Index

Index

Photographic Credits

For permission to reproduce the photographs in this book, grateful acknowledgment is made to the following:

Associated Press, 17; Gérard Décaux, 14 top; DR, 11 bottom, 12 top, 13, 17 bottom, 18 top, 19 top, 22 bottom right and left, 23 top and bottom, 27 top, 29 top, 30 top, 31 right; *Elle* / Henri Elwing, 15 top, 24 bottom; *Elle* / Michel Roi, 11 top; Louis Foucherand, 2 top, 3 bottom; *France/Dimanche,* 6 bottom right and left; Gamma/ Martine Pecoux, 26 bottom; Jacques Gomot, 10 top and bottom, 24 top; *Jours de France* / Fournol, 16; John Kobal Collection, 6 top, 12 bottom, 20 top, 22 top, 23 middle; Bernard Kouchner, 30 bottom; Madoulet, 8; Magnum/Bruce Davidson, 20 bottom; Michel Mako, 9 bottom; Chris Marker, 18 bottom, 25 both; The Estate of Yves Montand, 1 all, 2 bottom, 3 top, 4 both, 5 all, 6 top, 7, 14 bottom, 15 bottom, 19 bottom, 21, 27, bottom, 28, 31 top, 32; Alan Pajer, 26 top; Teddy Piaz, 9 top; Sygma, 29 bottom.

A NOTE ON THE TYPE

This book was set in Garamond, a typeface originally designed by the famous Parisian type cutter Claude Garamond (1480–1561). This version of Garamond was modeled on a 1592 specimen sheet from the Egenolff-Berner foundry, which was produced from types thought to have been brought to Frankfurt by Jacques Sabon (d. 1580).

Claude Garamond is one of the most famous type designers in printing history. His distinguished romans and italics first appeared in *Opera Ciceronis* in 1543–44. While delightfully unconventional in design, the Garamond types are clear and open, yet maintain an elegance and precision of line that mark them as French.

Composed by ComCom, a division of The Haddon Craftsmen, Inc., Allentown, Pennsylvania

Printed and bound by Fairfield Graphics, Fairfield, Pennsylvania

Photographic inserts printed by Halliday Lithographers, West Hanover, Massachusetts

Designed by Cassandra J. Pappas